THE OXFORD HANDBOOK OF

FILM AND MEDIA STUDIES

THE OXFORD HANDBOOK OF

FILM AND MEDIA STUDIES

Edited by

ROBERT KOLKER

OXFORD
UNIVERSITY PRESS

2008

OXFORD
UNIVERSITY PRESS

Oxford University Press, Inc., publishes works that further
Oxford University's objective of excellence
in research, scholarship, and education.

Oxford   New York
Auckland   Bangkok   Bogotá   Buenos Aires   Cape Town   Chennai
Dar es Salaam   Delhi   Hong Kong   Istanbul   Karachi   Kolkata
Kuala Lumpur   Madrid   Melbourne   Mexico City   Mumbai   Nairobi
São Paulo   Shanghai   Singapore   Taipei   Tokyo   Toronto

With offices in
Argentina   Austria   Brazil   Chile   Czech Republic   France   Greece
Guatemala   Hungary   Italy   Japan   Poland   Portugal   Singapore
South Korea   Switzerland   Thailand   Turkey   Ukraine   Vietnam

Published by Oxford University Press, Inc.
198 Madison Avenue, New York, New York 10016

www.oup.com

Library of Congress Cataloging-in-Publication Data
The Oxford handbook of film and media studies / edited by Robert Kolker.
p. cm.
Includes bibliographical references and index.
ISBN 978-0-19-517596-7
1. Motion pictures.   2. Mass media.   3. Interactive multimedia.
I. Kolker, Robert Phillip.
PN1994.O93   2008
791.43—dc22   2007047635

ISBN: 978-0-19-517596-7

1 3 5 7 9 8 6 4 2

Printed in the United States of America
on acid-free paper

Contents

....

CONTRIBUTORS

LEE BERGER is currently the president of the film division of Los Angeles–based Rhythm & Hues Studios. Rhythm & Hues provides high-end computer-generated character animation and visual effects for Hollywood motion pictures and television commercials. His company won an Academy Award for best visual effects in the 2007 film, *The Golden Compass*.

TOM BERNARD is the copresident and cofounder of Sony Pictures Classics, an autonomous division of Sony Pictures Entertainment, currently celebrating its fifteenth anniversary. Sony Pictures Classics distributes, produces, and acquires independent films from the United States and around the world.

JAY DAVID BOLTER is Wesley Chair of New Media and director of the Wesley New Media Center at the Georgia Institute of Technology. He is the author of *Turing's Man: Western Culture in the Computer Age* (1984); *Writing Space: The Computer, Hypertext, and the History of Writing* (1991, 2001); *Remediation* (with Richard Grusin, 1999); and *Windows and Mirrors* (with Diane Gromala, 2003).

WARREN BUCKLAND is senior lecturer in film studies, Oxford Brookes University, and author of *Directed by Steven Spielberg* (2006); *Film Studies* (2nd ed., 2003); *Studying Contemporary American Film* (with Thomas Elsaesser, 2002); *The Cognitive Semiotics of Film* (2000); and editor of *The Film Spectator* (1995) and *Complex Storytelling in Contemporary World Cinema* (2008). He is also editor of the journal *New Review of Film and Television Studies*.

JOHN T. CALDWELL is chair of film and television critical studies at UCLA. His books include *Televisuality: Style, Crisis, and Authority in American Television* (1995); *Electronic Media and Technoculture* (1995, editor); *New Media: Theories and Practices of Digitextuality* (2003, coeditor); and *Production Culture: Industrial Reflexivity and Critical Practice in Film/Television* (2008).

EVANS CHAN (www.evanschan.com), New York–based critic and filmmaker, is originally from Hong Kong. Chan's filmography includes four narrative features: *To Liv(e)* (1991), *Crossings* (1994), *Bauhinia* (2002), and *The Map of Sex and Love* (2001)—and five documentaries, including *Journey to Beijing* (1998), *Adeus Macau*

(2000), and *The Life and Times of Wu Zhong Xin* (2003). His most recent documentary, *Sorceress of the New Piano*, was released on DVD by Mode Records in 2008 and his filming of Tan's performance of George Crumb's *Makrokosmos I & II* can also be found on DVD. Chan has edited and translated (into Chinese) two books by Susan Sontag.

ANDREW FLIBBERT is an assistant professor in the Department of Political Science at Trinity College in Hartford, Connecticut. He is the author of *Commerce in Culture: States and Markets in the World Film Trade* (2007).

DAVID GOLUMBIA writes about and teaches cultural studies, digital media, and theories of language at the University of Virginia. He is author of *The Cultural Logic of Computation* (2009) from which his chapter is excerpted.

FRANCES GUERIN teaches in the Department of Film at the University of Kent. She is the author of *A Culture of Light* (2005) and a coeditor of *The Image and the Witness* (2007). She is currently completing a book on amateur film and photography from Nazi Germany, *Through Amateur Eyes*.

RICHARD HOLLANDER has been active in the effects industry for over twenty-five years, with work on such films as the *China Syndrome; Star Trek; Blade Runner; Titanic; Harry Potter and the Sorcerer's Stone; The Lion, The Witch, and The Wardrobe; Superman Returns;* and *The Golden Compass.* He cofounded VIFX, which later merged with Rhythm & Hues where he was president of the film division for eight years before joining PIXAR, Inc. as a producer. He has been awarded a Scientific and Technical Achievement Award from the Academy of Motion Picture Arts and Sciences and a CLIO for his work in computer-generated animation.

PETER JASZI teaches at the Washington College of Law of American University in Washington, D.C., where he also directs the Glushko-Samuelson Intellectual Property Law Clinic. He specializes in domestic and international copyright law. In 1994, he was a member of the Library of Congress Advisory Commission on Copyright Registration and Deposit. He is a trustee of the Copyright Society of the U.S.A. and a member of the editorial board of its journal. Since 1995 he has been active in the Digital Future Coalition, which he helped to organize. Alone and with Martha Woodmansee, he has written several articles on copyright history and theory; together they edited *The Construction of Authorship* (1994).

MARIANA JOHNSON is assistant professor of film studies at the University of North Carolina, Wilmington. She has published articles on French avant-garde and Latin American film and is currently working on a book about contemporary Cuban cinema.

ROBERT KOLKER is emeritus professor at the University of Maryland and lecturer in media studies at the University of Virginia. He is the author of many books, including *A Cinema of Loneliness: Penn, Kubrick, Scorsese, Spielberg, and Altman* (2000); *The Altering Eye: Contemporary International Cinema* (1983) (http://otal .umd.edu/~rkolker/AlteringEye); *Film, Form, and Culture* (2007); and *Media Studies* (2008).

GINA MARCHETTI is on the faculty at the University of Hong Kong. She is author of *Romance and the "Yellow Peril": Race, Sex and Discursive Strategies in Hollywood Fiction* (1994); and *From Tian'anmen to Times Square: Transnational China and the Chinese Diaspora on Global Screens, 1989–1997* (2006).

TARA MCPHERSON teaches courses in new media and popular culture in the University of Southern California's School of Cinema–TV. She is author of *Reconstructing Dixie: Race, Gender and Nostalgia in the Imagined South* (2003) and a coeditor of the anthology *Hop on Pop: The Politics and Pleasures of Popular Culture* (2003). She has edited *Digital Youth: Innovation and the Unexpected* (2008) (for the MacArthur Foundation) and recently launched *Vectors*, a new multimedia peer-reviewed journal (http://www.vectorsjournal.org). She is a member of the Academic Advisory Board of the Academy of Television Arts and Sciences Archives.

TOBY MILLER is professor of English, sociology, and women's studies, and director of the Program in Film and Visual Culture, at the University of California, Riverside. He is the author and editor of more than twenty books and has published essays in more than thirty journals and fifty volumes. His current research covers the success of Hollywood overseas, the links between culture and citizenship, and anti-Americanism.

DEVIN ORGERON is an associate professor of film studies at North Carolina State University, where he has taught courses on cinematic realism and the documentary. He also collects, shows, and writes about home movies from the 1940s to the 1970s. He is the author of *Road Movies: From Muybridge and Méliès to Lynch and Kiarostami* (2008).

MARSHA ORGERON is an associate professor of film studies at North Carolina State University. Her research interests include the star system and movie fan culture through the studio era; Sam Fuller, Ida Lupino, and other independent filmmakers of the 1940s and 1950s; home movies and industrial and educational films; and the intersections between film and other art forms such as literature. She is the author of *Hollywood Ambitions: Celebrity in the Movie Age* (2008).

MANJUNATH PENDAKUR is dean of the Dorothy F. Schmidt College of Arts & Letters, Florida Atlantic University. He worked in the Indian film industry prior to emigrating to Canada. His research interests are in the political economy of communication, ethnography, critical cultural theory, and third world cinema. He has done field research in the United States, Canada, Africa, and India. His current work focuses on globalization of the U.S. and Indian film industries and public policy. Pendakur's publications include *Citizenship and Participation in the Information Age* (edited with Roma Harris, 2002), and *Indian Popular Cinema: Industry, Ideology, and Consciousness* (2003).

BRIAN PRICE is assistant professor of film studies at Oklahoma State University. He is also coeditor of *Framework: The Journal of Film and Media Studies*.

JEANNENE M. PRZYBLYSKI is an artist, historian, and associate professor in the School for Interdisciplinary Studies at the San Francisco Art Institute. She has published widely on art, photography, and urban visual culture. Most recently she coedited *The Nineteenth-Century Visual Culture Reader* (2004).

JOSEPH CHRISTOPHER SCHAUB is an associate professor in the Communication Arts Department at the College of Notre Dame of Maryland. He is currently writing a book on contemporary Japanese popular culture.

WILLIAM URICCHIO is professor and director of comparative media studies at MIT and professor of comparative media history at Utrecht University in the Netherlands.

CRISTINA VENEGAS is assistant professor in film and media studies at the University of California Santa Barbara. Her teaching and writing focus on Latin American media, Spanish-language media in the United States, international cinema, and cultural studies. Her essays have appeared in various journals and anthologies, including a monograph dealing with cyberculture in Cuba. She has curated numerous film programs on Latin American and indigenous film in the United States and Canada. She is cofounder and artistic director (since 2004) of the Latino CineMedia International Film Festival in Santa Barbara, which is now copresented with the Santa Barbara International Film Festival.

PAUL YOUNG is director of film studies and assistant professor of English at Vanderbilt University. He is the author of *The Cinema Dreams Its Rivals: Media Fantasy Films from Radio to the Internet* (2006) and is currently writing *Mobilizing Pictures: Realism, Transformation, Early American Cinema*. His article, "Telling Descriptions: Frank Norris's Kinetoscopic Naturalism and the Future of the Novel, 1899," appeared in *Modernism and Modernity* (2007).

THE OXFORD HANDBOOK OF

FILM AND MEDIA STUDIES

INTRODUCTION

ROBERT KOLKER

Nondiscrete Objects

We are living in the late age of film. Jay Bolter (Chapter 1) quotes this remarkably prescient statement made by Paul Young in 1999.[1] Now that Hollywood has completely absorbed digital graphics technologies, swapping out most of the old, analog F/X tricks filmmakers had employed since the turn of the twentieth century, it is suddenly confronting its own antiquity. Perhaps Rupert Murdoch realized this when he decided not to update and rename 20th Century Fox after the start of the new millennium. Declining box office receipts, rising DVD rentals and downloads, new online distribution channels, increasing use of high-definition video recording to replace film on the production side and digital projection on the exhibition side, all signal the demise of traditional motion picture production and reception.

Yet the demise of the traditional is a constant in film and other media, as well as in the criticism of all media types. Media are defined by the fact that they change. "Convergence" is the current catchphrase to describe the cascade of all "old" media into the digital, but throughout their history, the businesses of media have been in a continual state of flux, of uncertainty, of accommodating new technologies and new audiences. Writing about media reflects this state of constant flux. Ideas change as their subjects do; methodologies evolve as new media forms develop; and the ways in which media are situated in critical discourse keep changing as well. Questions arise as we attempt to separate media in order to create stable objects to study; contexts shift as we attempt to define what constitutes a media "text": the work itself, a film or a television program; the businesses that create the work; the global processes of production, distribution, and reception that put the works in circulation?

Media objects—even the attempt to give them a generic name is difficult—are both discrete and nondiscrete simultaneously. Works of imagination, commodity items in the circulation of capital, cultural productions used by their consumers— they exist in their own spaces, the spaces of their creation, distribution, and reception, all of which also exist as subjects of critical inquiry. Film, television, photography, journalism, radio and recorded sound, advertising, and the new entities of the digital world are complete in themselves but at the same time completed only in the full context of the cultures that surround, create, and make use of them. This complexity is what this handbook addresses.

WHERE ARE MEDIA?
EXTENSIONS/MEDIATIONS/POLITICS AND CULTURE

Media are "extensions of man," as Marshall McLuhan subtitled *Understanding Media*, a book that itself became a media sensation in the mid 1960s. His serious, somewhat delirious study brought to the fore the inextricable relationship of media and culture, indeed pointed to the existence of media culture, after a long period of denial and downright hostility—not that there hadn't been important attempts to regard media as serious imaginative events. Film, certainly, received attention as "art." The poet Vachel Lindsay, writing about film art in his 1915 book, *The Art of the Moving Picture*, sought homologies with painting and sculpture. In *The Seven Lively Arts*, written in the early 1920s, Gilbert Seldes attempted a syncretic approach, looking at the prominent media of the time and offering cultural analysis, including an attempt to think through the phenomenon of celebrity. In a chapter entitled "An Open Letter to the Movie Magnates, Ignorant and Unhappy People," he wrote about the always precarious relationship between media business and its audience, and called for a deeper understanding of film itself:

> The Lord has brought you into a narrow place—what you would call a tight corner—and you are beginning to feel the pressure. A voice is heard in the land saying that your day is over. The name of the voice is Radio, broadcasting nightly to announce that the unequal struggle between the tired washerwoman and the captions written by or for Mr. Griffith is ended. It is easier to listen than to read. And it is long since you have given us anything significant to see.

You may say that radio will ruin the movies no more than the movies ruined the theatre. The difference is that your foundation is insecure: you are monstrously over-capitalized and monstrously undereducated; the one thing you cannot stand is a series of lean years. You have to keep on going because you have from the beginning considered the pictures as a business, not as an entertainment. Perhaps in your desperate straits you will for the first time try to think about the movie, to see it steadily and see it whole . . .

My suggestion to you is that you engage a number of men and women: an archaeologist to unearth the history of the moving picture; a mechanical genius to explain the camera and the projector to you; a typical movie fan, if you can find one; and above all a man of no practical capacity whatever: a theorist. Let these people get to work for you; do what they tell you to do. You will hardly lose more money than in any other case.[2]

Film studies answered Seldes's call many years after the fact. Serious critical engagement with other media followed. Soon the business of those "ignorant and unhappy people" became an object of study itself.

The Politics of Media Culture

These early attempts to extend film into the realm of art faltered in the face of a political culture whose force thwarted serious engagement. Seldes, a magazine editor, later became a media commentator, appearing on television during the 1950s, and continued his attempts at thinking seriously about media. But Seldes and other media critics had a difficult time in the immediate postwar period. The media were targets of the very popular culture they were part of, taking a bashing as cultural pariah, political subversive, despoiler of youth, inciter to sexual predation. The attacks were hardly new. The mock fear of moral destruction was always at hand. In the early days of radio and recorded sound, the strong influence of African American jazz on popular music exposed an always ready racism, which was itself a ready catalyst to warnings of moral decay. Here is the music chairwoman of the General Federation of Women's Clubs in 1921: "Jazz disorganizes all regular laws and order; it stimulates to extreme deeds, to a breaking away from all rules and conventions, and its influence is wholly bad. . . . The effect of jazz on the normal brain produces an atrophied condition . . . until . . . those under the demoralizing influence . . . are actually incapable of distinguishing between good and evil, between right and wrong."[3] The statement could be transposed word for word into the opprobrium poured on rock and roll in the mid-fifties, when African American music again catalyzed a musical form that would change popular music and popular culture for good and all. But racism was only one part of the large, ideological postwar campaign against media, waged against the most popular of the day—film—and the increasingly popular television. The campaign was both cultural and political.

The media object and political culture have never been separable. Much has been written about the government show trials on "communist infiltration" of the movie business, and the concurrent private "investigation" of television, all leading to the blacklisting of some of the most talented people in postwar media. The attacks of the House Committee on Un-American Activities (HUAC), beginning in 1947, and the publication of *Red Channels* in the early 1950s, were the beginning of the assertion of a general right-wing control of the political culture that continues to this day. Battered by World War II, appalled by the revelations of the Nazi concentration camps, scared by nuclear power, the culture seemed ready to accept the fact that it was now threatened from within as well as without, and that the things that people loved, from comic books to music to movies, were dangerous. It was mass media as mass cultural threat. It is important to recall, however, that HUAC tried to nose itself into Hollywood before this, in the early 1940s, and met with a lack of interest. After the war, the movie industry was in trouble on a number of fronts: audiences were diminishing; the Supreme Court had severed the vertical integration of product and exhibition, so that the studios no longer owned the theaters that exhibited their product; the studios' anger over the labor unrest during the war became a source for revenge. When HUAC returned to Hollywood in the late 1940s, the studios found the hunt for communist infiltration irresistible.[4] On the television side, a former FBI agent and a right-wing television producer, with some help from a supermarket owner, published *Red Channels*, a list of alleged left-wing entertainers. This bunch had only to threaten to remove the products advertised on these "communist" broadcasts from store shelves to scare the radio and television networks into submission.

The red scare and the excoriation of media were a clear result of a grab for power on all sides, part of the establishment of a conservative state in which industry would be protected above all else while the culture the industry produced was kept ideologically in line. As Jon Lewis pointed out, the collaboration of the movie studios with the government during the red purges was part of a process that moved them away from a paternalist model, in which each studio struggled with its talent and their unions, to a corporate model. "The new Hollywood we see in place today—a new Hollywood that rates and censors its own and everyone else's films and flaunts its disregard for antitrust legislation and federal communications and trade guidelines—is very much the product and the still-evolving legacy of the blacklist."[5] The same could be said of television. *Red Channels* provided what television and all media wanted and want still: an excuse that permitted control without blame, hegemony wrapped in righteousness.

Film and television were hardly the only targets. At mid-century, the U.S. Senate Committee on the Judiciary, which included such luminaries as Harley M. Kilgore, a founder of the National Science Foundation; Estes Kefauver, crime fighter and presidential hopeful; and James O. Eastland, racist and McCarthyite, investigated the effects of comic books on juvenile delinquency. Juvenile delinquency was itself an invention of 1950s culture, turning young people into yet another threat, providing a cause for fear and a subject for movies.[6] The report of the comic book committee reveled in the description of the things it claimed to abhor:

> It has been pointed out that the so-called crime and horror comic books of concern to the subcommittee offer short courses in murder, mayhem, robbery, rape, cannibalism, carnage, necrophilia, sex, sadism, masochism, and virtually every other form of crime, degeneracy, bestiality, and horror. . . . Many of the books dwell in detail on various forms of insanity and stress sadistic degeneracy. Others are devoted to cannibalism with monsters in human form feasting on human bodies, usually the bodies of scantily clad women.

The report assured us that comics are communist tools. However, a direct influence of comics on adolescent behavior and decaying morals cannot be proved. Despite this, the committee assured the country that "neither the comic-book industry nor any other sector of the media of mass communications can absolve itself from responsibility for the effects of its product."[7]

The struggle for political power over public morality, using the media as intermediary, continues. During the regime of George W. Bush, the religious Right continued to pressure the media. The Parents Television Council and the American Family Association make concerted efforts to barrage the Federal Communications Commission (FCC) with complaints about media content they find objectionable, or even media technologies that make them fearful. The Parents Television Council tends to describe the content in lip-smacking detail, even posting "objectionable" clips on its Web site. These and other right-wing lobbies, like Focus on the Family, have caused the FCC to enact the 2005 Broadcast Decency Enforcement Act, which allows it to levy massive fines against the already small, cautious moves the networks might take to make their programming reflect the world. The act carries forward the 1978 Supreme Court ruling, brought by the FCC and instigated by a radio broadcast of a bit by comedian George Carlin, that forbade the airing of "filthy words" at an indecent hour.[8]

Media producers often thrive when criticism of their content comes from the outside, allowing them to proclaim themselves innocent mediators of public taste. Too often, they fold in the face of pressure. During the Bush regime, right-wing groups created the pressure as government surrogates. During the fifties, media criticism was hardly the province of the government, or even the right wing. Public intellectuals, from left to right, criticized media as vulgar and vulgarizing. Magazine editor, film critic, and former Trotskyite Dwight MacDonald set the tone, midway between Theodor Adorno, the complex analyst of high and low culture, and the Senate comic book committee. MacDonald did not so much attack media as he did their audience. "The question of Masscult is part of the larger question of the masses. The tendency of modern industrial society, whether in the USA or the USSR, is to transform the individual into the mass man. . . . The masses . . . are not related *to each other* at all but only to some impersonal, abstract, crystallizing factory." That would be media. Masscult is "very, very democratic," in that it "all comes out finely ground indeed." For MacDonald, mass culture was as beyond redemption as was the finely ground mass that fed it. He invented another level of debasement to complain about, "Midcult." Here is mass culture masquerading as high. "In Masscult the trick is plain—to please the crowd by any means. But Midcult has it both ways: it pretends to respect the standards of High Culture while in fact it waters them down and vulgarizes them."[9]

FROM LOW BROW TO THE EXTENSIONS OF MAN

Serious media criticism emerges slowly from this complex mix of politics, cultural criticism, and generalized antipathy. The political-moral antipathies fueled by the cold war, and the not-so-vaguely racist phrenology of high-, middle-, and low-brow culture, all expressed an anxiety that power was moving not so much to the media producers (which was actually the case) but to the despicable, undiscerning masses who sopped up their products. Condemnation and concern for media's negative effects informed much discourse about media. But studied it had to be. The increasing use of statistical and sociological approaches, concentrating on the "effects" of various kinds of media on various audiences, an approach influenced by another immigrant intellectual, Paul Lazarsfeld, became a way of analyzing media by means of circumventing troublesome value judgments.[10]

All this helps to account for the reception accorded to McLuhan's *Understanding Media*. Here was informed, scholarly analysis that was not interested in condemnation, and was deeply concerned with media's *formal* structures. McLuhan understood that media were not a force that moved downward on culture, or even moved culture itself downward, debasing it in the process. Media were, like any form of expression, of our making, our history, our culture. They expressed us. They mediated the culture. McLuhan's "the medium is the message" became a catchphrase but caught a complex of ideas that enabled the serious study of its subject: content is what form expresses, and form itself is an intricate weave of the media object—a television program, a film, a computer game—the production forces behind it, and the reception of it. McLuhan and his work became media phenomena, well enough known that Woody Allen could give him a "cameo" in *Annie Hall* (1977).[11]

FILM STUDIES

McLuhan's star as media subject rose and fell; the seriousness with which he took his own subject was, quite independently, being picked up by film studies. Politics, style, and culture formed what was to become an important force in the critical analysis of media. In the United States, film studies was born partly of politics, partly of the very culture that allowed Woody Allen to put McLuhan in his film in the first place. Before the 1970s, film had separated itself from the "vulgarity" of mass media to become an admired form of art, celebrated, anticipated. The origins of film studies are enmeshed with the renaissance of international filmmaking that began in Europe after WW II. A complex series of events in postwar Europe invigorated European cinema: The Blum-Byrnes Accords in France created quotas for American films on French screens; the development of neorealism in Italy put film crews on the streets of the country's ruined cities. Neorealism revitalized film style; the Blum-Byrnes Accords were responsible for ossifying it.

In Italy, Roberto Rossellini, Vittorio De Sica, and their colleagues were confronting the collapse of Fascism by creating melodramas of survival in a mise-en-scène of tangible presence. The French response to the influx of American film was to create a literate and literary cinema, later called the "tradition of quality," somewhat static, very much studio bound, the opposite of the place-accurate, almost tactile mise-en-scène of the Italians. Responding to French ossification were a group of French filmmakers, who, seeing the works of the Italians, as well as catching up on many years of American film embargoed during the occupation, began a wholesale challenge to the givens of commercial film. The challenge came first in the form of criticism. This is significant because these writers, many of whom—Jean-Luc Godard, François Truffaut, Claude Chabrol, Eric Rohmer, among others—would turn to filmmaking by the late 1950s, continued the prewar movement of serious film discussion. They were shepherded by André Bazin, champion of neorealism, theorist of cinema's capacity for quiet observation, and promoter of film culture.[12] Together, they laid the ground for modern film theory.

American filmmaking had begun its own response to convention before the United States's entry into World War II. Orson Welles announced a change in vision in the deep-focused chiaroscuro of *Citizen Kane* (1941). Following on *Kane,* pulling in the existential ironies of hard-boiled detective fiction, saturated by the darkening of cultural vision during the war, film noir emerged. The French named it, and it became part of the revitalization of their national cinema, as it was of ours. The French also discovered the potency of a proper name. Viewing many American films released after the embargoes of the war, they recognized that a consistency of visual and narrative style could be categorized by director. Therefore, they nominated directors as the artistic force of a film, analyzed their styles, and, in so doing, pulled American film out of the mass of studio production and into the realm of artistic creation. They saw the trees in the forest, to borrow Andrew Sarris's image for the discovery of the film auteur.[13] Influences began crossing back and forth. Neorealist films created particular interest in the United States. One of them, Rossellini's "The Miracle," a contribution to an omnibus collection of short works (*L'amore*, 1948) created a spasm of censorship from the Roman Catholic Church, reminiscent of an earlier time that led to the institution of the internal censorship body called the Hays Office in the 1930s. While "The Miracle" was fought in the United States and neorealism in its home country (the Italian Christian Democrats had no use for the neorealists' grim representations, no matter how melodramatic they turned out to be), Hollywood meanwhile absorbed one aspect of the style that became a structural component of the breakdown of the studio system: the streets were substituted for the back lot. Hollywood announced it as realistic.

The French New Wave—the general rubric given those films by critics turned directors—absorbed everything it could. The neorealist movement, in the hands of such directors as Michelangelo Antonioni, Pier Paolo Pasolini, and the young Bernardo Bertolucci, matured into a modernist cinema, reflecting on its own means of image making, becoming an image cinema, and enlivened not only the act of filmmaking, but reception itself—calling on the viewer to become an active participant in reading and interpreting the image.[14] In the sixties and seventies, a film culture was born in the United States, and with it an excitement about the possibilities inherent in the cinematic imagination, and an elevation of that imagination that rose into academe and influenced Hollywood itself. This culture was fed by strong, leftist student movements, born of the cold war and the ongoing hot war against Vietnam. These movements found new modes of expression, new discursive relationships with media. The individuals within the movement may or may not have read McLuhan, but they believed and intuited that the medium is indeed the message. Filmmaking approached the status of writing, given a name and a face through the elevation of the director to the status of artist, becoming an academic subject mostly by the force of youngsters seeking a freshened curriculum.

Critical theory in general had reached a place of quietude in the early sixties. The entry of film studies brought with it a raft of theorizing that moved through and changed critical discourse across the board. As they did in filmmaking, the French led the way, while in the United States, native born theory, especially in gender analysis, had a powerful influence on rereading cinema and ultimately all media. In this collection, Brian Price (Chapter 2) reviews the waves and particles of film theory, exposing the connections among them (and the current reaction against them). Perhaps the overriding element of all late-twentieth-century theorizing is how thoroughly it politicized its subject, and, more accurately, how thoroughly it opened the inherent political structure of its subject. Studies of ideology, how film form, generic clusters, economic imperatives, and audience reception, established the links of power within the narrative image and between the image and the viewer.[15] This political imperative was at the root of the broader discipline of media studies.

Because filmmaking, observed from the business end, is deeply conservative and profit driven, the political imperative of media is focused in the power that comes from profit, and that profit depends on absorption and extension. From the production perspective, media are not—as McLuhan has it—"extensions of man"; rather, their audience is an extension of media. Under the rubric of "giving the audience what they want," media give themselves what they need—an expanding bottom line. To that end, they will do what is necessary to create an audience that will buy their products, even if it means, however indirectly, buying into critical theory. When mid-seventies films such as *The Godfather* (Francis Ford Coppola, 1972, 1974) and *Jaws* (Steven Spielberg, 1975) made a great deal of money, Hollywood was pleased to recognize their directors. When *Heaven's Gate* (1980), directed by Michael Cimino, cost United Artists its existence as an independent studio, Hollywood was happy to bump the director off, or at least restrict the name to moneymakers only, or at times create an auteur where none exists, as in the brief instance of M. Night Shyamalan, whose reputation rested on the popularity of one film, *The Sixth Sense* (1999).

FROM HISTORICAL FILM TO FILM AND MEDIA HISTORY

Media attempt to maintain a steady state, creating their audience by shifting conventions just enough to create illusions of originality, pulling back when the media producers themselves feel under siege. In 1970, 20th Century Fox released *MASH*, a film made by an unknown, and already not so young, Robert Altman. Mocking authority, mocking the steady, comfortable gaze and continuity cutting of the authoritative style of Hollywood convention, playing to the vital anti-Vietnam culture of the moment, the film was successful critically and commercially. The same year, the studio released a film about Pearl Harbor, called *Tora! Tora! Tora!* (Richard Fleisher, Kinji Fukasaku, and Toship Masuda). The film initially was to have some auteur appeal. Akira Kurosawa was to direct the Japanese sequences. This did not happen, and the resulting film stands as the anti-*MASH*: wooden, earnest, a recitation of government memos by a roster of Hollywood's aging players. Fox franchised *MASH* into a television series that ran for eleven years. Robert Altman (who had nothing to do with, and gained nothing from, the television series) was able to talk the success of his film into funding for a decade of imaginative, cinematically adventurous commercial failures. In 1985–86, Rupert Murdoch, Australian "media mogul," owner of European satellite stations, the London *Times*, and the *New York Post,* among many others, bought 20th Century Fox and started the Fox Network, whose cable news channel became the propaganda arm of the George W. Bush administration.

The logic of this brief case history exists not only in the movements of cinematic and televisual art, but in the equilibrium and the progress controlled by their producers. How much interaction can we observe between the products—the films, the television series—and the media producers? Was there a conscious attempt on Fox's part to balance *MASH* with *Tora! Tora! Tora!*? It is the work of contemporary film historians to explore Fox's archives—were they available to scholars—to find out what the aging Darryl Zanuck and his minions were thinking as the failing company was reaching the end of its independent existence. The spin-off of the television series presents another set of logics, of the taming of an anarchic film, turning it into the genre of workplace comedy, while still retaining some antimilitary edge. The tools of film studies expand into the larger texts of media cultures and economies.

The entry of Rupert Murdoch announces another narrative, the story of media acquisitions and globalization, variously interpreted as a homogenizing of media output to the detriment of national media and individual talent, and as an increased means of access to entertainment and information. Andrew Flibbert (Chapter 17) addresses the interactions of American, Latin American, and Middle Eastern media, noting that "the worldwide integration of the industry . . . calls into question the very concepts of 'national' and 'foreign' film production and trade." He finds a dynamic where Hollywood hegemony and local creativity contend without anyone permanently losing anything. Manjunath Pendakur (Chapter 15) explores the continued dominance of national Indian cinema, stressing its multiplicity and ability to exist alongside of American product within a complex economic web. These essays among others analyze the discourses of media power, where film and television, their production and reception, are more expressions of national interests or global power—fluid and always changing—and less individual works of imagination.

FILM VERSUS MEDIA

Toby Miller and Mariana Johnson (Chapter 8) clearly observe the expansion of film studies into large issues of economics and trade: "Because texts accrete and attenuate meanings on their travels as they rub up against, trope, and are troped by other fictional and social texts, we must consider all the shifts and shocks that characterize their existence as cultural commodities, their ongoing renewal as the temporary 'property' of varied, productive workers and publics, and the abiding 'property' of business people." Interesting within the history of film and media studies is that this insight comes relatively late, and in fact is offered by Miller and Johnson as a caution to the field. The reason is, as I have been indicating, that historically film studies started with a notion of film as an art object. I am not thinking of "art cinema" in particular, but of the decision made by film scholars, as their discipline was being formed, that a film could be considered a coherent, expressive text in itself, open to analysis on a number of levels. It had a history, was made up of definable genres, was perhaps the product of a single imagination whose hand and eye could be seen operating in a number of texts, formally and contextually of a piece. The "Hitchcocko-Hawksians," as the late 1950s–early 1960s French, English, and then American writers were called, promoted a textual history of film, provided a taxonomy based on directorial style, and looked at film as the visual narrative it is, stressing the ways in which their favored directors saw the world cinematically.

The politicization of film studies I discussed earlier—the recognition that the very form and reception of film were part of a larger ideological construct—was built on this conception of film as an art object. While the various ideological and structural analyses of the 1970s seemed to counteract this, pushing in and out of the cinematic text to find how it expressed or countered power, the base was still the film as analyzable object, even as its integrity was called into question by the expansion of the discipline into historical and economic contexts.[16] The study of other media almost always focused on the nexus of text, context, industry, culture, and ideology—cultural commodities, the polysemous complex, as John T. Caldwell (Chapter 11) points out, of multiple authorship, interrelated content, and a formal expression that speaks many voices.

MEDIA STUDIES

I am aware of the risk of setting up a false comparison between film and media studies for the sake of argument. I have already pointed to Gilbert Seldes's study of film as one medium within the cultural surround of the 1920s. The Frankfurt School examined media, film included, within larger, profoundly political and cultural contexts, work that pointed the way to media studies. Siegfried Kracauer's *From Caligari to Hitler* is—despite its tendentiousness—solidly grounded in the intersections of film and cultural-historical formations. Theodor Adorno and Max Horkheimer's *Dialectic of Enlightenment,* specifically the chapter "The Culture

Industry," had a major impact on our understanding of the ways media, politics, and corporate structures conspire. But "conspire" is the operative word in much of the work of the Frankfurt School: media as a kind of conspiracy, less a thing in itself than a representation of ways in which the dominant power manipulates the dominant culture, homogenizes it, makes it passive, even feminizes it. We recall Kracauer's "little shop girls go to the movies," along with Adorno's more sophisticated condemnation of the debasements of jazz.[17]

The Frankfurt School spoke from the position of high left-wing modernism, which observed contemporary culture collapsing in ruins and being reconstituted through an authoritarian structure, mediating the ruins into a chimera of control under the reality of fear. The dialectic was synthesized by positing the model of a high culture of creative intellectual force battling the darkness. The complexity of the model, however, was too much for the popularizers in the 1950s, who could not posit a dialectic, but only work up rage against the debasement of culture and announce the superiority of those observing the debasement. What was missing was something that early film scholars understood implicitly: people respond to the popular, the commercial, and the generic; they embrace it, share it, dwell within it through their imaginations, and even learn from it. The wholesale condemnation of that response has always been counterproductive at best. Needed were ways to address the response without condemnation.

Intellectual groundwork for this process was laid by Walter Benjamin, a peripheral member of the Frankfurt School, a writer of modernity whose curiosity led him to wander through the cultural byways of the first half of the twentieth century with a welcoming analytic mind. In his 1935 essay, "The Work of Art in the Age of Mechanical Reproduction," Benjamin developed a metaphor that has served to differentiate high art and mass media by emphasizing a complex binary: high art carries the signifier of uniqueness; mass art does not. Benjamin's metaphor of difference is "aura," a signifier not only of the unique, but of access and emotional response to the singular work. An original painting, for example, is auratic—one of a kind, carrying the barely mediated mark of its creator, urging the viewer to imagine the artist through the work. A television series has no aura. It is created by a number of individuals, each of whom has some input into the final product; it is based on formula and, like all visual narratives created with technology, made in pieces, edited together for best effect, and further fragmented by advertising. Reception of television programming varies in intensity, from attentive, even communal viewing to the use of television as part of the household environment. Reception of the mechanically reproduced works does not have the aura of communing with a singular masterpiece. "Communing" is replaced by "communal" and a sense of connection rather than reverence.

Benjamin did not understand loss of aura as cultural calamity. Quite the contrary, mechanical reproduction (Benjamin used film as his main example) was a democratic, progressive event, bringing imaginative works to an audience who had no access to auratic art. Through mass distribution, technologically reproduced art creates a receptive community linked by individuals' mutual contact with the reproduced work and an audience responding in kind. The result is that the mechanically reproduced work and its audience begin to intermingle, to respond to each other. The loss of aura is a loss of a boundary and the creation of a new imaginative space:

> Thus, the distinction between author and public is about to lose its basic character. The difference becomes merely functional; it may vary from case to case. At any moment the reader is ready to turn into a writer. As expert, which he had to become willy-nilly in an extremely specialized work process, even if only in some minor respect, the reader gains access to authorship.[18]

This understanding of interaction as opposed to passive reception would provide a break in the deadlock of masscult/midcult versus high art. It would permit critics to understand media as a complex dynamic among all parties, on all levels, allowing that media, even in potential, were a communal act and a socializing force, not a one-way slide into passivity.

Cultural studies emerged in the early 1970s from the work of the Birmingham Centre for Contemporary Cultural Studies, with a strong base in Benjamin's essay, Marxist materialism, in the work of Adorno, in Antonio Gramsci's theories of hegemony, and the work of Raymond Williams and Richard Hoggart. At its core was the insistence that culture is not the same as "cultured," and is the always changing complex of actions and responses, based in history, class, gender, and race. David Golumbia (Chapter 18) points out that the

> foundational theorists like [Raymond] Williams and Stuart Hall, along with Fredric Jameson, John Fiske, John Frow, and the authors in the [Lawrence] Grossberg, [Cary] Nelson and [Paula A.] Treichler *Cultural Studies* anthology, share a profound concern with the politics of our contemporary world, and understand cultural production, including not just media but technical production, as part of this culture, part of us.

The "foundational theorists" were set on accounting for a cultural textuality by discovering coherent sets of meaning-making processes within culture, the various subcultures that make it up, and the media that these subcultures choose and decode. Cultural studies, especially as it addresses the cultures of media, was a break both from the judgmental postures of early cultural and media critics, and from the empiricist methodologies that pretend a "value-free" statistical analysis of the "effects" of media on its audiences. On the contrary, cultural studies values all parts of the complex interactions of audience and media, seeking out the movements and conflicting pressures of ideologies manifested in the ways producers of culture code their artifacts and the consumers of culture decode them.[19] It understands culture and its media as a set of interacting discourses, influencing one another, with balances of power constantly shifting.

FILM AND MEDIA

I need to return for a moment to the boundary that still exists between film studies and media studies, marked by definition and the very nomination of their objects of study. No matter how far film studies has come in its investigations of the cultural, political, and economic contexts of its object, there lingers about film the aura of art. Cultural and media studies rarely nominate their objects as such. Intent on a textual analysis that includes the circuitry of production and reception, they indeed often pay attention to the imaginative text, the work itself that is part of the circulation. But this attention is contained within the larger project of interpretation and appropriation of media by its audience, of understanding imaginative works as commodities in a transnational flow and as mediators of daily life.

Traditional film studies starts with the individual work, genre, or director, and moves outward to larger issues of the ideologies of production and reception, to gender issues, to the effects of distribution on viewership, and increasingly to the ways globalization is affecting national cinemas, always attempting to solidify its ground in theory. Media studies starts with larger textual entities, sometimes isolating a media artifact—a genre of music, a television series, a social-networking site, a computer game—often analyzing these from the perspective of subcultural, audience-specific interaction. Perhaps film studies has never quite removed itself from the aura of art, and perhaps media studies still retains roots in methodologies of sociology and cultural history. But from these roots have come a variety of methodologies, of ways to reimagine imagination itself and the complexities that arise when imagination is put at the service of production and consumption.

CONVERGENCE

I have been using the terms "cultural studies" and "media studies" interchangeably, and surely they are deeply intertwined. Raymond Williams's discovery of the complexities of American television programming, which he developed into the foundational theory of "flow," certainly sealed the connection.[20] Film studies, while privileging the object of its study as art was, from its inception, aware that film had to be understood within a cultural context. Within the university, the three fields of study—culture, media, and film—are beginning to merge. Film, while a thriving discipline since its inception, has grown only slowly in terms of academic units that are devoted exclusively to its study. Like film studies, cultural studies most often exists within existing academic departments, embracing, often infiltrating, traditional disciplines. Media studies, partly as an administrative solution, partly as a way to establish a discipline that moves beyond statistical methodologies in order to situate media as a humanities-based discipline, is absorbing film and cultural studies as well as, in some instances, journalism and mass communications. At its best, the convergence provides an expanded base for theory and analysis and offers a more complex field of research.

Convergence, of course, is coded with a host of meanings outside the university: for media companies, it means an ongoing effort to wring profits from the transition of old analog forms of media to the digital. For consumers, convergence suggests that, as old media move to new, accessibility, portability, interaction, even possibilities for intervention, grow. But digital accessibility cuts all ways. Content producers as well as content users can interact, and the extent of a resulting surveillance becomes clearer daily. The much-prized freedom of digital interaction comes at an increasing price. The "freedom" of the Internet has raised consciousness about ownership and intellectual property, which have emerged as an important field of contending legal opinion.

Convergence puts a different kind of pressure on scholars, who traditionally depend on the stability of their objects of study to allow prolonged observation and analysis. Media scholars, however, are witness to old media forms being transformed by the new, and new media forms creating new audiences within a cultural complex that is itself being altered by its responses to the digital. Film scholars are at risk in the face of changing media. Celluloid-based filmmaking and distribution are coming to an end, and the old, physical carrier of film will turn into archival material. Film is moving toward digital recording and transmission so that, beyond the influence of digital effects within a film, large visual elements, the very quality of the way light is recorded on digital media as opposed to chemically based film, will alter. Even now, cinematographers are being urged by producers to introduce as little "style" as possible in their lighting in order to allow maximum manipulation during the digital phase of production, where every film is transferred to a digital file for editing and effects. Film reception itself is undergoing rapid change as distribution moves from the movie theater to the living room to the computer screen to the mobile phone.

Convergence and globalization work hand in hand, creating an expanding, shifting landscape in which boundaries of every kind liquefy and are transgressed. Globalization of media threatens, from one perspective, the creation of a corporate hegemony, a conquering of borders by business interests that will sweep up national differences and dilute them in a global media soup. From another, globalization will redefine national media, producing new imaginative works, new interactions of audience and media, new policies and politics. This movement, change, and liquidity make the media object, its history and production, its audience, hardly possible to pin down long enough for detailed study. Theory making, unless it begins with an explanation of change, becomes all but impossible. Recall the flurry of critical activity involving "hypertext" in the mid 1990s.[21]

Any collection of writing on film and media must take into account not only the complex array of issues in film and media, but also this rapidity of change. In this light, I have sought essays that survey their field as well as those that address current issues. Beginning with Jay Bolter's discussion of media remediation, that lays the groundwork for much of the discussion that follows, Brian Price (Chapter 2) offers a history of film theory, while essays by Jeannene Przyblyski (Chapter 5) and Devin Orgeron (Chapter 3) interrogate the image in photography and film. Some contributors reflect on the traditional differences in the critical and theoretical approaches to film and other media, or seek out the history of the immediate in order to provide footing. But any attempt to investigate the sheer complexity of the media landscape can at best point to some features and the connections among them. Taken together, these essays give an idea where the scholarship is and where it is going. I've constrained coverage—for the sake of space and coherence—to visual media: film (including documentary in Frances Guerin's encyclopedic history of the radical image in European documentary filmmaking in Chapter 4), television (William Uricchio provides a fascinating history of television before television in chapter 9, and in chapter 11 John Caldwell investigates the complex, often self-reflexive business practices of television), photography (in Chapter 5, Jeannene M. Przyblyski meditates on the move from traditional to digital photography, providing a political history of the media along the way), media celebrity (Marsha Orgeron's Chapter 6), and the digital. Indeed, many of the essays interrogate the complex nature of the image itself as mediator of politics, of ideology, of "reality." I have included three essays—David Golumbia's on computers and cultural studies (Chapter 18, an essay that examines the history, mythology, and sociology of digital in the world of realpolitik), Warren Buckland's on media pedagogy (Chapter 19), and Peter Jaszi's overview of intellectual property issues (Chapter 20)—to broaden the scope of media studies into adjoining areas of importance.

I have attempted to include matters of globalization through a number of paths. Toby Miller and Mariana Johnson (Chapter 8) examine one film, *Gilda,* as text and as part of a global context, interrogating the entire structure and methodology of media studies along the way. Andrew Flibbert (Chapter 17), complementing Cristina Venegas's encyclopedic essay on Latin America (Chapter 16), does a comparative analysis of film production and distribution in both the Middle East and Latin America. There are, as well, essays by Evans Chan, Joseph Schaub, Gina Marchetti, and Manjunath Pendakur (Chapters 12, 13, 14, and 15) that examine particular national cinemas and media in Asia and India.

Finally, I have included two essays in appendixes 1 & 2 by people in the field. Tom Bernard, copresident of Sony Pictures Classics, writes a brief history of the American independent film movement, and Lee Berger and Richard Hollander describe the methodologies of digital effects that are now at the base of all films we see. Their discussion of technique provides a basis for the theorizing of how CGI—computer generated imagery—influences our reception of film.

While each chapter in the collection is self-contained, each also points outward to larger issues, and all are finally deeply interrelated in their desire to understand media productions, media theory, and media culture. Paul Young (Chapter 7), for example, examines genre theory from film to computer games. Joseph Schaub (Chapter 13) investigates the current horror film cycle in Japan, pulling genre theory into an immediate expression of cultural angst. Tara McPherson (Chapter 10), writing on the popular TV series *24*, provides an understanding, from inside a particular series, of how television attempts to create an audience as well as spread its content into a variety of media, and moves, once again, from the media into the political sphere.

In June 2006, the cast of *24* was invited to appear at an event sponsored by the right-wing Heritage Foundation. Attendees included Michael Chertoff, head of Homeland Security, Supreme Court Justice Clarence Thomas, and Rush Limbaugh. It was entitled " '24' and America's Image in Fighting Terrorism: Fact, Fiction or Does It Matter?"—perhaps one of the more stunning examples of how the very people who govern us cannot extricate themselves from the media imaginary, and how we can never extricate the media from the political.[22]

NOTES

1. Paul Young, "The Negative Reinvention of Cinema: Late Hollywood in the Early Digital Age," *Convergence* 5 (1999): 24–50.

2. Gilbert Seldes, *The Seven Lively Arts* (New York: Harper & Brothers, 1924), 275–276.

3. Quoted by Michele Hilmes, *Radio Voices: American Broadcasting, 1922–1952* (Minneapolis: University of Minnesota Press, 1997), 47–48.

4. The best recent work on the studios, HUAC, and the blacklist is by Jon Lewis, " 'We Do Not Ask You to Condone This': How the Blacklist Saved Hollywood," *Cinema Journal* 39.2 (2000): 3–30. The standard work is Victor Navasky, *Naming Names* (New York: Viking Press, 1980).

5. Lewis, " 'We Do Not Ask You to Condone This,' " 4.

6. See James Gilbert, *Cycle of Outrage: America's Reaction to the Juvenile Delinquent in the 1950s* (New York: Oxford University Press, 1986).

7. *Comic Books and Juvenile Delinquency: Interim Report of the Committee on the Judiciary Pursuant to S. Res. 89 and S. Res. 190 (83d Cong. 1st Sess.)–(83d Cong. 2d Sess.)*, http://www.geocities.com/athens/8580/kefauver.html. *Mad* magazine publisher William M. Gaines played the comic book committee not unlike the way Bertolt Brecht played HUAC. Both understood the basic malevolent stupidity of the process. Gaines was happy to tweak the committee members with the communist card: "So the next time some joker gets up at a PTA meeting, or starts jabbering about 'the naughty comic books' at your local candy store, give him the once-over. We are not saying he is a Communist. He may be a dupe. He may not even read the *Daily Worker*. It is just that he's swallowed the Red bait—hook, line and sinker."

8. The Parents Television Council site is at www.parentstv.org. Focus on the Family is at www.family.org. The Supreme Court ruling—a very interesting document in the history of media policy—can be found at http://www.law.umkc.edu/faculty/projects/ftrials/conlaw/pacifica.html.

9. Dwight MacDonald, "Masscult & Midcult," *Against the American Grain* (New York: DaCapo Press, 1983), 6, 8, 20. An excellent survey of the place of media—film studies in particular—can be found in Jonathan Auerbach, "American Studies and Film, Blindness and Insight," *American Quarterly* 58.1 (2006): 31–50.

10. See, for example, Paul F. Lazarsfeld and Robert K. Merton, "Mass Communication, Popular Taste and Organized Social Action," in *Mass Culture: the Popular Arts in America*, ed. Bernard Rosenberg and David Manning White (Glencoe, IL: Free Press, 1957), 457–473.

11. Marshall McLuhan, *Understanding Media: The Extensions of Man* (Cambridge, MA: MIT Press, 1994).

12. See James Monaco, *The New Wave* (New York: Oxford University Press, 1976); Robert Kolker, *The Altering Eye: Contemporary International Cinema* (New York: Oxford University Press, 1983), otal.umd.edu/~rkolker/AlteringEye; Dudley Andrew, *André Bazin* (New York: Oxford University Press, 1978).

13. Andrew Sarris, "Notes on the Auteur Theory in 1962," in *Film Theory and Criticism*, 6th ed., ed. Leo Braudy and Marshall Cohen (New York: Oxford University Press, 2004), 561–564.

14. I'm playing very loosely on Deleuze's "time-image." See Gilles Deleuze, *Cinema*, 2 vols., trans. Hugh Tomlinson and Barbara Habberjam (Minneapolis: University of Minnesota Press, 1986, 1989).

15. The work of Louis Althusser was a key influence on the ideological analysis of film. See *For Marx,* trans. Ben Brewster (New York: Viking Books, 1970).

16. Key is the analysis of John Ford's *Young Mr. Lincoln* undertaken by the editors of the influential French journal *Cahiers du cinema*. It can be found in Bill Nichols, ed., *Movies and Methods*, vol. 1 (Berkeley: University of California Press, 1976), 493–529.

17. Siegfried Kracauer, *The Mass Ornament: Weimar Essays* (Cambridge, MA: Harvard University Press, 1995); Theodor Adorno, *Introduction to the Sociology of Music*, trans. E. B. Ashton (New York: Seabury Press, 1976). For an interesting study of Adorno's theories of radio, see Robert Hullot-Kentor, "Second Salvage: Prolegomenon to a Reconstruction of 'Current of Music,' " *Cultural Critique* 60 (2005): 134–169.

18. Walter Benjamin, "The Work of Art in the Age of Mechanical Reproduction," in *Illuminations*, trans. Harry Zohn (New York: Schocken Books, 1968), 232.

19. Norma Schulman, "Conditions of Their Own Making: An Intellectual History of the Centre for Contemporary Cultural Studies at the University of Birmingham," *Canadian Journal of Communications* 18 (1993). Stuart Hall's essay "Encoding/Decoding" is in *Media and Cultural Studies,* 2nd ed., eds. Meenakashi Gigi Durham and Douglas M. Kellner (Malden, MA: Blackwell Publishers, 2005), 163–173.

20. Raymond Williams, *Television: Technology and Cultural Form* (Hanover, NH: University Press of New England, 1974).

21. For example, George Landow, *Hyper/text/theory* (Baltimore: Johns Hopkins University Press, 1994).

22. Paul Farhi, "Calling on Hollywood's Terrorism 'Experts': Homeland Security Chief Compares Reality and '24,' " *Washington Post*, June 14, 2006; Maureen Dowd, "We Need Chloe!" *New York Times*, June 24, 2006.

CHAPTER 1

DIGITAL MEDIA AND THE FUTURE OF FILMIC NARRATIVE

JAY DAVID BOLTER

THE LATE AGE OF FILM

We are living in the late age of film.[1] "Late" does not necessarily mean "declining." Although no longer new or revolutionary, film remains tremendously successful in economic terms and influential in cultural terms. Film is late in the sense that it is an established medium (or series of media forms and genres) that is now being challenged by various digital media forms, especially computer games.

These digital forms do not constitute the first assault on the cultural and economic dominance of film. In the 1950s, another new medium, television, threatened to steal film's audience. In fact, although film attendance did decline for a few years, the industry not only survived that threat, but flourished in the following decades. Hollywood adopted a number of strategies to meet the challenge.[2] For example, the studios learned how to cooperate with the new medium of television by sharing plots and genres, by cross-promotion, and so on. At the same time, film adopted the new technologies of widescreen projection and color presentation, neither of which was available to broadcast television at that time. These technologies enabled film to claim that its representational practices were larger than life and at the same time more lifelike than the small, grainy, black-and-white images that the consumers could see in their living rooms. Filmmakers and the film industry were claiming that their product could still deliver an experience of greater authenticity, and ultimately greater reality, than television could.

The current challenge might eventually have the same outcome; that is, a rapprochement between film and digital media may yet be found. After all, in some cases, the same parent corporation (e.g., Sony) owns film studios (Columbia) and game companies (PlayStation), so there is an economic motivation to keep both late film and early new media profitable. Again there is crossover, as some films are made into computer games, and some games become the basis for films. At other times, however, the relationship seems to be antagonistic rather than cooperative, especially at the level of cultural reception. It is sometimes claimed that the game industry has now surpassed the film industry in economic importance, but that claim is based on a creative interpretation of the figures: it relies on comparing the box office receipts for film against the sales of games and game sets, while excluding the sale of movie DVDs and videocassettes. Nevertheless, the market for computer and video games is certainly vast and growing. These games are also gaining in cultural importance, but the influence of film remains both broader and deeper. Despite efforts to broaden the audience, the market for video games still consists largely of young adults, particularly young males.[3] Although genres of film are also marketed to individual demographic groups, the range of popular genres has something to offer to all age-groups, to most economic classes, and indeed to people of a wide variety of cultures around the world. Film remains on a par with television and the music industry in defining or mirroring cultural concerns. Thus, millions of film fans follow the intimate details of the lives of the stars, and our culture often speaks in a vocabulary drawn from successful contemporary films. Some film directors and producers, such as Steven Spielberg, James Cameron, and George Lucas, are themselves celebrities. By contrast, how many people, even among those who regularly play video games, can name a single game designer?

Film still plays a greater role than games in defining spectacle in our culture—that is, in constituting our collective sense of the real or the authentic. Film and television together define dominant models for constructing visual narrative. We might argue that they constitute our culture's principal representational style, the way in which we expect to experience space and time in and through media technologies. Any digital technology that aspires to present us with dramatic experiences (or even a new way of experiencing our physical world) must address the models offered by film and television. Computer and video game designers must (and do) draw on these models, even if they aspire to modify or surpass them.

REMEDIATION

My colleague Richard Grusin and I have attempted to describe the tension that exists between traditional media and newly introduced media as a relationship of "remediation."[4] Remediation is our name for the strategy by which designers in one medium (or media form or genre) position their work in relationship to other media (media forms, genres). This strategy is always characterized by some combination of homage and rivalry, as designers borrow the representational practices of another medium while at the same time insisting that those practices are inadequate or incomplete. Designers make an implicit and sometimes explicit claim that their new medium can capture the authentic or the real more effectively than the other medium can. Remediation can work in either direction: a new medium can borrow from an older one, or an older medium from a newer one. In a complex media economy such as ours, all the various media are busy borrowing from and refashioning one another.

It is clear that computer and video games are working to remediate film. The most straightforward kind of remediation is what Hollywood calls "repurposing"—transferring the characters and story line from a movie to a game, as has been done, for example, with *The Lord of the Rings* (Peter Jackson, 2001, 2002, 2003), *Harry Potter* (Chris Columbus, 2001, 2002; Alfonso Cuarón, 2004; Mike Newell, 2005; David Yates, 2007), and James Bond films. More significant is the borrowing of filmic techniques, such as the camera work and continuity editing that make up the Hollywood style. These techniques are most obvious in the so-called cut scenes in video games, in which the player cedes control to the system, which plays a short linear scene to advance the action or provide information that the player may need when he or she resumes control. Even when play resumes (and the camera is no longer fully under the system's control), some cinematic elements remain. Plot and characterization are borrowed from related film genres, and non-diegetic music provides continuity and momentum to the play action. Even extremely violent games such as the *Grand Theft Auto* series make considerable use of cinematic conventions. In *Grand Theft Auto: San Andreas*, for example, the game's goals are divided into missions, each of which is introduced with a cut scene. After the cut scene, the mission proceeds under the player's control, but if the player plays his or her role as expected, the mission will have the shape of an extended sequence in an action-adventure film. One reason for this borrowing of cinematic conventions is that decades of filmgoing have rendered these conventions natural for our culture: we have accepted this as the way to view the unfolding of a visual narrative. The typical filmgoer does not think about the 180-degree rule or eye-line matching; these practices have become transparent. Game designers use some (though by no means all) filmic conventions when they want to appropriate the sense of transparency and authenticity that film still conveys. At the same time, filmic narrative remains a model for dramatic treatment. Games that consciously remediate film and television offer the user (most often a teenage boy or young man) the opportunity to insert himself into a filmic world—with this "improvement": that the user becomes an active participant rather than a viewer whose gaze is manipulated by the director. Interactivity is put forth as the feature that games (and computer-mediated experiences in general) add to the grounding reality of filmic representation. When Janet Murray claims that games will be the film of the twenty-first century, what she means is that gamelike digital dramas will take over the cultural status that film enjoyed in the preceding century, because digital technology can add the dimension of interactivity to the repertoire of representational practices that popular film has already established.[5]

How does film respond to the challenge of digital media? Part of film's response is to work its own remediation, that is, to borrow and refashion the representational practices developed for and by digital media. In some cases filmmakers repurpose the characters and backstories of successful video games, such as *Mortal Kombat*, *Tomb Raider*, and *Resident Evil*. The film *Resident Evil: Apocalypse* (Alexander Witt, 2004), for example, is notable in the way it attempts to emulate the structure of the game. The film is even more episodic than most action-adventure movies; it is divided into action segments, in each of which the heroine has a goal, exactly like the missions or levels of a video game. As the heroine fulfills one mission, she learns of another that propels the action forward.

In general, mainstream film's most important remediation of digital media lies in its appropriation of visual effects. Computer graphics special effects have been a key element of Hollywood film for more than two decades. In most cases, however, the computer-generated effects are absorbed into the film's dominant, transparent style, in the sense that compositing is used to make the effects invisible to the viewer. For example, in *Titanic* (James Cameron, 1997), computer graphics are combined with models to make the sinking of the ship as "realistic" as possible, where realism is defined as the visual experience that would be produced if the sinking of a physical ship were filmed in live action. Sometimes the computer graphics are foregrounded, but still offered as natural. For example, in the *Jurassic Park* films, the dinosaurs, again combinations of animatronics and computer-graphic images, are meant to be as realistic as possible. The viewer of course knows that there are no velociraptors still alive on the planet, but the goal is to convince the viewer that if someone were to clone a velociraptor, this is how it would look. Although computer graphics are usually deployed in this "as if" mode—as a replacement for live-action filming—some filmmakers strive for other effects. In *The Matrix* (Andy Wachowski and Larry Wachowski, 1999), computer graphics are naturalized in another way: the violations of natural effects (such as the "bullet-time" shots and 360-degree tracks around arrested three-dimensional [3-D] figures) are justified by the fact that the characters themselves are living in a computer simulation of the world. The 360-degree effect—so popular that it has managed to become a cinematic cliché in the space of a few years—is a good illustration of stylistic remediation. Tracking the "camera" around the 3-D model is a technique known to computer graphics experts since the 1970s. (3-D-graphics specialists have themselves appropriated some of the vocabulary of film, most noticeably the term "camera" for the point to which the 3-D projections converge.) The track reinforces the corporeality of the model. In general, in interactive graphics programs, the user is allowed to explore and define the space by moving the camera (the technique that has become indispensable to the first-person-shooter video game). Now, 360-degree tracks were sometimes used in traditional (precomputer) film, for example, the famous tracking shot around James Stewart and Kim Novak in *Vertigo* (Alfred Hitchcock, 1958). But the tracking shot in *The Matrix* does not seem to refer to cinematic antecedents; instead, a young contemporary viewer is more likely to think in terms of video or computer games. Whereas film's method of defining space has always been under the control of the editor and director, computer games redefine cinematic space by requiring the player to take control of the camera and move in and through the space him- or herself. Thus, the camera movement in *The Matrix* recalls for contemporary viewers the kind of control of space that they would have in a game; it becomes a filmic attempt to remediate the interactivity of the game and the feeling of immersion that games are supposed to produce in the player. The film industry has experimented with various forms of immersive viewing beginning in the 1950s and continuing with IMAX today. IMAX has been more successful than earlier technologies but does not seem likely to replace the established widescreen formats. In any case, IMAX does not threaten mainstream filmmakers' concept of filmic space as long as the camera and therefore the audience's point of view remain under the filmmaker's control.

Despite their willingness to adapt some of the representational practices of new digital media, mainstream filmmakers and their production companies have been conservative when it comes to what they regard as the defining practices of camera work, continuity editing, and the temporal flow of the visual narrative. Through these techniques, the filmmaker asserts control of the space and the time of the viewer's reception, and this control is felt to constitute the authenticity of filmic representation. The avant-garde may continue to explore methods that refuse to take responsibility for the viewer's gaze, for example, by ignoring conventions of continuity editing or by refusing to move the camera at all, by looping film to disrupt the sense of flowing time, or by placing film in the context of an installation where it cannot command the undivided attention of the viewer. But such practices are exactly what pin the label of "avant-garde" on such filmmakers. Popular film still stakes its claim to authenticity on the traditional representational style.

Remediation is a process of rivalry between two or among several media forms. In this case, digital new media pay homage to film by treating filmic techniques and genres as the bases for their remediations, but these new media also claim to surpass film in the capacity to provide the viewer or user with an authentic experience.

New media theorists and practitioners often insist that the distinguishing feature of their new medium is the capacity to give the user a sense of agency, the ability to affect the represented world into which the user enters.[6] Mainstream filmmakers continue to insist that the essence of the filmic experience is the unfolding of a visual narrative under the control of the director and editor. The tension between mainstream film and mainstream digital media such as games comes from the fact that the filmmaker and digital designer are looking at the same problem from quite different perspectives. The digital designer wants to figure out how to introduce the experience of storytelling into the design without sacrificing the user's interactivity. Because this is the late age of film, the filmmaker's task is one of opposition: how to defend against the challenge that new media pose—how to borrow elements of digital compositing and graphics while at the same time defending the integrity of the film as a linear experience against the "threat" of interactivity. The questions are, Can filmic narrative ever be successfully combined with an interactive role for the user? And if so, Would that combination still be recognized as film? Although Hollywood acts as if these questions have already been answered (and the answer is no), in fact the contestation between new and old media continues. The possible interplay among the viewer or user, the narrative, and the visual space of representation will define the future of cinema as well as some of the most popular genres of computer games and other possible digital forms.

FILM AND THE DESIRE FOR
TRANSPARENT IMMEDIACY

What we might still characterize as the standard history of film envisions two defining moments, or what Gaudreault and Marion have called the "two births" of film.[7] The first came with the Lumière brothers' *actualités* (filming of everyday events), which made the implicit claim that this new medium could provide the viewer with an authentic and immediate experience of the physical world. From the outset, film could plausibly claim to fulfill the promise of a transparent medium even better than photography because of its capacity to represent the passage of time. William Uricchio has argued that the desire for a transparent medium of presence manifested itself in the late nineteenth and early twentieth centuries in fantasies for a prototelevision technology that would allow a viewer to experience a distant event or, better, a distant person as if present[8] (see Chapter 9). Because there was always a gap between the time of filming and the time of viewing, film could not really satisfy a desire for temporal presence—let alone copresent communication between two people. Nevertheless, film could offer the plausible illusion of erasing the spatial and temporal gap between recording and presentation. Such is the standard interpretation of the audience's reaction to *The Arrival of the Train at La Ciotat*: that this experience seemed "immersive," in the sense that the viewers felt themselves to be in the same space as the filmed image.[9]

The second, more protracted "moment" of birth for cinema was the development of narrative film over a period of years in the early twentieth century. This development can also be understood as an attempt to give the viewer the feeling of immediacy or presence through the power of storytelling. The idea was that the viewer would find the story compelling and would be absorbed by it, forgetting his or her physical surroundings and circumstances. To feel immersed in the story, however, the viewer had to accept the conventions of filmic narrative as natural. Some of the conventions—the narrative arc and patterns of characterization—were adapted from nineteenth-century melodrama and the novel. These conventions developed into the formulas of the various Hollywood genres (the musical, the comedy, the detective film, and so on) and became so stylized that they could be accurately described in how-to manuals addressed to would-be screenwriters.[10] The audience also had to learn to accept certain visual conventions realized through techniques of camera work and continuity editing, which developed in the period from 1900 to 1920. These techniques, which defined mainstream cinema and marginalized other possible representational styles, allowed film to lay claim to a sense of immediacy and therefore presence. To achieve presence, filmmakers chose the same route that novelists and dramatists had traveled for centuries. That is, we could say film retracted its original promise of showing viewers the quotidian, what had "really" happened in a particular place and time, and offered them instead an admittedly staged narrative, whose reality was heightened rather than diminished by the fiction and the filming conventions. It catered to the viewer's desire to give the quotidian the shape and meaning of an authored narrative—to a tacit assumption that our lives are or should be coherent stories. Of course this is an oversimplification of film history, because filmmakers never reneged entirely on the original promise. Documentary became an established genre. Furthermore, because narrative is in the eye of the beholder, even the Lumière *actualités* could be regarded as having an element of narrative: a train arrives at the station; workers leave a factory after a day's labor; and so on. Nevertheless, audiences perceived a great difference, a watershed with the advent of sustained "authored" narratives, and filmmakers such as D.W. Griffith were quite insistent that they were offering a new kind of cinematic experience in telling grand historical or contemporary stories.

Although film failed to satisfy the desire for copresence expressed in fantasies of prototelevision, it succeeded spectacularly in defining a filmic version of storytelling that large popular audiences experienced as presence. It is not surprising that film has become one of the two key models (along with television as it was deployed in the second half of the twentieth century) that interactive fiction and games designers and new media theorists refer to as they hope to achieve presence in a new medium. Designers refer to film because filmic narrative remains irrevocably connected in the popular imagination to the promise of transparent representation. This connection works both ways. Any stylistic choices by the filmmaker that threaten transparency also threaten to get in the way of the narrative and therefore make it less emotionally compelling. Furthermore, departures from plausible narrative will also eventually affect the illusion of transparency. For example, although the film *Three Kings* (David O. Russell, 1999) contains some MTV-like music interludes in what is generally a transparent representational style, these moments are probably not enough to break the illusion of what is essentially presented as a realistic and historically grounded story. (Because this is a film that wants to make a serious political point about American policy in the Persian Gulf War, it must make a claim to a historical foundation for its narrative.) On the other hand, similar but more thoroughly applied techniques in *Natural Born Killers* (Oliver Stone, 1994) move the film out of the realistic mode of representation. Breaks in continuity editing and camera work are ultimately probably more dangerous than breaks in the plausibility of the narrative or in realistic acting styles. If the filmmaker experiments with story line and characterization but maintains a conventional film style, then at worst the film is judged as a muddled or ineffective narrative, which has violated the expectations of its genre. Experiments with film style, however, can quickly transport the film out of the mainstream altogether into the category of the avant-garde. In general, as noted above, avant-garde film is marked by the opposite representational strategy, which we call "reflexivity," because the viewer is encouraged to reflect on the process of representation, the technical and cultural conditions that surround the making of the film.

DIGITAL MEDIA AND TRANSPARENT REPRESENTATION

The history of film has therefore suggested two strategies for the pursuit of transparent representation, both of which are now being reflected in genres or forms of digital media. The first is perceptual immersion, creating a visual (and auditory) space that is meant to surround the user and replace the physical world. This strategy in digital media corresponds to the everyday films of the Lumière brothers and others. Although these early films may have seemed miraculous at the time, the strategy of immersion depends on continued technological innovation to achieve more lifelike representations. For film, the introduction of sound was an obvious milestone, as were various color technologies. Mainstream film went through periods, however, when the technology remained fairly stable. The pursuit of new technologies of transparency was taken up again in the second half of the twentieth century, including not only the general adoption of widescreen and color formats in the 1950s but also, obviously, the brief 3-D craze of the early 1950s as well as Cinerama and IMAX.

In digital media, the desire for perceptual immersion finds its purest expression in the technology of virtual reality (VR). The success of VR technology is measured by the degree to which it can engender in the user the sense of presence, which happens to be the name of a computer science journal devoted to studying the effects of VR. In his key essays, "The Ontology of the Photographic Image" and "The Myth of Total Cinema," André Bazin established the criterion of fidelity to the temporal-spatial given as the technological basis for cinema.[11] Although VR specialists are unlikely to have read Bazin, they are in fact conceiving of their technology in much the same way. The legendary effect of the original showing of *La Ciotat* in 1895 (Méliès), when the audience apparently felt the need to get out of the way of the train on the screen, would be counted as the greatest success in VR. In fact, similar experiments (to see whether the user would react involuntarily to a virtual object that appears to be coming at him or her) have actually been proposed as a possible physiological measure of presence in VR.[12]

I have argued that film's second strategy for achieving transparency is through compelling narrative. Some digital media producers and artists have sought to emulate this strategy in film; that is, they have tried to adapt narrative or dramatic forms for presentation in digital media, usually on a computer screen (rather than in VR). But here the situation is complicated by the fact that the digital media designers do not look solely to filmic narrative for their remediations. In fact, attempts at digital story-based experiences have proceeded along at least two rather separate tracks, one drawn from literature and the other from film (and to some extent television).

From the late 1980s on, a relatively small number of authors have been creating literary works in hypertext systems for presentation on the computer screen. The reader of a hypertext sits at the computer and moves from one textual unit (paragraph, page) to another by following links, that is, by clicking on words in the text or typing short responses. The first literary hypertexts were almost exclusively verbal and were produced by creative writers, such as Michael Joyce and Stuart Moulthrop, who belonged to the tradition of literature rather than film.[13] A second generation of hypertexts combined static images, animation, video, and audio with verbal text and are sometimes called "hypermedia" rather than "hypertext." But even these hypermedia experiments, like the purely verbal hypertexts before them, principally remediate various forms of literary production in print: the printed novel, the short story, concrete poetry, perhaps the graphic novel, and so on. A movement toward kinetic or electronic poetry emerged in the second half of the 1990s and has continued into the 2000s (for example, the digital pieces of John

Cayley and Talan Memmott). All of these works have generally been regarded (rightly or wrongly) as expressions of a literary avant-garde, and they continue to command a relatively small audience of enthusiastic readers.

The digital remediations of visual narrative (film and television) also include what might be regarded as avant-garde forms: digital installation art featured at such festivals as Ars Electronica and ISEA. But it is video and computer games, hugely popular and economically important, that are defining the nature of visual story-based experiences in digital formats. Some game theorists deny that narrative is an important feature of games, and they are right that many computer and some video games do not meet the minimum requirements of a traditional narrative.[14] Others insist that current games constitute (or are the forerunners of) a new genre of narrative experiences.[15] Without making fine narratological distinctions, we can at least distinguish between narratives proper (acts of storytelling) and what are sometimes called "story-based" experiences. Although games are not narratives in the strict sense (because they do not generally have an explicit narrator or implicit narrative voice), it is clear that many of the most popular genres, including action-adventure and role-playing games, have backstories that motivate the action.

These genres of games are story based, although not narrative in the strict sense, because of an inherent conflict between narrative and the quality of "interactivity." The play of such games requires the moment-to-moment involvement and interaction of the user or player. Typically the user or player can visit a variety of places, control where he or she is looking, and choose from a variety of actions. This freedom of movement and action puts games at odds with their filmic models. In a film, the director or editor controls the viewer's gaze and attention: this control is what constitutes filmic narrative analogous to literary narrative. This kind of control is antithetical to the game, except in the so-called cut scenes mentioned earlier. The cut scenes are authorial precisely because the viewer's gaze is directed as in traditional film. There was an analogous conflict between narrative and interactivity in hypertextual literature. If the reader could choose to follow one link or another, then the author had to accept the loss of a degree of control over the temporal flow and perhaps the direction of the story. If narrative is the act of telling a story in a particular sequence and from a particular point of view, then it is important to ask whether there is such a thing as "interactive narrative."

It was probably inevitable that digital media enthusiasts would adopt interactivity as their principle of remediation, that is, as the "essential" quality that distinguishes digital media from film, television, and the printed book as cultural competitors. Since the work of Engelbart and Kay in the 1960s and 1970s,[16] the term "interactivity" has acquired a particular meaning in defining the relationship of the user to the software and hardware. The creation of the graphical user interface (GUI) was the key software technology that led to the development of the personal computer as a new medium of representation, and the GUI is based on the feedback principle, in which the software circles endlessly in an "event" loop waiting for the user to initiate an action to which it can respond. By directly manipulating the icons on the computer screen, the user comes to understand "interaction" in this sense as the essence of his or her experience with the computer as a medium.

Nevertheless, new media theorists' commitment to interactivity leaves them with a problem, because neither computer games nor more experimental media forms (such as interactive television and digital art) have been any more successful than earlier hypertext in reconciling interactivity and narrative. They hope that the user, reader, or viewer will be able to achieve presence by his or her participation in the story: the story becomes the user's world and is immediately present to the user. Presence would come through the engaging (human) qualities of the story itself, even without the illusionary technology of VR or 3-D graphics; in other words, it would be the same kind of presence that is ascribed to certain literary works and genres of the nineteenth and twentieth centuries. Some new media theorists speak of "storyworlds," connecting their aspirations directly to popular authors such as Tolkien or indirectly to literary fabulists such as Balzac or Faulkner. In addition to novels, of course, there have been a number of filmic storyworlds, usually adapted from novels and serving as the basis of a film series: the two recent great successes have been *The Lord of the Rings* and the *Harry Potter* series. But the term "storyworld" really only foregrounds the tension between the randomness of the lived world and coherence of a story as sanctioned by an authorial presence. The difference between a story and a narrative is after all the implied presence of the author. New media theorists will say that the "author" of a storyworld is the designer who puts the world together and gives its "rules." This author would be immanent in his or her world—a concept whose theological counterpart (that God is present in his or her world through his or her design) convinces no one except creationists these days.

Narrative film provided one solution to the problem of reconciling the story and the world, or rather an ongoing series of solutions through various techniques of editing and control. Literary narrative has likewise "solved" the problem many times since the rise of the novel. Although interactive narrative enthusiasts want to solve it again, they are caught in a dilemma. Their principal models are film (and to a lesser extent stage drama and the novel), but they are compelled to reject any of the solutions that these models offer. They want to reinstate the authorial voice—or the authorially sanctioned gaze—but they must also insist on the ability of the user to assert control over the action. They long for the transparent immediacy of film, and yet giving the user control over the action threatens to cast the user in the role of author, who must reflect on the structure of the action. If the user pauses to reflect (on his or her role of influencing or determining the story line), then the experience of transparency is jeopardized or lost altogether.

AURA

We can better understand the tension between narrative and interactivity by examining it from another (and very familiar) critical perspective—by evoking Walter Benjamin's concept of aura. In one sense, introducing aura into a discussion of the cultural work of film and digital media needs little justification. Aura is one of the most influential concepts that emerged from film criticism in the twentieth century, and it seems natural to ask what happens to aura in digital media that remediate film. In another sense, such a move adds complexity by introducing Benjamin's difficult dichotomy (auratic and non-auratic) into an argument already plagued by dichotomies (narrative/non-narrative, authorial/interactive). We will focus on the key–if enigmatic–characterization of aura in "The Work of Art in the Age of Mechanical Reproduction" as "a sense of distance no matter how near."[17]

Benjamin offered a specific technical argument to show how film diminishes aura by erasing the distance between the object of representation and the viewer. For Benjamin, the fundamental practice of editing works against the establishment of aura for film characters. The authorial camera makes what would otherwise be distant available to the viewer. As the camera penetrates the space of the action, the viewer can see around and ultimately through the film actors; Benjamin explicitly compares the camera to a scalpel as well as an X-ray machine. The viewer occupies the same space as the actors. Film actors lose the aura that still belongs to stage actors, who at least in a traditional theater are separated from the audience. Film engenders a crisis of aura by its very qualities as a technology of reproduction. We could argue, however, that there is an important limit to the film camera's capacity to destroy aura. The camera remains under authorial control, that is, under the control of the director and editor rather than the viewer. The penetrating gaze of the camera reasserts aura in the very act of diminishing it. The camera that dissects the actor and the space of the action does so at the behest of an authorial "presence," which remains distant, however near.

In other ways, too, the narrative character of Hollywood film works to reestablish aura. If control of the gaze through the work of the camera and editing is film's peculiar element of authorial control, the dialogue, action, and mise-en-scène all belong to the authorial tradition that film derives from stage drama. If the camera work is evidence of an authored gaze, the dramatic arc of the film, its wholeness as a story, is implicit evidence of an authorial voice. The playing out of the story is meant to capture the real, the authentic, as validated by the author (who is obviously other than the viewer him- or herself). For this reason, non-narrative cinema should have an easier time destroying aura. Although Benjamin appealed to the films of Chaplin as examples of non-auratic cinema, he would perhaps have been able to make a better case for Leger, Man Ray, or Buñuel. Avant-garde film is more determinedly non-auratic, especially when it undermines the coherence of the visual space as well as the story line of mainstream film. Although Benjamin argued that film would ultimately destroy the aura of art in the twentieth century, taken together, the narrative and associative, popular and avant-garde, film traditions have succeeded only in achieving a condition of crisis, in which aura is both negated and reaffirmed.

We can also see the crisis of aura extending to computer games and the hoped-for interactive narratives. Under the influence of film, though perhaps not intentionally, new media theorists and designers have reinscribed the crisis of aura in their pursuit of a media form that would be at the same time interactive and narrative. On the one hand, they want the user to enter a (graphically realized) storyworld, in which every place may be visited, and everything becomes available for manipulation. The player experiences virtual presence by taking control of the camera or rather becoming a camera that can explore and even change the world. In Benjamin's terms, the subject position of the player as "interactor" should diminish aura. In fact, by allowing the user to imagine direct intervention into the very fabric of the storyworld, the aura of proximity and presence is created.

On the other hand, the new media enthusiasts also want the player to experience a narrative—not just a mimetic world, but a coherent and organic line. The storyworlds they have in mind must make narrative sense. Such worlds are "authored," and the pleasure that the user experiences comes from interacting with the contours, the traces of that authority. To feel the controlling presence of an author is to experience what is distant, no matter how near. The very term "storyworld" embodies the tension between interactivity and authorship, because, insofar as a digital form becomes a world, it must lose a key quality of story (at least for a literate culture such as ours). As a digital experience increases the user's sense of presence, it must lose authorial presence.

CINEMA, DIGITAL MEDIA, AND THE CRISIS OF AURA

Digital narrative forms can never "solve" the crisis of aura that photography and film introduced. Even if the technical difficulties were removed, interactive games or dramas could not resolve the tension between interactivity and authority in favor of either an auratic or a non-auratic form that would meet all our culture's needs for visual representation. Instead, new media forms revive the crisis in new ways. There is no evidence, however, that our media culture needs or wants a resolution of the crisis of aura. Various popular media forms of film and television are quite successful at playing with the disappearance and reappearance of aura. Many of the most popular Hollywood blockbusters (e.g., the *Harry Potter* series, *The Lord of the Rings* trilogy) still offer eager audiences an aesthetic of transparency and authorial presence: they are high auratic. At the same time, some popular animated films—*Shrek* (Andrew Adamson, 2001), *Shrek 2* (Adamson, 2004), *The Incredibles* (Brad Bird, 2004)—combine 3-D graphics and filmic "camera work" with self-referential humor, quotation, and parody of film conventions in a style that must diminish aura. Music videos in general exploit film techniques that would once have been considered avant-garde and therefore non-auratic, and yet MTV remains extremely popular. Meanwhile, digital installation artists continue to experiment with the moving image in a variety of media forms in a way calculated to destroy aura. Instead of disappearing altogether, aura has now become a design parameter. Some genres generally aim for transparency and aura; others do not. Individual producers, designers, and filmmakers often feel free to adopt styles that are more or less auratic.

The heterogeneity of our current media culture should make us wary of predicting the future of either cinema or new digital forms. Nothing in the current situation, however, suggests that our culture wants to do away with traditional filmic or televisual forms in favor of one all-encompassing interactive digital medium. Instead, we seem to be adding more forms without eliminating the older ones, creating a broader spectrum for popular consumption. It does seem likely that all the various forms—linear and interactive, narrative and non-narrative—will eventually (perhaps soon) be stored and presented digitally. The desire for transparent representation and for auratic narrative remains strong, as is shown both by the continued popularity of traditional Hollywood films and by the attempt on the part of some new media specialists to reconcile narrative with interactivity. At the same time the popular interest in hybrid forms has probably never been greater.

The DVD is now emerging as a hybrid form that illustrates the variety of film's encounter with digital technology. At its core, the Hollywood DVD still offers the viewer a canonical version of the film in linear order; that is, what the viewer gets by pressing the play button on the remote control. But most DVDs also allow the viewer to intervene in the canonical order by choosing to begin at a particular scene, or by skipping ahead or back. Many DVDs include special features such as alternate endings, deleted scenes, directors' commentaries, and so on. These extra elements cluster around the sanctioned presentation of the film and enable the viewer to appropriate a limited degree of authority. Some DVDs go further, for example, the DVD for *Memento* (Christopher Nolan, 2000), a film that played with order and authorial control even in its theatrical version. The *Memento* DVD positions the viewer in an active role, almost like that of a game player; there is even a "cheat" (special code) that allows the viewer to reverse the order of the scenes in the film, which in fact restores them to chronological order. Currently there is a kind of ad hoc negotiation between the filmmakers and the viewer for control, and this negotiation captures perfectly the crisis of aura in which film and digital media are both implicated. The aura that was generated by the traditional narrative arc of melodrama is definitely threatened. The DVD may in fact become a key site at which film and digital media (especially digital games) test culturally satisfying constructions of tension between interactivity and narrative.

At the moment the DVD is still seen as a medium for presenting film, but it is worth considering whether the DVD may eventually develop into one or a series of forms that are no longer recognized as cinema. Richard Grusin argued that in an era of digital technology, film can no longer be regarded as a single, organic medium. Films such as the *Matrix* trilogy are no longer "complete" in their theatrical release; instead, they extend and complete themselves through Web sites and DVD releases of additional material and forms—in this case, for example, the Animatrix series that elaborates on the narrative provided by the live-action *Matrix* films. Grusin called this new hybrid condition the "cinema of interactions."[18] His phrase still suggests the primacy of cinema, but it is an open question whether our culture will continue to regard cinema as the appropriate name for this distributed network of digital media forms.

NOTES

I wish to thank Robert Kolker for his valuable suggestions and revisions. The argument offered here regarding late cinema as a remediation of digital technology is presented in a different form in Jay David Bolter, "Digital Technology and the Remediation of Cinema," *Intermédialités*, no. 6 (Remédier/Remediation) (2005): 13–26.

1. Paul Young, "The Negative Reinvention of Cinema: Late Hollywood in the Early Digital Age," *Convergence* 5.2 (1999): 24–50.

2. David A. Cook, *A History of Narrative Film*, 2nd ed. (New York: W.W. Norton, 1990): 478–506.

3. "Video Gaming: Chasing the Dream," *Economist*, August 6–12, 2005: 53–55.

4. Jay David Bolter and Richard Grusin, *Remediation: Understanding New Media* (Cambridge, MA: MIT Press, 1999).

5. Janet Murray, personal communication with the author, April 2005. Murray has made similar statements about the relationship of film to future game-story hybrids in a number of informal presentations. See also Janet Murray, "From Game-Story to Cyberdrama," in *First Person: New Media as Story, Performance, and Game*, ed. Noah Wardrip-Fruen and Pat Harrigan (Cambridge, MA: MIT Press, 2004): 2–11.

6. See, for example, Murray, "From Game-Story to Cyberdrama"; Janet Murray, *Hamlet on the Holodeck* (Cambridge, MA: MIT Press, 1997); Michael Mateas, "A Preliminary Poetics for Interactive Drama and Games," in *First Person: New Media as Story, Performance, and Game*, ed. Noah Wardrip-Fruen and Pat Harrigan (Cambridge, MA: MIT Press, 2004): 19–33.

7. André Gaudreault and Philippe Marion, "The Cinema as a Model for the Genealogy of Media," *Convergence*, no. 8 (2002): 12–18.

8. William Uricchio, "Phantasia and Technè at the Fin-De-Siècle," *Intermédialités*, no. 6 (2005): 27– 42.

9. For the standard interpretation of this cinematic event and his own revisionist view, see Tom Gunning, "An Aesthetic of Astonishment," in *Viewing Positions: Ways of Seeing Film*, ed. Linda Williams (New Brunswick, NJ: Rutgers University Press, 1995): 114–33.

10. For example, Syd Fields, *Screenplay: The Foundations of Screenwriting*, 3rd ed. (New York: Dell, 1994).

11. André Bazin, "The Ontology of the Photographic Image," in *Classic Essays in Photography*, ed. Alan Trachtenberg (1967; New Haven: Leete's Islands Books, 1980): 237–44; and "The Myth of Total Cinema," in *What Is Cinema?* vol. 1, ed. Hugh Gray (Berkeley: University of California Press, 1967): 17–22.

12. See T.B. Sheridan, "Musings on Telepresence and Virtual Presence," *Presence* 1.1 (1992): 120–26 and further issues of *Presence*.

13. See Michael Joyce, *Afternoon: A Story* (1987; Watertown, MA: Eastgate Press, 1990); and Stuart Moulthrop, *Victory Garden* (Watertown, MA.: Eastgate Press, 1991).

14. Markku Eskelinnen, "Towards Computer Games Studies," in *First Person: New Media as Story, Performance, and Game*, ed. Noah Wardrip-Fruen and Pat Harrigan (Cambridge, MA: MIT Press, 2004): 36– 44; also Espen Aarseth, "Genre Trouble: Narrativism and the Art of Simulation," in *First Person: New Media as Story, Performance, and Game*, ed. Noah Wardrip-Fruen and Pat Harrigan (Cambridge, MA: MIT Press, 2004): 45–55.

15. Murray, "From Game-Story to Cyberdrama"; also Henry Jenkins, "Game Design as Narrative Architecture," in *First Person: New Media as Story, Performance, and Game*, ed. Noah Wardrip-Fruen and Pat Harrigan (Cambridge, MA: MIT Press, 2004): 118–30.

16. For the work of these pioneers of the graphical user interface, see Michael Hiltzik, *Dealers of Lightning: Xerox Parc and the Dawn of the Computer Age* (New York: Harperbusiness, 1999).

17. Walter Benjamin, "The Work of Art in the Age of Mechanical Reproduction," in *Illuminations*, trans. Harry Zohn (New York: Schocken Books, 1968): 217–51. For a discussion of Benjamin and new media, see Jay David Bolter, Blair MacIntyre, Maribeth Gandy, and Petra Schweitzer, "New Media and the Permanent Crisis of Aura," *Convergence* 12.1 (2006): 21–39.

18. Richard Grusin. "DVDs, Video Games and the Cinema of Interactions," *Multimedia Histories: From the Magic Lantern to the Internet,* ed. James Lyons and John Plunkett (Exeter: University of Exeter Press, 2007): 222–234.

BIBLIOGRAPHY

Aarseth, Espen. "Genre Trouble: Narrativism and the Art of Simulation." *First Person: New Media as Story, Performance, and Game*. Ed. Noah Wardrip-Fruen and Pat Harrigan. Cambridge, MA: MIT Press, 2004: 45–55.

Bazin, André. "The Myth of Total Cinema." *What Is Cinema?* Ed. Hugh Gray. Vol. 1. Berkeley: University of California Press, 1967: 17–22.

———. "The Ontology of the Photographic Image." *Classic Essays in Photography*. Ed. Alan Trachtenberg. 1967. New Haven, CT: Leete's Islands Books, 1980: 237–44.

Benjamin, Walter. "The Work of Art in the Age of Mechanical Reproduction." Trans. Harry Zohn. *Illuminations*. New York: Schocken Books, 1968: 217–51.

Bolter, Jay David. "Digital Technology and the Remediation of Cinema." *Intermédialités* 6 (Remédier/Remediation) (2005): 13–26.

Bolter, Jay David, and Richard Grusin. *Remediation: Understanding New Media*. Cambridge, MA: MIT Press, 1999.

Bolter, Jay David, Blair MacIntyre, Maribeth Gandy, and Petra Schweitzer. "New Media and the Permanent Crisis of Aura." *Convergence* 12.1 (2006): 21–39.

Cook, David A. *A History of Narrative Film*. 2nd ed. New York: W.W. Norton, 1990.

Eskelinnen, Markku. "Towards Computer Games Studies." *First Person: New Media as Story, Performance, and Game*. Ed. Noah Wardrip-Fruen and Pat Harrigan. Cambridge, MA: MIT Press, 2004: 36–44.

Fields, Syd. *Screenplay: The Foundations of Screenwriting*. 3rd ed. New York: Dell, 1994.

Gaudreault, Andre, and Philippe Marion. "The Cinema as a Model for the Genealogy of Media." *Convergence* 8 (2002): 12–18.

Grusin, Richard. "The Cinema of Interactions: DVDs, Video Games, and the Aesthetic of the Animate." *Multimedia Histories: From the Magic Lantern to the Internet*. Ed. James Lyons and John Plunkett. Exeter: University of Exeter Press, 2007.

Gunning, Tom. "An Aesthetic of Astonishment." *Viewing Positions: Ways of Seeing Film*. Ed. Linda Williams. New Brunswick, NJ: Rutgers University Press, 1995: 114–33.

Hiltzik, Michael. *Dealers of Lightning: Xerox Parc and the Dawn of the Computer Age*. New York: Harperbusiness, 1999.

Jenkins, Henry. "Game Design as Narrative Architecture." *First Person: New Media as Story, Performance, and Game*. Ed. Noah Wardrip-Fruen and Pat Harrigan. Cambridge, MA: MIT Press, 2004: 118–30.

Joyce, Michael. *Afternoon: A Story*. Computer software. 1987. Watertown, MA: Eastgate Press, 1990.

Mateas, Michael. "A Preliminary Poetics for Interactive Drama and Games." *First Person: New Media as Story, Performance, and Game*. Ed. Noah Wardrip-Fruen and Pat Harrigan. Cambridge, MA: MIT Press, 2004: 19–33.

Moulthrop, Stuart. *Victory Garden*. Computer software. Eastgate Systems, 1991.

Murray, Janet. "From Game-Story to Cyberdrama." *First Person: New Media as Story, Performance, and Game*. Ed. Noah Wardrip-Fruen and Pat Harrigan. Cambridge, MA: MIT Press, 2004: 2–11.

———. *Hamlet on the Holodeck*. Cambridge, MA: MIT Press, 1997.

Sheridan, T.B. "Musings on Telepresence and Virtual Presence." *Presence* 1.1 (1992): 120–26.

Uricchio, William. "Phantasia and Technè at the Fin-De-Siècle." *Intermédialités* 6 (Remédier/Remediation) (2005): 27–42.

"Video Gaming: Chasing the Dream." *Economist*. August 6–12, 2005: 53–55.

Young, Paul. "The Negative Reinvention of Cinema: Late Hollywood in the Early Digital Age." *Convergence* 5.2 (1999): 24–50.

CHAPTER 2

THE LATEST LAOCOÖN: MEDIUM SPECIFICITY AND THE HISTORY OF FILM THEORY

BRIAN PRICE

To write a history of film theory is practically an exercise in irony. History itself is generally regarded as the new (and so far cheerfully durable) Messiah of film and media studies, the New Jerusalem for our heathen, theoretical hearts. Having found our way toward responsible, archival projects—thick descriptions of industrial practices, ticket sales, trade agreements, and demographics—we are meant to look back at theory as a quaint, somewhat embarrassing moment.

That theory has been consigned to the dustbin of history is nowhere more in evidence than in the names now given to it. In *Post Theory: Reconstructing Film Studies*, an anthology that played no small part in the precipitous decline of film theory, David Bordwell and Noël Carroll called it "Grand Theory," as if to mock past film theorists for framing their discussions of cinema "within schemas which seek to explain very broad features of society, history, language, and psyche."[1] Bordwell went even further, linking Grand Theory to a particular moment, offering us the term "1975 Film Theory," so as to indicate theories of cinema predicated on larger, and in his view specious, concerns with subject formation.[2] It is a designation no doubt intended to date and effectively deny the relevance of Laura Mulvey's hugely influential work of film theory, "Visual Pleasure and Narrative Cinema," which was first published in *Screen* that very year and has long since remained an object of fascination and empowerment for legions of students and scholars. And of course Bordwell had already prepared us for the end of theory in his *Making Meaning: Inference and Rhetoric in the Interpretation of Cinema*, a sweeping attack on the use of continental philosophy as a heuristic device, as a semantic field employed in a top-down manner for textual explication. In this work in particular, Bordwell laid to waste legions of scholars for what he took to be their confusion of theory and criticism; for offering, to cite one example, Lacanian readings of a Hitchcock film. Carroll ratified Bordwell's contention soon thereafter, wishing further to strip said scholars of the very imprimatur of film theorist: "If indeed it could be plausibly shown that the film *Every Man for Himself and God Against All* independently discovered the Lacanian scenario of the child's entry into language, then it would be Herzog and not his exegete who would count as theorist."[3] It does not matter who got there first—Jacques Lacan, Werner Herzog, or the theorist in question. Rather, continental philosophers, Lacan included, regularly engage with art as parallel philosophical texts; the art is of interest precisely because it *is* philosophical.[4]

In its place, Bordwell and Carroll call for more modest research programs, histories of style, and more "middle-level" empirical research projects (production histories, reception studies, formalist accounts of narrative style), or piecemeal theorizing—that is, theory that resists making totalizing claims about cinema and its social and psychic functions. Rather, we are supposed to act more locally, to wonder about the relationship between point-of-view editing and feelings of empathy, or to prove that we are hardwired, cognitively, to respond to certain cinematic conventions in definite, universal ways. Carroll suggested that film theory may well have been too preoccupied with film itself. He wrote, "What is often called classical film theory not only conceptualizes the activity as Film Theory, but as *Film* Theory—that is, as committed to medium specificity in such a way that whatever counts as theorizing about film must be connected to features of the medium that are thought to be uniquely or essentially cinematic."[5] In other words, Carroll sees one of the problems of film theory as residing, however paradoxically, in its preoccupation with the material properties of film itself. One might ask: What is the point of theorizing about cinema and its effects if the medium is in no way essential to theory? Likewise, Carroll asks that we "do" theory with a lowercase *t*, as if this diminution will encourage us to think in smaller, more practical terms.[6]

Bordwell and Carroll's critiques of theory are symptomatic of a larger turn from theory in academia and in the culture at large. *Post-Theory* has had a very noticeable effect on the field of film studies. There has been a paucity of theoretical work and a subsequent rise in historical work that resists making speculative claims about the larger implications of its subject. However, the turn toward history, and away from theory, is happening across the disciplines, a turn reinforced by an unforeseen glibness in Anglo-American culture more generally. One need only consider the now notorious *New York Times* obituary for Jacques Derrida, whose headline read, "Jacques Derrida, Abstruse Theorist, Dies at 74," as if to simultaneously announce and ridicule the death of a major philosopher who, by introducing the notion of deconstruction, "savaged" Western culture.[7] And when did the *New York Times*—so long the champion of modern art and cosmopolitan culture—render difficulty a defect? One might also have noticed, less than a year before Derrida's death, an article by Emily Eakins (the *Times'* resident translator of academic culture) on a major conference at the University of Chicago in April 2003 on the future of theory, entitled "The Latest Theory Is that Theory Doesn't Matter," replete with statements against theory by figures such as Sander Gilman and Stanley Fish.[8]

Why, then, the retreat from theory? And why should we look back at film theory if we are certain that it has no future?

In his recent work, *After Theory*, Terry Eagleton provided an answer to this first question in unflinching terms. Eagleton made the no doubt unpopular observation that the decline of theory from the 1990s to the present is coincident with the rise of fundamentalism in American political life. Fundamentalism implies an inflexibility toward meaning and belief, a staunch refusal to examine texts (or a variety of phenomena) from multiple and divergent points of view. As Eagleton himself has argued, the language of fundamentalism is in this very sense antitheory. He cites the rise of fundamentalist discourse in the wake of 9/11, where words such as "patriot," "evil," "freedom-loving," and, conversely, "freedom-hating" demonstrate a general intolerance for theory—that is, for ideas about the world that depart from easy, ready-made categories. Eagleton suggests that such words are:

> well-thumbed tokens which serve in the place of thought, automated reactions which make do for the labor of analysis. Such language is not necessarily mistaken in suggesting that some events are evil, or some men are bad, or that freedom is a capacity to be prized. It is just that the force of these terms is to suggest that there is absolutely no more to be said. Discussion must at all costs remain on the level of the ready tag, the moralistic outcry, the pious rejoinder, the shopworn phrase. Theory—which means, in this context, the taxing business of trying to grasp what is actually going on—is unpatriotic.[9]

The simplicity of Eagleton's definition of theory here, as the "taxing business of trying to grasp what is going on," is only apparent. To say that "I love freedom" is to assent to an orthodoxy and thus ask no questions about what lies behind both official explanation and appearances; to refer to a body of theory as 1975 film theory is to assert that there is nothing more to be said about it, nothing more to be gained by looking again. Eagleton's hypothetical "freedom lover" is antitheory precisely because he or she believes what he or she sees, what he or she is shown. By contrast, to have a theory is to speculate at once about what we *can* and what we *cannot* see, about the relay between the two. And while that wondering is in Eagleton's terms decidedly political, it does not need to be so.

For one, scientists routinely posit theories of things that cannot be seen; that must, in fact, rely on models to account for processes that elude the naked eye, to continually adjust those models to the flux of matter. Political theory works in a very similar fashion. Consider the following example from an essay entitled "An American View," written in 1940 by the eminent formalist art critic, Clement Greenberg. There, Greenberg argued that in order to successfully defeat fascism, America, France, and Britain would need to make a choice between capitalism and democracy, theorizing that fascism was a logical extension of capitalism.[10] Hitler, he proposed, was fascism's vicious avatar, not its root. Hence, to mount an attack against Germany in the name of Hitler would be to put an end to the current manifestation of fascism (highly necessary and very concrete), but not its future development (that which remains invisible). To do that, we would have to choose democracy over capitalism on the belief that the perpetuation of capitalism leads to fascism and to future acts of tyranny in the name of commerce. Greenberg's proposition is clearly theoretical, even grand. Rather than simply respond to what he sees in a dogmatic, orthodox vein (Hitler is evil; he must be stopped), he seeks a deeper explanation for how Hitler could even come into existence. Moreover, his proposal includes observable phenomena—Hitler's actions, his socioeconomic policy—and also relies on that which is neither readily nor wholly observable, namely, the link between capitalism and fascism. However, once connected through an act of imagination, the physical traces of that connection might very well come into focus. The tension that exists for the scientist between the phenomenal and the noumenal likewise exists for the theorist of culture and politics. To be antitheory is, in this sense, to be invested in the preservation of the status quo.

The decline of theory and the subsequent rise of empiricism must be understood as coincident not only with the rise of fundamentalism in American culture, but also with the increasing alignment of academia with commerce and the logic of corporate culture. As Eagleton pointed out, the general turn from theory has been marked by a not so surprising commitment to the concrete.

> Yet while this return to the concrete was a homecoming to be welcomed, it was, like almost all of human phenomena, not entirely positive. For one thing, it was typical of a society which believed only in what it could touch, taste and sell. For another thing, many of the more *recherché* ideas of earlier days were only apparently remote from social and political life. Hermeneutics, as the art of deciphering language, taught us to be suspicious of the glaringly self-evident. Structuralism gave us insight into the hidden codes and conventions which governed social behavior, thus making the behavior appear less natural and spontaneous.[11]

Eagleton's suggestion here is at least twofold. On the one hand, he is in agreement about the necessity of dealing with the concrete, but on the other hand, he is at the same time suspicious of the explanations that rely solely upon it insofar as we might thus deny ourselves powerful explanations for very complex phenomena. Moreover, our current preoccupation with the concrete has the whiff of the marketplace about it: that which can be touched can also be sold. Consequently, to deny theory its validity simply because it strays from the concrete is to renounce our efforts not only to understand the world in more complex terms but to limit ourselves to the task of simply describing what appears, or has appeared before. Theory not only seeks to explain the nature of an object (cameras, screens, stylistic elements) but is likewise concerned with understanding the ways in which those objects function in social, economic, and political ways. To have a theory about cinema is to want to understand not only how a particular object works, but also what the larger consequences, or precedents, of that functioning might be. And as Eagleton's work so strongly suggests, to return to theory is to make a return to not only having an idea about the world, but also offering suggestions about how that world might in fact be changed.

Film theorists have long been preoccupied by both the concrete and the immaterial, by *how* an object communicates and what might lie behind, or ahead of, that process of communication. In this sense, we should understand the history of film theory as being animated by two central impulses, both of which remain linked in very different ways: medium specificity and cultural politics. It is only recently that the latter has been on the wane. However, as this survey should suggest, the disappearance of the Grand Theory, as it has been so unjustly named, is only a recent and hopefully limited phenomenon. What, then, does it mean to be concerned with both medium specificity and cultural politics?

Medium Specificity

The concept of medium specificity derives from philosophical aesthetics, first popularized by the German dramatist and critic Gotthold Ephraim Lessing in 1769 with the publication of his *Laocoon; or, the Limits of Painting and Poetry*. Named after the prescient priest from classical mythology, who warned the Trojans against accepting the large wooden horse, correctly fearing that there was more to that object than met the eye, Lessing's book explores the defining, material differences between painting and poetry. As a concept, medium specificity involves the determination of that which is essential to a particular medium. What, the medium specificity theorist asks, can film do that none of the arts can? How does painting communicate differently than poetry?

Medium specificity has been most often hitched to modernism, especially early to mid-twentieth-century painting. Art critics such as Meyer Shapiro and Clement Greenberg, for instance, embraced the turn from representational painting toward abstraction. An abstract painting that forgoes the illusion of three-dimensional representation is said to be truer to the materiality of paint on canvas. A photograph can represent the world in mimetic fullness, whereas painting, if unfettered by the techniques of mimesis, can emphasize the flat surface of the canvas. Thus, to create an abstract painting is to utilize, rather than to attempt to conceal, the two-dimensional nature of the medium itself, to delight in the sensual qualities of surface instead of the optical illusion of depth. In this sense, medium specificity not only marks an effort to determine that which is unique to the medium itself, but as such becomes a guiding critical concept for the understanding of the work as art.[12] Modernist film theorists of the 1920s were especially interested in defining the essential characteristics of cinema so as to make cinema legible, culturally and institutionally, as art. Medium specificity tends to be both descriptive and propaedeutic. In identifying the essential characteristics of the medium, the medium specificity theorist not only provides a sense of what is unique to the medium, but also offers a sense of what should be done with it.

It could be argued that medium specificity, especially in its alignment with various forms of modernist production, tends toward the achievement and celebration of pure aestheticism: an art-for-art's-sake model that eschews larger cultural concerns. However, the effort to understand the unique functioning of cinema has long been wed to larger, and quite varied, questions about the cultural politics in which those forms are either embedded or which those forms seek to evade. It is a problem of which even the earliest theorists of film were well aware. Given this, I will argue that the history of film theory, as we know it, has been animated, and to some sense united, by questions of medium specificity. I will show that the development of film theory in the classical period is predicated on precisely such questions. And as such, those questions remain central to the development of film history up to the present moment, when the notion of medium itself is beginning to recede under the totalizing force of the digital image, as both idea and object.

CLASSICAL FILM THEORY: EARLY PIONEERS

Classical film theory is generally understood to represent the period of film theory from the birth of cinema, in the final years of the nineteenth century, to the 1950s. This period falls well before theory was institutionalized in the academy and subject to scholarly procedure. The earliest traces of film theory tend, as such, to be impressionistic accounts of this strange new medium—impressions that nevertheless point toward the central issues that will preoccupy film theorists throughout the twentieth century. One such important early effort was authored by the Russian writer Maxim Gorky, who sought to characterize his impressions of the new medium after witnessing a screening of Lumière films in 1896. In so doing, Gorky sounds as if he had been transported into a world strikingly real yet recognizable only, one suspects, from the pages of science fiction—but different still:

> Yesterday I was in the kingdom of shadows. If only you knew how strange it is
> to be there. There are no sounds, no colours. There, everything—the earth,
> the trees, the people, the water, the air—is tinted in grey monotone: in a grey sky
> there are grey rays of sunlight; in grey faces, grey eyes, and the leaves of trees
> are grey like ashes. This is not life but the shadow of life and this is not move-
> ment but the soundless shadow of movement.[13]

These opening remarks may well constitute the inaugural moment for film theory. Gorky's observations constitute a list of what is unusual about cinema, about what the medium seems to do that is as yet unrecognizable in relation to other media: paintings are rarely black and white; photographs do not actually move; the world on-screen resembles our own but emits no sound or color. And while Gorky does not seek to synthesize his observations into a more coherent theory of cinema, classical film theorists would soon attempt to connect their impressions of this emergent medium to larger theories about its unique functioning.

More specifically, Gorky's early remarks on the Lumière brothers are emblematic of both classical film theory's preoccupation with medium specificity and the cultural background of cinema's early proselytizers. As a writer, Gorky was obviously concerned to see what distinguished this new medium from his own. The evocations of science fiction in his description are in this respect telling, suggestive of his own efforts to puzzle out how this medium relates to literature— to what extent it goes beyond it, to what extent it overlaps it. Over the next twenty years, a wide variety of writers such as Vladimir Mayakovsky (who would also act in some early Russian films), Russian dramatist Vsevelod Meyerhold, Italian expatriate Ricciotto Canudo, French poet Rémy de Gourmont, and American poet and painter Vachel Lindsay would tease out the difference between cinema and the related arts.[14] Having identified that which is unique to cinema, these writers sought to establish a cultural legitimacy for cinema equal to the media in which they were already established. In this sense, the early body of film theory—in its most hyperbolic mode—is remarkable for the way in which it merges questions of medium specificity with the cultural politics of art institutions, especially insofar as it is authored by those already ensconced within those institutions. In theorizing what was unique about cinema, these writers sought to upset dominant cultural attitudes about cinema and to find a place for it in a variety of cultural institutions.

To give a sense of what this meant at the time, I will look more closely at the early and extensive contribution made by Vachel Lindsay and his pioneering book of film theory, *The Art of the Moving Picture*, first published in 1915.

Lindsay opens his treatise on cinema with a declaration of his intention to raise cinema to a higher level of appreciation: He inveighs in capital letters,

> Let us take for our platform this sentence: THE MOTION PICTURE ART IS
> A GREAT HIGH ART, NOT A PROCESS OF COMMERCIAL MANUFACTURE.
> The people I hope to convince of this are (1) the great art museums of America,
> including the people who support them in any way, the people who attend
> them, the art school students in the corridors below coming on in the same
> field; (2) the departments of English, of the history of drama, of the practice of
> drama, and the history and practice of "art" in that amazingly long list of our
> colleges and universities—to be found, for instance, in the World Almanac; (3) the
> critical and literary world generally. Somewhere in this enormous field, piled
> with endowments mountain high, it should be possible to establish the theory
> and practice of the photoplay as a fine art.[15]

Here Lindsay already identifies a major stumbling block for the cultural value of cinema: a distinction between high art and low art, elite culture and mass culture. Cinema's status as a mass art would preoccupy theorists for the rest of the century. Indeed, one of the major accomplishments of contemporary film and cultural theory has been to argue against the distinction itself, seeing, to cite just one example, the ways in which the Hollywood romantic comedy shares formal and thematic concerns with the most revered literary and philosophical texts.[16] However, in 1916 Lindsay sought to bring cinema to the museum and the university; to draw on the prestige of those institutions in order to confer a loftier status on cinema, rather than negotiate the terms of cultural power and prestige altogether. And he did so in an effort to complicate cinema's relation to its (putative) origin as a product of commerce and mass production.

With this goal in mind, Lindsay adopted a strategy that would become common to classical film theory, though it lacks the kind of rigor displayed by later theorists. On the one hand, he attempted to distinguish cinema from the other arts—to prove that it was more than merely a popular, and thus debased, imitation of other media; theater, most notably. For instance, Lindsay singled out cinema's capacity for rendering action and motion, for making possible the long outdoor chase, an element that could only be hinted at in theater. He likewise considered cinema unique in its capacity to depict crowds, or as he put it, "crowd splendor," so as to indicate not only the static, pictorial quality of massness, but the vicissitudes of the crowd experience. Lindsay also understood cinema as a uniquely intimate art form, owing to its capacity to situate the spectator in intimate spaces. For instance:

> The Intimate Film has its photographic basis in the fact that any photoplay in-
> terior has a very small ground plan, and the coziest of enclosing walls. Many a

worth-while scene is acted out in a space no bigger than that which is occupied by an office boy's stool and hat. If there is a table in this room, it is often so near it is half out of the picture or perhaps it is against the front line of the triangular ground-plan. . . . We in the audience are privileged characters. Generally attending the show in bunches of two or three, we are members of the household on the screen. Sometimes we are sitting on the near side of the family board. Or we are gossiping whispering neighbors, of the shoemaker, we will say, with our noses pressed against the pane of a metaphoric window.[17]

On the other hand, Lindsay contrasted this sense of intimacy with the absent fourth wall of the stage, where we are constantly reminded of the artifice of the space before us. Cinema, he implied, gives us a seat at the table. Better still, it allows us to occupy a variety of different seats at the table. Lindsay made this distinction to suggest that cinema is not a redundant form of theater, that it in fact offers an entirely different perceptual experience. The static view of the theatergoer is outdone by the perceptual multiplicity afforded by editing. As such, we can see the larger cultural dimension of Lindsay's argument, and medium specificity more generally, as it is ultimately an effort to prove cinema worthy of the mantle of art by virtue of its uniqueness. Moreover, in thinking about how cinema creates an experience of *being there* in the image, Lindsay's medium-specific claim contains the seed of suture theory, a largely psychoanalytical strain of film theory of the early 1970s interested in how cinema sews us, as spectators, into the fictional world on-screen—about which there will be more to say later. In other words, Lindsay here spoke merely of editing as the means toward an improved view—proof of cinema's advance over the static, distanced seat of the theatergoer.

Lindsay's ideas about the unique sense of intimacy made possible by cinema also entail a more philosophical claim about the medium. He added, "The Intimate Motion Picture is the world's new medium for studying, not the great passions, such as black hate, transcendent love, devouring ambition, but rather the half-relaxed or gently restrained moods of human creatures. It gives us our idiosyncrasies."[18] Cinema, in other words, was fit to depict not the universal themes of theater but the vicissitudes of human experience, our idiosyncrasies instead of that which might constitute us as a type. In this way, Lindsay conceived of cinema as more capable of rendering subjectivity than theater—raising important questions about the unique form of realism that would occupy film theorists of the classical period. But Lindsay's early theory of film is remarkable not only for its interest in what cinema alone can do, but also in its attempt to define the ways in which cinema should be understood as an amalgamation of all the arts. It was not enough to prove that cinema could communicate in terms unique to itself; rather, having distinguished it as such, classical film theorists were inclined to show that cinema's uniqueness also lies in its ability to contain the stylistics of all of the other media simultaneously. To this end, Lindsay offered chapters such as "Painting in Motion," "Sculpture in Motion," and "Architecture in Motion." We might suggest that Lindsay offered early on the view that cinema is inherently interdisciplinary, the consequences of which were many, and remain at the forefront of the academic acceptance of cinema today. For example, to demonstrate that cinema could do what sculpture could is to begin to trouble the distinction between high and low culture. If cinema could be shown to function in precisely the same ways as sculpture, then the gatekeepers of culture in both the museum and the university would have to admit cinema as an important art form. Here we can begin to see the ways in which medium specificity and cultural politics animate early film theory. The question "What is cinema?" leads to a larger renegotiation of the cultural politics of the museum and the academy, and an attempt to expand the institution of art. While the issues of class that regularly attend such distinctions would come to the fore later on, Lindsay's impulse to elevate cinema would remain integral to even the most radical, politically conscious film theory of the 1920s.

If we leap forward for a moment, we can see how influential this argument would become in 1954, with the publication, in *Cahiers du Cinéma*, of François Truffaut's "A Certain Tendency of the French Cinema." In this famous piece, Truffaut railed against the literary tendencies of the French Tradition of Quality, a generation of filmmakers whose works consist largely of adaptations of classic French literature. Truffaut protested most strongly against this generation's belief in the notion that stylistic equivalents between literature and film could be found, and that in this way cinema would be but a vessel for the transmission of classic literature and theater. Truffaut was opposed to the notion of a faithful adaptation. True cinema—cinema as art instead of mere recording device—could be made only by what he termed "a man of the cinema," that is, an auteur, who utilized the unique properties that distinguish cinema from related art forms.[19] The notion of medium specificity comes to inform the auteurist conception of cinema, and the effort to legitimize cinema as being of equal importance as the other arts in the wave of film theory that began in the 1960s.[20] Truffaut's young colleagues at *Cahiers du Cinéma*, who would go on with him to become the leading filmmakers of the French New Wave, all began their careers writing film criticism expressly in this auteurist vein. Indeed, the writings of Jean-Luc Godard, Eric Rohmer, Claude Chabrol, and Jacques Rivette were largely undertaken in an effort to create a pantheon of film artists and thus create an institutional space for the appreciation of their own filmmaking, which was soon to follow. While auteur theory has been repeatedly dismissed and significantly revised since the 1950s, it remains the most popular and frequent model for thinking about cinema in Western culture more generally. The increasingly ubiquitous film festival is, for instance, predicated on the notion of the auteur, whether as the site for the emergence of new auteurs or as the site of the unveiling of the works of our more celebrated auteurs. The theory itself may have receded, but we are living its future.

Even by the 1910s, though, the importance of theory to the institutional establishment of cinema extended beyond the domain of artists and writers, and would also appear within the confines of the academy. Just one year after the publication of Lindsay's work, Harvard professor of psychology Hugo Munsterberg published his groundbreaking book of film theory, *The Film: A Psychological Study* (1916). Munsterberg's work is important in a number of respects. Munsterberg represents the first serious, extensive consideration of cinema within the university—the very realization of one of Lindsay's hopes. But even more important, *The Film: A Psychological Study* represents an important merger of medium specificity and psychology, of a medium and a discipline that had only a nascent cultural value, but would become, well after Munsterberg's time, the central preoccupation of film theory, one instrumental to the academic legitimation of cinema studies.

At the core of Munsterberg's work is the idea that cinema is analogous to the mind. Cinema, Munsterberg posited, is freed from the conditions of time and space. As a result, our experience of cinema is analogous to thought. That is, when watching a film, we are witnessing a series of images disconnected from time and space, much in the way that thought involves reordering scenes of our own experience in a variety of different ways, irrespective of the time and place in which those scenes of experience actually occurred. For Munsterberg, cinema explains the functioning of the mind as much as it explains the logic of cinema. Munsterberg's theory of the relation between cinema and mind, of course, is predicated on notions of medium specificity. For instance, to make the claim that cinema, like the mind, is uniquely free of the conditions of time and space, Munsterberg considers the case of theater: "But theater is bound not only by space and time. Whatever it shows is controlled by the same laws of causality which govern nature. This involves a complete continuity of the physical events: no cause without following effect, no effect without preceding cause. This whole natural course is left behind on the screen."[21]

Munsterberg's theory depends on what he takes to be the weakened role of causality in cinema, which he likewise sees as a limiting fact of theater. Theater in this respect is too caught up with reality, with a linear experience of time and place.[22] It is important to note the way in which Munsterberg carefully considers the material properties of competing media in an effort to theorize the workings of the mind. He wrote, *"The photoplay shows us a significant conflict of human actions in moving pictures which, freed from the physical forms of space, time, and causality, are adjusted to the free play of our mental experiences and which reach complete isolation from the practical world through the perfect unity of plot and pictorial appearance."*[23] Munsterberg began in the mode of medium specificity, but then extended his observations toward psychology, finally suggesting a major psychic function of cinema—that as a medium cinema is particularly well suited to workings of the mind. His theory of cinema, like Lindsay's, is in service of the legitimation of cinema as an art form (its medium-specific claims) and as subject for psychological inquiry (what cinema can tell us about the mind). In this sense,

Munsterberg foretold the two major tendencies of film theory through the twentieth century: a concern with aesthetics, and a concern with the psychic effects of cinema. By the 1960s, the inquiry into the psychological effects of cinema became the basis for larger political questions about the role of cinema in the propagation of ideology—a period of theorizing that merged aesthetics, psychology, and politics, and would emerge, like Munsterberg, from within the halls of academe.

THE FILMMAKER AS FILM THEORIST

The pioneering work of Lindsay and Munsterberg was followed in the 1920s and 1930s by a marked proliferation of film theory, which is of particular interest as filmmakers themselves wrote most of it. Not surprisingly, the emergence of the filmmaker as film theorist in this period is marked by an amplification of the concern with medium specificity. As filmmakers, they had a vested interest not only in the cultural legitimacy of cinema itself, but also in the development of film technology, especially around the introduction of sound in the late 1920s. Likewise, in the prewar period, theory was, as Francesco Casetti has argued, essentially autochthonous.[24] Filmmakers were most often inclined to theorize their practice in relation to their own national cinemas. If films from other countries were considered it was to imagine how certain techniques could either be appropriated or pointed to as something to avoid. The films of D.W. Griffith, for example, would mean both things to Soviet filmmakers of the early 1920s. They served at once as examples of how to make montage and how to expropriate those forms for a decidedly different political end. The dominant tendency of the period is not toward universal theories of the cinema, but toward theories best suited to the achievements of a distinct national cinema, and often, to the construction or reinforcement of a national polity.

Yet, despite whatever national differences might intervene, the theoretical concerns of filmmakers in the 1920s and 1930s were very similar. For instance, filmmakers–film theorists of this period remained committed to theorizing the ways in which cinema could be distinguished from the other arts. As was the case of Sergei Eisenstein, some filmmakers were even inclined to theorize cinema as the very apotheosis of art. For instance, in an essay entitled "Laocoön," Eisenstein argued that "the *principle of cinema* is not something which dropped upon mankind from the heavens, but it is something that has grown out of the depths of human culture."[25] Eisenstein saw various art forms attempting to represent motion, noticing the ways in which painters across various periods attempted to imply motion in the frame, whether by featuring identical groups in different areas of the canvas, or, like the cubists, attempting to present multiple views of an object in one canvas; cinema, as a moving image, would perfectly realize this long-standing impulse of human culture to depict movement. Motion no longer needed to be implied; cinema *is* movement. Others saw the invention of cinema as the potential perfection of painting. For instance, the French painter and filmmaker Fernand Léger saw that these two media, cinema and painting, could merge if the limitations of each medium were overcome: "The error of painting is the subject. The error of cinema is the scenario."[26] Consequently, Léger reasoned, both needed to capture fragmented, or isolated, views of an object—images of an object made unfamiliar, and subsequently freed from the respective conditions of scene and story. Cinema would thus become painting, painting cinema, and it would do so through its unique capacity not just to depict, but to instantiate movement itself. Cinema's unique capacity to produce motion would likewise become the very thing that opened cinema to philosophical discourse by the end of the twentieth century, in the work of Gilles Deleuze and Alain Badiou especially.

Film theorists of the twenties and thirties remained interested in distinguishing cinema from the other arts. However, in this period, theorists also moved closer to considerations of film itself and how it functioned; *what*, in fact, it was. Subsequently, what we see across national borders is an interest in defining the major stylistic principles of cinema so as to explain their effect and often unearth their larger philosophical and political implications. Film theory of the 1920s and 1930s, then, can be said to be preoccupied with three central components: the shot, editing, and sound.

Twenties film theory, for example, is especially bound up with the theorization of the close-up, an element widely viewed as the defining characteristic of cinema—something, for instance, denied to theater, and which painting could do only without motion.[27] The close-up meant many things to many theorists in the 1920s. However, as early as the mid-1910s, the close-up gained especial attention from a concern with notions of *photogénie*.

The idea of *photogénie* emerged in France in the 1910s in the work of the pioneering film critic and theorist Louis Delluc.[28] However, French filmmaker Jean Epstein's writing on the close-up in the 1920s represents the major theorization of *photogénie*. Epstein defined *photogénie* as "any aspect of things, beings, or souls whose moral character is enhanced by filmic reproduction. And any aspect not enhanced by filmic reproduction is not photogenic, plays no part in the art of cinema."[29] Central to the achievement of *photogénie* for Epstein is the close-up and its perceived capacity for magnification. The unique quality of cinema resides in the close-up's ability to reveal some aspect of phenomena that would remain undetected by the naked eye. It becomes a tool uniquely capable of producing knowledge about the visible world. Along these same lines, Ricciotto Canudo marveled at cinema's ability to document change at the most microscopic level:

"What it [cinema] can already show us—for example, in slow motion studies of plant growth—is an affirmation of its stupendous capacity to renew the representation of life itself, fixing the instant by instant movement of beings and things."[30] Here, the close-up makes of the camera a kind of microscope; it makes visible something that would otherwise elude the eye.

This particular principle of *photogénie* likewise animates the early film theory and practice of the Soviet filmmaker Dziga Vertov. Vertov was also interested in the revelatory capacity of cinema, especially the close-up, and cinema's capacity to control time through slow motion. Central to Vertov's theory of the Kino-Eye, or the camera eye, is the notion that the camera itself was better than the human eye, as he proclaimed in "The Council of Three": "The main thing is this: The sensory exploration of the world through film. We therefore take as the point of departure the use of the camera as a kino-eye, more perfect than the human eye, for the exploration of the chaos of visual phenomena that fills space."[31] Like Epstein and Canudo, Vertov was fascinated by the notion of magnification: the cinema as a form of improved vision; the camera as a surrogate for the eye. As Annette Michelson has shown, Vertov's interest in the revelatory potential of cinema is also informed by politics:

> For Vertov, . . . the systematic development of the specificity of cinematic processes—of slow, accelerated, and reversed motion, of split screen, and of superimposition, those disjunctions, tensions and movements specific to cinema— were indeed harnessed in the services of revelation: but that revelation was a *reading*, a communist *decoding* of the world as social text, inseparable from the identification of class structure and class interests.[32]

Nowhere is this more in evidence than in Vertov's 1924 film *Kino-Eye*, in which he performed an extended reverse-motion sequence where a bull, slaughtered in a capitalist abattoir, regains his entrails through a process of slow motion. As the bull becomes whole, it is led backward to the socialist cooperative to which it properly belongs. Not only does cinema reveal phenomena, but it can also analyze and reorder it—all by virtue of tending to that which is specific to the medium itself— the close-up and reverse motion. The example of Vertov also suggests the extent to which questions of medium specificity worked in the service of politics during this period: the utilization of that which is unique to cinema is linked to a pedagogical project, to the education of the masses on the ills of capitalism. And indeed, for many Soviet filmmakers, cinema itself was considered a new language, an instrument necessary for the education of a largely illiterate Soviet peasantry on the virtues of the newly implemented Soviet state. For Vertov and many Soviet filmmakers of the 1920s, theory was inseparable from the construction of the Soviet state.

Theories of *photogénie* are not always expressed in explicitly political terms. However, the respective theories of *photogénie* proposed by Jean Epstein and Béla Balázs respectively, closely align it with the conditions of melodrama, which has its origin in the French Revolution, and suggests the extent to which we might consider the expanded visibility of the close-up as political at the very level of its material properties. For indeed, the privileging of gesture as something that rubs up against language, whether through excess or attrition, aligns it with melodrama's retreat from reason in a postsacred universe. In particular, *photogénie* is most often understood as an experience of having a close-up of the human face, of what it could reveal about a character's consciousness that exceeds language and other media of expressivity. Epstein, for instance, would make clear the expressive potential of the face in close-up:

> The close-up is the soul of cinema. It can be brief because the value of the photogenic is measured in seconds. Intermittent paroxysms affect me the way needles do. Until now, I have never seen an entire minute of pure *photogénie*. Therefore, one must admit that the photogenic is like a spark that appears in fits and starts. It imposes a decoupage a thousand times more detailed than that of most films, even American ones. Mincemeat. Even more beautiful than a laugh is the face preparing for it. I must interrupt. I love the mouth which is about to speak and holds back, the gesture which hesitates between right and left, the recoil before the leap, and the moment before the landing, the becoming, the hesitation, the taut spring, the prelude, and even more than all these, the piano being tuned before the overture. The photogenic is conjugated in the future. It does not allow for stasis.[33]

What one senses in Epstein is a tension between the official gesture the actor is in the process of performing and the sign of the real human being evincing some degree of consciousness alongside that gesture's realization, allowing for a complex mode of performance, a counterpoint between character and actor unthinkable on the stage for all but the privileged few seated in the orchestra pit.

Epstein's contemporary in Hungary, Béla Balázs, offered an even more nuanced conception of the face in close-up in his influential *Theory of the Film*. In many respects, Balázs is the great theorist of the close-up in the classical period, concerned as he was not only with what the face can express but also with the expressivities of the body in fragments—head, hand, toe. Balázs was particularly interested in the possibilities of nonverbal signification; with the tension between language and gesture. As in Epstein, the tension between what a character is supposed to perform and what the actor's face reveals apart from dialogue intrigued him especially; indeed, he considered the face itself to be more subjective than speech. "Close-ups," he wrote, "are often dramatic revelations of what is happening beneath the surface."[34] From here, Balázs went even further than Epstein to argue that the close-up itself gives access to a "polyphonic play of features," or rather the appearance on the face of potentially contradictory expressions, a "sort of physiognomic chord of a variety of feelings."[35] Balázs's theory of the face in close-up is remarkable for the way in which it details the uniqueness and complexity of cinematic performance. And in his use of a musical metaphor—the physiognomic chord—we can likewise detect the by now familiar appeal to larger cultural discourses about what constitutes art (if it is structurally analogous to music, cinema can be an art).

But as I have already suggested, this unique feature of cinema also realizes the full potential of melodrama. Peter Brooks has argued that the limitations of the melodramatic imagination are a product of the genre's eventual appearance in novelistic form, that is, in language:

> We must recognize that gesture in the texts that concern us is being mediated by the context of articulated language, that the generalized indications of the gestural sequence exist to be translated into specific verbal articulations of the gestural project. This translation may in part be performed by other persons on stage . . . , by the context of action in which the gesture occurs (which must to some degree be true of gesture in pantomime proper), and, necessarily, by the spectator, whose interpretations are represented by those messages suggested in the stage directions. The operative code is that of articulated language, which alone provides the possibility of interpretation and hence of meaning; gesture is in fact desemanticized, it is anaphoric, in Julia Kristeva's term, in that it points *toward* meaning.[36]

Brooks ultimately suggested that the spectator's work is not one of decoding, which implies a search for equivalence between gesture and word in a language system, but one of decipherment, a process by which we follow the continual shifts and movements of gesture that would be erased by the positing of a single term (i.e., sadness, happiness, etc.). Gesture, as amplified by the close-up, is anaphoric. It is resistant to any one meaning; it is always in excess of it. It is worth noting, along such lines, that melodrama itself was born of an interdiction against dialogue, of French national policy that afforded only the classical French theater, and its aristocratic audience, the dignity of the word.[37] And as we will soon see, this generation of filmmakers, theorizing the expressive potential of the shot in terms uncannily similar to melodramatic effect, would resist mightily the implementation of the sound film and the priority that it would give to language.

While Balázs and Epstein privileged the shot for its potential for magnification, other filmmakers–film theorists in the classical period were more inclined to consider editing, or montage, as the defining characteristic of film. Nowhere do we see the theoretical preoccupation with montage registered so strongly as in the classical period than in the Soviet Union in the 1920s. Dziga Vertov's constructivist musings on montage are emblematic of the period. For instance, thinking of what the new Soviet man should be, Vertov exclaimed, "From one person I take the hands, the strongest and most dexterous; from another I take the legs, the swiftest and most shapely; from a third, the most beautiful and expressive head—and through montage I create a new perfect man."[38]

Here, Vertov is extolling the virtues of what we have come to describe as the Kuleshov effect. Lev Kuleshov was filmmaker, theorist, and teacher to a generation of Soviet filmmakers in the early 1920s. The Kuleshov effect, for which he is most famous, refers to one of Kuleshov's early experiments with the psychological effects of editing. Kuleshov theorized that our emotional response to film is the result of not the single shot, the single expressive gesture, but the juxtaposition of shots in montage. His most famous experiment involved the great actor Mozhukin. Kuleshov is said to have taken a single shot of Mozhukin's face, to which, in three separate montage constructions, he followed the face with a shot of soup, a dead body, and a baby (reports of the images used in the actual experiment vary considerably). The result of Kuleshov's experiment is that the very same shot of Mozhukin's face produced three different emotional effects for the spectators tested: hunger, sadness, elation, respectively. Consequently, Kuleshov conceived of editing as the essential characteristic of the medium. A shot, in its own terms, was seen as inert, capable of communicating no definite meaning—a notion antithetical to Balázs's and Epstein's theory of the expressive fullness of the shot. For Kuleshov, the constructive principle of montage extends outward to a larger notion of creative geography, in which Kuleshov theorized the ways in which cinema creates a unified space out of elements that are otherwise distinct in the phenomenal world.[39] In his *Art of the Cinema*, for instance, Kuleshov spoke of shooting two actors walking down a Moscow street who meet, clasp hands, and look at the White House. By including a shot of the White House, Kuleshov made his actors appear to be not in Moscow, as they actually were, but in America.[40]

Kuleshov's insights about editing as the fundamental principle of cinema were greatly expanded and revised by his protégés in the Soviet Union—Dziga Vertov, Vsevelod Pudovkin, and Sergei Eisenstein most notably. Eisenstein's voluminous writings on montage are the most well-known and the most expansive. Eisenstein broke away from Kuleshov's conception of montage, rejecting the latter's tendency to privilege continuity over dialectical tension. In "The Dramaturgy of Film Form," Eisenstein argued that his conception entailed "defining an object exclusively in terms of its own external course," by its place in a seamless, causal narrative chain.[41] Like most of his peers in the 1920s, Eisenstein was guided by the logic of dialectical materialism, as when, for instance he celebrated conflict between shots: "*In my view montage is not an idea composed of successive shots stuck together but an idea that* DERIVES *from the collision between two shots that are independent of one another.*"[42]

Thus was born Eisenstein's most enduring claim that the meaning, or an idea, of a montage sequence emerges in the mind of the spectator and does not literally appear in the image. Shot A is juxtaposed with shot B, and then yields a new concept C, which does not literally appear on-screen. As Eisenstein saw it, in privileging conflict between frames, filmmakers would be better able to adhere to the Marxist dialectic and ultimately "form the right view by stirring up contradictions in the observer's mind and through the dynamic clash of opposing passions."[43] It is important to remember that not only is Eisenstein's conception of montage based on what the medium can uniquely accomplish—the ways in which the successive presentation of two opposing images can and must be completed in the mind of the spectator—but also, it is formulated in this way in an effort to think through the political ramifications of cinema at a material level. More specifically, Eisenstein was interested less in the illusion of continuity, which brings to the fore the medium's capacity for deception, than in the ways in which the spectator's process of intellection begins with discontinuity.

Eisenstein's departure from Kuleshov's theorization of cinema's essential capabilities points at once to a problem with and a solution to the idea of medium specificity itself. First and foremost, it suggests that medium specificity is not necessarily essentialist. Having arrived at what distinguishes one medium from another, a medium-specific theory does not thus imply technological determinism, as we will see most clearly when we discuss the work of André Bazin. Eisenstein's theorization of cinema is in no way monolithic, yet it was always expressed in terms of medium specificity, even where that involved a conscious appropriation of the means of other art forms. Rather, Eisenstein's concern with the defining material properties of cinema and the possible effects generated yielded a stunningly heterogeneous body of theory.

Likewise, Eisenstein's theorization of montage as the essence of cinema is by no means limited to the canonical, and simplified, formulation described above. For instance, Eisenstein's earliest conception of montage, known as "The Montage of Attractions," was bound very closely to Pavlovian reflexology. The montage of attractions, with its combination of shots selected for their potential physical response, was intended to reeducate the Soviet viewer at a bodily level, effecting bodily imitation in the spectator.[44] Montage here is less contemplative for the spectator than the view put forward a few years later in "The Dramaturgy of Film Form." And yet Eisenstein would later expand his interest in the intellectual component of montage in his late essays on vertical montage. In vertical montage, narrative emerges in the horizontal axis of montage (and that which is depicted on-screen), while the vertical axis is composed of visual motifs accumulated and brought to order in the mind of the spectator.[45] This later essay is especially emblematic of Eisenstein's interest in understanding cinema in relation to the other arts. For, as Eisenstein saw it, vertical montage was an essentially symphonic structure. Elsewhere, Eisenstein would describe montage as architecture, the accumulation of disparate shots in montage the rough equivalent of moving through the different spaces of a well-built structure, replete as that experience should be with varied tones, colors, and spatial relations.[46] In cinema, a series of disparate spaces travel past the body at rest. In an architectural space, the body moves through the space of permanent, though dynamic, forms.

To read Eisenstein at length is to witness a mind uniquely sensitive to change. Eisenstein's life and career are marked by his effort to think through system and structure. At the beginning of his career ("The Montage of Attractions"), Eisenstein was in search of a cinema, in its most material basis, that could produce a new

Soviet subject through enforced movement and reflex response. By the end of his career, and well under the thumb of Stalin and the terrors of the purge, Eisenstein became preoccupied with notions of ecstasy, intellectual montage, and inner speech; which is to say, with models of montage that run contrary to the uniformity of Soviet socialist realism. In other words, where once Eisenstein's theory was predicated on the creation of a new Soviet subject, by the 1930s Eisenstein privileged heterogeneity. Much of this heterogeneity is owed to the political pressures Eisenstein faced in the late 1930s and early 1940s, having by then been routinely accused of being an avant-gardist, elite intellectual whose obscurity was at odds with the needs of the Soviet state. This is, of course, just one sign of the political risk of theory, if by that we mean an understanding of a practice that counters or exceeds the logic of its avowed institutional and political function. However the shifts in Eisenstein's consciousness and beliefs might be articulated, though, it is worth noting that his theoretical practice remains steeped in medium specificity, which is less a contradiction in Eisenstein's thought than it is an insight into the ways in which privileging the unique aspects of cinema as a technology does not work to set a permanent course for the use and development of that technology. And as we will see, this tension lived by Eisenstein at an intellectual and political level is one that will inform the two major tendencies of film theory in the 1960s and 1970s: the attempt to define cinema as system (whether as a language or as a series of codes and conventions) and the desire to theorize a mode of resistance to the structuring tendencies of cinema along material lines.

With the coming of sound, technology and theory become closely entwined, and often at odds. Film theory of this period is littered with the battles between modernist filmmakers declaring the perfection of the silent cinema and filmmakers (and often producers and equipment engineers) defending the supposedly realist vocation of cinema through the implementation of synchronized sound. The experience of wonder recorded early on by Gorky would be no more.

Emblematic of this battle is a debate that took place in the 1920s between the French filmmaker René Clair and the dramatist and filmmaker Marcel Pagnol. As an avant-garde filmmaker, Clair was loath to hand cinema over to dramatists such as Pagnol, whom he considered to be incapable of recognizing cinema as anything more than a recording device. Clair's objection to sound was at least twofold. Most fundamentally, Clair was concerned that the new sound film would challenge the director's status as the author of the work. Now a scriptwriter (often a recognized dramatist) would be seen as the controlling agent of production. The prestige of cinema would disappear alongside the director's reputation as author.

However, Clair's larger concern had to do with what he perceived to be the potential redundancy of sound and image. In a synchronized cinema, an image of people clapping, for instance, would now be accompanied by the sounds of people clapping. In its place, Clair suggested three alternatives for maintaining an approach to cinema in the sound era that maintained what was unique to cinema. He wrote, "I distinguish three kinds of scenes in my film [*Sous les toit de Paris*, 1930]: a purely visual scene in which sound plays the role of orchestral accompaniment; another in which the images are made comprehensible by means of [natural] sound; and a third in which speech is used to produce a special effect or else to explain the action."[47]

Clair's prescription for a nontheatrical, nonsynchronized sound cinema draws, as he acknowledged in the essay, on an idea for a contrapuntal sound film that Eisenstein, Pudovkin, and Alexandrov elaborated in the Soviet Union in 1928. In "Statement on Sound," they theorized sound as something that could perfect, rather than defeat, montage and a modernist conception of cinema more generally. Sound gave the image an inertia it did not have in the silent period; it made the image less dependent on the other images in a montage chain—thus reducing the possibility of an intellectual cinema, of thinking the relation between images.[48] Consequently, Eisenstein and his coconspirators argued, "*The first experiments in sound must aim at a sharp discord with the visual images.* Only such a 'hammer and tongs' approach will produce the necessary sensation that will result consequently in the new creation of a new *orchestral counterpoint* of sound and images."[49] Clair's formula, while less infused with the language of dialectical materialism, is nevertheless consonant with the notion of a sound-image counterpoint, especially as it not only avoids redundancy (and in Clair's practice the separation of sound from image allows him to retain a mobile camera) but also allows sound to do more than merely serve dialogue. Noise, for instance, becomes a structuring possibility (or, perhaps more accurately, working without structure becomes possible).

Marcel Pagnol, Clair's antagonist, saw sound and ultimately cinema as a way of improving theater. In "The Talkie Offers the Writer New Resources" (1930), Pagnol addressed the class aspects of the contrapuntal sound film and the resistance to synchronization. For Pagnol, cinema afforded the dramatist a more complex use of language based on mechanical reproducibility. Noting how the dramatist has to write lines that can be delivered to a thousand people, he wrote, "And that's the problem for a writer in the theater: his subject, dialogue, and rhythmic structure have to be valid for a thousand spectators, who are already different in age, education, and intelligence, and none of whom will see the work from the same angle as his neighbor!"[50]

Cinema, by virtue of its mechanical reproducibility—by its capacity to give every audience member, regardless of class, age, or intelligence, the same view and sound—not only can rectify the gap between those variables but also can offer the dramatist a more subtle palette on which to construct his performance. Moreover, for Pagnol, sound cinema promised to restore regional dialects to film and thus properly promote a regional cinema. It should be noted that Pagnol relied on questions of medium specificity, just as much as Clair did, insofar as he saw cinema merging with theater to create a new unique art form that likewise promised to break down class barriers.

Along such lines, it is also worth noting that one of the great concerns of the modernist sound theorists of this period is the way in which language differences, by virtue of synchronization, would reduce the international circulation of their work. It is a problem of which Eisenstein, Pudovkin, and Alexandrov were especially aware; they saw the contrapuntal sound film as combating: "The *contrapuntal method* of structuring a sound film not only does not weaken the *international nature of cinema* but gives to its meaning unparalleled strength and cultural heights."[51] In other words, if noise, rather than speech, became a structuring principle for cinema, then images could retain their international currency without recourse to the imperializing tendencies of language; nor, ironically, would the films be restricted to their domestic markets.

Whether one sides with Pagnol or the modernists, it is worth noting the especially close relation classical film theory maintains with issues concerning the technological developments and the global circulation of cinema. In particular, film theory of this period is deeply committed to medium specificity in an effort to stem the tide of an industrial logic of realism that was working to commit cinema, as a medium, to a course of synchronization that would render it a theatrical, realist medium. And as historians of the transition era have noted, the development of sound technology along such lines had a deleterious effect on national cinemas (especially France's) that did not develop their own sound technologies in time to avoid paying the licensing fees to companies outside its own borders (the United States and Germany especially) that did.[52] What might appear to some as an innocuous debate about aesthetics and the true vocation of cinema is instead a culture of resistance to technological developments that would alter the course of national film industries, introducing and enabling the hegemonic force of American cinema as an instrument of cultural imperialism. This relation of film theory to politics—its interventionist character—would only be exacerbated in the postwar period.

THEORY IN THE POST–WORLD WAR II ERA

Despite the impassioned pleas of the avant-garde, sound cinema commenced on its path toward synchronization in the 1930s and has, with few but notable exceptions, only expanded on the promises of figures such as Pagnol, though most often without Pagnol's concerns about the relations connecting dialogue, language, and cultural specificity. Consequently, the forward march of realism over 1920s modernist cinema and film theory was not only a technological and economic victory, but also the reigning preoccupation of film theory in the postwar period.[53] Indeed, two of the most significant film theorists of the period, André Bazin and Siegfried Kracauer, developed theories of cinematic realism in the 1940s and 1950s that not only account for cinema in an advanced state of synchronized realism, but once again based those theories on questions of medium specificity.

André Bazin's vastly influential texts on cinema and realism were largely written in France between the mid-1940s and the late 1950s—a life and career cut short by his death at the age of forty in 1957. Bazin was cofounder of *Cahiers du Cinéma* and is often understood as the patron saint of the French New Wave and auteurism (despite his reservations about the latter). Both Bazin and Kracauer developed theories of realism that originated from conceptions of photography; indeed, both viewed cinema as an extension of photography—that is, as the medium that makes good on photography's promise to represent the phenomenal world in a faithful manner—and both linked this relationship to social and political implications.

Bazin's theory of realism begins in "The Ontology of the Photographic Image," wherein he celebrates the photographic image for its indexical properties.[54] Here, Bazin celebrated cinema for the existential bond that exists between signified and signifier; the causal relationship that exists between the object and the image. He wrote, "No matter how fuzzy, distorted, or discolored, no matter how lacking in documentary value the image may be, it shares, by virtue of the very process of its becoming, the being of the model of which it is the reproduction; it *is* the model."[55] The latter half of Bazin's claim has long been a source of controversy among theorists for the ways in which its euphoric prose implies that the photographic image almost renders representation itself obsolete (i.e., not an image of a chair, but the chair *itself*). Slightly less controversial is Bazin's insistence on photography's tie to the objects of the phenomenal world: no matter how distorted the print, the image it produces proves the existence of the object depicted; if the chair did not exist, neither would the image. Upon this fundamental claim rest a number of other claims essential to Bazin's theory of photography, and thus cinema: the photographic image preserves time; it offers us a form of improved vision (the faithfully reproduced object lets us see again, scan indefinitely, fully); it is a uniquely objective medium (no hand intervenes between what appears and what is recorded); *and* it frees "the plastic arts from their obsession with likeness."[56] The last of these claims announces most clearly the medium-specific nature of Bazin's theory. Since cinema is uniquely capable of representing reality, painting can move away from attempts at approximating reality and toward abstraction and subjectivity.[57] Consequently, Bazin's essays on cinematic realism work to adapt, and prescribe, cinematic techniques that fulfill the medium's true vocation of representing reality faithfully in space and time, and in so doing, hew closely to the industrial logic of cinema's development as a synchronized, narrative medium.

Many of Bazin's essays on cinematic realism work toward developing a theory of style as an extension of the indexical nature of the cinematic image, championing especially the deep-focus, long-take practices of Orson Welles, Jean Renoir, William Wyler, and the Italian neorealists. Consequently, Bazin's work is both theory *and* stylistic history. His evolutionary history of the medium is premised on distinctions between what he would describe in "The Evolution of the Language of Cinema" as a difference between "those directors who put their faith in the image and those who put their faith in reality."[58] Here Bazin wrote of the virtues of deep-focus, long-take filmmaking (those who have faith in an image, by which he means reality) over practices that manipulate images of the phenomenal world through editing, namely those of Soviet filmmakers of the 1920s and the classical Hollywood style, both of which direct what we see through a series of interpolated close-ups. By contrast, Bazin admired realist cinema for the ways in which it not only utilizes the indexical character of the photographic image (that is, it remains true to what makes the medium unique), but also conforms to the ways in which realist cinema can, at times, also reproduce the limitations of human vision through more elliptical editing strategies that seek to reproduce the same blind spots experienced by a character on-screen.[59] Bazin's interest in reproducing the limitations of human vision would seem to contradict his previously cited claim about the expansive character of the photographic image. However, these contradictions only underline the fecundity of Bazin's thought and its resistance to dogma. Moreover, what unifies his work above all is the search for a realist cinema, in all its vicissitudes, that weds stylistic achievement with indexicality and all that that may imply for models of spectatorship that allow the spectator the autonomy to select what he or she wants to see in an image, and by extension, the world. Despite his opposition to Soviet montage, Bazin was just as concerned with the autonomy of the spectator as Eisenstein.

Siegfried Kracauer's theory of realism, offered in *Theory of Film*, has many points of contact with Bazin's work, and is expressly articulated in medium-specific terms that are themselves based on a commitment to cinema's relation to the real: "films may claim aesthetic validity if they build from their basic properties; like photographs, that is, they must record and reveal physical reality."[60] The beauty of the photograph, Kracauer suggested, is owed to its capacity to make us "perceive the world we actually live in—no mean achievement considering the power of resistance inherent in habits of seeing."[61] Like Bazin, here Kracauer attempts to account for the ways in which film style is predicated on the medium's relationship to physical reality. However, he is less beholden to indexicality, per se. As long as film resembles reality, it can be said to have aesthetic validity; that is, it preserves its bond to the real even if the images are themselves not causally produced by it. Kracauer's theory thus encompasses both an indexical and an iconic conception of representation. For example, this is how Kracauer sees the cinema of René Clair. Citing from Clair's musicals from the transitional era—films shot on sets designed to resemble actual working-class Parisian neighborhoods—Kracauer argued, "[E]ven granted that they are drawn into an imaginary universe, this universe itself reflects throughout our real world in stylizing it. What dancing there is, seems to occur on the spur of the moment; it is the vicissitudes of life from which these ballets issue."[62] Clair's work blends what Kracauer described as the two dominant tendencies of cinema—the realistic and the formative—and thus remains true to a medium-specific conception of film as art. The images bear a close resemblance to the world, and more important, preserve a sense of chance, motion, and improvisation that is essential to both physical reality and cinema itself.

Kracauer's interest in binding cinematic art to the medium's natural ability to depict movement and chance is also, as Miriam Bratu Hansen has shown, what characterizes the social dimension of *Theory of Film*. Written in the 1950s, Kracauer's book at first seems like a departure from the social preoccupation of Kracauer's early work, *From Caligari to Hitler: A Psychological History of the German Film*, in which Kracauer very famously attempted to account for the rise of totalitarianism in German film of the 1920s. In this work, cinema gave concrete expression to ideology. However, while the political dimension of *Theory of Film* is less obvious, it is no less significant. As Hansen noted in her introduction to *Theory of Film*, Kracauer first conceived of the project in Marseilles in the early 1930s while waiting to flee Europe during the rise of the Nazis. Noting this fact of Kracauer's production, Hansen argued that his interest in chance as an essential property of the medium and a primary feature of realist cinema was born of his encounter with totalitarianism. She wrote, "The concept of chance, which affiliates Kracauer with both the surrealists and, proleptically, a figure like John Cage, emerges as a historicophilosphical alternative to the closed dramaturgy of fate or destiny (which Kracauer associates with Fritz Lang); in fact, chance alone offers a tiny window, at once hope and obligation, of survival, of continuing life after the grand metaphysical stakes have been lost."[63]

Hansen succinctly defined the political potential of realist theories (and thus cinematic practices) predicated on the terms of medium specificity. She suggested the ways in which Kracauer's attention to the material is predicated on a desire to alter that which cannot, at least as yet, be seen. For Kracauer, chance stands in opposition to structure, order, and ideology.

Despite the claims of autonomy and spectatorial agency that underlie these influential theories of realism, the impression of reality produced by cinema, and celebrated by Bazin and Kracauer, was revised by the more politicized generation of film theorists who came to prominence in the aftermath of May 1968 in France, elaborating what came to be known as "apparatus theory." By 1969, Jean-Louis Comolli and Jean Narboni had assumed the editorship of *Cahiers du Cinéma*, which had, following the massive shifts in French culture after May 1968, taken an explicitly politicized position. Where once *Cahiers du Cinéma* generated auteur analyses and stylistic histories in an effort to establish the cultural legitimacy of film as art, it now sought to understand cinema, following the work of Louis Althusser, as a state apparatus designed for the interpellation of subjects into dominant ideology; an apparatus that produces and fulfills desires in a transcendental subject. One still sees analyses of films in the pages of *Cahiers du Cinéma* during this period; however, the films analyzed were drawn from the Soviet cinema of the 1920s, Renoir's political cinema of the 1930s, and contemporary modernist cinema resistant, at a formal and material level, to the codes and conventions of dominant cinema. In this sense, *Cahiers du Cinéma* contributed to a larger cultural turn toward structuralism, post-structuralism, semiology, Marxism, and psychoanalysis that would dominate film theory in the 1970s in journals such as *Communications*, *Cinéthique*, and *Tel Quel* in France, *Screen* and *Framework* in the United Kingdom, and *Camera Obscura* in the United States.[64]

Apparatus theory, especially under the early and influential formulations of Christian Metz and Jean-Louis Baudry, can be distinguished first and foremost by its critique of the impression of reality produced by cinema, and celebrated by Bazin and Kracauer. It sees the cinema not as a window onto the world, but as an instrument of illusion and deception. In "The Apparatus: Metapsychological Approaches to the Impression of Reality in the Cinema," Baudry very famously described cinema as an extension of Plato's cave, wherein the production of reality on-screen is an illusion performed by the state in an effort to produce obedient subjects who desire only to see the illusions before them, who desire only the conditions of their own alienation. Cinema is understood to be the material realization of Plato's cave. Accordingly, the demystification of cinema as an apparatus—the turning toward the light and away from the pleasures that bind the subject to the will of the state and the expanding terrain of capital more generally—becomes the project of apparatus theory. On the one hand, this involves developing considerations, along Brechtian lines, of the cinematic strategies designed to expose the conventions of realism and the ways in which those conventions work to produce illusions of reality *and* a transcendental subject.[65] The strategies of demystification celebrated here are predicated on terms of medium specificity. To make a viewer aware of the process of signification is to encourage that viewer to become aware of the medium in its most material basis. To become subject to illusion, in the logic of apparatus theory, is to be unaware, in some sense, that one is watching a film.

On the other hand, the larger project of apparatus theory lies in its attention not only to the styles of mystification, but also to the larger psychic mechanisms at work in cinema, to that which makes the body itself an extension of the cinematic apparatus. Perhaps the greatest example of this effort is Christian Metz's "The Imaginary Signifier," first published in *Communications* and *Screen* in 1975. In this extensive essay, Metz wed Lacanian psychoanalysis to cinema, a relation that would guide film theory for decades to follow. In particular, Metz expanded the notion of what we refer to as the "film industry," to incorporate the ways it includes, as an industry, the cooperation between a libidinal economy (the pleasure of film and the codes, styles, and conventions that guarantee that pleasure) and a political one (cinema as a form of commerce that produces subjects in the name of the commodity and ideology). Included in Metz's formulation is a conception of criticism itself (especially auteurism) as a third machine, an arm of the apparatus that merely produces more talk about, and thus more pleasure from, the cinema. For Metz, criticism works to bring the spectator back to the cinema. Thus, apparatus theory took pleasure, and for that matter, art, as the primary problem of cinema. For instance, Metz was very suspicious of cinephilia as a sign of the success of cinema as an apparatus. He denounced his own passion for cinema and suggested that all theorists follow suit: "To be a theoretician of the cinema, one should ideally no longer love the cinema and yet still love it: have loved it a lot and only have detached oneself from it by taking it up again from the other end, taking it as the target for the very same scopic drive which had made one love it. Have broken with it, as certain relationships are broken, not in order to return to it at the next bend in the spiral."[66] This spiral, of course, runs from the cinephiliac moment of 1920s film theory through to *Cahiers du Cinéma* of the 1950s, as a celebration of the film artist who distinguished himself in expressly cinematic terms. For Metz, cinephilia was a necessary precondition for understanding the larger social and psychic functioning of cinema as a machine, but only once the theorist was no longer also a cinephile.

Nevertheless, Metz's theory is no less beholden to questions of medium specificity. While it may unmoor medium specificity from questions of what makes cinema an art, it considers it instead in relation to how cinema produces pleasure, and for what end. In Metz's broadened formulation, the mind and body of the spectator become extensions of the cinema; they are all a part of the same machine. For what Metz ultimately attempted to reveal is the way in which cinema will "disengage the cinema-object from the imaginary and . . . win it for the symbolic, in the hope of extending the latter by a new province: an enterprise of displacement, a territorial enterprise, a symbolic advance."[67] Along these lines, he theorized that the nexus of the cinematic apparatus is its unique capacity to utilize what he dubbed an "imaginary signifier." Metz's major claim here concerns the status of the signifier in cinema, as opposed to other media, most notably theater and the novel. But Metz offered a major overhaul of Bazin's ontology of cinema, and the idealist strain of Bazin's thought that weds technological progress to humanism. Whereas Bazin privileged an indexical view of the cinema, suggesting an existential bond between signifier and signified—the object and its appearance on film—Metz proposed that the signifier is only ever imaginary; that the signified, the image on-screen, is all that can be said to exist. For when the film is projected in a theater, the signifier is not actually present, even if it did cause the existence of the photograph itself. This, Metz reasoned, is a departure both from Bazinian theory, which holds that an image *is* the object, and from theater. For the latter, Metz provided the example of Sarah Bernhardt: "At the theatre, Sarah Bernhardt may tell me that she is Phèdre or, if the play were from another period and rejected the figurative regime, she might say, as in a type of modern theatre, that she is Sandra Bernhardt. But at any rate, I should see Sarah Bernhardt. At the cinema, she could make the same two kinds of speeches too, but it would be her shadow that would be offering them to me (or she would be offering them in her own absence). Every film is a fiction film."[68]

Every film is a fiction film because we have to imagine what we see before us as present, even if the figure does not assume a fictional identity. The cinema is always imaginary because only the signified, not the signifier, is present at the time of projection.[69] And because we have all lived the experience of the mirror stage, as defined by Jacques Lacan, we are psychologically prepared for a process of identification that depends on an image that is simultaneously present and absent. In Lacan's scenario, the infant sees himself in the mirror as a fully formed, autonomous individual, but only as an image, as other. Recognition in the mirror stage is predicated on misrecognition. Metz's spectator, by contrast, has lived through the mirror stage and thus does not actually mistake the character on screen for him- or herself. Nevertheless, Metz believed that cinematic spectatorship depends on disavowal and fetishism. Because we know that we are watching a film, we know that what appears is not real. And yet, we believe that it *is* real despite our knowledge that it is not. Thus, spectatorship takes on the character of the fetish: an object is adopted to cover a lack. That object can take the form of an interest in the machinery of cinema (a kind of techno-fetishism) or even an interest in style itself, including the ways in which the codes and conventions remain imprinted on our psyche. Either way, once the imaginary of the cinema aligns with the spectator's imaginary, identification begins. In this respect, identification takes place not with a character, but with the camera—a transcendental position of mastery that is further impelled by scopophilia and voyeurism. And once identification with the camera takes place—once the gaze of the camera is inhabited—the imaginary is given over to the symbolic order and its potential for social or political ordering.

The psychoanalytic aspect of apparatus theory so prominent here builds on the semiological investigations of cinema as a language that precedes it, which Metz also pioneered. To be sure, Metz's work in the 1960s, which appeared in translation in the United States in the 1970s, is rooted in investigations of the defining characteristics of film as language, especially as informed by structural linguistics and semiology.[70] Acknowledging throughout his work that film is not a language per se, Metz went on to try to describe the normative stylistic features of film, a typology of styles that constitute the Grand Syntagmatique.[71] Metz's investigations into what might constitute cinema as a kind of language, however analogously, reverberated in multiple ways. Metz's work of this period anticipates the neoformalist tradition of film study, especially as performed by David Bordwell, Janet Staiger, and Kristin Thompson in *The Classical Hollywood Cinema* (1985) and Bordwell and Thompson in *Film Art: An Introduction* (2004).

Closer to Metz's psychoanalytic conception of cinema as an apparatus, but equally concerned with the possibility of film as a language, is suture theory. Suture theory was first developed by Jean-Pierre Oudart in *Cahiers du Cinéma* in 1969 in an essay called "Cinema and Suture." In Oudart's pioneering formulation, suture is expressly concerned with the ways in which the spectator becomes a part of the chain of cinematic discourse. Oudart's theory of cinematic suture is largely adapted from Jacques-Alain Miller's Lacanian consideration of suture as an effect of linguistic discourse. As Kaja Silverman has put it, suture is, for Miller as well as Oudart, the "moment when the subject inserts itself into the symbolic register in the guise of the signifier, and in so doing gains meaning at the expense of being."[72] Though inspired by a linguistic model, Oudart imagined suture to be a way of understanding the unique function of cinema. The habit of linguistic thinking, Oudart reasoned, ultimately makes us consider one image as simply succeeding another in a linear fashion. However, the process of suture, which is essential to cinema as a medium, involves a process of presence and absence, a movement from image to spectator that should alter a simple conception of cinema as a mere succession of images. As Oudart saw it:

> prior to any semantic 'exchange' between two images . . . and within the framework of a cinematic *énoncé* constructed on a shot/reverse shot principle, the appearance of a lack perceived as Some One (the Absent One) is followed by its abolition by someone (or something) placed within the same field—everything happening within the same shot or rather within the same filmic space defined by the same take. This is the fundamental fact from which effects derive.[73]

Oudart's theory of suture is derived from a close consideration of the films of Robert Bresson. As such, it reflects an effort to understand a modernist, medium-specific conception of cinema that extends outward to a consideration of the way in which the spectator is figured as part of the film. This sentiment alone suggests the extent to which medium-specific theorizing remains a significant aspect of apparatus theory, even if, like the 1920s modernists before him, Oudart implemented it as a method of making judgments about art.[74] But as Daniel Dayan showed, suture might also represent the very way in which classical narration functions, by way of the shot/reverse-shot, to include the spectator within the world of the fiction and make him or her forget the edge of the frame, which would prevent cinema, as a system, from obtaining its ideological effect.[75] In this formulation, the conception of cinema as normative system becomes consonant with what Metz went on to articulate in more sweeping terms in "The Imaginary Signifier." However, it is an often overlooked fact that Metz himself acknowledged in "The Imaginary Signifier" that cinema is not simply *a* system; rather, there is what he described as a "structural and relational (but not necessarily exhaustible) order, and peculiar to a given film, not to the cinema, distinct from every code and combining several of them."[76]

Despite this nuance, Metz's work would come under attack for many years to come and from many different quarters for its systematicity, and for its effort to understand systematicity itself. Indeed, Metz, and apparatus theory more generally, remain at the center of the current animosity and skepticism about theory, and the attendant rise of historicism described at the outset of this essay. In this respect, one could argue with reference to Metz's own term that the historicist turn is simply the new manifestation of the "third machine." Where once criticism returned the spectator to the theater to see more, pay again, and have one's imaginary reshaped, the empirical historian could be said to document the success of cinema and media as a technology. Perhaps historicism itself is more prone than theory to technological determinism by virtue of its steadfast commitment to looking only at what appears.

Theory, of course, has not disappeared. However, the dominant strain of theory over the past decade has been marked, however paradoxically, by skepticism and positivism at once, by a commitment to science and reason, the twinned virtues of Enlightenment thought. On the one hand, cognitive film theory has set its sights on debunking the claims of psychoanalytic film theory. Stephen Prince, for example, has suggested that the trouble with psychoanalytic film theory lies in the fact that psychoanalysis is itself "a discipline without reliable data."[77] Cognitive film theory has likewise sought to understand the normative response to the normative features of film as innate, biologically determined, and often hardwired responses, as if the mind is not subject to environmental influence. David Bordwell has argued that the shot/reverse-shot structure is not an arbitrary convention utilized, as proponents of apparatus theory would have it, for its ideological effect. Rather, he described it as a "contingent universal," a practice adopted routinely across cultures for its adhesion to natural perception, that is, to the way in which we see the world, or try to see in the world more effectively in everyday life. The appearance of the shot/reverse shot in Senegal as well as France owes nothing to cultural imperialism but rather to the fact that different cultures agree and arrive independently at the shot/reverse-shot pattern simply because it makes the most sense. Of course, this makes cinema an extension of our biological functions in their most reduced form—art as an imitation of what the body can do without effort. A more philosophical theory, by contrast, seeks to understand the vicissitudes of thought, the mind in its most expansive form, not its capacity for consensus. Curiously, Bordwell's redefinition of the notion of convention seems especially suitable as a description of film as an apparatus: "There is another way to conceive of conventions [as opposed to the post-structuralist version]: as norm bound practices that co-ordinate social activities and direct action in order to achieve goals."[78]

Likewise, analytical film theory has set out to examine the logical fallacies of film theory in its continental manifestations.[79] Richard Allen's *Projecting Illusion*, for instance, marks an effort to uphold the concept of illusion so central to Baudry and Metz and apparatus theory more generally, but along more rational lines.[80] More specifically, he considers the Wittgensteinian notion of "seeing as," where one fastens on the image either as fiction or as medium (or nonfictional aspects of what appears in the image), but never simultaneously.

Of course, the cognitive and analytical branches of film have not been the only ones to critique apparatus theory. Feminist film theory of the 1970s was also, in many respects, critical of Metz and the generalized formulation of cinema as an apparatus. As Constance Penley has argued, the problem lies with the conception of cinema as a kind of bachelor machine designed to "represent the relation of the body to the social, the relation of the sexes to each other, the structure of the psyche, or the workings of history."[81] Penley suggested that feminist film theory has:

> found it more productive to ask whether this description [as opposed to questions about the concept of the apparatus itself], with its own extreme bacheloresque emphasis on homogeneity and closure, does not itself subscribe to a theoretical systematicity, one that would close off those same questions of sexual difference that it claims are denied or disavowed in the narrative system of the classical film.[82]

Could apparatus theory itself be a kind of third machine, a theoretical discourse that secures the logic of the very thing of which it is supposed to be critical? A great deal of important work within feminist film theory has been devoted to addressing the mischaracterizations of psychoanalytic theory within the theories of Metz and Baudry.[83]

However, as Penley herself has noted, much of the work of feminist film theory focuses on the matter of pleasure. And in this way, one of the major contributions of feminist film theory has been to bring us to a more complex understanding of the ways in which cinema as an apparatus is gendered, and what it means for women, in particular, to experience the pleasure necessary for that machine to function. If, as Metz has argued, cinema involves a kind of perceptual mastery aided by scopophilia and voyeurism, how do women figure in?[84] Does a woman take the same pleasure in occupying the gaze as a man? Does cinema function as such only for heterosexual spectators, or for white, heteronormative spectators?[85]

At the center of this inquiry, as well as its critique, is Laura Mulvey's vastly influential "Visual Pleasure and Narrative Cinema," published in the same year as "The Imaginary Signifier," but written in 1973. Like Metz, Mulvey developed a model of the classical cinema as an apparatus that depends on Lacan's conception of the relation between the imaginary and the symbolic in the workings of the mirror stage. For Mulvey, in particular, classical cinema is, in its most material basis, a machine involved in the production of pleasure, a pleasure that comes by way of the male gaze, the structuring look of mainstream cinema that extends from men looking at women on screen to the men and women who inhabit that gaze in the voyeuristic space of the cinema. Following Lacan, the male gaze is secured against the threat of castration, which the image of woman on screen is said to project. Thus, Mulvey wrote:

> The male unconscious has two avenues of escape from this castration anxiety: preoccupation with the re-enactment of the original trauma (investigating the woman, demystifying her mystery), counterbalanced by the devaluation, punishment or saving of the guilty object (an avenue typified by the concerns of *film noir*); or else complete disavowal of castration by the substitution of a fetish object or turning the represented figure itself into a fetish so that it becomes reassuring rather than dangerous (hence overvaluation, the cult of the female star).[86]

In this formulation, scopophilia and voyeurism are the alternate possibilities for producing pleasure where there might otherwise be displeasure, or, for that matter, terror. Scopophilia involves an appreciation of the fetish as beautiful (and thus all covering), while voyeurism involves the sadistic pleasure of "asserting control and subjugating the guilty person through punishment or forgiveness."[87] The codes and conventions of mainstream narrative film are thus understood as central to the process itself: the close-up, for example, emphasizes a part of the female body (a leg for the whole) and narrative itself provides the space for the confrontations and closure that constitute voyeuristic pleasure. And the theory is steeped in questions of medium specificity. Style and technology work to secure an illusion of perceptual mastery; even the space of the theater is seen as essential to the summation of voyeuristic pleasure: "the extreme contrast between the darkness in the auditorium (which also isolates the spectators from one another) and the brilliance of the shifting patterns of light and shade on the screen helps to promote the illusion of voyeuristic separation."[88] In the years since Mulvey's essay appeared, theorists have taken issue with this aspect of its formulation. But it is important for our purposes here to note the way in which style, exhibition, and the psychology of the spectators are understood as uniquely aligned in the cinematic apparatus.[89] The medium, in Mulvey's formulation, has been predetermined by the psychological dispositions of the spectator that are already in place prior to development of cinema, or one's first experience of it.

Despite the volumes of criticism that have followed Mulvey's essay since its first appearance (and its merits and defects), the theory itself has been remarkably enduring. It created a space for feminist film theory within the academy, and thus a space for female academics as well, that did not exist before. It continues to fascinate and awaken generations of students to the politics of pleasure, to the ways in which the experience of entertainment itself, which so many take as an unreflective given, is a socially determined process. And, of course, the liberating promise of the closing lines of the essay still resonate very strongly:

> The first blow against the monolithic accumulation of traditional film conventions (already undertaken by radical filmmakers) is to free the look of the camera

into its materiality in time and space and the look of the audience into passionate detachment. There is no doubt that this destroys the satisfaction, pleasure and privilege of the "invisible," and highlights the way film has depended on voyeuristic active/passive mechanisms. Women, whose image has continually been stolen and used for this end, cannot view the decline of the traditional film form with anything much more than sentimental regret.[90]

In 1975, this meant for Mulvey the consideration of cinema at a material, medium-specific level; in particular, it involved the promise of 16-millimeter film as a material readily available outside the dominant mode of production at a significantly reduced cost. The affordability of 16-millimeter film would allow filmmakers to make films that not only reflexively reveal the codes and conventions of dominant practice, but also circulate outside the channels of commodity culture, to produce films that are themselves incapable of merely supporting the apparatus and the commodity culture that feeds it. In this sense, Mulvey rehearsed the claims made by the film theorists of the 1920s at the introduction of sound. To develop a countercinema is to disrupt the dominant cinema that, like the unconscious, Mulvey said, is structured like a language.

Mulvey's interest in the relation between 16-millimeter film and the aesthetic and political possibilities it promises is worth retaining, even if the situation today is remarkably different (and even if the unconscious is not structured like a language). The kind of independent cinema called for by Laura Mulvey in 1975 became, in certain respects, the norm of the so-called indie boom of the late 1980s and 1990s, where, in the absence of a central studio system that gave rise to the classical narrative, narrative filmmakers of the most conventional stripe (from Stephen Soderbergh to Kevin Smith) produced films independently on 16-millimeter film so as to sell those films to major distributors (New Line Cinema, Miramax). That is to say, the low cost of the material itself did not necessarily produce a generation of avant-garde filmmakers. Rather, it ultimately reduced the risks for the corporations who would buy them, and who would thus no longer incur the larger risk of funding an entire production. By and large, the generation of independent filmmakers that emerged in the eighties and nineties, I would argue, use this medium familiar to the avant-garde (which often delights in the reduced clarity of the image and a tighter aspect ratio) to reproduce an aesthetic system (classical Hollywood) that had disappeared in its material, economic form. Certainly one might argue that a feature of postclassical filmmaking is the abandonment of classical style in favor of pastiche, reflexivity, and more heterogeneous stylistic devices. Indeed, there is no denying that reflexivity has become a central feature, a convention of contemporary production. More likely, the success of the global expansion of the film industry has been predicated by its adoption of the strategies of classical narration. The disruption of the clarifying procedure of classical narration thus remains a political imperative for filmmakers caught in the web of an international film culture that has expanded its reach while contracting stylistic and thus cultural difference.[91]

As this divergence of film theory and film history suggests, the movement of capital and the reorganization of global culture today demand that film theory extend beyond questions about what constitutes film as an art form, to what extent one medium differs from another, considering more closely *and* more broadly how that which constitutes cinema in its uniqueness works in cooperation with larger psychic, social, and geopolitical forces. This situation is only exacerbated by the fact that film itself, as a medium, is clearly on the decline. The digital image, at the level of production, distribution, and exhibition, has significantly complicated the questions asked by film theorists throughout the 1920s.

However, the emergence of the digital image has not foreclosed the kind of medium-specificity theory that we saw during the transition to sound, and for good reasons. For example, in "The Digital World Picture," Jean-Pierre Geuens (who is also a filmmaker and a film theorist) examined what he took to be the nihilistic features of the digital image. Drawing on a Heideggerian conception of technology, Geuens suggested that "the kind of technology we use circumscribes our view of the world, earmarking our access to it, ultimately shaping what we make of it."[92] As Geuens saw it, digital production does away with the heroics of production, the role that chance plays when actors, director, cameraman, and crew work together to film a scene in one continuous take. Furthermore, the green screen of digital production allows two people together in an image, despite shooting their respective moments of a conversation in total isolation.[93] Whereas Kracauer imagined the essence of cinema to reside in the production of movement—of a necessary chaos that stands in contradistinction to the structuring logic of fascism—the digital image is in Geuens's view nihilistic; it can only re-create the alienated conditions of its own production. Geuens was clearly bemoaning the loss of a Bazinian ontology, with its guarantee of an indexical bond between the image and the object that causes it. However, in doing so, he was nevertheless able to reveal what distinguishes the digital image as a medium. Indeed, medium specificity also seems to be at the heart of digital theory in its early manifestations, even when it is medium specificity itself that is said to be disappearing. Such is the case, for example, in Jay David Bolter and Richard Grusin's notion of remediation, in which new media are said to always imitate and absorb the strategies of other media in their pursuit of immediacy and liveness.[94] In Bolter and Grusin's formulation, medium specificity is an outmoded modernist strategy of disruption; remediation, by contrast, is the mode through which new technologies proliferate and race toward an increasing sense of immediacy. However, if we take Geuens's approach seriously, we see that it is offered very much in the spirit of opening a space for reflection, as Heidegger once tried to, before the coming to presence of technological domination. Thus, the comparative mode of medium-specificity theory that it represents allows us to see what the new medium otherwise seeks to efface. It brings into view the problems and contradictions of technology before they become standardized, which is to say, precisely at the moment when theory can become interventionist and future oriented.

For instance, one of the positive features of the digital image, in Geuens's view, is the portability of the digital camera, the instantaneity of its image in the moment of production, and the consolidation, by way of digital editing, of the filmmaking process around a single artist. In this sense, he claimed, it promises the realization of Astruc's "*caméra-stylo*." In 1948, the French filmmaker and film theorist Alexandre Astruc published "The Birth of a New Avant-Garde: La caméra-stylo." Astruc's guiding concept is that of the *caméra-stylo*, the camera pen. This metaphor, grounded as it is in a medium-specific conception of cinema, defined auteur theory a decade later. It proposes a form of filmmaking that no longer depends on the scriptwriter, where the director, by virtue of the portability of equipment, becomes the sole arbiter of structure and meaning.

Astruc inherited the problems of René Clair and other French modernist filmmakers before him, and set the pace for the French New Wave. Astruc's major theoretical intervention, however, has more to do with the ways in which the film artist will forge a unique relation between film and philosophy: "[A] Descartes of today would already have shut himself up in his bedroom with a 16mm camera and some film, and would be writing his philosophy on film: for his *Discours de la Méthode* would today be of such a kind that only the cinema could express it satisfactorily."[95] This medium-specific conception of cinema leads Astruc to a larger conception of the cinema as a new language, one as flexible as the written word, and yet which bears no structural relation to it (this is not unlike Mulvey's call for an avant-garde cinema). Indeed, if shed of its literary bias, the cinema will provide direct access to thought unmoored from the word. As Astruc argued, "By language, I mean a form in which and by which an artist can express his thoughts, however abstract they may be, or translate his obsessions exactly as he does in the contemporary essay or novel."[96]

Astruc, however, went much further than to argue that cinema can become a language of its own. For Astruc's language—the language of cinema—has no grammar, and thus not only becomes a vehicle of thought, but works to close the gap between cinema and philosophy:

> Every film, because its primary function is to move, i.e. to take place in time, is a theorem. It is a series of images which, from one end to the other, have an inexorable logic (or better even, a dialectic) of their own. . . . All thought, like all feeling, is a relationship between one human being and another human being or certain objects which form part of this universe. It is by clarifying these relationships, by making a tangible allusion, that the cinema can really make itself the vehicle of thought.[97]

Through movement, time, and editing (or, at least, its consecutive movements through and around objects and people), cinema makes propositional statements about the world, or about consciousness itself, free of systematicity. Each film, produced under the conditions of the *caméra-stylo*, has its own inexorable logic, as opposed to the logic imposed by the normative procedures of industrial production. For Astruc, like Munsterberg before him, cinema is thus figured as a vehicle for the autonomy of thought, and yet set against the procedures of dominant cinema that work to regulate perception and consciousness (which precede Munsterberg).

Thus, Astruc announced a path for theory that has been taken up more forcefully by philosophy. Gilles Deleuze's philosophy of cinema, which is predicated on its endless movements, reshaping, and groupings, shares Astruc's conception of cinema as a vehicle for thought and the production of concepts that move according to their own inexorable logic.[98] And in many respects, the level of specificity that is so central to Deleuze's philosophy of cinema is what has attracted so many to it as a way of thinking beyond the structural determinations of Metz and apparatus theory—the possible mutuality of the overwhelming determinations of apparatus theory with the apparatus itself. As Gregory Flaxman has written:

> for him [Deleuze] the specificity of cinematographic images invariably eludes the rigid determinations of any overarching schematism. The result is a philosophy whose rigor is always local, reflecting the emergence of rules immanent to each given 'zone of indetermination.' The concepts that theory develops 'must specifically relate to cinema,' Deleuze writes, and so the cinema itself is thereby made the mode for understanding the world, our world.[99]

In certain respects, Deleuze's philosophy moves in ways similar to medium-specificity theorizing of the 1920s, especially that of Epstein, Balázs, and Eisenstein. And it is no accident that *Cinema 1* is marked by an engagement with these very same figures. Given the landscape in which Deleuze's work on cinema emerged in the United States, it is worth noting that its concerns with the specificity of individual films differs sharply from the kind of calls for modesty made by the opponents of Grand Theory. Rather, and as Flaxman suggested, "*The Movement Image* amounts to a 'story of the universe'—a story the cinema induces but also one in which, on the other hand, the cinema itself plays the crucial role because its images allow us to go 'back up the path' along which the human world of molar perception develops and thus to glimpse the molecular universe about which Bergson writes."[100] Cinema, in Deleuze's philosophy, has always performed the kinds of philosophical investigations imagined by Astruc, and theorists of the digital image.

Of course, it remains to be seen whether the digital actually promises the realization of Astruc's autonomous *caméra-stylo*. At the level of practice, Jonathan Caouette's documentary *Tarnation* (2003), which features images recorded of his schizophrenic mother that he shot throughout his life on digital video and edited on Macintosh software, strongly suggests the possibility of digital cinema as a site for the autonomy of thought. But more important, medium-specificity theorizing, as I have indicated, is not simply a utopian procedure. For instance, as Geuens himself noted, while the digital image allows for new styles and new modes of production, the equipment itself has stylistic features (the "cinema effect," tinting) built into it that work to standardize vision at the level of the equipment itself; that is, normalizing features are already inscribed in a technology lauded for its democratizing qualities.

But this problem, finally—the possibility of autonomy within and against totalizing structures—is one for which theory has long been prepared. It demands that we continue to ask medium-specific questions, ones that nevertheless seek to understand a relation between what we can see and what cannot be apprehended visually. How does cinema function at a material level? What psychic and social effects might it have? And to what extent can theory imagine a mode of intervention? The questions may be similar, but the object of theory, and theory itself, are always shifting. Above all, theory itself must be concerned with futurity, which calls to modesty will never promote, precisely because the chastising imperatives of such claims are in many cases themselves an effort to secure a particular kind of future. We might thus take seriously how relevant Guy Debord's *Society of the Spectacle* now appears to us, more than forty years after its publication. It was, thankfully, no modest enterprise: "The spectacle cannot be understood either as a deliberate distortion of the visual world or as a product of the technology of the mass dissemination of images. It is far better viewed as a *weltanshauung* that has been actualized, translated into the material realm—a worldview translated into an objective force."[101]

Despite the seeming fulfillment of this scenario today, though, it is important to recognize in it that theory does not claim to foretell *the* future, but *a* future. Indeed, if a history of theory can tell us anything, it is that theory is meant to provide an opening for thought, which is necessarily divergent. Bazin and Metz might not agree, nor, for that matter, would Deleuze and Debord. If anything, the history of theory that I have outlined here, I hope, is not a story of succession—a long process of imitation, repudiation, and revision that leads us to a final understanding of what cinema *is*, in all its ontological unfolding. On the contrary, medium-specificity theorizing can be just the antidote to such deterministic enterprises. It just might, for instance, work to dismantle totalizing structures to create an opening that allows us to think and to see differently; to recognize structures that work to regulate thought and desire; to identify works of art, so uniquely constituted, that they move in step with philosophy itself. There is no right answer, even if some strike us as more reasonable than others. But that is a problem that only theory can address.

NOTES

....

1. David Bordwell, "Contemporary Film Theory and the Vicissitudes of Grand Theory," in *Post-Theory: Reconstructing Film Studies*, ed. David Bordwell and Noël Carroll (Madison: University of Wisconsin Press, 1996): 3.

2. Ibid., 14.

3. Noël Carroll, "Prospects for Film Theory: A Personal Assessment," in Bordwell and Carroll, *Post-Theory*: 43.

4. For a spirited defense of literature as theory, theory as literature, see Jean Michel Rabaté's *The Future of Theory* (London: Blackwell, 2002).

5. Carroll, "Prospects for Film Theory," 39.

6. For a very incisive critique of Bordwell and Carroll's interest in modesty, see Colin Davis, *After Poststructuralism: Reading, Stories and Theory* (New York: Routledge, 2004).

7. Jonathan Kandell, "Jacques Derrida, Abstruse Theorist, Dies at 74," *New York Times*, October 10, 2004.

8. Emily Eakins, "The Latest Theory Is that Theory Doesn't Matter," *New York Times*, April 13, 2003.

9. Terry Eagleton, *After Theory* (New York: Basic Books, 2003): 223.

10. Clement Greenberg, "An American View," in *The Collected Essays and Criticism*, vol. 1, ed. John O'Brien (Chicago: University of Chicago Press, 1986): 39.

11. Eagleton, *After Theory*, 53.

12. Indeed, modernist art criticism like Greenberg's often allowed it to be the very thing that guided qualitative distinctions between abstract works. The more an artist utilized his or her medium, the more distinctive the work and the likelier that it would be deemed art. Take, for instance, Clement Greenberg's statement of his preference of Miró, in 1941, over Léger and Kandinsky:

> Of the artists who have produced the best paintings of the last five years or so, without doubt one is Miró. . . . The show of his recent work at the Matisse Gallery impressed one with the extent to which the modern painter derives his inspiration from the very physical materials he works with. In spite of, and perhaps because of, the freedom it offers, canvas imposes upon the painter a style more or less proper to itself. . . . The coarse surface of the burlap has refreshed his invention, compelling him to tighten and compress his design in order to animate and set off the minuscule criss-cross pattern of the rough stitching. Since the burlap does not present a smooth surface, paint must be rubbed rather than brushed on, and so a new quality of "paintedness" is gained. Although the brisk reds, the blacks, yellow and livid whites are reminiscent of Miró's previous work, the result constitutes on the whole a new and brilliant phase in his development.

"Review of Exhibitions of Joan Miró, Fernand Léger, and Wassily Kandinsky," *Collected Essays and Criticism*, vol. 1: 63.

13. Maxim Gorky, "The Lumière Cinematograph," in *The Film Factory: Russian and Soviet Cinema in Documents, 1896–1939*, ed. Richard Taylor and Ian Christie, trans. Richard Taylor (Cambridge, MA: Harvard University Press, 1988): 25.

14. The list could be substantially longer, but see especially Vladimir Mayakovksy, "Theatre, Cinema, Futurism," 33–34; Vladimir Mayakovsky, "The Relation Between Contemporary Theatre and Cinema Art," 35–37; and Vsevelod Meyerhold, "On Cinema," 39; all in Taylor and Christie, *The Film Factory*; Rémy de Gourmont, "Epilogues: Cinematograph," in *French Film Theory and Criticism*, vol. 1, *1907–1929*, ed. Richard Abel (Princeton, NJ: Princeton University Press, 1988): 47–50; Ricciotto Canudo, "The Birth of a Sixth Art," in Abel, *French Film Theory and Criticism*, vol. 1, *1907–1929*.

15. Vachal Lindsay, *The Art of the Moving Picture* (New York: Liveright Corporation, 1970): 45.

16. Stanley Cavell's work on comedies of remarriage has been especially influential. See Stanley Cavell, *Pursuits of Happiness: The Hollywood Comedy of Remarriage* (Cambridge, MA: Harvard University Press, 1981).

17. Lindsay, *Art of the Moving Picture*, 47–48.

18. Ibid., 49.

19. François Truffaut, "A Certain Tendency of the Cinema," in *Movies and Methods*, vol. 1, ed. Bill Nichols (Berkeley: University of California Press, 1976): 229.

20. Truffaut's claim, which is medium specific, is also and oddly made in moral terms. A commitment to a medium-specific use of cinema is seen as a corrective to the perceived immorality of the Tradition of Quality. In other words, in trying to advance a medium-specific conception of the cinema, Truffaut not only cleared the way for cinema as a distinct art form, but also made unfashionable a generation of filmmakers whom, as a Catholic, he opposed on moral grounds.

21. Hugo Munsterberg, "The Means of the Photoplay," in *Film Theory and Criticism*, 6th ed., ed. Leo Braudy and Marshall Cohen (New York: Oxford University Press, 2004): 415.

22. Munsterberg's theory likewise anticipated the surrealists' interest in cinema in the 1920s for its unique capacity to blend images of physical reality with the imagination and to re-create the irrational quality of the dream. Unlike Munsterberg's, the early writing on film by the surrealists, especially Aragon and André Breton, tends more toward the manifesto, toward statements about how to make mainstream cinema a more radical experience than it intends to provide. See Paul Hammond's excellent collection of surrealist writing on the cinema, *The Shadow and Its Shadow: Surrealist Writing on the Cinema*, 3rd ed., ed. and trans. Paul Hammond (San Francisco: City Lights, 2000).

23. Ibid., 417 (Munsterberg's italics).

24. Francesco Casetti, *Theories of Cinema: 1945–1995*, trans. Francesca Chiostri and Elizabeth Gard Bartolini-Salimbeni, with Thomas Kelso (Austin: University of Texas Press, 1999): 9.

25. Sergei Eisenstein, "Laocoön," in *Eisenstein*, vol. 2, *Toward a Theory of Montage*, ed. Michael Glenny and Richard Taylor, trans. Michael Glenny (London: British Film Institute, 1991): 117.

26. Fernand Léger, "Painting and Cinema," in Abel, *French Film Theory and Cinema*, vol. 1, *1907–1929*: 373.

27. Emblematic of this generation's euphoric celebration of the close-up is the very name given to the journal devoted to cinema created in 1927 by the modernist writers H.D., Kenneth McPherson, and Bryher: *Close Up*. See *Close Up 1927–1933: Cinema and Modernism*, ed. Anne Friedberg, James Donald, and Laura Marcus (Princeton, NJ: Princeton University Press, 1998).

28. For more on Delluc, see Richard Abel's "*Photogénie* and Company," as well as the accompanying texts by Delluc, in Abel, *French Film Theory and Cinema*, vol. 1, *1907–1929*: 95–124.

29. Jean Epstein, "On Certain Characteristics of *Photogénie*," in Abel, *French Film Theory and Cinema*, vol. 1, *1907–1929*: 314.

30. Ricciotto Canudo, "Reflections on the Seventh Art," in Abel, *French Film Theory and Cinema*, vol. 1, *1907–1929*: 296.

31. Dziga Vertov, "The Council of Three," in *Kino-Eye: The Writings of Dziga Vertov*, ed. Annette Michelson, trans. Kevin O'Brien (Berkeley: University of California Press, 1984): 14–15.

32. Annette Michelson, "Introduction," in Michelson, *Kino-Eye: The Writings of Dziga Vertov*: xiv–xlvi.

33. Jean Epstein, "Magnification," in Abel, *French Film Theory and Cinema*, vol. 1, *1907–1929*: 236.

34. Béla Balázs, *Theory of the Film*, ed. Edith Bone (New York: Arno Press, 1972): 56.

35. Ibid., 64.

36. Peter Brooks, *The Melodramatic Imagination: Balzac, Henry James, Melodrama and the Mode of Excess* (New Haven, CT: Yale University Press, 1995): 71.

37. Ibid., chap. 4.

38. Vertov, "Council of Three," 17.

39. For an excellent account of the scientific character of Kuleshov's theory, see Vance Kepley, Jr., "The Kuleshov Workshop," *Iris* 4.1 (Fall 1986): 5–23.

40. Lev Kuleshov, *Kuleshov on Film: Writings of Lev Kuleshov*, trans. and ed. Ronald Levaco (Berkeley: University of California Press, 1974): 52.

41. Sergei Eisenstein, "The Dramaturgy of Film Form," in *Eisenstein Writings, 1922–1934*, trans. and ed. Richard Taylor (London: BFI Publishing, 1998): 163.

42. Ibid. (their italics).

43. Ibid., 161.

44. See Sergei Eisenstein, "The Montage of Attractions," in Taylor, *Eisenstein Writings, 1922–1934*: 33–38.

45. See especially Sergei Eisenstein, "Vertical Montage," in *Eisenstein*, vol. 2, *Toward a Theory of Montage*, ed. Michael Glenny and Richard Taylor, trans. Michael Glenny (London: British Film Institute, 1991): 327–399.

46. See Sergei Eisenstein, "Montage and Architecture," in Glenny and Taylor, *Eisenstein Writings*, vol. 2, *Toward a Theory of Montage*: 59–81.

47. René Clair, "Talkie Versus Talkie," in *French Film Theory and Criticism*, vol. 2, *1929–1939*, ed. Richard Abel (Princeton, NJ: Princeton University Press, 1988): 40.

48. Sergei Eisenstein, Vsevolod Pudovkin, and Grigori Alexandrov, "Statement on Sound," in Glenny and Taylor, *Eisenstein Writings, 1922–1934*: 114.

49. Ibid. (their italics).

50. Marcel Pagnol, "The Talkie Offers the Writer New Resources," in Abel, *French Film Theory and Criticism*, vol. 2, *1929–1939*: 55.

51. Eisenstein, Pudovkin, and Alexandrov, "Statement on Sound," 114 (their italics).

52. The industrial and political questions that surrounded the transition, internationally, are too numerous and too complex to adequately represent here. For more, see Douglas Gomery, "Economic Struggles and Hollywood Imperialism: Europe Converts to Sound," in *Film Sound*, ed. John Belton and Elisabeth Weiss (New York: Columbia

University Press, 1985): 5–24; Alan Williams, "Historical and Theoretical Issue in the Coming of Recorded Sound to the Cinema," in *Sound Theory/Sound Practice*, ed. Rick Altman (New York: Routledge, 1992): 126–137; Charles O'Brien, *Cinema's Conversion to Sound: Technology and Film Style in France and the U.S.* (Bloomington: Indiana University Press, 2005).

53. It is important to note, however, that modernist film theories built on questions of medium specificity do not disappear in the aftermath of World War II. Rather, they continued to flourish within the international avant-garde, especially in the writings of filmmakers such as Maya Deren, Stan Brakhage, Hollis Frampton, and Paul Sharits, to name but a few.

54. Bazin was not, of course, solely preoccupied with questions of realism. Dudley Andrew has shown that Bazin's work far exceeds his ideas about realism, that the entire corpus of his work, which far exceeds the essays anthologized in *What Is Cinema?* and with which Andrew is uniquely familiar, is marked not by its dogmatic consistency but by its heterogeneity. Andrew's recent work on Bazin, presented at the Chicago Film Seminar in December 2004, titled, "Philosophers and the Soul of Cinema, circa 1945," suggests that Bazin's reputation within the history of film theory has been determined by our lack of exposure to the entirety of Bazin's production. For the purposes of this essay only, my account of Bazin will stick closely to these more conventional accounts of his work; however, Andrew's claim suggests the very necessity of rethinking the way in which the history of film theory has been written.

55. André Bazin, "The Ontology of the Photographic Image," in *What Is Cinema?* vol. 1, trans. and ed. Hugh Gray (Berkeley: University of California Press, 1967): 14.

56. Ibid., 12.

57. This by now standard account of photography's impact on representational painting and the rise of modernism has been undergoing a series of revisions within art history over the past twenty years. See especially Jonathan Crary, *Techniques of the Observer: On Vision and Modernity in the Nineteenth Century* (Cambridge: MIT Press, 2001).

58. André Bazin, "The Evolution of the Language of Cinema," in Gray, *What Is Cinema?* vol. 1: 24.

59. See in particular Bazin's "An Aesthetic of Reality: Cinematic Realism and the Italian School of Liberation," in *What Is Cinema?* vol. 2, ed. and trans. Hugh Gray (Berkeley: University of California Press, 1971): 16–40.

60. Siegfried Kracauer, *Theory of Film* (Princeton, NJ: Princeton University Press, 1997): 37.

61. Ibid., 9.

62. Ibid., 43. There are many other examples to be seen. Short of documenting Kracauer's many examples, the reader is especially encouraged to look at his chapter "The Establishment of Physical Existence," in which he theorized numerous aspects of film style and genre, considering the ways in which they conform to the laws of physical existence. He offered, for example, a defense of the close-up as a realist strategy that harks back to the writing on the close-up from the 1920s, which we considered earlier.

63. Miriam Bratu Hansen, introduction to *Theory of Film*: xxii.

64. There are a number of excellent sources for a fuller view and consideration of apparatus theory. See especially D.N. Rodowick, *The Crisis of Political Modernism: Criticism and Ideology in Contemporary Film Theory* (Berkeley: University of California

Press, 1994); Philip Rosen, ed., *Narrative, Apparatus, Ideology* (New York: Columbia University Press, 1986); Teresa De Lauretis and Stephen Heath, eds., *The Cinematic Apparatus* (New York: St. Martin's Press, 1980).

65. See, for example, Peter Wollen's "Godard and Counter-Cinema: *Vent d'est*," in Rosen, *Narrative, Apparatus, Theory*: 120–129; also, Colin MacCabe, "Theory and Film: Principles of Realism and Pleasure," in Rosen, *Narrative, Apparatus, Theory*: 179–198.

66. Christian Metz, *The Imaginary Signifier: Psychoanalysis and the Cinema*, trans. Celia Britton, Annwyl Williams, Ben Brewster, and Alfred Guzzetti (Bloomington: Indiana University Press, 1982): 15. For an interesting reconsideration of Metz and cinephilia that is made in light of the attainability of film on video and DVD, see Jeffrey Sconce, "The (Depressingly) Attainable Text," *Framework: The Journal of Cinema and Media* 45.2 (Fall 2004): 68–75.

67. Ibid., 3.

68. Ibid., 45.

69. An important influence on Metz's notion of the imaginary, it should be noted, is to be found in the work of Edgar Morin, which in many respects serves as a bridge from early classical film theory to Metz. See Edgar Morin, *The Cinema, or the Imaginary Man* (Minneapolis: University of Minnesota Press, 2005).

70. For another example from the period, see especially Pier Paolo Pasolini, "The Cinema of Poetry," in *Movies and Methods I*, ed. Bill Nichols (Berkeley: University of California Press, 1976). Also, for a radical revision of the notion of film as language, see Edward Branigan's *Projecting a Camera: Language-Games in Film Theory* (New York: Routledge, 2006).

71. See in particular the essays collected in Christian Metz, *Film Language: A Semiotics of the Cinema* (New York: Oxford University Press, 1974).

72. Kaja Silverman, "Suture [Excerpts]," in Rosen, *Narrative, Apparatus, Theory*: 219.

73. Jean-Pierre Oudart, "Cinema and Suture," in *Cahiers du Cinéma, 1969–1972: The Politics of Representation*, ed. Nick Browne (Cambridge, MA: Harvard University Press, 1990): 47.

74. This, for example, is what Stephen Heath said about it in his stunning reading of suture, "On Suture," in *Questions of Cinema* (Bloomington: Indiana University Press, 1981): 91.

75. Daniel Dayan, "The Tutor-Code of Classical Cinema," in Braudy and Cohen, *Film Theory and Criticism*: 106–117. See also Nick Browne, "The Spectator-in-the-Text: The Rhetoric of *Stagecoach*," in Braudy and Cohen, *Film Theory and Criticism*: 118–133; also, Heath, "On Suture," and Silverman, "Suture [Excerpts]."

76. Metz, *The Imaginary Signifier*: 29.

77. Stephen Prince, "Psychoanalytic Film Theory and the Problem of the Missing Spectator," in Bordwell and Carroll, *Post-Theory*: 73.

78. David Bordwell, "Convention, Construction, and Vision," in Bordwell and Carroll, *Post-Theory*: 92.

79. For a good introduction to this tradition of film theory, see *Film Theory and Philosophy*, ed. Richard Allen and Murray Smith (New York: Oxford University Press, 1997).

80. Richard Allen, *Projecting Illusion: Film Spectatorship and the Impression of Reality* (New York: Cambridge University Press, 1995).

81. Constance Penley, "Feminism, Film Theory, and the Bachelor Machines," in *The Future of an Illusion: Film, Feminism, and Psychoanalysis* (Minneapolis: University of Minnesota Press, 1989): 57.

82. Ibid., 58.

83. See especially Joan Copjec, "The Orthopsychic Subject: Film Theory and the Reception of Lacan," in *Film and Theory*, ed. Robert Stam and Toby Miller (Malden, MA: Blackwell, 2000): 437– 455; Jacqueline Rose, "The Cinematic Apparatus: Problems in Current Theory," in De Lauretis and Heath, *The Cinematic Apparatus*: 172–186; Constance Penley, " 'A Certain Refusal of Difference': Feminism and Film Theory," in *The Future of An Illusion*: 41–54.

84. See, among many others, Gaylyn Studlar, *In the Realm of Pleasure: Von Sternberg, Dietrich, and the Masochistic Aesthetic* (Urbana: University of Illinois Press, 1988); D.N. Rodowick, *The Difficulty of Difference: Psychoanalysis, Sexual Difference, and Film Theory* (New York: Routledge, 1992); Mary Ann Doane, *The Desire to Desire: The Woman's Films of the 1940s* (Bloomington: Indiana University Press, 1987).

85. See, for instance, Manthia Diawara's "Black Spectatorship: Problems of Identification and Resistance," in Braudy and Cohen, *Film Theory and Criticism*: 892–900.

86. Laura Mulvey, "Visual Pleasure and Narrative Cinema," in *Visual and Other Pleasures* (Bloomington: Indiana University Press, 1989): 21.

87. Ibid., 22.

88. Ibid., 17.

89. For critiques and revisions of Mulvey's essay, see Gaylyn Studlar, *In the Realm of Pleasure: Von Sternberg, Deitrich, and the Masochistic Aesthetic* (New York: Columbia University Press, 1993).

90. Ibid., 26.

91. I developed this argument more fully in "Color, the Formless, and Cinematic Eros," *Framework: The Journal of Cinema and Media* 47.1 (Spring 2006): 22–35.

92. Jean-Pierre Geuens, "The Digital World Picture," *Film Quarterly* 55.4 (Summer 2002): 16.

93. Ibid., 21.

94. Jay David Bolter and Richard Grusin, *Remediation: Understanding New Media* (Cambridge: MIT Press, 1999); another influential medium-specific theory of the digital is Lev Manovich's *The Language of New Media* (Cambridge: MIT Press, 2001).

95. Alexandre Astruc, "The Birth of a New Avant-Garde: La caméra-stylo," in *The New Wave*, ed. Peter Graham (London: Secker and Warburg, 1968): 19.

96. Ibid.

97. Ibid., 20.

98. See Gilles Deleuze, *Cinema 1: The Movement Image*, trans. Hugh Tomlinson and Barbara Habberjam (Minneapolis: University of Minnesota Press, 1986); Gilles Deleuze, *Cinema 2: The Time Image* (Minneapolis: University of Minnesota Press, 1989).

99. Gregory Flaxman, introduction to *The Brain Is the Screen: Deleuze and the Philosophy of Cinema*, ed. Gregory Flaxman (Minneapolis: University of Minnesota Press, 2000): 9.

100. Ibid., 15.

101. Guy Debord, *The Society of the Spectacle*, trans. Donald Nicholson-Smith (New York: Zone Books, 1994).

BIBLIOGRAPHY

Abel, Richard, ed. *French Film Theory and Criticism.* Vol. 1. *1907–1929.* Princeton, NJ: Princeton University Press, 1988.

———. *French Film Theory and Criticism.* Vol. 2. *1929–1939.* Princeton, NJ: Princeton University Press, 1988.

Allen, Richard. *Projecting Illusion: Film Spectatorship and the Impression of Reality.* New York: Cambridge University Press, 1995. Allen, Richard, and Murray Smith, eds. *Film Theory and Philosophy.* New York: Oxford University Press, 1997.

Astruc, Alexandre. "The Birth of a New Avant-Garde: La caméra-stylo." *The New Wave.* Ed. Peter Graham. London: Secker and Warburg, 1968.

Balázs, Béla. *Theory of the Film.* Ed. Edith Bone. New York: Arno Press, 1972.

Bazin, André. *What Is Cinema?* Vol. 1. Ed. and trans. Hugh Gray. Berkeley: University of California Press, 1967.

———. *What Is Cinema?* Vol. 2. Ed. and trans. Hugh Gray. Berkeley: University of California Press, 1971.

Bolter, Jay David, and Richard Grusin. *Remediation: Understanding New Media.* Cambridge: MIT Press, 1999.

Branigan, Edward. *Projecting a Camera: Language-Games in Film Theory.* New York: Routledge, 2006.

Braudy, Leo, and Marshall Cohen, eds. *Film Theory and Criticism.* 6th ed. New York: Oxford University Press, 2004.

Brooks, Peter. *The Melodramatic Imagination: Balzac, Henry James, Melodrama and the Mode of Excess.* New Haven, CT: Yale University Press, 1995.

Browne, Nick, ed. *Cahiers du Cinéma, 1969–1972: The Politics of Representation.* Cambridge, MA: Harvard University Press, 1990.

Casetti, Francesco. *Theories of Cinema: 1945–1995.* Trans. Francesca Chiostri and Elizabeth Gard Bartolini-Salimbeni, with Thomas Kelso. Austin: University of Texas Press, 1999.

Cavell, Stanley. *Pursuits of Happiness: The Hollywood Comedy of Remarriage.* Cambridge, MA: Harvard University Press, 1981.

Copjec, Joan. "The Orthopsychic Subject: Film Theory and the Reception of Lacan." *Film and Theory.* Ed. Robert Stam and Toby Miller. Malden, MA: Blackwell, 2000: 437–455.

Crary, Jonathan. *Techniques of the Observer: On Vision and Modernity in the Nineteenth Century.* Cambridge: MIT Press, 2001.

Davis, Colin. *After Poststructuralism: Reading, Stories and Theory.* New York: Routledge, 2004.

De Lauretis, Teresa, and Stephen Heath, eds. *The Cinematic Apparatus.* New York: St. Martin's Press, 1980.

Deleuze, Gilles. *Cinema 1: The Movement Image.* Trans. Hugh Tomlinson and Barbara Habberjam. Minneapolis: University of Minnesota Press, 1986.

———. *Cinema 2: The Time Image.* Minneapolis: University of Minnesota Press, 1989.

Doane, Mary Ann. *The Desire to Desire: The Woman's Films of the 1940s.* Bloomington: Indiana University Press, 1987.

Eagleton, Terry. *After Theory.* New York: Basic Books, 2003.

Eisenstein, Sergei. *Eisenstein Writings, 1922–1934.* Trans. and ed. Richard Taylor. London: BFI Publishing, 1998.

———. *Eisenstein*. Vol. 2. *Toward a Theory of Montage*. Ed. Michael Glenny and Richard Taylor. Trans. Michael Glenny. London: British Film Institute, 1991.

Flaxman. Gregory, ed. *The Brain Is the Screen: Deleuze and the Philosophy of Cinema*. Minneapolis: University of Minnesota Press, 2000.

Friedberg, Anne, James Donald, and Laura Marcus, eds. *Close Up 1927–1933: Cinema and Modernism*. Princeton, NJ: Princeton University Press, 1998.

Geuens, Jean-Pierre. "The Digital World Picture." *Film Quarterly* 55.4 (Summer 2002): 16.

Gomery, Douglas. "Economic Struggles and Hollywood Imperialism: Europe Converts to Sound." *Film Sound*. Ed. John Belton and Elisabeth Weiss. New York: Columbia University Press, 1985: 5–24.

Greenberg, Clement. *The Collected Essays and Criticism*. Vol. 1. Ed. John O'Brien. Chicago: University of Chicago Press, 1986.

Hammond, Paul, ed. and trans. *The Shadow and Its Shadow: Surrealist Writing on the Cinema*. 3rd ed. San Francisco: City Lights, 2000.

Heath, Stephen. *Questions of Cinema*. Bloomington: Indiana University Press, 1981.

Kepley, Vance, Jr. "The Kuleshov Workshop," *Iris* 4.1 (Fall 1986): 5–23.

Kracauer, Siegfried. *Theory of Film*. Princeton, NJ: Princeton University Press, 1997.

Lindsay, Vachal. *The Art of the Moving Picture*. New York: Liveright Corporation, 1970.

Manovich, Lev. *The Language of New Media*. Cambridge: MIT Press, 2001.

Metz, Christian. *Film Language: A Semiotics of the Cinema*. New York: Oxford University Press, 1974.

———. *The Imaginary Signifier: Psychoanalysis and the Cinema*. Trans. Celia Britton, Annwyl Williams, Ben Brewster, and Alfred Guzzetti. Bloomington: Indiana University Press, 1982.

Morin, Edgar. *The Cinema, or the Imaginary Man*. Minneapolis: University of Minnesota Press, 2005.

Mulvey, Laura. *Visual and Other Pleasures*. Bloomington: Indiana University Press, 1989.

O'Brien, Charles. *Cinema's Conversion to Sound: Technology and Film Style in France and the U.S.* Bloomington: Indiana University Press, 2005.

Pasolini, Pier Paolo. "The Cinema of Poetry." *Movies and Methods I*. Ed. Bill Nichols. Berkeley: University of California Press, 1976.

Penley, Constance. *The Future of an Illusion: Film, Feminism, and Psychoanalysis*. Minneapolis: University of Minnesota Press, 1989.

Price, Brian. "Color, the Formless, and Cinematic Eros." *Framework: The Journal of Cinema and Media* 47.1 (Spring 2006): 22–35.

Rodowick, D.N. *The Crisis of Political Modernism: Criticism and Ideology in Contemporary Film Theory*. Berkeley: University of California Press, 1994.

———. *The Difficulty of Difference: Psychoanalysis, Sexual Difference, and Film Theory*. New York: Routledge, 1992.

Rosen, Philip, ed. *Narrative, Apparatus, Ideology*. New York: Columbia University Press, 1986.

Sconce, Jeffrey. "The (Depressingly) Attainable Text." *Framework: The Journal of Cinema and Media* 45.2 (Fall 2004): 68–75.

Studlar, Gaylyn. *In the Realm of Pleasure: Von Sternberg, Dietrich, and the Masochistic Aesthetic*. Urbana: University of Illinois Press, 1988.

Taylor, Richard, and Ian Christie, eds. *The Film Factory: Russian and Soviet Cinema in Documents, 1896–1939*. Trans. Richard Taylor. Cambridge, MA: Harvard University Press, 1988.

Truffaut, Francois. "A Certain Tendency of the Cinema." *Movies and Methods*. Vol. 1. Ed. Bill Nichols. Berkeley: University of California Press, 1976.

Vertov, Dziga. *Kino-Eye: The Writings of Dziga Vertov*. Ed. Annette Michelson, trans. Kevin O'Brien. Berkeley: University of California Press, 1984.

Williams, Alan. "Historical and Theoretical Issue in the Coming of Recorded Sound to the Cinema." *Sound Theory/Sound Practice*. Ed. Rick Altman. New York: Routledge, 1992: 126–137.

CHAPTER 3

....

VISUAL MEDIA AND
THE TYRANNY
OF THE REAL

....

DEVIN ORGERON

Alfred Hitchcock: I should like to ask you a question. Why has it become old-fashioned to tell a story, to use a plot? I believe that there are no more plots in the recent French films.

François Truffaut: Well, that isn't systematic. It's simply a trend that reflects the evolution of the public, the impact of television, and the increasing use of documentary and press material in the entertainment field. All of these factors have a bearing on the current attitude toward fiction; people seem to be moving away from that form and to be rather leery of the old patterns.

A.H.: In other words, the trend away from the plot is due to the progress in communications? Well, that's possible. I feel that way myself, and nowadays I'd prefer to build a film around a situation rather than a plot.

—François Truffaut, *Hitchcock*[1]

FILM AND THE PRIVILEGED RELATIONSHIP

While the conversational fragment quoted at the top of this essay was chosen half playfully, its prescience, not to mention its hindsight, are undeniable. Hitchcock, the cinematic storyteller, mourned the disintegration of what he called "plot," that convention-bound structure upon which "narrative" is hung. Truffaut, in an unusual moment of pragmatism devoid of his usual and often quite intoxicating cinematic romanticism, suggested that this "trend" was the result of "evolution" and the increasing speed with which *reality* might be transmitted. The topic passes quickly in the seminal book of interviews but, like the repressed, keeps returning in veiled form; and, more often than not, Hitchcock is the unlikely author of its return, continually questioning the value of what he referred to as "photographic reality" in favor of a tightly orchestrated, cinematic—one is tempted to say "Hitchcockian"—rendering. At the peak of one such moment, Hitchcock leveled the following highly instructive, perhaps slightly defensive argument: "[I]f you're going to show two men fighting with each other, you're not going to get very much by simply photographing that fight. More often than not the photographic reality is not realistic. The only way to do it is get into the fight and make the public feel it. In that way you achieve true realism."[2]

Hitchcock, emotional provocateur that he was, let his formalist slip show here, but did so with remarkable aplomb, bringing to the table a term that will guide our present line of inquiry. Invoking the notion of "true realism," Hitchcock suggested that the cinematic situation, in its remarkable flexibility, offers multiple "realisms," which he felt obliged to qualify. His, perhaps obviously, is "true," but in its wake one might imagine dozens of—to continue with Hitchcock's boxing metaphor— contenders. And, "true" or not, Hitchcock's brand of realism, at the time of the interviews, was falling dangerously out of fashion. Based as it is upon an economically derived logic of emotional returns—he was concerned with "getting" an emotional response and feared not "get[ting] very much"—Hitchcock's "illusionist" realism seems a tidy example of the manipulative, often placating nightmare that seventies and eighties structuralist film theory sought to exorcize. Realism, like reality itself, is inconstant, an idea the following pages will return to repeatedly.

Hitchcock and Truffaut's varying realist allegiances chart out with remarkable efficiency the directions in which the realist debate itself has moved. Truffaut, a student of French cinematic realist and *Cahiers du Cinéma* founder André Bazin, borrowed the language of his adoptive father figure, referring obliquely in the quote that opens this essay to Bazin's own Darwino-creationist rhetoric in "The Evolution of the Language of the Cinema," the highly influential and, for a decade or so, much maligned essay from *What Is Cinema?*[3] Bazin, who aligned himself and his theoretical framework against German Expressionism, placed Soviet montage somewhere near the middle of the ladder of cinematic perfection and suggested the primacy of the deeply composed long take, the pinnacle, in his estimation, of cinematic realism, which, for Bazin, is the pinnacle of the cinematic itself. Weaned on German Expressionism and influenced by the evocative power of montage, Hitchcock wondered, and provoked a similar sense of wonder in Truffaut, about the "truth" of simply setting up the camera to "record" an event or, for that matter, a nonevent, a process intricately tied, in his estimation, to the case of the disappearing plot. Perhaps unbeknownst to the master himself, Hitchcock's invocation of "photographic reality" is uncannily similar, though opposed philosophically, to "camera reality," the notion of that other giant among realist theoreticians, Siegfried Kracauer, who explored this concept in unflinching detail in his 1960 tome to the subject, *Theory of Film: The Redemption of Physical Reality.*[4]

The frequently returned-to subject in the Hitchcock-Truffaut interviews marks a critical, if popular, development within a debate that, while predating the cinema, has lingered within and around the cinema to the present day. The subject enjoyed a particular "vogue" in the 1960s and 1970s, around the publication of Truffaut's interviews with Hitchcock and the aforementioned major works by Bazin and Kracauer. Changing attitudes toward realism, in fact, have inspired most of the major cinematic movements studied in university film programs, resulting in a number of highly polemic and deeply volatile "manifestos," continuing to shape film theory as we understand and practice it today. Perhaps predictably, discussions of realism are once again prominent in our present age of verisimilar digital manipulation, popular documentaries, and that phenomenon we still insist on calling reality television. As we will see, Bazin's and Kracauer's theories were a response to a fundamental and far-reaching crisis in our cultural comprehension of reality; a reaction to a series of moments that seemed profoundly *unreal*. And, while our present "crisis" is more diffuse certainly than the Second World War, our understanding of "the real" is once again being challenged, in part by image-making industries that have perfected the illusion of access.

In its organizational strategies, this essay attempts to account for the cultural, critical, and theoretical history of "realism." While cinema is the focus, other visual media are referenced, in part because notions of cinematic realism still exert considerable power over other areas of our popular visual culture and in part because, as Truffaut's remarks from the 1960s indicate, those other visual media, in their immediacy, have impacted in considerable ways our mutating notions of cinematic realism. Additionally, for all of its shifts and turns, this history of cinematic realism continually casts André Bazin and Siegfried Kracauer in central rolls. Peter Matthews, in a 1999 *Sight and Sound* feature on Bazin called "Divining the Real," explained, in a manner that I think can usefully be applied to Kracauer as well, the critical position Bazin occupies within our field:

> Bazin, a rhapsodist of the cinema and a true believer in its perfectibility, had replied to his own sweeping question "what is cinema?" with a resounding affirmation—whereas the new breed of theorists answered it increasingly in the negative. In the wake of the 60s counterculture, film-studies departments across

Europe were transformed into hubs of self-styled revolutionary activity. Fuelled by the absolutist views of French structuralist Marxist Louis Althusser (who proclaimed the function of the mass media to be an endless replication of ruling-class values), radical academics came out not to praise cinema but to bury it. . . . It might almost be said that the whole Byzantine edifice of contemporary film theory sprang out of an irresistible itch to prove Bazin wrong.[5]

While Matthews's position, in its apparent and disturbing anti-intellectual, anti-political furor, is as reductive as the anti-Bazinian stance he questioned (far from burying the cinema, this emergent and radicalized theoretical school sought to explain its effects upon the viewer), its backbone remains critically rigid. In a turn of phrase Jean-Luc Godard would surely approve of, Matthews here implied a credo that is nearly impossible to dismantle: "No Bazin, No Cinema Studies" (where, of course, "No" might also be spelled "Know"). And, indeed, even when he is not named, the post-Bazin landscape of film theory has him in mind. Writing several decades after the fact and for a British magazine that, especially during "those" years, seemed the diametric opposite of *Screen* (the implied culprit in Matthews's selective history), what Matthews passes off as Bazin bashing, however, needs, like Bazinian thought itself, to be historicized. For, like Bazin's supposed "naïveté," his legendary faith in the indexicality of the image, structuralism (one could fill in just about any theoretical school here), was a response to the culture around it, to a specific set of historical prime movers. As I examine in this essay, Bazin's faith (and several readings of this term are appropriate here) in the image as an index for the real was as important to postwar Europe as, for example, Jean Baudrillard's apparent faithlessness is to our current and similarly critical historical moment. Bazin and Kracauer, then, form a realist hub from which a number of sometimes unlikely, seemingly oppositional theoretical spokes emerge. It is, of course, the cinema's hotly contested "privileged relationship" with the realm of the real that fuels this long-standing, at times contentious interest. In their attempts to historicize their understanding of this relationship, the cinema's foundational realists, Bazin and Kracauer, grounded their ideas in an understanding of the cinema's photomechanical roots.

WORTH A THOUSAND WORDS: REALITY AND THE PHOTOGRAPHIC INDEX

Predating Bazin's and Kracauer's ideas regarding the cinema's ties to the photographic process, and in many ways predicting the shape if not the tone of much realist theory to follow, is Marxist cultural critic Walter Benjamin's important and

highly influential 1935 essay "The Work of Art in the Age of Mechanical Reproduction."[6] As Miriam Hansen's remarkable 1997 introduction to Kracauer's *Theory
of Film* has illuminated, Kracauer and Benjamin had known each other since 1924,
had both drawn at various points in their careers from the well of the Frankfurt
School, and met and exchanged notes regularly during their exile years in Paris.[7]
Their influence on each other is as undeniable as perhaps the even more critical
impact of history on their philosophical approaches. Like Bazin, Benjamin and
Kracauer were keen to observe and record modernity's impact on the real, the
authentic, and the human. Created just before, from within, and just beyond
a historical moment of incalculable Fascist disruption to all three categories,
their writing, in both theme and style, reflects the crisis itself. Though they approached it differently, all three hoped to understand the mechanical arts and
their relationship—redemptive or destructive—to the real, the authentic, and the
human. This philosophical quest for all three critics begins with an examination of
photography, which they regarded as the cinema's most critical predecessor and
the single most important technological development of the twentieth century in
its ability to rearrange human psychology.

Benjamin's conviction that photography was the linchpin of modernity begins simply enough and in a mode of semi-oedipal evolutionary rhetoric (this
art form supersedes that one, and so on down the line), a genealogy that realist
approaches to the cinema will have difficulty shaking, as Truffaut's comments
suggest (he referred to the evolution of the "public" and Hitchcock to a "progress
in communications"). Benjamin wrote, "[O]nly a few decades after its invention, lithography was surpassed by photography. For the first time in the process
of pictorial reproduction, photography freed the hand of the most important
artistic functions which henceforth devolved only upon the eye looking into
a lens."[8]

More complex and, for the realist critics who proceed from him, more alluring, is Benjamin's notion of "aura" and its disappearance in the modern era.
Mechanical reproduction, especially what we may wish to refer to as "lens technologies" (a terminological choice that allows Benjamin's celluloid-based arguments access to the digital age), is doubly freighted. On the one hand, Benjamin
suggested, these technologies "free" the original from its specific historical and
physical location, allowing broad access and mass engagement with otherwise
"fixed" (i.e., exclusive, inaccessible) realities. On the other hand, this "freedom"
strips the original of its originality, its authenticity, or its "aura."

Benjamin remained uniquely and admirably flexible in his position on the vast
cultural changes brought on by these technologies, functioning like an especially
articulate though somewhat distant reporter on the twentieth century from his
own unique vantage point in 1935. The political implications of the phenomenon as
Benjamin described it, however, forced him to editorialize in a manner that has
had a profound impact on future approaches to realism in the cinema straight into

our present age. As surgically incisive as the lens technologies he described in its ability to cut to the heart of the matter,[9] Benjamin's argumentation reveals the potential—both positive and negative—of a newly liberated cultural practice and, in a manner that both Kracauer and Bazin later adopted, makes a plea for imagistic responsibility. Written on the precipice of the Holocaust, Benjamin's words prophetically warn against the highly aesthetic Fascist misuse of mechanical reproduction to overwhelm and placate the image-hungry masses.[10] Responding to the aftermath of such an abuse, postwar realist critics sought to reclaim and de-aestheticize reality and, in the process, liberate the viewer and democratize the viewing process. The deeply composed long take championed by Bazin, while itself an acknowledged convention, was an important counteraesthetic to these perceived abuses in its invitation to the spectator, its unique ability to create the illusion of precisely the type of perceptual choice stymied by Fascism.

Though Kracauer's *Theory of Film* was not published until 1960 (at the same time as Bazin's essays were first collected and published in French), his thinking about cinema and its relationship to the physical world long predates it. The year 1995 saw the publication, many years overdue, of Kracauer's earliest writings in a translated collection called *The Mass Ornament: Weimar Essays*.[11] Of particular interest in the collection is Kracauer's 1927 essay, "Photography," in which he lays the foundation for what would become a highly "medium-specific" understanding of the cinematic phenomenon.[12] Kracauer recognized, like Benjamin, a discernible, massive, and growing cult of the image, and feared the potential abuses of this cult. His much-discussed media specificity, his enumeration, in *Theory of Film*, of a set of photographic "affinities" and cinematic properties, are less an act of simple-minded polemical boundary building and more an act of basic and deeply personal historical necessity.[13] Although it is flawed and sometimes downright frustrating, there is a quiet and heartbreaking desperation in Kracauer's writing that Benjamin (fellow Jew, fellow exile, and in 1940 a tragic suicidal statistic) and Bazin (whom Jean Renoir, in his foreword to *What Is Cinema*, vol. 1, described as "a modest fellow, sickly, slowly and prematurely dying") somehow manage to escape in their own rhetorical flourishes.[14] Miriam Bratu Hansen, turning to Benjamin's letters from the period, credited this desperation to Kracauer's own fetishistic image absorption at the moment he thought was sure to bring his own and the world's destruction.[15] Kracauer found *salvation* in images, certain images, and hoped to share that salvation. This point is muted at best in the book as published in 1960, removed as that moment seemed from the specific history to which Kracauer's ideas were actively responding. Hansen's extensive research into what she called Kracauer's "virtual book," one that was begun decades prior to the 1960 publication, restores much of this history and needs to be kept in mind when approaching Kracauer's work, which is a response to and account of cinema, most certainly, but one, like Benjamin's, that cannot help but be deeply colored by the moment from which it emerged.

Key to Kracauer's understanding of the cinema are its ties to the photographic. The book's first chapter, "Photography," an updated and reconceived version of a 1927 essay, begins with a statement that, standing alone, accounts for the almost immediate and quite lengthy flogging the book and its author would receive from the critical community. Kracauer wrote that "[t]his study rests upon the assumption that each medium has a specific nature which invites certain kinds of communications while obstructing others."[16] Then, mapping out a well-researched, logical, and highly convincing history of the photographic medium, Kracauer developed the pivot upon which his entire theoretical structure would sway: "Throughout the history of photography there is on the one side a tendency toward realism culminating in records of nature, and on the other a formative tendency aiming at artistic creations. Often enough, formative aspirations clash with the desire to render reality, overwhelming it in the process. Photography, then, is the arena of two tendencies which may well conflict with each other. This state of things raises the aesthetic problems to which we now must turn."[17]

Kracauer suggested, then, that the lens (photographic and, by extension, cinematic), is uniquely fitted to and capable of the accurate representation of physical reality. Certain photographic images might be ranked as more or less "photographic" depending on their reverence for the physical world. Predictably enough, this logic extends to the cinema as well, "evolving" as it does from the photographic.

Bazin made a similar argument in "The Ontology of the Photographic Image" but established in even greater detail a key comparative factor that is implied but muffled in Kracauer's analysis. Again, we are deep in the sometimes quite uncomfortable trenches of medium-specific warfare, but Bazin's attention to the "two ambitions" of painting (Kracauer would have called them tendencies) and the concentration of those ambitions toward their more "subjective" and mediated pursuits as photography established its realist *objectivity* lends to Bazin's argumentation a difficult to deny, seemingly *ordained* orderliness.[18] Capitalizing on the dual valences of the French term for lens, *objectif*, Bazin suggested that photography "does reality better" and with less subjective human intervention, a skill set that ultimately liberated painting from its realist confines and allowed it to pursue its natural but momentarily interrupted path. At the end of the essay he wrote that "photography is clearly the most important event in the history of the plastic arts. Simultaneously a liberation and a fulfillment, it has freed Western painting, once and for all, from its obsession with realism and allowed it to recover its aesthetic autonomy."[19]

The implied narrowness of these convictions is legendary, spawning a generation of critical debate. What Benjamin, Kracauer, and Bazin each recognized (and, undeniably, overemphasized), however, is the mechanical difference that separates the lens-based arts from other representational endeavors. Benjamin offered a warning that was picked up by Kracauer, who seemed to search for and find images that retain some trace of the "authentic." He praised these while leveling an aesthetic and political attack against images that do not. This critical strategy, for Kracauer, began in earnest in his 1947 book *From Caligari to Hitler: A Psychological History of the German Film*. Here he laid bare his conviction that history and cinema affect each other, and that certain aesthetic concerns *enrich* (for better or worse) the sociopolitical soil. In his preface, Kracauer stated, "It is my contention that through an analysis of the German films [*sic*] deep psychological dispositions predominant in Germany from 1918 to 1933 can be exposed—dispositions which influenced the course of events during that time and which will have to be reckoned with in the post-Hitler era."[20] This comment, the book from which it arises, and a reanalysis of Kracauer's career itself, in other words, suggest the commonalities between Kracauer's work and the wave of Athusserian structuralism that seemed to bury him. Kracauer (though the issue is often recessed) understood all too personally the political implications of image making and its societal effects. Images *can* placate, *can* mobilize, *can* naturalize ideology. Kracauer's faith, a faith we might link to Bazin's, in a certain set of images created in the name of spectatorial democratization is what sets the realist position apart.

From Caligari to Hitler and *Theory of Film* stand as the initial pieces in the larger picture of Kracauer's proposed post-Hitler reckonings. They are attempts to deal with the aftermath of the Second World War and the future of the image. But Kracauer's prefatory remarks reveal a metaphorical subtlety his supporters and critics have hitherto ignored, a subtlety that takes us back to the idea of photography and the chemical-mechanical properties so central to these initial realist theoretical endeavors. Kracauer hinted at, through his choice of words and by virtue of his obsessive returns to the topic itself from 1927 onward, the historically *revealing* power of analysis and its own photographic nature. The bath of analytical attention, Kracauer suggested (or hoped), *exposes* the sometimes hidden contours of history. There is a conviction here, one our present generation needs to reckon with, that history, blurred as it is by its own cultural artifacts, is slow to reveal itself, mutates over time, and threatens its own disappearance. This fact—not simply a belief—is one that our realist critics actively railed against in their search for a preservational form and an aesthetic equal to it. In this quest, one is reminded of the photographer's quest in *Blow-Up*, Michelangelo Antonioni's 1966 cinematic reflection on photographic fidelity and its effect on the psyche. We might imagine our critics, like the photographer, in the darkroom (or the darkened room) awaiting an explanation for the inexplicable, waiting for history itself to *develop*.

EARLY CINEMA AND "THE REALIST TENDENCY"

This emphasis on the cinema's relationship to photography, on its mechanical backbone, and on its ability or, more radically, its *predestination* to capture and preserve is especially relevant to what we might call the cinema's prehistory. Kracauer's "encyclopedia" of the cinematic medium, as Benjamin called it,[21] in fact, moves from the photographic, in its first pages, to the early cinematic in the second chapter, called "Basic Concepts," focusing on and to some degree canonizing for future generations of film scholars the turn-of-the-century works of the Lumière brothers and Georges Méliès. Kracauer situated the brothers on the realistic or photographic side of his thesis and the fantasist Méliès on the formative or theatrical side, faulting the latter for what he took to be his use of "photography in a pre-photographic spirit—for the reproduction of a papier-mâché universe inspired by stage traditions."[22]

Kracauer's famous and at times overwhelming desire to dichotomize film history lies at the heart of his critical undoing and explains, for example, Dudley Andrew's accusation, in *The Major Film Theories*, that *Theory of Film* represents "a huge homogenous block of realist theory."[23] Still, his "this is cinematic and that is not" rhetoric, however reductive, reveals an important moment when cinema's future direction seemed to hang in the balance and when either direction seemed tenable. As I examine here, his dedication to a cinematic practice rooted in what he calls "the realistic tendency" would have a profound impact on the cinematic movements that arose from his and Bazin's influence. Kracauer wrote, "If film grows out of photography, the realistic and formative tendencies must be operative in it also. . . . Their prototypes were Lumière, a strict realist, and Méliès, who gave free rein to his artistic imagination. The films they made embody thesis and antithesis in a Hegelian sense."[24]

The seductive ease of Kracauer's categories has, of course, been called into question. However, once again, the occasional subtlety of Kracauer's ideas themselves underscores his own awareness, his own commitment to "balance" or, to follow with the Hegelian line referenced above, his belief that cinema in its most harmonious state is neither *thesis* nor *antithesis* but a delicate (if tilted toward the realist) *synthesis* of these originary tendencies. Like the primary cinematic texts they often engage with, theoretical ideas are canonized, a process that often involves the endless quotation of and confrontation with the idea itself in its most basic, most volatile, most polemical state. Theorists of what we might effectively refer to as the *Screen* years—because that British journal was the seedbed of antirealist cinematic theorizing in the seventies and early eighties—were made nervous, I suspect, by the genuine ambivalence of realist theory, an ambivalence that

Figure 3.1 An example of Kracauer's "realist tendency":
the Lumières' *The Baby's Meal* (1895).

itself reflected the realist position. Theories of cinematic realism remind us, in their very rhetorical strategies, that "reality" rarely provides simple "this" or "that" options. Peter Matthews, speaking once again of Bazin but in a manner that applies to Kracauer as well, wrote, "[P]rofessional intellectuals who jumped on Bazin's alleged incoherence also underrated the profoundly dialectical nature of his thinking. To put it another way, they were stone-blind to Bazin's poetic genius— his ability to hold contrary terms in a state of paradoxical suspension that transcends mere theory and approaches mystical understanding."[25] Here, as before, Matthews's own anti-intellectual venom veils the vital heart at the center of his argument. Bazin's and Kracauer's theoretical maneuvers replicate the cinematic virtues they promote in their ability to allow the beholder (the viewer, the reader) an opportunity to think for him- or herself; we might refer to this as a sort of "deep-field" theoretics. For his own part, Kracauer, toward the end of "Basic Concepts," wrote that "everything depends on the 'right' balance between the realistic tendency and the formative tendency[,] and the two tendencies are well balanced if the latter does not try to overwhelm the former but eventually follows its lead."[26] Bazin, in an essay called "Bicycle Thief" in the second volume of the *What Is Cinema* collection, arrived at a similar conclusion, writing that " 'realism' can only occupy in art a dialectical position—it is more a reaction than a truth."[27] For Kracauer, early cinema afforded few opportunities for such balance and was categorically divided.

Recent examinations of early cinema have upset Kracauer's seemingly simple dichotomy. They have made the artifacts of early cinema an especially hot object

Figure 3.2 An example of Kracauer's "formative tendency":
Méliès's *A Trip to the Moon* (1902).

within cinema studies, focusing quite often on the very questions of realism that Kracauer seemed to take for granted, questions of what constituted "the cinematic" even as it was establishing itself. Tom Gunning's highly influential and much referenced "The Cinema of Attraction: Early Film, Its Spectator and the Avant-Garde" (1986) is an excellent case in point and remains a central and guiding text for a new wave of cine-historical archivists interested in exploring the impulses driving pre-1906 cinematic modes in a decidedly less impressionistic fashion. Gunning, in fact, did not see the moment Kracauer described as a moment swaying between "realism" and "narrative"—a common enough way of understanding Kracauer's distinctions, though Kracauer himself never used the term "narrative" and seemed more concerned with a very particular *kind* of artifice—and recognized instead a certain commonality between the two supposed poles. Gunning argued that, rather than accepting the polarity of Lumière and Méliès, one might "unite them in a conception that sees cinema less as a way of telling stories than as a way of presenting a series of views to an audience." He called this earlier conception of cinema "the cinema of attractions."[28] In borrowing the notion of "attractions" from Sergei Eisenstein, loaded as it is with all of its fairground baggage, Gunning hoped to "underscore the relations to the spectator that . . . later avant-garde practice shares with early cinema: that of exhibitionist confrontation rather than diegetic absorption."[29] In Gunning's estimation, the allure the cinema held for the pre-1906 spectator lay neither in its "realist" recording function nor in its whimsical narrative abilities but, rather, in its stark and largely technologically based "newness."

Mary Ann Doane's 1996 "Temporality, Storage, Legibility: Freud, Marey, and the Cinema" focuses on the precinematic motion experiments of Etienne-Jules

Marey, detecting in this work another kind of "realist" impulse, one which, like Freudian analysis, hoped to find and make legible the otherwise imperceptible reality hiding beneath the seen or the spoken. Doane suggested that, in this, Freud and Marey might both be considered scientists engaged in an attempt to isolate moments. Hinging as it does on issues of temporality and the capturing and reading of these "moments," "[c]inema presents the illusion—and the commercially successful illusion—of what Marey could only dream about, the possibility of a continuous and nonselective recording of real-time. In concealing the division between frames, it refuses to acknowledge the loss of time on which it is based. From Marey's point of view, there is a double deception at work here: the lie that truth resides in visibility, in what the eye can see, and the pretense that the cinema replicates time perfectly, without loss."[30]

Doane cast both Marey and—by a leap of imagination—Freud as precinematic realists who would, in their concern over those lost bits of time and the cinematic act of deception, *resist* the cinema for its built-in illusionist nature, its ability to look complete in the midst of its sleight of hand. To Doane, this line of reasoning "[a]nticipates Kracauer's anxieties about photography's and film's inscription of a spatial and temporal continuum without gap, of a 'blizzard' or 'flood' of images."[31] She suggested, further, that "time is produced as an effect, at least in part to protect the subject from the anxieties of total representation generated by the new technological media.[32] Classical film theory grows in response to precisely this anxiety with regard to the photo-cinematic index and its treatment of both space and time. Both classical categories, the realists on one side and what Noël Carroll has called the "creationists" on the other, are aware of the cinema's deception, its innate and unconquerable "illusionist" qualities.[33] The options seem to be to dig more deeply into reality or, conversely, to disrupt the cinema's realist ease and plentitude through aggressive and authorial formal techniques that simply cannot be taken for granted and that underscore the illusion itself. Neither is so simple and, by the 1970s, both exploded.

CLASSICAL FILM THEORY, ITS OBJECTS, AND ITS OBJECTIONS: SOVIET MONTAGE, GERMAN EXPRESSIONISM, AND ITALIAN NEOREALISM

As Noël Carroll and others have noted, what we now refer to as "classical" film theory experienced a significant division with the advent of sound.[34] Interestingly, this rift occurred along the terrain of cinematic realism, and the aftershocks of these massive and opposed theoretical plates butting against one another are still being felt. The late silent period, the era of both Soviet montage and German Expressionism, aligned its energies in an effort to escape the mere "recording" of reality of which the photo-cinematic arts were accused. The period was marked by artistic invention and authorial control and a demonstrable desire to "elevate" what was perceived to be a mechanical novelty to new *artistic* heights. Moving against the idea of medium specificity—the notion that certain forms are best suited to certain tasks—silent film *artists* manipulated the mechanical aspects of their form, fractured the reality their tool was believed capable of recording, and foregrounded cinematic expressiveness in a manner they equated with other expressive forms.

Rudolf Arnheim emerged at this end of the divide, promoting a notion of the cinema's *artistic* potentialities transcending, in his estimation, objective fidelity. Refuting the widespread and medium-specific belief that photography, and by extension the cinematic arts, were denied access to the temple of artistic creation on largely technological grounds, Arnheim—an art historian—posited a notion of cinematic expression that descended in marked ways from his understanding of the other arts, chiefly painting.

Though his seminal text, *Film as Art*, was not published until 1957, like Kracauer's work, it represents decades of critical thought.[35] In fact, much of the book—the portions most frequently cited and reprinted—were adapted from an earlier text, *Film als Kunst*, which was translated into English under the title *Film* in 1933. Still, in a fashion that would be repeated throughout film theory's brief history, there is a feeling that Arnheim's ideas arrived on the scene a bit late; film theory, with few and important exceptions, seems to operate about a decade behind the medium whose path it traces. This Johnny-come-lately feeling is all the more pronounced in Arnheim's case insofar as the book makes an argument for the silent film, suggesting that the so-called technological advances within the cinematic medium (sound, color, etc.) have, in fact, stunted its *artistic* growth. Film as art, in other words, has become an impossibility under the weight of technologically achieved and culturally demanded verisimilitude.

At the beginning of this chapter I indicated the degree to which Truffaut's and Hitchcock's positions encapsulate several decades' worth of theoretical thought. It is worth noting that, though he most certainly adapted, learning to embrace both sound and color (and, if only for a moment, three-dimensional technology), Hitchcock maintained the Arnheim party line throughout his career. Consistently citing his highly "realist" 1957 film *The Wrong Man* as a temporary detour, Hitchcock was a famous and self-proclaimed antirealist (at least as that idea was popularly understood). In a telling fragment toward the end of the revised edition of the interviews, Truffaut innocently asked if Hitchcock was in favor of the teaching of cinema in the universities. Hitchcock's answer is indicative of his position and of the realist debate as it stood at that historical juncture. He responded, "Only on the condition that they teach cinema since the era of Méliès and that the students learn how to make silent films, because there is no better form of training. Talking pictures often served merely to introduce the theater into the studios. The danger is that young people, and even adults, all too often believe that one can become a director without knowing how to sketch a décor, or how to edit."[36]

Like Hitchcock, Arnheim was interested chiefly in the expressive and subjective (read "artistic") manipulation of mise-en-scène (German Expressionism is object choice number one) and a similarly authorial use of editing (Soviet montage becomes object choice number two). Though he was a latecomer, Arnheim is an exemplar of the "film as art" position, a position previously held by Sergei Eisenstein, Lev Kuleshov, V.I. Pudovkin, Hugo Munsterberg, Béla Balázs, and others. Later, though with some solid and often very articulate realist hesitancy, Maya Deren and a new, postsurrealist generation of cinematic avant-gardists would guard the same line.

On the other side of the divide are the realist theorists, Bazin and Kracauer most notably, who praised what they perceived to be the sound cinema's innate realist abilities. In an argumentative line perfectly opposed to Arnheim's, Bazin, in "The Myth of Total Cinema," went so far as to claim that the cinema, as such, had yet to be invented,[37] a philosophical move that bristled the hairs of the high-art, antisound theorists of the era in its suggestion that sound was a *progressive* step on the ladder of cinematic perfection.

Perhaps because of the unified logic of his approach and his ability to point directly to the thematic and aesthetic embodiment of his theoretical ideal, Bazin has become the theoretical voice of cinematic realism. Bazin admired and wrote extensively about postwar Italian cinema—Italian neorealism—and his admiration revolved around a fundamental set of aesthetic, moral, and political values upheld in those films. Though he enumerated the "basic" neorealistic qualities he admired, qualities that are similarly enumerated in Cesare Zavattini's own demands for a revitalized Italian cinema, Bazin's concerns are less strongly tied to subtleties in acting (and, indeed, the use of nonactors), the mere fact of shooting on location, or the neorealistic predilection for the contemporary. Indeed, Bazin's ideas, though opposed philosophically to the Freud/Marey thesis in their effort to find redemption in certain corners of the cinematic, seem to arise from the same temporal and spatial logic that elicited such fear (as Doane would have it) from, for instance, Sigmund Freud and Etienne-Jules Marey. It is the neorealistic attention to spatial depth and temporal duration that, for Bazin, is the cinema's salvation. Writing specifically of neorealism's oppositional treatment of time, Bazin argued that

> it is perhaps especially the structure of the narrative which is most radically turned upside down. It must now respect the actual duration of the event. The cuts that logic demands can only be, at best, descriptive. The assemblage of the film must never add anything to the existing reality. If it is part of the meaning of the film, as with Rossellini, it is because the empty gaps, the white spaces, the parts of the event that we are not given, are themselves of a concrete nature: stones

which are missing from the building. It is the same in life: we do not know everything that happens to others. Ellipsis in classic montage is an effect of style. In Rossellini's films it is a lacuna in reality, or rather in the knowledge we have of it, which is by its nature limited.[38]

Bazin's ideal aesthetic, it seems, is an aesthetic of skilled authorial self-effacement. This logic opposes, for example, Arnheim's notion of "film as art" in its practiced denial of the artistic function. Critics and supporters have pointed to the religious undertones in Bazin's reasoning, his fear that cinematic artistry would result in a dangerous form of demagoguery and a problematic denial of reality's grandeur. Style, in the Bazinian realm, is trickery, and so the main stylistic units of the form (the shot and the cut) must adopt a seemingly more "democratic" nature. It is, in fact, neorealism's allowance for perceptual choice that Bazin valued, though he was keen to advertise his awareness that this democratic approach itself is a stylistic choice. The structuralist dread over realism, of course, was aimed at a different set of ideologically grounded and numbing aesthetic choices, largely the creation of the Hollywood machine. For Bazin, cutting only to change location, a less plotted elliptical structure, and a deep and expansive compositional approach *replicate* the experience of actual, daily existence. Like Kracauer, Bazin espoused the cinema's unique ability to replicate.

This theoretical mode is all the more interesting given its results. In discussing Arnheim's "film as art" thesis and its faith in and lament over the passing of the silent cinema, I mentioned the curious fact of film theory's perpetual and rarely fashionable "lateness." Film and film theory rarely walk hand in hand. Trends in the one rarely reflect similar activity in the other. Bazin and Kracauer are even more remarkable in this respect. Published at the beginning of the 1960s, their ideas seemed in perfect keeping with a cinematic culture, in fact a popular culture more generally, that was increasingly and enthusiastically dispensing with the artifice in which previous generations had luxuriated. Postwar children were coming of age and responding to that singularly defining event in a defiant language, and that language, at its base, was principally a realist language forged from a theoretical fire some in the critical community mistakenly saw as simple, reactionary, or overtly puritanical.

New Waves, New Realisms, and the Bazinian/Brechtian Imprint

The "recent French films" to which Alfred Hitchcock referred somewhat mischievously in the quote that opens this essay, films Truffaut himself was "guilty" of making, were the offspring of a newly forming interest in cinematic authorship (a theoretical notion often associated with, credited to, or blamed on André Bazin, who remained ambivalent and occasionally opposed to it) and a continuing postwar, Italian-influenced interest in cinematic realism. In fact, the appeal, the shock, the fleeting "newness" of the French New Wave stem, at least in part, from the never entirely comfortable fit of its varied inheritances. Rejecting one "tradition of quality," some of the soon-to-be filmmakers among the *Cahiers du Cinéma* critics (Jean-Luc Godard and François Truffaut most notably and most vehemently) embraced another, though they were careful to lionize its outsiders for what they discerned as their authorial mark: Samuel Fuller, Nicholas Ray, Robert Aldrich, and the like. Following close on the heels of their Italian predecessors (Truffaut, in fact, even served as assistant to Rossellini for two years, working on three of the director's unreleased films), they were equally energized by that movement's commitment to and exploration of reality.

Their theoretical influences were similarly held in contradiction. On the one hand, Bazin, the movement's spiritual father, gave them the courage to intelligently and honestly explore their own generation for all its faults, its ugliness, and its postwar desperation; he offered them their neorealist inheritance. Alexandre Astruc, on the other hand, whose 1949 essay "The Birth of a New Avant-Garde: La Caméra Stylo" (literally "The Camera Pen") suggested to this group of then journalists and eventual filmmakers the artistic and expressive potential of the form they held dear.[39] It was self-effacement on the one hand and self-propulsion on the other; that perhaps oddly, German émigré Bertolt Brecht would "mediate."

Though his own literal and theoretical interactions with the cinematic medium were rather scarce, it was Brecht's politically responsive and responsible, not to mention aesthetically generated and authorially reflexive, notion of realism, albeit a different kind of realism, that appealed to many of the filmmakers who would come to be known as the French New Wave. Realism, for Brecht, was not fixed or permanent but, rather, free and mobile. Less a "window on reality," Brechtian realism was a window on the conventions we use to express reality. Later popularized and made cinematic by Godard and others in the New Wave, Brecht's "distanciation" methods, or "alienation effects," were mechanisms by which the audience (in Brecht the theater audience, later the cinematic spectator) is made aware of the constructedness of the proceedings. Rather than being comforted and, perhaps, duped, the audience (which Brecht imagined as populist) would be critically activated and made aware of the mechanics of their *potential* undoing. Reliant as it is upon the audience and an awareness of that body, Brecht's brand of realism was necessarily flexible. In "The Popular and the Realistic" he articulated the evolutionary nature of realism in the following manner: "Our conception of *realism* needs to be broad and political, free from aesthetic restrictions and independent of convention. *Realist* means: laying bare society's causal network / showing up the dominant viewpoint of the dominators / writing from the standpoint of the class which has prepared the broadest solutions for the most pressing problems afflicting human society / emphasizing the dynamics of development / concrete and so as to encourage abstraction."[40]

Brecht stated later that "[r]eality alters; to represent it the means of representation must alter too. Nothing arises from nothing; the new springs from the old, but that is just what makes it new."[41] The filmmakers of the French New Wave embraced Bazin's notion of realism during what had become an increasingly, perhaps overwhelmingly, imagistic era (one that had seduced them). This was an era that had just passed though the furnace of the Second World War (a war that, as Kracauer told us, was fueled by its own image-making machines), and sought a realist form that would, at the same time, account for its own artificiality. This brand of self-reflexivity would balance the seemingly contradictory impulses of a giving in to the cinema's recording capabilities and exploiting its artistic and expressive possibilities. Most critically, this temperate brand of "exploitation" would absolve the filmmakers from the accusation that their artistry was *exploiting* their audience. The combination of these theoretical impulses would result in a charged cinema grounded firmly in the present, stripped of the illusionism of its predecessors. In our current and largely uncritical realist furor, we would do well to consider Brecht's warning, which seeks not to erect rules and criteria but, rather, to enforce a state of perpetual and intelligent flexibility. Brecht argued that "the criteria for the popular and the realistic need to be chosen not only with great care but also with an open mind. They must not be deduced from existing realist works and existing popular works, as is often the case. Such an approach would lead to purely formalistic criteria, and questions of popularity and realism would be decided by form."[42]

Brecht's line of argument returns us, once again, to the evolutionary language of Hitchcock and Truffaut, and of Kracauer and Bazin before them. Brecht's language, however, has been divested of the "naturalist" implications of his fellow realists, focusing instead on a notion of social "evolution." The quotes here serve to remind us of the fact that Brecht steered clear of the term itself and thereby escaped being critiqued for an uncritical faith that passing years and the changes they necessitate bring "progress," drawing us nearer to the dream of aesthetic perfection. Colin MacCabe's 1974 *Screen* essay, "Realism and the Cinema: Notes on Some Brechtian Theses," attempts to make sense out of the perceived "competing" realities contained within the "classic realist text" (CRT, as it came to be known, mirroring similarly abbreviated structures of dominance, such as the ISA, or the ideological state apparatus).[43] In a theoretical leap that would quickly be criticized (by David Bordwell, among others) or replicated (in the pages of *Screen* and elsewhere), MacCabe examined the parallels between "realist" nineteenth-century novels and, to him, similarly constructed, similarly dominant Hollywood films.

In MacCabe's analysis, the cinematic image track promises "truth" in the same way the narrating voice in fiction does. Hierarchically, in its abundance, in its apparent transparency, the image track is what MacCabe referred to as the "metalanguage." This "metalanguage" rises above other "discourses" (MacCabe used the packed language of the theoretical strains that inform his logic) contained within the structure and conservatively shuts down ambiguity. For many, the lack of ambiguity in MacCabe's *own* assertions provided evidence of a sort of *theoretical metalanguage* or set of metalanguages at work within film studies in the 1970s that, strangely, seemed to fly directly in the face of Brecht's own considerably less doctrinaire approach. This becomes all the more puzzling given the cinematic object of scrutiny in MacCabe's analysis, the immensely popular 1974 Alan Pakula film, *Klute*, in which an apparent contradiction between the narrational "said" of the film and the "seen" sends MacCabe reeling.

David Bordwell, in an insightful reading of MacCabe's brand of structuralism, suggested that the ambiguous ending of *Klute* is open to a range of possible readings and that neither image nor sound track emerges as privileged.[44] In retrospect, it seems the image-sound disconnect MacCabe wants so badly to read "metalinguistically" is a reflection of that era's immersion in and preoccupation with psychoanalysis, a topic thematically addressed within the film. As Doane reminded us, Freud's project was, in part, to bring "the real" (read "repressed") to the surface. Though I would not care to defend this position, it is entirely possible, given Brecht's model for flexibility, that for a moment in the seventies, *Klute*'s "realism" might well have been *subversive*, not dominant and repressive.

In any case, MacCabe's contribution to the realist question, compact though that contribution seems, had an enormous and lasting effect on the cine-theoretical community and resulted in a deeply factional wave within the academy, dividing film scholars into camps of neo-Bazinians to one side (Stanley Cavell is perhaps most notable among these), and what Noël Carroll refers to as "cine-Brechtians" on the other. While the turf they fought over was not limited to issues of realism, many of the key battles were. The furor over these opposed philosophical positions is all the more curious when we recall that their *combined* force resulted in one of film history's most interesting and most critically engaged movements. To some degree, Noël Carroll's career has been an attempt to make sense out of these positions in what he might, rather hopefully, refer to as the post-theoretical age.

THEORETICAL DIRECTIONS

Several decades in the making, the realism debate was clearly moving in a number of directions by the 1970s. Definitions and terminology proliferated, and major systems of understanding aligned against others. MacCabe, in fact, opened "Realism and the Cinema" with a statement that reverberates within the pages of *Screen*:

"One of the difficulties of any discussion about realism is the lack of any really effective vocabulary with which to discuss the topic."[45] Raymond Williams, with less dismay and a more powerful desire to arrange the history, opened "A Lecture on Realism" (1977) similarly: "It should be clear at the outset that except in the local vocabulary of particular schools, realism is a highly variable and inherently complex term. In fact, as a term, it only exists in critical vocabulary from the mid-nineteenth century, yet it is clear that methods to which the term refers are very much older."[46] This definitional confusion and the virtual quagmire it resulted in, coupled with the debate's long-standing history in a number of non–English speaking countries, led to the publication of a necessary but highly unusual attempt at international and historical synthesis, Christopher Williams's *Realism and the Cinema: A Reader*. Like MacCabe and Raymond Williams before him, Christopher Williams began with the admission that "[d]iscussion of realism, in film as in other art forms, tends to be tortuous or circular."[47] This statement is true enough, I think, though Williams does not fight very hard against it.

The book, published by Routledge in association with the British Film Institute in 1980, is noble in its efforts. It culls from a wide range of sources—Williams called them "fairly representative statements by film-makers, critics, and theoreticians . . . place[d] side by side so as to bring out their similarities and contradictions"[48]— and herein lies the book's usefulness and its damnation. A "reader" in the truest sense of the word, this highly selective anthology takes its reader through a quotational history of the realist question: first John Grierson, Eisenstein, Dziga Vertov, Zavattini, Bazin, Kracauer. It also anthologizes some of the key moments in the (as of 1980) contemporary state of the realist debate, and devotes, delightfully and perhaps oddly, a good deal of space to Eric Rohmer's musings on the topic, in both article and interview form. Perhaps more than anything else, the book illustrates the continued relevance of the topic of realism and the need to think beyond the confines of documentary, on the one hand, and what is sometimes called classical theory (and attempts to confront it), on the other.

Through an examination of the theoretical ideas attending both fiction and nonfiction filmmaking and through placing those theories "side by side," Williams foregrounded the conventions governing both. This increased awareness of documentary conventions and a significant shift in our cultural understanding of "documentary" itself has, in fact, resulted in realism's second dawning. Theories of "realism," when applied to fiction film, may finally be exercises in defining various ways of representing and understanding what is not "real" at all. But what happens when we turn to the documentary, which is, apparently at least, the representation of reality? The documentary has spawned its own line of critical argument, which has recently merged with theories of realism applied to fiction filmmaking.

Erik Barnouw's *Documentary: A History of the Non-Fiction Film*, originally published in 1974 and updated nearly every decade, ushered in a new interest in realism, focused, as it had been in the days of Robert Flaherty and Dziga Vertov, on documentary practice.[49] Bill Nichols's 1991 *Representing Reality* and, later, his *Introduction to Documentary* helped lay the foundation for a new theoretical framework that would be enhanced both by other scholarly efforts, chiefly Brian Winston's 1995 *Claiming the Real* and, perhaps more critically, a host of new politically, aesthetically, and morally innovative films from filmmakers as diverse as Marlon Riggs, Trinh T. Minh-ha, Errol Morris, Ken Burns, Ross McElwee, and the seemingly ubiquitous Michael Moore.[50]

While the relevance of the series moves well beyond the notion of "documentary," the highly influential Visible Evidence series, edited by Michael Renov, Fay Ginsburg, and Jane Gaines, and published by the University of Minnesota Press, has certainly revitalized serious thought within that category, helping since its emergence, alongside the Visible Evidence conferences from which the series arose, to push the boundaries of documentary studies while reassessing previous boundaries. The series' editorial mission statement is a revealing document. Found on the frontispiece of a number of the earlier volumes in the series and a featured element in their catalog descriptions, it reads, "Public confidence in the 'real' is everywhere in decline. This series offers a forum for the in-depth consideration of the representation of the real, with books that engage issues that bear upon questions of cultural and historical representation, and that forward the work of challenging prevailing notions of the 'documentary tradition' and of nonfiction culture more generally."

As a rallying cry for a generational wave of scholarship, these lines could not be more effective. The books promise to challenge and to engage, and have done so without fail, volume after volume. With each new volume, however, I have puzzled over the presumed access the editors have to the ins and outs of public confidence, wondering at the irony of a public whose confidence in the "real" (quotes and all) has waned. From all indications, our culture seems all too willing to accept certain packaged forms of the real, usually with the utmost confidence, or at least with a degree of passivity that would have alarmed the likes of Benjamin and Kracauer.

My sense of wonder is partly soothed by the assurance Jane Gaines gives in her introductory essay, "The Real Returns," to the anthological volume 6 in the series, titled *Collecting Visible Evidence*. Gaines wrote, "To return to documentary is to return again to cinematic realism and its dilemmas. To look back at film theory from the 1950s to the 1970s is to think about the way cinematic realism, first heralded as a technological triumph, became a philosophical problem."[51] Gaines acknowledges here the larger philosophical questions raised by a series on documentary film practice, a set of questions revolving once again around the real and the possibility, in any case, of documenting that reality. In a section of the introduction titled " 'Reality' in Quotation Marks," she extended a bit further, recognizing the critical importance of a flexible and multiply significant notion of realism. She did this by highlighting her (and the series') theoretical indebtedness:

To some degree, there is really only one way to read the pioneer thinkers Bazin and Kracauer—that is, as though they are capable of employing several notions of "realism" and "reality" at once. André Bazin is then seen as one of the more adept negotiators of these concepts, simultaneously able to give the impression that realism is both achieved through artifice and unproblematically expressed, and able to create the sense that "reality" is found as well as constructed. The critic who said that "some measure of realism must always be sacrificed in the effort of achieving it" can hardly be construed as a naïve realist. Also, in Siegfried Kracauer's famous assertion that "what the camera captures is more real than reality itself" one finds a subtle comment on aesthetics whereby the construction surpasses and even comments on its own constructedness. Putting the emphasis in Kracauer's famous statement on the "more real" instead of on the "reality itself" produces a comment on the plurality and the contingency or the relativity of realities.[52]

Gaines, in a move that has become increasingly popular, increasingly necessary, has put a postmodern spin on our formative realist thinkers, a spin that reflects our continuing battle with notions of the real and once again foregrounds the continuing relevance of Bazin and Kracauer in the midst of a new century's realist concerns. Gaines moreover appreciates and utilizes, both in this statement and in her own work, an open critical methodology.

In part due to our contemporary desire to define, redefine, and undefine it, the lion's share of contemporary realist thought has focused squarely upon documentary, which, as the Visible Evidence series indicates, is now a far more flexible category than it was even a decade ago when Barnouw and Nichols were charting out its territory and carving out a critical methodology. This wave of theoretical attention, accompanied by and predicated on major shifts within the culture itself, has provoked carrier waves with more broadly defined intentions reaching more deeply into our ceaseless desire to understand the mediation of reality.

Stephen Prince, in his important 1996 *Film Quarterly* essay "True Lies: Perceptual Realism, Digital Images and Film Theory," picked up where Kracauer and Bazin, for reasons having to do with their historical moment, left off. Prince, recognizing the challenges to previous theories of realism posed by digital technologies, proposed an alternate model, one that, he suggested, "produces[s] a better integration of the tensions between realism and formalism in film theory."[53] While his highly useful notion of "perceptual realism" overemphasizes the naïveté of his theoretical predecessors' indexical adherence, a presumed naïveté that presided over the academic burial of Kracauer and Bazin and which can be debunked or supported with similar ease, it is also a theoretical construct that provides useful avenues into media stretching far beyond Prince's own digitally centered thesis. Historicizing and then drawing from formalist and realist theories, Prince articulated the manner by which digitally rendered images might be read as "referentially fictional but perceptually realistic."[54] Centered as it is on spectatorial perception and a sliding scale of acceptable degrees of spatial verisimilitude,

Prince's model, like Brecht's, involves the viewer in the process and remains a relevant theoretical understanding of digitized reality-scapes even as those processes themselves have evolved into our present moment.

Like Prince's contribution, Julia Hallam and Margaret Mashment's *Realism and Popular Cinema* (2000) is concerned primarily with what we might rather simplistically refer to as contemporary "mainstream" realist traditions and offers a fresh evaluation of popular cinema's realist modes.[55] In spite of attempts to historicize and contextualize, though, and in spite of its much needed attention to British and Commonwealth cinemas in particular, the much-needed book's theoretical spine seems thin, especially with regard to the definitional quandaries the realist debate inevitably inspires. Its close readings of individual films as they hover around specific topical concerns serve to revitalize the realist question, focusing it once again on films that run the risk of being taken for granted or, for that matter, taken at their word.

It is almost a cliché for a theoretical overview to end with a section on postmodernity. It has become something of a scholarly punctuation mark, functioning rather like a highly self-aware ellipsis signifying eminent and continuing change, and this entry can scarcely escape the temptation. Postmodern theory has, to be certain, focused squarely on the palpable "crisis" the real finds itself in at century's end (and, for that matter, century's beginning), and the delicate position the real finds itself in corresponds directly to our culture's increased and often unthinking reliance on the mediated. Writing of realism in the postmodern era, Jean-François Lyotard argued that "capitalism inherently possesses the power to derealize familiar objects, social roles, and institutions to such a degree that the so-called realistic representations can no longer evoke reality except as nostalgia or mockery, as an occasion for suffering rather than for satisfaction. Classicism seems to be out in a world in which reality is so destabilized that it offers no occasion for experience but for ratings and experimentation."[56]

Lyotard, underestimating the powerful ambivalence in Benjamin's formulation, took issue, arguing, "[T]hat the mechanical and the industrial should appear as substitutes for hand or craft was not itself a disaster—except if one believes that art is in its essence the expression of an individuality of genius assisted by an elite craftsmanship."[57] In Lyotard's estimation, the mechanical processes simply maintained a trajectory that had already been undertaken. What Lyotard might refer to as classical realism has been replaced in our era by an economically driven *eclectic realism*, an idea Jean Baudrillard would expand upon and, to use Lyotard's own phrase, "wallow" in. Lyotard wrote, "By becoming kitsch, art panders to the confusion which reigns in the 'taste' of the patrons. Artists, gallery owners, critics, and public wallow together in the 'anything goes,' and the epoch is one of slackening. But this realism of the 'anything goes' is in fact that of money; in the absence of aesthetic criteria, it remains possible and useful to assess the value of works of art according to the profits they yield. Such realism accommodates all tendencies, just as capital accommodates all 'needs,' providing that the tendencies and needs have purchasing power.[58]

In some ways the pop-theoretical response to Lyotard's project, a project that digs deeply into the status of science, technology, the arts, and "information" more generally, Jean Baudrillard's sometimes beautifully truncated prose is even more spirited in its attention to the media and its transformation of the world as we *might have* known it. In *Simulacra and Simulation* (1994), he began the chapter "The Implosion of Meaning in the Media" with a near haiku-like plea that unravels into a post-McLuhanian treatise on the status of the real. He simply wrote, "We live in a world where there is more and more information, and less and less meaning. Consider these hypotheses."[59] In a phraseological move typical of Baudrillard, one that would be adopted by the popular culture that rose in his wake, Baudrillard wrote, "The hyperreality of communication and of meaning. More real than the real, that is how the real is abolished."[60] Baudrillard's *America* (1986) is a testament to the veracity of this statement and a painfully accurate (though Baudrillard expresses little of this pain) account of a country that, if it was ever real, is slipping outside of that realm swiftly.[61]

It is the unfair and still-to-be-played-out legacy of postmodern theoretics that it has somehow single-handedly killed, as if such a murder were possible, the real, or at least the idea of it. As is abundantly clear from the preceding, however, the real has never been a stable entity. Its temperature, as well as our temperature toward it, is in a constant state of flux. What theories of postmodernity have so poetically illustrated, however, is that our particular historical moment—let us say the last three decades, what we once, with a hesitant wink of romance, called the "information age" and what now we are at a loss to name—finds humanity at a philosophical crossroads. Bazin and Kracauer each, along with the world, shaken by the trauma of the Second World War and the impossibilities it spun into truth, found in the cinema a chance at liberation that would move along with and beyond the Allied efforts to enact the same. In a similar, less culturally specific moment of crisis, Jean-François Lyotard, Jean Baudrillard, and a host of other postmodern theorists have provided fewer salvational models to embrace, remaining more cautiously observational.

The self-conscious aftermath of this theoretical activity has manifested itself in an occasionally interesting cinematic reaction that is concerned, primarily at the thematic level, with the disintegration of reality. The cinema of David Cronenberg, in fact, has been treading this thematic ground for several decades; his 1999 *eXistenZ* is only the most obvious iteration of this concern in its ponderings over virtual reality. *The Matrix* series (Andy Wachowski and Larry Wachowski, 1999–2003) and the work of Philip K. Dick (which seems to have a choke-hold on a generation of young, educated readers) are similarly concerned, the former wearing its postmodern theoretical pedigree quite proudly (a cut to Neo opening, not reading, *Simulacra and Simulation* caused a veritable swoon among its cadre of academic viewers). David Fincher's *Fight Club* (1999) and the Chuck Palahniuk novel that inspired it are both terse but desperately humane responses to the same post-real impulse and manage to wade far more intelligently (certainly more intelligently than they have been given credit for) through the detritus of the contemporary in an unsuccessful search for a soul grounded in reality. Spike Jonze (*Being John Malkovich* [2000], *Adaptation* [2003]) and Michel Gondry (*Eternal Sunshine of the Spotless Mind* [2004], *The Science of Sleep* [2006], *Be Kind Rewind* [2008]) have adopted a similar stance, occasionally eschewing even the digital and technological effects that mark their age and adopting a more organic, maybe even anachronistic and deeply ironic position in response to reality's shift under the weight of technology.

Jonze and Gondry, in fact, signal a middle ground in the realist dilemma that is met on even more extreme terms in the highly doctrinaire cinematic challenge posed by Lars Von Trier, Thomas Vinterberg, Søren Kragh-Jacobsen, and Kristen Levring, the authors of the DOGME-95 manifesto and its attending rules, known as "The Vow of Chastity." David Cook suggested that these documents "were designed to liberate the cinema from its bondage to illusionist dramaturgy and bourgeois romanticism (and, thus, auteurism)."[62] The documents themselves, which have in their turn been highly romanticized, also express in no uncertain terms the authors' awareness that they (and cinematic culture as a whole) stood at the brink of profound change. Arising in the midst of what Cook called "a technological revolution driven by the proliferation of digital video,"[63] the DOGME movement recognized the potential (positive and negative) of technological innovation and, in an act of post-Bazinian, post-Kracauerian realist media specificity, laid the groundwork for a redemptive (albeit painful) exploration of reality. Foregrounding the manner by which digital technology might reveal rather than transform the real, these filmmakers and others after them were and are engaged in an act of redemption resembling, in many ways, the attempts of their predecessors: Umberto Barbaro and Cesare Zavattini's call for a new Italian cinema, Astruc and Truffaut's call for a new French cinema, the Oberhausen Manifesto's call for a rearranged and more vital German cinema, and so on.

In the midst of this grassroots realist activity, though predating it, stands the work of Iranian filmmaker Abbas Kiarostami. Like so many of his generation, Kiarostami's eyes were opened by Italian film from the 1940s, and his career since the 1970s has been an attempt to adapt and rework that language. Once he had gained notoriety (chiefly from Jean-Luc Godard, who would later come to distrust his work) for *Where Is the Friend's House?* (1986), Kiarostami's long-standing desire to explore and disrupt notions of cinematic realism began to take shape. *Where Is the Friend's House?* which was essentially a neorealist melodrama about a missing homework assignment, was followed in 1988 by *Homework*, a closely related and highly self-conscious documentary about homework and child abuse in contemporary Iran. This pair of films and the more famous "Koker-Trilogy"—a trio of films formed by *Where Is the Friend's House? Life and Nothing More* (1992), and

Through the Olive Trees (1994)—find the filmmaker "blurring the boundaries," to borrow Nichols's term, between documentary and fiction filmmaking. This balancing act is typified in his 2002 film *Ten*, which uses two digital video cameras mounted on the dashboard of a moving car to record ten highly improvisational conversations between a young, recently remarried woman and her passengers. Though not preceded by the DOGME "certificate," Kiarostami's film embodies that movement's precepts.

Scholarly and semischolarly attempts to grapple with questions of the real have, in recent years, run slightly behind cinematic endeavors to explore it, in part, I suspect, because of the increased theoretical sophistication of the films themselves, which render a body of critical literature redundant, at best. That literature itself has assumed a Baudrillard-influenced core; in short, we are returned again and again to the topic of media saturation and the homogenization of contemporary experience. On the semischolarly side of things, Neal Gabler's *Life the Movie* (1998) picks up where historian Daniel Boorstin's *The Image: A Guide to Pseudo-Events in America* (1961) left off, updating and expanding Boorstin's thesis for a new media era and articulating the degree to which our contemporary culture simply is an *entertainment culture*—an undifferentiated mass of constructed events that increasingly resemble generic motion pictures.[64]

Growing in some ways out of Bill Nichols's 1994 *Blurred Boundaries: Questions of Meaning in Contemporary Culture*, Joel Black's *The Reality Effect: Film Culture and the Graphic Imperative* (2002) remains the most original, most useful, and

Figure 3.3 Mania, the driver in Kiarostami's *Ten* (2002), regards the road ahead. Shot on video using a camera mounted to the dashboard of the almost constantly moving vehicle, Kiarostami's film is an exercise in stripped-down, though at times tensely dramatic, realism.

most dynamic contemporary book on the subject.[65] Less concerned with establishing rules, conventions, parameters, or criteria of realism (as many of his predecessors were required to do), Black's analysis is a sweeping, delicately handled, and at times elegantly written account of the intersections between visual media (in all of its contemporary forms, though focused on film) and our mutating notions of "the real." Succinct, well researched, and precise, Black's analysis makes Baudrillard look like a philosophical impressionist (a title that, I suspect, Baudrillard himself could redeem). Black's introduction opens with a quotation from Don DeLillo's *The Names*, which captures the spirit of his examination and, regrettably, of the century: "The Twentieth Century is *on film*. It's the filmed century. You have to ask yourself if there's anything about us more important than the fact that we're constantly on film, constantly watching ourselves. The whole world is on film, all the time. Spy satellites, microscopic scanners, pictures of the uterus, embryos, sex, war, assassinations, everything."[66]

Black's analysis is at its most sophisticated when it explores the fluid line "separating" reality and movies, provocatively illustrating how each comes to bear on the other. Though revolving around a smart selection of comparative case studies, Black's study of what he terms the "Reality Effect" moves knowingly against a preceding generation's understanding of the film scholar's task: "Not only is film more than a medium of art or entertainment, then, but it plays a key role in shaping viewers' notions of 'reality' itself. As a result, it is often no longer meaningful or even possible to categorize movies into the traditional dichotomy of fictional films and documentary—or 'nonfiction films,' as they are now called."[67] By refusing to categorize and limit, and perhaps even suggesting the irrelevance of such enterprises, Black's study remains fascinatingly "open" and suggestive, applicable as his ideas are to a wide range of cultural and cinematic phenomena.

Ivone Margulies's 2003 collection, *Rites of Realism: Essays on Corporeal Cinema*, makes similar inroads.[68] Margulies's work on Chantal Ackerman and John Cassavetes along with her current research on the politics of cinematic reenactment position her close to the center of the contemporary debate over realism.[69] A thoughtful and far-reaching assemblage of essays, *Rites of Realism*'s task is to move the debate itself outside of the sway of the indexical image and toward the realm of what Margulies terms "performative realism." Beginning with Bazin's "Death Every Afternoon," the collection also serves to remind us that, while the fact has been buried under a generation of scholarship bent on ignoring it, the formative realist thinkers themselves were similarly cautious, aware, and skeptical of the illusion of simple referentiality. Focused on films whose key terms are bodily, films that "stubbornly resist the notion of duplication," the essays in the anthology invite the reader to reconsider the cinema's and perhaps even their own relationship to the real, forecasting the turns the debate might take as we journey more deeply into the twenty-first century.[70]

Though the question of realism has never disappeared from the critical radar altogether, renewed attention at both the cinematic and critical levels has brought the debate into the present century, a century that faces a whole set of new representational and philosophical challenges. We are at a strange juncture in our still infantile cinematic history, a juncture that calls into question the very word "cinematic." And yet our options are as old as the medium. Digital technology, like cinematic technology before it, is capable of creating (as it typically does in the mainstream) a new wave of "cinematic attractions," to borrow language used by Gunning to discuss films of a century prior. Spectacular, new, unique, and visually overwhelming, this phenomenon is, however, about as far from the avant-garde spirit as can be imagined. These films sell momentary bursts of verisimilar fantasy, and fall, often sans the narrative dexterity, on the formative side of Kracauer's table. In contrast, digital technology seems to provide increased and more immediate—and, seemingly, though falsely, less "mediated"—access to the real, a technological twist that has resulted in an even greater level of saturation as moving-image makers have become ubiquitous. Banality, in this century, sells almost as much as "attraction," perhaps because the banal itself is the *latest* attraction. This newness is wearing thin; for some, it was pretty thin to begin with. If Hitchcock was puzzled over the New Wave's interest in the quotidian, our present state of affairs would cause him genuine anxiety. And if progress in communication is commensurate with a move away from narrative, perhaps we should wish to pause as well.

NOTES

1. François Truffaut, *Hitchcock*, rev. ed., with the collaboration of Helen G. Scott (New York: Simon & Schuster, 1983), 203.

2. Ibid., 265.

3. André Bazin, "The Evolution of the Language of the Cinema," in *What Is Cinema?* vol. 1, trans. Hugh Gray (Berkeley: University of California Press, 1967), 23–40.

4. Siegfried Kracauer, *Theory of Film: The Redemption of Physical Reality* (Princeton, NJ: Princeton University Press, 1997).

5. Peter Matthews, "Divining the Real," *Sight and Sound* (August 1999): 25.

6. Walter Benjamin, "The Work of Art in the Age of Mechanical Reproduction," in *Illuminations*, ed. Hannah Arendt, trans. Harry Zohn (New York: Schocken Books, 1969).

7. Miriam Hansen, introduction to Kracauer, *Theory of Film*, xiv.

8. Walter Benjamin, "Work of Art," 219.

9. Ibid., 233.

10. Ibid., 241–242.

11. Siegfried Kracauer, *The Mass Ornament: Weimar Essays*, ed. and trans. Thomas Y. Levin (Cambridge, MA: Harvard University Press, 1995).

12. Siegfried Kracauer, "Photography," in *The Mass Ornament*, 47–64.

13. Kracauer, *Theory of Film*, 18–20, 27–40.

14. Jean Renoir, foreword to Bazin, *What Is Cinema?* vol. 1, v.

15. Hansen, introduction to Kracauer, *Theory of Film*, xiv–xv.

16. Kracauer, *Theory of Film*, 3.

17. Ibid., 11–12.

18. André Bazin, "The Ontology of the Photographic Image," in *What Is Cinema?* vol. 1, 11–13.

19. Ibid., 16.

20. Siegfried Kracauer, *From Caligari to Hitler: A Psychological History of the German Film* (Princeton, NJ: Princeton University Press, 1947), v.

21. Cited by Hansen in the introduction to Kracauer, *Theory of Film*, xiv.

22. Kracauer, *Theory of Film*, 33.

23. Dudley Andrew, *The Major Film Theories* (London: Oxford University Press, 1976), 106.

24. Kracauer, *Theory of Film*, 30.

25. Matthews, "Divining the Real," 25.

26. Kracauer, *Theory of Film*, 39.

27. André Bazin, "The Bicycle Thief," in *What Is Cinema?* vol. 2, trans. Hugh Gray (Berkeley: University of California Press, 1971), 48.

28. Tom Gunning, "The Cinema of Attraction: Early Film, Its Spectator and the Avant-Garde," *Wide Angle* 8.3–4 (Fall 1986): 64.

29. Ibid., 66.

30. Mary Ann Doane, "Temporality, Storage, Legibility: Freud, Marey, and the Cinema," *Critical Inquiry* 22.2 (Winter 1996): 336–7.

31. Ibid., 343.

32. Ibid.

33. Noël Carroll, *Philosophical Problems of Classical Film Theory* (Princeton, NJ: Princeton University Press, 1988), 96.

34. Ibid., 95–97.

35. Rudolf Arnheim, *Film As Art* (Berkeley: University of California Press, 1957).

36. Truffaut, *Hitchcock*, 335.

37. André Bazin, "The Myth of Total Cinema," in *What Is Cinema?* vol. 1, 21.

38. André Bazin, "De Sica: Metteur en Scène," in *What Is Cinema?* vol. 2, 65–66.

39. Alexandre Astruc, "The Birth of a New Avant-Garde: La Caméra Stylo," in *The New Wave*, ed. Peter Graham (New York: Doubleday, 1968), 17–23.

40. Bertolt Brecht, "The Popular and the Realistic," in *Brecht on Theatre: The Development of an Aesthetic*, ed. and trans. John Willett (New York: Hill and Wang, 1992), 109.

41. Ibid., 110.

42. Ibid., 112.

43. Colin MacCabe, "Realism and the Cinema: Notes on some Brechtian Theses," *Screen* 15.2 (1974): 7–27.

44. David Bordwell, *Narration in the Fiction Film* (Madison: University of Wisconsin Press, 1985), 18–20.

45. MacCabe, "Realism and the Cinema," 7.

46. Raymond Williams, "A Lecture on Realism," *Screen* 18.1 (Spring 1977): 61.

47. Christopher Williams, ed., *Realism and the Cinema: A Reader* (London: Routledge, 1980), 1.

48. Ibid., 3.

49. Erik Barnouw, *Documentary: A History of the Non-Fiction Film*, 2nd rev. ed. (New York: Oxford University Press, 1993).

50. See Bill Nichols, *Representing Reality: Issues and Concepts in Documentary* (Bloomington: Indiana University Press, 1991), and *Introduction to Documentary* (Bloomington: Indiana University Press, 2001). See also Brian Winston, *Claiming the Real* (London: BFI Publishing, 1995).

51. Jane M. Gaines and Michael Renov, eds., *Collecting Visible Evidence*, Visible Evidence 6 (Minneapolis: University of Minnesota Press, 1999), 1–2.

52. Ibid., 3–4.

53. Stephen Prince, "True Lies: Perceptual Realism, Digital Images and Film Theory," *Film Quarterly* 49.3 (Spring 1996): 29.

54. Ibid., 32.

55. Julia Hallam and Margaret Marshment, *Realism and Popular Cinema* (Manchester, Manchester University Press, 2000).

56. Jean-François Lyotard, *The Postmodern Condition: A Report on Knowledge*, trans. Geoff Bennington and Brian Massumi (Minneapolis: University of Minnesota Press, 1984), 74.

57. Ibid.

58. Ibid., 76.

59. Jean Baudrillard, *Simulacra and Simulation*, trans. Shelia Faria Glaser (Ann Arbor: University of Michigan Press, 1994), 79.

60. Ibid., 81.

61. Jean Baudrillard, *America*, trans. Chris Turner (London: Verso, 1986).

62. David Cook, *A History of Narrative Film*, 4th ed. (New York: W.W. Norton, 2004), 569.

63. Ibid., 568.

64. See Neal Gabler, *Life the Movie: How Entertainment Conquered Reality* (New York: Alfred A. Knopf, 1998), and Daniel J. Boorstin, *The Image: A Guide to Pseudo-Events in America* (1961; New York: Atheneum, 1987).

65. Bill Nichols, *Blurred Boundaries: Questions of Meaning in Contemporary Culture* (Bloomington: Indiana University Press, 1994), and Joel Black, *The Reality Effect: Film Culture and the Graphic Imperative* (New York: Routledge, 2002).

66. Quoted in Black, *Reality Effect*, 1.

67. Black, *Reality Effect*, 7.

68. Ivone Margulies, *Rites of Realism: Essays on Corporeal Cinema* (Durham, NC: Duke University Press, 2003).

69. Ivone Margulies, *Nothing Happens: Chantal Ackerman's Hyperrealist Everyday* (Durham, NC, Duke University Press, 1996), and Ivone Margulies, "John Cassavetes: Amateur Director," in *The New American Cinema*, ed. John Lewis (Durham, NC: Duke University Press, 1998), 275–306.

70. Margulies, *Rites of Realism*, 1.

BIBLIOGRAPHY

Andrew, Dudley. *The Major Film Theories*. London: Oxford University Press, 1976.

Arnheim, Rudolf. *Film As Art*. Berkeley: University of California Press, 1957.

Astruc, Alexandre. "The Birth of a New Avant-Garde: La Caméra Stylo." *The New Wave*. Ed. Peter Graham. New York: Doubleday, 1968: 17–23.

Barnouw, Erik. *Documentary: A History of the Non-Fiction Film*. 2nd rev. ed. New York: Oxford University Press, 1993.

Baudrillard, Jean. *America*. Trans. Chris Turner. London: Verso, 1986.

———. *Simulacra and Simulation*. Trans. Shelia Faria Glaser. Ann Arbor: University of Michigan Press, 1994.

Bazin, André. *What Is Cinema?* Vol. 1. Trans. Hugh Gray. Berkeley: University of California Press, 1967.

———. *What Is Cinema?* Vol. 2. Trans. Hugh Gray. Berkeley: University of California Press, 1971.

Benjamin, Walter. "The Work of Art in the Age of Mechanical Reproduction." *Illuminations*. Ed. Hannah Arendt, trans. Harry Zohn. New York: Schocken Books, 1969: 217–251.

Black, David Alan. "Cinematic Realism and the Phonographic Analogy." *Cinema Journal* 16.2 (Winter 1987): 39–50.

Black, Joel. *The Reality Effect: Film Culture and the Graphic Imperative*. New York: Routledge, 2002.

Boorstin, Daniel J. *The Image: A Guide to Pseudo-Events in America*. New York: Atheneum, 1987.

Bordwell, David. *Narration in the Fiction Film*. Madison: University of Wisconsin Press, 1985.

Brecht, Bertolt. "Alienation Effects in Chinese Acting." *Brecht on Theatre: The Development of an Aesthetic*. Ed. and trans. John Willett. New York: Hill and Wang, 1992: 91–99.

———. "The Film, the Novel and Epic Theatre." *Brecht on Theatre: The Development of an Aesthetic*. Ed. and trans. John Willett. New York: Hill and Wang, 1992: 47–51.

———. "The Modern Theatre Is the Epic Theatre." *Brecht on Theatre: The Development of an Aesthetic*. Ed. and trans. John Willett. New York: Hill and Wang, 1992: 33–42.

———. "The Popular and the Realistic." *Brecht on Theatre: The Development of an Aesthetic*. Ed. and trans. John Willett. New York: Hill and Wang, 1992: 107–115.

Carroll, Noël. *Engaging the Moving Image*. New Haven, CT: Yale University Press, 2003.

———. *Philosophical Problems of Classical Film Theory*. Princeton, NJ: Princeton University Press, 1988.

Cavell, Stanley. *The World Viewed: Reflections on the Ontology of Film*. New York: Viking Press, 1971.

Comolli, Jean Louis. "Machines of the Visible." In *The Cinematic Apparatus*. Ed. Teresa De Laurentis and Stephen Heath. New York: St. Martin's Press, 1980: 121–143.

Cook, David. *A History of Narrative Film*. 4th ed. New York: W.W. Norton, 2004.

Corner, John. "Presumption as Theory: Realism in Television Studies." *Screen* 33.1 (Spring 1992): 97–102.

Deren, Maya. "Cinematography: The Creative Use of Reality." *Daedalus: Journal of the American Academy of Arts and Sciences* 89:1 (Winter 1960). Reprinted in *Film Theory and Criticism*. New York: Oxford University Press, 2004: 187–198.

Diawara, Manthia. "Black American Cinema: The New Realism." *Film and Theory: An Anthology*. Ed. Robert Stam and Toby Miller. Boston: Blackwell, 2000: 236–256.

Doane, Mary Ann. "Temporality, Storage, Legibility: Freud, Marey, and the Cinema." *Critical Inquiry* 22.2 (Winter 1996): 313–343.

Gabler, Neal. *Life the Movie: How Entertainment Conquered Reality*. New York: Alfred A. Knopf, 1998.

Gaines, Jane M., and Michael Renov. *Collecting Visible Evidence*. Visible Evidence 6. Minneapolis: University of Minnesota Press, 1999.

Gledhill, Christine, and Linda Williams. *Reinventing Film Studies*. London: Arnold, 2000.

Gunning, Tom. "The Cinema of Attraction: Early Film, Its Spectator and the Avant-Garde." *Wide Angle* 8.3–4 (Fall 1986): 62–70.

Knight, Deborah. "Reconsidering Film Theory and Method." *New Literary History* 24.2 (Spring 1993): 321–338.

Kracauer, Siegfried. *From Caligari to Hitler: A Psychological History of the German Film*. Princeton, NJ: Princeton University Press, 1947.

———. *The Mass Ornament: Weimar Essays*. Ed. and trans. Thomas Y. Levin. Cambridge, MA: Harvard University Press, 1995.

———. *Theory of Film: The Redemption of Physical Reality*. Introduction by Miriam Bratu Hansen. Princeton, NJ: Princeton University Press, 1960.

Lyotard, Jean-Francois. *The Postmodern Condition: A Report on Knowledge*. Trans. Geoff Bennington and Brian Massumi. Minneapolis: University of Minnesota Press, 1984.

MacCabe, Colin. "Realism and the Cinema: Notes on some Brechtian Theses." *Screen* 15.2 (1974): 7–27.

Matthews, Peter. "Divining the Real." *Sight and Sound* 9.8 (August 1999): 22–25.

Nichols, Bill. *Blurred Boundaries: Questions of Meaning in Contemporary Culture*. Bloomington: Indiana University Press, 1994.

———. *Introduction to Documentary*. Bloomington: Indiana University Press, 2001.

———. *Representing Reality: Issues and Concepts in Documentary*. Bloomington: Indiana University Press, 1991.

Prince, Stephen. "True Lies: Perceptual Realism, Digital Images and Film Theory." *Film Quarterly* 49.3 (Spring 1996): 27–37.

Renov, Michael. *The Subject of Documentary: Visible Evidence 16*. Minneapolis: University of Minnesota Press, 2004.

Truffaut, François. *Hitchcock*. Rev. ed. With the collaboration of Helen G. Scott. New York: Simon & Schuster, 1983.

Williams, Christopher. "After the Classic, the Classical and Ideology: The Differences of Realism." *Reinventing Film Studies*. Ed. Christine Gledhill and Linda Williams. London: Arnold, 2000: 206–220.

———, ed. *Realism and the Cinema: A Reader*. London: Routledge, 1980.

Williams, Raymond. "A Lecture on Realism." *Screen* 18.1 (Spring 1977): 61–74.

Winston, Brian. *Claiming the Real*. London: BFI Publishing, 1995.

....

CHAPTER 4

RADICAL ASPIRATIONS HISTORICIZED: THE EUROPEAN COMMITMENT TO POLITICAL DOCUMENTARY

....

FRANCES GUERIN

Kino-eye as the possibility of making the invisible visible, the unclear clear, the hidden manifest, the disguised overt, the acted nonacted; making falsehood into truth.
Kino-eye as the union of science with newsreel to further the battle for the communist decoding of the world, as an attempt to show the truth on the screen—Film-truth.

—Dziga Vertov[1]

This is not just a film; it is a conscious attempt to change the world.
—Keith Sanborn of *The Society of the Spectacle*

Western and Eastern European television played a major role in the revolution that culminated in the destruction of the Berlin Wall in October 1989. The media were not necessarily responsible for the mass dissent and revolution: Gorbachev and perestroika, the Solidarity demonstrations in Gdansk, the essays of Václav Havel in Czechoslovakia, are among the many complex political, social, and cultural events that led to the collapse of the communist dictatorships of Eastern and Central Europe in the 1990s. Nevertheless, both print and audiovisual media were central to the unfolding of events. Even if the media turned these events into a spectacle that gave the events an imaginary quality, it was only thanks to the media coverage of swelling dissent across Eastern Europe that Czechoslovakians and East Germans had the confidence to set the revolutions in motion in late 1989. In the months and years that followed, there were at least three instances in which the struggle and victory of the people against political oppression were dependent on television, radio, and the Internet.[2] In Romania, Serbia, and more recently Ukraine, not only did the people's self-liberation involve the mass media, but the revolutionaries overturned their governments when they appropriated the media and fought back with the very same tools that had hitherto oppressed them.

In this essay, I propose that media images were more than inspiration and more than enabler of the events in Timisoara and Bucharest in November 1989, Belgrade in the early 1990s, and Kiev in 2004. The often hastily produced, not especially experimental local images realized the Marxist aspiration for liberation through moving-image representation that was first explored in the cinematic experiments of the 1920s radical documentary. It becomes evident through my discussion that this realization does not necessarily accord with the vision of Marx and his early twentieth-century intellectual followers. Indeed, figures such as Dziga Vertov, Bertolt Brecht, and György Lukács could not and would not subscribe to my proposal that representations of the late-twentieth-century revolutions are the material reality of their aspirations. While these contemporary situations represent victories for late capitalism over a nevertheless outdated and untenable form of socialism, Marxist materialism cannot be directly imposed on them. Similarly, as we shall see, the role of the image is far removed from the inverted reflection conceived of and extended from Marx and Engels's *German Ideology* into twentieth-century conceptions of the revolutionary image. Nevertheless, the examples of the revolutions in Eastern and Central Europe, the overturning of governments that stifled all movement—both literal and abstract—witness the victory of the people over the systems that oppressed them. And these revolutions were realized through the control of the production, distribution, and exhibition of the image. Whatever the political troubles and disappointments that followed these revolutions, the events themselves must be considered victories for the mass-produced image.

In the wake of World War I and on the eve of World War II, the political documentary cinema in Europe found energy and purpose in its belief that the cinema aesthetic harbored the agency to incite social and political change in the masses. In the 1920s in the Communist Soviet Union, these aspirations were reached for by filmmakers such as Dziga Vertov and Esfir Shub; in Britain in the 1930s, by John Grierson and, to a lesser extent, Alberto Cavalcanti. In Germany, filmmakers and dramaturges such as Erwin Piscator and Bertolt Brecht were committed to similar projects. The anti–Spanish Civil War films of Dutchman Joris Ivens were being made in a similar spirit. In their different ways, these filmmakers manipulated the cinema aesthetic to challenge the reigning structures of social and political domination. In the same historical period, documentary filmmakers on the right also pursued radical modes of filmmaking in the interests of social intervention. Famously, Leni Riefenstahl's creative documentaries might easily be placed in the same aesthetic if not political tradition as those of Vertov, Grierson, and Ivens. Like *Enthusiasm* (Leni Riefenstahl, 1931) and *Kuhle Wampe* (Slatan Dudow and Bertolt Brecht, 1931), political documentary films such as *Triumph of the Will* (Leni Reifenstahl, 1934) are underlined by an ideological principle and driven by a commitment to audience mobilization. However, *Triumph of the Will* is neither activist nor interested in overturning the social status quo through a people's revolution. The distinction of the films that I situate as predecessors to the images of the Eastern European revolution is their twin commitment: First, they incite revolutionary action in their designated audiences. Second, they achieve this action through experiments with the film aesthetic. Whether it be in image composition, editing, or sound-image relations, the politically committed documentary as it has become known[3] is concerned with disturbing the viewing process through the creation of a radical aesthetic. While the images that overthrew the governments of, for example, Ceauşescu, Milošević, and Yanukovich were not aesthetically radical, they shared the common Marxist belief among the filmmakers I discuss in this essay that the aesthetic has the capacity to agitate an audience and to propel it into a self-interested revolution. Ideally, then, the Marxist revolution would overthrow traditional industrialist-worker hierarchies, or a permutation thereof. Even when doubts are raised about the adequacy of the image to meet such ends, there is always a fundamental belief in its possibility. It was only at the end of the twentieth century, when the Marxist project of political modernism was all but abandoned, that these dreams were realized, however transmuted the form, however idealized the vision.

This essay moves beyond observations on the uniqueness of the politically committed documentary, and seeks an answer to the question, "What happened to the political documentary of 1920s and 1930s Europe?" Although I embrace one possible answer to the question of where the genre has migrated to and, perhaps most important, where it is today, this answer is in no sense definitive, or schematic. Mine is only one perspective, and it is a perspective motivated by my underlying concern for the fate of the aesthetic in successful political image making today. Moreover, when I reflect on the politically committed documentary as the ancestor of the television, Internet, and video images that toppled these Central and Eastern European regimes, I seek out examples that engage in issues of the aesthetic via their exploration of medium specificity. The 1920s and 1930s documentary filmmakers turned to the technological, to the moving image, to realize the modernist aspirations for social change. I trace a single strand of filmmaking that takes up this challenge begun by artists such as Vertov and his Soviet compatriots. Ultimately, despite the contemporary pursuit of the same questions through new media such as the digital, today's image makers have discovered—often inadvertently—that the politicization of an audience through moving images is not the result of aesthetic exploration. Rather, as I argue in relation to the centrality of the moving image in the people's revolutions of Eastern Europe, it is primarily through the people's access to—often via specific modes of distribution and exhibition—and uses of the image that these moving images garner their power to revolutionize.

The idiosyncrasy of the history I trace must be signaled from the outset. The aesthetic and political successors of the 1920s and 1930s European documentarists, and the ancestors of the late 1990s revolutionaries, are found most immediately in 1960s and 1970s European art cinema. In particular, we find the commitment to social change through an audience's interaction with a radical aesthetic in the political modernism of the works of, for example, Jean-Luc Godard and Alexander Kluge. It is also identifiable in documentaries, particularly in 1970s French films such as Guy Debord's Society of the Spectacle (1973) or in Germany in the late 1980s and early 1990s films of Harun Farocki. The 1920s and 1930s radical documentary tradition is conventionally thought to lead through cinema verité and direct cinema.[4] However, I focus on the journey of the modernist political aesthetic through the Marxist-leftist filmmaking in postwar Europe because this is the path that is illuminated when history is perceived through the lens of the images imbricated in the Eastern European revolutions. Thus, I am writing a history that must be read backward as well as forward, a double motion that takes its cue from how history is read and understood.

The European films I discuss that were made prior to the collapse of the Eastern European dictatorships are all "privileged microcosm[s] in which to observe dialectical thinking at work."[5] In different ways, each insists that Marxist principles lend themselves to a restructuring of our vision of society. The films maintain, for example, that social and class conflict is given material form or made visible in the sensuous qualities of the film aesthetic. Similarly, a conflict between the work of art and the historical-social reality that surrounds it is always the assumption on which the formal experimentation is founded. In turn, these beliefs are based on the Marxist philosophy that it is possible to see one's own role, one's own labor, in the actual process of commodity production if one sees it reflected in an image. The real world begins as a projection of the ideological: the social role of the film is driven by the belief that it can expose the ideological and cultural constructions that are made to appear natural. Lastly, the works I discuss all believe that to raise consciousness through art will lead to collective organization of opposition.[6] While this deep political commitment to a process of dialectical thinking and the role of the image within this thinking may not be apparent in the media images of the recent revolutions, their end result of opposition is.

By the third and final section of this essay, I come full circle to explain the use of television and other digital media in the people's revolutions of the former Communist bloc, specifically, the victories in Romania, Serbia, and more recently, Ukraine, as a particular contemporary evolution of the politically committed documentary. Therefore, these images are elucidated as the inheritors of their century's most radical filmic experiments. At the same time, they enable clarification of the filmic tradition that precedes them. None of these revolutions were realized via the aesthetic dreams of the idealist documentarians of the 1920s and 1930s. Moreover, they were not the only instances in which the popular revolution was dependent on the image, the events of the so-called Velvet Revolution in Georgia being an obvious example. However, the three chosen instances represent striking examples of revolutions brought about through the agency of an image that exposes the beclouded relations on which social order is built. These revolutions were both fueled and articulated by the technological image. Therefore, despite the formal compromise, the image as social object became instrumental to a radical political turnaround. At last, as these dictatorships collapsed, we saw the moving image simultaneously represent and spawn social revolution. These revolutions realized the aspirations for the image that had remained at the theoretical level in the first half of the twentieth century.

IMAGE AND IDEOLOGY

More than twenty years ago, Thomas Waugh termed the films I discuss here "the committed documentary."[7] Waugh's term for this vein of films that provoke action against state oppression has had lasting resonance among critics. He demarcated the parameters of the committed documentary when he said that it is both ideologically motivated and activist in its position. It is "[a] specific ideological undertaking, a declaration of solidarity with the goal of radical socio-political transformation. . . . I mean a specific political positioning: activism, or intervention in the process of change itself. To paraphrase Marx, a committed filmmaker is not content only to interpret the world but is also engaged in changing it."[8]

As Waugh went on to argue, the films themselves do not make the revolution but, rather, can be appropriated as " 'working tools' for those who can."[9] By extension, the committed documentary is designed for a popular audience. While activism by small groups of leftist intellectuals should be the rightful goal of all cultural workers, the committed documentary is at least designed for, if not taken up by, a broader audience. We must allow that the films do not always realize their goal of connecting with a broad, popular audience. Nevertheless, it is their intention that both defines their commitment to radical political change and is of primary concern to my investigation.

Waugh did not explicitly address the centrality of a radical aesthetic to the committed documentary because he had moved beyond the moment when it was assumed that intervention could be made only through a modernist image. This historical distance gives us a different perspective on the agency and effectiveness of the radical image. Unlike Waugh, who was writing in the early 1980s, our privileged perspective is helped by the waning attachment to Marxist theory as a template for social change. The radical aesthetic and the revolutionary intention are intricately woven together in the 1920s and 1930s political documentaries and in their post–World War II successors. Then, in the contemporary television and digital images of provocation, the relationship takes on a different form: the radicality of the image is no longer a priority. I argue that this absence of a radical aesthetic in the contemporary examples of politically committed documentary images is indicative of a more general shift in the cultural attitude toward the image and its political engagement. Thus, the contemporary shift away from the formal emphasis will be as instructive as those elements it sustains and develops.

Before turning to individual examples of the politically committed documentary in the 1920s and 1930s, I must address the modernist attachment to the technically produced image as the forum for agitation and potential revolution. We find the belief in the transformative capacities of the moving image everywhere in the theoretical writings of the interwar period. One of the most oft-quoted examples is found in Walter Benjamin's reflections on the capacity of the mechanically produced image to alter the reality and perception of time and space in the historical world. Benjamin believes that as the product of the modern world, the technically produced image opens up our experience of this same world.[10] However, Benjamin was not a lone genius: his ideas were developed in a climate of euphoria around the potential of the image. Germany's Siegfried Kracauer, France's Jean Epstein and René Clair, and the Soviet Union's Vertov and Sergei Eisenstein were among the better-known examples of the many thinkers and image makers concerned with the liberatory potential of the image.[11] This burgeoning faith in the capacity of the moving image was vigorously expressed by writers, critics, dramaturges, and social commentators all over Europe in the interwar period. For filmmakers and theorists of the image alike, the belief in the power of the technically produced image was a belief in the capacity of the modernist image to transform reality. If historical modernity was characterized by a world in which the temporal and spatial parameters were transformed by the second industrial revolution, the modernist image both contributed to and was able to represent this transformation. Through its appeal to the transformed world around it, the modernist image, for which the cinema was the most likely candidate, articulated its own production within and contribution to this world. The coherence among products of a Europe experiencing huge political and social upheavals following the devastation of World War I was located in the fragmentation and interruption so unique to the modernist aesthetic.

This participation in the contemporaneous modernity was often characterized by the modernist imperative to disturb the viewing practices hitherto dominated by "bourgeois art" for a "bourgeois audience." In keeping with the modernist impulse to shock, critics and commentators praised the power of the film image to fragment and question the hermetically sealed worlds of fantasy and contemplation of the nineteenth-century painted image and, in its wake, the commercial film modeled on the continuity of the nineteenth-century narrative.[12] While painting and literature tended toward an audience of educational or social privilege, it was believed that the production, distribution, and exhibition processes of film were democratic. Film was a medium made by the people for the people: illiterate, geographically isolated workers could access the cinema as easily as the wealthy, educated cosmopolitan elite. Unlike the other arts, the cinema was all-inclusive and could be used to wake up the European masses and urge them to assume agency in their social and political futures.[13] As I argue in this essay, the celebration of the radical image as generator of truth and freedom gradually dissipated as the century progressed.

Nevertheless, the skepticism toward the radical aesthetic is no barometer of the faith in the image itself to communicate the truth. The examples I discuss from Televiziunea Română, Radio B92, and the images of the Orange Revolution show a deep, seemingly intractable skepticism and iconoclasm toward the image. However, the wisdom of the revolutionary use of the image in Eastern Europe lies in the recognition that it is not the image per se that must be rejected—not all images continue to lie. Rather, as the images that powered the overturn of the dictatorships in Romania, Yugoslavia, and Ukraine demonstrate, it is the government manipulation of the television image in particular that corrupts, lies, and condemns its people to servitude. The oppositions in each of these countries produced images in which there was no question of their veracity. In short, they were exhibited and distributed as real and were received as windows on the world of the insurgencies. They were quite simply received as documentations that "occupy the same moment and place as the event they record." As Barbara Kershenblatt-Gimblett argued of the voluminous images of the World Trade Center attacks,[14] "they become part of the event in the very moment of their creation." Within the discursive fields of the digital and Steadicam footage of the Eastern European revolutions, there is no question that the images are authentic, immediate, and accurate. This is not to say that they were not manipulated; rather, they were disseminated and received as authentic. The loss of faith in the (modernist) image is powerfully transposed to a documentary aesthetic marked by its synergy with the event it portrays. As I argue in the final section, there is nothing new or radical about this aesthetic—it was conceived at least forty years prior to the revolutions in question. The innovation of the images involved in the liberation from dictatorships in Romania, Serbia, and Ukraine was located in the practicalities of how they were trafficked through the turbulent times and spaces of political and social upheaval.

THE RADICAL DOCUMENTARY AESTHETIC OF THE 1920S AND 1930S

It is important to remember that the cinema was not alone in this search for the political aesthetic in Europe between the two world wars. This was a time when the modernist realist image in its many forms was believed to harbor the potential to agitate. The photomontage of John Heartfield, the architectural design of Vladimir Tatlin, the poetry of Vladimir Mayakovsky, and the constructivist and realist theaters of Vsevolod Meyerhold, Brecht, and Erwin Piscator all believed in the formal agency of art to arouse the masses and prompt them to political action. This enthusiasm for and belief in the image had much to do with the store put in the technological image's ability to speak to the masses. Not only could the technologically reproducible image reach the masses through its mass distribution, but, for many European avant-garde artists and filmmakers, the mass-produced image was accessible because of the public's assumed identification with an industrial mode of production.[15] Similarly, despite the uncertain political and economic climate in Europe and, in particular, the exponential development of capitalism, this was a time when Marxist thought motivated the revolutionary imagination. Europe was unstable, and as its artists and thinkers turned to idealists and would-be dictators in the search for economic and social stability, they identified the imperative to put technology to different uses and to imagine alternative social orders.[16]

In the cinema, the interpretation and implementation of the modernist belief in the political agency of the image took many different forms. Within the parameters of politically committed documentary films, there are as many variations again. I limit my discussion here to a number of the major exponents of different kinds of political filmmaking, namely, the search for truth in the films of Dziga Vertov and John Grierson, with some reference to those of Joris Ivens. The striking differences in the respective aesthetics are instructive, as is their coherence through a common commitment to the search for truth in and through the modernist realist image. However disparate their particular brands of realism, they were in all cases driven by an aversion to the illusory, classical realism of continuity editing nurtured by Hollywood. This does not mean that the filmmakers were adverse to Hollywood films per se. Rather, their frustration was with the illusions produced by a particular mode of filmmaking that had its roots in Hollywood and, more likely, by the version that had come to dominate screens in their own countries. However, beyond this, the social and political climates in which the filmmakers worked made demands that resulted in products with few commonalities. In turn, the social and political discourses espoused by the respective films are multiple.

Dziga Vertov is usually acknowledged as the father of political documentary. His belief in and euphoric celebration of the possibilities of cinema were founded on the Communist Party's call to build a Communist reality, that is, a materialist, socialist everyday life, through a marriage of art and life.[17] Like so many of his contemporaries in the postrevolutionary Soviet Union and European countries in the 1920s and 1930s, Vertov believed that the cinema was the medium most suited to the needs of the new society. The cinema had the capacity to see the world anew, to catch "life unawares."[18] Having used the all-seeing, objective eye of the camera, the Kino-eye, to capture the epistemological certainty of daily life, Vertov maintained that this material should be organized (through editing). The construction of the film fragments through editing was Vertov's way of reaching beneath the surface of the phenomenological world, of making the invisible world visible. As he points out in the epigraph to this essay, the visible world revealed to the naked eye by the camera is the decoded Communist reality. And once decoded, it is, in turn, ready to be lived. According to Vertov, the material, mechanical production of facts on a film screen married art and life. Thus, the cinema perfectly coupled aesthetic thought and the emergent industrialization, giving Soviet workers, intellectuals, and manufacturers alike the opportunity to grasp and build the phenomenological world of the present and future.

As critics before me have argued, Vertov filmed the stereotypes of capitalist industrialization and its representation only to destroy the illusion of the freedom they offer. We see this process in action when, for example, Vertov broke the illusion of the manufacturing process through exposing the gaps between different forms of labor—worker and industrialist—and between manufactured goods and their agricultural beginnings. In turn, the intervals between different levels of production are mimicked in the intervals between shots, between film fragments, and between film phrases. That is, Vertov broke the illusion of the continuity and coherence of cinema in an attempt to raise the consciousness of the viewer to the level of a class vision, a social vision. This social vision is characterized by a transparent understanding of the modes and processes of daily industrial life. Annette Michelson argued that in a film such as *Enthusiasm* (1931), sequences in reverse motion of a woman going to market to buy loaves of bread that are, in turn, transformed step by step through the editing process back into loaves of bread being made in a bakery, expose the otherwise invisibility of the worker's role in production, delivery, and consumption. This process is exposed through the simultaneous undoing of the cinema as an instrument of illusory stories.[19] The woman's backward motion and the cinema's reversal of time in *Enthusiasm* come together to lift the veil on what is otherwise hidden behind the narratives of modern industrialization. Like the raw material of film stock, the raw material of life would determine the nature and construction of the Communist reality of the present and future Soviet Union. For all Vertov's emphasis on form and experimental cinematic technique, we can see from this particular example that the content of the individual image is critical to the agitation of the audience. The juxtaposed images were carefully chosen for the communication of meaning.[20]

Vertov did not address the practical effects of his filmmaking. This was not his concern; he was merely fulfilling the dictates of the party, which chose cinema to spearhead the new Communist reality. Nevertheless, Vertov's belief in the power of the radical cinematic image to lead the way toward a political and social future Soviet Union was unswerving. Vertov saw in the cinema an industrial mode of artistic production that, unlike any other before or after it, had the capacity not only to mimic the patterns and processes of daily life. The cinema went one step further, one step deeper, when it peeled away the surface reality of industrial life and exposed its constituent components through their reorganization in the most modern of creative media. However, it is only at a theoretical level that the artist or filmmaker was one in a number of workers who would set the conditions of building a new way of life.

In keeping with his focus on the theoretical principles of his filmmaking, Vertov did not write extensively on the identity or experience of the audience in his brand of political filmmaking. It was a revolutionary filmmaking that was more successful in theory. Nevertheless, the intended audience for films such as *Enthusiasm* or *The Man with a Movie Camera* (1929) was all-encompassing and national in scope: it was the Soviet "masses," all of those people who were to find freedom in this new way of life being offered by the Communist reality. Even though the audiences of Vertov's films are said not to have understood the films as he intended, audience involvement was significant to Vertov's theory. As the Soviet Union transitioned from an agrarian to an industrial economy, the technological image's reflection through a dialectical composition of the conditions of production was crucial to the desired coming together of the imagined audience. Industrialists, workers, peasants, intellectuals, and artists alike were addressed as a mass whose social situation was reflected in the tensions and resolutions of the image. This presence of the audience to the creative process was also a fundamental motivation of Vertov's belief—again, even if only in theory—in the collective process of filmmaking. It was imagined that the audience could come together in life as individual spectators did before the image of fragmentation to produce the new Soviet reality.

Like Vertov, John Grierson was committed to using the relatively new medium of cinema as a means to educate and enlighten the masses to the desires of the state for a socially integrated and harmonious society.[21] However, Grierson was working in a very different political and social climate, in which there was no pretense of unity across class division. He was more interested in raising the standard of living for the workers, educating them as a means to create harmony among the social classes. Britain in the 1930s was enjoying the increased benefits of industrialization; however, it still experienced extreme poverty, with the concomitant social problems of ill health and poor housing. Extending the principles of the bourgeois public sphere, Grierson believed that documentary film was a way of informing the working classes, of opening up a dialogue between the state and the citizen, of creating a bridge between citizen and community, that would offer each individual an awareness of his or her place in everyday life and of the responsibilities of "good citizenship." In short, film was a tool used to educate and inform the people as a community, and to create enlightened citizens.[22]

Despite their different audiences, film was an attractive medium for Grierson for many of the same reasons that it was for Vertov and the Kino-Eye: it was the ideal means to inform the public of the desires of the state. Not only did Grierson appropriate some of the aesthetic principles of Soviet, and in particular Vertovian, montage, as the founder and leading exponent of the British documentary film movement, he was also attracted to the use of this industrial mode of production for its appeal to the masses rather than the individual, public rather than private life, and the ability of the documentary film to dramatize the relationship between man and his community.[23] Again, the conception of the "mass" was instrumental to the filmmaker's vision. Also like Vertov's, Grierson's was a cinema of public responsibility and enlightenment, not irresponsible entertainment.

Notwithstanding the flaws in Grierson's ideological vision of documentary cinema—a coherent voice imposed from above rather than reached through collective struggle, a nonconsensual production and regulation of public working-class life by a middle-class intellectual—he was progressive in his belief that the people are inseparable from their real social and physical environments. Drawing on nineteenth- and early-twentieth-century French paintings by, for example, Jean-François Millet, Gustave Courbet, and Honoré Daumier, Grierson turned to the city streets, slums, markets, and factories and raised the voices of the people at one with, rather than against, the background of their environment. Like Vertov, Grierson and his fellows in the documentary film movement were not interested in factual or evidential accuracy of working-class life. They were committed to representing a moral reality. In the interests of capturing the moral value of this life, Grierson's cinematic project was to make the ordinary strange, even beautiful. His vision was romantic and exotic in its insistence on infusing the image with an emotional depth and integrity. Thus in films such as *Drifters* (1929) and those of the documentary film movement more generally, such as *Nightmail* (Harry Watt and Basil Wright, 1936) or *Song of Ceylon* (Wright, 1934), the fishermen, postmen, and indigenous workers move gracefully and purposefully in long shot, in perfect harmony with the work they perform. Together with the centrality of action as narrative force, Grierson and his followers insisted on the use of montage as a means to eschew psychological realism. The characters and their movements were distanced, observed in long shot, and yet their movements managed to dictate the rhythm and tone of the cutting. Grierson used montage as a system of interdependence and integration to create multiple relationships among the workers, their mode of production, and their produce in a Britain of rigid class distinction and colonial rule.

It is clear from even this short exposition that there was always a tension between the sociological and the aesthetic experimentation in Grierson's work. Indeed, his moral intentions and the poetic realism that overcame the coldness and objectivity inherent to the documentary aesthetic were incompatible. Similarly, the supposed audience for Grierson's films was in fact alienated from them. Working-class people could not recognize the toil and harshness of their working conditions in the fluent, lyrical camera work, the poetic editing, and the rich sound track. Like audiences throughout the Western world, British workers who experienced the pleasures of the cinema at this time wanted entertainment and escape from their labor, not education about its satisfactions. Despite these shortcomings, Grierson's insistence on the possibility of integrating the workers with their environment and their social world through the aesthetic manipulation of the radical documentary form was cinema resolutely in the interests of public education and social agitation. Grierson believed even when his audiences did not. Grierson's theories may have been more convincing in theory than in practice, but what remains impressive about them is the continued reflection of social and cultural conditions in the experimental form of the aesthetic. This interest in the aesthetic dissipated as the twentieth century moved toward its close.

While the late work of Joris Ivens follows paths similar to those of Vertov and Grierson, there are also marked differences, perhaps the most significant being that even though Ivens was a European filmmaker working in the traditions of European radical documentary filmmaking, his best-known work in this field was made for a Depression-era United States amid the 1930s militant climate of the intellectual Left.[24] Similarly, Ivens's work was successful because of its engagement with publicity strategies that were, in turn, bound to the motives and processes of American industry. However, the success of *The Spanish Earth* (1937), a film made in the hope of garnering American support for the Spanish Civil War, casts the efforts of European political documentary filmmaking in a new light. The life of this film emphasizes that the actual results of Vertov's and Grierson's documentary agitation were not necessarily as important as the theoretical conception. Similarly, from the vantage point of history, Ivens's filmmaking as it functioned within the field of American capitalism might today be understood as a European digression that set the template for the success of 1990s Eastern European people's revolutions.

Like Vertov and Grierson, Ivens is a leading example of the commitment to film truth as a vehicle for the incitation to political change between the world wars. Again, for Ivens, a cinematic truth is "not just seeing things," but rather a "[penetration of] the facts," an analysis of the relations among the various elements of the revolutionary struggle in Spain. More akin to Grierson and the British documentary film movement, easily the most important relationship for Ivens was the coexistence of the Spanish peasants and the Spanish earth. Ivens believed that a representation of the unity with the land, and the people's struggle to own that relationship, would mobilize the empathy and ire of the American audience. This belief is quite different from the Marxist belief in the rights of the proletariat to own his labor in the face of the ruling classes. For Ivens, the relationship to the land was driven not by the economic imperative of capital, but by a spiritual connection. Before exploring this relationship, Ivens was committed first to penetrate and analyze the social, economic, and historical structures that obscured the harmony between peasants and the land.[25] Ivens was heavily influenced by Soviet *Novy lef* filmmaker Esfir Shub, whose film *The Fall of the Romanov Dynasty* (1927) was made entirely from footage found in the collection of Czar Nicholas II. Like Shub, Ivens believed in the dramatic manipulation of his footage for compilation: his was an aesthetic of expressiveness created through complex editing, voice-over commentary, and frequent restagings with acute attention to the mise-en-scène. Also heir to Dziga Vertov, as Waugh argued, Ivens searched for maximum audience impact, leading him to pillage particularly provocative scenes from local newsreels.[26]

Bill Nichols astutely aligned Ivens's work with the thought of Lukács, due to their common attachment to a narrative-based realism. Ivens departed from the use of a machine-inspired modernism, which fragments the temporality and spatiality of representation. Like Lukács's theory of realism, Ivens's work may trumpet narrative continuity, but it is not in search of a seamless, coherent, and illusory world. On the contrary, as Nichols asserted, Ivens's theory and aesthetic are squarely in line with the policies and beliefs of the Communist parties in Europe and the United States in the 1930s and 1940s.[27] For Ivens, the assembly line and forms of mechanization are not the undisputed emblems of human production. This, together with his emphasis on the worker's affinity to the land—a relationship of harmony and continuity—led Ivens to his chosen realist aesthetic. Ivens was also well aware of the alienating effects of radical form on the popular narrative, and though he did experiment with form in his earlier European avant-garde films, for example, *Rain* (1929), his political work of the 1930s did away with the canted angles, the blurred mise-en-scènes, dialectical crosscutting, and any other techniques that might lose the audience's attention. Instead, Ivens's narratives

were carefully structured into cause-and-effect sequences, the sound effects creatively interwoven with meticulously drawn images in an attempt to encourage
processes of identification. Nichols described Ivens's narrative aesthetic as being
inspired by the move away from a focus on industrial production. This belief
"pushed Ivens toward the doubled temporality and space of narrative (the experiential time of representation and the historical time represented), the voice, its
grain, and the embodied presence of man as well as those processes of identification, transference and persuasion made available through realist representation."[28] In turn, this brand of narrative realism enables Ivens's documentary films
to do more than simply see the world. Rather, the world they depict is presented
as the basis of a new level of consciousness.[29] This "heightened consciousness"
stems from familiarity and recognition, followed by empathic involvement, experienced by the viewer.

In the well-known *Spanish Earth*, Ivens intercut classically composed shots of
the workers' irrigation of the land, soldiers trudging through the landscape on their
way into action with the alternating sounds of bomb blasts, repeating rifles, and
carefree traditional tunes cohering them. The voice-over of Hemingway's text
explains the proximity of bombing to the village of Fuenteduena, where the land
was irrigated. Finally, we see the land being torn apart by war in long shot. When
the film turns a microscopic eye on the process of war, the narrative of Republican
success comes to the fore: recruitment, rifle assembly, occupation of the villages,
formation of the people's army, the "clenched fist of the Republican Army,"
speeches given by the leaders, "a nation forged in the name of its soldiers," and so
on. This is the story of the continuity of civilian, military, and revolutionary
struggle, and the rewards that are reaped from these struggles. The film's formal
choices are conventional, often because the footage is redeployed from old newsreels that chose long shots, minimal camera movement, close-ups in the interests
of advancing the narrative, and square angles.[30]

The story of the individual soldier Julien is intercut with the narrative of struggle to hold on to what belongs to the Spanish people—the earth. Through Julien, as
we reflect on his face in close-up, and follow his movements home after battle, we
are led into the world of family, loved ones, the importance of community, and the
devastation brought to these values and relationships by fighter and Junker planes.
In these passages, not only does the film focus on Julien, but his character takes us to
the streets of the towns and villages now populated by dead, wounded, and
homeless people, the victims of war. As the village continues to work to bring water
to nourish the land, the government troops rush to win it back from the enemy that
has destroyed it. Ultimately, the people's struggle is won and there is great hope
for the further development of the land and the Spanish people's synergy with it.

For all of the sophistication of Ivens's aesthetic, it is safe to say that the success
of his brand of political filmmaking lay squarely in the publicity campaign that
accompanied the screening of *The Spanish Earth* in the United States. The handling

of the film marked a crucial shift in the effectivity of the left-wing documentary. Further, it is no coincidence that this shift took place in the United States, in a political economy in which marketing and publicity were key to the success of any product, especially film. By taking the concerns of documentary cinema across the Atlantic, Ivens's film introduced the importance of publicity, distribution, and exhibition into the realization of the politically committed documentary's goal. *The Spanish Earth* began as an attempt to bolster American support for the Republican cause. Most notably, the film was introduced to the White House by journalist Martha Gellhorn, and this led to its public mention by her friend Eleanor Roosevelt.[31] Roosevelt urged her husband to lift the embargo against equipment and goods for Spain, and criticized the State Department for its unwillingness to help the Loyalists. Similarly, the film's publicity campaign included photos of Joan Crawford[32] in the attempt to garner the support–both for the film's commercial distribution and in the form of donations to the Republican cause. Despite the reluctance of the Hollywood majors to distribute *The Spanish Earth*, the publicity led to sellout premiers, private fund-raisers, critical applause, and, the real measure of success, public support in the United States for the people's cause in the Spanish Civil War.[33] Thus, in the films of Ivens—and around the same time, the New Deal films of Pare Lorentz (*The Plow That Broke the Plains* [1936]; *The River* [1937]—we find the political documentary's groundbreaking foray into the arena of commercial media. In spite of Ivens's careful construction of the image, and his meticulous working of the score and voice-over narration, the revolution is made in the publicity and distribution of film as a mass medium. The particular truth discovered through aesthetic innovation cannot hope to lure the audience into political action if it does not reach its intended audience. We will see the importance of modes of distribution and exhibition not only rekindled, but elevated to the sine qua non of the images of Central and Eastern European revolution.

Ivens's artistic choices in *The Spanish Earth* were critical to the garnering of audience sympathy with the cause. Ivens's emphasis on a continuously unfolding narrative was instrumental to the appeal of the film to a large audience. It was a narrative form that could be easily consumed and assimilated by an audience awaiting politicization. Thus, the marketing and publicity for *The Spanish Earth* was joined by a narrative form used in commercial filmmaking to realize political success. These distinctions from the work of Vertov and Grierson underline the European documentary avant-garde's commitment to the theoretical possibilities of the image. Similarly, the case of *The Spanish Earth* might be discursively placed as a precursor to the ultimate successes of the documentary image in the revolutions in Eastern Europe. By the time of the 1989 European revolutions, even Ivens's self-conscious Marxist aesthetic form had lost its prominence as key to the aspiration for liberation from repressive social and political regimes through images. The modes of production, distribution, and exhibition took over as the engine of the politically committed image.

THE POSTWAR PERIOD

In the postwar period, the properly Marxist project of sociopolitical transformation through an audience action inspired by a radical aesthetic migrated to a
number of different spaces. The pre–World War II work of Joris Ivens and Pare
Lorentz continued into the postwar period and, as Nichols demonstrated, into
the newsreels of filmmakers such as Leo Hurwitz. However, during the immediate process of rebuilding Europe, cultural production did not prosper. It was
only in the 1960s and 1970s, the period of great cultural revolution in Europe, that
realist filmmakers took up the mantle passed to them by the likes of Vertov and
Grierson. Indeed, the impetus to challenge the authority and power of the state
through the agency of the image found its most potent postwar examples in the
work of the New Wave European art cinemas of the 1960s and 1970s. What is
striking about these works is that not only did they challenge the given political and
social realities, but they also complicated the role of aesthetic. They did this by
questioning the images put forward by the mass media, a mass media understood
as the contemporary public sphere. Thus, filmmaker-theorists such as Alexander
Kluge, Jean-Marie Straub and Danièle Huillet, and Jean-Luc Godard and
Guy Debord, among others, agitated by interrogating the status of the images
that dominated public discourse. In doing so, these filmmakers added another
layer of reflection to the already complex relationship between the image and the
social world.

While the works of each of these filmmakers reflect their specific historical
environments and, more particularly, the concerns of their nations, they always
convey a firm belief in the possibility of social revolution. French filmmakers such
as Godard and Debord were immersed in the French Left, which nurtured a love
affair with Leninist-based socialism in its most general sense. The Cultural Revolution in China, Che Guevara in Cuba, and the struggle for socialism in Burma
were the touchstones of this radical work of film-as-theory and theory-as-film.
Contemporaneous with events such as the publication of Louis Althusser's *For
Marx* and *Reading Capital*, the first stirrings of the youth revolution, and the Six
Days' war in the Middle East, and in the wake of uprisings in Prague and Budapest,
filmmakers Godard and Debord brought innovation and a searing critique of
capitalism and its institutions to these movements. This was a historical moment
of hope in and commitment to social revolution. T.J. Clark and Donald Nicholson-
Smith said of Debord and his fellow Situationists International members, "It
was the 'art' dimension, to put it crudely—the continual pressure put on the
question of representational forms in politics and everyday life, and the refusal
to foreclose on the issue of representation versus agency—that made their politics the deadly weapon it was for a while. And gave them the role they had in
May 1968."[34]

The cinema, like the automatization of production work, left the workers free to do other things, namely, as Lukács would have it, to contemplate.[35] And according to this thinking, freed from the strictures of reification, the worker would be free to revolt and, consequently, enjoy the liberation otherwise reserved for the bourgeoisie. That is, the films of Godard, Debord, and other young French radicals of the late 1960s and early 1970s found audiences of intellectuals who, through exposure to self-reflexive cinematic strategies, were encouraged to see their own role in the oppression of those they were being called upon to liberate.

In Germany in the 1960s there was no less of a revolutionary spirit among filmmakers. Tired of the lies and corruption of the generation before them, Kluge and his fellow Young German filmmakers were determined to expose the lies of those in power and to forge a new public sphere of communication and cooperation, in short, a new form of political and social democracy. Kluge and his colleagues not only reacted to the conservative cultural policies and products of Adenauer's post-Nazi Germany; they were also caught in the throes of social revolution that was both national and international in scope. Although the events of the Korean War and, subsequently, the war in Vietnam were not explicitly examined in their films, these events weighed on the search for a more educated and articulate German people. Films such as Kluge's *Die Patriotin* (*The Female Patriot*, 1979) were also among the many components in the widespread debate that overtook German intellectual and creative circles regarding what to do with the unspoken—or denial of—criminality of the nation's recent past. In this sense, the Baader-Meinhof Gang's contemporaneous revolutionary activities were kindred spirits with films that searched for answers through representational means.[36]

That all of the films I discuss in this section are not traditionally conceived documentaries is both significant and not. The significance lies in the fact that some of the most provocative examples of revolutionary agitprop cinema in the postwar period also challenged the traditionally conceived distinctions between documentary and fiction. Like their 1920s and 1930s documentary predecessors, filmmakers such as Godard and Gorin, Kluge, and Straub and Huillet are committed to the incitation of change in a revolutionary audience, however imagined and achieved through a radical aesthetic. However, in addition, these filmmakers recognized the necessity of questioning the validity of their own images. Because the truth status of the cinematic image is always at stake in a revolutionary cinema, these filmmakers foregrounded this problem and forced audiences to question not only the reality that was given them by existing social structures but also the communication of that reality in the films themselves. Kluge's interrogation of history and the discourses of historical representation in *Abschied von Gestern* (*Yesterday's Girl*, 1966) and his contribution to *Deutschland im Herbst* (*Germany in Autumn*, 1978) can, therefore, be conceived of as legitimate descendents of, for example, Brecht's *Kühle Wampe*. First, however, we must turn to the French films.

Letter to Jane (Jean-Luc Godard and Jean-Pierre Gorin, 1972) arguably harbors some of the strongest ties to the agitational films of the 1920s and 1930s, and raises issues that would become central to the intellectuals' role in Central and Eastern Europe in the late eighties and early nineties. Indeed, all of Godard's work of this period, work eventually done in collaboration with Jean-Pierre Gorin under the aegis of the Dziga Vertov label, was working in these same directions. *Le weekend* (*Weekend*, 1967), *Vent d'est* (*Wind from the East*, 1971), and *Tout va bien* (*All is Well*, 1972) all work to expose what the filmmakers believe to be the so-called political dominant's ideological manipulation of representation. In spite of the failure of their attempts to reach their designated audience, these films still claimed to enlist the factory worker in the struggle against industrial capitalism. Godard and Gorin's films were specifically addressed to those workers who were oppressed by the unyielding political and social structures that had produced post–World War II prosperity. They were also supposedly designed to open dialogue between the intellectual and the factory worker in the anticipation of revolution. However, in reality, these films were made in a climate of intense reflection and contemplation on the role of the intellectual in the wake of 1968. Despite the apparent commitment to the worker audience, they were more accurately conceived as self-interested ruminations made to provoke intellectual audiences to continue consideration of their responsibility to the revolution. In this sense, the films of this period are indeed post-1968 treatises that strove to continue the important collaboration of workers and intellectuals that had been ignited in the student revolutions. Godard and Gorin took the Dziga Vertov appellation as an indicator of their commitment to social and political revolution, but they never imagined that their work would agitate and change on the vast national level that had been Vertov's aspiration. The exhibition history of their films testifies to this. The films were usually shown in schools, cinémathèques, and, only occasionally, the factory workplace.[37] Even with more focused target audiences, these films never had the impact that might be assumed from the theoretical reflections.

Letter to Jane was filmed as an appendix to, a reflection on, the filmmakers say, an apology for *Tout va bien*. The film focuses on an image of Jane Fonda that first appeared in *L'Express*. Fonda is depicted listening to Vietnamese in Hanoi. The American star is in the foreground and in focus, while the one Vietnamese man who faces the camera is in the background and blurred by his distance from the camera. The other Vietnamese figures have their backs to the camera. The film explores the way the media imagines Hollywood stars in its enthusiasm to mask the reality of, in this case, the Vietnam War. Godard and Gorin exposed Fonda's image, its framing, its dominance of and privilege in the frame, its expression, its relationship to the Vietnamese people. They were especially concerned to point out the high degree of mediation and contradiction used to mask the political reality of the situation in North Vietnam. According to *Letter to Jane*, the image communicates no information about the Vietnam War and an abundance about Jane

Fonda's star persona. For example, through a montage of stills from the history of Hollywood and other filmmaking traditions, *Letter to Jane* equates Fonda's expression with, among others, that of her father when he looks at the unfortunate black people in *Young Mr. Lincoln* (John Ford, 1939) and that of Joan of Arc as she hears the verdict of the court that announces her punishment in *The Passion of Joan of Arc* (Carl Theodor Dreyer, 1928). Likewise, the connection is made between Fonda's face in the *L'Express* photograph and her face when she looks at the Donald Sutherland character in *Klute* (Alan Pakula, 1971). Through this montage of still images, Godard and Gorin argued that the image of Jane Fonda in the *L'Express* photograph bears an expression that has been used throughout the history of Hollywood and other filmmaking traditions for any number of different emotions expressed in myriad contexts.[38] The film argues that if the intellectual and, in particular, the filmmaker are to have a role in the revolution, it is necessary to question and find new answers to the mechanisms of representation. Ultimately, *Letter to Jane* claims it is time to listen to the oppressed workers or, in this case, the Vietnamese, and discern how the political situation affects them. Photographs of Jane Fonda in *L'Express* go no way toward this goal because the situation in Vietnam is absent from an image in which the star persona of the Hollywood actress effectively oils the machines of capitalist oppression.

The political charge of films such as *Tout va bien* and *Vent d'est* is ignited through both the form and the content of the image. In these films, the minimalist parameters of the film camera are paramount to Godard's insistence that the viewer probes all that he or she otherwise takes for granted: the framing, the composition, the relationship between pro-filmic and represented, the diegetic movement, and so on. Thus, in *Tout va bien* we cannot forget the uninterrupted single-take tracking shot at the supermarket. The extended, single-take shot in long shot abrogates narrative development and pleasure and forces us to see from a distance and confront the absurdity of American consumer capitalism. In the so-called Marxist western, *Vent d'est*, the familiar Godardian static camera is accompanied by the equally familiar struggle of sound and image, and by intertextual appropriation of literary and philosophical sources and their critical analysis, in a film that is considered a primer of Marxist theory converted into action. The characters—more like human participants—discuss the deployment and effectiveness of sounds and images in the Marxist struggle in long shot while a man and woman sit motionless, chained together in a field in high-angle long shot. The couple is particularly interested in the use of representation in the analysis of a mining strike. Should, for example, an image of Stalin be used in the struggle? The question is particularly relevant given the capitalists' use of Stalin's image as a sign of repression. What, therefore, does this image mean from the revolutionary perspective? Simultaneously, *Vent d'est* analyzes Stalin's representation and the different meanings it has been given. Thus, Godard and Gorin demystified the image of the heterosexual couple in narrative cinema in an effort to militate against bourgeois notions of representation. Simultaneously, the film attempts to have an impact outside of representation when, later on, it enters into an examination of the necessity of action. For example, a voice-over narrator reminds us that it is not enough to read *Das Kapital* when a union delegate selects the book from Miss Althusser's book stall. Rather, the man must know how to use it. Action is always the goal of the revolutionary representation.

The radicality of the Godard-Gorin image manipulation can be observed through its juxtaposition with the aesthetic interruptions of their namesake, Dziga Vertov. Godard and Gorin's long, static takes in which very little appears to happen, the separation and contention of sound and image, the repetition of cutaways to extra-textual references, are all very different from the fast-paced, rhythmical editing that politicized the apparently complacent viewing experience in the 1920s. The most important difference comes when Godard and Gorin pry open the modes of visual representation and the construction of meaning. The first step toward the revolution is, according to the filmmakers, to strip away the formal facade that masks the truth of the image even in the documentary.[39] In *Letter to Jane*, the moving image is laid open to interrogation by a film that comprises a collation of still photographs. Furthermore, the editing of these still images is exposed when on a couple of occasions an unseen hand slides one photograph into the frame so that it replaces the one already there. Perhaps most disturbing to the spectator is the periodic cut to a blank screen. This device prompts careful listening of the voice-over narration's critical discourse on the deception of the photograph, the disingenuity of the production, distribution, and reception of the star as political vehicle, and the importance of finding a visual language through which to enable the voices of the Vietnamese.

Whatever the shortcomings of films such as *Letter to Jane*, this and the other Dziga Vertov films marked a significant step for the history of political documentary filmmaking. Even though the films did not enjoy a revolutionary agency, they moved ever closer to the core motivation of political domination and the potential role of the image in its overturn. Godard and others working in the late 1960s and early 1970s understood that the Marxist project demanded a self-reflective interrogation of the production, exhibition, and distribution of the moving image. The work of these filmmakers extended the concerns of their pre–World War II ancestors when, for the first time, the politically agitational film theorized its own collaboration in the process. This complicity had to be acknowledged before it could become possible to use the same images as tools in the struggle for political freedom. In this sense, the work of European postwar political documentarists might become visible as a precursor to the images that were instrumental in liberation from forty-five years of socialist dictatorships. Before exploring this connection in more depth, it is worthwhile to trace the further unfolding of this tradition.

In the same historical moment, but from a different perspective, Guy Debord and the Situationists International made a film version of Debord's well-known manifesto, *Society of the Spectacle* (1973). In a strategy favored by documentary filmmakers since Shub's reappropriation of the films of Czar Nicholas II, Debord *"détournes"* film and image fragments from a variety of sources: Hollywood movies, soft-core pornography, instructional films, television commercials, news-reels, and Eastern bloc feature films. These fragments of moving images are inter-woven in an indeterminate logic with written texts, often philosophical quotations ranging from Dante to von Clausewitz. Film fragments, still images, and textual wisdoms are then overlaid by the voice-over of Debord reading his book, *Society of the Spectacle.* In yet another layer, music by the eighteenth-century composer Michel Corette is entwined with the voice-over to add a rich sound track to the dense visual compilation. This complex amalgam of words and images is *détourné*—hijacked, embezzled, corrupted—into a narrative performance that seeks to negate the "bourgeois conception of art and culture" as it is realized in "the society of the spectacle."

For Debord and his collaborators, the image as "spectacle" was born of a capitalist society that had witnessed the progressive shift within production toward the provision of consumer goods and services. Concomitant with their coloniza-tion of everyday life, culture and its images had become meaningless, replete with a confusion of values, disorienting, and repeated ad infinitum. In short, they were the enemy of revolution.[40] Where bureaucracy had appropriated words and images to fuel its ideology, Debord's form of reappropriation, or subversive *détournement*, is a restitution of words and images to their rightful context as agents in the Marxist struggle for liberation from such oppression. Debord's is an anarchic practice that commences with the reinstatement of the historical or materialist dimension to language and images. If the ideological language of power steals and "attacks language and reduces its poetry to the vulgar prose of its information," the revolutionary critique recuperates the language of power and transforms it into its weapon.[41]

Thus, for example, in *Society of the Spectacle* a short fragment bombards our senses with an overload of visual and aural stimuli. The confusion and density of our sensory experience mimics the language of ideological manipulation. How-ever, Debord reinfused the otherwise superficial discourses with polemical per-suasion through juxtaposition and endless layering. Footage of Richard Nixon in conversation with Chairman Mao is intercut with soaring views from the cockpits of helicopters flying over the jungles of Vietnam. In turn, these fragments sit side by side with an officer delivering a eulogy, dense traffic moving through past landmarks of urban Paris, a hysterical crowd at a rock concert, and the familiar faces of the Beatles waving to the crowds as they come off a plane, singing, drumming, playing. A series of stills of an all-but-naked Marilyn Monroe is jux-taposed with a man throwing V-Day leaflets from a window, riot police, and Vietnamese lying dead on the side of the road or being tortured on the streets. Hitler then takes his long walk to the podium at the Nuremberg rally, Khrushchev waves from his balcony, and then a war-torn landscape is seen from a point of view inside a tanker. These never-ending, historically, geographically, and politically disparate images continue. They are then overlaid with Debord's voice citing the thesis we already know from his book.

> The spectacular false struggles of the rival forms of separate power are also real, in that they translate the unequal and conflict-laden development of the system, the relatively contradictory interests of the classes or of the subdivisions of classes that recognize the system, and define their own participation in its power. These diverse oppositions can present themselves in the spectacle, by completely different criteria, as absolutely distinct forms of society. But in terms of their actual reality as particular sectors, the truth of their particularity resides in the universal system that contains them: in the unique movement that has made the planet its field, capitalism. . . . The concentrated spectacular belongs essentially to bureaucratic capitalism, while it can be imported as a technique of state power over more backwards mixed economies, or in certain moments of crisis of advanced capitalism.

The intensity of these visual and aural stimuli make the task of viewing, synthesizing, and understanding an impossible one.[42] The narration may describe and interpret the images, but its extent and density preclude a comfortable viewing experience. *The Society of the Spectacle* endlessly reiterates the thesis (without antithesis) that the "real is inverted in ideology, that ideology, changed in its essence in the spectacle, passes itself off for the real, that it is necessary to overthrow ideology in order to bring back into its own."[43]

Although the film of *The Society of the Spectacle* appeared dated by the time it was released in 1981, it marks a significant development in the trajectory I am tracing. Once again, following the tendency of its interwar predecessors, it is more successful as a philosophical statement. And its statement focuses on the political imperative of the image as counterspectacle: *The Society of the Spectacle* sees the double bind of the image where it is both "repugnant" and redemptive. And yet, Debord must concede the ultimate triumph of the spectacle in the twentieth century when he signaled the collapse of the Berlin Wall in 1989 as "a contemporary media event" repeated ad infinitum as the sign of modern progress. For Debord, this event marked the end of all possible redemption. He asked ironically, "How can the poor be made to work once their illusions have been shattered, and once force has been defeated?"[44] Sadly, or perhaps appropriately, Debord did not live to see the demythification of the bureaucratic colonization through the dissembling of media power in Serbia and Ukraine. The identity of Eastern Europe may have been dissolute, as Debord noted in 1992; however, it would also become redefined through a popular appropriation of the media. This direct involvement of the "masses" such that the audience literally shared in the production of the image would become the critical difference in the successful revolutionary documentary. But first, Alexander Kluge's relationship to the image takes us one step closer to the political documentary realism that we witnessed at the end of the last century in the Eastern European revolutions.

Kluge's work further challenges the traditional conceptions of the documentary already questioned by the French political filmmaking of the 1970s. His films straddle the line between documentary and fiction through their energetic interweaving of archival footage, newly shot images, dramatic re-creations, and interviews. Typically, the "documentary" sequences in films such as *Abshied von Gestern* are staged, and the fictionalized sequences depict actual events; thus, the films deliberately resist easy categorization as one or the other. Nevertheless, if we remember that my concern is to foreground the relationship between aesthetic and political agency, the challenge to more conservative categories comes as a welcome complication. In addition, Kluge's work leads the discussion in the direction of new media. Kluge was among the first of his postwar, 1960s generation of filmmakers to recognize the limitations of film as a political medium. Kluge's beliefs and awareness here are, in part, due to the historically intimate relationship between film and television production and exhibition in postwar Germany.[45] After the mid-1980s his conscious decision to air his 16-millimeter films on television only is a concrete manifestation of the philosophical underpinnings of his position. Kluge recognizes the importance of television as a way to reach the masses. He is both devoted to the film aesthetic as the harbinger of social democracy, and convinced of the centrality of television for garnering an audience:

> We are involving ourselves in the new private TV medium, and we will make cinema there. We are bringing film history into it. . . . We are making programs that offer film stories to a large majority of the population. We're influencing TV very powerfully, but we want eventually to reestablish the cinema. We will come through television to cinema again and won't leave 35mm. It's not necessary. It's the best material, because it provides the best information, even for television. But for the moment we can only get to a general audience through television.[46]

Kluge's understanding of television and his readiness to bring television and cinema together in an effort to have a social impact on an audience prefigure the type of political images that witnessed and contributed to the fall of Communism at the end of the last century. Similarly, they present themselves here as the germ of a sophisticated way of thinking about the relationship between new and old media in the twentieth century as it has been theorized by leading thinkers in the field. Lastly, like Godard and Debord, Kluge is committed to countering the superficial images that are propagated by the commercial media. Like his colleagues in France, Kluge believes that to alert and radicalize his viewers he must fragment and distort the image as a way to unsettle them and, consequently, provoke thought. Furthermore, like Godard and Debord, Kluge is driven by the Marxist project to use the technological image politically. He thinks it is the ideal way to expose what his teacher, Theodor Adorno, identified as the way systemic apparatuses schematize and standardize in the economic interests of capital.[47] Kluge, as one of the great modernist filmmakers, believes that the form of the film can be manipulated through productive fragmentation and conflict. This formal experimentation supposedly wrests film away from the debilitating grasp of the culture industry and gives it back to the people. Through this gesture of handing back, Kluge rewrites, or refilms history. Thus, there are multiple reasons for seeing Kluge's films as stepping-stones along the path from the political documentary of the interwar period to those that witness and engage in the fall of Communism, those that actually effect the change that was so desired. After Adorno, Kluge continued the commitment to a Marxist project that urgently sought the collapse of capitalism. It was a collapse that he believed could be realized via the moving technological image aesthetic.

Kluge's aesthetic also departs in significant ways from that of his French colleagues. Most significantly, he does not believe in the cause-and-effect relationship of the image to the revolution. For Kluge, the image itself does not directly produce the action that is so coveted among audiences. Rather, he believes it is necessary to critique the image that persuades and "interpolates" the bourgeois individual. Thus, his goal is undergirded by an impulse to criticize, a deep skepticism toward the bourgeois propagation of images. Kluge knows that the only way to get people to think and to engage with social politics is to ensure that they think about the way its opinions are formed in the first place. Film and the moving image could never change a government, but they can change the representations that are produced by and of that government. From there, the moving image is able to provoke thought and reflection, which will, in turn, hopefully slowly erode the bourgeois institutions that entrap us.[48]

To meet these ends, Kluge tells stories. He is interested not in documentaries or fiction narratives per se but, rather, in a form that hovers somewhere between the two. Although the films differ significantly across his oeuvre, they never sit comfortably within either the linear (or nonlinear) informational narratives of social realist documentary, or the coherent narratives of commercial fiction filmmaking.[49] Kluge believes, like Brecht before him, that the disinterested spectator must find pleasure as well as intellectual challenges in films. Through their formal manipulations, films must inspire humor, irony, and delight, responses that, in keeping with Brecht, are free of immersion in an illusory world. The spectator will then respond with fantasies and thoughts that produce the film in his or her head. Kluge's modern fables are not so much unfinished as they are incomplete, awaiting the imagination of an audience to complete them. The imagination of the audience is crucial to Kluge's Marxist practice because of its philosophical commitment to the countering of reason and instrumentalization. For all the differences among the films, this principle of the film in the spectator's head remains constant across Kluge's work.[50]

Kluge's aim is, ultimately, to create through cinema a counterpublic sphere in which communication can begin to evolve.[51] As Miriam Hansen explained, the public sphere that Kluge's cinema seeks to counter is familiar to us from other Marxist film practices of the twentieth century.

> As a medium that organizes human needs and qualities in a social form, the existing public sphere maintains a claim to be representative while excluding large areas of people's experience. Among the media that increasingly constitute the public sphere, the cinema lags behind on account of its primarily artisanal mode of production (in Germany, at least), preserving a certain degree of independence thanks to state and television funding. This ironic constellation provides the cinema with a potential for creating an alternative, oppositional public sphere within the larger one, addressing itself primarily to the kinds of experience repressed by the latter. Thus the cinema's intervention aims not only at the systematic non- or misrepresentation of specific issues—eg. family, factory, security, war and Nazism—but also the structure of the public sphere itself.[52]

The intended political agency of Kluge's films differs from the agitational, revolution-provoking work of Godard and Debord in still other ways. Kluge's aesthetic is never an incitation to aggressive opposition or action. Form is always in the name of intellectual and emotional enlightenment. A counterpractice provoking straightforward active resistance would, of course, stay locked within the logic of systematization that oppresses. It is only through an experience that transcends conventional modes of thought and action that creative and constructive paths of resistance can be discovered. Kluge's mode of filmmaking and its desired effect are forcefully captured in his contribution to *Deutschland im Herbst*, arguably one of his most political films.

Deutschland im Herbst is a compilation of short films by eight teams of filmmakers; it is a collective response to the kidnapping and murder of Hanns-Martin Schleyer, and the subsequent deaths of three of the Baader-Meinhof members some months later. The film does not seek to resolve the suspicions surrounding the deaths, but, rather, wanders through issues such as the silent and invisible mechanisms of state repression, a social fabric permeated with violence at every level of public and private experience, the confusion and complexities, blame and responsibility, of German history. Although it is difficult to discern where the work of one filmmaking team ends and the next begins, Kluge's contributions are periodically made obvious, not through his style, but through the presence of Gabi Teichert, a character who appears again in *Die Patriotin* two years later.

In one such sequence, following a series of still paintings, we meet Kluge's history teacher trudging through a romantic, snow-covered landscape with a spade. She is off to dig up German history, or perhaps "to make a shelter for World War III" in search of "prehistoric remains." Whatever her purpose, Gabi's work will unearth many contradictions. We join her in the bath after documentary footage of Field Marshal Erwin Rommel who was killed with poison by the state in 1944. We witness the ceremonious, public mourning of his funeral courtesy of the Deutsche Wochenschau: it is a state-led response blanketed in a mood of grave sorrow that is echoed in the funeral of Hanns-Martin Schleyer. The state's duplicity is as unfathomable when shown in the black and white of these 1944 archival treasures as it is in the color of 1970s newscast footage. Through a series of yet more images we are also told of the suicide of Franz der Kaiser (Archduke Franz Ferdinand), another episode in Germany's history of violence, its violent history. By the time we return to Gabi in the bath, the voice-over tells us she "got into trouble with the authorities" because her version of history was not suitable for the classroom. The layers of contradiction that Gabi has unearthed and obviously professed become increasingly incredulous and unacceptable through Kluge's matter-of-fact editing. Following Gabi's appearance, the film moves through archival footage of the slaying of the prince of Serbia in 1938 by the German Secret Service, the high mass of Schleyer's state funeral, and the arrest of a Turkish man who happens to carry a gun outside the church in which the funeral takes place. This mélange of documentary footage, fictional restagings, archival footage from the past and the present, Germany and abroad, joins to force us to see the contradictions, the repression, the pomposity of official versions of German history.

The fragmented nature of Kluge's segment of *Deutschland im Herbst* is repeated at the level of the film as a whole: the film is an anthology of documentary and fictional passages comprising a fractured narrative. This is not to encourage further aggression toward the state, nor is it to condone the cause of the Baader-Meinhof Gang. Rather, Kluge and the other contributors to *Deutschland im Herbst* ask that their audience see history and politics in a different way. The film is a searing indictment of governments and politicians that, through its very exposure of the injustice of these powers, will give way to systemic change. However, we note that neither Kluge nor Gabi has a solution to the contortions of history and the abuse of power. This would be to stymie a forward motion of history as it is conceived by the people who live it, namely, the German audience. Kluge offered the contradictions of the past and the injustices of the present as a trigger to the audience's intellectual and emotional imaginings of how to rethink the past with the goal of avoiding its repetition in the future.

Kluge is quick to admit that his aesthetic is iconoclastic. He has little regard for the emotional persuasion of Hollywood filmmaking and is skeptical of most other images in capitalist society. In the short episode from *Deutschland im Herbst* we find the continual juxtaposition of one fragment, undoing the apparent meanings of the next. Thus, having seen the rhythmical and sensuous stock footage of the death and funeral of the prince of Serbia, accompanied by a voice-over that pries open the duplicity of the state that both murders and celebrates the foreign statesman, we have nothing but suspicion for the reverence paid to the live broadcast of Schleyer's funeral on closed-circuit monitors before a silent floor of workers at the Daimler-Benz factory. Nevertheless, Kluge, like Godard and Debord, is committed to finding redemptive capacities of the image. And redemption is found, as he has reiterated throughout his forty-five-year career, in the mind of the spectator. It is the film in the viewer's mind that ultimately has the capacity to change the social and political fabric of German society.

Perhaps most important for my history of radical European filmmaking, Kluge is always interested in extending the distribution of his films. Kluge brings to this history an audience that theoretically reaches far beyond those ever imagined by his predecessors. Since the 1980s, Kluge has worked and continues to work in private commercial television. Due to the very specific configuration of public and private television production in Germany, and the relations between them, Kluge has managed to exploit the "rifts, rivalries, and contradictory interests within and between private industry and governmental spheres" to create "counterinstitutions and an 'oppositional public sphere.' "[53] Since the mid-1980s, not only has Kluge carved out a space within the entertainment-style programming of private broadcasting, but he has also developed an aesthetic that befits the medium in which he now always works. As Peter Lutze explained, Kluge transforms his cinematic style of appropriation, interruption, fragmentation, and repetition to find an aesthetic that "simultaneously mimics the television style, flouts its conventions, and reveals its constructedness." Lutze described an example from *The Blind Director*, Kluge's 1985 made-for-television film: fragments and stills from archival films from distinct and recognizable historical moments are taken out of their logical order, repeated, segmented, and so on, in an attempt to subvert the form of a television serial.[54] In addition, the television films explore the possibilities of digital and video technologies.

The aesthetic is central to the politics of Kluge's television films, because it challenges audience expectations, always alerting the viewer to the processes of, in this case, the production of film and the consumption of television. However, the force of Kluge's work is as attributable to its mode of dissemination. His films are sandwiched among porn films, sports games, and American-style headline news on private television. Kluge's "cultural window," as it is called, has a duration of no more than thirty minutes; thus, it finds an unsuspecting audience through its very broadcast conditions. Once this audience's attention is caught, the films challenge their complacency particularly as it is manifested in their relationship to images. Despite his persistent animosity toward commercial mainstream image making, Kluge's move into television signals the imperative to adopt the media form that best reaches the eyes of those who are to instigate the revolution. It may not be a revolution with hammers and sickles; however, it is a revolution in which the modernist image is the springboard to undoing the power and knowledge base that are thought to be central to continued oppression and social retardation. Kluge's is a practice in which distribution is critical to the realization of a participating spectator—at least this is how the films function theoretically.

For all of these exciting inroads into exploiting the agitational potential of the television medium, even though Kluge's films enjoy this unprecedented access to a national audience, their practical impact is negligible. In this sense, Kluge's audience continues the ever-decreasing trend of European radical political documentary that began with the vast national reach of Vertov and dwindled to the audience of academics found by *Letter to Jane*. Kluge's televisual experiments might be aired on commercial television, but their contentiousness is never more than a theoretical statement. Siegfried Zielinski explained the paradoxical situation of Kluge's films, which are made possible by one of the world's leading commercial organizations, and yet, they have no audience:

> Kluge made clever use of a loophole in the terms of the broadcasting licenses awarded to these private channels [SAT1 and RTLplus] whereby they are obliged to allow third parties access to programming if they wish to occupy terrestrial frequencies. In the Japanese advertising agency DENTSU, Kluge found a partner to finance his televisual experiments. . . . Slotted between the prime time feature film and late night striptease shows or a sex magazine, it really is intimate television, for a club of audiovisual gourmets, with ratings around zero.[55]

Thus, the politically committed documentary in Europe moves ever closer to its demise when it becomes so elite that it loses its audience.

In one last example of political postwar documentary filmmaking, Harun Farocki's practice consciously celebrates its marginalization as the sine qua non of political radicality. Farocki shares the bloodlines of Kluge and, before him, Adorno. As a political documentarist, only recently brought to audiences outside Germany, Farocki inhabits the visual spaces colonized by power to question the role of the image in the perpetuation of that power. Again, Farocki is a devoted Marxist image maker who is both skeptical of the past use of images and yet continues to examine them in search of clarification and new perspectives on the world. Thus, like his predecessors, he explicitly despoils the image to reveal his implicit belief in the agency of the image. Like Kluge and Godard, Farocki takes a step back from the image and mobilizes a modernist aesthetic of distortion, interruption, separation of sound and image, and culling of secondhand images only to dissemble their coherence. Farocki's focus on the multiplicity of perspectives that comprise the truth of the radical aesthetic necessitates the questioning of his own intervention in its production. He interrogates his authority to render visible the material conditions of the world before the camera. This level of reflexivity moves beyond the didacticism characteristic of Godard's work, and Kluge's preference to diffuse this didacticism through collective authorship. Through his own self-effacement, Farocki actively strips the image of the illusions behind which all power relations might hide. Again, we must keep in mind that this is a theoretical position only.

Together with Kluge's television programs, Farocki's films extend into the post-Marxist, postindustrialized world of the closing stages of the twentieth century, the 1990s. In this particular economy, the commodity had become further abstracted and the technologized image no longer spoke against a background of social reality. Instead, in Farocki's world, the image was recognized as the reality itself. It was all we had. While Vertov and Grierson believed that the image had the power to change the world in its midst, and the postwar filmmakers understood that this would be realized only through a critique of the representations of this reality, for Farocki, the social world and representation became the same thing: we had reached a historical moment when to watch events on television was to see and experience them at first hand. As Jonathan Beller argued, not only is looking at a screen a form of labor,[56] but to follow the logic of Farocki's films, history, memory, power, and knowledge are always staged in the battle for visions and images. In the powerful civic movements of late-twentieth-century Europe we saw this merging of reality and representation literally enable the transition to a post-communist era.

Much of the time in Farocki's work, film and the technological image are handled as a historical hieroglyph. They always represent a historical perspective from which we can learn of the spaces and places at which power is secreted, and ideology is institutionalized. And even if the said images are from a past that seems remote, as we saw in *Deutschland im Herbst*, the mistakes of today are only ever a repetition of those of the past.[57] This is because, for Farocki, the image is always a displacement of time, history and identity, power and knowledge. Similarly, no image is ever benign: the same principles that underline the taking of scientific photographs, the invention of the camera obscura, even the perspectival formulations of Albrecht Dürer, also motivate the persecution of victims such as the Jews in the hands of Nazi Germany, or Algerian women photographed for the first time in 1960 at the order of French military. Without losing sight of the singularity of this history of images, images of history, we can recognize that they are threaded together in an examination of their shared exploitation close to the opening of *Bilder der Welt und Inschrift des Krieges* (*Images of the World and the Inscription of War*, 1988).

The primary distinction between Farocki's images and those of Godard and Kluge, for example, is his constant foregrounding of who sees, who speaks, and how those eyes and voices are reiterated everywhere in the histories secreted by the same images. Thus, Farocki's films are about looking: his own films usually look at others' perceptions in an attempt to create a space from which his audience might see anew. To achieve these ends, Farocki's films join the descendents of Shub's brand of political documentary. Farocki characteristically reuses and re-presents images of all media from the archives and dustbins of history: amateur images, educational and industrial films, silent film treasures, broadcast television, footage from surveillance cameras, still images turned into icons. And these secondhand images are typically "de-aestheticized" through Farocki's own manipulation—cropping, extreme close-ups that decontextualize, multiple repetitions and transfers, vertical layering, and other forms of distress. All of his documentaries are

accompanied by an unemotional, informational voice-over that binds the fragments in a narrative that exposes how images are used to perpetuate political,
economic, and institutional power.[58] Every level of the status, production, distribution, redistribution, storing, and perception of images is probed in Farocki's
complex, often contradictory works.

Farocki's best-known film outside Germany, *Bilder der Welt und Inschrift des
Krieges*, demonstrates all of these qualities. At the end of a comparatively long
sequence that pauses to examine the use of photographs for the daily operation,
documentation, and memory of the concentration camp at Auschwitz-Birkenau,
the film examines the exchange of looks and their performance in a single photograph. The image, evidently taken by a soldier, depicts the arrivals at the camp,
specifically focusing on the all-too-recognizable process of selection. As Farocki's
camera cuts to a variety of perspectives, a woman walks past, perhaps into the shot,
and she returns the look of the soldier behind the camera. It is, as the female voice-
over explains to us, a photograph that marks the preservation of the woman—her
image is now one of the most widely distributed of photographs at Auschwitz—
and her simultaneous destruction. Like the still images of Allied reconnaissance
missions—what the camera sees in this image is instantly marked for destruction.
Her very presence before a camera, in a line awaiting selection on the ramp at
Auschwitz, signals her impending death. The following image is that of a woman
having makeup applied; she is also preserved and destroyed in this deceptively
harmless gesture. Sometime later in the film, the same photograph of the selection
line at Auschwitz is reinserted—to illustrate yet another form of exploitation: the
human being as labor power. While work is the sole destiny in Auschwitz 1944,
the only means of survival, it is also the ultimate murderer when the body and soul
are pushed beyond their limits. And through unique modes of juxtaposition, for
Farocki, the labor of the concentration camp is a close relative of the exploitation
of the worker in the factory.

Adding a further layer of contradiction to the story of Farocki's practice, his
1992 film that documents the fall of the Ceauşescu regime in Bucharest in 1989,
Videogramme einer Revolution (*Videograms of a Revolution*, 1992), locates the realization of the Marxist aspiration for a revolutionary image. However, the revolution is spawned not by Farocki's film, but by the media and home movie footage
he culls. Farocki appropriates the televisual images that contributed to the eventual
freedom of Romania from the noose of Ceauşescu's dictatorship. Similarly, he
weaves them as "videograms" into his finished product. However *Videogramme
einer Revolution* itself characteristically remains on the margins of mass movement.[59] In turn, the key to mass mobilization is not found in a meticulous construction of the television and amateur video images. Rather, it comes through the
twin avenues of the coarseness and spontaneity, thus authenticity, of the homemade image and its distribution. Most important, while the aesthetic of new
technology does not bring innovation to the revolution, the limitlessness of its

distribution possibilities does. Thus, if we take our cue from the revolutionary image identified by Farocki, the realization of the Marxist aspiration for a radical image that will provoke mass confrontation and overturning of the system necessitates a shift away from the attachment to the radical, supposedly antibourgeois aesthetic as a tool of direct political organization.

Godard's claim in *British Sounds* (1968) could well come from the pen of Harun Farocki: "[I]f a million prints are made of a Marxist-Leninist film it becomes *Gone with the Wind*." While Farocki is quick to integrate all media including the digital into his visionscape, his works reach even fewer viewers than those of Kluge. Although they are slowly being made available for home video usage, they have historically been relegated to European film festivals and specialist screenings at (predominantly German) art-house venues. Their small audience of intellectuals, usually already in the know, casts these would-be tools of the revolution as boutique productions. Equally as esoteric, Farocki does not even offer his films for consumption as commodities—this would remove their cutting edge. He sees no way out of the impasse: to enter into the arena of commercial film and television is to subscribe to its politics. The limited distribution of films such as *Bilder der Welt* leaves Farocki hovering on the margins, his films barely known outside the European festival circuit. In this sense, Farocki's image-making practice moves farther away from the Marxist goal of an image that instigates the masses in revolt. And yet, Farocki's interrogation of the multifarious meanings, the realities and ambiguities, uses and misuses of images in the public sphere, effectively strips away illusion such that we are brought face-to-face with the historical truth—however performative—of the image. Again, we see the paradox of this vein of Marxist filmmaking in its most naked form.

All of the filmmakers I have discussed believe that the image can be appropriated, taken out of the hands of the powerful and put in the service of revolution. In turn, this is underwritten by a belief in the radical possibilities of the image, where the effects are experienced beyond the film frame. As I have argued, the project was, until the so-called people's revolutions of 1989, a failed one. Like the Marxist struggle it sought to incite, the experimental aesthetic of interruption in the struggle for revolutionary change and liberation never realized its aspiration. This aspiration, particularly in film, was closely tied to a Marxist materialism that believed in the potential of the image to invert the dominant ideology. This would be realized through the same logic as the Marxist dialectic, which strives to invert the labor-power relations that ensure the subservience of the worker to the industrialist. When the Marxist concept of sociality that moves toward revolution became no longer viable in the 1980s, the attachment to an image that had the mirror agency was also necessarily rejected.[60] It was however, a fortuitous rejection. Even though no political model for social change was put in the place of classical Marxist thought, the image still triumphed in the face of increasing disillusionment with the oligarchies of Eastern and Central Europe.

The Revolution in Eastern and Central Europe

The late-twentieth-century revolutions fought and won in and through images were not enabled by conscious formal manipulation of an image of interruption as it was historically conceived. In this sense, they were not, strictly speaking, Marxist images, and neither did they follow the dialectical thinking that believes that exposure of the obfuscatory mechanisms of the image as ideological object is necessarily carried out at the level of the aesthetic. On the contrary, even though the aesthetic was important, its construction was only innovative because of who produced it and the ways it was used. The role of the revolutionary image in the downfall of Eastern European socialism can be held up as a historical articulation of W.J.T. Mitchell's assertion that the political and ideological force of the image lies not in its aesthetic, but in the uses to which it is put. It is the values we place on images, the beliefs and expectations we invest in them, and the conversations we have about images that are the real mirrors of visual meaning.[61] We may now be aware of the deceptions involved in the production and dissemination of the revolutionary images. However, my argument rests on their effectivity to mobilize an audience; therefore, the fact that people trusted the evidentiary truths of what they saw on television is all that matters.

If Harun Farocki's films and their processes of distribution represent one end of the spectrum of contemporary political filmmaking, the television and new media coverage of the Eastern European revolutions might be placed at the other end. The success of the image in the popular overthrow of Communist regimes lies in its access to modes of distribution that have come hand in hand with the ostensible democratization of information enabled by computer and digital technologies. Together with the declining faith in a Marxist conception of revolution, the documentary image underwent its own redefinitions in the 1980s and 1990s in particular. Quite simply, new media technologies put the production and distribution of the image in the hands of the people in a way that was never possible with film, due to its industrial and material constraints. At least in theory, and in the former Eastern bloc in practice, anyone with a camera could make and disseminate documentation of events deemed newsworthy.[62] Gone was the imperative to counter ideological structures through aesthetic manipulation of their representations. In the 1990s, it became possible to appropriate these representational spaces prior to their domination by the powers that be. And the resulting images made with handheld camcorders and digital recorders were immediate, hastily put together, and, thus, opened up new definitions of the radical documentary aesthetic.

It comes as no surprise to find revolutions played out through the media in Romania, Serbia, and Ukraine. In each of these cases, the revolution meant the overthrow of a totalitarian regime. In each state, the media was at the center of the respective regime's domination. The revolutionaries had no choice: to arrest power, they had to seize the instruments with which this power was exercised. The Ceaușescu regime, which had lasted twenty-five years in Romania, was the first of these empires to topple. Even though the Communist media did not report the revolt against the Ceaușescu regime that began in the western, multiethnic city of Timisoara in mid-December 1989, Hungarian radio and television did. It was only a matter of time before the news spread—if only through the Romanian media's silence around what was obviously going on—to Bucharest and the rest of the country. When the struggle for power between the Ceaușescu loyalist Securitate and the dissident army-backed citizens was ignited, it was done so at the site and on the screens of Televiziunea Română. The occupation of the station and the appearance of dissidents, actors, film directors, intellectuals, playwrights, and poets on television screens meant the victory of the revolution.[63]

The images broadcast by the newly formed National Salvation Front were not interested in the past sixty years of theorizing about the moving image, the intricacies of realist representation, and the ethical responsibility of truth claims on film. Gone also was the importance placed on the filmmaker as artist exploring the political possibilities of moving visual images. Instead, images as supposedly transparent windows onto the reality of events as they happened became privileged as the purveyors of political truth. Romanian audiences sat glued to their television sets, were fed and believed the horrors of the Ceaușescu reign: torture chambers, the Ceaușescus' haul of gold, the weapons of ideological and political manipulation that were presented as evidence of the monstrous nature of their ruler. As would become characteristic of the footage that convinced the people to rise up in resistance to their oppression, it was the mistakes, the repetitions, the shakiness of the handheld camera in the crossfire of the unfolding of history that guaranteed authenticity. People believed and were motivated to respond politically to the images they saw because they were raw, immediate, and flawed, not because they were carefully put together according to an intellectual logic. Similarly, people were invited to come into the station and speak the truth of their experience under this brutal Communist rule. The voice of the people was raised and spoke the reality of their repression while their fellow countrymen sat at home and watched the events unfold on their television sets. Peter Gross explained it thus: "Peasants, priests, doctors, engineers, students, homemakers, military personnel, factory workers, former prisoners in the Communist gulag, all were given their few seconds of fame or at the very least brief, first and last ever national exposure. Never before and not since have the broadcast media been ruled by the politics of inclusion and been truly democratized media."[64]

Simultaneously, the fate of Nicolae Ceaușescu and his wife, Elena, was broadcast in minute detail. Their capture, trial, and execution, and their contorted bodies lying wasted against a wall, were staged and performed for the benefit of the viewer at home. At the same time that viewers were feasting on the live, around-the-clock broadcast of the continued fighting between the Securitate and the army inside and outside the television station, no doubt was left in their minds that the dictator who had purveyed a repressive social, political, economic, and cultural Romania was finally gone.

Shortly after New Year in 1990, doubts and criticisms began to be cast over the sincerity and authenticity of the information broadcast by Free Televiziunea Română. As has been argued since, the transmitted material was manipulated by the nationalists to ensure their support against the villainous Communist regime.[65] Nevertheless, whether the material was prescripted, manipulated to cast the future government in a favorable light, or distorted to garner popular support, there is no dispute: this was a revolution in and through television. In addition, the broadcast images may not have been as spontaneous and "real" as was claimed through their presentation, but they were, nevertheless, received as authentic documents of the social and political convulsions. At the time, there was absolutely no question of the veracity of these images—what was taking place was doing so simultaneously before the eyes of a nation. It was live, it was real, and people were experiencing their oppression as they immersed themselves in the images of Ceauşescu's past brutality, the present of his downfall, and the future possibilities of democratic freedom. Gone was the claim for a politicized aesthetic form. The ostensibly naive claim that the television camera re-presents uncompromisingly the reality of what lies before it in real time was enough to call these people to revolution. Similarly, unlike the politically committed documentary of the first half of the century, the documentary cameras of Televiziunea Română literally gave the people the opportunity to own the image, to be involved in its production, and to see themselves as its addressee. Romanian people of all walks of life were never alienated from any level of the moving image: they were in the studio filming and being filmed, they were at home watching, thus taking part, and they were vociferously determining what they saw. The fact that this was all very carefully staged is significant, but not directly so for the purposes of my argument. What matters is that the people believed in the authenticity of their involvement in the television revolution, the revolution in television. And what matters is that it was a revolution utterly imbricated with the production, dissemination, and exhibition of the moving image, a moving image over which the people were given full command.

While the rest of Central and Eastern Europe was living out its revolution, in 1989 Slobodan Milošević was consolidating his power in Yugoslavia. Like that of Ceauşescu before him, Milošević's stranglehold over his people was fueled by his control and manipulation of the media. Nevertheless, unbeknownst to Milošević, the revolution that would overthrow him was simultaneously in the making in downtown Belgrade. Radio B92, the only independent radio station in Serbia, was granted a temporary permit to broadcast on an FM frequency in an otherwise government-monopolized media.[66] B92 began as a funky, experimental local music station with brief news flashes run by young cultural intellectuals. As time went on, it expanded into a film and video production unit and a music label that strove for transparency in opposition to the lies of the criminal dictatorship. Without the government recognizing the significance of its international reach, B92 also established an Internet center and service provider, OpenNet.org, in 1994 as a part of its operation. Ironically, supported by a telephone line from the Telecommunications Ministry[67] and Web space from a provider in Amsterdam, B92 offered Internet access to a wealth of independent media, human rights groups, and academics in Yugoslavia.[68] Although Milošević quickly put a stop to B92's live radio broadcasts of election frauds and demonstrations of opposition to the government, Radio B92 began broadcasting around the clock over the Internet through OpenNet.org. This allowed people to download information and pass it on through all possible means of communication, primarily the ever-expanding Internet and landline telephone. News of what was going on across the country, including, eventually, ethnic cleansing, reached the international community, and by the time Milošević loyalists took over B92 in 1995, it was too late. Not only had the independent voices of democracy proliferated across the Internet using other providers that had by this time been set up in Serbia, but Radio B92 had successfully attracted the attention of the international community. During the Kosovo war, the Milošević regime made attempts to appropriate the B92 Web site; however, ultimately, the power of the Internet was too great even for the dictator. The continued widespread dissemination of information with the help of Amsterdam spawned the government's loss of control of public perception, and, ultimately, the downfall of the Milošević regime. Milošević's stranglehold over the imagination of the Yugoslavian people was no longer sustainable without absolute control over the media.

Once again, the images transmitted over the Internet were presented as formally unsophisticated: quite clearly, they were made by pointing a camera and rolling the film. Like the images of demonstration and violence in Romania, the truth of Milošević's brutal reign was found in the content of images shown through shaky camera movements, hastily constructed frames, and barely edited footage. Again, the apparent coarseness of the images was the guarantee of their depiction of reality as it took place. Due to B92's establishment of multiple independent radio stations and Internet sites, access to the production of images was greater in Serbia than it had been in Bucharest. It was not necessary to go into B92's headquarters to ensure the broadcast of one's story. Anyone could film what they saw and, no matter their whereabouts in the country, the images had maximum audience exposure. The possibilities opened up by Radio B92 in Serbia were one example in which the Internet had truly democratized access to information. Every government gesture to regain its control over public information was reciprocated with the resistance's mobilization of yet more images through yet another Web site. Once again, to invoke Mitchell's assertion that the handling of images, not the images themselves, must answer for the social, and in this case, political role they play, it is only thanks to the indeterminacy and immediacy of the Web that a revolution can be fought using images as weapons. For all of its shortcomings, computer technology has put the production, distribution, and exhibition of images in the hands of the people, thus decentralizing the access to all phases of the revolutionary image. Most important, the immateriality of these images ensures that they cannot be harnessed by censorship. Although, to be sure, it is naive and irresponsible to celebrate the unqualified emancipation of the Web and Internet communication, the revolution in Serbia and the overthrow of the Milošević regime are nevertheless concrete examples of what can be achieved if its form is exploited to its full potential.

By the time of the "Orange Revolution" in Kiev in November 2004, which saw protests against election fraud, the deposition of Victor Yanukovich, and the election of Viktor Yushchenko, the line between mass revolution and television had been fully erased. The opposition knew in advance that election fraud was inevitable—how else could Yanukovich, the Kuchma- and Kremlin-backed candidate, win the vote in the face of the known dissension that had already been voiced in the west and center of the country?[69] Ordinary citizens with their camcorders were called to volunteer at polling stations to film the goings-on that Yushchenko's team knew would take place. Yuri Kolivoshko, a thirty-something property developer, took his camcorder to the polling station and explained his role in exposing the fraud:

> "I'm the kind of person who believed that things had been decided on our behalf a long time ago, that's all, and whether I went to vote wouldn't make any difference to me or Ukraine." Once Kolivoshko had voted, like millions of others, he began to believe that Yushchenko's movement offered a chance of change. "In the second round of voting I worked as an observer at a polling station until 6am. My task was to monitor violations, and I filmed everything. Then I went to Kiev, with the clothes on my back."[70]

The images of people such as Kolivoshko discovered such incredulities as "pens filled with disappearing ink, so that ballots would appear blank after they were cast" in areas where support for Yushchenko was high.[71] What was seen on these monitors was then fed to the people via Channel Five, Ukraine's only opposition television station. Once again, the people were either glued to their television sets at home or followed the public call to gather in Independence Square in Kiev to protest the injustice of their government. Similarly, the events at Independence Square, including the rock concert and speeches by opposition leaders, were also broadcast to people at home, who were experiencing the revolution from their armchairs.

Before the visual documentation of the massive criminal voter fraud, awareness of the corruption and brutality of the Kuchma government was growing. In turn, objective information of its activities was communicated far and wide through the Internet. As had been the case in the former Yugoslavia, civic protest and social convulsion may have already been in the making, but the agitation was fully enabled through the rapidly emerging Internet news sites.[72] Perhaps the most resounding truth to ignite public protest in Kiev was the leaking of audiotapes linking Kuchma to the murder of Georgiy Gongadze. The headless body of Gongadze, a journalist who specialized in writing about corruption in high places, was found in the woods outside Kiev in November 2000.[73] The tapes were uploaded to the Internet immediately after they were leaked by one of Kuchma's bodyguards, and the people responded animatedly by taking to the streets in search of justice and democracy. Once the voice of opposition logged onto the Web, all possibility of maintaining monopoly control over the media was lost to the dictatorship. Ukrainian students, intellectuals, and shopkeepers had learned the potential of the Web from earlier Eastern European protests, and they did not hesitate to flood these spaces with evidence and information to garner support for their candidate and his people's revolution.

As had been the case with the exposure of government corruption in Romania, there was no question cast over the large-scale fraud shown by the people's camcorders. Similarly, the effectiveness of the image as evidence, both on television and on the Web, was built on its immediacy, the presence of the camera at the event as it was lived. This immediacy took a number of forms that drew as necessary on old and new documentary conventions. For example, the direct cinema-like "rawness" of footage such as the slow, unedited unfolding of events filmed in real time at Independence Square was of utmost importance to its conviction. In addition, the more recent invention of highly-pixilated "surveillance" images from monitors present at polling stations was just as crucial to the received authenticity of the images. Sound techniques were also deemed important: the crackling, not always discernible voices of Kuchma in conversation with government officials—in short, all of the signifiers of amateur, uncensored audio and visual footage—were the stamp of authenticity that cast these sounds and images as the inspiration for political action. There was no place for complex theorizations of the relationship between the image and the historical world in this triumph for democracy. The all-important factor was the accessibility of an image made by the people and for the people who defined and were defined by the overthrow of their government.

It remains to speculate, however tentatively, on why faith in the capacity of the radical aesthetic to interrupt the viewing process and incite the spectator to action against the political status quo has diminished. There are a number of cultural and intellectual shifts that refuse the possibility of a return to the modernist belief in the liberatory aesthetic. First, various discourses in cultural studies in the 1980s testified to the misguided assumption that the illusory world of the coherent moving image is a conservative bourgeois indulgence. Feminist film critics, for example, convincingly demonstrated that the images of the classical Hollywood film were just as available for the pleasure of female viewers as they were for the heterosexual, white male in the audience.[74] And as the 1980s progressed, reception studies consistently demonstrated the appeal and the potential emancipation of so-called oppressive images to otherwise oppressed audiences.[75] By extension, this rejection of the hermetically sealed audiovisual narrative as oppressive led to a rejection of the notion that the formal fragmentation or interruption of the viewing experience necessarily politicizes. In fact, again and again, it has been shown that formalism is a symptom of artistic elitism and alienation from the masses.

Second, today the radical film aesthetic has been appropriated by the mainstream to the extent that experimentation in moving image technology is usually found in other media, particularly in single-channel video and digital media.[76] When experimentation does occur, it usually remains on the margins, as is the case with Farocki's culled images. Third, as evidenced by the examples of Romania, Serbia, and Ukraine, film is no longer the medium of the masses. On a philosophical level, the worker and the masses have shown that they are not wedded to the mode of film production as a mirror image of their own role within the processes of industrial manufacture. To repeat Beller, labor today is produced through looking at a screen, rather than standing on a production line. The late-twentieth-century revolutions took place at a historical moment when "the people" were more appropriately conceived as an emergent middle class. In all cases, it was the intellectual, the student, the independent businessperson, or, as Timothy Garten Ash and Timothy Snyder observed, "the owner of a beauty parlor,"[77] who formed the substance of the street-led revolutions. The shifts and development of industrial and postindustrial labor are likewise accompanied by growth in other media of visual communication: television, home video, computers, and the World Wide Web, all of which resolutely reconfigure access and relationships to images. And in all cases, it was their access to the production, distribution, and reception of their own images that guaranteed change.

For all of the new media developments, and their potential to empower people and relieve social and political oppression, if we accept the links between the European politically committed documentary and the images of socialist revolution, then within this discursive field, new technologies take few aesthetic risks. And when they do venture into unpredictable territory, it is always contained by the socially sanctioned space of the television or the computer screen. That is, all aesthetic experimentation is protected from audience fallout by the mode of distribution and exhibition. The images of revolution are indeed captured by new media that have developed the tools of the 1920s political documentaries of social revolution. However, the preferred aesthetic of contemporary revolution mimicked without apology the fly-on-the-wall strategies and philosophies developed by 1960s filmmakers such as D.A. Pennebaker. Today, even where the digital has entered the public sphere in conjunction with political upheaval—for example, in its conjoint efforts with smart bombs in the first Iraq war, or in the amateur digital pictures taken by soldiers in the Abu Ghraib prison—the political is not pinned to aesthetic experiment. In the case of the Abu Ghraib images, the key to their potency lies in their access and distribution over the Internet and as analog photographic images. There is nothing compositionally or aesthetically innovative about what are otherwise snapshots of a day at work in Abu Ghraib. Whether their reproduction comes to fuel Iraqi protest against the unwanted presence of the United States, the American Left's interrogation of our relationship to an unnecessary war, or the authorities' indictment and conviction (or not) of those involved and responsible for the abhorrent acts of violation, the images are significant because of their ad infinitum reproduction and widespread distribution.[78]

The presence of the amateur and media cameras at the unfolding of events in the Eastern European revolutions produced the impression of immediate experience that has been guaranteed by broadcast television for years. Similarly, as we know, these images were superficial illusions that films such as Godard's *Letter to Jane* went to great efforts to expose as fallacious 35 years ago. The apparent retrograde aesthetic of these images does not, however, make them any less sophisticated as visual constructions designed to arouse public ire and political action. On the contrary, as I have argued, they are highly complex barometers of the radical intellectual and cultural shifts—and the role of the moving image within these shifts—which have enabled these "conscious attempts" to change the world.

NOTES

My thanks go to Elizabeth Cowie for conversations in the early stages of writing this essay. Thanks also to Joe McElhaney for his discussions, bibliographic leads, and editorial suggestions. Robert Kolker also contributed insightful editorial interventions.

1. Dziga Vertov, "The Birth of Kino-Eye," in *Kino-Eye: The Writings of Dziga Vertov*, ed. Annette Michelson (Berkeley: University of California Press, 1984), 41–42.

2. The alternative argument is that the media made these events into a movie, and when the illusions wore off as restructuring began, the élan of modern capitalism was the empty space behind the revolutions. Accordingly, within this argument, the stakes for the image are low, whereas I understand them to be higher than they ever were throughout the twentieth century.

3. The term "politically committed documentary" was given to the types of documentary I discuss by Thomas Waugh almost twenty years ago. See Thomas Waugh, "Introduction: Why Documentary Filmmakers Keep Trying to Change the World, *or* Why People Changing the World Keep Making Documentaries," in *Show Us Life: Toward a History and Aesthetics of Committed Documentary*, ed. Thomas Waugh (Metuchen, NJ: Scarecrow Press, 1984), xi–xxvii.

4. Brian Winston, "Direct Cinema: The Third Decade," in *New Challenges for Documentary*, ed. Alan Rosenthal (Berkeley: University of California Press, 1988), 517–29.

5. Frederic Jameson, *Marxism and Form: Twentieth-Century Dialectical Theories of Literature* (Princeton, NJ: Princeton University Press, 1971), xi.

6. Karl Marx and Frederick Engels, *The German Ideology*, ed. C.J. Arthur (New York: International Publishers, 1970).

7. Waugh, op. cit.

8. Ibid.

9. Waugh, "Introduction," xiv.

10. Walter Benjamin, "The Work of Art in the Age of Mechanical Reproduction," in *Illuminations*, ed. Hannah Arendt, trans. Harry Zohn (New York: Schocken Books, 1968).

11. Siegfried Kracauer, *Theory of Film: The Redemption of Physical Reality* (Oxford: Oxford University Press, 1960); Jean Epstein, "For a New Avant-Garde," in *French Film Theory and Criticism*, vol. 1, *1907–1929*, ed. Richard Abel (Princeton, NJ: Princeton University Press, 1988), 349–52; René Clair, "Rhythm," in Abel, *French Film Theory*, 368–69; Richard Taylor (ed.), *S.M. Eisenstein: Selected Works* (London: BFI, 1988–1996).

12. T.J. Clark, *The Painting of Modern Life: Paris in the Art of Manet and His Followers* (New York: Knopf, 1985).

13. Again, this belief comes through in the writings of filmmakers, film commentators, and film critics from the period, most notably, Soviet and German works. See, for example, Richard Taylor (ed.), *The Film Factory: Russian and Soviet Cinema in Documents* (Cambridge, MA: Harvard University Press, 1988); Fritz Güttinger (ed.), *Kein Tag ohne Kino: Schriftsteller über den Stummfilm* (Frankfurt: Deutsches Filmmuseum, 1984).

14. Barbara Kershenblatt-Gimblett, "Kodak Moments, Flashbulb Memories: Reflections on 9/11," *Drama Review* 47.1 (Spring 2003): 26. I am grateful to James Polchin for pointing me in the direction of Kershenblatt-Gimblett's work on these photographs.

15. Christoph Asendorf, *Batteries of Life: On the History of Things and Their Perception in Modernity*, trans. Don Reneau (Berkeley: University of California Press, 1993).

16. See Frederic Jameson, *Marxism and Form: Twentieth-Century Dialectical Theories of Literature* (Princeton, NJ: Princeton University Press, 1971), for an excellent discussion of the modernist commitment to a revolutionary aesthetic form.

17. Anatoli Lunacharsky, "Speech to Film Workers," "To the Party Conference on Cinema from a Group of Film Directors," and "Party Cinema Conference Resolution: The Results of Cinema Construction in the USSR and the Tasks of Soviet Cinema," in Taylor, *Film Factory*, 195–97, 205–15.

18. See Dziga Vertov, "The Same Thing from Different Angles," in Michelson, *Kino-Eye*, 57. See also, Dziga Vertov, "The Factory of Facts," in Michelson, *Kino-Eye*, 58–60.

19. Annette Michelson, introduction to Michelson, *Kino-Eye*.

20. We also know from the work of filmmakers such as Walter Ruttmann and Jean Vigo, both of whom were influenced by Vertov and used these same techniques, that responsibility for political mobilization does not rest solely with montage.

21. Grierson's work came as a culmination of historical attempts in Britain to achieve social integration following the fracturing of the social world after the Industrial Revolution in the late nineteenth century. Ian Aitken, "The British Documentary Film Movement," in *The British Cinema Book*, ed. Robert Murphy (London: BFI, 1998), 58–67.

22. While there are discrepancies between Negt and Kluge's notion of the bourgeois public sphere and Grierson's belief in cinema, I am referring here to only Grierson's belief, not the reality of his films.

23. John Grierson, "The Course of Realism," in *Footnotes to the Film*, ed. Charles Davy (London: Lovat Dickson for Readers' Union, 1938), 137–61.

24. Ivens arrived in the United States in December 1936 from his native Holland.

25. Joris Ivens, *The Camera and I* (New York: International Publishers, 1969). See also Thomas Waugh, " 'Men Cannot Act Before the Camera in the Presence of Death': Joris Ivens's *The Spanish Earth*," in *Documenting the Documentary: Close Readings of Documentary Film and Video*, ed. Barry Keith Grant and Jeannette Sloniowski (Detroit, MI: Wayne State University Press, 1998), 136–53. Waugh gave a particularly useful overview of the various stages of the film: its making, aesthetic, distribution, and reception.

26. Waugh, " 'Men Cannot Act,' " 144– 45.

27. Bill Nichols, "The Documentary and the Turn from Modernism," in *Joris Ivens and the Documentary Context*, ed. Kees Bakker (Amsterdam: Amsterdam University Press, 1999), 153.

28. Ibid., 150.

29. Ibid., 153–54.

30. Ivens discussed the logic of the editing in *The Spanish Earth* and emphasized the anticipation of the audience's feelings toward the images as the keys to successful propaganda. See Joris Ivens, "Documentary: Subjectivity and Montage (1939)," in Bakker, *Joris Ivens*, 250–60.

31. Joseph Lash, *Eleanor and Franklin* (New York: W.W. Norton, 1971), 737– 42.

32. Crawford was among the prominent artists with whom Ivens forged connections in the United States. Ivens was looked up to as someone who had realized the aspirations of Roosevelt's New Deal: to develop associations between artists and farmers, laborers, miners, and the unemployed. Ivens found favor and support from sources as diverse as Crawford, Paul Robeson, Orson Welles, Greta Garbo, Clifford Odets, and Joseph Losey. References to his friends and associates are scattered throughout Bakker, *Joris Ivens*.

33. See Thomas Waugh, "Joris Ivens' *The Spanish Earth*: Committed Documentary and the Popular Front," in Waugh, *Show Us Life*, 126–28.

34. T.J. Clark and Donald Nicholson-Smith, "Why Art Can't Kill the Situationist International," *October* 79 (Winter 1978): 29.

35. See Georg Lukacs, *History and Class Consciousness: Studies in Marxist Dialectics*, trans. Rodney Livingstone (Cambridge, MA: MIT Press, 1971).

36. See the collection of documents of the *Historikerstreit* in *Forever in the Shadow of History?* trans. James Knowlton and Truett Cates (Atlantic Highlands, NJ: Humanities Press, 1993). On the political programs of the Red Army Faction, see Stefan Aust, *The Baader-Meinhof Group: The Inside Story of a Phenomenon*, trans. Anthea Bell (London: Bodley Head, 1985).

37. For a discussion of the role of film within the student revolutions, see Sylvia Harvey, *May '68 and Film Culture* (London: British Film Institute, 1980).

38. It is worth noting that the filmmakers' juxtapositions are not convincing. The expressions of all these actors are in fact extremely varied.

39. The Dziga Vertov Group's films *British Sounds* and *Pravda* (both 1969) scrutinize the form of the documentary and particularly the form's claim to truth through provision of images to accompany the truth of the sound track.

40. Guy Debord and Gil J. Wolman, "Methods of Detournement" in *Situationist International: Anthology*, ed. Ken Knabb (Berkeley, CA: Bureau of Public Secrets, 1981), 8–14.

41. Mustapha Khayati, "Captive Words: Preface to a Situationist Dictionary," in Knabb, *Situationist International*, 170–75.

42. The task of the non–French speaking viewer is even more difficult because the subtitles supply yet another layer of information in this already crowded scene. We are required to look, listen, and read.

43. "How Not to Understand Situationist Books," in Knabb, *Situationist International*, 265–66.

44. Guy Debord, preface to *The Society of the Spectacle*, 3rd ed. (New York: Zone Books, 1995), 10.

45. On the new German cinema's dependence on television in West Germany, see Thomas Elsaesser, *New German Cinema: A History* (New Brunswick, NJ: Rutgers University Press, 1989).

46. Stuart Liebman, "On New German Cinema, Art, Enlightenment, and the Public Sphere: An Interview with Alexander Kluge," *October* 46 (1988): 29. See also Alexander Kluge, "Why Should Film and Television Cooperate," trans. Stuart Liebman, *October* 46 (1988): 96–102.

47. Theodor Adorno, "The Schema of Mass Culture," in *The Culture Industry*, ed. J.M. Bernstein (London: Routledge, 1991), 53–84. This essay, only recently translated into English, was originally conceived as an extension of the "Culture Industry" chapter of *The Dialectic of Enlightenment*. See also Theodor Adorno and Max Horkheimer, "The Culture Industry: Enlightenment as Mass Deception," in *The Dialectic of Enlightenment*, trans. John Cumming (New York: Continuum, 1993), 120–67, and Theodor Adorno, "Culture Industry Reconsidered," in Bernstein, *The Culture Industry*, 85–92.

48. Liebman, "On New German Cinema," 34.

49. Miriam Hansen, "The Stubborn Discourse: History and Story-Telling in the Films of Alexander Kluge," *Persistence of Vision*, no. 2 (Fall 1985): 19–29.

50. This idea finds a particularly articulate embodiment in *The Blind Director* (1985), in which Kluge's familiar formal manipulations follow a director with a camera that cannot see.

51. Kluge developed this concept in his philosophical work with Oskar Negt, *Offentlichkeit und Erfahrung: Zur Organisationsanalyse von buergerlicher und proletarischer Oeffentlichkeit* (Frankfurt am Main: Suhrkamp, 1972). See Miriam Hansen, "Alexander Kluge, Cinema and the Public Sphere: The Construction Site of History," *Discourse*, no. 6 (Fall 1983): 53–74.

52. Miriam Hansen, "Alexander Kluge," 57–58.

53. Peter Lutze, *Alexander Kluge: The Last Modernist* (Detroit, MI: Wayne State University Press, 1998), 179–200 (quotation on 181).

54. Ibid., 187–89.

55. Siegfried Zielinski, "*Fin de Siècle* of Television," in *Cinema Futures: Cain, Abel or Cable? The Screen Arts in the Digital Age*, ed. Thomas Elsaesser and Kay Hoffmann (Amsterdam: Amsterdam University Press, 1998), 82.

56. Jonathan L. Beller, "Kino-I, Kino-World: Notes on the Cinematic Mode of Production," in *The Visual Culture Reader*, ed. Nicholas Mirzoeff (London: Routledge, 1998), 61.

57. Thomas Elsaesser, "Working at the Margins: Film as a Form of Intelligence," in *Harun Farocki: Working on the Sightlines*, ed. Thomas Elsaesser (Amsterdam: Amsterdam University Press, 2004), 99.

58. On the intricacies of Farocki's stylistic manipulations and their political ends, see Thomas Elsaesser, "Political Filmmaking After Brecht: Harun Farocki, for Example," in Elsaesser, *Harun Farocki*, 133–53.

59. Within Farocki's discourse—both filmic and written—the videogram is, as the word suggests, a symbolic representation of ideas within a much larger system. Here, the television image as videogram represents the values of the political system that produced it.

60. Cornelius Castoriadis, "Marx Today: An Interview," *Thesis Eleven*, no. 8 (1984), 124–32; Johann Arnason, "Reflections on the Crisis of Marxism," *Thesis Eleven*, no. 1 (1980), 29–42.

61. W.J.T. Mitchell, "The Rhetoric of Iconoclasm," in *Iconology: Image, Text, Ideology* (Chicago: University of Chicago Press, 1990), 160–208.

62. A significant event, often cited as marking the shift to the "people's" command of representations of visible evidence, is that of George Holliday's video recording of Rodney King's beating in Los Angeles in 1989. Whatever the complicated history of the Holliday footage, as images that produced social unrest, and effectively, changed the face of race relations in the United States, their connections to the role of "people-produced" images in the Eastern and Central European revolutions are salient.

63. Peter Gross, "Mass Media in Revolution," in *Mass Media in Revolution and National Development: The Romanian Laboratory* (Ames: Iowa State University Press, 1996), 29–52. See also Hubertus von Amelunxen and Andrei Ujica (eds.), *Television, Revolution: das Ultimatum des Bildes, Rumänien im Dezember 1989* (Marburg: Jonas, 1990).

64. Gross, "Mass Media in Revolution," 35.

65. This is perhaps most convincingly demonstrated before our eyes in Farocki and Ujica's film *Videograms of a Revolution*.

66. For an excellent summary of the history of B92, see Drazen Pantic, "B92 of Belgrade: Free Voices on the Airwaves and the Internet," in *Reporting the Post-Communist Revolution*, ed. Robert Giles, Robert Snyder, and Lisa DeLisle (New Brunswick, NJ: Transaction, 1999), 201–6.

67. Veran Matic and Drazen Pantic, "War of Words: When the Bombs Came, Serbia's B92 Hit the Net," *Nation*, November 29, 1999, 34–35.

68. Ibid., 203.

69. The west and central regions are the ones that were annexed from Poland by the Soviets.

70. Daniel Wolf, "Revolution in the Making," *Guardian Weekly*, May 31, 2005.

71. Adrian Karatnycky, "Ukraine's Orange Revolution," *Foreign Affairs* 84.2 (March–April 2005): 37.

72. Ibid., 43. See also Timothy Garton Ash and Timothy Snyder, "The Orange Revolution," *New York Review of Books*, April 28, 2005.

73. For English transcripts of the tapes, see http://www.brama.com/survey/messages/4121.html accessed March 21, 2008.

74. This work commenced in the late 1970s in response to the psychoanalytical criticism of the *Screen* theorists, including that of Laura Mulvey. See, for example, Paveen Adams and Elizabeth Cowie (eds.), *The Woman in Question: m/f*, October Books (Cambridge, MA: MIT Press, 1990).

75. Ien Ang's work on the reception of the soap opera *Dallas* was groundbreaking in this field. See Ien Ang, *Watching Dallas: Soap Opera and the Melodramatic Imagination*, trans. Della Couling (London: Methuen, 1985).

76. Good examples of artists and image makers who continue to push the boundaries of the moving image aesthetic and meaning include Bill Viola and Gary Hill. Also, the Labyrinth Project, conceived and directed by Marsha Kinder at the Annenberg Center for Communication, University of California, explores the parameters of digital media. See http://college.usc.edu/labyrinth/ accessed March 21, 2008.

77. Ash and Snyder, "The Orange Revolution."

78. Seymour M. Hersh, *Inconvenient Evidence: Iraqi Prison Photographs from Abu Ghraib* (New York: International Center of Photography, September 2004).

BIBLIOGRAPHY

Abel, Richard (ed.). *French Film Theory and Criticism.* Vol. 1, *1907–1929.* Princeton, NJ: Princeton University Press, 1988.

Bakker, Kees (ed.). *Joris Ivens and the Documentary Context.* Amsterdam: Amsterdam University Press, 1999.

Elsaesser, Thomas. *New German Cinema: A History.* New Brunswick, NJ: Rutgers University Press, 1989.

———(ed.). *Harun Farocki: Working on the Sightlines.* Amsterdam: Amsterdam University Press, 2004.

Giles, Robert, Robert Snyder, and Lisa DeLisle (eds.). *Reporting the Post-Communist Revolution.* New Brunswick, NJ: Transaction, 1999.

Grierson, John. "The Course of Realism." *Footnotes to the Film.* Ed. Charles Davy. London: Lovat Dickson for Readers' Union, 1938.

Jameson, Frederic. *Marxism and Form: Twentieth-Century Dialectical Theories of Literature.* Princeton, NJ: Princeton University Press, 1971.

Knabb, Ken (ed). *Situationist International: Anthology.* Berkeley, CA: Bureau of Public Secrets, 1981.

Ivens, Joris. *The Camera and I.* New York: International Publishers, 1969.

Lutze, Peter. *Alexander Kluge: The Last Modernist.* Detroit, MI: Wayne State University Press, 1998.

Michelson, Annette (ed.). *Kino-Eye: The Writings of Dziga Vertov.* Berkeley: University of California Press, 1984.

Mirzoeff, Nicholas (ed.). *The Visual Culture Reader.* London: Routledge, 1998.

October 46 (1988). Special issue on Alexander Kluge.

Rosenthal, Alan (ed.). *New Challenges for Documentary.* Berkeley: University of California Press, 1988.

Taylor, Richard (ed.). *The Film Factory: Russian and Soviet Cinema in Documents.* Cambridge, MA: Harvard University Press, 1988.

———. *S.M.Eisenstein: Selected Works.* London: BFI, 1988–1996.

Waugh, Thomas (ed.). *Show Us Life: Toward a History and Aesthetics of Committed Documentary.* Metuchen, NJ: Scarecrow Press, 1984.

CHAPTER 5

LOSS OF LIGHT: THE LONG SHADOW OF PHOTOGRAPHY IN THE DIGITAL AGE

JEANNENE M. PRZYBLYSKI

It is a point most eloquently and exhaustively made by Geoffrey Batchen in his book, *Burning with Desire*, that photography was willed into being in 1839 because its need was so deeply and widely felt that the medium appeared already enveloped in an aura of inevitability.[1] According to Batchen, between 1790 and 1839, no fewer than twenty people from seven European countries either theorized the possibility of photography, or dabbled in some aspect of its chemical and optical processes, or claimed some credit for its discovery. Ultimately, two men are most often named as photography's "fathers." One was an English country gentleman who conducted scientific experiments, produced delightful landscape sketches, and wrote learned treatises when not managing his estate in Lacock, England. The other was a Parisian theatrical entrepreneur and purveyor of dioramas and other entertainments of the "*son et lumière*" variety, who had obtained much of the technical where-withal from a starry-eyed and otherwise impractical inventor from the provinces. This nexus between the purity of scientific investigation in the positivist age and the cutthroat pursuit of novelty in a nascent culture of commodities was no less a set of enabling conditions for the invention of photography than the optical lenses and light-sensitive plates with which the first cameras were equipped.

The question is whether the same aura of inevitability can be claimed for digital media, which to the extent that they have been predicated on the "look and feel" of chemically based processes of photography and film might still be best understood as merely extensions of them—even as these new media have finally begun to outstrip their photographic ancestors in defining our expectations of visual quality and the pervasiveness of images in a persistent "society of the spectacle."[2] Or perhaps this question is not far-reaching enough. So here is an even more extreme assertion to put to the test: to the extent that digital media might represent a radical departure from (or rupture in) these processes, perhaps the most that can be said is that, unlike photography, they have all too often seemed to be inventions in advance of their applications, or rather media in search of their own ontology and language—the conventions by which they would become, in themselves, meaningful.

This last assertion matters because our understanding of photography and its commanding role in a broader cultural imaginary is largely based on arguments about what we have come to accept as its ontological character. That is, although most of us can point to memorable and meaningful photographic images either from history (the battlefields of nineteenth-century Gettysburg or Republican Spain or postcolonial Vietnam, a "Victory" kiss shared by a sailor and his girl in Times Square, President John F. Kennedy agonizing over the Bay of Pigs in the Oval Office) or from our personal lives (insert your own family or professional moments here), the memorableness and meaningfulness of these images are strongly framed by attributes that we ascribe to "photography" itself and rely upon it to consistently deliver—its capacity as a surrogate eyewitness, its quality as an objective document, its ability to fix a passing instant as a permanent image, its almost haptic presence as a fingerprint-like trace, its knack for neatly taking its place in an archival structure of knowledge and power.

To be sure, the visual conventions of the medium and a broader cultural literacy in reading them, as this essay is at some pains to demonstrate, were cultivated over time (not to mention the technical refinements that made photography faster, sharper, more portable, durable, easily reproducible, able to represent the world in "living" color and moving pictures). But even so, there was and remains something about the deep cultural resonance of the photographic convergence of optics and chemistry that seems to exceed a simple account of its technological development and use—whether as an art form in its own right or as an instrument of other disciplines of information gathering, organization, and dissemination. Indeed what remains significant is that these uses were largely anticipated by a contemporary culture that rushed headlong into their embrace in advance of their technical implementation, and has yet to abandon its romance with photography despite the ceding of chemical effect to digitally encoded information, or the eclipse of optical truth by digital manipulation. Or to put it another way: it is not simply that a modern positivist, capitalist, and industrializing

European culture willed photography into being in the nineteenth-century, but that there is something about a modern culture so entrapped in the experience of its own contemporaneity (as figured by the twin cults of technological innovation and the commodity form) that—even more profoundly—it needed and continues to need photography to have an ontological authority. The French sociologist and semiotician Roland Barthes confessed to just such an "ontological desire" to define the medium once and for all when sorting through some photographs that were particularly meaningful to him. His desire gave rise to one of the most influential books on the medium, *Camera Lucida*, a brilliant and paradoxical meditation on the apparent fixity of the photographic image as evidence of "that-which-has-been" and the troubling indeterminacy of the photographic sign as a kind of evidentiary residue broken photographically loose from its moorings in the real world.[3]

The longing for certainty and a persistent unsureness about exactly what has been made certain, through photography: this is a short way of saying that the central ontological question about photography is also a question about episte-mology, and particularly about the form of human world making and knowing that we call history. As this essay is primarily concerned to show, we continue to understand history itself as a primarily visual and photographic record of the past—to the point where it seems impossible to speak of the experience of history, of historical consciousness and the historical artifact, without speaking at the same time of the photography of history.[4] When the Weimar philosopher and cultural historian Walter Benjamin went trolling through the already obsolete manifesta-tions of nineteenth-century modernity (shopping arcades, the twinned figures of the urban flaneur and the prostitute, the *grands boulevards* of Paris, the bourgeois obsession with the domestic interior—all hailed as historical manifestations of "progress" in their times) to create a genealogy for the contemporary crisis of his-torical experience occasioned by the rise of fascism in the 1930s (also hailed, by some, as a historical manifestation of "progress" in *its* time), photography, with its instantaneous "flashes" of illumination, its "secret heliotropism," and its ability to bring history to a "standstill," became not just a governing metaphor but the most powerful instantiation of his conception of historical consciousness.[5] Another cultural critic of the same era, Siegfried Kracauer, argued that "the world itself has taken on a photographic face" in a desperate attempt to remember a present that is always slipping through its fingers—even as the evidence of presentness accu-mulates with apparent comprehensivity in the dead, denatured and meaningless pages of the photographically illustrated mass press.[6] History, argued in these terms, becomes the image of contemporaneity as it recedes from an ever-advancing, unforeseeable future of disastrous proportions. This is Benjamin's figure of the "angel of history," who flies in the face of a future continually piling in (photo-graphic?) ruins at her feet,[7] or Kracauer's trenchant (and cryptic) observation that "photography is the *go-for-broke game* of history."[8] But as even the briefest reference to these seminal authors begins to suggest (more about them later), photography—and film as well—not only become the instruments of a culture of forgetfulness, erasure, "gaps," and disappearances on which modern authoritarian regimes depend, but also are the potential instruments of cultural redemption by allowing multiple, contestatory histories to emerge from rereading and retelling the unruly inexhaustibleness of the photographic and filmic archives.

Redemption is something we are so clearly still waiting for, which may also explain why we find photographic thinking so difficult to abandon. So when we cast a backward-looking eye on the early decades of photography in order to explain something about our experience of visual culture in a twenty-first-century digital age, we want to ask ourselves, as Benjamin might have, What is it about photography that continues to inform—however retrospectively, and even in the fact of its very obsolescence—our contemporary sense of visuality and culture? And even more important is a question that neither Benjamin nor Kracauer nor Barthes could have fully imagined (although there is some glimmer of it in Barthes's various linkages of photography and colonialism in *Mythologies* and elsewhere): What is it about the broad cultural investment in photography and an ontological view of its ideological role that has facilitated the enlargement of its scope of command from its foundations in a primarily European or European-influenced cultural imaginary to an increasingly global, transactional phenomenon?[9]

William Henry Fox Talbot, photography's English inventor, debuted the new medium in a photographically illustrated book, self-published in 1844 with the title *The Pencil of Nature*.[10] For Talbot, the "natural" authority of the photographic image was a function of its foundations in a process born of scientific research, whereby the light reflecting off objects in the world was "seen" through a disembodied, glass "eye" and transcribed onto a chemically coated, light-sensitive surface—in Talbot's case, a paper negative—so that with only the smallest amount of human intervention (pointing the camera and exposing the plate), nature did the rest. The world appeared to draw *itself* in comprehensive and undiscriminating detail. Talbot recognized that the process had value for art—not only in the reproduction of art objects but in the artful composition of landscape scenes (both are featured in *The Pencil of Nature*). He also immediately foresaw its value for the law. A caption accompanying the image of a collection of porcelain bric-a-brac suggested that the photograph might also be produced as evidence in the case of theft or breakage.[11]

Talbot closely guarded the patent rights for his invention, thereby suppressing its exploitation in the marketplace despite the considerable advantages of a photographic process that not only reproduced the world with stunning faithfulness but was also itself potentially infinitely reproducible. The "Talbotype" and its close relation, the calotype, would largely become the province of "amateurs" and arty types with an affinity for its pictorial effects.[12] On the other side of the English

Channel, Louis Jacques Mandé Daguerre, photography's French inventor, could not provide the same feature of infinite reproducibility—the equally eponymously named "daguerreotype" process produced a single direct positive onto a silver-coated metal plate. But Daguerre's photographic technique was made freely available to all comers courtesy of the French government, ensuring that its commercial exploitation would be widely and almost immediately felt, taken up by a host of small-time entrepreneurs whose visions of the medium's potential were far less high-minded than Talbot's.[13] The French poet Charles Baudelaire remarked in his review of the Salon of 1859 that despite other endeavors to which photography was being diligently applied in its early years, the medium's greatest contribution to society might well be in the pornography industry.[14] And it was no wonder: porn, like the law, is another application where the closeness of vicarious proximity to the real thing matters.

The staging of photographic "skin-shots" aside, the most widespread early commercial application of photography was in the field of portraiture, where the photographic portrait quickly usurped the role of the painted portrait, and especially the painted miniature, as a treasured family keepsake, signifier of privileged social status, medium of self-invention, and insurance that one's image would not be lost to posterity (indeed, many portrait photographers were former miniature painters who could see the writing on the wall). The daguerreotype was soon superseded by the more inexpensive tintype, which preserved much of the wondrous, mirrorlike detail that gave daguerreotypes an almost holographic presence, but in slightly flimsier, "flatter" form. As paper-based negatives gave way to glass, the resulting sharper image made this process appealing for portraiture as well. In 1854, the merchant-turned-actor-turned-painter-turned-daguerreotypist A.A.E. Disdéri patented the carte-de-visite process. By bracketing six or eight exposures on a single glass plate, Disdéri could offer his customers more poses, cheaper prices, *and* the possibility of unlimited multiple prints.[15] Between 1848 and 1871, the number of photography studios in Paris alone grew from thirteen to four hundred. The rest, as they say, is history.[16]

The carte de visite offered anyone with the money in his or her pocket the chance to purchase a public face, but it is worth emphasizing that this opportunity did not extend to everyone. The cost of a session in Disdéri's photography emporium was a modest fifteen francs, but this was at least three days' wages to the legions of day laborers, laundresses, street cleaners, and shopgirls that kept a city like Paris moving on a daily basis.[17] Instead, in the nineteenth century, photographic immortality was a solidly bourgeois phenomenon, perfectly suited to a class of society that valued a close congruence between cost and value ("what you see is what you get"), anchored its ideological authority in the immanent effects of the "real" (even if reality is, as it is with photography, only an illusion), and self-identified with a modern culture of innovation, entrepreneurialism, leisure, and spectacle—in which photography played a pervasive role.[18]

Figure 5.1 A.A.E. Disdéri, *Monsieur Kalergis* (1859), uncut sheet of eight carte-de-visite photographs (author's collection).

But more than that, not only did photography give the middle classes a central place in the visual economy of contemporary life (and, by extension, a place in the visual archive that would accumulate out of the ephemera of contemporary experience); it also gave them the *same place* as that occupied by royalty, politicians, prestigious authors and artists, and celebrities of a more mundane stripe, from actresses to athletes—images of whom were featured in the windows of the carte-de-visite photography studios, where they could be purchased to take their place right next to the photo of cousin Jacques or sister Marie in the photo albums that quickly became fixtures in middle-class homes. Indeed, to sort through the vast archive of carte-de-visite likenesses of nineteenth-century bankers, soldiers, shopkeepers, businesspeople, petty officials, and matrons and their children, whose names have long been forgotten, is to watch a group of people self-consciously try on the role of a dominant culture by tucking a hand in a well-padded waistcoat, coyly framing cheek with fingertips, presenting one's heir proudly to the world. This simulation of the poses of power (this play of social *like-ness*) within the frame of the new representational system of photography is the source of claims about its "democratizing" effect. In its capacity as a "celebratory" medium, it "leveled up" the social relations of an economically and culturally ascendant bourgeoisie, evening the playing field between it and those it perceived as its betters—by reason of birth, achievement, or sheer good luck.

But the same medium, in the same form, could also discipline the social hierarchy in repressive ways, "keeping down" those whose inscription into the new photographic order was not necessarily voluntary, but imposed. Photographic portraiture had other applications beyond the personalized souvenir. The individual identities recorded through photography could be sorted according to other taxonomies and classification systems than social status and the self-elected pleasure of seeing oneself become an image. If the family album was the celebratory manifestation of photographic practice and its power to memorialize the unique, photographically recorded subject, then the police file, the medical case book, and the ethnographic field journal were also increasingly populated with photographs in the nineteenth century. These other, adjacent fields of photographic presentation claimed a comparable power not to commemorate, but to pathologize, criminalize, and dehumanize by transforming individual subjects into representative specimens. The radical elaboration and standardization of the disciplines of social classification, identity management, and tracking in modern times might be regarded as the other side of photography's Janus-like face, similarly enabled by the camera's capacity for putting people in their place.

Or so it seems now. The history of photography as a "disciplinary" system rests on the intersection between two ways of understanding and positioning the medium, one focusing on the optical process of making photographs, and the other on the material disposition of the photographic artifact. In the first case, the affinity between photographic exposure and surveillance is emphasized, especially the degree to which an Enlightenment-based culture that regards sight as the dominant sense for experiencing and knowing the world has ideologically enlarged the field of vision to the point where it can be characterized as a "scopic regime"—a nexus of power and knowledge that situates all subjects within the condition of always being seen. In the second case, the status of the photograph as a unit of visual data is taken up as a key factor in the medium's ready inscription in the schemes of broad classification upon which modern knowledge systems are based—a concomitant "archival regime," if you will. This view of photography has been predicated on the work of Michel Foucault—both his historical study of modern systems of punishment (most particularly the eighteenth-century invention by Bentham of the panopticon—a mode of prison architecture meant to instill in the prisoner a self-imposed belief in his constant surveillance) and his poststructural, genealogical accounts of the ordering of knowledge.[19] The case for photography as the privileged representational system under the disciplinary conditions of modernity has been argued most powerfully via Foucault by Marxist-influenced thinkers such as Allan Sekula (himself a practicing photographer) and John Tagg, both of whom have been concerned with demonstrating photography's role in empowering the bourgeoisie *at the expense of* pathologizing the weak or mentally ill, scapegoating the poor, marginalizing racial and ethnic difference, and (bound up in all of these other endeavors) identifying the face of criminality.[20]

And yet, what seems most interesting to me about the various nineteenth-century attempts to mobilize photography as an instrument of disciplinary authority is that the camera was, at least initially, a not-so-perfect tool for fixing social identity—its optical authority too easily challenged by the same performative fiction of the pose upon which the middle-class photographic portrait relied for its celebratory aura. The stability of the photographic portrait as a verifiable data unit in any classificatory system required not only archival context (and this was still no guarantee that the photograph could not slip from one context to another) but an at least marginally compliant subject. In the United States, J. T. Zealy was commissioned by naturalists at Harvard University to photograph the physiognomy of the African slave population of the American South. The resulting daguerreotype images of men and women, naked from the waist up, presented in full face and profile, are among the closest things to a truly forensic photographic practice in the nineteenth century, but they are also powerfully haunting, poignant evidence of a group of people so thoroughly and completely subjected that they perceive themselves—at least at that moment—to have no other choice than to submit to the camera. The same cannot be said of others, clinging to the periphery of the dominant culture, who still thought they might have a fighting chance. In England, the psychiatrist Hugh Diamond began to photograph his subjects as part of his clinical studies—these seated portraits, many of them in three-quarter view, are more striking for the touching efforts of their subjects to emulate normality, precisely as a perceived function of the conventionalized poses of bourgeois photographic portraiture, than they are for any utility in identifying their illness (for this, they need captions: "Convalescence after Acute Melancholia," "Apoplectic Mania. Infanticide," "Puerperal Mania").[21] In France, the first bureau of police photography in the world was opened in 1874. This official institutionalization of photographic practice sprang largely from an entrepreneurial initiative in 1871, however, when a small-time carte-de-visite photographer named Eugéne Appert wheedled his way into the vast makeshift prison camps outside of Paris, where thousands of suspected participants in the revolutionary Paris Commune were being detained, by offering a deal that was appealing to all parties: every accused Communard who sat for his camera would receive copies of his or her photograph, the authorities would also get prints, and Appert himself would retain copyright for other uses and commercial distribution.

The Communards posed as they would have themselves remembered—some somber and dignified, some still displaying their youthful idealism, some still defiant in their revolutionary fervor. And their images were seen as people wanted to see them: a mother concerned for her son saw evidence that he had survived the commune's bloody repression; a police officer saw yet another suspect to finger; a complacent bourgeois, safe again at home in his Parisian living room after the recent "insurrection," saw the face of the mob who had ruled Paris during the commune's tenure. Photographic practices during and after the Paris Commune offer a compelling view of the troubling mobility of social identity as seen through the camera in the nineteenth century, and the heroic efforts mobilized by the dominant culture to stabilize its persistent subjectivity. A carte-de-visite photograph in a police file might well be adequate proof of criminal status; outside that file, it could be a treasured family heirloom.[22] The problem was that slippage from celebratory to disciplinary registers—and back again—was always a possibility, as was the chance of evading the "system" altogether. In the 1880s and 1890s, the canny criminal had to be physically restrained to have his or her photograph legibly made—a shake of the head could render the image useless to the authorities (and it is worth noting that in the early years of photography, exposure times could be so long that so also did the bourgeois gentleman niche his head into a supporting vise to achieve a sharper image). The French bureaucrat Alphonse Bertillon would not codify the mug shot as a reliable system of criminal identification until the end of the century. Even then, his success depended on both standardizing a system of photographic conventions *and* devising a workable filing system.[23] By now the coercive aspects of photographic identification have become so deeply internalized that, whether at the Department of Motor Vehicles or the local police station, there is no need to "make" anyone assume the pose.

So when we look at early portrait photography and the applications that accumulated around it, we can see the medium being pressed to do a job, its potential grasped if not fully realized, in advance not only of its technical capabilities but also of the representational cues and ways of reading and understanding the photographs that would help to secure photographic meaning within the frame. If this was the case with the photographic ordering of social identity, then it was equally so in terms of the photographic documentation of culturally significant events, whose place in a collective perception of historical consciousness was anticipated well before the technology existed to reproduce actual photographs in the mass media.

Visually speaking, the task of giving an image to history belonged largely to painting for the first half of the nineteenth century, while contemporary events were largely the domains of engraving and lithography, broadsheets, mass-produced prints, and, increasingly, the illustrated press. Indeed this functional distinction also carried with it a sense of hierarchy, distinguishing the collectively valuable, lasting lessons of history properly speaking from the easily disposed-of visual ephemera of everyday life and the "news." Photography may not have played the role for which it is so often credited in the death of painting as a realist enterprise—although it

Figure 5.2 Eugéne Appert, *M. Vitet,*
pétroleur (*M. Vitet, Arsonist*), 1871, carte-
de-visite photograph (author's collection).

certainly challenged artists from Monet to Picasso and beyond to imagine painted
practices of mimesis and illusionism differently.[24] But it *was* implicated in the
eclipse of history painting as a privileged mode of representing and memorializing
the annexation of significant events from present experience to collective memory.
To put it another way: On the one hand, to look at the nascent history of modern
art in the nineteenth century is to trace a story of artists from Jacques-Louis David
to Gustave Courbet and Edouard Manet engaged in a project of producing painted
allegories of historical subjects that became realer and realer until the mere fact of
contemporaneity seemed to take on an allegorical/historical charge. On the other
hand, beginning to define the emergent conditions of modernity in the nineteenth
century includes tracking the collapse of historical experience into the representational system of "current events," where topicality, ephemerality, immediacy,
and obsolescence—the certainty that today's top story would be supplanted by

tomorrow's late-breaking disaster or scandal—ensured that forgetting was as much a part of the modern historical process as remembering.[25] These two trajectories converge under the sign of photography.

The centrality of photography to an evolving reconfiguration of historical experience was thus intimately related to the elaboration of a mass press whose commercial viability depended on the claims of objectivity that would make its journalistic offerings acceptable to the broadest possible audience.[26] The news could be good business, but it was better business if the perception of bias or a partisan point of view did not narrow your customer base and, more important, the potential customer base of the advertisers who were increasingly subsidizing your print runs. The illustrated press was not filled with photographs in the mid-nineteenth century—this would need to wait for the development of photogravure technology in the 1890s. But it was filled with engravings "after" photographs, as well as with invocations of "photography" as assurances of the factuality of its narrative reports and news items. In this way, the mass press sought in photography a mode and model of a marketable objectivity that operated both materially and metaphorically, resting on cultural perceptions of photography's ability to pose as a scrupulously dispassionate witness and the mechanistic, literal veracity that was attributed to it (Talbot's "pencil of nature" redux). Just as important, however, photography offered the press a means to update its own ideological authority in a modern economy of image systems—placing its products cheek by jowl in the constellation of mediated experiences by which modernity, as a function of the confounding of the dividing line between the appearance of objectivity and the distraction of spectacle, was coming to be defined.

In other words, just as the photographic portrait rested at the intersection of the celebratory and disciplinary uses of the medium (which turned out to be not distinct and different discourses at all, but rather two sides of the same discursive coin), so also did the photography of history depend on blurring the discourses of information and entertainment—all the better to produce the passive, alienated spectator/consumer who, as the chief devotee of the commodity form, also ensured the commodity's intractable persistence in a future that could be reliably guaranteed to its chief investors to look ever the same. No one said it better than the twentieth-century cultural critic, filmmaker, and "Situationist" Guy Debord: "The spectacle is capital accumulated to the point where it becomes an image."[27] He might have gone on to say that, under modern conditions of production, that image, both figuratively and literally, has appeared photographically more often than not. As photography became the preferred language of the news (the stories we tell ourselves to make sense of the world), so it also became the preferred language of advertising (the dreams we sell ourselves to escape from the world), confusing the distinction between the historically significant and the merely fashionable, and lulling the spectator within a seductive and mesmerizing realm that contained equal helpings of both. It was the essential, systematic sameness of these two image repertories that produced the future as "eternal return," conjuring a sensation of progress as déjà vu that always seemed to place the modern subject back where he or she had started.[28]

But as with photographic portraiture, this conclusion gets us ahead of the game. Photography in the nineteenth century was largely a studio practice dependent on cumbersome machinery, long exposure times, and finicky, often hit-or-miss processes of developing and fixing images. In order for it to take its place as the preferred medium of journalistic reportage (and the privileged image of history-as-mediated-spectacle), it had to find its way first to the streets and battlefields where history was being made, and then to the newspapers, journals, and print shops where the news was promoted and consumed. In the Crimean theater of 1855, when English and French troops allied themselves with the Turks in a dispute with the Russians over control of the Holy Lands, English photographer Roger Fenton traveled with not only a heavy, tripod-mounted camera and an assistant and two servants to help him set it up, but also a mobile darkroom, rigged from a horse-drawn wine merchant's van. On commission from a London print dealer, and with the support of Prince Albert, who hoped to mobilize support for an increasingly unpopular war, Fenton produced a portfolio of more than three hundred large-format prints featuring posed scenes of life at camp, portraits of military leaders, and genre studies of the exotically costumed Turkish troops. By providing images of the war that highlighted its orderly professionalism and the stiff-upper-lip stoicism of the British soldier rather than hardship and carnage, these photographs were intended to provide a counterbalance to the relentless antiwar stories appearing in the press. To accomplish this work of photographic persuasion, Fenton and his sponsors counted on the camera's authority of presence, which was a function of both its perceived objectivity *and* its novelty value as a journalistic tool. And to the degree to which Fenton's photographs have taken their place as images of historical record, the selective eye of the photographer was aided and abetted by limitations of the equipment itself—although mid-nineteenth-century photographs were often described as "instantaneous images," capturing action as it happened was well beyond their scope. Indeed, one of Fenton's few photographs of the battlefields themselves, and not coincidentally, one of his most celebrated photographs, poetically entitled "Valley of the Shadow of Death" (this was the war of Tennyson's famous "The Charge of the Light Brigade"), was not only taken after the fact. Just as Fenton staged his camp vignettes, this photograph reputedly owed its artful composition to a little strategic repositioning of the spent cannonballs and other wreckage found at the scene.[29]

A few years later, troops of roving photographers sponsored by photographic entrepreneurs Mathew Brady and Andrew Gardner, among others, followed the battles of the U.S. Civil War from 1861 to 1865 with much the same equipment, and much the same investment in the historical and commercial value of photography's ability to make things real to its viewers. "Brady never misrepresents," claimed one popular journal, while another newspaper observed that Brady's photographs "will do more than the most elaborate descriptions" to perpetuate the concrete memory of the war.[30] The rich trove of photographs produced during the Civil War also manifests the same nineteenth-century disregard for the uncorrupted status of the photographic "document," but with much less Victorian circumspection regarding the horrors of battle (or, as the French would have it, much more American fascination with gore and sensationalism). For "Harvest of Death," a photograph taken on the battlefield of Gettysburg in 1863 and reproduced in Gardner's *Photographic Sketch Book of the War*, photographer Timothy O'Sullivan moved not cannonballs but corpses to create one of the war's most haunting images. O'Sullivan's photograph may not be "true" to the literally immediate effects of actual battle (and the time lag between the battle itself and its packaging as a photographic view is indicated not only by the ability of the photographer to rove the scene to adjust the evidence in its aftermath, but also by the visibly bloated condition of the bodies themselves), but it nonetheless speaks to what the cultural critic Paul Virilio has identified as one of the most radical convergences of historical consciousness under the conditions of modernity—that is, the interdependence of the technologies of modern, mechanized warfare and modern modes of image making.[31] Just as the photographs of Brady and company represented to a fascinated American public a new, high-tech approach to war reporting (and these photographs not only were seen as prints and engraved reproductions, but also viewed in three dimensions as stereoscopic cards), the massive and mass casualties of the Civil War represented in some of those photographs (seven thousand dead and more than thirty thousand wounded at Gettysburg alone) were the result of new long-range and rapid-fire artillery. On a more practical level, consider this: in the nineteenth century, collodion was used as a form of photographic emulsion, in wadding for field ammunition, and in dressings for wounds.

As even this brief look at photography and war in the nineteenth century begins to suggest, questions about the status of the photograph as historical document must be situated not only in the context of the emergent conditions of modern journalism and modern novelty entertainments, but also in the context of the intimate relationship linking photographic reportage, propaganda, and photographic fakery. The photograph's perceived immediacy, and its power to declare "that-which-has-been," gave it almost instantaneous credibility as a privileged image of official record, even as the apparent transparency of the medium, the viewer's ability to vicariously "look through" the camera to somewhere else, became the ontologically cast basis for its ideological (and propagandistic) authority. And small wonder: as Louis Althusser has argued so eloquently, "transparency" is the condition of ideology at its most persuasive, when it has become so naturalized within a given society that its most powerful cultural fictions appear as truths that "go without saying." Photography slipped into this role of ideological naturalizer with an ease that belied its technical limitations and ensured that the steady pressure of official support and consumer demand would drive its technical refinement for generations to come.[32] Yet not only does photography's point of view appear as apparently unmediated; it is always already partial—partially sighted in its monocular authority and partially blind (to everything outside the frame and everything that happened before and after the exposure), and this partialness "always already" (to evoke another Althusserian turn of phrase) positions every photograph as a "faked" representation of a greater reality, to some degree. The fragmentation of reality through photography, its rupture of the continuous flow of time into isolated moments, and its shattering of any sense of a historical continuity between past and present (replacing it instead with a seemingly endless supply of isolated incidents of "present-ness," riddled with so many gaps between them that they could be stitched back together arbitrarily or at will) are also facets of its ontological and, hence, ideological positioning.[33]

One of the best opportunities to grapple with this paradox involves returning to Eugene Appert and to the photographic prison portraits he produced in the aftermath of the Paris Commune of 1871. To a great extent, the commune was France's equivalent "civil war," and its suppression, carried out with great dispatch during a single week in May 1871, left more than forty thousand dead in the streets of Paris and many of the city's familiar monuments and neighborhoods burned to the ground. The commune also left a compelling photographic record. Perhaps spurred by the commercial success of American war photographers, Parisian photographers took to the streets en masse (Disdéri even had his own photographic van), producing hokey tableaux of the Communards posing on the barricades in March of 1871, newsy before-and-after shots of the Communards' ceremonial toppling of the Vendôme column in early May, portfolio after portfolio of the "ruins of Paris," and even some grisly photographs of Communard corpses. So many bodies lay in the streets and the weather was so unseasonably warm that spring that fears of cholera compelled mass burials in advance of identifying the dead. It was hoped that photography might, retrospectively, do the job.

Aside from the photographs of the Vendôme column, what these photographers did not produce, however, were images of the most notorious events of the commune—events that, through breathless "eyewitness" accounts and engraved images supposedly rendered "on the spot," the newspapers and illustrated journals had been busily packaging into a shocking and semiofficial chronology, beginning with the summary execution of two French generals by the Communard insurgents, extending through the detention and murder of the archbishop of Paris, and a mass slaughter of clerics, cops, and suspected spies on the rue Haxo in the commune's waning days, and culminating with the torching of Paris by a fearsome and largely mythic (it would turn out) band of *pétroleuses*, or female arsonists. This is where Appert stepped in. By cutting and pasting the faces of "real, live" Communards (the ones he had photographed in jail) into after-the-fact restagings of the crimes they had supposedly perpetrated, on the very sites where those events had taken place, Appert produced an ingenious and enduring suite of photomontages entitled "Crimes of the Commune," in which the partial truth value of the altered images (those particular people! those exact places!) allowed viewers to consume their fictions (look what they did! they deserve to be punished!) as if they were real. Not only did such fictions satisfy the public taste for sensation, catastrophe, and culpability (and affirmed, because they reflected, that which the public had already been primed to consume as the "news"); they also upheld the official story that the commune was not a "civil rebellion" at all, but a mob uprising that demanded severe repression rather than reconciliation.

I have argued elsewhere and at length that as much as fakes, which they certainly were, and nasty ones at that (although I am not sure that most people at the time would not have known that, or at least would have relished them as much for their novelty as for their evidentiary value), Appert's photomontages might be better understood as some of the first "moving pictures": they are a manifestation

Figure 5.3 Eugéne Appert, *Massacre des dominicains d'Arcueil* (Massacre of the Dominican priests of Arcueil) (1871), photomontage (author's collection).

of the desire that photographs fulfill a potential as animated images that was foreseeable if not yet able to be realized.[34] This argument insists on historically locating the consumer of Appert's photographs within nineteenth-century habits of image viewing and knowledge gathering (and, hence, world making), and so historically locating Appert's photomontage and re-photography technique in the same family of impulses as the numerous "pre-cinematic" devices for enhancing and animating two-dimensional imagery, both pre-photographic and photographic, that bridged nineteenth-century research into optical perception and the nineteenth-century refinement of spectacular entertainments—including thaumatropes, phenakistoscopes, zoetropes, and stereoscopes.[35] All of these devices worked in some way to isolate image fragments, and then to reassemble them into the illusion of a greater "whole" that appeared more perfectly lifelike and seamless, and, in some cases, even appeared to be in motion. Just one year after Appert's "Crimes" appeared, and on the other side of the world, in California, another photographer, Eadweard Muybridge, would decisively redefine the conditions of modern visuality in a fractured and hetereogeneous field of optical stimulation and visual information by pioneering a process of high-speed, multiple-exposure photography that would lead to the first "movies."[36]

In the spring of 1872, railroad baron, philanthropist, and racehorse owner Leland Stanford commissioned Muybridge to help put to rest an ongoing debate: does a trotting horse ever have all four feet off the ground? Muybridge's motion studies were a positivist solution to the problem of how to test a hypothesis when the supporting evidence occurs faster than the human eye can perceive. By isolating the horse's movement into a series of "stopped-action" still photographs, Muybridge and Stanford could see that, yes, indeed, there is one moment when all hooves are suspended in midair. But by mechanically projecting the still photographs on a screen in rapid succession, the photographically stilled horse could be magically put back in motion. Muybridge's "zoopraxiscope," as he called it, was a precursor of the modern film projector, although cinematic technology properly speaking would be invented by other people and elsewhere (around 1895, machines for projecting filmic images were invented independently in four major industrialized countries: France, England, Germany, and the United States; the first major film companies—American Biograph, Lumière Brothers, Pathé Brothers, etc.—appeared shortly thereafter).[37] But Muybridge's studies of human and animal motion—birds flying, horses galloping, men turning somersaults, and women dancing—opened up a world of suggestive possibility for both the documentation of contemporary life and the narrative telling of stories.[38] Within the space of a decade, film studios were cranking out newsy reels of politicians and parades, *and* concocted scenes of military charges, little domestic dramas, vaudevillian physical comedy acts, and fantastic trips to the moon. Imaginatively speaking, early films offered their fascinated spectators the vicarious temporal experience of going around the world and beyond, even as they helped to position them, as viewing subjects, in a system of images, information, money, and power conspiring to ensure that, more often than not, they were not going anywhere at all.

Fast forward to 2006. Walking through the gardens of the new Letterman Digital Arts Center in San Francisco, one of the first things you come across (after a statue of Yoda) is a bronze sculpture of Muybridge himself, bent over his moving-picture machine. And it is no wonder. Over the last one hundred and some-odd years, cinematic reality has, of course, come to look more and more real. And yet the thrill of experiencing cinematic illusion as if it was real that is delivered digitally today by Lucas's Industrial Light and Magic company is not qualitatively different from the effects sought by early filmmakers at the end of the nineteenth century (as Lucas and company well know). Then and now, people will pay good money for the pleasure of having their eyes fooled by the camera (and, increasingly, the computer), and whether the pleasure of that foolery involves filming an actual train that appears to rush toward the audience, or causing a digitally imported cow to fly out of the vortex of a digitally concocted tornado, the end result is a question more of refining the process than of changing the product. The sensation produced in the audience by this "cinema of attractions," as film historian Tom Gunning would have it, remains the same—a pleasurable gasp of surprise, an instinctive flinch from the illusion of danger, a feeling of awe: "How did they do that?"[39]

At the same time, the advent of digital media—despite their manipulative possibilities—has not lessened but rather increased the dependency of a global, networked society on those very same media to provide a "real-time" picture of the view from elsewhere. Electronic media, satellite technology, and the Internet have partnered to bring the world closer and to transmit world-making events more immediately—to the point where the question of "instantaneity" has come down to the microsecond. In this light, it is worth remembering that Muybridge's California produced both Hollywood's dream factory and the digitized information revolution instigated in Silicon Valley.[40] And insofar as both can trace their antecedents to photographic practices and ways of thinking, the conjunction of information and entertainment, truth and trickery, entrepreneurial innovation and newsstand or box office sales, making images and making history, is an old story.

CODA

June 9, 2006: Three photographs are spread out on my desk, all from the front pages of today's newspapers, all concerning the U.S. raid on a house in the Iraqi town of Hibhib that killed Al-Qaeda leader Abu Masub al-Zarqawi. One photograph was provided to the Associated Press by the U.S. military. It shows a series of satellite images tracking the deployment of two five-hundred-pound bombs dropped from the sky onto the target site. One photograph is set in U.S. Army headquarters in Baghdad, where Major General William Caldwell, dressed in army fatigues, displays a large, gilt-framed photograph of al-Zarqawi's battered corpse at a news conference. And one photograph shows us the arms and torso of a young civilian who has picked through the rubble of al-Zarqawi's "hideout" to discover a tattered magazine photo of U.S. president George Bush, which he holds up for the camera. These last two images were made by professional news photographers working for international news agencies Reuters and the Associated Press. As they did in the twentieth century, these news agencies continue to provide the majority of images by which we know the world, dominating a global market that spans both print and online media. But as this array of photographs suggests, these pro-fessional photojournalistic images are often supplemented by technical images, which have become part of the popular vocabulary of journalistic documentation and evidence. And they are also enabled by a photographically oriented mass culture that enacts again and again a kind of photographic *mis-en-abyme*, image layered upon image: the Iraqi boy who recognizes that the fragmentary portrait of a U.S. president is a culturally significant emblem of bitterly contested imperialism; the chillingly old-fashioned bounty-hunter's scene staged by the army, which harks back further than the corpse photographs from the U.S. Civil War or the Paris Commune to a pre-photographic, premodern disciplinary regime where punish-ment was a public spectacle, and the heads of one's enemies were displayed on pikes for all to see.[41] The world appears caught in a photographic circuit where reality is indistinguishable from representation (and mechanical satellite and sur-veillance photographs, more often than not released by self-interested "official" sources, are fully complicit in this circuit as well).

First, we must recognize that the triumphalist view of digital media that would position them as a paradigm shift in our ways of perceiving and knowing the world is predicated on an argument about the "death of photography" that is strikingly reminiscent of the moment when photography came on the scene amid cries that "painting was dead."[42] To be sure, the technical death of a photography based on light-sensitive chemicals does to no small degree appear to be decisive (as indeed it was for miniature paintings and for engravings of topical images in the nineteenth century). Within the space of a decade, photographic materials giants such as Kodak and Ilford have largely gone out of the business of manufacturing black-and-white films and printing papers; small camera and photographic-processing businesses have disappeared from neighborhood shopping districts; photography programs in art schools no longer require classes in darkroom printing; and professional shops have been absorbed into the electronics and software depart-ments of big media stores. Perhaps the defining historical event of our age—the terrorist attacks of September 11, 2001—was collectively experienced as a media event according to the conventions of literal instantaneity (the global "real time" and "live feeds" of CNN and MSNBC); the implosion of any distinction between distance and proximity when the world is experienced so immediately as representation; and the collapse of any division between the news value of professional and amateur images that have come to define our expectations of digital media. It is estimated that more than two-thirds of news photographers on the scene in New York were shooting digitally that day, uploading their images from nearby delis and drugstores. Newspapers, wire services, and magazines selected not only from the digital work of the pros in illustrating their stories, but also from images e-mailed and posted on Web sites by a host of shell-shocked bystanders whose instinctive reaction to unimaginable catastrophe was to reach for their cameras. September 11 was "a true test of digital photography in recording history," said one photographer, "and it definitely passed the test."[43]

And yet, my local digital photography "lab" has announced a new capability to print digital photographs with the black-and-white tonal gradations of fine silver-based processes, suggesting that the look of "analog" photography retains its celebratory value. At the same time, not only does photography threaten to become more (and not less) pervasive as a privileged mode of surveillance, but the instrumental value of surveillance photographs often seems exceeded by the imaginative, almost Homeric power associated with their blindly dispassionate scrutiny—think only of the haunting surveillance camera "before" stills released of the London Underground bombers passing through the turnstiles in 2005. And when it comes to crime, forensic science may be increasingly dependent on the decoding of invisible DNA traces, but the popular packaging of forensics as entertainment in the form of television dramas such as *CSI: Crime Scene Investigation* continues to frame the spectacle of computer-driven crime solving with an almost ritualistic appeal to the good old positivism of the photographic era: confronted with evidence of the most grisly and perverse mayhem, the investigators always begin by shining a flashlight in the darkness and snapping pictures. DNA analysis may provide conclusive proof, but to the police, the truth still looks like a photograph.

So while the digital age may have found it easy to dispense with silver nitrates and chemical "fix," it has not found it so easy to dispense with the ethical and cultural place of photography as a system of representation, a mode of truth telling, and a way of knowing the world. It is a commonplace by now to insist—and often with a shudder of foreboding or some conspiracy theory–tinged mutterings of doom and gloom—on the fictional character of the digitally mediated sign. But as this essay's long look backward at the beginnings of photography has been at pains to demonstrate, that fictional value was always present *in potentia*. In other words, nineteenth-century photography may have been premised on the perceived truthfulness of the photographic image, but a culture already "burning with desire" for a photographic regime willed its truth value into broadly accepted, ontological status by vigorously policing its fictional value—transforming the pose into the mug shot, condensing a multiplicity of stories into an official history, contextualizing the waywardness of the photographic sign with the grafted-on support of the journalistic caption or the bureaucrat's filing system. Digital media may begin from a fascination with the mutability of the information-based image, but a society premised as much on symbol production as on the production of goods needs its truths nonetheless, and interested parties (the state and the media, the self-perpetuating structures of global capital) continue to do what it takes to enforce them, no matter how much of a rear-guard photographically authorized effort this might be.

This is why overemphasizing the manipulative possibilities of the digital image seems the least interesting aspect in any attempt to define the ontological character of its paradigm-shifting capacities. The digitally enhanced or doctored image (the image from nowhere, as it were, that like the perfect commodity appears without a "fingerprint" and bearing no trace of the material relations that formed it) is the most predictable manifestation of its potential: it fulfills rather than undoes a promise latent in the invention of photography for the future of commodity relations in general. It is no surprise that this promise is most obviously capitalized on in the entertainment and publicity industries, where the apparently limitless "magic" of digitally produced movies (a *Poseidon Adventure* with no water! a *Pirates of the Caribbean* with no pirates!) is matched only by the downright weirdness of contemporary, digitally souped-up advertising (which, if anything, demonstrates just how limited an imagination Salvador Dalí really had). This is why so much early digital art has seemed so uncompelling—it tells us nothing that we do not already know through the latest ad campaign, and its futuristic messages (cyborgs! hybridity!) are scarcely more appealing.

Instead, as I have argued, where photography is concerned, ontological claims emerged in full confrontation with the medium's constraints, and when it comes to digital media, one of these constraining, or limit, factors might well be the persistent memory of photography itself. This may be why—in the midst of the digital revolution—history painting has been enjoying something of a resurgence as a critical practice thanks to the investment of contemporary artists in photographically based practices that are oddly "nineteenth century" in their tactics. Take the work of Gerhard Richter, for example, whose *October 18, 1977* (1988) series on the deaths of the Baader-Meinhof group of political extremists derives the weight of cultural significance from the slurried gloom of grainy news photographs, enlarged and depleted to the point where painting becomes a kind of erasure, producing public memory as both tenacious (precisely located in the evidentiary quality of the photograph as "that-which-has-been") and hopelessly degraded.[44] Or take William Kentridge's comparable practice of "undrawing," in which the artist works in place on the same sheet of paper to draw and erase images that will be photographed using a single-frame animation technique.[45] The resulting epic short films, including *Ubu Tells the Truth* (1996–97) and *Tide Table* (2003), have a jittery, kinetoscopic quality to them (even when they are seen as video projections, you can almost hear the ghost sound of film clattering through sprockets). Their memorialization of the violent history of contemporary South Africa (the stark injustice of apartheid, the unchecked devastation wrought by HIV/AIDS) builds its emotional scale through a process that seeks not only to give allegorical images to the immediate past but, through drawing, erasing, drawing, and filming, to deny the apparent seamlessness and inevitability of the present moment. In a Kentridge film, no matter how riddled with "gaps," it is always possible to glimpse how we got from "here" to "there."

There is much more to say about both of these artists. But what is important for now is the way both practices not only "use" photographs or photography, but employ painting and drawing in a self-conscious, relational way to how photography and film work as modes of representation and ways of remembering and tracing time. In both cases, the linkage of retrograde technologies and systems of photographic representation with even more retrograde representational technologies and systems (painting and drawing themselves) strikes me as far more interesting than the seamless and saturated hyperrealism with which a Jeff Wall, say, or a Gregory Crewdson has attempted to photographically "update" the practice of history painting as "real allegory." In brief, all of this is to insist upon the value of a Benjaminian perspective on the possibilities for critique and questioning that are embedded in the tactical deployment of forms and practices of contemporaneity that have just been rendered obsolete, and so have shed their ideological "transparency" for the opaque look of the out-of-date. To rush headlong into the embrace of the state of the art runs the risk of appearing merely fashionable—or worse.

June 9, 2006: Three photographs are spread out on my desk, all from the front pages of today's newspapers, all concerning the U.S. raid on a house in the Iraqi town of Hibhib that killed Al-Qaeda leader Abu Masub al-Zarqawi. I look at them completely situated in a present I can see no way out of—no way out of escalating war, and no way out of the escalating twin threats of terror and an ever-widening, corrosive regime of self-policing that we continue to buy into with unsettling, dismaying ease. The often-acknowledged seduction of a satellite or target-system view of war is one strategy to create this buy-in. Its distancing, abstracting power "disappears" the impact of violence on the ground, replacing it with a screen experience that reduces war to the appearance of an arcade game. And yet the unreal reality of these dispassionate documents raises the specter of other reality checks. Within hours of al-Zarqawi's death, speculation about the authenticity of his corpse photograph began to build: how could his body not have been pulverized in such a heavy attack? And what does it mean for an Iraqi child to turn the victor's gesture deployed by the U.S. military in exhibiting al-Zarqawi's corpse photograph on its head, by turning a tiny, tattered photograph of a world leader into a kind of wanted poster and a promise of future retribution? All of these anxieties circulate around a larger one: the acknowledgement that, like it or not, representations such as these may be nothing more than the reality of the world we live in. The three images on my desk are ongoing, compelling evidence that the battle begun at the World Trade Center on September 11, 2001, and carried to Iraq by U.S. troops in 2003, continues to be fought to a significant degree as a war of representations that in their relation to spectacle and the "colonization of everyday life" as the twin mechanisms of "business as usual" also bear a continued relation to photography as the medium through which those relations have been at least partially enacted.[46]

Second, and finally, we must recognize that the term "enacted" is key. If there is no turning back from a digital regime, if the representations it engenders in all of their fragmentary, mutable, ephemeral relations to truth and falseness are here to stay, then the transactional aspect of digital media—its ready insertion, both officially and unofficially, into established circuits of exchange and circulation, and the call-and-response forms of address it enables within those structures (print and electronic media, the Internet, etc.)—might well be not just the source of its utility within dominant cultures and systems of power but the potential for its critical undoing, re-enabling multiple, dispersed micro-contestations of the truth, whether "real" or "manipulated." In one way, the radically enlarged globalness of a photographic imagination in the digital age is predicated on an old dialogue between amateur and professional technologies and practices that was a much more socially localized phenomenon in the nineteenth century (the portable box camera, commercially produced roll film, and the snapshot all appeared in the 1890s; like the photographic portrait in the 1850s and 1860s, they were, at least initially, largely techniques of bourgeois self-imaging). And yet it exceeds the parameters of this dialogue to the extent that the look of professionalism and technical competency in modes of digital image making and display is the easiest thing of all to try on. Web sites, blogs, electronic newsletters, the home video that makes it onto the evening news, the classified documents pirated on the Internet, the marginalized group that builds its own home (page)—all of these suggest how profoundly digital media have troubled and may continue to trouble the balance of social relationships as constituted under the conditions of spectacle. Yes, officialdom still takes up the most space, but it does so under duress, in full-blown paranoia at the specter of its truth splintering into truths—incidental, unofficial, vernacular, militant. Do not put away your battered copy of *The Society of the Spectacle* yet—it seems even more relevant now than when it was written.

In this regard, the art historian T. J. Clark has advocated that we take Debord's writings not as a salvo against representation as such (and most emphatically not as the staging of a dialectics between mere "representations" and the affirmation of "lived experience") but as a model for proposing "certain tests for . . . truth and falsity in [the] representational regimes" within which we are always, already compelled to live. "Why is it so difficult," Clark asked,

[t]o think (and demand and construct) "representation" as plural rather than as singular and centralized: representations as so many fields or terrains of activity, subject to leakage and interference between modes and technologies, and constantly crossed and dispersed by other kinds of activity altogether: subject, as a result, to retrieval and cancellation—to continual reversals of direction between object and image, and image and receiver? Why should a regime not be built on the principle that images are, or ought to be, transformable (as opposed to exchangeable)—meaning disposable through and through, and yet utterly material and contingent; shareable, imaginable, coming up constantly in their negativity, their non-identity, and for that reason promoted and dismantled at will? "History," to take up one of Debord's favorite quotations from Lukács, "is the history of the unceasing overthrow of the objective forms that shape the life of man."[47]

This is one of *my* favorite quotations from Clark's many writings on the question of representation, painted and otherwise, under the conditions of nineteenth- and twentieth-century modernity, and so I quote it at length in place of a conclusion. It reads as well at the present moment—whether or not we take any comfort in naming this moment as postmodern or post-photographic.

"The tradition of the oppressed teaches us that the 'state of emergency' in which we live is not the exception but the rule," wrote Walter Benjamin in 1940, as the consolidation of fascist powers and the escalating conflict in Europe drove Benjamin first from Berlin to Paris, and then from Paris to Marseille. "We must attain to a conception of history that is in keeping with this insight."[48] Now more than ever, in the current "state of emergency," we can ill afford to be passive spectators in a digitally produced dreamworld. The full investment of our age in digital media demands the active, engaged, skeptical viewer (who is also a maker of images and a writer) called for so presciently in Benjamin's essays of the 1930s and Debord's of the 1960s and 1970s. Then again, as their essays also serve to remind us, we were never exempted from this critical obligation. It is not simply that photography persists beyond its dependence on light-based processes, or even past its particular incarnation as a technology of optics and chemistry, but that we may have been on the wrong track all along—failing to see the extent to which an Enlightenment culture that equated "seeing" with "believing" was to be photographically eclipsed by a new dark ages.

NOTES

1. Geoffrey Batchen's *Burning with Desire: The Conception of Photography* (Cambridge: MIT Press, 1997) remains one of the most compelling accounts of photography's origin story/stories.

2. The application of the term "spectacle" to the visual conditions of modernity is most often credited to Guy Debord. See Debord, *Society of the Spectacle,* trans. Donald

Nicholson-Smith (Cambridge: MIT Press/Zone Books, 1994). One of the best position-ings of the term with respect to the visual culture of the nineteenth century remains T. J. Clark, *The Painting of Modern Life: Paris in the Art of Manet and His Followers* (Princeton, NJ: Princeton University Press, 1984), esp. 9–10.

3. Roland Barthes, *Camera Lucida: Reflections on Photography*, trans. Richard Howard (New York: Hill and Wang, 1981).

4. Eduardo Cadava has written a beautiful, meditative study on this aspect of photography. See *Words of Light: Theses on the Photography of History* (Princeton, NJ: Princeton University Press, 1997).

5. A short list of seminal essays for the history of photography by Walter Benjamin includes "The Work of Art in the Age of Mechanical Reproduction," "A Little History of Photography," "The Author as Producer," and "On the Concept of History" (also fre-quently translated as "Theses on the Philosophy of History"). All may be found in the five-volume collection edited by Michael Jennings et al., *Walter Benjamin: Selected Writings*, trans. Edmund Jephcott et al. (Cambridge, MA: Harvard/Belknap Press, 1996–2003), which also includes *The Arcades Project*, Benjamin's unfinished genealogy of nineteenth-century modernity. For a critical/bibliographic discussion of the centrality of Benjamin's work to the study of the history of photography, see Jeannene Przyblyski, "History Is Photography: The Afterimage of Walter Benjamin," *Afterimage: The Journal of Media Arts and Cultural Criticism* (September–October 1998): 8–11. For a critical/bibliographic dis-cussion of the centrality of Benjamin to the practice of history, see Vanessa R. Schwartz, "Walter Benjamin for Historians," *American Historical Review* (December 2001): 1721–43.

6. Siegfried Kracauer, "Photography," in *The Mass Ornament: Weimar Essays*, ed. Thomas Y. Levin (Cambridge, MA: Harvard University Press, 1995), 59.

7. Walter Benjamin, "On the Concept of History," in Jennings et al., *Walter Benjamin*, vol. 4, *1938–1940*, 392.

8. Kracauer, "Photography," 61. Also of interest is Siegfried Kracauer, *Theory of Film: The Redemption of Physical Reality* (Princeton, NJ: Princeton University Press, 1960).

9. See Roland Barthes, *Mythologies*, trans. Richard Howard (New York: Noonday Press, 1972), especially the short essay "The Great Family of Man," 100–102, and the pages on a magazine image of a French African soldier in "Myth Today," 116–127. Eleanor M. Hight and Gary D. Sampson, eds., *Colonialist Photography: Imag(in)ing Race and Place* (London: Routledge, 2002), provides a useful selection of essays exploring the relation of photography to empire building in detail.

10. William Henry Fox Talbot, *The Pencil of Nature*, reprint ed. (New York: Da Capo Press, 1969).

11. Talbot, *Pencil of Nature*, comments to Plate III, "Articles of China."

12. Richard Brettell et al.'s *Paper and Light: The Calotype in France and Great Britain, 1839–1870* (Boston: David R. Godine and the Art Institute of Chicago, 1984), provides a useful overview.

13. François Arago, "Bill Presented to the Chamber of Deputies, France (June 15, 1839)," trans. in *Photography in Print: Writings from 1816 to the Present*, ed. Vicki Goldberg (New York: Simon and Schuster, 1981), 31–35.

14. Charles Baudelaire, "Salon of 1859," trans. in Goldberg, *Photography in Print*, 124.

15. See Elizabeth Anne McCauley's comprehensive *A. A. E. Disdéri and the Carte de Visite Portrait Photograph* (New Haven, CT: Yale University Press, 1985).

16. One of the best comprehensive studies of the commercial exploitation of photography in France remains Elizabeth Anne McCauley, *Industrial Madness: Commercial Photography in Paris 1848–1871* (New Haven, CT: Yale University Press, 1994).

17. André Rouillé, "Les images photographiques du monde du travail sous le Second Empire," *Actes de la recherche en sciences sociales*, no. 54 (September 1984): 42.

18. The best and most cogent book on the historic affinity of the bourgeoisie to photography remains Gisèle Freund's *Photographie et société*, originally published in 1974 and later published as *Photography and Society* (Boston: Godine, 1980). This book forms the foundations of such later, critical, and revisionist histories of photography as that of John Tagg, whose chapter "A Democracy of the Image" in *The Burden of Representation: Essays on Photographies and Histories* (Amherst: University of Massachusetts Press, 1988), 34–59, follows Freund very closely. One of the most systematic sociological analyses of photography as a class-based cultural system can be found in Pierre Bourdieu, *Photography: A Middlebrow Art*, trans. Shaun Whiteside (Stanford: Stanford University Press, 1990).

19. Michel Foucault, *Discipline and Punish: The Birth of the Prison*, trans. Alan Sheridan (New York: Vintage Books, 1979), esp. 195–228. See also Foucault, *The Archeology of Knowledge and the Discourse on Language,* trans. A. M. Sheridan Smith (New York: Pantheon Books, 1972), and Foucault, *The Order of Things: An Archeology of the Human Sciences* (New York: Random House, 1970).

20. A good selection of his essays can be found in Allan Sekula, *Photography Against the Grain* (Halifax, Nova Scotia: Press of Nova Scotia College of Art and Design, 1984). See also Tagg, "A Democracy of the Image," and Shawn Michelle Smith, *American Archives: Gender, Race, and Class in Visual Culture* (Princeton, NJ: Princeton University Press, 1999).

21. See Adrienne Burrows and Ivan Schumacher, *Portraits of the Insane: The Case of Dr. Diamond* (London: Quarter Books, 1990).

22. On photographic portraiture and the Paris Commune, see Jeannene Przyblyski, "Revolution at a Standstill: Photography and the Paris Commune of 1871," *Yale French Studies* 101 (2001): 54–78.

23. On Bertillon, see Allan Sekula, "The Body and the Archive," *October* 39 (Winter 1986): 3–64.

24. Paul Delaroche, among other painters, supposedly foresaw the death of painting in the invention of photography. What is certain is that many former painters found jobs in the new industry. See Helmut Gernsheim, *The Origins of Photography* (London: Thames and Hudson, 1982), 45.

25. Paul de Man has described this as modernity's "ability to *forget* whatever precedes a present situation." See "Literary History and Literary Modernity," in his *Blindness and Insight*, 2nd ed. (Minneapolis: University of Minnesota Press, 1983), 142–165.

26. Richard Terdiman presented an influential account of this process in *Discourse/Counter-Discourse: The Theory and Practice of Symbolic Resistance in Nineteenth-Century France* (Ithaca, NY: Cornell University Press, 1985), 117–148. For a collection of essays that builds on Terdiman's insights, see Dean de la Motte and Jeannene Przyblyski, eds., *Making the News: Modernity and the Mass Press in Nineteenth-Century France* (Amherst: University of Massachusetts Press, 1999).

27. Debord, *Society of the Spectacle*, 24.

28. The concept of "eternal return" is at the core of Walter Benjamin's excavations of the conditions of modernity in the *Arcades Project*. See especially "The Exposé of

1939," in *The Arcades Project,* trans. Howard Eiland and Kevin McLaughlin (Cambridge, MA: Belknap/Harvard University Press, 1999), 25–26. One of the best books to explore the implications of the *Arcades Project* as an archeology of modern historical consciousness is Susan Buck-Morss, *The Dialectics of Seeing: Walter Benjamin and the Arcades Project* (Cambridge: MIT Press, 1990).

29. For a broader view of Fenton's work, consult Gordon Baldwin et al., *All the Mighty World: The Photography of Roger Fenton, 1852–1860* (New York: Metropolitan Museum of Art, 2004).

30. These quotes are taken from Alan Trachtenberg's excellent essay, "Albums of War," in his essential *Reading American Photographs: Images as History, Mathew Brady to Walker Evans* (New York: Hill and Wang, 1989), 72.

31. See Paul Virilio, *War and Cinema: The Logistics of Perception,* trans. Patrick Camiller. (London: Verso, 1989).

32. On ideology and transparency, see Louis Althusser, "Ideology and Ideological State Apparatuses (Notes Toward an Investigation)," in *Lenin and Philosophy and Other Essays,* trans. Ben Brewster (New York: Monthly Review Press, 1971), 127–188.

33. Kracauer wrote most persuasively about history experienced, photographically, as "gaps." See "Photography," 49ff.

34. Jeannene Przyblyski, "Moving Pictures: Photography and the Paris Commune of 1871," in *Cinema and the Invention of Modern Life,* ed. Leo Charney and Vanessa R. Schwartz (Berkeley: University of California Press, 1995), 253–278.

35. One of the best books on this subject remains Jonathan Crary, *Techniques of the Observer: On Vision and Modernity in the Nineteenth Century* (Cambridge: MIT Press, 1990). For a more materialist view of the constellation of "spectacles" in which nineteenth-century photographic practices should be located, see Vanessa R. Schwartz, *Spectacular Realities: Early Mass Culture in Fin-de-Siècle Paris* (Berkeley: University of California Press, 1998).

36. Like photography itself, credit for the stop action process was claimed by more than one inventor. Muybridge's French counterpart was Etienne-Jules Marey. For more on Marey, see Marta Braun, *Picturing Time: The Work of Etienne-Jules Marey (1830–1904)* (Chicago: Chicago University Press, 1992).

37. For a thoroughgoing history of early cinema, albeit told from an American perspective, consult Charles Musser, *The Emergence of Cinema: The American Screen to 1907* (Berkeley: University of California Press, 1990).

38. For a compelling account of Muybridge's invention in the context of his times, see Rebecca Solnit, *River of Shadows: Eadweard Muybridge and the Technological Wild West* (New York: Viking Penguin, 2003).

39. See Tom Gunning, "The Cinema of Attractions: Early Film, Its Spectator and the Avant-Garde," in *Early Cinema: Space Frame Narrative,* ed. Thomas Elsaesser (London: British Film Institute, 1990): 56–62.

40. On this point, see Solnit, *River of Shadows,* 6.

41. For an account of discipline as spectacle, see Foucault, *Discipline and Punish,* 3–72.

42. Timothy Druckery and Fred Ritchin have been two of the strongest advocates for this point of view. See Fred Ritchin, *In Our Own Image: The Coming Revolution in Photography (How Computers Changed Our View of the World)* (New York: Aperture, 1999), and Timothy Druckery, ed., *Electronic Culture: Technology and Visual Representation*

(New York: Aperture 1996). For another, more detailed examination of claims about the "death of photography," see "Epitaph," in Batchen's *Burning with Desire*, 206–216.

43. Mark Glaser, "A New Image: Why Pros Go Digital," *New York Times*, October 18, 2001.

44. On this series, see Robert Storr, *Gerhard Richter—October 18, 1977* (New York: Abrams/Museum of Modern Art, 2001).

45. On Kentridge, see Neal Benezra et al., *William Kentridge* (New York: Abrams, 2001).

46. There are many places to look for such an analysis. As a starting point, I suggest Retort (Iain Boal et al.), *Afflicted Powers: Capital and Spectacle in a New Age of War* (London: Verso, 2005), which has the benefit of rigorously bringing Debord's concept of the "spectacle" forward to the present moment. See in particular "The State, the Spectacle, and September 11," 16–37.

47. T. J. Clark, foreword to Anselm Jappe, *Guy Debord* (Berkeley: University of California Press, 1999), ix–x.

48. Benjamin, "On the Concept of History," 392.

BIBLIOGRAPHY

Althusser, Louis. *Lenin and Philosophy and Other Essays*. Trans. Ben Brewster. New York: Monthly Review Press, 1971.

Baldwin, Gordon, et al. *All the Mighty World: The Photography of Roger Fenton, 1852–1860*. New York: Metropolitan Museum of Art, 2004.

Barthes, Roland. *Mythologies*. Trans. Richard Howard. New York: Noonday Press, 1972.

———. *Camera Lucida: Reflections on Photography*. Trans. Richard Howard. New York: Hill and Wang, 1981.

Batchen, Geoffrey. *Burning with Desire: The Conception of Photography*. Cambridge: MIT Press, 1997.

Benezra, Neal, et al. *William Kentridge*. New York: Abrams, 2001.

Benjamin, Walter. *The Arcades Project*. Trans. Howard Eiland and Kevin McLaughlin. Cambridge, MA: Harvard University Press/Belknap, 1999.

Bourdieu, Pierre. *Photography: A Middlebrow Art*. Trans. Shaun Whiteside. Stanford, CA: Stanford University Press, 1990.

Braun, Marta. *Picturing Time: The Work of Etienne-Jules Marey (1830–1904)*. Chicago: Chicago University Press, 1992.

Brettell, Richard, et al. *Paper and Light: The Calotype in France and Great Britain, 1839–1870*. Boston: David R. Godine and the Art Institute of Chicago, 1984.

Buck-Morss, Susan. *The Dialectics of Seeing: Walter Benjamin and the Arcades Project*. Cambridge: MIT Press, 1990.

Burrows, Adrienne and Ivan Schumacher. *Portraits of the Insane: The Case of Dr. Diamond*. London: Quarter Books, 1990.

Cadava, Eduardo. *Words of Light: Theses on the Photography of History*. Princeton, NJ: Princeton University Press, 1997.

Charney, Leo, and Vanessa R. Schwartz, eds. *Cinema and the Invention of Modern Life.* Berkeley: University of California Press, 1995.

Clark, T. J. *The Painting of Modern Life: Paris in the Art of Manet and His Followers* Princeton, NJ: Princeton University Press, 1984.

Crary, Jonathan. *Techniques of the Observer: On Vision and Modernity in the Nineteenth Century.* Cambridge: MIT Press, 1990.

Debord, Guy. *Society of the Spectacle.* Trans. Donald Nicholson-Smith. Cambridge: MIT Press/Zone Books, 1994.

de la Motte, Dean, and Jeannene Przyblyski, eds. *Making the News: Modernity and the Mass Press in Nineteenth-Century France.* Amherst: University of Massachusetts Press, 1999.

de Man, Paul. *Blindness and Insight*, 2nd ed. Minneapolis: University of Minnesota Press, 1983.

Druckery, Timothy, ed. *Electronic Culture: Technology and Visual Representation.* New York: Aperture, 1996.

Elsaesser, Thomas, ed. *Early Cinema: Space Frame Narrative.* London: British Film Institute, 1990.

Foucault, Michel. *The Order of Things: An Archeology of the Human Sciences.* New York: Random House, 1970.

———. *The Archeology of Knowledge and the Discourse on Language.* Trans. A. M. Sheridan Smith. New York: Pantheon Books, 1972.

———. *Discipline and Punish: The Birth of the Prison.* Trans. Alan Sheridan. New York: Vintage Books, 1979.

Freund, Gisèle. *Photography and Society.* Boston: Godine, 1980.

Gernsheim, Helmut. *The Origins of Photography.* London: Thames and Hudson, 1982.

Glaser, Mark. "A New Image: Why Pros Go Digital," *New York Times*, October 18, 2001.

Goldberg, Vicki, ed. *Photography in Print: Writings from 1816 to the Present.* New York: Simon and Schuster, 1981.

Hight, Eleanor M., and Gary D. Sampson, eds. *Colonialist Photography: Imag(in)ing Race and Place.* London: Routledge, 2002.

Jappe, Anselm. *Guy Debord.* Berkeley: University of California Press, 1999.

Jennings, Michael, et. al. *Walter Benjamin: Selected Writings.* Trans. Edmund Jephcott et al. 4 vols. Cambridge, MA: Harvard/Belknap Press, 1996–2003.

Kracauer, Siegfried. *Theory of Film: The Redemption of Physical Reality.* Princeton, NJ: Princeton University Press, 1960.

———. "Photography," in *The Mass Ornament: Weimar Essays.* Trans. Thomas Y. Levin. Cambridge, MA: Harvard University Press, 1995.

McCauley, Elizabeth Anne. *A. A. E. Disdéri and the Carte-de-Visite Portrait Photograph.* New Haven, CT: Yale University Press, 1985.

———. *Industrial Madness: Commercial Photography in Paris, 1848–1871.* New Haven, CT: Yale University Press, 1994.

Musser, Charles. *The Emergence of Cinema: The American Screen to 1907.* Berkeley: University of California Press, 1990.

Przyblyski, Jeannene. "History Is Photography: The Afterimage of Walter Benjamin." *Afterimage: The Journal of Media Arts and Cultural Criticism* (September–October 1998): 8–11.

———. "Revolution at a Standstill: Photography and the Paris Commune of 1871." *Yale French Studies* 101 (2001): 54–78.

Retort (Ian Boal, et. al.). *Afflicted Powers: Capital and Spectacle in a New Age of War*. London: Verso, 2005.

Ritchin, Fred. *In Our Own Image: The Coming Revolution in Photography (How Computers Changed Our View of the World)*. New York: Aperture, 1999.

Rouillé, André. "Les images photographiques du monde du travail sous le Second Empire," *Actes de la recherche en sciences sociales*, no. 54 (September 1984): 42.

Schwartz, Vanessa R. *Spectacular Realities: Early Mass Culture in Fin-de-Siècle Paris*. Berkeley: University of California Press, 1998.

———. "Walter Benjamin for Historians." *American Historical Review* (December 2001): 1721–43.

Sekula, Allan. *Photography Against the Grain*. Halifax, Nova Scotia: The Press of Nova Scotia College of Art and Design, 1984.

———. "The Body and the Archive." *October* 39 (Winter 1986): 3–64.

Smith, Shawn Michelle. *American Archives: Gender, Race, and Class in Visual Culture*. Princeton: Princeton University Press, 1999.

Solnit, Rebecca. *River of Shadows: Eadweard Muybridge and the Technological Wild West*. New York: Viking Penguin, 2003.

Storr, Robert, *Gerhard Richter—October 18, 1977* (New York: Abrams/Museum of Modern Art, 2001).

Tagg, John. *The Burden of Representation: Essays on Photographies and Histories*. Amherst: University of Massachusetts Press, 1988.

Talbot, William Henry Fox. *The Pencil of Nature*. New York: Da Capo Press, 1969.

Terdiman, Richard. *Discourse/Counter-Discourse: The Theory and Practice of Symbolic Resistance in Nineteenth-Century France*. Ithaca, NY: Cornell University Press, 1985.

Trachtenberg, Alan. *Reading American Photographs: Images as History, Mathew Brady to Walker Evans*. New York: Hill and Wang, 1989.

Virilio, Paul. *War and Cinema: The Logistics of Perception*. Trans. Patrick Camiller. London: Verso, 1989.

CHAPTER 6

MEDIA CELEBRITY IN THE AGE OF THE IMAGE

MARSHA ORGERON

The star challenges analysis in the way it crosses disciplinary boundaries: a product of mass culture, but retaining theatrical concerns with acting, performance and art; an industrial marketing device, but a signifying element in films; a social sign, carrying cultural meanings and ideological values, which express the intimacies of individual personality, inviting desire and identification; an emblem of national celebrity, founded on the body, fashion and personal style; a product of capitalism and the ideology of individualism, yet a site of contest by marginalized groups; a figure consumed for his or her personal life, who competes for allegiance with statesmen and politicians.

—Christine Gledhill, ed., *Stardom: Industry of Desire*[1]

Figure 6.1 In Oliver Stone's *Natural Born Killers* (1994),
Mickey and Mallory get celebrity treatment on a mocked-up
cover of *Newsweek*. Wayne Gale's sensationalistic television
program *American Maniacs* recycles the image in this
celebratory montage.

PART I. CRITICAL TERRAIN

The Canonization of Star Studies

In his 1994 cine-treatise on the mania of media celebrity, *Natural Born Killers*, Oliver
Stone represented his outrageously murderous duo of Mickey (Woody Harrelson)
and Mallory (Juliette Lewis) as MTV-era media darlings. They begin their spree with
Mallory's lecherous father (Rodney Dangerfield), whose abuse of his family is
imagined in an "*I Love Lucy*"–style flashback complete with a painfully inappropriate
laugh track. Their violent career escalates as they slay their way across the country,
"always leaving one survivor" to tell the story of their homicidal escapades and to
ensure that the eagerly anticipating world hears their stories. Fetishized by ratings-
hungry news agencies and worshipped by an unthinking cult of the media-numbed,
the pair learn to play to the cameras with unlikely ease, making dupes—and

corpses—of almost everyone around them as they gleefully emerge from the blood-soaked narrative in another sitcom-like hallucination of perverse domestic bliss.

Media celebrity in the late twentieth century, the film argues, is not only ridiculous; it has become dangerous. Stone surveyed the media landscape and found inanity, excess, and morbidity. Mickey and Mallory seem on the one hand absurd caricatures and on the other completely plausible modern-day celebrities. They are a crude culmination of a century of moving-image-nurtured fame, which began in the United States with twenty-second kinetoscope glimpses of both anonymous and known performers (such as actress May Irwin and Sandow the Strongman), and which has proliferated to a point of near untenable dispersion and occasionally indiscernible justification in the current Internet age.[2]

A rapidly growing body of scholarship has attempted to study and theorize both the history and the current environs of media fame in which Stone situated his protagonists. Converging under the broad, inviting umbrella of celebrity or star studies, the field has attracted scholars from film and media studies, psychology, sociology, literary studies, women's studies, legal and political studies, history, cultural and American studies, anthropology, and so on. Star studies offers scholars a hook on which to hang any number of critical issues, as Christine Gledhill's generous definition of stardom that opens this essay indicates. The sustained multidisciplinary interest in celebrity derives from its embodiment of so many diverse ideas not only worthy of critical investigation but urgently requiring it, as Stone's film makes clear.

As the term's cosmological origins would suggest, classical-era stardom (the concept mutates after the collapse of the studio system) is conceptualized partly in terms of *distance*. The romantic and celestially grand bodies on screen communicate with the spectator both within the moment of cinematic exhibition and outside of this moment as the star's off-screen persona accrues symbolic weight. During the golden age, formidable forces of promotion conspired to craft the star image. Contemporary stars, however, exist in quite another orbit; deprived of the rigorously protective, all-encompassing forces of the studio system, they are subject to virtually unaccountable and intensely aggressive media outlets that seek to document every moment in the lives of the celebrity du jour, especially, it seems, the embarrassing, humiliating ones. With such differences in mind, Leo Braudy associated stars with "spiritual transcendence," but the celebrity with "material success," suggesting the degree to which the idea of celebrity is more closely associated with the shallow enterprises of the passing headline, the mundane intimacy of television, and the rapidity and indiscriminate nature of postmodern mediation (one need only think again of Stone's hideous progeny).[3] For Daniel Boorstin, writing in 1962, the modern-day celebrity, made so by the media for a variety of reasons great and small, is a tautological and empty concept: "*a person who is known for his well-knownness* . . . He is the human pseudo-event."[4]

Despite these associational differences, stardom and celebrity are both defined by excess. Boorstin argued that stage actors were evaluated on the basis of their ability to interpret a play, but "the sign of a true star was in fact that whatever he appeared in was only a 'vehicle.' "[5] The star's value, in other words, exceeds her performance; in fact, stars exist largely outside of the moment of performance, be it film or theater. Actors become stars, as Christine Gledhill suggested, "when their off-screen life-styles and personalities equal or surpass acting ability in importance."[6] However, the liberal application of the term "star" to virtually anyone in the public eye—Robert Allen and Douglas Gomery point out its use for athletes, soap opera actors, and musicians—has the effect of draining the concept of its historical meaning and impact.

Some scholars have attempted to differentiate between stardom and celebrity by considering issues of power that extend beyond box office or ratings. The Italian sociologist Francesco Alberoni in "The Powerless 'Elite' " (1962) maintained that one of the ironies of the celebrity is the limited political power that comes with such incredible visibility. Traditionally, Alberoni asserted, the most visible members of a culture were also agents of proportional power, decision making, and influence. Citing Max Weber's definition of charisma as a quality affording influence over others, Alberoni wondered why "the charismatic element of 'stardom' does not get transformed into a power relationship?"[7] Of course, Alberoni could not have anticipated the emergence of such actors-turned-politicians as Ronald Reagan and Arnold Schwarzenegger, nor the ways that television would eventually compel politicians to behave like publicity-hungry celebrities in their own right. Stars of Hollywood's emergent era—the likes of Mary Pickford and Charlie Chaplin, for example—eventually controlled their own careers and their own films, moved in elite social and political circles, could pay for extravagant houses and conspicuous luxuries that few others in the culture could, and possessed a significant international presence. But one need only remember the politics that led to the refusal to readmit Charlie Chaplin to the United States in 1952 to glimpse the limits of stardom's influence and the degree to which politics affects, shapes, and even at times limits the supposed power of stardom.

If power fails to adequately differentiate between stars and celebrities, it also seems insufficient to point to media specificity—movies versus television—as the distinguishing criterion, which John Ellis did in *Visible Fictions* (1982) when he claimed that stars are a specifically cinematic phenomenon because television's immediacy and familiarity work against stardom's enigmatic status. Tabloids, celebrity journalism, and the myriad of celebrity and gossip Web sites suggest that, at least in the current day, television and movie performers, politicians and musicians, and headline makers of all sorts hold increasingly equivalent and perhaps even progressively undifferentiated power and allure over audiences, if only for their proverbial fifteen minutes.[8]

The categorical slipperiness here—star and celebrity certainly, but in other contexts personality, superstar, and megastar—exists because our conceptions of these terms are ever shifting, responding to changes in the culture, in the media,

Figure 6.2 Even a seemingly omnipotent star like Charlie Chaplin—
who held on to his silence a full decade into sound production, until the
musical finale of *Modern Times* (Charlie Chaplin, 1936)—was rendered
powerless during the anticommunist fervor of the 1950s.

and in the celebrated themselves. Media celebrity is not, of course, itself a modern phenomenon. Nor do its origins reside solely in the technologies of the moving image: film, television, and—increasingly—the Internet. It is rooted in past centuries and was, in its earliest manifestations, especially indebted to innovations afforded by the invention of the printing press and its capacity for disseminating words and images in books, newspapers, and magazines. As Leo Braudy demonstrated in his seminal *Frenzy of Renown* (1986), the image was the central currency of fame as it was disseminated first through literature, theater, and public monuments; then painting and engraved portraits; and finally photography, movies, and television (Braudy completed his study before the Internet became the latest tool in the fame game). But it is the movie star that has most held captive the imagination of scholars in the field, and it is Hollywood that most visibly and seductively rationalized the process of star making.

Much of celebrity studies has, for these and a number of other industrial, cultural, and political reasons, revolved around American film stardom, especially of the emerging period (the first decades of the twentieth century) into the classical era (primarily the 1930s and 1940s). The earliest literature about stardom was popular—fan magazines, for example—offering details about lifestyles and often-fabricated biographical information about the celebrated. This material was primarily written for, and occasionally even by, the fans themselves; its most palpable effects were on the stars who were made and sometimes unmade by it, and the producers and exhibitors of their films who stood to profit by it. Into this largely

Figure 6.3 Like many of the movie fan magazines, which helped to nurture the public's mania for stars, *Picture-Play* included a regular section of star portraits for its readers' "collections." Mary Miles Minter—who would later become famous for her involvement with William Desmond Taylor prior to his murder in 1922—was given star treatment in the November 1919 issue.

celebratory literature entered the work of historians, sociologists, and anthropologists who, beginning in the 1920s and often—but not always—with the aim of purging the phenomenon of its uncritical populism, investigated Hollywood's denizens, corporate structure, and product.[9]

While anthropologists, sociologists, and historians were publishing their first accounts of how movie stars changed the business of the film industry, cultural theorists began to address stardom's ideological impact. The most coherent of these theories emerged from the Frankfurt School, whose "members" vehemently critiqued the power of the media and of celebrities as agents of capitalism with significant control over presumably passive audiences. Theodor Adorno and Max Horkheimer in "The Culture Industry" (1944) and Herbert Marcuse in *One Dimensional Man* (1964) pointed to celebrities as agents of containment and placation. The Frankfurt School scholars pointed out, at an especially relevant historical moment, the possible dangers of media celebrity; however, they also underestimated the potential resistance of media spectators and overestimated the effectiveness of those trying to manipulate audiences, as later scholars have amply demonstrated.[10]

For a number of these practitioners of cultural studies—Edgar Morin and Daniel Boorstin among them—there is something sinister in the project of celebrity culture. Boorstin, who was concerned less about movie stars than about the general status of celebrity in American culture in *The Image* (1962), argued that the media—television, movies, radio, newspapers, and magazines—conspire to create the illusion that "fame—well-knownness—is still a hallmark of greatness," a notion Leo Braudy in essence affirmed some twenty years later.[11] Boorstin did not conceal his attitude toward this state of affairs, suggesting that the prevalence of "artificial fame" is an unfortunate misstep; it is, perhaps, one that we now are currently confronted with in the omnipresence of so-called reality television and the flurry of pseudo-stars (to employ language indebted to Boorstin) it produces. Heroes, for Boorstin, are a kind of lost object, replaced by celebrity, which can too easily and indiscriminately be fabricated and proliferated. Andy Warhol witnessed and exploited a similar phenomenon around the same time, but Boorstin did not possess Warhol's delight in the perversity of this state of affairs. Rather, Boorstin was convinced that the constant media bombardment of the day—a trickle by today's standards—both made and destroyed celebrities through oversaturation, resulting in a situation—or a condition—in which "celebrities die quickly but they are still more quickly replaced," creating an ever-increasing supply as the years go by.[12] Situating movie stars within this "world of pseudo-events," Boorstin was suspicious of the ways in which stars spawn other pseudo-events—like fan clubs and film premieres—in a seemingly endless cycle of unreality that dangerously distracts us from more pressing and politically urgent realities.[13]

Although Boorstin did not perform sustained analyses of such pseudo-events as fan magazines and clubs, nor any specific case studies of the stars themselves, these areas of investigation became, for a post-1960s generation of scholars, key to determining the ideological significance of stars. While early historical accounts of stardom included in the histories by Lewis Jacobs, Benjamin Hampton, and Leo Rosten veered away from *analyzing* the myriad insinuations of stardom into popular culture, Boorstin set the stage for future generations of scholars who sought to explore stardom's cultural implications, not just to narrate the terms of its existence or to condemn the culture out of which it was emerging. By the late 1970s and 1980s, a significant body of work was appearing about the mediation of stars and, conversely, concerning their influence on mass culture.[14] This new generation of scholars had varied allegiances to film history, cultural studies, semiotics, and emerging theoretical strains such as feminism, psychoanalysis, and Marxism.

The 1979 publication of Richard Dyer's *Stars* is one of the benchmark moments in this era of the discipline's history, partly because its appearance signaled that stardom had "arrived" as a valid subset of film and media studies. Utilizing theories of sociology, semiotics, and cultural studies, Dyer established the legitimacy of star studies by enumerating the scholarly and political value of stars in relation to other aspects of culture and identity. Dyer laid out a formal approach by which to read "star texts," the signifiers of stardom, which include films, advertisements, publicity, magazines, and television. Dyer's mantra, in *Stars*, is that culture and ideology go hand in hand, and that stars matter precisely because they embody the confluence of the personal with the political. By analyzing star texts and contexts, Dyer suggested a way that the critic can tease out the ideological contradictions that divergent spectators might encounter when interacting with any element— from page to screen—of star construction. With the publication of his follow-up work, *Heavenly Bodies* (1986)—which used case studies of Marilyn Monroe, Paul Robeson, and Judy Garland to reclaim the audience as a site of resistance by emphasizing the degree to which it is "disparate and fragmented" and "not wholly controlled by Hollywood and the media"—Dyer paved the way for studies of both the construction and the reception of star images to proceed.[15]

Justifying, defining, laying claim to, and establishing critical boundaries for understanding stars—as exampled by Dyer's work, and by scholars such as Anthony Slide, Janet Staiger, and Charles Musser in film history—were tasks undertaken in earnest by the late 1970s. Concerns over establishing critical authority, over distancing star studies from star adoration, were reflective of a larger tendency toward the serious consideration of identity and politics within the humanities at a historical moment when few lines of inquiry seemed as frivolous or as suspect as "star studies." The works of these scholars aided in the legitimization of the field at a time when history and theory were collectively sharpening their approaches.

Staiger's "Seeing Stars" (1983), for example, is indicative of this critical formalization of star studies because it pauses, and reviews, reflects on, and rethinks the ways film historians had been telling the story of stardom; in other words, its concerns are both historical and methodological. Staiger rehearsed the major star evolutionary theories and pointed out the ways that certain narratives were being reproduced without question as the histories accumulated.[16] She stepped back from the archival details to look at the broader picture of stardom's history, urging historians to consider, for example, the theatrical star system as a key precedent to the burgeoning cinematic star system, as well as to ask "whether or not the audiences were also seeing stars."[17]

The most important response to Staiger's plea for a re-historicization of motion picture stardom came in the form of Richard deCordova's authoritative *Picture Personalities: The Emergence of the Star System in America* (1990). In it deCordova documented the emergence of the "picture personality," a phenomenon he defines as being created by audiences who were making their own connections between performers in different roles and then seeking out knowledge about these performers. Arguing that there is "a more complex logic in the rise of the star system," one that resists the seductiveness of the "good simple story" that had so often been repeated, deCordova questioned and amended many of the interpretations of the star chronology.[18] To date, deCordova's history remains the most convincing account of stardom's emergence. He insisted that the star system, emphasized here above the individual star, cannot be understood simply by narrating a chain of major star-making events because this fails to acknowledge the complexity of this system; the "events," in other words, do not simply speak for themselves. DeCordova's scholarly care for the unfolding star narrative took the field a long way from such popular book-length studies as Alexander Walker's 1970 *Stardom*, important in its own right (and own time) for attempting to resuscitate then-obscure stars such as Rudolph Valentino, Lillian Gish, and Douglas Fairbanks. DeCordova restructured the way that the emergence of stardom was understood and recognized, while also mandating a kind of historical rigor absent from the popular literature.

Although the academic field of star studies emerged in the post-studio era, with a particular interest in the era preceding it, its largely retrospective focus has not yet adequately accounted for the myriad shifts that have transpired in the post-studio age, especially in terms of the latest generation of diversified, global media stars. So much had star studies focused on star history that it was not until the 1990s that the first significant upsurge in critical attention focused on the contemporary star situation, or on star systems generated outside of Hollywood. Joshua Gamson's *Claims to Fame: Celebrity in Contemporary America* (1994), for example, blends interviews with celebrity-industry workers and observations of celebrity-based settings in 1990s Hollywood—in the mode established by Leo Rosten sixty years prior—to assess the current production and reception of celebrity, how people in the late twentieth century "*interpret and use* celebrity images."[19] Following the path laid out by Alberoni, P. David Marshall's *Celebrity and Power: Fame in Contemporary Culture* (1997) approaches the current celebrity-making industries of the movies, music, television, and politics in an effort to discern the ways that "power is articulated through the celebrity."[20] Both scholars are indebted to the works in history and cultural studies preceding them, but they looked to the present and future instead of the past to fill the significant need for understanding how celebrity has been altered in the late twentieth and early twenty-first century, the era that bequeathed us the fictional Mickey and Mallory and their many nonfictional celebrity counterparts. In doing so, they—and a number of other scholars who have turned their attention outside of Hollywood's domain—have begun to fill in the many gaps that remain in our understanding of the global media celebrity phenomenon.

A Star System Is Born

An argument can be made that movie stars legitimated and elevated the American film industry, enabling the kind of growth necessary for the creation of the most successful mass-entertainment enterprise of the early twentieth century. The arrival and escalation of movie stardom coincided with and, I would argue, was instrumental in the transition of moviemaking from a geographically diffuse, economically unorganized, somewhat haphazard enterprise to a consolidated, organized, localized, and coherent business structure soon to be ruled by a few corporate giants. The American movie star system's emergence is attributable to a complex series of conditions and motivations, not all of them economic but certainly having significant financial consequences. As much as the rationalization of a star system by the nascent studios intended to create a methodology, of sorts, for the making of stars, it was never a system that intended to homogenize; rather, the emerging system operated on the principles of differentiation, and stars were being used to distinguish (in every sense of the word) producers' products from one another.

The cinema's first producers, in the 1890s, did not place their "performers" in the privileged position they would hold in later years. Audiences of cinema's first decade were most fascinated with the apparatus itself, with its ability to magically reproduce the "real." Coming to see actualities, early cinema spectators were lured by the medium's ability to capture and reproduce different places, people, and events, and were especially intrigued by the enchanting qualities of movement itself.[21] "Actors," such as they were, were more often than not unprofessional recruits for the camera, bystanders caught by the camera's wandering eye, or temporary loans from the "legitimate" stage or vaudeville. Films were not marketed in the near-star-auteurist way they would be by the late 1920s and 1930s—"Garbo's latest," "Valentino in"; rather, they were sold and marketed by manufacturer name (Biograph, for example).

Coincident with these earliest "flickers," however, was an atmosphere in which an abiding interest in, and perhaps even a mania over, celebrity was making itself apparent. The twentieth century began equipped with an increasingly forceful and celebrity-mad press, which reflected a reorientation of moral standards (privacy, for example, had been a major tenet of Victorian culture) and the urbanizing modernization of recreational behavior and lifestyles; it is possible, then, to view American movie stardom as a continuum growing out of the culture's sustained beliefs in exceptional individualism combined with a burgeoning interest in celebrity and fascination with media visibility.[22] Movie stardom's precedents were set in nineteenth-century theater and vaudeville, themselves outgrowths of eighteenth-century innovations in publicity.[23] The term "star" was used as early as 1830 to refer to an "exceptional performer" of the stage,[24] and in the early 1900s the theater, vaudeville, and opera "all operated to a large extent on the basis of a star system, in which the personal magnetism of a particular performer often outweighed other considerations of artistic talent, or the value of the drama or music."[25] Despite the existence of such time-tested models for performance recognition and marketing, however, motion picture performers in the first decade of American filmmaking were not named in film credits, which did not yet exist; nor did their names appear in publicity.[26] When celebrity was being touted in connection with the new medium in the early 1910s, in fact, it often extended past those on-screen performers to the fame of the films' well-known authors, who provided the story material for filmmakers when sustained narrative films came into vogue and even, on occasion, to emerging star-directors such as D.W. Griffith.

It was not until 1907 that a sustained tendency toward fiction filmmaking, regular film-acting employment, and trade press coverage of film actors converged to create a climate in which certain performers began to garner recognition from the public. Over the course of 1909 and 1910, when intertextual connections between screen performances were being made by these audiences, information began circulating in the press that allowed the public to learn about the actors' professional lives, but not (yet) their personal lives. A January 5, 1910, article in *The Moving Picture World* notes "a new method of lobby advertising" by the Kalem company that included photographs of "principal actors" for "lobby display."[27] The article partly explains the novelty of this mode of promotion by claiming that acting "professionals" frequently tried to "shield their identity," fearing "that their artistic reputations would suffer." Ten months later, the same magazine would acknowledge that the "better known moving picture actors and actresses are known to the public at large," but that "the rank and file, however, are not," using this lack to make a plea for "each picture or reel [to] be preceded by the full cast of characters . . . with the names of actors and actresses playing the parts."[28] Actors were, in other words, becoming objects of curiosity and sites of knowledge, encouraging the hierarchical conditions for stardom. The movies already seemed to foster an ongoing relationship between spectators and performers that was unlike prior relationships built around similar entertainment contexts, most obviously in terms of market penetration and regularity.

In response to the public's desire to see more of movie actors offscreen, in February of 1911 the *New York Telegraph* added a motion picture section to its Sunday editions that included portraits of movie players;[29] this is also the date of publication for *Motion Picture Story Magazine*, which became a fan magazine largely in response to readers' pressures for it to move beyond its initial film promotional (versus star promotional) role. By the early teens, as deCordova asserted, "the question of the player's existence outside his or her work in film became the primary focus of discourse."[30] In answer to a growing public interest in knowledge about stars' lives, and prompted by the industry's recognition that such interest could be exploited to help ensure the success of their enterprises, stories about the personal lives of movie actors began to proliferate—as did the number of publications that carried these stories—throughout the teens and twenties.

With a substantial mass media now revolving exclusively around film stardom, the exploitation of the star commodity became a practicable part of filmmaking and marketing. Around this time Carl Laemmle made an oft-cited contribution to the process of star making, one that has been widely understood as a—if not *the*—foundational event in most of the histories of stardom's birth, however problematically. Laemmle recruited Biograph actress Florence Lawrence—then known to the public only as the "Biograph Girl"—away from the powerful Trust company on behalf of his Independent Motion Pictures (Imp). Several months later a series of ads publicized his new star, by reproducing first the image—but not yet the name—of his new performer in the trades in December 1909, and then both name and image in January 1910. In March of 1910 Laemmle began a new campaign countering alleged reports of the death of his star, and although these death reports have never been found, his advertisements proclaimed that Florence Lawrence—no longer a nameless player—was alive and well.[31] This public star-naming campaign culminated in April 1910, when Lawrence personally appeared in St. Louis to once-and-for-all squelch the rumor concerning her untimely demise, signaling a highly visible instance of deliberate star publicity in the tradition of P.T. Barnum–style sensationalism.

The Florence Lawrence incident, invoked by virtually all scholars of stardom's history as a turning point in the evolution of movie stardom, is not an isolated episode and cannot, on its own, account for the "birth" of the star system. Richard deCordova has produced the most compelling rereading of the Florence Lawrence/Imp affair, not to invalidate the event but to reject "the singular and supposedly initiatory appeal of Florence Lawrence" without regard for "the broader context within which actors became well known."[32] He read Lawrence's emergence as signaling the existence of an intermediary figure between the movie performer and the full-fledged star, pointing out that the marketing of her "picture personality" began well before her naming changed the stakes of this familiarity.

Indeed, by the end of 1910 numerous companies—including Trust members—were starting to promote their stars, suggesting a confluence of market conditions and strategies to which Laemmle was, no doubt, responding, however innovatively.[33] The Lawrence incident, then, is indicative of a larger trend toward recognizing and publicizing performers to market the film product, which was itself becoming more reliant on the prestige of its literary sources alongside the prominence of its players. In June 1910 a photograph of Florence Turner, the "Vitagraph Girl," was described in captions as "A Motion Picture Star" alongside a story about her in the *New York Dramatic Mirror*; by 1910, stock company photographs were being displayed in theater lobbies; "Broncho Billy" Anderson was starring in westerns that bore his nickname in mid-1910; and the Famous Players Film Company was founded in 1912 with the intent to produce "Famous Players in Famous Plays," as their slogan put it, which contributed to elevating the status of film performance through prestige productions associated with theatrical greats.[34]

Movie stars were thus becoming widely recognizable as such by the second decade of the twentieth century. Star packaging and promotion were developed and refined over the course of the teens, during which time fan magazines worked in concert with producers to construct and sell a breed of performer whose appeal could far transcend their brief appearances in the space of theatrical exhibition. As actors became fetishized by mass audiences, they could regularly be encountered in the mainstream press as well as at public appearances (which were, of course, covered by the press in the emerging pseudo-event cycle to which Boorstin pointed) or in direct studio publicity (in the form of autographed photographs, fan clubs, and correspondence). Performers became essential economic determinants in the production and exhibition process, and as the studio system was codified over the course of the 1920s, they came to inform every element of a film's production, from genre to budget to distribution. The contractual nature of star employment under the studio system, at its peak in the 1930s and 1940s, allowed for the ownership of stars' images, performances, and even behavior, both on-screen and off. The genius of this system, to borrow a phrase from André Bazin and Thomas Schatz, was the impressive manipulation of the economic value of the star through the realization of the fantastic, erotic, romantic, identificatory, deistic, and on occasion even antagonistic personal relationship audiences had grown to have with the stars.

Global Star Systems

Hollywood is often casually assumed to have a monopoly on stardom's history, but it is worth recalling that the early years of film exhibition did not always find America in the foremost position of film production or distribution. France, England, and Italy were also dominating powers in the cinema's first decades. Their films—and their performers—greatly influenced the nature of the American film product, performance style, and even star handling. Many "foreign" luminaries lit up the silver screen both in their countries of origin and abroad: Max Linder and Sarah Bernhardt from France, Alma Taylor from England, and Italian divas such as Francesca Bertini and Lydia Borelli, just to name a few. In recent years scholarly attention has taken note of the truly global nature of stardom, moving from Hollywood as the center of celebrity studies out to include television and other mass-media personalities, politicians, musicians, as well as formerly neglected international stars. It is true that by the 1930s Hollywood stars disproportionately resonated outside of American borders, often—and for a variety of reasons—occupying center stage in the hearts and minds of spectators around the globe. Although the opposite exchange transpired, if perhaps with less regularity and intensity, the Hollywood star has always been at the center of academic star studies.

Scholarly attention has only recently, however, begun to shift beyond the dominant Hollywood orbit. Book-length studies on stardom in Britain, Spain, and India—to name a few—begin to answer questions about stardom outside of the United States, as well as to explain the industrial practices of other national cinemas with regard to the use and treatment of star performers, and the impact of American stars on other national cinemas. Due to the disproportionate attention that has been paid to Hollywood stardom, there exists an odd lacuna that has shrouded the stars of other nations whose cinemas—as in the case of Britain—have been widely studied in virtually every other way. The work of historical explication—how a certain nation's film performers came to be known, how they were publicized, how the public reacted to them, how they were treated by the producers and corporations who employed them, and so on—is crucial to informing a more balanced understanding of the global impact of film stardom.

As the American film industry dominated the global market in the 1920s and beyond, national cinemas often modeled their star systems on Hollywood's. It is often this context, then, that must be kept in mind when looking at stardom beyond Hollywood. In the case of Britain, where only two studios could compete with the big eight of Hollywood, seven-year contracts, publicity stills, and high (but not nearly as-high) salary practices were born of Hollywood emulation.[35] But British film stars—Bruce Babington refers to them as "indigenous stars"—require a total rethinking of Hollywood-based star theory for a variety of reasons: British films tend to be ensemble pieces rather than star vehicles; publicity in Britain was not as furious as it was in Hollywood; British theater was considered of greater importance (intellectual and otherwise) than cinema; and acting was considered of primary magnitude in the evaluation of a star's status.[36] In France, where the industry was not dominated by large corporate film studios in the 1930s, star contracts of the American variety were not the standard and, therefore, French stars did not have the same degree of carefully handled promotion during America's, or France's, golden age.[37]

Without considering the national contexts of stardom, we remain myopic to systems that operate outside of—or even in opposition to—the Hollywood model. Even when Hollywood was the unrepentant model for other industries, which is not surprising given the status of that industry's films in the world market during the studio era in particular, cultural specificity complicates the simple adoption of that system around the globe. Bombay stars did model themselves on their Hollywood counterparts such as Charlie Chaplin, Douglas Fairbanks, and, later, Elvis Presley, largely as a consequence of Hollywood films' dominance for middle-class Indian spectators through at least the late 1950s.[38] But without an intimate knowledge of India's cultural and national history, it would be impossible to understand such phenomena as Indian male stars' disproportionate salaries, which are at least double that of their female counterparts; or early Indian women stars' reluctance to be photographed because of Hindu and Muslim taboos about women's public exposure; or the Indian star's decidedly greater political power when compared to their Hollywood counterparts, which allows them a degree of freedom unthinkable for any other member of the culture.[39]

Whereas Indian cinema's star system might parallel, or even exceed, that of Hollywood, it may be impossible to identify a star system, as we understand it, in Spain, which has had a proportionately small and only sporadically international presence. While not full-fledged in comparison to the American standard, Spain's star system can, however, be detected in the value of actors' names to producers, as well as in the considerable media attention given to celebrities and the significant role film viewing plays in everyday life.[40] The nuances of national stardom, whether in relation to Hollywood or not, contain essential revelations about the cultures in which they are created and consumed, and about patterns of exhibition and viewing. The fact that numerous national star systems have not yet received significant—if any—treatment in the form of books or even articles suggests a vast area of potential growth in the field in terms both of understanding star history and of better grasping its contemporary state.

Part II. Theoretical Directions

The first half of this essay maps out the terrain of star studies to orient the reader with the basic elements and history of the field; this half charts three major directions that star studies has taken, largely in the post-Dyer years. The scholarship about media celebrity is diffuse in terms of both its breadth and its disciplinary focus. The subject is widely applicable, its contexts variable and complex. Having already acknowledged the interdisciplinarity of star studies—which Dyer's landmark work established from the outset—we can identify three organizational umbrellas that seem capable of categorizing much of the work of the field. Beyond the scholarship involving star history, which in fact weaves its way throughout all of the other scholarship, work on stars might be conceived of as occupying three major categories of thought dealing with (1) the work of stardom, which engages with issues of labor and performance; (2) star texts, which follow the lines laid out by Richard Dyer to analyze how stars are constructed, represented, disseminated, and consumed; and (3) identity politics, which works to understand the ways that stars function in relation to issues of race, class, gender, sexuality, and ethnicity, both in terms of star representation and in terms of spectatorship and reception. The sections that follow briefly map out these major theoretical currents that constitute this still-evolving field, with full awareness that these categories are themselves much more discrete than the interdisciplinary scholarship practiced by most scholars in the field, whose work typically defies such rigid segmentation.

The Work of Stardom

Richard Schickel, writing in the 1960s, claimed that "movie stars are not basically actors, although many of them demonstrate mimetic gifts of a high order. They are, simply, empty vessels who indicate to us the kind of fantasies with which they and their superiors in the production hierarchy want us to fill them."[41] Schickel's imagining of stars outside of the realm of labor is representative of much of the pre-1980s scholarship on stars, which tended to evince an understanding of stardom as a product of the studio's labor, if acknowledging that labor was involved in the process at all. Stars have more typically been conceived of as laborless icons, when quite the opposite is true: the work of being a cynosure may be concealed, but it is hardly labor free. In fact movie stars are actors well beyond the limited time they spend in front of the cameras; their obligations to perform and to, in essence, live their lives *as stars* is elided by Schickel's estimation, which is indicative of the tenor of much of the scholarship written about movie stardom.

The *work* of acting seems, in fact, to be one of the more impenetrable aspects of the field, and this certainly points to the fact that stardom is part of a labor division that intends to valorize—and reward—only a small portion of those who collaborate on the moviemaking process. Published in 1941, Murray Ross's pioneering *Stars and Strikes* made some of the first strides in considering the impact of celebrity on Hollywood's corporate and labor practices, attempting to make a certain aspect of star actors' work visible; but only recently have scholars interrogated star studies' assumptions about the relationship between stardom and labor, and about the labor of stardom, with the first significant body of critical work emerging in the late 1980s and early 1990s. Scholarship has so focused upon the celebrity components of stardom, it might be argued, that it has often failed to acknowledge the literal work of the stars themselves.

Despite Alberoni's thesis about the relative disempowerment of stars, many stars have had a significant influence on public opinion as well as on the shape of the industry itself. Stars affected, during the golden age, the studio's treatment of all of its actors, not just the elite few who had been elevated to stardom. Stars played a crucial role in Hollywood's labor history, especially in relation to the rise of the Screen Actors Guild and the battles over the salary control provisions of the National Recovery Administration.[42] These struggles reveal that stars had significant influence over their employers, however limited by the letter of their contracts, which in some cases enabled all unionized actors—ranging from day players to extras, stuntmen, and freelance players—to make gains during the contentious 1930s.

Throughout their existence, then, stars have sought to justify not simply the fruits—which are always highly visible—but the *labor* of their labor. Stars could exert their limited contractual will, typically by refusing to work (James Cagney's, Bette Davis's, and Olivia de Havilland's struggles at Warner Bros. in this vein are well-known). By depriving the studios of their labor, they could hold sway over the moguls and the studios that sought to control them on paper, in turn impacting studio resources and, therefore, production. In one of the best-known and most dramatic incidents of star labor history, escalating salaries and a desire for greater autonomy compelled a collective of stars—the founders of United Artists, Mary Pickford, Charlie Chaplin, Douglas Fairbanks, and the star-director D.W. Griffith—to form their own corporation to accommodate their status and to allow them to profit more directly from their unparalleled audience draw.[43] Star work and our cultural understanding of it, then, have had a significant practical effect on the business and output of Hollywood more generally.

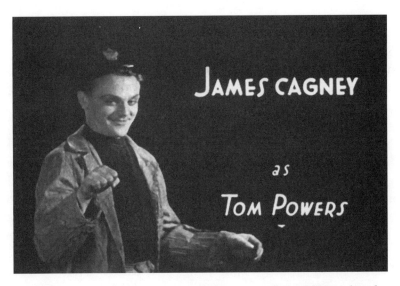

Figure 6.4 James Cagney's legendary efforts to use his celebrity—here he appears in the credit sequence for *The Public Enemy* (William A. Wellman, 1931)—as leverage against what he felt were restrictive long-term contracts at Warner Bros. resulted in years of legal and publicity battles.

The ways that work and stardom intertwine, and the ways that stardom often obscures the nature of labor in the industry, first came to the critical fore in the high-theory dominated 1980s. Certain theorists, most prominently Barry King and later Danae Clark, have attempted to disabuse scholars of the notion that stardom is divorced from traditional conceptualizations of labor. Stardom, the argument goes, is a job that fits into the labor hierarchy of the studio system, albeit one at the apex of that hierarchy. Stardom is rarely discussed as work per se, but the star is part of a much larger matrix of labor, production, distribution, and consumption. King, in fact, argued that "stardom is a strategy of performance that is an adaptive response to the limits and pressures exerted upon acting as a discursive practice in the mainstream cinema," demonstrable by examining "the cultural economy of the human body as a sign; the economy of signification in film; and the economy of the labour market for actors."[44]

However alluring this conceptualization is, performing the study of non-star actors' labor is decidedly more difficult and is especially complicated by the fact that most surviving evidence of actors' labor—films, records, press accounts, biographies, and the like—pertains almost exclusively to the stars, and not to secondary personnel. This is coupled with the unsettling fact that the little "evidence" that does remain cannot help but compound the overvaluation of "the star image." Star studies have thus traditionally neglected the labor issues behind stardom and acting in favor of a model in which a star—one of the chosen few—is studied with nominal attention to the labor required of that position.[45]

It is possible, however, to remedy this state of affairs by unmasking the labor that we often presume is made invisible in the star-making process. Rita Hayworth, as a recent study of labor and stardom by Adrienne McLean suggests, is precisely one of those stars who begs to be understood in the context of stardom as labor. Hayworth's ethnicity was discussed openly in print media throughout her career, as was the occasionally agonizing work—from hairline electrolysis to dance lessons—it took for the actress to become star material. The work of becoming a star, in other words, was foregrounded over the course of Hayworth's career, as were the star's origins. As McLean put it, "contra the assertions of Danae Clark and others about the 'erasing' of an actor's previous identity, name, and personal history during his or her ascent to stardom, the half-Spanish Margarita Carmen Cansino was always present in Rita Hayworth as a star text."[46] Furthermore, the work of stardom is—in Hayworth's and in many other a star's case—revealed to be much more than filmmaking; it is, in fact, the work of star making and star being that is revealed as rigorous here. The contradictions borne by stars—the fantastic with the everyday, the perfect with the flawed, the seeming effortlessness with the effort—are, in some instances, a crucial rhetorical tool used to get audiences to appreciate the work required of becoming a star (not born, one might say, but made).

However, the fact that stardom as labor is in a constant state of retreat in the critical literature merely points up our cultural fascination with stars as they exist *outside* of the realm of the practical, the knowable, the accounted for. Despite its vivid presence every time we watch a film, another manifestation of star labor—film acting, the most seemingly accessible aspect of the star—suffers from a similar elusiveness.[47] Star performances are, after all, the thing that allows stars to exist, and star images, which circulate constantly, are incomplete without films, which are themselves only occasional.[48] We might analyze transitions in performance style—for example, the compensatory acting style of silent film stars or the physically frenetic performance style of the 1920s flapper—but how these conventions relate to ideas of stardom remains undertheorized. Film performers function, as James Naremore pointed out, on multiple levels: "as actors playing theatrical personages, as public figures playing theatrical versions of themselves, and as documentary evidence."[49] Without each element, stars are incomplete, and by analyzing the layers of star performance—diegetic and extratextual, as Dyer advised—we can, at minimum, perceive the construction of the star text. However, the work of the star is often lost in this explication of star textuality, which has become a much more conventional—and concrete, and *seemingly* objective—way of dealing with the signifiers of stardom.

Star Texts: Construction and Consumption

In *Stars*, Dyer handled issues of labor and performance obliquely, favoring an analysis of the star text that has become paradigmatic to the discipline. During the studio era, stars were handled by studio heads, who worked in concert with well-oiled publicity departments to disseminate the star product as efficiently and widely (and profitably) as possible. But stars, both then and now, are of course reliant on a host of other collaborators in the process of becoming and staying: costumers, makeup artists, and directors; the media and the agents who feed stories to them; and, of course, the fans who perceive them in relation to their own imaginations and desires. Although promotion and publicity, as concepts, are often blurred, promotion is that which emanates from the star and his or her "camp," while publicity is that which generates from the media, often (but not always) well outside of the star's (or studio's) control. Through product tie-ins, advertising campaigns, and the like, the Hollywood studios certainly tried to make a science of predicting and guiding spectatorial response through the marketing of their stars. The aim, then, in the scholarly pursuit of the star is largely to understand how "extraordinary" stars are disseminated to the "ordinary" public, how stars are used to compel audiences to behave, largely as consumers.[50] As Andrew Britton pointed out, "the importance of publicity and promotion consists in the fact that they *seek* to define an orientation to the star—not that they succeed."[51] In other words, the construction and consumption of star promotion are necessarily distinct categories, each revealing more, perhaps, about their maker and consumer than about the stars themselves.

Promotion and publicity are not, of course, unique to the motion picture industry, nor to the motion picture star; however, Hollywood in particular refined the processes of selling its product through the promotion of its stars. By the 1930s, all of the major studios had public relations departments that worked to test their up-and-coming stars through print media; to develop mutually beneficial relationships with advertisers; and to keep their current roster of screen favorites in the public eye by writing puff pieces for the newspapers and fan magazines, providing photographs, and working with exhibitors prior to and during the release of new films. Promotion provides the key narrative elements of the star text— stories of youth and hardship, romance and disappointment—that material upon which the public feeds to gain a perceived intimacy with the star. But, as Richard Dyer and many others have argued, this fabrication of knowledge fails to ever bring us closer to the star's "true" identity; rather, it provides consumers with a seductive illusion of proximity, something on which to chew but which can never sustain.

Promotion can take many forms—from advertising to magazine puff pieces to cutting the ribbon at a supermarket. Some scholars, such as Simon Dixon in "Ambiguous Ecologies: Stardom's Domestic Mise-en-Scène," have used the nuances of the star text to study the attempts at narrative cohesiveness of star marketing in the golden age, and the ways that these signs are often organized around gender and ideology. Dixon's title refers to the "part dwelling, part location" nature of the star home in the golden age, with the star residing in a place that might be defined somewhere between "privacy and exhibition."[52] Mining the star home-tour issues of *Photoplay* and *Architectural Digest*, Dixon rethought the star home in the context of star exhibition, here in the case of prominent male stars such as Edward G. Robinson and James Cagney. The star home evolves out of the demands of set design intended to create a mise-en-scène reflective of the mood and message of the unfolding "real life" narrative at hand. A star's home is less a "place" and more a "location," ready for public display.[53] Like other elements of the star's life during the studio era, the star's home and home life become part of the exhibition of personality, part of the marketing strategy worked out by publicists, the stars, and the media.

As a twentieth-century phenomenon, Hollywood stars were made to appear a new breed of American success story: luxury was compensation for a life lived in the spotlight, one begun humbly if not poorly—or so the story usually went— suggesting the everyman or everywoman lurking within the mansions and beneath the furs. Constructing stars as symbols of the success of the American dream was both a political necessity, more urgently at some times than others, and a practical means for sustaining the desirability and likeability of what were both immensely valuable and volatile assets. As Lary May has put it, stars were intended to be "the models, not the enemies, for the middle class," and therefore needed to appear both extraordinary and yet not incompatible with the ranks of the everyday.[54] But this goal was no assurance of a sympathetic relationship between stars and the public. The star narrative—well documented in the media—includes the acquisition of the signifiers of true stardom: the houses, cars, lifestyle, and so forth. It also typically includes the trappings and failures, the squandering and the excesses, the divorces and the scandals, the depression and the anxiety, even the murders, overdoses, and suicides. The moral of the story is usually that stardom is no guarantor of happiness, an ironic moral given the fact that the star system can be understood as the "basic leverage for audience involvement," as Andrew Tudor put it.[55] Perhaps that is the key to stardom's ambiguous success: it is at once a seemingly ideal and flawless condition, and simultaneously nearly always on the verge of crumbling into ruin, seeming to signify caution for the rest of us out there in the dark to stay clear of such devastating and frequently humiliating twists of fate.

However divergent and frequently conflicting, the audience's reactions to stardom contain perhaps the most crucial residue of the efficacy and effects of stardom. Despite this, the media audience presents a host of problems for the scholar of celebrity. In her introduction to *The Adoring Audience*, Lisa Lewis asked why fans have been overlooked or dismissed as research subjects given their status as "the most visible and identifiable of audiences."[56] The answer resides both in the difficulty of this kind of research and its inherent flaws. Some of the earliest academic work in this area, which appeared in the 1970s, when psychoanalytic and feminist scholars, in particular, began to theorize the nature of spectatorship and the spectator's relationship to stars and the roles they played, sought to avoid the problem of the "real audience" by creating a theoretical one. Laura Mulvey's "Visual Pleasure and Narrative Cinema," which used psychoanalysis alongside textual analysis to produce an idea of theoretical—and necessarily speculative—spectatorship to understand how certain female stars and characters signified within Hollywood narratives, sparked a wave of such criticism. Although perhaps more about the psychosexual politics of roles than about the stars themselves, Mulvey's argument about the patriarchal, punishing nature of classical Hollywood cinema makes certain assumptions about stardom that fail to account for the extratextual and lived-body nature of stardom that would later inform the audience work of such scholars as Jackie Stacey.

Indeed, work in reception can be approached through a variety of methodologies, ranging from the theoretical (Mulvey), to the empirical (Jackie Stacey), to elements of the former combined with the study of archival and historical documents (Miriam Hansen and Gaylyn Studlar, the latter practicing a kind of historical archaeology in *This Mad Masquerade*). Dealing with actual audience members and their memories and experiences of film stardom is perhaps the most seductive and most problematic of these approaches. The preeminent study using audience responses to stardom—as opposed to theoretical formulations about spectatorship and reception, or interpretations of promotions aimed at audiences—is Jackie Stacey's *Star Gazing* (1994). Stacey, a British professor of sociology, attempted to remedy the paucity of attention given to Hollywood stars by feminist scholars outside of textual analysis by polling more than three hundred British women filmgoers, located through advertisements in two popular women's magazines, about their memories of Hollywood stars during the 1940s and 1950s. Audience research comes with its own difficulties—audience memories are especially subject to any number of empirical flaws (selectiveness, forgetfulness, etc.)— of which Stacey is fully aware. But the results yielded valuable revelations, and Stacey used them to make an argument about "white British women's fantasies about glamour, Americanness and about themselves."[57]

Stacey's study interweaves filmgoers' responses with analysis and theory, although the theory and the practice sometimes appear to be at odds with each other. Using repeated references by her respondents to the careers of Bette Davis and Joan Crawford, for example, Stacey demonstrated that ideals such as confidence and worldliness were frequently considered to be crucial elements of these star texts, so that these stars were not just physical ideals but behavioral ideals. Stacey concluded that "powerful female stars often played characters in punishing patriarchal narratives, where the woman is either killed off, or married, or both, but these spectators do not seem to select this aspect of their films to write about. Instead, the qualities of confidence and power are remembered as offering female spectators the pleasure of participation in qualities they themselves lacked and desired."[58] This interpretive terrain is markedly different from that produced by the generation of theorists before Stacey. The most valuable aspect of Stacey's study is her use of "lived" examples to rethink theoretical ideas such as psychoanalytic models of identification.

But Stacey's work, an exemplar of audience research, is not without its flaws. Bruce Babington, in *British Stars and Stardom* (2001), severely criticized Stacey for neglecting British stars in favor of Hollywood stars, and especially for ignoring responses she received to questions about British celebrities in order to emphasize respondents' adulation of Hollywood stars. Although Babington read this as symptomatic of a larger problem with British film historians favoring American stars over British, he was most irked by Stacey's repression, of sorts, of her own respondents' affinities for such notable British performers as Margaret Lockwood. What Stacey attempted to do, however imperfectly, was to assess the processes and consequences of star consumption: how those on-screen and offscreen texts are digested by those who opt to consume them.

Consumption is one of the central theoretical conceits in the study of stardom and fandom, that element of the star system on which its functionality depends. Because stars cannot simply be plucked from the populace and imposed on a public, despite the numerous efforts to do so, they must be made into something so desirable that it elicits mass interest and participation. This cannot be achieved solely in the brief moments of exhibition, in part because that is an exchange with very limited elements of audience participation and self-involvement. To compensate for this, the industry developed modes of interactive culture—fan magazines, star search contests, fan correspondence—with which to encourage a more engaged and energized fan experience, ultimately fostering a cumulative relationship between fan and future ticket buyer. As Miriam Hansen explained, "film spectatorship epitomized a tendency that strategies of advertising and consumer culture had been pursuing for decades: the stimulation of new needs and new desires through visual fascination."[59] Spectatorship was, in other words, recast as consumption, and this consumption revolved almost entirely around the stars.

For example, in the 1930s, prior to a film's release, photographs or sketches of the fashions worn by actresses were used by manufacturers so that advertising and merchandising tie-ins would be awaiting female consumers at the time of the film's premiere.[60] This, of course, served multiple purposes, the main function of which was to make the star all the more consumable even offscreen. Mass-marketed fashions or even homemade copies allowed "normal" people to engage with a tangible element of stardom, to feel intimate with those heavenly bodies if only in a symbolic way. These interactions were always of a highly personal nature, for the act of consumption—be it in the theater or with a fan magazine, a knockoff dress, or even a star-endorsed beauty product—brings the corporate construction of the star text home, individualizes that which was always intended for the masses. Star consumption is, therefore, an act imbued with politics of a personal nature. Elements of race, gender, sexuality, class, and ethnicity come to the fore in such cinematic and post-cinematic acts, and this foregrounding produces some of the more exciting and important territory for star studies to explore.

Identity Politics

Acknowledging, of course, that it is a gross oversimplification and that many other mechanisms are of equal importance, the "subject" of star studies is fascinatingly and frustratingly "human," in spite of industrial attempts to regulate that humanity. As the previous section suggests, in fact, the star system as such grew out of the industry's desire to mediate between star bodies and spectatorial bodies, to maximize control, to minimize loss. Humanity, however, is notoriously unruly, and in the 1970s theoretical and critical attempts to account for the points of rupture began to circulate within the field, growing in some ways out of literary models for reader response and a newly invigorated interest in the politics of identity. Guiding many of these approaches is a central question still swirling around attempts to negotiate the Hollywood product: in its highly suspect mode of "universal" address, in its regulated and equally limited creation of ideal spectators who will behave ideally, what are we to do with the uninvited and the alienated? Similarly, what is at stake when the calculations go haywire, when even the ideal spectator

Figure 6.5 Operating well outside of Hollywood's economic sphere, Oscar Micheaux cultivated his own star system with regular performers such as Evelyn Preer, who appeared in a number of Micheaux films and is pictured here in the role of Sylvia Landry from *Within Our Gates* (1919).

misbehaves, or behaves in a manner that is less than ideal? The questions are as difficult to answer as they are important.

It is impossible to adequately conceive of stardom without understanding the ways that identity politics inform star making, marketing, and consumption. It will not come as a surprise, for example, that black actors were largely excluded from stardom in mainstream Hollywood throughout the golden age. Dominant racial politics informed casting, which relegated African Americans to roles as servants, slaves, and entertainers. Race films—directed, for example, by Oscar Micheaux or Spencer Williams—had their own star constellations, but these films did not circulate widely outside of the racially segregated exhibition practices of the Jim Crow era. Karen Alexander has argued that, for black people, cinema is "iconically impotent," but this fails to account for the complexity of raced spectatorship, and the contradictory appeal of the white Hollywood star system.[61] As James Baldwin made clear in his meditation on his own cinematic coming of age, *The Devil Finds Work*, the awe of seeing movies as a black spectator in the golden age is necessarily mingled with the shame generated by Hollywood's largely retrograde racial representation.

In the 1960s, black stars were allowed to ascend in Hollywood as part of an effort to recapture a steadily declining box office, resulting in a slew of mannered civil rights conscious films such as *Guess Who's Coming to Dinner?* (Stanley Kramer, 1967) starring Sidney Poitier, and markedly less polite films such as *Sweet Sweetback's Baadasssss Song* (1971), starring and directed by Melvin Van Peebles.

Race—not unlike gender, ethnicity, sexuality, and class—informs every element of filmmaking and spectatorship, influencing the business and the politics of representation and reception. Richard Dyer's chapter on Paul Robeson's stardom during the 1924– 45 period in *Heavenly Bodies* asks a series of questions that still require scholarly answering within this context, and which might be applied to any of the categories of identity listed above: "How did the period permit black stardom? What were the qualities this black person could be taken to embody, that could catch on in a society where there had never been a black star of this magnitude? What was the fit between the parameters of what black image the society could tolerate and the particular qualities that Robeson could be taken to embody? Where was the give in the ideological system? . . . What was the price that had to be paid for a black person to become such a star?"[62]

As Dyer acknowledged in his case studies involving race, gender, and sexual identity, all of his subjects experienced alienation from their star identities, which functioned to reproduce ideas about race, gender, sexuality, and class with which their performers were often at odds. Both performers and spectators, however, can behave in unruly ways, undermining the seeming efficacy of dominant forms of representation. As Andrea Weiss pointed out in " 'A Queer Feeling When I Look at You': Hollywood Stars and Lesbian Spectatorship in the 1930s," the actual sexual identity of actresses in the golden age was less important than the way they were perceived by audiences, allowing for—in Weiss's example—lesbian spectators to read into and beyond the films they were watching. Weiss took the kind of theoretical work done by Mulvey in a different direction to argue that gossip and rumor so inform "the unrecorded history of the gay subculture," that "what the public knew, or what the gay subculture knew, about these stars' 'real lives' cannot be separated from their 'star image.' "[63] Moments like that of Marlene Dietrich kissing a woman in *Morocco* (1930) have become iconic lesbian moments claimed by an audience who refuses to obey the narrative provided to them, which almost always recuperates such on-screen deviancies within the context of heterosexuality (or, I would add, comedy). Weiss saw spectatorship as less bound up in a singular interpretation of filmic narrative, opening up the possibility for subversive readings of movie characters and stars based on personal spectatorial issues of identity and, in turn, identification.

Such subversive readings can go beyond on-screen performance and spectatorship to inform the writing of history as well. If race and sexuality are operative forces in the often-suppressed narratives of film production, so too is gender. We may revisit history through the lens of a star's identity politics to see, for example, Ida Lupino's tenure as one of the studio system's only female directors directly as an outgrowth of her status as a frustrated Warner Bros. star, an actress trapped by a studio favoring male stars and genres. As Lupino navigated the publicity landscape as a novelty woman director in the late 1940s and early 1950s, her former star status enabled a public banter that, in turn, facilitated her career move into the strictly male domain of directing.

Looking to an earlier moment in film history, Jennifer Bean in "Technologies of Early Stardom and the Extraordinary Body" attempted to remedy "the conspicuous absence of early women stars" in the scholarly histories by turning to "a pantheon of unusual female stars collectively known as 'those daring missies of the movies.' "[64] Bean claimed that the cinema's first "en masse celebrities"—Pearl White is an exemplar, but there were dozens of adventurous female heroines that were, among other things, serial stars in the teens—should compel us to reassess the birth of stardom: "Rather than a fixed galaxy of stars associated with 'great' auteurs and the bid for bourgeois respectability," Bean asserted, "we find an entirely different constellation of figures associated with thrilling modern film genres and praised for their superlative physical and psychical stamina."[65] These adventurous actresses do not fit neatly into the chronology of stardom, but it is their incongruity—mingling athleticism with beauty, bravery with feminine charms, fantasy with realism—that suggests a new framework through which we can more perceptively understand the layered variety of stardom's earliest years. The suppressed elements of star history may be resuscitated by looking to the past through the politically aware lenses afforded by advances in theories of identity that have evolved over the course of the past forty years.

The myriad variations on identity politics, in other words, can be a productive lens through which to view star history, politics, and spectatorship. It is impossible to view stardom, as Richard Dyer and many others have noted, without an awareness of the personal implications wrought by that institution for the lives and psyches of a variety of spectators with widely divergent aspirations. The political urgency of understanding stardom in these contexts should be apparent if only because stardom is always geared toward the masses and is therefore necessarily reflective, however problematically and untidily, of mass desire. Difference is, as my earlier discussion of Rita Hayworth suggests, always mediated in the process of star making, sometimes in surprising ways. Stars can and should be used as cultural markers that enable the mapping of personal politics. Such critical work allows us to see the variable resonances of stardom as they are exchanged across the lines that, at least in theory, demarcate personal identities.

A Discipline Unbound

As should be evident from even the preceding and highly selective cartographic history, what might best be thought of as the formative base for celebrity studies has been anything but monolithic. Richard Dyer, who occupies the center—but not, by any means, the beginning—of this history, pulled together several key threads within the nascent field in an organized, critical, and highly influential manner. The seductiveness of his model and a nearly decade-long need to reca-pitulate or take issue with it yielded numerous subdisciplinary pursuits, which fork out from Dyer's understanding of stardom as a phenomenon of both production and consumption. Star studies has made its longest and most revolutionary strides in the post-*Stars* years, which saw a shift both in the theoretical models employed and, perhaps even more crucially, in the objects of inquiry itself. Recent work in the field has continued to unearth neglected elements of celebrity, to fill in the blanks—the neglected sites—of stardom's history and legacy. Subdisciplines revolving around issues of race, nation, sexuality, gender, labor, and audience reception have become especially energized sites of inquiry in this larger project of understanding stardom's past and future.

There are still significant areas in the field that require scholarly attention, as has been pointed out throughout this essay. Digital technology and the Internet remain perhaps the most undertheorized of stardom's recent developments. These technologies have radically altered the possibilities of star performance, which no longer needs to be tied to a living actor being filmed before a camera. Star mar-keting and publicity have changed as well. A new kind of celebrity self-mediation exists today—celebrities can, of course, have their own Web sites on which they may post competing versions of stories being reported in the press, daily updates, photographs, and the like—and we seem to find ourselves in an era in which the control of star images is even more decentralized and uncontrollable than ever before.[66] Anyone—fans, detractors, publicists, corporate sponsors—can create a Web site or post information or images about a star's life. A Google search for Julia Roberts, for example, finds hundreds of fan sites (some claiming to be the "best," the "official," or the "unauthorized"—see, for example, www.aboutjulia.com), photo archives, links to eBay, where Julia Roberts memorabilia is being auctioned off, chat rooms, promotional links asking quiz questions about whether or not fans like the names Roberts bestowed upon her children, domestic grosses on her films, Julia Roberts screensavers, archives of interviews and quotes, tips on how to make your hair look as good as Julia's, a Julia Roberts essay about the books that inspire her from Oprah Winfrey's "Oprah's Books" pages, and so on.

Absurd? Yes. Harmless? Perhaps. There are consequences of overinvesting certain members of our culture with collective fantasies and ideals, as well as re-warding them with material gains of such seemingly impossible magnitude. If heroes rise to the top by doing deeds worthy of our admiration, stars have much less to keep them perched on the summit, with consequences both for them and for their admirers and detractors. Stardom has often afforded a kind of permissibility for those who attain it to behave in ways that are outside of the bounds of the rest of society, fostering a disparity in which "they" do not have to act like the rest of "us." While it is unfair and decidedly untrue to claim that this inequality has gotten worse than it was twenty, or forty, or sixty years ago, it is reasonable to argue that the most dramatic consequences of such elevation are clearly bound to the seemingly untouchable, however illusorily, place we have, over the course of the past century, put our stars.

Now more than ever we seem to be at a crossroads in terms of our understanding of the unprecedented and multiple mediations of celebrity with which we are confronted on a daily basis. As my brief discussion of Stone's *Natural Born Killers* with which this essay opened should indicate, celebrity itself appears to have mutated to a kind of boiling point. With the collapse of the studio system in the 1950s and 1960s in concert with the arrival and proliferation of television, video, tabloids, and the Internet as the major creators, conduits, and diffusers of celebrity, we can no longer point to the kind of localized, concerted efforts to construct star images that were present in the golden era. Today celebrity matters precisely because it reveals so many different things about culture and political climate, the entertainment and information industries that produce that culture, and the individuals who consume and otherwise react to that culture. The discipline of star studies has a kind of boundlessness that is both fascinating and frustrating. Oliver Stone and his improbably like-minded predecessors—Boorstin, Adorno, Horkheimer, Morin—suggest that our overevaluation of the unextraordinary, or even the shamefully unworthy, has placed us in a precarious position in which reality and decency are slipping quickly out of our grasp, lost in a flurry of meaningless celebration and mediation. If they are right, then there is more urgency than ever to the task of star studies.

NOTES

1. Christine Gledhill, ed., *Stardom: Industry of Desire* (New York: Routledge, 1991), xiii.

2. This is not to say that Sandow and Irwin were recognized as "movie stars" in the 1890s. As Richard deCordova pointed out, "although personalities from other fields (particularly politics) were presented in documentary 'views' from a very early date, they were not in any strict sense of the term movie stars." Richard deCordova, *Picture Personalities: The Emergence of the Star System in America* (Chicago: University of Illinois Press, 1990), 23. Having said this, it is still the case that Thomas Edison and Edwin S. Porter turned to known personalities, performers, and public figures for a number of their early kinetograph films, motivated on some level by certain assumptions about what might appeal to the earliest moving-image audiences.

3. Leo Braudy, *The Frenzy of Renown* (New York: Vintage Books, 1986), 554.

4. Daniel Boorstin, *The Image* (New York: Atheneum, 1962), 57.

5. Ibid., 158.

6. Gledhill, *Stardom*, xiv.

7. Francesco Alberoni, "The Powerless 'Elite': Theory and Sociological Research on the Phenomenon of the Stars," trans. Denis McQuail, in *Sociology of Mass Communications*, ed. Denis McQuail (Middlesex: Penguin, 1972), 79.

8. For recent work on the relationship between celebrity and scandal, gossip, and tabloid culture, see Elizabeth Bird, *For Enquiring Minds: A Cultural Study of Supermarket Tabloids* (Knoxville: University of Tennessee Press, 1992); Gail Collins, *Scorpion Tongues: Gossip, Celebrity and American Politics* (New York: William Morrow, 1998); and Adrienne McLean and David Cook, *Headline Hollywood* (New Brunswick, NJ: Rutgers University Press, 2001).

9. See, for example, Terry Ramsaye, *A Million and One Nights: A History of the Motion Picture Industry* (New York: Simon and Schuster, 1964; originally published in 1925); Benjamin Hampton, *A History of the American Film Industry* (New York: Dover, 1970; originally published in 1931 as *A History of the Movies*); Herbert Blumer, *Movies and Conduct* (New York: Macmillan, 1933); Lewis Jacobs, *The Rise of the American Film* (New York: Teachers College Press, 1939); Leo Rosten, *Hollywood: The Movie Colony, The Movie Makers* (New York: Harcourt, Brace, 1941); and Hortense Powdermaker, *Hollywood the Dream Factory: An Anthropologist Looks at the Movie-Makers* (Boston: Little, Brown, 1950).

10. For example, see Jackie Stacey, *Star Gazing* (New York: Routledge, 1994); Andrea Weiss, " 'A Queer Feeling When I Look at You': Hollywood Stars and Lesbian Spectators in the 1930s," in Gledhill, *Stardom*; and Richard Dyer, *Stars* (London: British Film Institute, 1982; originally published in 1979).

11. Boorstin, *The Image*, 47.

12. Ibid., 64.

13. Ibid., 154–160.

14. Jane Gaines, Charles Eckert, John Ellis, Christine Gledhill, and Miriam Hansen are among those who made substantial contributions to star studies in this period. Their articles and books appear in this essay's bibliography.

15. Dyer, *Stars*, 4. A number of authors after Dyer, such as Robert Allen, have applied Dyer's guiding methodology to approach the study of a particular star, in Allen's case for an insightful reading of Joan Crawford. Robert Allen, "The Role of the Star in Film History," in *Film Theory and Criticism*, ed. Leo Braudy (New York: Oxford, 1999). Still others have critiqued Dyer's methodologies, including Pam Cook in her critical response to *Stars*, "Star Signs," *Screen* 20 (Winter 1979–80): 80–88; Danae Clark in her labor-centered critiques, which include a plea to re-term "star studies" "actor studies" to reduce the "elitism of text-based analysis concerned only with stars": *Negotiating Hollywood: The Cultural Politics of Actors' Labor* (Minneapolis: University of Minnesota, 1995), 119; and Barry King, who alleged that Dyer failed "to define stardom as a form of agency deriving from the site of production," which "mirrors the governing imperative of the capitalist media": "The Star and the Commodity: Notes Towards a Performance Theory of Stardom," *Cultural Studies* 1 (May 1987): 148.

16. The histories Staiger referred to are by David Cook (in his 1981 *A History of Narrative Film*), Lewis Jacobs (in *The Rise of the American Film*, 1968), Benjamin Hampton (in his 1931 *History of the American Film Industry*), Anthony Slide (in "The Evolution of the Film Star," 1974), and Richard deCordova (in a conference paper given at a 1982 Ohio University Film Conference).

17. Janet Staiger, "Seeing Stars," *Velvet Light Trap* 20 (1983): 13.

18. deCordova, *Picture Personalities*, 6.

19. Joshua Gamson, *Claims to Fame: Celebrity in Contemporary America* (Berkeley: University of California Press, 1994), 5.

20. P. David Marshall, *Celebrity and Power: Fame in Contemporary Culture* (Minneapolis: University of Minnesota Press, 1997), ix.

21. Tom Gunning has theorized these early years in terms of a cinema of attractions, suggesting that early moviegoers went to theaters precisely to see events, novelties, spectacles, things that would excite their curiosity along the lines of what they might see at a fairground. Tom Gunning, " 'Now You See It, Now You Don't': The Temporality of the Cinema of Attractions," in *Silent Film* (New Brunswick, NJ: Rutgers University Press, 1996), 73.

22. For more on this turn-of-the-century environment, see Charles Ponce de Leon, *Self-Exposure: Human-Interest Journalism and the Emergence of Celebrity in America, 1890– 1949* (Chapel Hill: University of North Carolina Press, 2002), 33–44.

23. See Raymond Williams's "The Romantic Artist," in *Culture and Society: 1780–1950* (New York: Columbia University Press, 1958), and Leo Lowenthal's *Literature, Popular Culture, and Society* (Upper Saddle River, NJ: Prentice Hall, 1961) for more on the evolution of mass culture and its relationship to fame, particularly of the literary variety, in the eighteenth and nineteenth centuries.

24. Jib Fowles, *Starstruck: Celebrity Performers and the American Public* (Washington, DC: Smithsonian Institution, 1992), 10.

25. Eileen Bowser, *The Transformation of Cinema: 1907–1915* (New York: Simon and Schuster, 1990), 106.

26. Bowser pointed out that a May 1909 film, Vitagraph's *Oliver Twist*, uses a credit title "years before they were commonly used" when the actress Elita Proctor Otis first appears in the film. Ibid., 107.

27. "Photographs of Moving Picture Actors: A New Method of Lobby Advertising," *Moving Picture World*, January 5, 1910, 50.

28. "The Actor—Likewise the Actress," *Moving Picture World*, November 12, 1910, 1099.

29. Charles Musser noted this date in "The Changing Status of the Actor," in *Before Hollywood: Turn-of-the-Century Films from American Archives* (New York: American Federation of Arts, 1986).

30. deCordova, *Picture Personalities*, 98.

31. Gorham Kindem and Richard deCordova have separately documented their futile searches for this evidence.

32. deCordova, *Picture Personalities*, 55.

33. Anthony Slide demonstrated that despite allegations that the Biograph Company refused to name its stars, the popular press was writing about its actresses by name at least since 1911.

34. See Bowser, *Transformation of Cinema*, 113–114, 171, 225–227.

35. See Geoffrey Macnab, *Searching for Stars: Stardom and Screen Acting in British Cinema* (New York: Cassell, 2000), 173.

36. See Bruce Babington, ed., *British Stars and Stardom from Alma Taylor to Sean Connery* (New York: Manchester University Press, 2001).

37. For an account of the French star system, see Ginnette Vincendeau, *Stars and Stardom in French Cinema* (London: Continuum, 2000).

38. See Vijay Mishra's *Bollywood Cinema: Temples of Desire* (New York: Routledge, 2002), 126.

39. See Behroze Gandhy and Rosie Thomas, "Three Indian Film Stars," in Gledhill, *Stardom*. Originally published in *Wide Angle* 6 (1985): 108–109.

40. See Chris Perriam, *Stars and Masculinity in Spanish Cinema: From Banderas to Bardem* (New York: Oxford, 2003), 2–3.

41. Richard Schickel, *The Stars* (New York: Dial Press, 1962), 16.

42. For more on this, see Ross's *Stars and Strikes: The Unionization of Hollywood* (New York: Columbia University Press, 1941).

43. Tino Balio's *United Artists: The Company Built by the Stars* (Madison: University of Wisconsin Press, 1976) discusses the birth of this company and its relationship to its founders' celebrity status.

44. Barry King, "Articulating Stardom," *Screen* 26 (1985), 27.

45. Danae Clark challenged this tendency in *Negotiating Hollywood* (1995) by distancing herself from the concept of star studies to "destabilize the concept of 'star' and to interrogate the very premises upon which 'star studies' traditionally rests" (ix) and by turning her critical gaze toward "the politics of actors' labor." Echoing, in some ways, Laura Mulvey's influential 1975 psychoanalytic treatise—which sought the "destruction of pleasure as a radical weapon" (15) to foreground the masochism of female spectatorship—Clark presented a provocative rethinking of stars as *the* privileged site of scholarly interest, which consigns "workers further down in the labor hierarchy" to the neglected, invisible place capitalism intends them to occupy. Mulvey, "Visual Pleasure and Narrative Cinema," in *Visual and Other Pleasures* (Bloomington: Indiana University Press, 1989), xii. Originally published in 1975.

46. Adrienne McLean, *Being Rita Hayworth: Labor, Identity, and Hollywood Stardom* (New Brunswick, NJ: Rutgers University Press, 2004), 11.

47. Charles Affron's gracefully written *Star Acting: Gish, Garbo, Davis* (New York: E.P. Dutton, 1977) is one of the first contributions to the critical literature on star performance. Jeremy Butler's more recent *Star Texts: Image and Performance in Film and Television* (Detroit, MI: Wayne State University Press, 1991) anthology includes writings about acting from film and theater directors, playwrights, screen theorists, and interpretive film scholars that develop multiple angles from which to approach the subject, and to suggest directions for future work in the field. Roberta Pearson's *Eloquent Gestures: The Transformation of Performance Style in the Griffith Biograph Films* (Berkeley: University of California Press, 1992) addresses silent screen acting, especially of the melodramatic variety, and Robert Sklar's *City Boys* (Princeton, NJ: Princeton University Press, 1992) analyzes performance, typecasting, and publicity in relation to three male Warner Bros. stars, James Cagney, Humphrey Bogart, and John Garfield.

48. For more on this, see John Ellis, *Visible Fictions: Cinema: Television: Video* (London: Routledge, 1982).

49. James Naremore, "The Performance Frame," in *Star Texts: Image and Performance in Film and Television*, ed. Jeremy Butler (Detroit, MI: Wayne State University Press, 1988), 108.

50. John Ellis pointed out the dual function of the star image as both "an invitation to cinema" (a form of advertising) and an embodiment of "an impossible paradox: people who are both ordinary and extraordinary" (an ideological function) (97).

51. Andrew Britton, *Katharine Hepburn: Star as Feminist* (New York: Columbia University Press, 2003), 15.

52. Simon Dixon, "Ambiguous Ecologies: Stardom's Domestic Mise-en-Scène," *Cinema Journal* 42.3 (Winter 2003), 81.

53. Ibid., 82.

54. Lary May, *Screening Out the Past: The Birth of Mass Culture and the Motion Picture Industry* (New York: Oxford University Press, 1980), 233.

55. Andrew Tudor, *Image and Influence* (New York: St. Martin's Press, 1974).

56. Lisa Lewis, *The Adoring Audience: Fan Culture and Popular Media* (New York: Routledge, 1992), 1.

57. Jackie Stacey, *Star Gazing* (New York: Routledge, 1994), 17.

58. Ibid., 158.

59. Miriam Hansen, *Babel and Babylon: Spectatorship in American Silent Film* (Cambridge, MA: Harvard University Press, 1991), 13.

60. For more on this, see Charles Eckert, "The Carole Lombard in Macy's Window," in *Fabrications: Costumes and the Female Body*, ed. Jane Gaines and Charlotte Herzog (New York: AFI, 1990); and Jane Gaines and Charlotte Herzog, "Puffed Sleeves Before Tea-Time: Joan Crawford, Adrian and Women Audiences," in Gledhill, *Stardom*; originally published in 1985.

61. Karen Alexander, "Fatal Beauties: Black Women in Hollywood," in Gledhill, *Stardom*, 54.

62. Richard Dyer, *Heavenly Bodies* (New York: Routledge, 2004), 65–66.

63. Weiss, " 'A Queer Feeling,' " 283, 286.

64. Jennifer Bean, "Technologies of Early Stardom and the Extraordinary Body," in *A Feminist Reader in Early Cinema*, ed. Jennifer Bean and Diane Negra (Durham, NC: Duke University Press, 2002), 404.

65. Ibid., 407.

66. Paul McDonald sees the Internet not as a threat to the star system, but rather as a decentralized—and, I would add, democratized—continuation of star promotion. *The Star System: Hollywood's Production of Popular Identities* (London: Wallflower, 2000), 114–115.

BIBLIOGRAPHY

Adorno, Theodor, and Max Horkheimer. "The Culture Industry: Enlightenment as Mass Deception." *Dialectic of Enlightenment*. New York: Continuum, 1987. Trans. John Cumming from original publication, 1944.

Affron, Charles. *Star Acting: Gish, Garbo, Davis*. New York: E.P. Dutton, 1977.

Alberoni, Francesco. "The Powerless 'Elite': Theory and Sociological Research on the Phenomenon of the Stars." Trans. Denis McQuail. *Sociology of Mass Communications*. Ed. Denis McQuail. Middlesex: Penguin, 1972, 75–98. Originally published in *Ikon*, 12.40 (1962).

Alexander, Karen. "Fatal Beauties: Black Women in Hollywood." *Stardom: Industry of Desire*. Ed. Christine Gledhill. London: Routledge, 1991.

Allen, Jeanne. "The Film Viewer as Consumer." *Quarterly Review of Film Studies* 5.4 (1980): 481–501.

Allen, Robert. "The Role of the Star in Film History." *Film Theory and Criticism*. Ed. Leo Braudy. New York: Oxford University Press, 1999.

Allen, Robert, and Douglas Gomery. *Film History: Theory and Practice.* New York: Knopf, 1985.

Anderson, Mark Lynn. "Shooting Star: Understanding Wallace Reid and His Public." *Headline Hollywood.* Ed. Adrienne McLean and David Cook. New Brunswick, NJ: Rutgers University Press, 2001, 83–106.

Auerbach, Jonathan. *Male Call: Becoming Jack London.* Durham, NC: Duke University Press, 1996.

Babington, Bruce, ed. *British Stars and Stardom from Alma Taylor to Sean Connery.* New York: Manchester University Press, 2001.

Balio, Tino. *United Artists: The Company Built by the Stars.* Madison: University of Wisconsin Press, 1976.

Barbas, Samantha. *Movie Crazy: Fans, Stars, and the Cult of Celebrity.* New York: Palgrave, 2001.

Barthes, Roland. "The Face of Garbo." *Mythologies.* Trans. Jonathan Cape. New York: Hill and Wang, 1972. Originally published in 1957.

Basinger, Jeanine. *Silent Stars.* New York: Alfred A. Knopf, 1999.

Bean, Jennifer. "Technologies of Early Stardom and the Extraordinary Body." *A Feminist Reader in Early Cinema.* Ed. Jennifer Bean and Diane Negra. Durham, NC: Duke University Press, 2002, 404–443.

Bingham, Dennis. *Acting Male: Masculinities in the Films of James Stewart, Jack Nicholson, and Clint Eastwood.* New Brunswick, NJ: Rutgers University Press, 1994.

Bird, S. Elizabeth. *For Enquiring Minds: A Cultural Study of Supermarket Tabloids.* Knoxville: University of Tennessee Press, 1992.

Blumer, Herbert. *Movies and Conduct.* New York: Macmillan, 1933.

Boorstin, Daniel J. *The Image.* New York: Atheneum, 1962.

Bowers, Q. David. "Souvenir Postcards and the Development of the Star System, 1912–1914." *Film History* 3 (1989): 39–45.

Bowser, Eileen. *The Transformation of Cinema: 1907–1915.* New York: Simon and Schuster, 1990.

Braudy, Leo. *The Frenzy of Renown.* New York: Vintage Books, 1986.

Britton, Andrew. *Katharine Hepburn: Star as Feminist.* New York: Columbia University Press: 2003. Originally published in 1984.

Butler, Jeremy, ed. *Star Texts: Image and Performance in Film and Television.* Detroit, MI: Wayne State University Press, 1991.

Byars, Jackie. "The Prime of Miss Kim Novak: Struggle Over the Feminine in the Star Image." *The Other Fifties: Interrogating Midcentury American Icons.* Ed. Joel Foreman. Chicago: University of Illinois Press, 1997.

Clark, Danae. *Negotiating Hollywood: The Cultural Politics of Actors' Labor.* Minneapolis: University of Minnesota Press, 1995.

———. "The Subject of Acting." *Stars: The Film Reader.* Ed. Lucy Fischer and Marcia Landy. New York: Routledge, 2004, 13–28.

Collins, Gail. *Scorpion Tongues: Gossip, Celebrity, and American Politics.* New York: William Morrow, 1998.

Cook, David. *A History of Narrative Film.* New York: Norton, 1981.

Cook, Pam. *The Cinema Book.* New York: Pantheon, 1985.

———. "Star Signs." *Screen* 20 (Winter 1979–80): 80–88.

deCordova, Richard. "The Emergence of the Star System in America." *Stardom: Industry of Desire.* Ed. Christine Gledhill. New York: Routledge, 1991, 17–30.

————. *Picture Personalities: The Emergence of the Star System in America*. Chicago: University of Illinois Press, 1990.

de Leon, Charles Ponce. *Self-Exposure: Human-Interest Journalism and the Emergence of Celebrity in America, 1890–1940*. Chapel Hill: University of North Carolina Press, 2002.

Dixon, Simon. "Ambiguous Ecologies: Stardom's Domestic Mise-en-Scène." *Cinema Journal* 42.3 (Winter 2003): 81–100.

Dyer, Richard. *Heavenly Bodies*. New York: Routledge, 2004. Originally published in 1986.

————. *Stars*. London: British Film Institute, 1982. Originally published in 1979.

Eckert, Charles. "The Carole Lombard in Macy's Window." *Fabrications: Costumes and the Female Body*. Ed. Jane Gaines and Charlotte Herzog. New York: AFI, 1990, 100–121.

————. "Shirley Temple and the House of Rockefeller." *Stardom: Industry of Desire*. Ed. Christine Gledhill. London: Routledge, 1991. Originally published in *Jump Cut* 2 (July–August 1974).

Ellis, John. "Star/Industry/Image." *Star Signs: Papers from a Weekend Workshop*. London: BFI Education, 1982.

————. *Visible Fictions: Cinema: Television: Video*. London: Routledge, 1982.

Finney, Angus. *The State of European Cinema: A New Dose of Reality*. London: Cassell, 1996.

Fischer, Lucy, and Marcia Landy. *Stars: The Film Reader*. New York: Routledge, 2004.

Fowles, Jib. *Starstruck: Celebrity Performers and the American Public*. Washington, DC: Smithsonian Institution Press, 1992.

Fuller, Kathryn. *At the Picture Show: Small-Town Audiences and the Creation of Movie Fan Culture*. Washington, DC: Smithsonian Institution Press, 1996.

Gaines, Jane. "Costume and Narrative." *Fabrications: Costume and the Female Body*. Ed. Jane Gaines and Charlotte Herzog. New York: AFI, 1990, 180–211.

————. "From Elephants to Lux Soap: The Programming and 'Flow' of Early Motion Picture Exploitation." *Velvet Light Trap* 25 (1990): 29–43.

————. "The Queen Christina Tie-Ups: Convergence of Show Window and Screen." *Quarterly Review of Film and Video* 11 (1989): 35–60.

————. "War, Women, and Lipstick: Fan Mags in the Forties." *Heresies* 5 (1985): 42–47.

Gaines, Jane, and Charlotte Herzog. " 'Puffed Sleeves Before Tea-Time': Joan Crawford, Adrian and Women Audiences." *Stardom: Industry of Desire*. Ed. Christine Gledhill. London: Routledge, 1991. Originally published in 1985.

Gamson, Joshua. *Claims to Fame: Celebrity in Contemporary America*. Berkeley: University of California Press, 1994.

Gandhy, Behroze, and Rosie Thomas. "Three Indian Film Stars." *Stardom: Industry of Desire*. Ed. Christine Gledhill. London: Routledge, 1991. Originally published in *Wide Angle* 6 (1985).

Geraghty, Christine. "Re-Examining Stardom: Questions of Texts, Bodies and Performance."*Reinventing Film Studies*. Ed. Christine Gledhill and Linda Williams. London: Arnold, 2000.

Giles, David. *Illusions of Immortality: A Psychology of Fame and Celebrity*. New York: St. Martin's Press, 2000.

Gledhill, Christine. *Stardom: Industry of Desire*. London: Routledge, 1991.

Gunning, Tom. " 'Now You See It, Now You Don't': The Temporality of the Cinema of Attractions." *Silent Film*. New Brunswick, NJ: Rutgers University Press, 1996), 73.

Gustafson, Robert. "The Power of the Screen: The Influence of Edith Head's Film Designs on the Retail Fashion Market." *Velvet Light Trap* 19 (1982): 8–15.

Hampton, Benjamin. *History of the Movies.* New York: Dover, 1970.

Hansen, Miriam. *Babel and Babylon: Spectatorship in American Silent Film.* Cambridge, MA: Harvard University Press, 1991.

Haskell, Molly. *From Reverence to Rape: The Treatment of Women in the Movies.* Chicago: University of Chicago Press, 1987. Originally published in 1974.

Jacobs, Lewis. *The Rise of the American Film.* New York: Teachers College Press, 1939.

Jenson, Joli. "Fandom as Pathology: The Consequences of Characterization." *The Adoring Audience: Fan Culture and Popular Media.* Ed. Lisa Lewis. New York: Routledge, 1992, 9–30.

Kerr, Catherine. "Incorporating the Star: The Intersection of Business and Aesthetic Strategies in Early American Film." *Business History Review* 64.3 (Autumn 1990): 383–410.

Kindem, Gorham. "Hollywood's Movie Star System: A Historical Overview." Carbondale: Southern Illinois University Press, 1982.

King, Barry. "Articulating Stardom." *Screen* 26 (1985): 27–50.

———. "The Star and the Commodity: Notes Towards a Performance Theory of Stardom." *Cultural Studies* 1 (May 1987): 145–161.

———. "Stardom as an Occupation." *The Hollywood Film Industry.* Ed. Paul Kerr. New York: Routledge, 1986, 154–184.

Klaprat, Kathy. "The Star as Market Strategy: Bette Davis in Another Light." *The American Film Industry.* Ed. Tino Balio. Madison: University of Wisconsin Press, 1976.

Leff, Leonard. *Hemingway and His Conspirators: Hollywood, Scribners, and the Making of Celebrity Culture.* New York: Rowman and Littlefield, 1997.

Lewis, Lisa, ed. *The Adoring Audience: Fan Culture and Popular Media.* New York: Routledge, 1992.

Lowenthal, Leo. *Literature, Popular Culture, and Society.* Upper Saddle River, NJ: Prentice Hall, 1961.

Lusted, David. "The Glut of Personality." *Stardom: Industry of Desire.* Ed. Christine Gledhill. London: Routledge, 1991. Originally published in *TV Mythologies.* Ed. L. Masterman. 1984.

Macnab, Geoffrey. *Searching for Stars: Stardom and Screen Acting in British Cinema.* New York: Cassell, 2000.

Mann, Denise. "The Spectacularization of Everyday Life: Recycling Hollywood Stars and Fans in Early Television Variety Shows." *Star Texts: Image and Performance in Film and Television.* Ed. Jeremy Butler. Detroit, MI: Wayne State University Press, 1991. Originally published in *Camera Obscura* 16 (January 1988).

Marshall, P. David. *Celebrity and Power: Fame in Contemporary Culture.* Minneapolis: University of Minnesota Press, 1997.

May, Lary. *Screening Out the Past: The Birth of Mass Culture and the Motion Picture Industry.* New York: Oxford, 1980.

McDonald, Gerald. "Origin of the Star System." *Films in Review* 4 (November 1953): 449–458.

McDonald, Paul. "Reconceptualising Stardom." *Stars.* New ed. Ed. Richard Dyer. London: BFI, 1998.

———. *The Star System: Hollywood's Production of Popular Identities*. London: Wallflower, 2000.

McLean, Adrienne. " 'New Films in Story Form': Movie Story Magazines and Spectatorship." *Cinema Journal* 42.3 (Spring 2003): 3–26.

———. *Being Rita Hayworth: Labor, Identity, and Hollywood Stardom*. New Brunswick, NJ: Rutgers University Press, 2004.

McLean, Adrienne, and David Cook. *Headline Hollywood*. New Brunswick, NJ: Rutgers University Press, 2001.

Mellencamp, Patricia. "Situation Comedy, Feminism, and Freud: Discourses of Gracie and Lucy." *Star Texts: Image and Performance in Film and Television*. Ed. Jeremy Butler. Detroit, MI: Wayne State University Press, 1991. Originally published in *Studies in Entertainment: Critical Approaches to Mass Culture* (1986).

Mishra, Vijay. *Bollywood Cinema: Temples of Desire*. New York: Routledge, 2002.

Monaco, James. *Celebrity: The Media as Image Makers*. New York: Delta, 1978.

Morin, Edgar. *The Stars*. Trans. Richard Howard. New York: Grove Press, 1960. Originally published in 1957.

Mulvey, Laura. "Visual Pleasure and Narrative Cinema." *Visual and Other Pleasures*. Bloomington: Indiana University Press, 1989. Originally published in 1975.

Musser, Charles. "The Changing Status of the Actor." *Before Hollywood: Turn-of-the-Century Film from American Archives*. With Jay Leyda. New York: American Federation of Arts, 1986.

Naremore, James. "The Performance Frame." *Star Texts: Image and Performance in Film and Television*. Ed. Jeremy Butler. Detroit, MI: Wayne State University Press, 1991. Originally published in *Acting in the Cinema* (1988).

Ndalianis, Angela, and Charlotte Henry, eds. *Stars in Our Eyes: The Star Phenomenon in the Contemporary Era*. Westport, CT: Praeger, 2002.

Negra, Diane. *Off White Hollywood: American Culture and Ethnic Female Stardom*. New York: Routledge, 2001.

Orgeron, Marsha. "Making *It* in Hollywood: Clara Bow, Fandom, and Consumer Culture." *Cinema Journal* 42 (Summer 2003): 76–97.

———. *Hollywood Ambitions: Celebrity in the Movie Age*. Middletown, CT: Wesleyan University Press, 2008.

Pearson, Roberta. *Eloquent Gestures: The Transformation of Performance Style in the Griffith Biograph Films*. Berkeley: University of California Press, 1992.

Perriam, Chris. *Stars and Masculinities in Spanish Cinema: From Banderas to Bardem*. New York: Oxford University Press, 2003.

Powdermaker, Hortense. *Hollywood the Dream Factory: An Anthropologist Looks at the Movie-Makers*. Boston: Little, Brown, 1950.

Prizogy, Ruth. "Judy Holliday: The Star and the Studio." *Columbia Pictures: Portrait of a Studio*. Ed. Bernard Dick. Lexington: University of Kentucky Press, 1992.

Ramsaye, Terry. *A Million and One Nights: A History of the Motion Picture Industry*. New York: Simon and Schuster, 1964. Originally published in 1925.

Renov, Michael. "Advertising/Photojournalism/Cinema." *Quarterly Review of Film and Video* 11 (1989): 1–21.

Roberts, Shari. " 'The Lady in the Tutti-Frutti Hat': Carmen Miranda, a Spectacle of Ethnicity." *Cinema Journal* 32 (1993): 3–23.

Rodden, John. *The Politics of Literary Reputation*. New York: Oxford University Press, 1989.

Ross, Murray. *Stars and Strikes: Unionization of Hollywood*. New York: Columbia University Press, 1941.

Rosten, Leo. *Hollywood: The Movie Colony, The Movie Makers*. New York: Harcourt, Brace, 1941.

Schickel, Richard. *Intimate Strangers: The Culture of Celebrity*. New York: Doubleday, 1985.

———. *The Stars*. New York: Dial Press, 1962.

Sedgwick, John. "The Comparative Popularity of Stars in Mid-1930s Britain." *Journal of Popular British Cinema* 2 (1999): 121–127.

Sklar, Robert. *City Boys: Cagney, Bogart, Garfield*. Princeton, NJ: Princeton University Press, 1992.

Slide, Anthony. "The Evolution of the Film Star." *Films in Review* 25 (1974): 591–594.

———. "The Fan Magazines." *The Stars Appear*. Ed. Richard Dyer MacCann. Lanham, MD: Scarecrow Press, 1992, 259–264.

Stacey, Jackie. *Star Gazing*. New York: Routledge, 1994.

Staiger, Janet. "Seeing Stars." *Velvet Light Trap* 20 (1983): 10–14.

Stamp, Shelley. *Movie-Struck Girls*. Princeton, NJ: Princeton University Press, 2000.

Studlar, Gaylyn. *This Mad Masquerade: Stardom and Masculinity in the Jazz Age*. New York: Columbia University Press, 1996.

———. "The Perils of Pleasure? Fan Magazine Discourse as Women's Commodified Culture in the 1920s." *Silent Cinema*. Ed. Richard Abel. New Brunswick, NJ: Rutgers University Press, 1996, 263–299.

Tudor, Andrew. *Image and Influence: Studies in the Sociology of Film*. New York: St. Martin's Press, 1974.

Vincendeau, Ginette. *Stars and Stardom in French Cinema*. London: Continuum, 2000.

Vincent, William. "Rita Hayworth at Columbia, 1941–1945: The Fabrication of a Star." *Columbia Pictures: Portrait of a Studio*. Ed. Bernard Dick. Lexington: University of Kentucky Press, 1992.

Walker, Alexander. "Elinor Glyn and Clara Bow." *The Stars Appear*. Ed. Richard Dyer MacCann. Lanham, MD: Scarecrow Press, 1992, 199–258.

———. *Stardom: The Hollywood Phenomenon*. New York: Stein and Day, 1970.

Weiss, Andrea. " 'A Queer Feeling When I Look at You': Hollywood Stars and Lesbian Spectatorship in the 1930s." *Stardom: Industry of Desire*. Ed. Christine Gledhill. London: Routledge, 1991.

Willis, Andy, ed. *Film Stars: Hollywood and Beyond*. London: Manchester University Press, 2004.

Wyatt, Justin. *High Concept: Movies and Marketing in Hollywood*. Austin: University of Texas Press, 1994.

Yacowar, Maurice. "An Aesthetic Defense of the Star System in Films." *Quarterly Review of Film Studies* 4 (1979): 39–52.

....

CHAPTER 7

FILM GENRE THEORY AND CONTEMPORARY MEDIA: DESCRIPTION, INTERPRETATION, INTERMEDIALITY

....

PAUL YOUNG

Like Alex de Large from Stanley Kubrick's *A Clockwork Orange* (1971), who appropriates Beethoven's "Ode to Joy" to fit his own needs, film theorists long ago snatched the lexicon of genre from literary theory in order to describe the subtypes of narrative film. Clearly, the value of this analogy has its limits; for one thing, film genre theorists are not dangerously psychotic (it says here). Nevertheless, our droogie Alex does offer an object lesson in the potential consequences of poaching a theory designed to analyze genres in a medium other than film. After withstanding the Ludovico Treatment, which conditions him to feel intense revulsion when classical music plays, Alex plugs his ears against an aural onslaught of his once-beloved Ludwig Van and attempts to "snuff it"—that is, to commit suicide by throwing himself out a third-story window. Now, at the turn of the cinema's third century, film genre theory seems desperate enough to attempt a defenestration of its own.

FILM GENRE THEORY AND CONTEMPORARY MEDIA   225

The problem is that genre theory has reached the limits of the premises we pinched from Aristotle and Northrop Frye, but nevertheless refuses to give them up. Beginning in the mid-seventies, film theorists mined literary theory to describe film genres, the films that derive from them, and the expectations and interpretations of them that viewers (supposedly) share. But genre theory has become increasingly sore in precisely the spot that Rick Altman once called most "worthy of a good scratch": the tautological nature of historical genre criticism.[1] To paraphrase Edward Buscombe, we cannot form a generic corpus without criteria, but we cannot articulate those criteria without assuming a corpus.[2]

This paradox did not go unnoticed. In the seventies, a few scholars like Stephen Neale attempted to push beyond the limitations of textual taxonomy. Following the lead of the Birmingham School of cultural studies, Neale examined genre as an anthropological phenomenon as well as a textual one.[3] In this view, each film genre produced by a major film industry (Hollywood being the prime, and too often the only, example cited) can be broken down into a set of practices and negotiations that take place at specific points in the circuit of communication: production, reception, critique. Neale's work and the intensive theorization of the musical, the western, and film noir in the 1970s and 1980s generated stunning insights about how spectators' genre knowledge not only assesses generic meaning but creates it.[4]

But the anthropological turn did not put to rest the field's faith that, underneath all the social activity *about* genres lay *the genres themselves*, objectively discoverable and real. Contemporary film genre theory still dreads confronting the question that scholarship on the cultures of genre has rendered no less pertinent, and indeed more glaring than ever in our avoidance of it: could it be that genres as such do not actually exist—that all we have of film genres is our certainty, as critics, viewers, or filmmakers, that they are really out there somewhere, perhaps simply waiting in a Platonic heaven, along with perfect love and perfect geometric shapes, for us to discover their true natures once and for all?

In his magisterial book *Film/Genre*, Rick Altman attempted to answer this underexamined question, but his response is tinged with what I can only describe as definitive doubt. Written after years during which Altman faithfully interrogated the assumptions of every genre theorist he could find (including himself), *Film/Genre* argues that What We (Really) Talk About When We Talk About Genre is not textual types, conventions, myths, or rituals, but power—the critic's power to promote an agenda by demonstrating that a genre exists and identifying its conventions in a definitive way.[5] Description of a genre's "core" conventions drapes an aura of empirical certainty around genre theory, making it seem as though a film such as *Stagecoach* or *The Searchers* (John Ford, 1939, 1958) distinctly, homogeneously, and even definitively expresses a single genre. In addition, an emphasis on description elides the distinction between so-called historical genres (the types invented and reproduced by Hollywood via such discursive acts as dedicated production units and, of course, films) and critical genres (the types invented and reproduced by film critics via critical writing, edited essay collections, conference panels, and the like). Since, whether they admit to it or not, film critics tend to regard historical genres as more legitimate objects of study than critical ones, this elision works in the critics' favor. Even the act of listing representative genres—say, for instance, the western, the women's melodrama of the 1940s, the musical— fronts an implicit claim that a genre called "the women's melodrama of the 1940s" is as legitimate as the two historical genres that bracket it. This critical tendency poses problems because it makes all genre description—the raison d'être of genre theory as practiced by literary theorists—into a suspicious act, tainted by self-interest rather than the critical generosity that film genre theory has cultivated since the early 1970s.

If Altman is correct, not only about film genres but (as he contended) also about genres of drama, literary fiction, television, and presumably every other aesthetic and/or mass-cultural medium, then it seems that the clock of genre theory, to paraphrase the introduction to Altman's 1984 essay "A Semantic/ Syntactic Approach to Film Genre," has not only struck thirteen but has unwound its spring altogether.[6] Having pulled back the curtain of empirical certainty to reveal an all-too-corporeal wizard who decrees genres at will, Altman appeared to have brought the epoch of film genre theory to a close.

Grateful as we must be for Altman's enlightening and disturbing book, however, one can scarcely close the covers on *Film/Genre* without muttering, "Not so fast." Like any other discourse, from political ideology to familial mythology, "film genre" will not disappear simply because we refuse to believe in it. As a concept, genre still maintains a good deal of historical, material, and discursive force, not only in film criticism and theory but also in global film and video production, the blogosphere of media fandom (meaning the Internet sites, chat rooms, and journals dedicated to science fiction, Japanese anime, and the like), advertising, everyday conversations, and the shelving protocols through which Borders, Tower Records, and Blockbuster communicate their holdings to their customers. And "new" media studies fields such as ludology—the study of computer games and game play—have followed film studies' early example of exploiting genre analysis to both invent and legitimate their disciplines.

The current stalemate between genre description and genre anthropology offers a unique opportunity to reconsider how genre theory might define a critical objective that is both less mystified in general, and more descriptive of the *inter-medial* character of genres in the mass audiovisual media. In this essay, I combine a brief assessment of genre theory in the twenty-first century with an attempt to plot a plausible course for the future of genre studies across the media studies disciplines. I hope to demonstrate that the most pressing question I have already posed—How can we reconcile the descriptive imperatives of genre criticism with the anthropological tasks of current film genre theory?—intersects rather unexpectedly, and quite productively, with a question that the contemporary moment of digital media makes equally urgent: How can we analyze genre discourses in specific media today without slighting the myriad effects of media synergy on those discourses?

The earliest film genre critics in the United States used the idea of genre to defend high art from the encroachment of mass culture.[7] Unlike the singular, expressive works crafted by individual artists, commercial films were generated according to a template, allowing rapid dissemination and easy differentiation among the westerns and sex melodramas of the silent era, which were joined by musicals, gangster films, and other apparently inane or sordid genres with the coming of sound. To their harshest critics, film genres seemed to have been cranked out of factories like broadcloth or sausages. But by the late 1960s (and, one could argue, as early as the 1930s and 1940s in the writings of a few critics such as Robert Warshow), the new academic field of cinema studies had transformed genre into a much more positive critical framework, in which film genres became visible as signifying systems akin to language as described by Saussure, and ideology as analyzed by Althusser (and buttressed by Lacanian psychoanalysis). Far from simply junk culture, argued the new wave of genre critics, film genres participated in the construction of cultural myths about everything from nationalist ideology to class mobility and gender roles. They also provided a ritual space, the movie theater, in which those myths were collectively maintained, night after night and film after film.

In 1970, Edward Buscombe aligned film genre studies explicitly with the literary project of identifying genre's ideal forms. He even went so far as to borrow the terms "outer form" and "inner form" from René Wellek and Austin Warren's *Theory of Literature*, which allowed him to concretize the cues that prompt viewers to feel that they know a genre film when they see it. A barren Arizona landscape and other visible cues constitute the outer form of a western, for example, while such comparatively abstract conventions as plot (cowboy seeks revenge for death of family members), the stock relationships among stock characters (cowboy and schoolmarm, cowboy and Indians, cowboy and cattle rustlers), and themes (the "garden versus desert" dichotomy) constitute the inner form.[8]

Obvious as this critical maneuver seems by the twenty-first century, Buscombe offered his contemporaries a novel and systematic way to approach film genre that mirrors empirical science in that it divides its attention between noumena and phenomena, essences and accidents. Thomas Schatz later defined the distinction between the ideal of a genre and the examples that seem to add up to that ideal as the distinction between *film genres* and *genre films*: "Whereas the genre exists as a sort of tacit 'contract' between filmmakers and audiences," Schatz wrote, "the genre film is an actual event that honors such a contract. To discuss the Western genre is to address neither a single Western film nor even all Westerns, but rather that system of conventions which identifies Western films as such."[9]

Thus, while Howard Hawks's *Red River* (1948) may express the western genre, it is not identical to the genre itself. Rather, it manifests a subset of the conventions of outer and inner form. This subset is by nature far from complete, perhaps varying wildly from the viewer's expectations at certain points, but sufficient for the experienced viewer to recognize a genre, and take pleasure (or umbrage) at the film based on the degree to which it fulfills the viewer's cherished expectations. If the monster does not get destroyed at the end of a horror film, even in an obviously impermanent way that opens the door to a possible sequel, the audience will likely find the film unsatisfying or even irritating; genre filmmakers rarely stray too far from conventional forms of closure. But if, for example, the monster breaks with behaviors conventional for that type of monster and becomes even more terrifying thereby—as when a zombie suddenly breaks into a dead run in Danny Boyle's *28 Days Later* (2002)—the audience is likely to be grateful, for while a sprinting zombie defies the precedent set by undead movie corpses since George A. Romero's original *Night of the Living Dead* (1968), it satisfies another precedent set by the most successful articulations of this particular body genre: it scares the hell out of viewers.[10]

Here we come upon a contradiction, which Altman found worrisome in 1984, between the goals of syntax-focused critics who prefer small pools of "definitive" genre films with traditional plots, themes, and characterizations, and the goals of critics whose faith in semantic cues allows them to admit a much larger number of films to the canon. As an example of the distinction, consider Altman's own thought experiment, which pits an optimistic semantic critic against an exclusionary syntactical critic, and ends (however accidentally) by giving the latter the last word: Diegetic songs do not automatically make Elvis movies count as musicals![11] Such critical confrontations must either stop at once for lack of a shared theory of what makes a genre film what it is, or bicker endlessly at cross-purposes. And yet, we cannot avoid such bickering if what genre theory expects to critique, analyze, and/or evaluate is *texts*—that is, genre films—and their relation to the film genres on which they rely and to which they contribute. We cannot avoid it, that is, unless we have recourse to a tertiary term (or terms) beyond "semantics" and "syntax," a term "outside" the outer form, exterior to the text, even to the genre with which the text wrestles.

Treating textual description as an end in itself mystifies the historical specificity of generic definitions by following Aristotle's example of discussing genre criticism as a taxonomic, even zoological pursuit. In this fantasized natural world of arts and letters, genres erupt spontaneously; it remains only for the critic to catalog them according to an enlightened protocol that accounts for similarities and differences.[12] As lions and bobcats share a genus but differ in species traits, so tragedy and epic each fall under the Aristotelian genus "poetry" but differ mightily in particulars. Tragedy, for example, concentrates on character psychology, while epic throws its weight into depicting quasi-historical events in minute detail.

Similarly, westerns and screwball comedies narrate their stories in similar ways, but distinguish themselves by semantics (the western's taciturn male hero and his long-suffering beloved; the screwball comedy's bickering couple) and syntactical conventions (the western heroine allows her hero to take care of the serious business of violence, while the screwball heroine perpetrates comic violence herself). Few readers would dispute the accuracy of these descriptions. But to a great extent, our acceptance of them is in itself genre criticism's greatest (and most embarrassing) victory over our analytical sensibilities. If we agree that these parenthetical comments portray accurately the genres I have named, we tacitly endorse the zoologist's view of genre, in which the ideal form precedes our discovery of it, and genre films themselves provide us with no more than Platonic accidents (such as the western-screwball hybrid *Rio Bravo* (Howard Hawks, 1959), which we might too easily "explain" by recourse to its auteur: Howard Hawks worked in both genres, so with *Rio Bravo* he is simply giving us two genres for the price of one).

In 1984, Altman sought to resolve the paradox by appealing to genre *history* to determine when and how a genre achieves a balance of "semantics" and "syntax" sufficient for audiences to recognize it. His attempt at balance, however, did not prevent Altman from nearly excluding *The Wizard of Oz* (Victor Fleming, 1939) from his own corpus of musicals on the grounds that it breached its contract with the musical—and the musical's audience—by shunning the formation of a romantic couple.[13] In *Film/Genre*, he completed the about-face from such descriptive traps begun by his semantic/syntactic theory and his preliminary focus on genre history. Here Altman offered a "semantic/syntactic/pragmatic theory" of genre that describes neither genre films nor film genres, but only the processes by which critics, producers, and other interpreters of genres arrive at their criteria and their reservoirs of films: "Each genre is simultaneously defined by multiple codes corresponding to the multiple groups who, by helping to define the genre, may be said to "speak" the genre. When the diverse groups using the genre are considered together, genres appear as regulatory schemes facilitating the integration of diverse factions into a single social fabric."[14] This is a brilliant redefinition of *descriptive* genre analysis: what he proposed to describe is genre-driven *behavior*, not genres themselves, because the latter exist only insofar as they are generated by the former.

Instead of rejoicing in his epistemological discovery, however, Altman looked on the results of his pragmatic investigation with equal parts cynicism and remorse. When he asserted that even the smallest group of viewers exerts remarkable force on genre discourses, he cast what some critics might call a moment of political possibility as a fall from grace, the disbandment of a universal community of genre viewers. His lost community of "common bodily and social coherence" sounds more like a nostalgic fantasy than a description of actual, historical participants in the negotiation process that is film genre.[15] If genres have no stable identities, it seems, then generic communities are similarly doomed to a purgatory of flux: "Now all we have left is bodies facing in the same direction." His tertiary term, changed from genre history to the history of genre *interpretation*, has collapsed under the weight of Altman's nostalgia for sing-along sessions around the family piano.

Nevertheless, Altman's semantic-syntactic-pragmatic approach scrapes a fundamental truth down to the bone for a new generation of theorists: genres cannot be located "in" texts alone, as recognizable genetic patterns can be located in any cell of any organisms belonging to the same *genus* (a Latin root for "genre," and, as Altman remarked, a misleading root in that it attributes natural, essential properties to cultural genres and their "evolution"). Instead, genres emerge from the descriptions of existing texts that producers, viewers, and critics produce on their own and in collaboration with one another. Even though the producers have greater power than the other groups to broadcast their generic definitions—that is, by airing their interpretations of a given genre through films, TV programs, music videos, and games—none of these groups has a greater claim to authority over a genre's description than the others.[16] Producers multiply genre cues for any given film in order to maximize their audiences; viewers collate and circulate their own sense of a genre's conventions to argue their superior status as interpreters; and critics buttress the importance of their central interests by "proving" (or merely assuming) that a certain genre unquestionably exists, then defining its conventions, its history, and its ideological refraction of its historical moment based on that assumption.

And yet, description of the "old," textual sort continues in other fields, including television studies and ludology. Its persistence suggests that genre description still serves some indispensable purpose. Indeed, typical labels of some kind seem, at least at first blush, more critically necessary than ever, as new types proliferate among both new and old media along with the new formats, new delivery systems, and indeed new media that change patterns of production, consumption, and—yes—the experience of mass-media genres in subtle but ultimately incalculable ways. I discovered firsthand how difficult it is to give up faith in the objective existence of genres when, while researching this essay, I went to the local Electronics Boutique to purchase a spectrum of PlayStation 2 (PS2) games. My goal was to take them home, play them, and use Altman's semantic-syntactic approach to "find" the different genres they represented. I quickly discovered that I had subconsciously planned my purchase based on generic categories the existence of which I assumed long before heading out to the mall: racing games, street-driving games, puzzle games, fighting games, space-battle games, first-person shooters, God games, and the like popped into my head so regularly as I looked around that I had to jot them down for fear I would forget them all. At this point I realized the trap in which I had landed, and wondered, surely genre study cannot do without such lists when developing analytic frameworks for emerging media forms. Inundation with unfamiliar media objects demands a search for similarities and differences among the various box images and descriptions. I made up these categories because they were useful to me at that moment, as I struggled to get my bearings in an unfamiliar mass-cultural universe. To break down this horizon of game experience into types in this way is to inch toward insights about what users expect from these myriad artifacts, and what the artifacts, in turn, expect of them.

So what is to be done, if genre theory cannot live on textual categorization alone but clearly cannot live without it? One tack I recommend as a beginning is to be wary of confusing the social negotiation of textual meaning with textual or generic essences. I made exactly this error when I walked into the game shop, though it turned out to be an instructive error, for it made me more aware of how quickly generic essentialism can insinuate itself into our understanding of new media products. In his collection *The Medium of the Video Game*, Mark J. P. Wolf had an Electronics Boutique moment of his own when he applied basic tenets of film genre analysis, particularly the essence-accidents distinction forwarded by Buscombe and Schatz, directly to video games.[17] The result is a list of categories that are by turns intuitive and infuriating. Wolf counted clear beginnings and clear endings as traits of "narrative" games in some cases (adventure games, for example) but excluded from the "narrative" category other games with what seem equally clear beginnings, endings, and developments over time (such as *Pac-Man*, with its goal to clear maze after maze of dots and avoid enemies whose speed and dexterity increase with each new maze, and its parallel goal—as important to my friends and me in the early 1980s as clearing yet another maze—of getting to the "cartoons" that appear every few screens as a reward for weary wrists).[18]

The problem that such a taxonomy poses for video game genre studies is that Wolf *prescribed* genres in the guise of *describing* them, and thereby (accidentally) privileged a singular, unproblematized hermeneutic over all other possible definitions, systematic or otherwise. He thereby sidestepped the conservative consequences of his own intervention for future interpretations of the artifacts in question. Wolf lifted his theory from critical essays and books written more than two decades ago, without adjusting their findings in response to the differences between games and narrative films. The result is that he emphasized the importance of categorization as an end in itself over the player's generic *experience* of the games.[19] Even the film theorists most oriented by cultural studies find the certitude of taxonomy difficult to resist; Stephen Neale's more recent introductory text on Hollywood genres devoted nearly a third of its pages to descriptions of each "major" genre and its historical divergences from its classical definition. He thereby risked perpetuating assumptions about the natures of these genres that seem outdated and even quaint after more than three decades of intergeneric pastiche.[20] Altman's pragmatic approach demands that we ask of Neale and Wolf the same nagging questions: *For whom* does a text "belong" in a genre? *For whom* does a genre equal a definite set of semantics and a consistent arrangement—a syntax—of those elements?

Now, asking these questions does not mean that we have to stop typifying films, games, TV programs, or other mass-media artifacts. It does mean, however, that we cannot exclude our own critical and theoretical acts of typification from anthropological scrutiny. Each analysis is merely one expression of genre knowledge among many, one that subverts the very idea of "pure" genre categories (rather than strategic) as surely as does a horror-movie blogger, a midnight movie aficionado, or an author of *Star Wars* fiction for fellow writer-fans. Compare my knee-jerk, semantic-syntactic list of video game genres to one formulated by Sam Miller, a student in my undergraduate Film Theory course, in response to an e-mail that asked, "What are the major video game genres today?":

> When discussing genre in video games, I think it is important to distinguish between games where the player controls one character and games where the [player] controls multiple characters. I have separated my list that way.

Individual control

> Player as outlaw: Max Payne, Grand Theft Auto [series]
> Player as sportsman: Golf, Billiards, Cards
> Player as problem/puzzle solver: Tomb Raider
> Player as nurturer: Black and White, Lemmings
> Flight simulation: Microsoft's Flight Simulator
> Racing simulation: Grand Turismo, Nascar
> Player as part of team: Counterstrike, Team Fortress
> Player as part of online community (especially Role Playing): Everquest
>   (fantasy), Sims (reality)

Team control

> Player as General (Realtime): StarCraft, Command and Conquer; Historical
>   General: Age of Empires, Lords of the Realm
> Player as coach of team: NBA Live, MLB
> Player as leader of military squad [in a single-player game]: Rainbow 6,
>   Delta Force[21]

Sam's corpuses differ from mine in that they reduce film studies' cherished categories of syntax and semantics to near irrelevance. In their stead, Sam posits a taxonomy driven by a feature that makes video games technologically and textually distinct from film: not Wolf's somewhat indistinct category of *interactivity*, but rather the *type of interface* that allows the player to "interact" with the game.

I will return to Sam's insight about the interface momentarily, but for now I want simply to recognize the analytical suppleness of Sam's taxonomy compared to the heuristic I applied at the Electronics Boutique, and to try to account for the superiority of the former. Knowing video games from the perspective of a longtime massively multiplayer (MMP) gamer (who currently identifies himself as "retired"), Sam offers a heuristic that gets straight to the heart of the unique experiences of playing games that differ from one another in ways only a gamer (or a programmer) could identify so intuitively, and he thereby promises more complex insights into how game genre knowledge gets used than my cinema-bound methodology could have delivered. A document like Sam's exemplifies our chance to recast the search for genre's origins as an anthropological task. Mass-cultural genre theory has long claimed for viewers or listeners the status of cultural producers by dint of their position as a nexus where genre history and individual experience meet new genre texts in the present. This is a potent analytical idea in a time of increased, digitally driven synergy among the audiovisual media.

Rather than move directly on to discerning a "grammar" for genres and how they work, following the structuralist-linguistic strain of textual criticism that Schatz employed in 1981, we might better expand on the unusually rich questions about genre reception that such an approach catalyzes. I would now like to concentrate not on *what* it is, exactly, about films or other media texts that Schatz recommends we "appreciate," but rather on the forms that the appreciation takes in the twenty-first century's audiovisual landscape.

On this count, we can learn much from Altman's previous attempts to reconcile divergent opinions about genres—not only their characteristics but also their historical development and the kinds of relationships they forge among producers, users, and other users. Altman argued in *Film/Genre* that neither semantic nor syntactic description, nor any combination thereof, benefits the critic unless she sacrifices the fool's errand of discovering an empirically certain description of a genre. His "semantic-syntactic-pragmatic" approach, by contrast, attempts not to taxonomize texts, but to taxonomize genre taxonomists of all stripes—to describe the processes of description undertaken by distinct groups to will a genre into existence:

> Instead of looking primarily down the chain of meaning towards texts, morphemes and phonemes, pragmatic analysis must constantly attend to the competition among multiple users that characterizes genres. . . . Always assuming multiple users of various sorts—not only various spectator groups, but producers, distributors, exhibitors, cultural agencies, and many others as well—pragmatics recognizes that some familiar patterns, such as genres, owe their very existence to that multiplicity.[22]

If taxonomizing the taxonomizers is our goal, we can and probably should begin by scrutinizing ourselves—the critics—and our rather undistinguished history of using genre, to quote *North by Northwest*'s Roger Thornhill, "like a flyswatter," to distinguish ourselves as scientific witnesses to a phenomenon that swallows the proletariat in illusions of their own discerning tastes. No matter which group's definition of genre it addresses, the semantic-syntactic-pragmatic approach does not limit itself to recognizing when or where or who exercises the power. Instead, it taxonomizes "taxonomy" as a meaning-making *process*. And it has the ability to investigate genre knowledge as a circulating idea by taking that idea's temperature at various points where genre "happens"—that is, where users meet texts.

The more critics focus on industrial and/or consumer "versions" of genre corpuses instead of attempting to form their own "definitive" canons, the greater the complexity with which they can model the interpretive matrices by which genre's users navigate their respective terrain. In film genre study, the emphasis on corpus construction has tended to dismiss generic hybridization as a marginal phenomenon. Television studies, however, has managed to learn from film studies' mistakes and has instead produced meticulously researched accounts of how the network imperatives to link production and scheduling to the viewer demographics associated with different times of day generate the algorithms that distinguish sitcoms from variety shows, daytime soaps from prime-time soaps, and newscasts from news magazines.[23] Producers prefer diverse genres because they differentiate product, a crucial marketing tool when mass-cultural products resemble one another as closely as classical films do. Genre is just as crucial for television, considering that programs run all day and all night and cannot retain viewers unless channels, even specialized ones like Comedy Central, provide variations on a theme like "comedy." Comedy Central shows movies and reruns of sketch comedy shows, but it also produces its own lines of (outrageously comic) game shows (*Distraction*), (outrageously comic) news shows (*The Daily Show* and its spin-off punditry program), and (outrageously comic) cartoons like *South Park*. Cartoon Network shows reruns of *Baby Looney Tunes*, a numbingly innocuous show featuring infant versions of Bugs Bunny and other Warner Bros. characters, early in the morning, while *Ed, Edd, and Eddy* and *Teen Titans* spew nose-blowing humor and light, consequence-free violence in the early evening hours, leaving the once-canceled Fox network series *Family Guy* to find a new home among surrealistic and prurient recombinations of old Hanna-Barbera cartoons (*Sealab 2021*, *Harvey Birdman: Attorney at Law*) and bloody but sophisticated Japanese anime (*Cowboy Bebop*) that fill out the Adult Swim schedule.

Such distinctions also hold in cinema, where film genres are one means through which Hollywood hails, and constructs, distinct markets among its viewers. However, Altman has suggested that genres have always, and indeed only, operated for Hollywood producers as sets of *cues* that could be manipulated and intermingled at various textual levels—the film itself, publicity narratives and advertising copy, posters and other still images—in order to *multiply* its audiences, not to send restrictive signals to them about the conventions to which a film would adhere. He has found a number of examples of studios switching among conventional semantic and syntactical cues in the course of publicizing a single film: as a biopic, a tragic romance, an adventure story, a courtroom drama. Whereas corpus assembly tends to portray hybrid genre texts as oddities that nevertheless proliferate, Altman portrayed them as the beating heart of genre sensibility. For producers as they interpret genres, genre is not so much a body of films or even a stable syntax or code as it is a form of bait. Bits and pieces of various genres can be intermingled—and are—in order to make the dish palatable to all stomachs. The producers of *Die Hard* (John Tiernan, 1988), for example, may well have determined to multiply the film's generic references to appeal to the broadest possible spate of spectators. Following Altman's discussion of this "producer's game," students in my Film Genres course at the University of Missouri-Columbia, when given the assignment to choose one "classic" Hollywood genre referred to by *Die Hard* and argue for its presence based on the semantic and syntactic conventions commonly identified with the genre, found references to the western, the screwball comedy, the women's film (which in this case assures its female viewers by proxy that they cannot have their careers and Bruce Willis, too), the horror film, and at least two or three others entangled together as densely as a root ball at the bottom of a houseplant that urgently needs to be repotted.[24]

The proliferation of such newer media as the video game, however, and Hollywood's keen interest in attracting gamers to theaters and DVDs, has made the rules of the producer's game more difficult to predict, though the efforts to figure them out are made quite apparent by game adaptations like *Mortal Kombat* and *Lara Croft: Tomb Raider*. *Final Fantasy*, the video game, is more or less a swords-and-sorcery adventure game with connections to other adventure-puzzles as recent as the *Myst* series and as old as the text-based computer game from the 1980s, *Adventure*, and its visual counterpart on the old 4K (!) Atari 2600 game deck. But when *Final Fantasy* was adapted into a fully digitally animated film, its science fiction plot bore almost no resemblance to the game; only a few of the characters and the idea of "spirits" were taken from game to movie. This interpretation reflects, among other things, Hollywood's marketing concerns: a film had to be made that would appeal to an audience broader than just the aficionados of the game. While video games regularly rake in more domestic gross than many films, the games cost as much as fifty to sixty dollars per unit when new, meaning that the audience need not be nearly as large as the required audience of a theatrically released film to be certified a hit.

Casting the translation of texts and genres across media as *readings* of those texts and genres brings us to the consumer's place in the negotiation of meaning. Specifically, what if genre criticism were to approach *media themselves* in generic terms—terms in which the user's genre recognition revolves around such issues as the modes of textual engagement specific to a given medium? To do so, it seems to me, points toward a solution to the problem that the *Final Fantasy* movie poses to genre theory: that is, how to account theoretically for, first, the calculated "over-spill" of one medium's text into another medium in our particular era of corporate media synergy, and second, the determinant role played by genre in the conception and consumption of the products of that overspill. Such an approach would not preclude the study of traditional genres and the patterns of reception they court (or in this context, perhaps the term should be "subgenres"—the science fiction film as a subgenre of narrative film; the God game and first-person-shooter as subgenres of deck or PC games; and so on). But an intermedial notion of genre knowledge and its circulation would describe how media producers produce, media consumers consume, and media analysts analyze the pleasures, meanings, and ideologies that media products express and illuminate.

Tom Schatz's astute condensation of the intertextual dialectic of novelty and familiarity still holds for films, in which the arrangement of familiar semantics and syntax presumes a "user" who engages these arrangements interpretively. The condensation sounds as clear, simple, and accurate now as it did in 1981, and runs like this: "As critics, we understand genre films because of their similarity with other films, but we appreciate them for their difference."[25] But what if we were to rewrite this apothegm thus: "As *multi-media users*, we understand *one medium's texts* because of their similarity with *another medium's texts*, but we appreciate them for their difference"? Restating the question shifts the focus of genre theory toward what it means, for example, to *view* Harry Potter in one medium and *play as* Harry Potter in another. Such transfers of characters from acted events to modes of being represent the emergence of a distinct typology for the digital era, one that demands description as well as historicization.

The intermedia road is not the easy one, to be sure, because to take it the critic must force him- or herself to place into scare quotes the questions that tradition demands the genre theorist ask: What matters most to our ability to recognize and analyze genres, the outer form of characters, settings, and conventional objects, or the inner form of conventional plots and themes? Do genre films represent a social and community-building ritual comparable to the church-raising dance in John Ford's *My Darling Clementine* (1947), or a tried-and-true delivery system for ideologies that serve social order and the film industry's capitalist interests equally well? And, in the first place, where do film genres—or any genres, for that matter—come from; what determines their patterns of development?.

However, the semantic-syntactic-pragmatic approach does not limit itself to recognizing when or where or who exercises the power. It investigates genre knowledge and its circulation by taking that idea's temperature at various points where genre "happens"—that is, where users meet texts. Where critics once mobilized genre to curse the "lurid" forms of culture both perpetrated on and perpetuated by the demonized masses, it could also be mobilized in the other direction, redemptively, to refer to an entire *medium*, as Aristotle began the study of genres by isolating epic, lyric, and drama as types—types that we might now call *aesthetic* media. The tendency to lump all "generic" production together as mindless reiteration of mindless conventions for mindless consumers has been translated into a less condemnatory, more critically productive strategy in the past, by proto–Birmingham School cultural critics who took an interest in the experiential contours of "popular art." In 1916, Hugo Münsterberg, the prominent psychologist and philosopher who sneaked into movies at the risk of damaging his reputation, discovered in cinematic editing not the visual reproduction of "outer reality" but a representation of space and time faithful to the "inner reality" of attention and cognition as demonstrated by transitions from shot to reverse-shot, long shot to close-up, event to simultaneous event, and the like.[26]

If we accept Altman's view that "genre" refers to a site where textual and historical-cultural meanings are negotiated, we now need to consider each technological medium separately as a quasi-generic means of *delivery*, and consider "genre difference" to be (first and intermedially, though by no means for good and all) a matter of *interfacing*, of modes of consumption—between viewer and television program, player and video game, spectators and movies, phone user and downloadable *Shrek 2* game for the cell phone. With the definition of such terms as "narrative" and even "textuality" in doubt among theorists of digital media, categories such as *simulation* and *interactivity* have come to envelop not only the imagination of new media but the sensibilities surrounding television, cinema, and popular music via the Web, iPod, and MP3 technologies, and streaming audio-video through DSL and cable connections. The forms spawned by these newer technologies depend, as Wolf makes clear, on "interaction" of various kinds for their very substance as products; interface with the environment offered by the game centers the textual experience itself, making a discussion of "consumption context" and genre knowledge—genre, in this case, meaning the video game medium—as central to any discussion of textual types and knowledge-appreciation contexts as *Red River* and *Unforgiven* (Clint Eastwood, 1992) are to prior discussions of the western.

Not all theorists of video games, particularly those who refer to their field as ludology, agree with Wolf on this point. On the one hand, the ludologist Espen Aarseth, always concerned with defending the boundaries of his field from marauding hordes of literary and film critics, expressed deep frustration with how non-ludologists use the term "interactive" to describe digital experiences. Interactivity is generally defined as that quality of games, hypertext, and other "ergodic" artifacts—which Aarseth defines as artifacts that (unlike written fiction) require what he calls "nontrivial effort" on the reader's part "to allow the reader to traverse the text"—which gives users the ability to manipulate those artifacts. For Aarseth, however, interactivity is no more than a sexy-sounding cipher that media studies scholars and hysterical digital utopians throw around instead of actually analyzing ergodic objects.[27] On the other hand, for gamers like Sam Miller and another Vanderbilt undergraduate, Michael Costello, interactivity refers to the spectrum of interfaces by which gamers appropriate and manipulate game worlds, and as such it denotes a crucial generic prompt. Michael goes so far as to claim that developers of new games take types of player-game interface, such as the massively multiplayer structure of *Halo*, more seriously as precedents to follow than they do semantic-syntactic types like the western, science fiction, and the like.

From this last perspective, a sports game like Electronic Arts's *Madden NFL 2005* has more in common with a PC chess program than it does with an MMPG (massively multi-player game) like *Halo* for the Xbox, or a four-player PS2 science fiction game. Since *Madden* and computer chess base their game-play conventions and rules on games played in physical reality and do their best to replicate those experiences, both are *simulations*. And popular interfaces beget more games with similar interfaces, not necessarily similar iconography or plots. A popular science fiction MMPG spawns not more science fiction games but more MMPGs, in hopes of replicating (but not fully duplicating) the prior program's game-play experience (kinds of teamwork, modes of creating new spaces or new alliances, communication among players, status of avatars when players go off-line, etc.). Similarity and difference take on their most significant meanings from look-and-feel issues, game rules, and ways of "entering" the game's world, not from semantics or even necessarily from syntax, at least if we define "syntax" in terms of recurrent plots (which MMPGs render nonlinear as far as the premises of the game allow, if not altogether unpredictable) or character traits and the relationships those traits generate (since individual players have a large degree of control over self-representation and behavior patterns, however much these elements might be overdetermined by a player's devotion to specific *Star Wars* characters, say, or such character types as "self-interested rogue with heart of gold," "bold but vulnerable regent," "wide-eyed idealist with enormous potential for heroic deeds," etc.).

What genre theory could most productively do next, it seems to me, is repurpose the semantic-syntactic-pragmatic approach to account for various kinds of borrowing across the institutional borders of textual production, address, and reception represented by individual media—cinema, broadcast TV, cable, prerecorded video, deck-bound video games, PC MMP games, and so forth. The benefit of doing so is to describe the intermedia character of genre knowledge, a historically important factor in genre discourses that nevertheless remains woefully undertheorized. This approach would recognize the overtly intermedia character of the contemporary processes by which critics, producers, and users typify audiovisual products without (ideally at least) overrepresenting or underrepresenting the discrete characteristics of each medium's products. Further investigation of video game genres is an obvious point of departure, because video games borrow genres from film and TV (science fiction, reality programming, televised football). The software suppliers for the mass-market game decks like the Sony PlayStation 2, Nintendo GameCube, and Microsoft Xbox cobble together new and distinct genres out of film genres like science fiction, war, and action movies with blinding speed and regularity. Both PC and Internet gaming and the wired versions of game-deck software (Xbox and PlayStation decks have had telephone and USB digital modem jacks installed for some time) also offer MMP games like *Quest* and *Star Wars: Battlefront* that expand the sharing of the two-to-four-player game-deck experience to the far corners of the Web. The universe of audiovisual genre has expanded along with the software lines available for digital gaming.

But what patterns do these forcible borrowings from other media—that is, interpretations of other media's texts—follow, if any? Here are three exemplary categories, which I posit as opening moves toward a description of the uses of genre in digital media discourse. Following the lead of Sam and Michael, the main categorical criterion is the type of interface between digital games and other media forms. Whereas gamers focus on the literal interface that gives the user access to the game, its world, and its rules of play, I am poaching the term "interface" as a metaphor, a flexible heuristic that allows us to account for the distinct differences among video game producers' *remediation* processes—that is, their processes of appropriating other media's forms.[28] Jay David Bolter and Richard Grusin characterized remediation as "the representation of one medium in another" and argued that "remediation is a defining characteristic of the new digital media."[29] However, if we reconsider remediation through the model of genre pragmatics, we must track a different quality of remediation than Bolter and Grusin do. While they assess various levels of remediation along an axis running between self-reflexive hypermediacy and hypermediated transparency, I propose a multiaxis model on which each distinct video game could be plotted as a point, perhaps reflecting its more or less *narrative* qualities, its more or less direct adaptations of another medium's *genres*, and its more or less literal adaptations of another medium's *distinct properties*—meaning modes of representation, modes of address, and, of course, modes of interface. While I do not have the space here to firm up these axes and begin plotting those points, I offer here three preliminary categories of adaptation that this "pragmatic-intermedial" approach to game genres allows us to see.

The first category I propose is *direct adaptation of a specific property from one medium into another medium*. When Fox licenses *The Simpsons*, its long-running cartoon sitcom, for a series of deck video games (*Road Rage, Hit & Run*) that allow the player to explore a virtual Springfield by car while running over its citizens (accidentally, of course), or elderly TV sitcoms and cop shows reappear as film franchises or one-offs (*Mission: Impossible, The Brady Bunch, Starsky & Hutch*), the parallel versions of the property share textual information and textual references. Nevertheless, each new expression of a text in a different medium differs from the others in that it requires distinct practices of consumption and use while borrowing such information as characterization and possible plot lines from the "first" version. Game adaptations of movies and television programs, as well as television adaptations of film properties, adapt their source texts in spotty ways that reflect the borrowing medium's conventional approaches to the semantics and syntax of the poached text's game, approaches that (it seems to me) have by now become generic, that is, conventions of syntax, themselves. Most games adapted from films focus on one or more action sequences or derive basic game premises from the movie in question, such as goals, geography, and laws of (meta)physics. In the *Matrix Online* MMPG, set after the death of Neo (Keanu Reeves) in *The Matrix: Revolutions*, Neo's followers share his powers over time and space and carry on his battle against the machines.

The second category is *indirect adaptation of a genre that originated in a different medium*, such as when a video game borrows a premise, semantics, and/or syntax from a recognizable film or TV genre rather than a licensed property like *The Matrix*. Game designers and PR staffs mobilize generic iconography and other signifiers to beckon fans of a genre in one medium, such as western films, to accept its incarnation in another medium, like TV's *Gunsmoke* or Rockstar Games' *Red Dead Revolver* for the PlayStation 2 and Xbox (2004). Programmers tend to adapt elements from the other medium's genre in playful ways that call attention to the semantic and syntactic conventions of that genre. Like most mass-market video games today, the original *Tomb Raider* game (Eidos, 1996) for the PlayStation 1, an adventure puzzle game that lifts its cave-and-archaeological-dig settings and its international intrigue master plot from action-adventure films like *Raiders of the Lost Ark* (Steven Spielberg, 1981), peppers two- to five-minute dramatic scenes (which the player cannot play, only watch) throughout the game play. These "cinematics," as they're called in the industry, perform at least two functions specific to electronic games: they provide context and information about the player's challenges and goals, and they carry on *Pac-Man*'s tradition of giving the player a chance to catch his or her breath and adjust a carpal-tunnel brace.

But video game cinematics also invite players to mobilize their semantic and syntactic expectations about mainstream cinema in general. Lara Croft is as agile, smart, movie-star beautiful, and eager for challenges as any goal-driven Hollywood protagonist. She and the player receive her mission not from a written rule book

Figure 7.1 Frame enlargement from the opening cinematic of *Red Dead Revolver* for PlayStation 2 (Rockstar Games, 2004) (author's collection).

like those that accompany *Monopoly* boards and Atari 2600 game cartridges from the early 1980s, but from a mysterious group of people with whom she clearly has a past. While receiving her assignment, Lara offers the player a few knowing glances using close-ups, a cinematic narration device that offers us visual omniscience and character identification while planting a mystery yet to be solved, thus holding our attention on the game's "plot" in high Hollywood style. The cinematic then cuts to a swirling "camera" movement that establishes a new setting, a snowy and isolated mountain range. At this point, the cinematic ends and the gamer begins, clumsily at first, to jog, climb, and shoot her way through a cavern teeming with wolves and bats. Like the standard Hollywood protagonist, Lara and the gamer have multiple goals to reach that are nonetheless bound together—in this case, finding the treasure and staying alive.

The implications of such subtle intermedial overlap for adapted-genre games are far from clear. Espen Aarseth and Markku Eskelinen have adamantly dismissed the possibility that games are narratives or even "texts" in the sense that literature and film studies attaches to these terms, and have more recently spoken out against discussing anything experienced "outside" the game, from other media's textual forms to everyday life, as if it affects players' experience of individual games in any way.[30] And yet it seems clear from *Red Dead Revolver*, puzzle-adventure games like *Tomb Raider*, and zombie first-person shooters like *Silent Hill* that adapted-genre games cannot tip their hats to specific borrowed genres via iconography (semantics) and plotlines (syntax) without also inviting the "old" medium's generic sensibility and the transduction of that sensibility into the experience of the game. These games literally banish cinematic storytelling elements to the cinematics and just as literally link players' continuing gaming pleasure—that is, the game avatar's survival—to their skills at manipulating an interface structure of a certain kind rather than their ability to recall key scenes from *A Fistful of Dollars* (Sergio Leone, 1964). Yet we cannot ignore the possibility that the same games invite gamers to let their generic expectations of, say, the western seep into the experience of game play. After all, *Red Dead Revolver* maintains western icons and character relations from start to finish, and returns again and again to western-styled cinematics that mark the return to a "genre movie" world as a reward for surviving the game levels.

My sense that players of such indirect adaptation games shift imaginatively between game play and film genre reverie would not please the ludologists, who base their distinction between "narrative," or "text," and "game" on what the user does with a game at the moment of reading/using/consuming it, as opposed to what one does with a television program, a film, a book, or a digital hypertext novel. Granted, their sense of what one "does" with media constructs is limited rather excruciatingly to one's immediate experience of those constructs, and describes those experiences only in immediate and literal terms; Eskelinen and Aarseth never discuss intermedia sensibility of games or other cybertexts without sniffing indignantly about the film and literature studies barbarians who stand at the gate of a field with intent to colonize. To a certain degree they are correct to note that film and literature theorists have barreled into game theory without accounting fully for fundamental differences in textuality and users' engagement with those textualities. Theorists on either side of this debate, however, speak of the medium on the other side of the fence as if it were simpler, quainter, and indeed more vulgar than their own—much as social critics once looked down on all films as "generic" because they were films.

One such discussion of connotation centers on the bust of Lara Croft and the heterosexual male gaze it seems built to attract or construct (just as that bust is pieced together out of digital polygons). Eskelinen asserts that it gets the critic no closer to describing the experience of a video game just to notice this or that game's closeness in theme or visual content to another mass-cultural text, even if the "closeness" in question is provided by as vexed an icon as the impossibly proportioned, fetishistically attired female body.[31] Yet these writers come off sounding dismissive at best (such terms as "naive" and "fallacious" appear in their essays in reference to humanists even more often than such terms as "resisting" and "beating") and hypocritical at worst. These media metacritics are perfectly willing and able to read "literary" critics' responses as "texts" with connotations and discursive functions much deeper than their authors will admit, but utterly unwilling to discuss anything but intentional determinants of meaning when discussing the modes of ergodic literature, games, and the like, not to mention their own written critiques of semiotics and narrative theory as applied by humanists to video games.[32]

To be fair, film spectatorship theory began in earnest in the late 1960s by making idealist generalizations of a similar sort. I would go so far as to say we cannot ask adequate versions of metatextual, intermedia questions without examining and analyzing the game experience (in this case) extensively. And yet Aarseth undercuts terms like "interactivity" on syllogistic grounds rather than on grounds of cultural usefulness—as a descriptor that programmers, gamers, and theorists use to describe certain gaming experiences—and they know their own definitions well, because they use those definitions to communicate their gaming experiences, frustrations, and pleasures with one another. Here are a few remarks on those experiences, culled from Amazon.com's *Red Dead Revolver* sales site comments board:

> Red Dead plays like an arcade shooter. You play as one of a few different characters, but mostly the main protagonist, Red. With a variety of weapons (which can be upgraded throughout the game) you take down waves of opposition in a number of gritty Western movie-style settings. A ghost town, a graveyard, up in the mountains, on a train, on a ranch, etc. . . . I felt Rockstar could have done much more with this title. There are times where you run around town between chapters with no real purpose. Let me get myself in trouble at the Saloon with a bar brawl, or end up in a Quickdraw shootout because I hit on some saucy barmaid that some other tough unwashed thug is interested in.[33]

Taking place in the Wild West (and borrowing heavily from the types of movies of this time period), Red Dead Revolver allows us to do something most of us adults have always dreamt about as kids . . . walk in the shoes of a gunslinger. Best of all, we can still walk away in the same shape we were in before playing the game, and not full of holes.[34]

Judging from these comments, historical definitions of "the western" as generic ideal have limited the spectrum of what can be *thought* about *Red Dead Revolver* by players and programmers alike! The reviews I cite above oscillate between interactive pleasures and cinematic ones, such as identifying with the cinematic western hero and expecting a greater number of iconic settings and standoffs, more immediately and fluidly than one can click a hypertext link. One wonders how long Aarseth will continue to tell users to stop processing their experiences as "interactivity" because they're missing the point of the medium, and what he hopes to accomplish by doing so. As Henry Jenkins wrote in his critique of the "unduly polemical" ludologists, any critic who discusses the role (or lack thereof) of narrative in the video game must do more than pay lip service to game experience from the user's multimediated, multigenred experience as compared to the experience of narrative in (ideally) unilinear texts such as films and novels. She must focus not only on "whether games tell stories" and were intended to do so by their programmers, but also on "whether narrative elements might enter games at a more localized level." In the "transmedia storytelling" modes adopted by contemporary filmmakers and television producers as well as game designers, rather than "each individual work being self-sufficient," "each work contribute[s] to a larger narrative economy."[35]

This idea brings us into my third category of intermedia generic textual interpretation/production, *adaptations of other media's capabilities.* As Aarseth noted, many digital media theorists writing in the 1990s assumed that digital media and interactivity transform the entire experience of media spectatorship. This becomes a problematic assumption when we consider how little the social and institutional parameters of many media experiences have changed over time. Digital projection of "films" in movie theaters neither promises nor delivers the kind of text-to-consumer relationship that video games and DVD movies foster with their consumers, namely, an interactive—or more precisely, ergodic—experience.[36] Nevertheless, the entrance of digital technologies into formerly analog consumption sites also opens an imaginative channel through which media users *fantasize* that the game transforms their access to the genre of the western film. The gamers I quote above, whose avatars sport ten-gallon hats and beard stubble, fantasize their Xboxes as interfaces to a wholly imaginary game-film experience, in which they both vicariously watch iconographically and syntactically "western" events, and actively perform themselves into the world of the western film genre—a world that is all representation and all simulation at the same time.[37]

In the less ethereal regions of the digital age, *privatized* digital delivery systems for cinematic and televisual content, as well as for games of all sorts and for social communication, do materially change the social and spatial relations among media users and media content. Often they accomplish this feat simply by dint of the shifting levels of public or private consumption that digital media make available. Each new system—from the home DVD-CD player to its portable counterpart, from the continually upgraded home game deck to the portable Game Boy and its progeny, from the camera phone to the PDA with Web browser—may not deserve to be called a *new* medium in its own right, because each one borrows and cobbles together features that used to "belong" to the others. These newer media develop their own textual subtypes that might or might not be termed "genres" depending on how closely one associates "genre" with "stories and storytelling": types of games, types of narratives, types of interactive experiences that seem ill suited to the label of "narrative" at all (including, but not limited to, blogs dedicated to topics like wrestling, film franchises, and politics; Webcam-centered "reality" sites that range from the performatively erotic to the hyperbolically mundane; hypertext narratives; interactive Flash cartoons), and types of cell phone downloads (ring tones, puzzle games, and the like).

As Bolter and Grusin argued, remediation runs in both directions—from "old" media to "new," as when the media just mentioned recast familiar forms (games, stories, etc.) to broach the multimedia landscape, and from "new" to "old," as producers for established media look to novel media genres and interfaces to attract their audiences anew.[38] "Reality" television series like *Fear Factor* and *Supernanny* seem so ordinary already, long after the premiere of *Survivor*, that it is easy to forget how much their creation appeals to our knowledge, whether firsthand or reported by other sources, of Webcam hookups over the World Wide Web. Both reality TV and quasi-docu-sitcoms like *The Office* and *Fat Actress* also fit the broadcasting and cable industries' interest in hybridizing novel media experiences—not only Webcam voyeurism but also the Digital Video filmmaking revolution and its resurrection of "unsteadycam" as an acceptable "media noise"—with its own core genres.[39]

Intermedial borrowings seem peculiarly obvious in current mass media at both the textual and generic levels because they happen so often and coincide so conspicuously with the release of new "genre" films. Spectacular films in which action and special effects take center screen inevitably generate directly adapted video game tie-ins, while a popular cycle of a specific Hollywood genre (such as science fiction in the late 1970s) incites development of indirect television adaptations (such as the original *Battlestar Galactica*, *Buck Rogers*, and the short-lived Buck Henry sitcom *Quark*, in which Richard Benjamin plays an interstellar garbage man[40]). What is less obvious, thanks to film studies' reverence for stable definitions of genres, is that the borrowings follow the patterns of appropriation and (re)definition that Altman described as themselves generic; in other words, according to the semantic-syntactic-pragmatic approach, "genre" names the processes of definition undertaken by users at all levels of a media industry who value such definitions.

Altman's redefinition not only allows us to track the history of genres in a more rigorously materialist way; it also offers to cast new theoretical light on the migration of genres across media. Too many studies of the Hollywood western cite the dime novel as its extracinematic source but scarcely consider the much more difficult question of how a genre of the written word became a visual and later an audiovisual one in a medium with rules of representation and industrial imperatives all its own: "Even when a genre already exists in other media, the film genre of the same name cannot simply be borrowed from non-film sources[;] it must be recreated."[41] Looked upon this way, a "borrowed" genre becomes more than simply an adaptation; it can be made visible as an intermedia contact point, ripe with clues about how this "re-creation" process alters the extracinematic genre in question just as each new western film, critical review, and "ordinary" viewer's response has the potential to shift, however subtly, the winds of the western's generic definition. The western became a recognizably consistent film type no earlier than 1906, despite the number of potted genre histories that claim Edwin S. Porter's *The Great Train Robbery* (1903) as the unproblematic "smoking gun" film of the genre. Between 1903 and the end of the decade, as Charles Musser has amply demonstrated, the films that many historians and genre critics unproblematically call "westerns" actually rolled together "several unrelated genres" already recognized by American viewers and critics, such as the railway travel film and the crime film.[42]

If genre theory—and genre theories of television, computer games, cell phone downloads, and new media yet to be developed—might avoid snuffing itself by focusing more tightly on the cultural processes of genre definition in general, and intermedial genre bending in particular, then my allusion to *A Clockwork Orange* at the beginning of this essay provides me here at its end with an allegory of a different sort: like Alex de Large dreaming of "ultra-violence" as he listens ecstatically to Beethoven, the historical interpreters of genre—genre theorists included—poach genres and amend them to serve their immediate needs, thus infusing them with unexpected connotations that hang tenaciously to the genres in their users' memories without revamping utterly the structures, conventions, or meanings they had previously expressed. If users want to communicate about or through those genres over time, they cannot simply snuff themselves if new iterations of the genres appear monstrous to them. Instead, they must ask whether, how, and why the genres have dropped some conventions and picked up others—and also whether, how, and why their own experience, like Alex's after the Ludovico treatment, has changed their reactions to the very same products of those genres that they had once evaluated so differently. *The Band Wagon* (Vincente Minnelli, 1953) and *The Searchers* may not change from year to year; the score for Beethoven's Ninth and the rules and geography of *Grand Theft Auto III* remain constant. But our acquaintance with the genres to which they belong shifts with every new musical or western produced, every classical symphony heard for the first time, every new *Grand Theft Auto* sequel played, and played again, and again.

If we were to investigate the effects of *media* definitions on audiovisual artifacts that hop the fence between "old" media and "new" media with the same apparatus with which Altman advises us to approach the effects of *genre* definitions on new genre films and our thinking about them, we would gain a fresh anthropological perspective on intermedial adaptations. From this perspective, the noun "medium" names not a technology but rather the processes by which a *definition* of any given medium gets negotiated, and also the pivotal roles played by direct and indirect adaptations of one medium's genre by another medium altogether. Robert Rodriguez's film of Frank Miller's *Sin City* (2005), adapted from the latter's graphic novels and codirected by Miller, reminded me that fundamental questions about how elder genres make the jump into unfamiliar media have yet to be answered. Thanks to Rodriguez's home-cooked computer graphics and his fervor to re-create Miller's hyperstatic sensibilities as a graphic designer and cartoonist, *Sin City* translates comic book panels taken directly from Miller's books into dynamic but nearly immobile frames, composed of thickly rendered angles and stark contrasts among black, white, and the few primary colors (mostly red blood and the sickly skin of a mutated villain known as That Yellow Bastard). And yet this style of frame composition, which when rendered by Miller's pen infuses his pages with a dynamism rarely seen in comics, appears weirdly static when committed to (digital) film. In this diegetic universe of moving images that scarcely move, actors have no recourse to the expression of character motivation over time. They must rely instead on one facial expression and one bodily stance at a time, mirrors of the poses that Miller has already drawn onto his characters.

This is not to say that graphic novels and comic books have fewer modes of expression at their disposal, or that those modes are inferior to those available to the cinema. It is only to say that *Sin City*'s attempt at direct translation from one medium into another highlights with special clarity the potential of examining media's relationships to other media just as Altman recommended we examine relationships between genre films and film genres, as well as relationships among genres: with attention simultaneously paid to semantic, syntactic, and pragmatic expressions of a given medium's capabilities, its conventions of representation and address, and its limitations when compared with and contrasted to the medium from which it borrows a property or a generic sensibility. Following this train of thought, the film version of *Sin City* is a singular interpretation of "the graphic novel" using film; it is also, and at the same time, a singular interpretation of "the graphic novel film," which differs from other adaptations of comic books, such as

Batman, *Spider-Man*, and *X-Men*, in that it does not stop at imitating costumes, mise-en-scène, and plot and character points from the comics series in question; it appropriates, as literally as possible, the static character of the graphic novel's conventions of narrating stories with pictures.

If the logic of intermedial adaptation seems ungeneric, please recall that the pragmatic approach privileges the *how* of generic production over the *what*, that is, generic thinking and its results over generic product and its empirically verifiable textual parameters. Consider the parallel between the diverse possibilities of interpreting "The western" via westerns—the loping pace and poetic violence of *My Darling Clementine* (John Ford, 1946), the physical brutality and stylistic exaggeration of *The Wild Bunch* (Sam Peckinpah, 1969), the cartoonish pastiche of moments from other westerns in Sam Raimi's *The Quick and the Dead* (1995)—and the equally diverse possibilities of interpreting "the graphic novel" via film. Particularly from the perspective of intermedia philosopher Friedrich Kittler, *Sin City* could be perceived as a failed experiment, because it attempts to *translate* the iconography and visual syntax of graphic novels directly and literally *into* filmed images, rather than *transducing* them *for* film. In other words, a "proper" *cinematic transduction* of the *Sin City* graphic novel, as opposed to Rodriguez's and Miller's attempt to *translate* it into a film, would squeeze from Miller's iconic drawings (such as a static image of a huge man emerging from a shattered tenement door with arms outstretched surrounded by the contorted bodies of policemen seemingly hanging in the air) a set of encoded, *signified meanings* (the huge man has broken his own door down with tremendous force, sending cops flying in every direction), which the filmmakers would have to determine how to express using moving images without sacrificing altogether the iconic qualities that make Miller's graphic novel unique, even among other graphic novels.[43]

No one disagrees that "genre" refers not simply to rules, but to textual possibilities that find expression through the individual producer, consumer, or critic's engagement with a set of rules *as that producer, consumer, or critic understands them*. It is for this reason that I see the semantic-syntactic-pragmatic approach as particularly rich soil for the ludologists to cultivate in collaboration with film and media genre theorists. To do so would prod both camps to recognize the unique technological and discursive parameters of the other camp's central medium, and at the same time to obtain from genre theory's emphasis on "playing by/against the rules" a more generous sense of user *play*—the kinds of experimental, intermedia interpretation in which all media users engage, however subconsciously, while playing, viewing, reading, discussing, and making mass-media artifacts. Michel de Certeau hinted that games focus not merely on rules and play, but on the "relatability" of both rules and specific gaming events to other subjects. While games themselves provide a sketch of what tactical responses to socially implemented "necessities" can be thought in a given cultural moment (consider *Monopoly*, created during the Great Depression, and the discourses on poverty, wealth, and governmental economic intervention within which its players must operate), the relatability of games offers players countless opportunities to narrate the triumphs and failures of their game tactics—and, by extension, the vagaries of their social tactics—to one another with a high degree of social sanction and a low degree of risk.[44] Thinking through video games and genre knowledge gives media studies an enriched position from which to recognize how knowledge gets mobilized in such tactical ways, to appropriate mass-culture forms while subverting some of their intended meanings and ideological codes, in the cultures of "old" media. The kinds of knowledge that film and TV genres represent have always involved shared, ritualized interpretations of everything from science fiction to medical melodrama, beginning with mimeographed fanzines and conventions (perhaps most notably surrounding the *Star Trek* phenomenon as early as the series' second season, when fans lobbied successfully for a third year of new episodes).

One might be tempted to claim that digital media have come to fulfill one of film genre theory's most utopian claims, derived from a combination of structural linguistics and the generous view of mass culture's political possibilities maintained by Raymond Williams and Stuart Hall: at last, it seems, mass media have caught up with the premise expressed by Schatz, Wright, and others that "genre" makes *all* media texts more or less interactive at both the informatic and sociological levels. At the informatic level (that is, the level of the user's engagement with a text or cybertext), the consumers of such otherwise "closed" narrative texts as novels, television series, films, and comic books bring their sense of a genre's conventions to bear on their evaluations and interpretations of these texts. At the sociological level, these consumers engage in extratextual conversations about texts based on generic codes, and arguably all such subjects imagine they belong to an interpretive community that shares their own foreknowledge, even if they never make contact with that community.

But it would be imprudent to proclaim that digital interactivity has come to destroy conventional film genre theory by fulfilling its most democratic wishes. Interactive media have much to teach theorists of genre in "non-interactive" media such as film and television, but text-centered genre theory also serves to remind us of the ideological dimension of genre's imagined communities. Choosing to watch or not watch films of a certain genre, after all, is not in itself equivalent to voting for it, nor do a video game's sales figures necessarily inspire producers to replicate the characterizations, visual style, plot arc, or political overtones of a viewer's favorite game. Realizing that essentialist and text-centered thinking about genre still carries a good deal of clout among users of all stripes also equips us to analyze the determinism that characterizes much theoretical writing about the future of digital media, in which digital artifacts limp along in relative disgrace because new media designers cannot manage to create characters or plot events compelling enough to make their users feel they are embedded in a familiarly satisfying media genre, such as the psychological novel or the classical narrative film.[45] I'm not being pejorative here, but rather pointing out how, like the atomized users who populate Altman's dystopia of contemporary genre culture, independent interpretive communities say the darnedest things, and those communities listen much more attentively to their own members than they do to the academics who "describe"—that is, prescribe—the textual conventions and readerly practices "proper" to a given genre or a given medium.

As a parting example, one that offers a glimpse of the diversity of forms through which ideas of genre get spoken, let me offer a synecdoche for what I began by calling Altman's "definitive doubt"—not to make you desperate enough to snuff it, but to pass along my impression of the irreverent richness of contemporary articulations of genericity. This game menu, which appears in the PS2/Xbox game *Atari Anthology* (2004), envisions an array of video game genres that span an entire galaxy. Genres and subgenres are represented by constellations of stars fashioned into stand-alone video arcade machines, starships, and other icons. Compared to "the musical" and "horror" in film or "soap opera" and "sitcom" in television, such categories as "Arcade Favorites," "Mind Games" (which takes the form of a brain) and "Space" strike the old-school genre critic as lacking in consistent logic. What links arcade games except the places one plays them? *Outlaw* was an arcade game first, so why is it lumped into the "Action" category instead of "Arcade at Home"? Is checkers really a "mind game" compared to chess?

But like the capricious animal taxonomy from Jorge Luis Borges's "The Analytical Language of John Wilkins" as interpreted by Michel Foucault, these

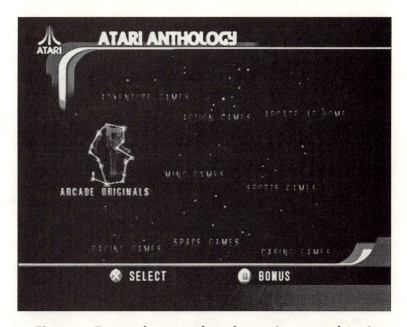

Figure 7.2 Frame enlargement from the opening menu of *Atari Anthology* for PlayStation 2 (Atari 2004) (author's collection).

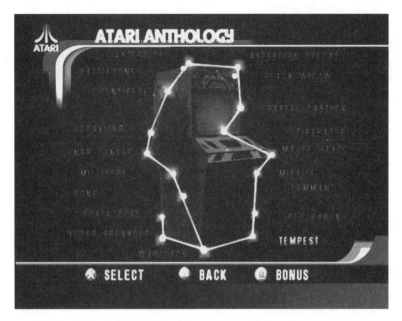

Figure 7.3 Frame enlargement from secondary menu of *Atari Anthology* for PlayStation 2 (Atari 2004) (author's collection).

constellations provide an index of how differently genre is *thought* by video game cultures than by traditional genre theory.[46] Hobbled neither by film studies' theoretical precedents nor by the ontological assertions of the ludologists, such genre experts as programmers, critics, and gamers choose labels like "Arcade Favorites" that mark the social and geographical functions of game types. Surely these ideas about what genre is and how it works are as challenging and as rife with potential for analysis as any ideas articulated by retoolings of familiar semantics and syntax.

Even such a well-trod concept as "semantics" gains an unexpected valence in the *Atari Anthology* universe. By separating the grossly artifacted home games of the late 1970s from the sleeker "vector-graphics" arcade games of the same era (the space-rock-blasting *Asteroids*, the tank game *Battlezone*, the abstract shoot-'em-up *Tempest*), *Atari Anthology* pays lip service to the technological differences between home and arcade games even as it hails specific player groups: it invites the older audience to play the "home arcade" games out of nostalgia, while warning younger players that they may find their crudeness amusing or off-putting. It also invites users to participate in the continuing production of private and public space as distinct, and even to infuse memory with spatial history. By re-creating, blow for blow, game-play options and even game-cabinet art for *Asteroids* and *Tempest*, *Atari Anthology* returns me to the Westdale Mall arcade where I used to feed these machines quarters by the roll. The effect is as startling as passing a plate of madeleines past Proust's Marcel: I am *there*, teasing and being teased by my friends who spend

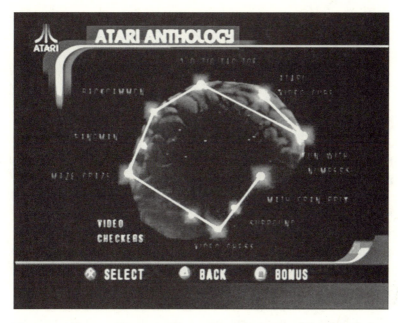

Figure 7.4 Frame enlargement from secondary menu of *Atari Anthology*
for PlayStation 2 (Atari 2004) (author's collection).

more money and play better than I, with the difference being that I wonder now
what we were really fighting about—class difference, social superiority, dexterity, or
perhaps simply the opportunity to fight about something that did not involve parents, school, or adolescent romance. By grouping "Arcade Favorites" together, *Atari
Anthology* has enabled me to revisit my experience of time period, social interaction,
and public space and behavior between 1979 and 1982, one game at a time.

Atari Anthology's historiographic, geographic zodiac of gaming history also
allows us to recognize that, in digital media cultures, typification hinges on
technological change and the culture's awareness of the social meanings of that
change. Each year the video game industry trumpets the arrival of a new deck, a
new format (handheld, Blackberry or similarly styled units that make the single-
screen Game Boy Advance look like a transistor radio crossed with a bulky flip
phone), or at the very least a new innovation (the bongo-drum controller for the
GameCube's *Donkey Konga*, the dance pad user interface). Sales imperatives, such
as the drive to invent new markets, provide the impetus for these changes more
than the users' collective desire for "better" experiences (more hyperreal in
graphical or interactive terms), though the latter helps to both mask and fulfill the
push of the former toward technological development.

The main menu from a similar anthology, *Midway Arcade Treasures* (2003),
addresses the bad faith of this discourse of progress in a particularly telling way by
portraying the exploration of video game history as an archaeological dig into the

pyramids of Egypt. As an anthology of classic games from one of the most successful arcade game producers, *Midway Arcade Treasures* exploits this image to trumpet the superiority of the new home game decks over the "ancient" arcade machines that represented the state of the art in the early 1980s. In those hoary days of yore, cabinets the size of truncated pinball tables were required to shield vulnerable hardware from aggressive gamers; in the sleek and miniaturized present, twenty-four of those very games have been compressed onto a single DVD-ROM for use in a machine that runs $149.95 retail and is smaller and lighter than a laptop computer. The pseudo-historical account of gaming history portrayed by the menu of *Treasures* is "deployed, like games [themselves], in a space outside of and isolated from daily competition, that of the past, the marvelous, the original." But such tales as the one this menu tells are "also, more discreetly, living museums" of the *tactics* that members of a culture use to get by in everyday life, "the benchmarks of an apprenticeship."[47] Following Certeau's lead, we could productively translate *Treasures*'s conceit into a general statement on video game history that befits the Egyptomanic iconography of the menu: we live in a fabulous present of life-like, three-dimensional video game worlds, yet can take nostalgic pleasure in archiving the technological past because, like archaeologists who dig up the tombs of long-dead pharaohs, we have nothing to fear from the past and everything to learn.

Figure 7.5 Frame enlargement from opening title of *Midway Arcade Treasures* for PlayStation 2 (Midway 2003) (author's collection).

My hope is that media theorists will take gamers' unique definitions of genre seriously, as signs of an experiential language of genre that is worth developing—a language that could be projected back onto the histories of genres in other mass audiovisual media in something more productive than merely analogical terms. The *Atari Anthology*'s vision of game icons twinkling in the cosmos presents a suggestive metaphor of "genre" as a constellation: purely organic and "already there," like the stars in the sky, and simultaneously a product of nothing more or less than interpretation. Theodor Adorno wrote that astrologists exploit the rational descriptions of the stars' positions and movements offered by a legitimately empirical science, astronomy, to grant themselves explanatory and predictive authority over the puny human individual: "A veneer of scientific rationality has been fused with blind acceptance of indemonstrable contentions and the spurious exaltation of the factual."[48] Westerners have long perceived the Greco-Roman zodiac as a set of irrefutable and eternal shapes, and equally long ago left the pseudo-scientific "reading" of their meanings to soothsayers and newspaper columnists. The game-cabinet shapes of the Atari zodiac, however, remind us that the true nature of constellations is their contestability across cultures and even among individuals, who regularly attribute entirely different sets of animals, gods, and heroes to the star formations they see. The Atari zodiac models a galaxy of genre, to be sure, but it also makes visible an unexplored universe of genre theory, in all the triangulations among genres, and among diverse media, that genre communities employ to label their artifacts. The dialectical quality of this image borders on the diacritically sublime, for it articulates certainty and doubt, clarity and indistinctness, naturalness and artificiality all at once—sure signs that a genre, and a set of audiences eager to disassemble and reassemble it, wait nearby.

NOTES

1. See Stephen Neale, *Genre* (London: British Film Institute, 1980). The "good scratch" metaphor comes from Rick Altman, "A Semantic/Syntactic Approach to Film Genre" (1984), in *Film/Genre* (London: British Film Institute, 1999), 216.

2. Edward Buscombe, "The Idea of Genre in the American Cinema" (1970), in *Film Genre Reader III*, ed. Barry Keith Grant (Austin: University of Texas Press, 2003), 14.

3. Neale, *Genre*.

4. For a few examples of varying proximity to Neale's blend of structural anthropology, semiotics, and Althusserian ideological theory, see the essays by Jim Collins, Richard Dyer, and Jane Feuer in *Genre: The Musical*, ed. Rick Altman (London: Routledge/BFI, 1980); Will Wright, *Sixguns and Society: A Structural Study of the Western* (Berkeley: University of California Press, 1975); the revised edition of *Women in Film Noir*, ed. E. Ann Kaplan (London: BFI, 1980); and Frank Krutnik, *In a Lonely Street: Film Noir, Genre, Masculinity* (London: Routledge, 1991).

5. Altman, *Film/Genre*, esp. chap. 5.

6. Altman, "A Semantic/Syntactic Approach," 216.

7. See John G. Cawelti, "The Question of Popular Genres Revisited," in *In the Eye of the Beholder: Critical Perspectives in Popular Film and Television*, ed. Gary R. Edgerton, Michael T. Marsden, and Jack Nachbar (Bowling Green, OH: Bowling Green State University Popular Press, 1997), 70.

8. See Buscombe, "The Idea of Genre," 13–19. Buscombe is much clearer about what he means by outer form than what he means by inner. Here I have borrowed Altman's (1984) distinction between genre *semantics*—the objects, people, sounds, and other nominative characteristics of a genre's universe—and genre *syntax*—the repeatable yet flexible systems of arrangement among semantic elements in space and time—in order to clarify the applicability of Buscombe's concepts.

9. Thomas Schatz, *Hollywood Genres: Formulas, Filmmaking, and the Studio System* (Boston: McGraw-Hill, 1981), 16.

10. For a discussion of "body genres" and the horror film's specific appeal to viewers' visceral expectations, see Linda Williams, "Film Bodies: Gender, Genre, and Excess," in Grant, *Film Genre Reader III*, 141–149.

11. See Altman, "A Semantic/Syntactic Approach," 217. Or consider how a semantically oriented critic who would call any film that features a spaceship "science fiction" might react when confronted by a critic from the more exclusive syntactical school, who might call films with spaceships in them "science fiction" only if their plots emphasize the joys of discovery in outer space over the terrors of the unknown. For an enlightening discussion of such a confrontation from the latter point of view, see Bruce F. Kawin, "Children of the Light" (1986), in Grant, *Film Genre Reader III*, 324–345.

12. Altman, *Film/Genre*, 21–22, 49, 101.

13. See Rick Altman, *The American Film Musical* (Bloomington: Indiana University Press, 1987), 36.

14. Altman, *Film/Genre*, 208.

15. Ibid., 205.

16. "Genres begin as reading positions established by studio personnel acting as critics, and expressed through film-making conceived as an act of applied criticism." Altman, *Film/Genre*, 44.

17. Mark J. P. Wolf, "Genre and the Video Game," in *The Medium of the Video Game*, ed. Mark J. P. Wolf (Austin: University of Texas Press, 2001), 113–134.

18. This is not to say that *Pac-Man* tells a story (although the more generous narrative theories suggest it might), but rather to say that Wolf's very loose definition of "narrative" does not in itself offer the reader the means to form an opinion. At the very least, narrative analysis requires following the lead of the Russian formalists and like-minded theorists such as Tzvetan Todorov and Gérard Genette in distinguishing a narrative's *story*—the narrated events as the reader, viewer, or player assembles them from the text or artifact at hand—from its *narration*, or *plot*—the discursive acts performed by or through the artifact that communicate the story's events. For overviews of the debates on what constitutes narrative in film, see André Gaudreault, "Film, Narrative, Narration: The Cinema of the Lumière Brothers," *Early Film: Space-Frame-Narrative*. Ed. Thomas Elsaesser with Adam Barker (London: British Film Institute, 1990)68–75 in which the author argued that any "statement [that] relates . . . a real or fictitious action," such as a given

cinematic shot, is a narrative; and Tom Gunning, *D. W. Griffith and the Origins of American Narrative Film: The Early Years at Biograph* (Urbana: University of Illinois Press, 1991), chap. 2.

19. Dudley Andrew doubts that genre "theory" counts as a theory at all, because (at least in its mid-seventies incarnation, as he described it then) its aim is to return to individual texts in order to evaluate them; unlike theories about the aesthetic nature of film, for example, genre theory seemed to have no end in itself. See Andrew, *The Major Film Theories* (New York: Oxford University Press, 1976), 4–5.

20. See Steve Neale, *Genre and Hollywood* (London: Routledge, 2000), esp. "Major Genres," 51–149. For an account of generic hybridization that follows up brilliantly on Fredric Jameson's "Nostalgia for the Present" argument about postmodern Hollywood, see Jim Collins, "Genericity in the Nineties: Eclectic Irony and the New Sincerity," in *Film Theory Goes to the Movies*, ed. Jim Collins, Hilary Radner, and Ava Preacher Collins (New York: Routledge, 1993), 242–263.

Film noir provides an excellent example of a critically productive "critical" genre that in its time forked the road of the gangster film into domestic melodrama, crime drama, police procedural, and others, all while attracting labels like "melodrama" from *Variety*, the *New York Times*, and other important organs of mainstream movie criticism—never the label given it by French critics of the 1940s. Film noir metamorphosed into a *production* genre only in the 1970s, after screenwriter and critic Paul Schrader consolidated the rising buzz of noir recognition into a key essay, "Notes on *Film Noir*" (1972). Realizing the impossibility of taking a taxonomic view of this genre that was not one, James Naremore led off his indispensable book, *More Than Night*, with "the history of [the] idea" of film noir. See Naremore, *More Than Night: Film Noir in Its Contexts* (Berkeley: University of California Press, 1998), 9–39.

21. Sam Miller, private e-mail correspondence with the author, February 16, 2005. Used with permission.

22. Altman, *Film/Genre*, 210.

23. See, for example, Jane Feuer, "Genre Study and Television," in *Channels of Discourse, Revisited*, ed. Robert C. Allen (Chapel Hill: University of North Carolina Press, 1992), 138–159, and Susan Murray, " 'I Think We Need a New Name for It': The Meeting of Documentary and Reality TV," in *Reality TV: Remaking Television Culture*, ed. Susan Murray and Laurie Ouellette (New York: New York University Press, 2004), 40–56.

24. On the Producer's Game and the "composite strategy" that Joel Silver undertook when planning the production of *Die Hard*, see Altman, *Film/Genre*, 47.

25. Schatz, *Hollywood Genres*, 36.

26. Hugo Münsterberg, *The Photoplay: A Psychological Study* (1916), in *Hugo Münsterberg on Film*, ed. Allan Langdale (New York: Routledge, 2002), esp. 79–88.

27. Espen Aarseth, *Cybertext: Perspectives on Ergodic Literature* (Baltimore: Johns Hopkins University Press, 1997), 47–51.

28. See Jay David Bolter and Richard Grusin, *Remediation: Understanding New Media* (Cambridge, MA: MIT Press, 1999), 44–50.

29. Ibid., 45.

30. Espen Aarseth, "Genre Trouble: Narrativism and the Art of Simulation," in *First Person: New Media as Story, Performance, and Game*, ed. Noah Wardrip-Fruin and Pat Harrigan (Cambridge, MA: MIT Press, 2004), 49–51; Markku Eskelinen, "Towards Computer Game Studies," in Wardrip-Fruin and Harrigan, *First Person*, 36–38.

31. Aarseth, response to Stuart Moulthrop's online response to "Genre Trouble," in Wardrip-Fruin and Harrigan, *First Person*, 49.

32. Evaluating "whether [semiotics] can provide a viable theoretical foundation for the study of cybernetic textuality," Aarseth wrote that "[f]or semiotics, as for linguistics, texts are chains of signs and, therefore, linear by definition. . . . The new [ergodic, i.e., multilinear] constructions [such as hypertext narratives/experiences] consist of 'interactive dynamic' elements, a fact that renders traditional semiotic models and terminology, which were developed for objects that are mostly static, useless in their present, unmodified form" (*Cybertext*, 26). This syllogism, which exemplifies the argumentative logic employed throughout *Cybertext*, skips over not only the vigorous modifications made to semiotic definitions of "text" when applied (by Aarseth's bugbear Roland Barthes, for example) to the signifying processes of photographs and other nonlinear or quasi-linear media objects, but also the attention semiotics traditionally pays to the nonlinear system of signification itself, in which icons, indexes, and symbols become more or less arbitrarily connected to concepts or *signifieds* through conventional use, use that ultimately depends on *differences* among symbols to ensure their discreteness from one another. It is difficult to imagine why, if Aarseth wished to wrest ergodic literature from semioticians for good, he did not address Ferdinand de Saussure's legacy for literary and media studies anywhere in *Cybertext* (he concentrated solely on the tenets of Charles Sanders Peirce, in similarly syllogistic fashion).

33. W. C. Bryant, customer review of *Red Dead Revolver*, 5 May 2004, http://www.amazon.com/exec/obidos/tg/detail/-/B0001ADAME/qid=1117038641/sr=1-1/ref=sr_1_1_etk-vg/002-5020132-6424819?v=glance&s=videogames&n=468642, accessed 14 May 2005.

34. gAmE_bOi, customer review of *Red Dead Revolver*, 5 May 2004, in ibid., 14 May 2005.

35. Henry Jenkins, "Game Design as Narrative Architecture," in Wardrip-Fruin and Harrigan, *First Person*, 120, 121, 123.

36. John Belton, "Digital Cinema: A False Revolution" (2002), in *Film Theory and Criticism*, 6th ed., ed. Leo Braudy and Marshall Cohen (New York: Oxford University Press, 2003), 905–906.

37. For examinations of the material effects of collective fantasies about media on their use and development, see Carolyn Marvin, *When Old Technologies Were New: Thinking About Electric Communication in the Nineteenth Century* (New York: Oxford University Press, 1988), and Paul Young, *The Cinema Dreams Its Rivals: Media Fantasy Films from Radio to the Internet* (Minneapolis: University of Minnesota Press, 2006), introduction and chap. 1.

38. See Bolter and Grusin, *Remediation*, esp. 46–48.

39. Television shows like the now-canceled *Talk Soup* and VH1's more recent *I Love the 90's* and *Best Week Ever* provide a kind of user's guide to new television genres and subgenres for viewers uncertain about the conventions and expectations they foster. They also demonstrate that textuality is never the only thing at stake when media invoke and evoke genres. Genre typification tends, as do gender, class, and race stereotypes, to mobilize "proper" audiences for specific genres based on social prejudices. See Laurie Ouellette and Carolyn Anderson, "Reading the Talk Show: The Politics of *Talk Soup*," in Edgerton, Marsden, and Nachbar, *In the Eye of the Beholder*, 154. See also Susan Murray and Laurie Ouellette, eds., *Reality TV: Remaking Television Culture* (New York: New York University Press, 2004).

40. "*Quark,*" Internet Movie Database, http://www.imdb.com/title/tt0077066/
?fr=c210ZT1kZnxodD0xfGZiPXV8cG49MHxxPXF1YXJrfG14PTIwfGxtPTUwMHxod
G1sPTE_;fc=1;ft=20;fm=1 (1 July 2005).

41. Altman, *Film/Genre*, 35.

42. Ibid., 34–35. Altman's source here is Charles Musser, "The Travel Genre in 1903–1904: Moving Towards Fictional Narrative," in *Early Cinema: Space-Frame-Narrative,* ed. Thomas Elsaesser with Adam Barker (London: British Film Institute, 1990), 123–132.

43. See Friedrich A. Kittler, *Discourse Networks 1800/1900,* trans. Michael Metteer, with Chris Cullens (1985; Stanford: Stanford University Press, 1990), 273–274.

44. Michel de Certeau, *The Practice of Everyday Life,* vol. 1, trans. Steven Rendall (Berkeley: University of California Press, 1984), 21–24.

45. For a crucial opening move in this discussion of digital narrative's development into an art form commensurate with drama and literary fiction (with all the ideological underpinnings this art envy entails), see Janet Murray, *Hamlet on the Holodeck: The Future of Narrative in Cyberspace* (New York: Free Press, 1997), esp. chap. 10. For a critique of Murray's work as "narrativistic colonialism," see Espen Aarseth, "Genre Trouble: Narrativism and the Art of Simulation," in Wardrip-Fruin and Harrigan, *First Person,* 45–55, esp. 49. For a discussion of "cinema envy" among game designers, see Young, *The Cinema Dreams Its Rivals,* chap. 5.

46. See Michel Foucault, *The Order of Things: An Archaeology of the Human Sciences* (1966; New York: Vintage, 1973), xv.

47. Certeau, *The Practice of Everyday Life,* 22–23.

48. Theodor W. Adorno, "The Stars Down to Earth: The *Los Angeles Times* Astrology Column" (1952–53), in *The Stars Down to Earth and Other Essays on the Irrational Culture,* 2nd ed., ed. Stephen Crook (New York: Routledge, 2001), 159.

BIBLIOGRAPHY

Aarseth, Espen. "Genre Trouble: Narrativism and the Art of Simulation." Wardrip-Fruin, *First Person,* 45–55.
———. *Cybertext: Perspectives on Ergodic Literature.* Baltimore: Johns Hopkins University Press, 1997.
Adorno, Theodor W. *The Stars Down to Earth and Other Essays on the Irrational Culture,* 2nd ed. Ed. Stephen Crook. New York: Routledge, 2001.
Altman, Rick. *The American Film Musical.* Bloomington: Indiana University Press, 1987.
———. *Film/Genre.* London: British Film Institute, 1999.
———, ed. *Genre: The Musical.* London: Routledge/British Film Institute, 1980.
Andrew, Dudley. *The Major Film Theories.* New York: Oxford University Press, 1976.
Belton, John. "Digital Cinema: A False Revolution." 2002. *Film Theory and Criticism.* Ed. Leo Braudy and Marshall Cohen. 6th ed. New York: Oxford University Press, 2003. 905–906.
Bolter, Jay David, and Richard Grusin. *Remediation: Understanding New Media.* Cambridge, MA: MIT Press, 1999.

Buscombe, Edward. "The Idea of Genre in the American Cinema." 1970. Grant, *Film Genre Reader III*, 12–26.

Cawelti, John G. "The Question of Popular Genres Revisited." Edgerton, Marsden, and Nachbar, *In the Eye of the Beholder*, 67–84.

Certeau, Michel de. *The Practice of Everyday Life*. Vol. 1. Trans. Steven Rendall. Berkeley: University of California Press, 1984.

Collins, Jim. "Genericity in the Nineties: Eclectic Irony and the New Sincerity." *Film Theory Goes to the Movies*. Ed. Jim Collins, Hilary Radner, and Ava Preacher Collins. New York: Routledge, 1993. 242–263.

Edgerton, Gary R., Michael T. Marsden, and Jack Nachbar, eds. *In the Eye of the Beholder: Critical Perspectives in Popular Film and Television*. Bowling Green, OH: Bowling Green State University Popular Press, 1997.

Eskelinen, Markku. "Towards Computer Game Studies." Wardrip-Fruin and Harrigan, *First Person*, 36–38.

Feuer, Jane. "Genre Study and Television." *Channels of Discourse, Revisited*. Ed. Robert C. Allen. Chapel Hill: University of North Carolina Press, 1992. 138–159.

Foucault, Michel. *The Order of Things: An Archaeology of the Human Sciences*. New York: Vintage, 1973.

Gaudreault, André. "Film, Narrative, Narration: The Cinema of the Lumière Brothers," *Early Film: Space-Frame-Narrative*. Ed. Thomas Elsaesser with Adam Barker. London: British Film Institute, 1990.

Grant, Barry Keith, ed. *Film Genre Reader III*. Austin: University of Texas Press, 2003.

Jenkins, Henry. "Game Design as Narrative Architecture." Wardrip-Fruin and Harrigan, *First Person*, 118–130.

Kaplan, E. Ann, ed. *Women in Film Noir*. 3rd ed. London: British Film Institute, 1999.

Kawin, Bruce F. "Children of the Light." Grant, *Film Genre Reader III*, 324–345.

Kittler, Friedrich A. *Discourse Networks 1800/1900*. Trans. Michael Metteer with Chris Cullens. Stanford: Stanford University Press, 1990.

Krutnik, Frank. *In a Lonely Street: Film Noir, Genre, Masculinity*. London: Routledge, 1991.

Marvin, Carolyn. *When Old Technologies Were New: Thinking about Electric Communication in the Nineteenth Century*. New York: Oxford University Press, 1988.

Münsterberg, Hugo. *Hugo Münsterberg on Film*. Ed. Allan Langdale. New York: Routledge, 2002.

Murray, Janet. *Hamlet on the Holodeck: The Future of Narrative in Cyberspace*. New York: Free Press, 1997.

Murray, Susan. " 'I Think We Need a New Name for It': The Meeting of Documentary and Reality TV." *Reality TV: Remaking Television Culture*. Ed. Susan Murray and Laurie Ouellette. New York: New York University Press, 2004. 40–56.

Musser, Charles. "The Travel Genre in 1903–1904: Moving Toward Fictional Narrative." *Early Cinema: Space-Frame-Narrative*. Ed. Thomas Elsaesser with Adam Barker. London: British Film Institute, 1990. 123–132.

Naremore, James. *More Than Night: Film Noir in Its Contexts*. Berkeley: University of California Press, 1998.

Neale, Stephen. *Genre*. London: British Film Institute, 1980.

———. *Genre and Hollywood*. London: Routledge, 2000.

Ouellette, Laurie, and Carolyn Anderson. "Reading the Talk Show: The Politics of *Talk Soup*." Edgerton, Marsden, and Nachbar, *In the Eye of the Beholder*, 149–165.

Schatz, Thomas. *Hollywood Genres: Formulas, Filmmaking, and the Studio System.* Boston: McGraw-Hill, 1981.

Wardrip-Fruin, Noah, and Pat Harrigan, eds. *First Person: New Media as Story, Performance, and Game.* Cambridge, MA: MIT Press, 2004.

Williams, Linda. "Film Bodies: Gender, Genre, and Excess." 1991. Grant, *Film Genre Reader III*, 141–149.

Wolf, Mark J. P. "Genre and the Video Game." *The Medium of the Video Game.* Ed. Mark J. P. Wolf. Austin: University of Texas Press, 2001. 113–134.

Wright, Will. *Sixguns and Society: A Structural Study of the Western.* Berkeley: University of California Press, 1975.

Young, Paul. *The Cinema Dreams Its Rivals: Media Fantasy Films from Radio to the Internet.* Minneapolis: University of Minnesota Press, 2006.

CHAPTER 8

GILDA: TEXTUAL ANALYSIS, POLITICAL ECONOMY, AND ETHNOGRAPHY

TOBY MILLER AND MARIANA JOHNSON

Gilda tries to get her dignity back through sex, Johnny through power—the same trophies many of us seek at Yale, the former on couches and the latter in classrooms.

   —Eve Tushnet, editor in chief, *Yale Free Press* (1999)

Will this get me a job?
Is TV bad for you?
How do we get that show back on?

    —Questions posed by undergraduate majors
       in film and media studies.

An intramurally oriented, Anglo-dominated textual determinism has dominated film and media studies for decades.[1] It is our contention that scholars of film and media studies should become more self-consciously interdisciplinary in their means, and public in their focus, following the examples of many other text-based critics across the humanities who have retrained themselves and now contribute to public-cultural debate.[2] If practitioners remain embedded in the old ways, they risk a disciplinary myopia that diminishes their ability to innovate as researchers, and argue as public intellectuals. Money, law, policy, production, content, distribution, exhibition, and reception are all equally relevant to the study of the screen. Research from multiple disciplinary and international contexts can expose the interrelationships among these categories along the spectrum of audiovisual production.

In this essay, we question the efficacy of contemporary mainstream film and media studies' dominant modes of analyzing texts, then investigate alternatives from political economy and media anthropology, seeking to blend economic and ethnographic insights with textual analysis. These methods offer a radical historicization of cultural context, supplementing the examination of textual properties and spectatorial processes with an account of *occasionality* that details the conditions under which texts are made, circulated, received, interpreted, and criticized. The life of any popular or praised text is a passage across space and time, a life remade again and again by institutions, discourses, and practices of distribution and reception. Cultural historian Roger Chartier proposed a tripartite approach to textual analysis, that is, reconstruction of "the diversity of older readings from their sparse and multiple traces"; a focus on "the text itself, the object that conveys it, and the act that grasps it"; and an identification of "the strategies by which authors and publishers tried to impose an orthodoxy or a prescribed reading on the text."[3] This grid from the new cultural history turns away from reflectionism, which argues that a text's key meaning lies in its overt or covert capacity to capture the zeitgeist. It also rejects formalism's claim that a close reading of sound and image cues can secure a definitive meaning. Because texts accrete and attenuate meanings on their travels as they rub up against, trope, and are troped by other fictional and social texts, we must consider all the shifts and shocks that characterize their existence as cultural commodities, their ongoing renewal as the temporary "property" of varied, productive workers and publics, and the abiding "property" of businesspeople.

The essay concludes with an example of such an approach, applied to the career of the classic film noir, *Gilda* (Charles Vidor, 1946).[4] Our Yale correspondent quoted above illustrates how key screen texts are taken up as guides for living, far beyond the imagination of the armchair critic, as when Ivy League scions use *Gilda* to conceptualize their quest for "vast sums of money and power."[5] For their part, the anonymous undergraduates from anonymous universities, also quoted above, are questioning film and media studies from a less Olympian perspective. Bearing in mind the importance of serving these lusty young leaders and followers of the future, we come to renew textual analysis with economic culturalism, not to bury it.

PROBLEMS WITH THE STATE OF PLAY

Film and media texts have always led lives that extend beyond their frames, inspiring dialogue, debate, antagonism, and even moral panic. There is a long history linking textual analysis to the screen in public culture. In the silent era, ethical critic Vachel Lindsay referred to "the moving picture man as a local social force . . . the mere formula of [whose] activities keeps the public well-tempered."[6] Because film had the power to stimulate and regulate public life, it was both a threat and a boon to intellectuals and reformers. Various forms of social criticism connected moviegoing to gambling and horse racing, but some social reformers looked to the medium as a potential forum for moral uplift. If the screen could drive the young to madness, it might also provoke responsibility.[7] Motion Picture Association of America bureaucrat Will Hays regarded the industry as an "institution of service" that riveted "the girders of society."[8] These girders were erected over the bodies of others, of course, as critics have pointed out through acute, social-movement-linked textual analysis. In 1921, the Great Wall Motion Picture Studio was founded in New York by Chinese expatriates angered by U.S. industry and government neglect of their complaints about Hollywood representations of Chinese characters. It proceeded to produce films for export home as well as for the U.S. market.[9] The following year, Mexico embargoed imported U.S. films because of the repugnant "greaser" genre, and was supported by other Latin American countries, Canada, France, and Spain.[10]

But these forms of criticism, closely articulated to national and diasporic cultures and immigrant concerns, were soon supplanted as sources of knowledge for students and scholars by academic professionalism. Like the other emergent audiovisual media of the twentieth century, the cinema was quickly mined by sociology and psychology, where obsessions with propaganda and perception gave scientific and/or reactionary professors the opportunity to serve churches, businesses, and governments. Consider the Payne Fund studies' research into the cinema's effects on young people in the 1930s.[11] These pioneering scholars boldly set out to gauge youthful emotional reactions by assessing, for example, "galvanic skin response."[12] Examining how movies influenced children's attitudes to race and sex, playground conduct, and sleeping patterns, the Payne fundees inaugurated mass social science panic about young people at the cinema. They were driven by academic, religious, and familial iconophobia in the face of large groups of people who were engaged by popular culture, and seemed able to elude the control of father, state, and ruling class.

Payne Fund concerns about the impact of the popular on young citizens inspired decades of remorseless media-effects work, a source of publicly funded nutrition to generations of psychologists via the U.S. model of social order through behavioral scientism, through seven decades of obsessive attempts to correlate youthful consumption of popular culture with antisocial conduct. The pattern is that whenever new communications technologies emerge, children are immediately identified as both pioneers and victims, endowed by manufacturers and critics with immense power and yet immense vulnerability. This was true of 1920s "Radio Boy" amateurs, seeking out signals from afar, and it was true of 1990s "Girl Power" avatars, seeking out subjectivities from afar. They are held to be the first to know and the last to understand the media—the grand paradox of youth, latterly on display in the "digital sublime" of technological determinism, as always with the superadded valence of a future citizenship in peril.[13] After the Second World War, the social sciences had begun the less lucrative and reactionary task of studying the film industry as a social institution, with the anthropology of Hortense Powdermaker[14] and the sociology of J. P. Mayer[15] calling for counterknowledge among the population. Powdermaker coined the expression "The Dream Factory," which has since passed into public discourse.[16] Regrettably, their work was eclipsed academically by the more instrumentally propitious arena of positivism, as cold war–style social science received greater material benefits and policy influence than critical ethnography.[17]

And as for textual analysis, the Catholic Church engaged debates about the role of the film critic when Pope Pius XII issued *Miranda Prorsus: Encyclical Letter on Motion Pictures, Radio and Television* in 1957, stating that ". . . Catholic Film critics can have much influence; they ought to set the moral issue of the plots in its proper light, defending those judgments which will act as a safeguard against falling into so-called 'relative morality,' or the overthrow of that right order in which the lesser issues yield place to the more important." The right kind of textual analysis could obviously mold good Catholic subjects. And indeed, textual analysis has become an ecumenical, even secular method of producing citizens, as per the missions of literary criticism and speech communication.[18] As part of liberal education, the mission of cultivating ethically self-styling subjects includes screen analysis as part of its armature, alongside ethical criticism and other techniques.

In keeping with this history, we are routinely told with pride about film and media studies' interdisciplinarity, which purportedly prepares it to participate at a high level intellectually, and a powerful one publicly. Yet a productive dialogue with public culture remains stifled, because the current orthodoxies of our field preclude us from contributing very much. Consider the following recent cases as tests of film and media studies' contribution to debate. Ask yourself which forms of knowledge—and objects of analysis, including texts—might have added to our capacity to respond to (or initiate) relevant inquiry and commentary, and what it says about our politics that *every* major issue of public concern about film and media remains essentially unaddressed by our discipline:

- A 1999 content analysis published by the American Medical Association (AMA) examined feature-length animation films made in the United States between 1937 and 1997 and their association of legal but damaging recreational drugs with heroism.[19] The study received significant public attention, with endorsement by the AMA itself, a widely attended press conference, numerous media stories, and formal replies from Disney, which clearly felt provoked. Similar interest surrounded the 2001 release of findings that despite the film industry and "big" tobacco companies agreeing to a voluntary ban on product placement in 1989, the incidence of stars smoking cigarettes in Hollywood films since that time had increased eleven-fold, mostly to get around bans on television commercials, while use in youth-oriented films had doubled since the 1998 Master Settlement Agreement between the tobacco companies and forty-six U.S. states. In addition to placing their products on film and television, the industry also provided stars with free cigarettes and cigars, encouraging them to smoke in public and during photographic and interview sessions as a quid pro quo.[20] In response, the American Lung Association staged a public relations campaign on the topic to coincide with the 2002 Academy Awards, seeking to embarrass the industry to include warnings in its film ratings about tobacco use, alongside alcohol advisories. Major campaigns and studies have also been undertaken by the Massachusetts Public Interest Research Group and the University of California, San Francisco Medical School. Film and media studies contributed not a jot to this textual research, or subsequent public debate.

- In 2002, the Tisch School of the Arts at New York University, where we have both worked, received a formal note from the Motion Picture Association advising that copyrighted films were being illegally distributed onto a computer assigned to someone in that school's bureaucracy. Administrators did not turn to the Department of Cinema Studies for advice on the legal, political, educational, textual, audience, technological, or privacy implications of the downloading and its surveillance by the association—and rightly so. We would have had nothing to offer.

- In the United States today, literally millions of people are petitioning the Federal Communications Commission about the impact on democracy and textual diversity of media ownership, control, access, and content. Yet large public events run by our vibrant media-reform and media-justice movements feature virtually no one from U.S. film and media studies as speakers or audiences.[21]

U.S. and British film and media studies are condemned to near irrelevancy in the public sphere of popular criticism, state and private policy, and social-movement critique. Our mistake was to set up a series of *nostra* early on about what counted as knowledge, then police the borders. This is a standard disciplinary tactic. It is very familiar rent-seeking conduct—effective as a form of gatekeeping, but *in*effective as a means of dialogue.

The particular *données* barely need rehearsal, but here is the binary of film and media studies' good and bad objects:

Good Object	Bad Object
Psychoanalysis central	Psychology unsubtle
Spectatorship sexy	Audience unimportant
Archive acceptable	Laboratory louche
Criticism canonical	Ethnography extraneous
Auteur interesting	Wonk wearisome
Textual analysis alpha	Content analysis crude

Media studies is sometimes said to be more sociocultural than film studies in its inclinations and methods, but is this really correct? U.S. media studies takes it as something of a given that the mainstream media are not responsible for—well, anything. This position functions as a virtual nostrum in some research into, for instance, fans of television drama or sport, who are thought to construct connections with celebrities and actants in ways that mimic friendship, make sense of human interaction, and ignite cultural politics. This critique commonly attacks opponents of television for failing to allot the people's machine its due as a populist apparatus that subverts patriarchy, capitalism, and other forms of oppression. Commercial television is held to have progressive effects, because its programs are decoded by viewers in keeping with their own social situations. That might suggest an attack on dominant ideology, but where is the evidence? Counterhegemonic activities are supposedly apparent to scholars from their perusal of audience conventions, Web pages, discussion groups, quizzes, and rankings, or by watching television with their children—very droll. But can fans be said to resist labor exploitation, patriarchy, racism, and U.S. neo-imperialism, or in some specifiable way make a difference to politics beyond their own selves, when they interpret texts unusually, dress up in public as men from outer space, or chat about their romantic frustrations? And what does it suggest about the subversive potential of a scholarly approach that privileges these consumer practices—to such an extent that it has taken hold in the first world at a moment when media policy fetishizes deregulation and governing at a distance?

The strand of U.S. media studies we are questioning emerged from venerable UK-based critiques of cultural pessimism, political economy, and current-affairs-oriented broadcasting. These critiques originated in reaction to a heavily regulated, duopolistic broadcasting system—1970s Britain—in which the BBC represented a high-culture snobbery that many leftists associated with an oppressive class structure. It is not surprising that there was a desire for a playful, commercial,

noncitizen address. As these accounts of television made their Atlantic crossing to
the United States, where there was no public-broadcasting behemoth in need of
critique, lots of not-very-leftist professors and students were ready to hear that
U.S. audiences learning about parts of the world that their country bombs, in-
vades, owns, misrepresents, or otherwise exploits were less important, and even less
political, than those audiences' interpretations of actually existing local soap operas, wrestling bouts, or science fiction series. For its part, in the United Kingdom,
where deregulation has latterly opened up the television landscape to more commercial endeavors, as per the United States, the original critique of documentary
seriousness looks tired—and when added to new forms of academic and governmental codification of media studies, it has arguably depoliticized much research there, as well, with scholars and students plumbing their own pleasures and
preoccupations.

This is not to gainsay important achievements in film and media studies. Analysts have sought to account for and resist narrative stereotypes and exclusions—
to explain, in Richard Dyer's words, "why socialists and feminists liked things
they thought they ought not to,"[22] and why some voices and images are excluded
or systematically distorted. This difficulty over pleasure, presence, and absence
accounts for film theory being highly critical of prevailing representations, but
never reifying itself into the puritanism alleged by critics of political correctness.
The diversity of latter-day film anthologies makes the point clear. Contemporary black film volumes divide between spectatorial and aesthetic dimensions,[23]
queer ones identify links between social oppression and film and video practice,[24]
and feminist collections engage differences of race, history, class, sexuality, and
nation, alongside and as part of theoretical difference.[25] The implicit and explicit Eurocentrism, masculinism, and universalism of earlier analyses have been
questioned by social movements and third and fourth world discourses that
highlight exclusions and generate new methods.[26] At the same time, U.S. binaries of black and white, straight and gay, continue to characterize much critical
work.

Crucial elements continue to be left out of today's dominant discourse of film
and media studies—the major journals,[27] book series, professional associations,
and graduate programs. Our anecdotes about health, copyright, and media reform
point to the disconnection of film and media studies from *both* popular *and* policy-
driven discussion of films. This irrelevance flows from a lack of engagement with
research conducted outside the textualist and historical side to the humanities. For
example, humanities work on stardom seldom addresses research on that topic
from the social sciences. Adding this material to the textual, theoreticist, and
biographical preferences of humanities critics could offer new kinds of knowledge
about, for instance, the impact of stars on box office, via regression analysis, and of
work practices, via labor studies.[28]

WHAT ELSE COULD BE DONE?

Film and media texts are part of a multiform network of entertainment, via the Web, DVDs, electronic games, television, telephones, and multiplexes. The brief moment when cinema could be viewed as a fairly unitary phenomenon in terms of exhibition (say, 1920 to 1950) set up the *conceptual* prospect of its textual fetishization in academia, something that became *technologically feasible* with videocassette recorders—just when that technology's popularity compromised the very discourse of stable aestheticization! Now that viewing environments, audiences, technologies, and genres are so multiple, the cinema is restored to a mixed-medium mode. No wonder some argue that "a film today is merely a billboard stretched out in time, designed to showcase tomorrow's classics in the video stores and television reruns,"[29] or that cinema is an aesthetic "engine driving . . . interlinked global entertainment markets."[30] And television? *Alias* continued its run on network television in the United States not because of high ratings, but because it posted the highest-ever DVD sales for drama programming.

The U.S. federal government's official classification of screen production[31] includes features, made-for-television films, television series, commercials, and music videos—and so should film and media studies' "official classification." We need to acknowledge the policy, distributional, promotional, and exhibitionary protocols of the screen at each site as much as their textual ones: enough talk of "economic reductionism" without also problematizing "textual reductionism"; enough valorization of close reading and armchair accounts of human interiority without ethical and political regard for the conditions of global cultural labor, and the significance of workers, texts, and subjectivities within social movements and demographic cohorts; enough denial of the role of government; enough teaching classes on animation, for instance, without reference to effects work, content analysis—and an international political economy that sees an episode of *The Simpsons* decrying globalization, when the program has itself been made by non-union animators in Southeast Asia. These issues—cultural labor, industry frameworks, audience experiences, patterns of meaning, and cultural policy—should be integral.

We need to view the screen through twin theoretical prisms. On the one hand, its texts can be understood as the newest component of sovereignty, a twentieth-century cultural addition to patrimony and rights that sits alongside such traditional topics as territory, language, history, and schooling. On the other hand, screen texts derive from a cluster of culture industries. They are subject to exactly the rent-seeking practices and exclusionary representational protocols that characterize liaisons between state and capital. We must ask:

- Is film and media studies serving phantasmatic projections of humanities critics' narcissism, or does it actively engage cultural policies and social-movement politics?
- Do the popular media give the people of the world what they want, or do they operate via monopoly-capitalist business practice?
- Is alternative/state-supported screen culture expanding the vision and availability of the good life to include the ability of a people to control its representation on screen?
- Is that "alternative" culture merely a free ride for fractions of a comprador, cosmopolitan, or social-movement bourgeoisie?
- To what extent do national television systems and cinemas engage their rhetorical publics?
- What place does labor have in giving culture value?
- How can film and media studies intervene in the public sphere?

To understand the screen and its audiences in the contemporary world and engage with the complex, intersecting questions raised above, film and media studies can take advantage of diverse disciplinary approaches to the study of culture by confronting the ways in which film and media texts collide with the concerns of economics, cultural policy, and media, communication, and cultural studies. There is an increasing need for those working within the field to recognize the ways in which these different approaches are intertwined and can be placed into productive dialogue with one another. Scholarship that interprets an individual film text's formal properties, for instance, should be concerned with how changes in technology or the labor process have influenced stylistic trends. From that insight follow several related, though rarely pursued, questions:

- Where does this technology come from, geographically speaking?
- How do policy and trade laws affect its availability and use?
- What kind of labor by producer and audiences does it require?
- Who is doing that work, where, and with what impact?

Some of these questions are addressed by recent developments in ethnography. Whereas cultural anthropology largely avoided the media in the past,[32] the transnational spread of electronic technology has led to the deconstruction of old ideas about place and culture, and a new alertness to the social worlds of the media and the workings of power within them that determine the production, content, and circulation of texts. Anthropologists have adapted cross-cultural ethnography and concerns for everyday life to the study of media practices worldwide via a materialist method that rejects the putative divisions of top-down versus bottom-up, of economy versus experience.[33]

Media Worlds: Anthropology on New Terrain[34] charts various critical anthropological perspectives that are now being brought to the study of media, addressing a broad range of contexts: indigenous video production and political activism, subject formation, cultural politics of nation-states, social analysis of institutional sites of production, transnational media flows, and the social life of technology. This willingness to address both the self-determined image production of disen-franchised groups (for example, Kayapo cultural performance in Brazil) and the social structures underlying dominant media institutions (such as the homoge-nization and branding of *Latinidad* by powerful Spanish-language television networks in the United States) demonstrates the "simultaneity of hegemonic and anti-hegemonic effects."[35] It also shows that media ethnography can transcend narrow audience studies, such as uses-and-gratifications research that quizzes hyperspecific audiences about their likes and dislikes without regard for larger, culture-crossing structures of power and meaning. Ethnographies of media look at the production, distribution, and consumption of film and other media as they travel through a variety of circuits and spaces. In doing so, the approach brings attention to media environments and practices that may appear "off the grid," situated outside the arenas in which film and media theorists typically operate.

For example, U.S. films are allotted various generic descriptions for use in specific markets. What could a static textual criticism tell us about the content of *Bram Stoker's Dracula* (Francis Ford Coppola, 1992) when it circulates differently in various parts of the world? For the British release, Columbia TriStar arranged a fashion extravaganza for journalists to encourage talk about a new Goth look, leading to a spot on the BBC's *Clothes Show*, and stories in *Harpers and Queen* magazine that located the meaning of the film in white urban style.[36] *Dances with Wolves* (Kevin Costner, 1990) was sold in France as a documentary-style drama-tization of Native American life, and *Malcolm X* (Spike Lee, 1991) was promoted there with posters of the Stars and Stripes aflame.[37] *Sliver* (Phillip Noyce, 1993), which was shown in the United States with four minutes cut by Paramount cen-sors, was promoted overseas as "The film America didn't see," returning twice its domestic revenue in foreign sales.[38] Whereas U.S. trailers for *Moulin Rouge!* (Baz Luhrmann, 2001) featured a syrupy moment of terpsichory between lovers, Japa-nese audiences were provided a death-bed scene, due to their alleged interest in tragedy as honor.[39] *Pearl Harbor* (Michael Bay, 2001) was promoted in Japan as a love story rather than the blend of righteous revenge and forgiving passion that provided a domestic focus elsewhere. Its trailer showed a Japanese airman warning children to take cover.[40] After *Minority Report* (2002) failed domestically, director Stephen Spielberg and star Tom Cruise traveled everywhere they could to recoup a seemingly unwise investment via personal appearances in the auteur reaches of Europe, amidst new commercials that made the film "not like schoolwork." The overseas release of *The Sweetest Thing* (Roger Kumble, 2002) included a segment considered too touchy for U.S. audiences: a performance number called "The Penis Song," which featured the female leads singing "You're too big to fit in" at their restaurant.[41] *Master and Commander: The Far Side of the World* (Peter Weir, 2003) was sold by Fox to transnational audiences by linking it to the 2003 men's Rugby World Cup. Star Russell Crowe appeared on the Fox Sports World cable channel, interspersed with footage of rugby games and his performance in the film, talking about how rugby was both a metaphor and a technique for male bonding on the set. This was also a means for the network to cross-promote the movie with its coverage of sports spectacles. These key paratexts—guides to the meaning of "the film"—are accessible via a blend of political economy and ethnography.

The global South experiences Hollywood films in an entirely different context. Jeff Himpele[42] has followed the life of such texts in La Paz, Bolivia, from their debut at the elite theater in the city *centro*, then up the surrounding canyon walls, where they play at various popular movie houses frequented by Aymara immigrants and their families. All the while, pirated video copies multiply and circulate. Using interviews with distributors and theater owners working in the city, Himpele demonstrates how print quality and exhibition map onto Bolivian social structure, with increases in altitude corresponding to indigenous identity and decreased social rank. Film exhibition is an extension of historical modes of distributing difference ingrained in colonial, race, and class hierarchies. Distribution in La Paz is a "spatializing practice," delineating difference and constructing social imaginaries. Certain genres of film become associated with imagined zones of people, and each zone gets access to "new" releases at different times, depending on its perceived social, political, and economic status.

Although official distribution itineraries can be undermined by the proliferation of pirated videocassettes, early access to new releases is only one component of cultural capital's prestige value. There is a certain status in renting from the commercial video store, just as there is prestige associated with which movie theater one attends. Himpele's willingness to follow both dominant and subaltern circulation practices is significant, because it neither valorizes the pirated circulation for upsetting structural inequalities, nor focuses solely on the reproduction of dominant ideology as a one-way, uncontested process. His methodology, marked by an expanded category of "appropriate" research sites, accounts for the resistance and negotiation that take place between presumed industry control and consumer practice—"how" a text accretes and abandons meaning in its travels. The focus on distribution is a necessary move away from research that dwells purely on how consumers create meaning with cultural objects. Such studies skip over the circulation process altogether, as though reception and criticism were the only sites for analysis.[43] And while some film-studies work is dedicated to distribution and exhibition in the United States,[44] it is more valuable for concretizing the history of moviegoing than making connections between circulation and textual meaning. It does not appear to have influenced textual analysts to loosen their moorings and become more nimble.

Political-economic-ethnographic approaches that "follow the thing" bring attention to the ways that media texts and commodities change in meaning and value depending on where and when they are viewed and consumed. Anthropology is also of value to film and media studies because it brings attention to audiovisual practices in the third world that are rarely included in common paradigms of national, postcolonial, or "third cinema." For instance, the Nigerian video film industry has been growing for more than a decade and a half and is now a US$45 million-a-year business, with more than four hundred low-budget narrative feature films released annually. These locally produced films are shot on video and receive no state sponsorship. The homegrown industry has grown so economically powerful that it is referred to as Nollywood[45] and is shaping the media culture of Anglophone and, increasingly, Francophone Africa. In Ghana and Kenya, especially, production companies are trying to keep up with and imitate the Nigerian model, a blend of supernatural horror and *telenovela*-influenced melodrama that addresses the economic challenges of an emergent cosmopolitanism, even as it makes the country one of the world's major traders in digital media.[46] Of course, multinational capital is also present. It is no surprise that in Nigeria, British American Tobacco handed out cigarettes to spectators as part of its 2002 "Rothmans Experience It Cinema Tour," which also offered viewers theatrical facilities far beyond the norm and new Hollywood action adventure.[47]

The other force dominating Nigerian screen culture is Bollywood. Brian Larkin's research on the global reach of Hindi film shows that, in Nigeria, Hindi film rivals and even marginalizes Hollywood, offering a "third space" between Islamic tradition and Western modernity that exerts a powerful influence over Hausa popular culture. Larkin pointed out the difficulty in finding a space for this kind of research within existing disciplinary hierarchies, writing that "the popularity of Indian films in Africa has fallen into the interstices of academic analysis, as the Indian texts do not fit with studies of African cinema; the African audience is ignored in the growing work on Indian film; the films are too non-Western for Euro-American-dominated media studies, and anthropologists are only beginning to theorise the social importance of media."[48] And one would be hard-pressed to find these films representing "African cinema" at international festivals or embassy screenings. Their popularity raises questions not only about what constitutes "authentic" African cinema (or whether such a category is even useful) but about the limitations of models that fail to recognize the regional power and influence of locally produced popular forms.

Fortunately, studies of transnational cultural flow are becoming more common. The popularity and, in some cases, dominance of Hindi film in a variety of locales—Egypt, Kenya, Japan, Nigeria, and South Asian diasporic communities around the world—as well as the international popularity of *telenovelas* in places like China and Russia, are being addressed by scholars from diverse disciplinary backgrounds.[49] The proliferation of transnational media currents has prompted Michael Curtin to argue that the study of "media capitals" presents a more viable contemporary alternative to methodologies centered on the nation-state.[50] Cities such as Mumbai, Cairo, and Hong Kong are financial centers of transnational media production and distribution. Each has evolved its own logics and interests, which do not necessarily correspond to those of any nation-state. By researching the cultural geographies of such media capitals, scholars can attend to the complex spatial and temporal dynamics of a globalized media world. The study of media capitals is not simply about acknowledging the dominance of a place. It must unravel, for instance, how Hong Kong negotiates its status as a cultural and economic nexus for Chinese social enclaves around the world, as well as its marginal position vis-à-vis both China and the West. For Curtin, a media capital is a relational concept; it examines different kinds of flow (economic, cultural, and technological) that are radically contextualized at multiple levels (local, national, and global). Consider the case of Miami. It has become the third-largest audiovisual production hub in the United States after Los Angeles and New York, and perhaps the largest Latin American hub.[51] This was achieved not by happenstance or convenience of location, but through very deliberate policy. The Miami Beach Enterprise Zone offers incentives to businesses expanding or relocating there that include property tax credits, tax credits on wages paid to enterprise zone residents, and sales tax refunds. The Façade Renovation Grant program provides matching grants to qualifying businesses for the rehabilitation of storefronts and the correction of interior code violations. As a consequence of this promotional activity, Miami-based culture industries generated about US$2 billion in 1997, more than any entertainment capital in Latin America, and boasted a workforce of ten thousand employees. By 2000, volume had increased to US$2.5 billion. Other counties in the region are also wooing the entertainment industries. To diminish the difficulties that producers and film companies encounter with the numerous municipalities in the area, Miami-Dade's Film Commission coordinates assistance to film and television business throughout South Florida.[52] Miami's status as a media capital has even been promoted during three-minute segments on TV Martí, the U.S.-government-funded, Cuban-exile-run enterprise that sends anti-Castro propaganda to the island, selling media cosmopolitanism as an index of democracy and freedom. Understanding the identity of a screen text produced or circulated under such circumstances necessitates viewing it in the light of global media urbanism and the role of state and capital.

Arjun Appadurai argued that as ethnic groups migrate, they dissolve the spatial boundaries of nation-states that circumscribe reified notions of culture. Ethnographers and media scholars alike must adapt to this changing landscape by focusing on the cultural dynamics of deterritorialization, and the defining roles played by the media in transnational life. With their endless presentation of possible lives, the media make fantasy a social practice for people throughout the world. "Fantasy" in this case does not refer to the escapist experiences often associated with viewing film and television. Rather, Appadurai sees such imaginative engagements as having profound social, cultural, economic, and political ramifications that may play both transformative and conservative roles in maintaining, asserting, and re-creating diasporic cultural identities. Images of "home" mobilize different expressions of exilic identity, from cultural conservation and social cohesion to extreme nationalism.[53]

The syncretic cultures created by diasporic communities are mobilized in different ways to serve a variety of interests. For some, media representations of the homeland may educate younger exile generations about traditional culture. Marie Gillespie's study of London Punjabi media practices, for example, shows how elders take the viewing of Hindi films with their children and grandchildren as an opportunity to convey a sense of their past in India.[54] For others, nostalgic imagery can fuel chauvinistic nationalism. There was controversy and even violence among exiled audiences in 1990 when their image of Iran was challenged during a film festival devoted to postrevolutionary cinema at the University of California, Los Angeles.[55] And diasporic Vietnamese in Southern California picketed a video store for fifty-three days in 1999 because its owner, Truong Van Tran, had displayed a picture of Ho Chi Minh in his Little Saigon shop.[56]

Today's most vibrant political-economic-ethnographic studies of film and other media move beyond textual parameters to show the diverse critical uptakes and social worlds in which production, distribution, and reception occur. As such, they intervene in larger discourses: the status of the nation-state as the framework for understanding culture; issues of cultural imperialism and local autonomy; the political economy and social lives of media institutions; and the complex dynamics of transnational media circulation and consumption. The cross-cultural approach that characterizes much ethnographic methodology also mirrors recent developments in international cultural studies. Eurocentric tendencies are being redressed with work that not only is cross-culturally and transnationally oriented, but recognizes the contributions of scholars who have been doing such work for decades in Latin America and Asia.[57]

None of this is to argue for the *irrelevancy* of interpreting texts. But attention to their occasionality, their movement through time and space, must recognize the contingency of texts, their protean malleability—*and* their form, *provided that this is understood as itself conjunctural*, via "discursive analysis of particular actor networks, technologies of textual exchange, circuits of communicational and textual effectivity, traditions of exegesis, commentary and critical practice." In other words, the specific "uptake" of a text by a community should be our focus; but not because this reveals something essential to the properties of screen texts or their likely uptake anywhere else or at any other time. We can discern a "general outline" of "interests," applied to specific cases only "upon a piecemeal and local inspection."[58]

To demonstrate the ways in which the political-economic and culturalist methods we have been describing can be productively combined with textual analysis, we now adopt an approach that tracks the life of the commodity sign via an examination of *Gilda*. Our desire is not to demonstrate each aspect of what we described above. Rather, we seek to follow the text's six-decade career of use. A classic film noir and canonical film-studies text, *Gilda* has been the subject of much elegant criticism, but criticism that has been rather monistic in its preoccupation and focus. Our analysis, which incorporates a materialist history of the film's meaning and life, reveals *Gilda* to be about spaces as much as psyches, something that emerges in its travels and citations as well as its form and style.

GILDA

Conventionally understood in film and media studies as a sexual drama, *Gilda* has been analyzed again and again in ways that pay insufficient heed to history and location, so taken are its critics with sex. The narrative backdrop to the film is that Ballin Mundson (George Macready) runs a casino in Buenos Aires. It provides money-laundering services for a global tungsten cartel run by German Nazis. Mundson himself is "an Hitlerian presence,"[59] his facial lesion suggesting an aristocratic German past. The casino and the cartel represent a return to international domination, for as he says, "a man who controls a strategic material can control the world," which is "made up of stupid little people." Mundson repeatedly disappears into "the interior," a mysterious site beyond urban norms, and he is reluctant to celebrate the end of the war. Two of his associates are central to the film: a new and much younger wife, the eponymous Gilda (Rita Hayworth), and a new and much younger personal nondigital assistant, Johnny Farrell (Glenn Ford).

There are numerous signs that Mundson and Farrell do the bad thing together in off screen space, such as uncharacteristically lengthy glances between the two and references to "gay life." Ford claimed that he and Macready "knew we were supposed to be playing homosexuals"[60] in a world that film-studies scholar Dyer imagined as "caught between gayness, in no way portrayed positively, and sadomasochism."[61] It also seems probable that Johnny and Gilda *used* to do the bad thing, as part of the backstory. When added to Gilda's repeated efforts to elude the control and physical constraints of men, these signs have rightly fascinated feminist and queer critics.[62] And their investment in psychoanalysis is encouraged and interpellated by the script's zealously obedient Freudianism:[63] Gilda "complains" that "I can never get a zipper to close. Maybe that stands for something"; she taunts Johnny's closeness to Ballin ("Any psychiatrist would tell your thought-associations are revealing"); Mundson has an ebony walking stick that turns into a blade and is his "little friend"; he insists to Johnny that "I must be sure that there is no woman anywhere"; and Johnny tells him, "I was born the night you met me." For the likes of noir historian Frank Krutnik, *Gilda* is "perhaps the high-watermark of 1940s erotic displacement."[64]

And "perhaps" it is. But that much-studied eroticism—or its watermark—has a geohistorical lineage beyond World War II and male-female-male triangulation, a history and a future beyond the boundaries of the film and its Freudianism that could undoubtedly enrich our understanding. For example, Hayworth embodied a new Hollywood aesthetic of difference—won at a price. Her "real" name was Margarita Carmen Delores Cansino, and her parents were New York dancers, her father a Spanish Sephardim. After the family moved west, Margarita was dancing at fifteen at the Agua Caliente (hot water) Jockey Club just north of the U.S.-Mexican border, a favored locale for gangsters and film producers, where she was transmogrified by a Hollywood mogul into Rita, and placed in several pictures as "the Dancing Latin." Her dark hair was dyed auburn, and she underwent two years of electrolysis to raise her hairline from a supposedly Latina look to what were deemed Anglo norms. Columbia Pictures executive Harry Cohn adopted her as his protégée and instructed producer Virginia Van Upp to manufacture a starring vehicle for her; thus, *Gilda*.[65] Hayworth's sultry torch-singer activities and exotic dancing in the film made her famous. A study of working-class women in Chicago in the mid-1950s found that she represented "luxury and glamour . . . a dashing hero . . . more concerned with the now than with the future" and sexual availability: "She'd like a man that could give her anything she wants. . . . She just wants to show off Rita Hayworth."[66] No wonder that when an atomic bomb was tested in the Bikini atoll, it was named Gilda and carried images of Hayworth.[67] French T-shirts depicted her as "*La vedette atomique*" (the atomic scout)—a sign of the volcanic power associated with her semiosis in the film.

While film studies tends to overlook *Gilda*'s connections to the economic and the geopolitical, references to these trends are abundant in the film, aptly understood by the *Village Voice* as "the most prominent big-business-as-underworld noir."[68] Place is very consequential here. Argentina is the most European of all non-European nations because of its population growth from 1880 to 1920, which drew principally on migration from Spain, Italy, Russia, and Central Europe. With the addition of immigrants from nearby Latin American countries, it also became the most urban country in the hemisphere, as rapid economic expansion between 1870 and 1930 ushered in a significant middle class and infrastructural development. But the Depression eroded the country's export markets in wool, grain, and beef, and fractured the society. This led to fifty years of populist/authoritarian regimes and dictatorships, and a concentration of wealth in elites. A coup in 1930 put the middle class, the military, and the traditional oligarchy in power. Argentina became the centerpiece of Nazi espionage in Latin America, with a spy ring established there in 1937 that also embarked on propaganda, assessing U.S. cultural exports and recruiting fellow travelers. Successive unstable regimes followed until a further coup in 1943 led by Fascist sympathizers, notably Juan Perón and his wife, Eva—she of *Evita* (Alan Parker, 1996) in which Madonna strips with her gloves as per Hayworth in *Gilda*.[69] In 1944, Argentina finally ended diplomatic relations with Germany, and arrested some of its spies.[70]

The Peróns dominated the political stage by the end of World War II. In 1946, he became president, leading a bulky, awkward coalition of right- and left-wing workerist populism cobbled together from the urban proletariat, the lower-middle class, and rural workers.[71] Perón's decade in power saw the nation become a "preferred haven for tens of thousands of Nazi war criminals and fellow travelers." These included the notorious SS medical researcher, Josef Mengele, and Holocaust administrator Adolf Eichmann. Many departed Nazis went on to fruitful careers as advisers to right-wing dictatorships across Latin America. They brought with them large sums of money, much of which was deposited in accounts under Eva Perón's control, and there were crucial links to Siemens, the German electronics multinational. Meanwhile, Argentina's application to join the United Nations, resisted by the Soviet Union because of the nation's late decision to turn against Fascism, was railroaded through by the United States, anxious to add to the list of client states that would give it a majority in the new body.[72] As part of the cold war, the U.S. government blended a few anti-Fascist criticisms of Perón (a consequence of his anti-Gringo rhetoric) with a large-scale program of aid to ex-Nazis.[73]

Johnny's first line of dialogue in the film, as the camera tilts slowly upwards to show the *gringo* street gambler's thrown dice, is extra-diegetic narration, and it speaks to the attitude of the United States toward Latin America from both ruling-class and petit-bourgeois levels: "To me a dollar was a dollar in any language. . . . I didn't know much about the local citizens." When two Nazis later dismiss him as "the American Indian," meddling where he is not welcome, Johnny proudly avows that this is his fate—manifest destiny goes global. Johnny's makeover from surly swindler to glamorous gambler is achieved blithely: "By the way, about that time the war ended," he offers in voice-over as a contextual counterpoint to the promise of transcendence implied in his oath to Mundson that "I was born last night." His character is as distant from time and space as his textual analysts.

Mundson's casino, where he goes to work, is a "massive South American house of sin."[74] A sign of fabulous, corrupt modernity, the casino is for all the world an engine room of pleasure and deceit, its huge rooms whirring with the sound and vision of spinning wheels, milling crowds, shimmering gowns, and dazzling lights. It represents the uneven modernity of Latin America, as tradition and development overlap in both contradictory and compatible ways. Buenos Aires comes alive in *Gilda* as a bizarre amalgam of sordid street life, glittering wealth, and winding, perennially dark streets. Mundson is like a James Bond villain in his perverse gaze on revelers from a concealed aerie, his manipulation of other conspirators, and his determination to achieve international and interpersonal conquest. And the setting calls up Bondian sequences of excess for the latter-day viewer.

"You can't talk to men down here the way you would at home. They think you mean it," says Johnny to Gilda. When a gigolo dances with Gilda, he asks her where she learned to dance. Her reply—"America"—draws puzzlement: "This is not America?" The retort is perfect—the casual arrogance of appropriating the word "America" to stand for the United States is problematized. She goes on to use racial difference to inscribe sexual desire: "I always say there's something about Latin men. For one thing they can dance. For another thing . . ." She gives him her phone number. Johnny, who is excluded from the conversation because he is not *hispano hablante*, demands to know what was said. She deceives him, saying that she'd instructed the boy to "hang up if a man answers." There is no translation for the audience, so most U.S. viewers are placed in the same position as Johnny. They must rely on the translation of a woman who is being set up as simultaneously unreliable and desirable, at least by his lights. Yet her name signifies as *palabra de honor* (word of honor) in Spain.[75]

This high-tensile mix of eroticism references hot Latinism mediated through the painfully and painstakingly de-Latinized Hayworth, as well as major world events. It has left a deep historical trace. The contemporary leftist Mexican newspaper *La Jornada* included Johnny slapping Gilda as one of its remarkable fiftieth-anniversary events,[76] while Madrid's *Expansión* metaphorized technology stock declines of late 2000 with reference to her[77] and *Urban Latino* magazine nominated Hayworth alongside Che Guevara among the sixteen sexiest Latin historical figures in 2001, thanks to her part in the film.[78] When Madonna sang that "Rita Hayworth gave good face" in her song "Vogue," there is little doubt that she was alluding to this most famous of sexualized characters, and Pink Martini's 2001 album *Sympathique* pays tribute to the role. The popular periodical *Entertainment Weekly* put Gilda at number 21 in its 2002 list of "The 100 Greatest Performances Ignored by Oscar," and in 2004 the American Film Institute included Hayworth saying "If I'd been a ranch, they would have named me the Bar Nothing" amongst the four hundred most memorable lines of cinema.[79]

The film's cultural intertextuality is crucial to any evaluation of its "meaning." *Down to Earth* (Alexander Hall, 1947) brings back Macready's cane and Hayworth's dance, and *Gilda* is also a promotional intertext to Orson Welles's *The Lady from Shanghai* (1948), from the use of male voice-over and triangulation of desire through to setting and music.[80] *The Bicycle Thief* (Vittorio De Sica, 1948) sees the protagonist making his way around town putting up sections of the *Gilda* poster, affirming his nation's poverty and indexing its obligation to accept Yanqui culture as part of the Marshall Plan.[81] Macready reprises his part in a 1966 episode of *The Man from U.N.C.L.E.*, "The Gurnius Affair." He plays a leftover escapee Nazi living in Central America whose plans for global domination are colored by the intense delight he takes in the sadism of his junior underlings. That classic liberal moment of contemporary Hollywood, *The Shawshank Redemption* (Frank Darabont, 1994), is based on Stephen King's short story "Rita Hayworth and the Shawshank Redemption."

Tim Robbins's tunnel excavation from unjust and brutal imprisonment is secreted behind a classic *Gilda* poster.[82] Nicole Kidman's role in *Moulin Rouge!* was an homage to Gilda, as were characters from André Engel's latter-day version of Igor Stravinsky's *Rake's Progress* and David Lynch's *Mulholland Drive* (2001).[83]

In 1998, a yellow item worn by Hayworth in the film fetched 20,000 francs ($3,571.00) at auction.[84] Her black satin strapless evening dress became perhaps the most famous of all Hollywood garments, complete with interior harness, *grosgrain* beneath the bust, three stays, and plastic bars softened with a gas flame and placed around the top, thus defying the tendency of such items to fall.[85] Saks Fifth Avenue offered a short version of the gown in 2001,[86] when the "Gilda look" became au courant in London via "a heavy, pale pancake foundation applied with a sponge, and lashings of pale powder," definition thanks to mascara and eyebrow pencil, blue-red lipstick with a brush, and Vaseline for gloss; the hair relied on Titian reds and golden chestnuts plus medium rollers, topped off with beer or tea to set it.[87] The Gilda style was de rigueur at Naomi Campbell's St Tropez birthday party during the 2004 Cannes Festival, and Edinburgh's *Evening News* could imagine nothing better to enliven Hogmanay.[88] Rumors that the proverbial "little black dress" was on the way "out" that year quickly led to rear-guard actions, based on the certainty that the Gilda look made "[m]en's jaws drop, from shock and awe,"[89] while Garnier's summer 2005 cosmetics line was headed by a British *Big Brother* presenter made up to resemble the role. Watching the film was even recommended to restore the joys of flamenco dancing to a shell-shocked United States after September 11, 2001. It continued to fascinate the Valencia smart set, and invigorated costumes for Comédie Française Molière revivals and 2005–6 Parisian prêt-à-porter.[90] The U.S. Alzheimer's Foundation sold a Gilda doll in 2000, and held its 2004–5 New Year's Ball with Gilda look-alikes stalking the room, recalling Hayworth's finest hour and later illness. No wonder that Ridley Scott, looking back forty years to his childhood memories of the movie, said, "[T]hat's where I fell in love with Rita Hayworth. . . . Those were the days when you could sit and watch the film twice, and I refused to leave. It was quite an adult movie." As Sharon Stone put it, "Sometimes I think she got Alzheimer's because she so desperately wanted to forget being Gilda."[91] For Spanish viewers of the 1970s, seeing the semi-striptease performance of "Put the Blame on Mame" was a newish sensation—Franco-era censors had cut the original beyond recognition, and the Roman Catholic Church had picketed what remained.[92]

This life after the text is available to a nimble materialist history, but seemingly not to the always-already known world of psychoanalysis. Both the geopolitical setting of U.S. foreign and cultural policy and the latter career of the film text elude Anglo-Yanqui critics. Film and media studies can do better. This means not jettisoning texts, but pluralizing and complicating them—understanding them as moments that spin their own tales of travel and uptake, as essentially unstable entities that change their composition as they move across time and space.

When it comes to key questions of texts and audiences—what gets produced and circulated and how it is read—film and media studies must embark on an analysis of hysteresis that looks for overlapping causes and sites. In search of appropriate models or exemplars, we have turned to a political-economic ethnography/ethnographic political economy to reinvigorate textual analysis and perhaps give the undergraduate students we quoted at the beginning of this essay some tools for living in media culture. Gilda and Johnny deserve at least that much.

NOTES

1. We are discussing humanities-based film and media studies as practiced in Britain, the United States, and satellite white-settler colonies such as Australia, Aotearoa/New Zealand, Israel, and Canada.
2. Think of George Yúdice, Andrew Ross, John Hartley, and Rob Nixon, to name just four.
3. Chartier, 1989: 157, 161–63, 166.
4. Charles Vidor, 1946.
5. Tushnet, 1999.
6. Lindsay, 1970: 243.
7. Greene, 2005.
8. Hays, 1927: 29.
9. Hu, 2003: 51–52.
10. De Los Reyes, 1996: 29–31.
11. May and Shuttleworth, 1933; Dale, 1933; Blumer, 1933; Blumer and Hauser, 1933; Forman, 1933; Mitchell, 1929.
12. Wartella, 1996: 173.
13. Mosco, 2004.
14. Powdermaker, 1950: 12–15.
15. Mayer, 1946: 24.
16. As of May 2005, a Google search for the term generated more than 46,000 references.
17. Simpson, 1996.
18. Hunter, 1988; Miller, 1993; Greene and Hicks, 2005.
19. Goldstein et al., 1999.
20. Laurance, 2001; Mekemson and Glantz, 2002; Ng and Dakake, 2002.
21. There are a few exceptions, such as Constance Penley.
22. Dyer, 1992: 4.
23. Diawara, 1993.
24. Gever et al., 1993; Holmlund and Fuchs, 1997.
25. Carson et al., 1994.
26. Shohat and Stam, 1994; Carson and Friedman, 1995.
27. Though we honor *Jump Cut*.

28. See references in Miller et al., 2005: 49n5, which provides some material used here, as does Miller, 2003.

29. Elsaesser, 2001: 11.

30. Prince, 2000: 141.

31. Department of Commerce, 2001: 14, 16n12.

32. Two notable exceptions are Powdermaker's Hollywood ethnography (1950), and Sol Worth et al.'s (1997) work with Navajo filmmakers in the 1960s.

33. Ginsburg et al., 2002; Askew and Wilk, 2002; Bird, 2003; for ethnomethodological stances, see Jalbert, 1999.

34. Ginsburg et al., 2002.

35. Ginsburg et al., 2002: 23.

36. Austin, 2002: 127.

37. Danan, 1995: 131–32, 137.

38. Augros, 2000: 159.

39. Eller and Muñoz, 2002.

40. Eller and Muñoz, 2002; Smith, 2002.

41. Groves, 2002.

42. Himpele, 1996.

43. But see Bolin, 1998.

44. Gomery, 1992; Hark, 2002.

45. Ironically, the description was coined in Gringolandia but is now begrudgingly embraced in the South.

46. Larkin, 2005; Ginsburg et al., 2002; Haynes, 2000.

47. Bates, 2003.

48. Larkin, 2001: 353.

49. Ginsburg et al., 2002; Larkin, 2001, 2004.

50. Curtin, 2003.

51. Many in the Western Hemisphere regard Miami as a Latin American city.

52. Miller and Yúdice, 2002: 80.

53. Gillespie, 1995; Kolar-Panov, 1997; Schein, 2002; Sinclair and Cunningham, 2000.

54. Gillespie, 1995.

55. Naficy, 1993.

56. Shore, 2004.

57. Abbas and Erni, 2005.

58. McHoul and O'Regan, 1992: 5–6, 8–9.

59. Higham and Greenberg, 1968: 46.

60. Quoted in Russo, 1987: 78.

61. Dyer, 1993: 71.

62. Doane, 1991: 99–118; Dyer, 1993: 70–71.

63. Christopher, 1997: 141.

64. Krutnik, 1991: 51.

65. Muller, 1998: 96–97.

66. Elkin, 1955: 99, 103–4, 106.

67. Muller, 1998: 98; Inclan, 2005.

68. "Red Harvest," 2002.

69. Savagliano, 1997: 163.

70. Polmar and Allen, 1989: 54.

71. Vacs, 2002: 400, 402–5.
72. Paterson, 1992: 35.
73. Lee, 2000: 109–13.
74. Higham and Greenberg, 1968: 46.
75. "Gilda," 2001.
76. Steinsleger, 1998.
77. Caro, 2000.
78. "EEUU-Hispanos," 2001.
79. Bierly et al., 2002; Spiegelman, 2004.
80. McLean, 2004: 130, 150.
81. Trumpbour, 2002; Pauwels and Loisen, 2003.
82. Vilar, 2002.
83. Frois, 2001; Roux, 2001; Ebert, 2001.
84. Tariant, 2001.
85. Vallance, 1997; Horwell, 1997.
86. "Modern Classics," 2001.
87. Polan, 2001.
88. Davidson, 2003.
89. Woods, 2004.
90. Ayuso, 2003; Torres, 2003; "La chronique théâtrale," 2005; Champenois et al., 2005.
91. Quoted in Tilley, 1998.
92. Vilar, 2002; Fortes, 2004; "Red-Hot Lavinia," 2005.

BIBLIOGRAPHY

Abbas, Ackbar, and John Nguyet Erni, eds. 2005. *Internationalizing Cultural Studies: An Anthology*. Malden: Blackwell.

Appadurai, Arjun. 1991. "Global Ethnoscapes: Notes and Queries for a Transnational Anthropology." *Recapturing Anthropology*. Ed. Richard Fox. Santa Fe, NM: School of American Research Press, 191–210.

Askew, Nelly, and Richard R. Wilk, eds. 2002. *The Anthropology of Media: A Reader*. Malden: Blackwell.

Augros, Joël. 2000. *El Dinero de Hollywood: Financiación, producción, distribución y nuevos mercados*. Trans. Josep Torrell. Barcelona: Paidós.

Austin, Thomas. 2002. *Hollywood, Hype and Audiences: Selling and Watching Popular Film in the 1990s*. Manchester: Manchester University Press.

Ayuso, Rocio. 2003. "Hollywood-Flamenco." *Spanish Newswire Services* 15 November.

Bates, James. 2003. "Warner Douses Smoking Promo." *Los Angeles Times* 5 March.

Bierly, Mandi, Scott Brown, Bob Cannon, and Steve Daly. 2002. "Overlooked: The 100 Greatest Performances Ignored by Oscar." *Entertainment Weekly* 29 November: 41–72.

Bird, S. Elizabeth. 2003. *The Audience in Everyday Life: Living in a Media World*. New York: Routledge.

Blumer, Herbert. 1933. *Movies and Conduct*. New York: Macmillan.

Blumer, Herbert, and Philip M. Hauser. 1933. *Movies, Delinquency and Crime.* New York: Macmillan.

Bolin, Göran. 1998. *Filmbytare: Videovåld, kulturell production & unga män.* Umeå: Boréa Bokförlag.

Caro, Susana F. 2000. "La city culpa la volantilidad." *Expansión* 13 October.

Carson, Diane, and Lester D. Friedman, eds. 1995. *Shared Differences: Multicultural Media and Practical Pedagogy.* Urbana: University of Illinois Press.

Carson, Diane, Linda Dittmar, and Janice R. Welsch, eds. 1994. *Multiple Voices in Feminist Film Criticism.* Minneapolis: University of Minnesota Press.

Champenois, Sabrina, Françoise Santucci, and Olivier Wicker. 2005. "Le bruit et la fourrure." *Libération* 5 March: 37.

Chartier, Roger. 1989. "Texts, Printings, Readings." *The New Cultural History.* Ed. Lynn Hunt. Berkeley: University of California Press, 154–75.

Christopher, Nicholas. 1997. *Somewhere in the Night: Film Noir and the American City.* New York: Henry Holt.

Curtin, Michael. 2003. "Towards the Study of Spatial Flows." *International Journal of Cultural Studies* 6.2: 202–28.

Dale, Edgar. 1933. *The Content of Motion Pictures.* New York: Macmillan.

Danan, Martine. 1995. "Marketing the Hollywood Blockbuster in France." *Journal of Popular Film and Television* 23.3: 131–40.

Davidson, Gina. 2003. "Play Goddess for a Hollywood-Style Hogmanay." *Evening News* 18 December.

De Los Reyes, Aurelio. 1996. "El Gobierno Mexicano y las películas denigrantes, 1920–1931." *México Estados Unidos: Encuentros y desencuentros en el cine.* Ed. Ignacio Durán, Iván Trujillo, and Mónica Verea. Mexico City: Universidad Nacional Autónoma de México, 23–35.

Department of Commerce. 2001. *The Migration of U.S. Film and Television Production.* Washington, DC.

Diawara, Manthia, ed. 1993. *Black American Cinema.* New York: Routledge.

Doane, Mary Anne. 1991. *Femmes Fatales: Feminism, Film Theory, Psychoanalysis.* New York: Routledge.

Dyer, Richard. 1992. *Only Entertainment.* London: Routledge.

Dyer, Richard. 1993. *The Matter of Images: Essays on Representations.* London: Routledge.

Ebert, Roger. 2001. "No Logic." *Toronto Star* 3 November: C3.

"EEUU-Hispanos de la Renta, Che Guevara y Khalo entre los Latinos más 'sexy.' " 2001. *Spanish Newswire Services* 20 February.

Elkin, Frederick. 1955. "Popular Hero Symbols and Audience Gratifications." *Journal of Educational Sociology* 29.3: 97–107.

Eller, Claudia, and Lorenza Muñoz. 2002. "The Plots Thicken in Foreign Markets." *Los Angeles Times* 6 October: A1.

Elsaesser, Thomas. 2001. "The Blockbuster: Everything Connects, but Not Everything Goes." *The End of Cinema as We Know It: American Film in the Nineties.* Ed. Jon Lewis. New York: New York University Press, 11–22.

Forman, Henry James. 1933. *Our Movie Made Children.* New York: Macmillan.

Fortes, Susana. 2004. "Infiernos." *El País* 14 February: 2.

Frois, Emmanuele. 2001. "Avec 'Moulin Rouge,' le cineaste australien présente une co-médie musicale qui abat les frontières du temps et des genres." *Le Figaro* 3 October.

Gever, Martha, John Greyson, and Pratibha Parmar, eds. 1993. *Queer Looks: Perspectives on Lesbian and Gay Film and Video*. New York: Routledge.

"Gilda." 2001. <usuarios.iponet.es/dardo/revista/gilda.html>.

Gillespie, Marie. 1995. *Television, Ethnicity and Cultural Change*. London: Routledge.

Ginsburg, Faye, Lila Abu-Lughod, and Brian Larkin, eds. 2002. *Media Worlds: Anthropology on New Terrain*. Berkeley: University of California Press.

Goldstein, Adam O., Rachel A. Sobel, and Glen R. Newman. 1999. "Tobacco and Alcohol Use in G-Rated Children's Animated Films." *Journal of the American Medical Association* 28.12: 1131–36.

Gomery, Douglas. 1992. *Shared Pleasures: A History of Movie Presentation in the United States*. Madison: University of Wisconsin Press.

Greene, Ronald Walter, and Darren Hicks. 2005. "Lost Convictions: Debating Both Sides and the Ethical Self-Fashioning of Liberal Citizens." *Cultural Studies* 19.1: 100–26.

Greene, Ronald Walter. 2005. "Y Movies: Film and the Modernization of Pastoral Power." *Communication and Critical/Cultural Studies* 2.1: 20–36.

Groves, Don. 2002. "Rejigged Marketing Helps U.S. Pics Soar." *Variety* 28 October–3 November: 14.

Hall, Stuart. 1990. "Cultural Identity and Diaspora." *Identity: Community, Culture, Difference*. Ed. Jonathan Rutherford. London: Lawrence and Wishart, 222–37.

Hark, Ina Rae, ed. 2002. *Exhibition, the Film Reader*. London: Routledge.

Haynes, Jonathan, ed. 2000. *Nigerian Video Film*. Athens: Ohio University Press.

Hays, Will. 1927. "Supervision from Within." *The Story of the Films as Told by Leaders of the Industry to the Students of the Graduate School of Business Administration George F. Baker Foundation Harvard University*. Ed. Joseph P. Kennedy. Chicago: A. W. Shaw Company, 29–54.

Higham, Charles, and Joel Greenberg. 1968. *Hollywood in the Forties*. London: Tantivy Press; New York: AS Barnes.

Himpele, Jeff. 1996. "Film Distribution as Media: Mapping Difference in the Bolivian Cinemascape." *Visual Anthropology Review* 12.1: 47–66.

Holmlund, Chris, and Cynthia Fuchs, eds. 1997. *Between the Sheets, in the Streets: Queer, Lesbian, Gay Documentary*. Minneapolis: University of Minnesota Press.

Horwell, Veronica. 1997. "The Talk of the Gown." *Manchester Guardian Weekly* 4 May: 24.

Hu, Jubin. 2003. *Projecting a Nation: Chinese National Cinema Before 1949*. Hong Kong: Hong Kong University Press.

Hunter, Ian. 1988. *Culture and Government*. London: Macmillan.

Inclan, Ramon. 2005. "Ecos del ayer." *La Opinión* 8 May.

Jalbert, Paul L., ed. 1999. *Media Studies: Ethnomethodological Approaches*. Lanham, MD: University Press of America.

Kolar-Panov, Dona. 1997. *Video, War and the Diasporic Imagination*. London: Routledge.

Krutnik, Frank. 1991. *In a Lonely Street: Film Noir, Genre, Masculinity*. London: Routledge.

"La chronique théâtrale." 2005. *L'Humanité* 9 May: 20.

Larkin, Brian. 2001. "Indian Films and Nigerian Lovers: Media and the Creation of Parallel Modernities." *The Anthropology of Globalization: A Reader*. Ed. Jonathan Xavier Inda and Renato Rosaldo. Malden: Blackwell, 350–78.

Larkin, Brian. 2004. "Piracy, Infrastructure, and the Rise of a Nigerian Video Industry." *Global Currents: Media and Technology Now*. Ed. Tasha G. Oren and Patrice Petro. New Brunswick, NJ: Rutgers University Press, 159–70.

Larkin, Brian. 2005. "Report on Nollywood Rising Conference." Unpublished paper.

Laurance, Jeremy. 2001. "The Habit Hollywood Just Can't Stub Out." *Independent* 5 January.

Lee, Martin A. 2000. *The Beast Reawakens.* New York: Routledge.

Lindsay, Vachel. 1970. *The Art of the Moving Picture.* New York: Liveright.

May, Mark A., and Frank K. Shuttleworth. 1933. *The Social Conduct and Attitudes of Movie Fans.* New York: Macmillan.

Mayer, J. P. 1946. *Sociology of Film: Studies and Documents.* London: Faber and Faber.

McHoul, Alec, and Tom O'Regan. 1992. "Towards a Paralogics of Textual Technologies: Batman, Glasnost and Relativism in Cultural Studies." *Southern Review* 25.1: 5–26.

McLean, Adrienne L. 2004. *Being Rita Hayworth: Labor, Identity, and Hollywood Stardom.* New Brunswick, NJ: Rutgers University Press.

Mekemson, C., and S. Glantz. 2002. "How the Tobacco Industry Built Its Relationship with Hollywood." *Tobacco Control* 11: 181–191.

Miller, Toby. 1993. *The Well-Tempered Self: Citizenship, Culture, and the Postmodern Subject.* Baltimore: Johns Hopkins University Press.

Miller, Toby, and George Yúdice. 2002. *Cultural Policy.* London: Sage.

Miller, Toby, Nitin Govil, John McMurria, Richard Maxwell, and Ting Wang. 2005. *Global Hollywood 2.* London: British Film Institute.

Miller, Toby. 2003. *Spyscreen: Espionage on Film and TV from the 1930s to the 1960s.* Oxford: Oxford University Press.

Mitchell, Alice Miller. 1929. *Children and the Movies.* Chicago: University of Chicago Press.

"Modern Classics." 2001. *In Style* October: 221.

Mosco, Vincent. 2004. *The Digital Sublime: Myth, Power, and Cyberspace.* Cambridge: MIT Press.

Muller, Eddie. 1998. *Dark City: The Lost World of Film Noir.* New York: St. Martin's Griffin.

Naficy, Hamid. 1993. *The Making of Exile Cultures: Iranian Television in Los Angeles.* Minneapolis: University of Minnesota Press.

Ng, Crystal, and Bradley Dakake. 2002. *Tobacco at the Movies.* Boston: Massachusetts Public Interest Research Group.

Paterson, Thomas G. 1992. *On Every Front: The Making and Unmaking of the Cold War.* Rev. ed. New York: W. W. Norton.

Pauwels, Caroline, and Jan Loisen. 2003. "The WTO and the Audiovisual Sector: Economic Free Trade vs Cultural Horse Trading?" *European Journal of Communication* 18.3: 291–313.

Pius XII. 1957. *Miranda Prorsus: Encyclical Letter on Motion Pictures, Radio and Television.* <www.vatican.va/holy_father/pius_xii/encyclicals/documents/hf_p-xii_enc_08091957_miranda-prorsus_en.html>. Accessed March 21, 2008.

Polan, Brenda. 2001. "Rita Hayworth was the Ultimate Feelgood Girl for Feelbad Times." *Daily Mail* 19 November: 43.

Polmar, Norman, and Thomas B. Allen. 1989. "The Decade of the Spy." *US Naval Institute Proceedings* May: 104–8.

Powdermaker, Hortense. 1950. *Hollywood, the Dream Factory: An Anthropologist Studies the Movie Makers.* Boston: Little, Brown.

Prince, Stephen. 2000. *History of the American Cinema.* Vol. 10, *A New Pot of Gold Under the Electronic Rainbow, 1980–1989.* New York: Charles Scribner's Sons.

"Red Harvest." 2002. *Village Voice* 9–15 October: 114.

"Red-Hot Lavinia Takes It Lying Down." 2005. *Daily Star* 26 April: 10.

Roux, Marie Aude. 2001. "The Rake's Progress, descente en enfer dans le grand music-hall de la vie." *Le Monde* 24 November.

Russo, Vito. 1987. *The Celluloid Closet: Homosexuality in the Movies*. Rev. ed. New York: Harper and Row.

Savagliano, Marta. 1997. "Evita: The Globalization of a National Myth." *Latin American Perspectives* 24.6: 156–72.

Schein, Louisa. 2002. "Mapping Hmong Media in Diasporic Space." *Media Worlds: Anthropology on New Terrain*. Ed. Faye Ginsburg, Lila Abu-Lughod, and Brian Larkin. Berkeley: University of California Press, 229–44.

Shohat, Ella, and Robert Stam. 1994. *Unthinking Eurocentrism: Multiculturalism and the Media*. New York: Routledge.

Shore, Elena. 2004. "Ho Chi Minh Protests." *Pacific News Service* 11 May.

Simpson, Christopher. 1996. *Science of Coercion: Communication Research and Psychological Warfare, 1945–1960*. New York: Oxford University Press.

Sinclair, John, and Stuart Cunningham. 2000. "Go with the Flow: Diasporas and the Media." *Television & New Media* 1.1: 11–31.

Smith, Roger. 2002. "Why Studio Movies Don't Make (Much) Money." *Film Comment* 38.2: 60–62.

Spiegelman, Arthur. 2004. " 'Wait a Minute, You Ain't Heard Nothin' Yet': CBS Show Will Pick 100 Greatest Movie Lines." *National Post* 19 November: PM8.

Steinsleger, José. 1998. "El 98." *La Jornada* 6 January.

Tariant, Eric. 2001. "La vogue des affiches de cinema." *Le Monde* 9 April.

Tilley, Steve. 1998. "Kinder, Gentler Sharon Stone at 40." *Edmonton Sun* 10 October: 33.

Torres, Monica. 2003. "El mito de 'Gilda' revive en el calor de la noche valenciana." *El País* 31 July: 1.

Trumpbour, John. 2002. *Selling Hollywood to the World: U.S. and European Struggles for Mastery of the Global Film Industry, 1920–1950*. Cambridge: Cambridge University Press.

Tushnet, Eve. 1999. "Rita Hayworth at Yale, or Education Is for the Weak." *Yale Free Press*.

Vacs, Aldo C. 2002. "Argentina." *Politics of Latin America: The Power Game*. Ed. Harry E. Vanden and Gary Prevost. New York: Oxford University Press, 399–435.

Vallance, Tom. 1997. "Obituary: Jean Louis." *Independent* 25 April: 18.

Vilar, Iván Bono. 2002. "Gilda: La Diosa del Amor." <www.eldigoras.com>.

Wartella, Ellen. 1996. "The History Reconsidered." *American Communication Research— The Remembered History*. Ed. Everette E. Dennis and Ellen Wartella. Mahwah, NJ: Lawrence Erlbaum, 169–80.

Woods, Vicki. 2004. "Requiem for Black." *National Post* 1 May: SP3.

Worth, Sol, John Adair, and Richard Chalfen. 1997. *Through Navajo Eyes*. Albuquerque: University of New Mexico Press.

CHAPTER 9

TELEVISION'S FIRST SEVENTY-FIVE YEARS: THE INTERPRETIVE FLEXIBILITY OF A MEDIUM IN TRANSITION

WILLIAM URICCHIO

Television's early history has tended to be overwritten by two factors: assumptions regarding the primacy of film as a moving-image medium, and thus the notion of television as a mix of film and radio; and the coordinated efforts of the electronics industry and governments in the late 1940s and early 1950s, each with their own agendas, to stabilize the medium. The result has been a certain "taken-for-grant-edness" regarding television's history that is strikingly at odds with the complicated and reasonably well-documented developmental histories of other media ranging from the book to film. But more than simply impoverishing our notion of television as a medium, this view has also had an impact on our understandings of sister media such as the telephone and film, and it has deprived us of a potentially useful model through which to consider aspects of media development and convergence. If we look back to television's first decades, before it achieved its conceptual and institutional stability and its culturally dominant definitions, we might better assess the medium's potentials and thus be in a position to learn from, to paraphrase Carolyn Marvin, an old medium when it was new.[1] Among the benefits of such an approach, this essay argues, are the opportunities it affords to reflect on the horizon of expectations facing the film medium's early developers, and to rethink some of our historiographic assumptions regarding media genealogies.

TELEVISION'S ORIGINS

Locating an appropriate entry point to a medium's history is a task complicated by the problem of determinacy.[2] If we work backward from a fully baked concept of television as we know it today to its point of origin, we risk replicating a dominant and frequently told success story and, in the process, missing the many alternatives and dead ends from which the winning construction emerged. However, if we begin with a wide spectrum of approaches to a particular concept of a medium (in television's case, something as loose as "seeing at a distance"), then our framing of the medium becomes determining. Scholars of early film history have been concerned with these issues for some time, framing and reframing the genealogy of their medium and the processes by which a bundle of possibilities gave way to a dominant cultural construction.[3] In the case of television, notwithstanding the important contributions of scholars such as R.W. Burns, Brian Winston, Siegfried Zielinski, George Shiers, Albert Abramson, and others, historical efforts have been considerably less energetic, providing only the weakest of orthodoxies, and an even weaker set of alternative constructions.[4] Fortunately, there seems to be a relatively clear moment at which something like the *televisual* entered both the popular imagination and the patent record, giving us at least a plausible starting place. To locate this moment, we must reach back considerably further than the birth of commercial or national broadcasting efforts in the years immediately following the Second World War. Television, long seen as something of a fusion of film (the visual component) and radio (the broadcasting component), might profitably be repositioned within a trajectory of technologies that sought to connect two distant points in real time, that is, with technologies such as the camera obscura, telescope, telephone, and telegraph before it.[5] But such a view assumes a clear definition of the object under scrutiny—something that in television's case is complicated.

WHAT IS TELEVISION?

André Bazin asked a similar question regarding cinema, discussing the ontology of the photographic image and employing the metaphor of a death mask as part of his attempt to understand film's (and photography's) physical relationship to the visible world. Bazin's reference is at odds with a far more appropriate metaphor for television, the telescope, and offers an apt reminder of the film medium's embalmed character. Television, at least as it was originally imagined and for most of its first seventy-five years, was about the ephemeral act of seeing, of extension and instantaneity, of visually connecting disparate locations in real time. Indeed, we can find the lingering traces of this meaning in the German word for television, *Fernseher* (literally "far-seer" like its English counterpart, "tele-vision"), a term that during the nineteenth century and earlier referred to the telescope. Of course, our contemporary notions of television are complicated by temporal disjunctions, whether in the form of storage media such as videotape and DVDs, or government-mandated delays in live broadcasting (just as contemporary notions of film are complicated by digital production, distribution, and exhibition technologies). One can go back at least to the invention of the telephone to see well-developed conceptions of the medium that would later bear the name "television." One might even argue that a conception of the medium took hold in the last quarter of the nineteenth century that would in crucial ways determine the distinctions among moving-image media. Inspired by the telephone, early notions of the televisual assumed that moving pictures would be seen simultaneously with their production, that is, that the medium would serve as something like an *electronic* camera obscura, or telescope, bringing spatially distant scenes into direct visual proximity with the viewer.

From 1876 onward, a well-developed notion of television as a "live" moving-picture medium offered a counterpart to the "stored" moving images seen, for example, with Reynaud's projecting praxinoscope, Edison's kinetoscope, and eventually, in 1895, with what we today celebrate as projected moving pictures. The difference between these two basic approaches to moving-picture technology was in some senses the same as that between the telephone and the gramophone. Both mediated the grain of the voice from sender or recorder to receiver, and both created an illusion of presence and even liveness. But only the telephone, like the period's sense of television, linked subject and object in real time; the gramophone, like the film medium, was by definition temporally disjunctive. Although we have since lost sight of the period's distinctions, the period itself elaborated upon the differences between these two approaches to moving imagery. Indeed, the range of evidence is such that one could argue that film, when it finally emerged, appeared as something of a disappointment (or at best a compromise) to those expecting simultaneity with their moving images—a view with serious implications for our understanding of early screen practice.

TELEVISION'S HISTORIES

That the media landscape has been in constant upheaval is a given, but the inter-actions of media and publics can be apprehended only if we can sort out differences among media forms. A look back at media's history as well as at their present state shows that even this basic issue has its difficulties. Technological convergence has posed a great challenge, as evidenced by 1920s recording technologies (film-based sound systems; Baird's television on wax disks) or contemporary digital technol-ogies (film and video special effects, editing, sound work, exhibition). In these cases, the materiality of a particular medium has been displaced to a material base associated with another medium. Depending on how media definitions are con-structed, such twists as the replacement of film's photochemical base by an elec-tromagnetic or digital-optical base may be seen as having little bearing on film as a cultural practice, or may be seen as threatening the very ontological underpinnings of film and video media. Tracing the cultural reception of these transformations, however, at least offers a clue to the conceptual impact of shifting technological forms and the manner by which (new) media identities take form. This is particu-larly clear in the case of television, a medium, even before its institutional con-solidation around 1950, that was related to telephone, radio, and film technologies; that drew upon journalistic, theatrical, and (documentary) filmmaking practices; that was variously understood as domestic like radio, public like film, or person-to-person like the telephone; that was live and recorded, high definition (more than two thousand lines) and low, large screen and small. Television, before its mid-century governmental and industrial takeover, took many forms and promised even more. Indeed, the medium's undulations today, with interactive and on-demand services, large flat screen, small cell phone and iPod displays, and a variety of storage platforms and live video services, are not so much new as reminders of the medium's long-term flexibility.

Although one can track the idea of live moving-image transmissions back to the distant past (early claimants range from the ancient Egyptians to Saint Claire of Assisi), we can speak about the televisual in a specific sense with the coming of Bell's telephone in 1876. The telephone sparked an anticipatory interest in visual systems that could share the instrument's ability to link distant locations point to point in real time. This consensus took the form of verbal and graphic descriptions in both the scientific and popular press, as well as technological invention and patenting. For their inspiration, the authors of these reports and inventors of these new devices drew not only upon the telephone, but also upon the telegraph, especially the picture-telegraph that had been in service since the 1850s, the magic lantern, photography, and, after its introduction in 1878, the gramophone. En-dowed as the devices were with names such as the "electronic camera obscura," the "telectroscope," "telephonoscope," "electrical telescope," and so on, their explicitly intermedia character was apparent. Although a wide range of possibilities were described, most shared several characteristics: an explicit integration of the liveness and point-to-point links offered by the telephone; a projected two-dimensional visual display (in a rectilinear or oval frame) informed by the magic lantern and photography; and an interface through which spectators could interact with "live" moving-picture images of their interlocutors in real time. As we shall see, this vision was additionally enlivened by a clear sense of genre and a full-blown taxonomy of applications.

The supporting evidence for this imagined television apparatus can be found in many domains. In June 1877, *L'année scientifique et industrielle* included a description of a telephone-like device attributed to Alexander Graham Bell that supposedly sent images over a distance. Within two years of Bell's invention, a now famous cartoon appeared in *Punch* that showed a girl in Ceylon speaking on the telephone with her parents in the United Kingdom by way of a wide-screen "telephonoscope" attributed to Edison and Bell.[6] By 1883, Albert Robida would provide his full-blown science fiction description of the "telephonoscope" (a description to which we will return), an audiovisual technology that could bring distant entertainment into the living room, serve as a means of surveillance, and function as a real-time face-to-face communication medium.[7] Robida's "prediction" of television, like the prognostications of some of his contemporaries, offers a striking instance of technological anticipation, but it also speaks to the long history of ideas, urges, and attempts that infuse our most recent understanding of "new" media.[8] Thanks to these inaccurate reports and science fiction fantasies, simultaneity, a quality the popular imagination already defined by and experienced in the telephone, was understood as an attribute that a visual medium could possess as well.

What can we learn from these early visions of the new medium of television? Robida's text offers a good example. As already suggested, it elaborates on a variety of scenarios for the telephonoscope, a display device that uses a large, oval-shaped (and sometimes rectangular) flat glass screen to show (distant) live events. A cousin of the telephone both nominally and mechanically (for it can facilitate two-way communications together with the telephone, in addition to offering one-way audiovisual access), the telephonoscope, in one scenario, permits a colonist posted in Indochina to talk with and see his family back home (a function that Robida entitled "*la suppression de l'absence*"). In another scenario, we read of the difficulties of attending the theater (from coach hiring, to inclement weather, to the poor sight lines of nineteenth-century theater boxes). The telephonoscope permits theater lovers to stay at home, and, from the comfort of their living rooms, have front-row access to the stage action as it unfolds. Robida also elaborated on the informational function of the device (world news, shown live as it happens); its role in the public sphere (billboard-sized public television displaying the day's events); and its potential for surveillance and voyeurism (as a telephonoscope "mistake" offers a group of men visual access to a woman as she undresses).

Robida's description includes an array of televisual functionalities that we have either seen deployed (live entertainment and CNN-style live global news coverage, surveillance) or have long been promised (television-telephone service, now finally available in our cell phones and Webcams). He understood the medium both as a one-to-one communication system and as a broadcasting system, and he situated reception both in the privacy of the home and in public settings. The defining elements of his imagined audiovisual medium are liveness, movement, and the capacities for interaction and (apparently) immersion. Many of these notions would be drawn upon by the following waves of new media. In articulating his ideas, Robida made use of existing media—the then six-year-old telephone, of course, but also a notion of visual display partially derived from the magic lantern (or perhaps more appropriately, the camera obscura).

The year following the publication of Robida's book (1884), Paul Nipkow, working in Germany, patented the disk that would be the heart of mechanical-optical television systems into the late 1930s—the *elektrisches Teleskop*. Although the name for Nipkow's device is also intermedially referenced to an existing technology (the telescope that provided the metaphor for the early television medium)—this time visual instead of the more familiar reference to the audio technology of the telephone—in fact his mechanical reference is to an audio technology. Nipkow's disk is remarkably similar to the polyphone system developed in Leipzig in the 1880s, a mechanical contemporary of the gramophone in the form of a music box system in which the software consisted of a perforated metal disk. Nipkow created his image dissector by perforating a similar metal disk in a spiral pattern, standing it on end, and giving it a spin, in the process effectively transforming the polyphone's digital musical software into analog (scanned) television hardware. Like Robida, Nipkow situated his new medium in terms of existing technologies—a reference to visual extension in real time (the telescope) and a mechanical homage to an audio medium (the polyphone) linked to a telephone or telegraph line. In his later years, Nipkow circulated a creation myth, recalling his student days, when far from home and wanting to be with his family for the Christmas holidays, he came up with the idea for "television." Like the 1877 *Punch* cartoon, Nipkow sought to develop a medium capable of live extension, interaction, virtual presence, and communication.

If the televisual enjoyed a period of rich development as both an imaginary and patented technology shortly after the invention of the telephone, certainly the material base that it held in common with the telephone also enjoyed a long prehistory—at least as long as the one we attribute to the film medium. For example, Daguerre's and Fox Talbot's very different 1830s photographic experiments, milestones central to cinema's development, might be paralleled to Samuel Morse's 1837 demonstrations of an electronic telegraph; Reynaud's projecting praxinoscope or Eadweard Muybridge's zoopraxiscope, both from around 1879, might be paralleled to Bell's voice telephone of 1876. Edison's and the Lumières' earliest patents for the moving-picture camera and projector might be paralleled to the 1884 patent for Paul Nipkow's *elektrisches Teleskop*. These paired milestones in photographic and electrical technologies suggest the rough contours of two genealogical traditions that help to distinguish the very different provenances and projects of television and film. But our media histories have not always been attentive to these differences or their implications and have tended at times to blur the distinctions. In this sense, Charles Francis Jenkins's phantascope stands as an emblem of the conflation that helped to obscure these two traditions. Nearly one hundred years ago, as projected moving pictures first graced the screen, Jenkins introduced two very different devices under the same name: a moving-picture system codesigned with Thomas Armat, and a television-like system that promised, but so far as we know, failed, to transmit simple shapes. The motion-picture device had a significant impact and has been inscribed in our histories as the vitascope; the televisual device, a visionary failure, had no impact, and was long overshadowed by its twin's success and Jenkins's poor choice in naming.

This genealogical distinction renders visible the notion of simultaneity, a defining characteristic of nineteenth- and early twentieth-century television. Although much of our consideration of moving-image systems has tended to focus on visual representation (with the acoustic enjoying something of a boom at the moment as well), the temporal has been rather neglected. Yet one can trace a long-term interest in technologies of simultaneity—an interest that created television in the first place, and that remains very much alive within today's media systems (although, ironically, rarely television). Eighteenth-century optical telegraph systems, nineteenth-century wired and wireless telegraph and fax machines, and the twentieth century's radio, television, and Internet all in their various ways attempted to facilitate simultaneous communication over distant spaces, and thus extensions of the subject. Just as important, all shared certain developmental and discursive traits. The literature on these technologies usually attributes the development of technological infrastructures to military interests, and accordingly inscribes the use of simultaneity for communication, mapping, and surveillance within this offensive or defensive framework. But a less appreciated motive to stimulate technologies of simultaneity had to do with the construction of national identity and the modern state. Patrice Flichy argued, for instance, that the idea of France as unified nation in the nineteenth century owes much to a conception of instant access to its farthest corners, and thus the simultaneity of state power and knowledge over the complete geographical domain.[9] Arguing from a transnational perspective, Stephen Kern has found that the infrastructures of simultaneity were crucial for such practices as the establishment of universal time—practices easily repositioned within Foucault's notion of the microtechnologies of discipline characteristic of the modern era.[10] From the viewing subject's relation to the image, to pragmatic military concerns, to tangible articulations of the nation-state, to the Western discipline of uniform temporality, a wide range of ideological strategies have been embedded in the various technologies of simultaneity. These projects suggest something of the specificity that the project of live television brought with it, and the implications of the temporal distinctions between our two moving-image systems, one "live" and the other "stored."

WHO INVENTED TELEVISION?

The question of invention, often posed and sometimes answered, misses the point. As has been suggested, the conceptual modeling of the medium's *dispositif* and its technological realization is dispersed across time and national setting. That said, television's numerous histories tend to answer the question, and to do so in an emphatically nationalistic way (perhaps in keeping with the nationalist project to which communications systems have long been shackled). Although several scholars such as Abramson, Shiers, and Winston offer detailed chronicles of the complex interworkings of individuals, concepts, literature, patents, and industrial contexts that eventually resulted in what we today consider television, the majority of the medium's historians have told the tale in terms that fit national narratives. Thus, in the Soviet Union, Boris Rosing's important work in St. Petersburg provided the conceptual spark; while in France it was Barthélemy and Belin; or in Germany, Nipkow, Karolus, Ardenne, and the Hungarian Von Mihaly; or in Britain, Campbell-Swinton and Baird; or in the United States, Jenkins and Farnsworth, and so on. Depending on the precise definition of the medium, the focus on concept, prototype, or industrially sanctioned "invention," the story of television can be (and has been) molded to fit local market demands. Those scholars advocating a "social constructivist" approach to technological development—in which the larger interactions among individuals, industries, regulatory frameworks, governmental ministries, engineers, the press, and publics give form to a culturally specific constellation of technology and its applications—offer a far more nuanced assessment of "invention." Scholars such as Wiebe Bijker and Trevor Pinch have consolidated the theoretical frameworks for such an approach, and others such as Brian Winston, Michele Hilmes, and William Boddy have explored different facets of television's development and its intermedia positioning through this lens.[11]

The question of invention is thus vexed conceptually, as the social constructivists show, and in terms of requiring a stable and moderately linear configuration of the medium, which television lacks. Television, as a concept and a technology, has positioned itself among related media (e.g., telephone, camera obscura, image telegraph), conceptual frames (e.g., communication, entertainment, journalism, surveillance), and national developments (with most Western nations and Japan contributing important patents and technological insights). Its conceptual development seemed fully baked by the late nineteenth century, but its technological deployment as a mass medium would follow radio's (and that with a considerable lag) in the mid-1930s. This long gestation period combined with the political-economic position of the electronics industry in the 1930s, and the precedent of radio as a "mass medium," served to raise the stakes of nationalist claims for the medium's invention and encouraged both national and corporate specificity in the medium's development. The efforts of the Radio Corporation of America (RCA) in the United States, EMI-Marconi in Britain, Telefunken in Germany, and counterparts in other lands to lay claim to the medium's invention and to ally themselves with the increasingly nationalistic discourse of their governments in the late 1930s and 1940s had a profound impact on the medium's conceptualization and deployment, and seems to linger in our histories and assumptions regarding the medium. While we quite rightly celebrate the various efforts of Philo Farnsworth (electronic dissection), John Logie Baird (color, 3-D, and recording technologies in the late 1920s), René Barthélemy (1,042-line high-definition transmission), and others, television's highly controlled development from the 1930s onward has significantly compromised constructions of the medium's history and attributions.

RETHINKING MEDIA SEQUENCE: TELEVISION BEFORE FILM?

The attempt to recover the distinctive genealogical traditions behind television and film raises a number of questions having to do with their intermedia contexts and, as suggested, time. Stephen Kern has offered a compelling portrait of the competing notions of temporality vying for dominance in fields such as philosophy, psychology, and physics during the last quarter of the nineteenth and the beginning of the twentieth century. This period is widely considered to mark a significant shift in Western perception and representation, as evidenced by the period's arts and technologies and the discourses they generated. The contested nature of time as both fragmented and continuous found expression in, among other things, early notions of television and film—media that took shape within this crucible and helped to give it tangible form. For the purposes of this essay, we can simply make a quick heuristic distinction between two contrasting traditions of thinking about time: as fragmented but creating the illusion of continuity; and as a continuous and unified present, creating the illusion of progression and development.[12]

Nineteenth-century photographers such as Muybridge, Etienne-Jules Marey, and Thomas Eakins embraced the analytic potentials of fragmentation, seeking to subdivide the flow of life and submit it to scientific scrutiny. A later generation of motion analysts, epitomized by Frank Gilbreth, would use film to break down motion and analyze the logics of body movement and workflow with the goal of maximizing efficiency. This tradition of conceiving time as fragmented and atomized is heavily, but certainly not exclusively, indebted to the mechanical and analytic traditions of the eighteenth and nineteenth centuries, in which motion could be dissected and reactivated. This view, which in fact can be traced back to pre-Socratics such as Democritus and the atomists, has a metaphoric relationship to our thinking about the film medium. Although we appear to see continuous motion on the screen, in fact we are witnessing a rapid succession of still images. The twentieth-century version of this model of temporal fragmentation repositions the phenomenon in terms of modernity. Stephen Kern and David Lowe, for example, see film's ability to speed up time, to freeze it, or even to reverse it as emblematic of the modern (and the relative), as well as of twentieth-century thinking about time.[13] The contrasting notion of time conceived as a continuous present, as flow, as seamless, is something that tends to derive from the agrarian past (cyclically flowing time and solid-state being, reaching back to pre-Socratics such as Parmenides of Elea) and is exemplified in the electrical age by technologies such as the telegraph, telephone, and television. It, too, makes a claim for the modern, not only technologically, but in the context of the international time treaties that were signed at the beginning of the twentieth century, and in relation to processes like global flows, networks, simultaneity, and indeed, the synchronicity associated with our increasingly computer-mediated present.[14]

These two notions of time, one fragmented and the other continuous, one admitting access to the discrete shards of time and the other bound into an eternal present, played out their long pas de deux with the fin de siècle media of television and film. Most discussions of the horizon of expectations that greeted the film medium do not include such elements as extensiveness with the lived world and the "now" of the viewing process. But if we go so far as to shift photography from the exclusive and defining condition for the moving picture, we might begin to ask very different questions about the cultural space film entered. What if the film medium had in fact entered a cultural moment that included continuity and not only fragmentation, electricity and not only photography, liveness and extension rather than simply storage and reflection? What if film appeared to a world that was prepared for moving images in the form of television?

One might expect that against this horizon of expectations, the film medium would have been deployed in ways consistent with the promise of television. There are, of course, a number of ways to understand the distinct production practices of the film medium's first decade, including its remediation of photographic, theatrical, and music hall and circus traditions, and scholars of early cinema have explored these as explanatory possibilities. But the televisual also offers a plausible formative influence, and thus a way to read some of the distinctive attributes of period between 1895 and 1903–5. If the temporal distinctions between television and film outlined above can be accepted, and if the metaphors for television as a connector with life as it happens are to be taken seriously, then one might expect a filmic mimicking of television to take a form that emphasized liveness, presence, and a true "window on the world."

Judging by many early humorous and probably exaggerated reports, the claim that at least for some audiences, early cinematic practices succeeded in confusing audiences as to the status of the image (live or stored? present or absent?) seems if not certain, at least well publicized. Films such as *Uncle Josh at the Picture Show* (1902) together with anecdotal (often apocryphal) reports about early audiences behaving as though screen images had the same ontological status as the viewers themselves suggest that the issue of the film medium's convincing level of verisimilitude was open for discussion.[15] What is curious is the longevity of this story for more than a decade after the first Paris screening.[16] Might we read this persistent tale as evidence of the motion picture industry's attempt to situate its products within a discourse of liveness? Might we see it as proof of the audience's expectation of images that were co-extensive with the lived world? Such readings may be just as appropriate as the more familiar attribution of alleged audience shock to the new heights in visual realism achieved by the film medium, or the explanation that certain naive audiences could not distinguish between movement and presence.

Astonishment may also account for the preponderance of nonfiction in early film production and exhibition, a preponderance that made speaking of the screen as a "window on the world" entirely reasonable.[17] As our knowledge of early cinema grows, it becomes clear that the signifying practices—particularly with regard to editing—operating in nonfiction differed from those deployed in fiction films. Nonfiction films seemed generally to have resisted the sorts of editorial fragmentation that characterized their fictional counterparts—a tendency that became more evident as the medium developed and fictional films grew ever-more fragmented. Single-shot street scenes, panoramic shots taken from the fronts of trains, and unbroken gazes at waves pounding rocks on the shore could easily have been read in their time as live; the films' arrangements of time and space (coherent and generally unbroken; or if containing multiple shots, nonanalytic in keeping with the metaphor of a window on the world) potentially simulated a televisual viewing experience in the same manner that the panorama simulated the experience of the panopticon. We might, too, consider certain terminological markers that appear in the early years of the film medium: the use of the *actualité* for nonfiction, a term loaded with meanings, one of which is temporal; or American Mutoscope and Biograph's 68-millimeter *Living Postcards*; or the transition, circa 1903, from the *actualité* to "canned" drama that declares the shift from the seemingly live to the emphatically stored (not to mention the insistence on Greek and Latin invocations of liveness—bioscope, vitagraph, animatograph, *lebende Bilder*, etc.). Such nomenclature, like the dominance of the *actualité* and the persistence of the Lumière effect, can be read as claims to a quality of liveness consistent with the long-awaited moving-image medium of television that graced the popular imagination for the twenty years preceding the first film exhibitions.[18]

INTERPRETIVE FLEXIBILITY

Robida's musings and Nipkow's patent helped to shape early thinking about television's possibilities, with other developers contributing to the mix along the way. Although many of the components for what would emerge as working television were in place by the turn of the century, the medium remained largely a tinkerer's fantasy until the late 1920s, when technologies such as radio, capitalization from government and industry, and demand in the form of (among other things) cinema sound systems, all converged. The late 1920s and early 1930s are notable as much for the battles between individual inventors and corporations (Farnsworth vs. RCA; Baird vs. EMI) as for the struggle over technological norms (optical-mechanical; electronic scan lines) and the developmental plurality of television's very conception.

The clearest examples can be found in Germany, which first introduced daily public television service in Berlin in March 1935.[19] By this point, independent British inventor John Logie Baird, finding little enthusiasm for his ideas from the BBC, formed an alliance with German partners and joined the Fernseh Company. But Baird and partners faced parallel difficulties in Germany. The 1936 Olympics were the testing grounds for the nation's two competing television systems: Fernseh's Nipkow-based mechanical interfilm system and Telefunken's electronic iconoscope system. Telefunken, part of a global RCA licensing network that included Baird's British competitor, EMI, won the standards battle in Germany just as EMI triumphed in Britain (and RCA dominated in America). There seemed to be a distinct pattern to the reduction of television's technological plurality, matching the technological need for standardization and an industrial desire for concentration.

In this period of general consolidation, television's conceptual contestation played itself out with greater variation in Germany than elsewhere, providing an excellent example of the flexibility that, despite periods of suppression, would remain a key trait of the medium. Thanks to a series of often-bitter struggles among political factions, governmental ministries, and interested corporations, television found itself pulled into at least four different directions. The electronics industry, in the midst of a national campaign to put a radio in every German home, un-surprisingly backed a radiolike notion of television: a household appliance that could bring the events of the outside world into the living room, and that like radio would thrive on live informational and mixed-form entertainment broadcasts. To this end, a relatively inexpensive "people's television receiver" was developed by the electronics companies, replicating the successful principle of the "people's radio" and anticipating similar sales.

This view was contested by Joseph Goebbels and Eugen Hadamovsky of the Propaganda Ministry together with the socialist wing of the Nazi Party, all of whom felt (for very different reasons) that television should be seen outside the home in collective, public settings, serving as something of a surrogate for film with the added capacity to show live sports and political events. The Propaganda Ministry felt that collective settings were more conducive to persuasion, and the socialist wing of the NSDAP (National Socialist German Workers Party) felt that television should be free for all until receivers were so cheap that working-class families could afford them. Accordingly, television halls, most accommodating forty viewers but in some cases (equipped with large-screen interfilm display) up to eight hundred, sprang up around Berlin and, for a time, Paris as well.

A third notion of television saw it as a two-way communication medium linked to the telephone, harkening back to the earliest visions of the medium. Accordingly, a nationwide television-telephone network was established with fa-cilities in major city post offices, with service stretching from Nuremburg to Hamburg, and Cologne to Leipzig. Finally, the Air Ministry developed television for the purposes of both reconnaissance (using high-definition prototypes of up to two thousand scan lines) and telepresence (visual guidance systems for bombs, rockets, and torpedoes in the form of mini–television cameras and remote con-trols). Although mini-cameras were actively produced for these "media" and testing was carried out, it seems as though this use of television did not see active deployment in the field. Each of these systems was deployed, each had corporate and governmental backers, and each gave form to a distinctive definition of tele-vision's capacities—whether representational or functional. Moreover, each was embedded in particular technological prototypes and medial *dispositifs*—radio, film, telephone, and telepresence, in turn constructing distinctive notions of in-terface, audience, and notions of effects. If nothing more, this episode demon-strates that the *postwar* certainty of television's place in the home, its status as a domestic technology, was by no means the only option for the medium before the war's end.

The German case is interesting for many reasons, not the least, its overriding interest in radio and television broadcasting as a means of using technologies of simultaneity to construct the nation. From the late 1920s into the late 1930s, German broadcasting authorities urged both the electronics industry and con-sumers to put "a radio in every house" by coordinating the design and pricing of the "people's receiver." The campaign was a massive success with the public, and it encouraged broadcasting journalists and engineers alike to theorize the potentials and implications of a public defined by a technology. Various media technologies were seen as part of an elaborated system that could help to extend the viewer beyond the site of his or her physical embodiment, to extend real-time participation in distant events, and in the German case, to redefine the *Volkskoerper*. This notion sought to make use of a temporal capacity lacking in the moving-image medium of film (although the period's film-distribution practices, particularly with regard to newsreels, seem to have privileged carefully synchronized and widespread release, suggesting a high degree of coordination even if simultaneity was impossible).

One striking example of how television's embrace of simultaneity would reposition if not eliminate the power of the storage medium of film—and in the process help to construct a new form of subjectivity—appeared in a top secret report produced by the German Post Ministry in 1943. The Post Ministry had long been engaged in a bitter conflict with the Propaganda Ministry, a conflict based on the culture clash between career civil servants (the Post) and NSDAP hacks (Propaganda). With the Post responsible for television's apparatus and technology-intensive live broadcasts, and Propaganda responsible for programming, disputes were inevitable over everything from time allocation to the sharing of radio license fees. Late in the war, however, senior officials at the Post Ministry drew up a secret plan for post-victory Europe that they felt would render the Propaganda Ministry redundant. The plan called for a live cable television news network to connect "Greater Germany" and the occupied territories. Round-the-clock live television news, the Post's domain, after all, would simply do away with the need for premeditated propaganda and filmed programming. The live connection between the leadership and its followers, the extension of nation through shared event, would constitute the new Germany's neural network, constructing the new *Volkskoerper*. This scenario, with its rather chilling implications, clearly illustrates the perceived differences in temporality, connectivity, and presence between the media of television and film alluded to earlier in the essay with the genealogical distinctions between the two technologies.

The specificities of the German case notwithstanding, the point is that at this stage of its development, television enjoyed considerable conceptual flexibility and was highly responsive to its media environment. It was a medium that could have taken very different directions from that which we today take for granted. True, in national contexts like the United States, where corporations such as RCA (NBC) and Columbia (CBS) enjoyed a particularly influential position, television was promoted almost exclusively within the radio paradigm (and in this sense, it is indeed ironic to find such plurality in a totalitarian state); nevertheless, the medium's potential to be configured in many different ways was explored even there. The ultimate dominance of the radio model had far-reaching consequences. On the one hand, television was in some circles conceived of as the "completion" of radio, the next step in a teleologically driven evolution process by which the senses were extended, allowing wireless participation and a modicum of control in distant places. On the other hand, media-conceptual issues such as a (state and corporate) preference for one-way rather than two-way communication; regulatory issues such as the division and allocation of the broadcast spectrum; content issues such as program formats; and economic models (whether commercial, state, or public) were all derived from the model radio provided in the late 1920s. In nations such as the United States, the period was crucial for the suppression of the medium's plurality and the consolidation of its modeling, and for revealing the nature of the pressures that forged this new medium as it was prepared for public consumption.

CONCLUSION: INTERMEDIALITY REVISITED

As the German case illustrates, television's interpretive flexibility took the form of intermedia alliances. Although the telephone has, from 1877 until the present, remained its most persistent if underdeveloped partner, film has provided the most visible site of intermedia collaboration. In 1940, the Balaban and Katz Theater Corporation, a company with roots going back to 1908, when it operated nickelodeons in Chicago, acquired a license for an experimental television station in the Windy City. By this point a subsidiary of Paramount, Balaban and Katz repositioned itself from an early adopter in the commercial film business to a forerunner in the commercial television business. Its parent company, Paramount (with Barney Balaban as president), owned several television stations outright and partnered with the Dumont network, an early commercial television company, in the ownership and development of others. Together, they would soon own four of the United States' first nine television stations, with competitors such as Fox, Warner Bros., and Loews-MGM each attempting to purchase stations and television-based technologies of their own. If television initially provided a significant component in the horizon of expectations that greeted film in 1895, and if some early television systems relied on interfilm technologies for production and in some cases exhibition, the 1930s and 1940s witnessed a different strategy, with the film industry attempting to deploy television technology in ways that served its core business.

Michele Hilmes has provided an extremely useful overview of these interactions, two of which are of particular note in thinking about television's ever-changing relationship with cinema.[20] As is evident from the German example, one model essentially brought television into the cinema theater. This model found widespread interest as late as the early 1950s, as cinemas brought live sports, major political events, and news to the big screen. Indeed, as early as 1939, some cinemas specializing in newsreels used large-screen television projections to enhance the timeliness of reports, again, with sports serving as an important driver. By the 1940s, although RCA's technology dominated, several Hollywood companies either invested in large-screen television projection technologies such as Paramount's Scophony system, or acquired the rights to such technologies, such as 20th Century Fox's rights to the Eidophor system. Like the timing of the large automated dance-hall organs that emerged shortly before loudspeaker technology began to find a market share, these large-screen applications of television appeared shortly before domestic television's second wave. Both technologies, the large dance-hall organ and the large television screen, found their prospects reduced to niche markets as the domestic model of television (and the dance-hall use of loudspeakers) took hold in the public's imagination and households.

The film industry, meanwhile, continued to explore ways of exploiting its products through the television medium. Subscription and pay-per-view emerged as viable alternatives, again with film companies either developing their own or partnering with existing technologies that could provide and regulate home exhibition. The Skiatron Corporation's Subscribervision, Paramount's Telemeter, and Zenith's Phonevision all offered ways of bringing films to the home through television (and revenues to Hollywood by way of tracking systems), but these technologies, too, were effectively put on hold by a combination of several factors. Despite these attempts to selectively meld television content into the cinema and cinematic content into television, in fact both efforts largely failed due to legal and regulatory reasons. In 1948, a Supreme Court decision (*United States v. Paramount Pictures, Inc.,* 334 U.S. 131) affirmed the antitrust cases brought against the major American film studios a decade earlier, triggering a reorganization and divestment of studio-owned cinemas. The film industry's attempts to use subscription television as an alternate distribution channel were stimulated by the decrees and eventually fell victim to them. The courts held that the film industry could not branch out into television distribution without violating the terms of the antitrust settlement. Similarly, the fate of television in the cinema and the joint partnership of Dumont and Paramount were undone by the broadcasting regulations of the Federal Communications Commission (FCC), which enforced rules against market dominance and effectively interpreted Paramount's cinemas as part of Dumont's broadcast network. The FCC effectively barred television from integrating with film exhibition.

Although the logics in both cases were regulatory, the results would keep "liveness" from entering the cinema, and, for a few years anyway, kept television from relying on "stored" programming. Despite the regulatory regimes that disciplined the boundaries of each medium (and that delayed the deployment of technologies that we today take for granted), the situation remained fundamentally complicated. For example, when forced to divest its cinemas, Paramount sold its holdings to radio and television (the American Broadcasting Company) now under the direction of one of its former employees (Leonard Goldenson, former head of United Paramount Theaters), thus giving the film-television relationship yet another twist. Television would continue its pas de deux with the film industry, eventually emerging as a major site of exhibition (whether through direct broadcast or subscription television or video on demand), as a key means of promotion, and as an explicit corporate partner as the twentieth century grew more convergent.

Lynn Spigel opens Chapter 4 of her *Make Room for Television* with a quote from television director Gary Simpson taken from a 1955 book on how to direct television. Simpson's definition speaks to the continued belief in liveness and "seeing at a distance" as defining components of the television medium: "Mr. Public views that television set in his home as a 20th Century electronic monster that can transport him to the baseball game, to Washington D.C., to the atomic blast in Nevada—and do it NOW. The viewer is inclined to accept it as his window to the world, as his reporter on what is happening now—simultaneously. The miracle of television is actually Man's ability to see at a distance while the event is happening."[21]

This definition would slowly lose its relevance as television increasingly relied on film and videotape, on reruns and the economic logics of syndication and the "rear end." On broadcast television, liveness became the stuff of Super Bowls and World Cup playoffs, of disasters and national rituals, even here (in regulatory settings such as the United States), eventually being outlawed in order to permit the censorship of unexpected events.[22] Live television survives in the margins, where it can be found in the restricted sphere of surveillance and medical applications, Webcams, and cell phones. But the latest intermedia alliances between television and the mobile phone or television and the Internet suggest a continuity of the larger flexibility and responsiveness that dominated the medium's history. The question is whether—and in what form—the long-term conceptual concerns that have bound definitions of television together will rebound as the stability of the medium, imposed since the 1950s by governments and the electronics industry, gives way to new articulations of the televisual.

NOTES

1. Carolyn Marvin, *When Old Technologies Were New: Thinking About Electric Communication in the Late Nineteenth Century* (New York: Oxford University Press, 1988).

2. Hayden White has perhaps most elegantly called attention to the implications of where we choose to begin and end our historical narratives in his *Metahistory: The Historical Imagination in Nineteenth-Century Europe* (Baltimore: Johns Hopkins University Press, 1973). Television in this regard is exemplary. Seen from the perspective of the dawn

of the broadcast era in the years following World War II, the medium's history might be read as a textbook case of collaborative efforts between industry and government stabilizing a "new" technology, with a precedent medium, radio, providing the main organizational and programming parameters for its deployment. The intervening years would then be positioned as both a confirmation of the wisdom of this original model and a testament to the slow but steady refinements of media technology (tubes to chips), interface (dial to remote control), and synergetic potential (ranging from delivery and storage systems to programming sources). But if we begin our story at a different point, the historical trajectory leads to quite another set of insights.

3. Consider the post-Brighton turn in early film studies, a development that has proven remarkably productive over the past twenty years.

4. See R.W. Burns, *Television, An International History of the Formative Years* (London: Institution of Electrical Engineers, 1998); Albert Abramson, *The History of Television, 1880–1941* (London: McFarland, 1987); Herman Hecht, *Pre-Cinema History: An Encyclopaedia and Annotated Bibliography of the Moving Image Before 1896* (London: BFI/Bowker/Saur, 1993); George Shires, *Early Television: A Bibliographic Guide to 1940* (London: Garland Publishing, 1997); Brian Winston, *Misunderstanding Media* (Cambridge, MA: Harvard University Press, 1986); Siegfried Zielinski, *Audiovisions: Cinema and Television as Entr'actes in History* (1989; Amsterdam: Amsterdam University Press, 1999).

5. Conceptually, the sixteenth-century development of the camera obscura can be argued as a direct conceptual predecessor to television, but for the purposes of this essay, the televisual is deployed in a more literal sense. See William Uricchio, "Technologies of Time," in *Allegories of Communication: Intermedial Concerns from Cinema to the Digital*, ed. Jan Olsson and John Fullerton (Eastleigh: John Libbey, 2004): 123–138.

6. George du Maurier, "Edison's Telephonoscope (Transmits Light as Well as Sound)," Almanac for 1879, *Punch* 75 (December 9, 1878).

7. Albert Robida, *Le vingtième siècle* (Paris: G. Decaux, 1883).

8. Erkki Huhtamo, "From Kaleidoscomaniac to Cybernerd: Notes Towards an Archaeology of Media," in *Electronic Culture: Technology and Visual Representation*, ed. Timothy Druckery (London: Aperture Press, 1996): 297–303.

9. Patrice Flichy, *Tele. Geschichte der modernen Kommunikation* (1991; Frankfurt: Campus Verlag, 1994).

10. Stephen Kern, *The Culture of Time and Space: 1880–1918* (London: Weidenfeld and Nicholson, 1983); for Michel Foucault, see especially *Discipline and Punish* (1975; New York: Vintage Books, 1979).

11. W. Bijker, T. Hughes, T. Pinch, eds., *The Social Construction of Technological Systems* (Cambridge, MA: MIT Press, 1989); William Boddy, *Fifties Television: The Industry and Its Critics* (Urbana: University of Illinois Press, 1990); Michele Hilmes, *Hollywood and Broadcasting: From Radio to Cable* (Urbana: University of Illinois Press, 1990).

12. In the West, we can distinguish between two broad approaches to the definition of time: one approach defines time as a structure, as either fragmented or as flow; the other defines time as an experience, as past or present. For discussion about the pre-television era, I have collapsed the two. The photographic character of film necessarily implies a temporal state of "pastness," while, for the purposes of my argument, I am taking the televisual to be "present" (ignoring the recorded nature of much contemporary television). This distinction is a crucial one with important implications for a larger discussion of the media.

13. Donald Lowe, *History of Bourgeois Perception* (Chicago: University of Chicago Press, 1983).

14. Manuel Castells, for example, defined globalization in temporal rather than spatial terms, paying particular attention to the near-simultaneity of information circulation. See Manuel Castells, *The Rise of the Network Society* (Cambridge: Blackwell, 1996).

15. This tale is a long-running trope in media history, evident from late-eighteenth-century drawings of Robertson's *Phatasmagorica* (where audience members are shown flailing the illusion-filled air with walking sticks) to cartoons about terrified "rubes" and "bumpkins" in the cinema as late as 1913.

16. See Stephen Bottomore's *I Want to See This Annie Mattygraph: A Cartoon History of the Coming of the Movies* (Gemona: Le Giornate del Cinema Muto, 1995), esp. 44–53.

17. For a compelling alternate view of this phenomenon, see Tom Gunning, "An Aesthetic of Astonishment: Early Film and the [In]Credulous Spectator," in *Viewing Positions*, ed. Linda Williams (New Brunswick, NJ: Rutgers University Press, 1995).

18. W. Uricchio, "Aktualitäten als Bilder der Zeit," *KINtop: Jahrbuch zur Erforschung des frühen Films* 6 (1997): 43–50.

19. The claim is complicated by the fact that Germany's initial efforts in fact differed little from what was being broadcast in the United States, England, and other countries on an experimental basis. Nevertheless, the Reich's broadcasting service represented a collaboration between industry and the state that continued largely unbroken until the last months of the war, and was responsible for significant innovation on both programming and technological fronts. For an overview, see William Uricchio, "Television as History: Representations of German Television Broadcasting, 1935–1944," in *Framing the Past: The Historiography of German Cinema and Television*, ed. Bruce Murray and Christopher Wickham (Carbondale: Southern Illinois University Press, 1992): 167–196.

20. Michele Hilmes, *Hollywood and Broadcasting: From Radio to Cable* (Urbana: University of Illinois Press, 1990).

21. Lynn Spigel, *Make Room for Television: Television and the Family Ideal in Postwar America* (Chicago: University of Chicago Press, 1992), 99, citing William J. Kaufman, ed., *How to Direct for Television* (New York: Hastings House, 1955), 13.

22. During the February 2004 broadcast of America's Super Bowl halftime show, the live airing of Janet Jackson's "wardrobe malfunction" caused the FCC to mandate a time delay on all future broadcasts, effectively outlawing "liveness."

BIBLIOGRAPHY

Abramson, Albert. *The History of Television, 1880–1941*. London: McFarland, 1987.

Bijker, W., T. Hughes, and T. Pinch, eds. *The Social Construction of Technological Systems*. Cambridge, MA: MIT Press, 1989.

Boddy, William. *Fifties Television: The Industry and Its Critics*. Urbana: University of Illinois Press, 1990.

Burns, R.W. *Television: An International History of the Formative Years*. London: Institution of Electrical Engineers, 1998.

Castells, Manuel. *The Rise of the Network Society*. Cambridge: Blackwell, 1996.

Gunning, Tom. "An Aesthetic of Astonishment: Early Film and the [In]Credulous Spectator." *Viewing Positions*. Ed. Linda Williams. New Brunswick, NJ: Rutgers University Press, 1995.

Hecht, Herman. *Pre-Cinema History: An Encyclopaedia and Annotated Bibliography of the Moving Image Before 1896*. London: BFI/Bowker/Saur, 1993.

Hilmes, Michele. *Hollywood and Broadcasting: From Radio to Cable*. Urbana: University of Illinois Press, 1990.

Huhtamo, Erkki. "From Kaleidoscomaniac to Cybernerd: Notes Towards an Archaeology of Media." *Electronic Culture: Technology and Visual Representation*. Ed. Timothy Druckery. London: Aperture Press, 1996. 297–303.

Kern, Stephen. *The Culture of Time and Space: 1880–1918*. London: Weidenfeld and Nicholson, 1983.

Marvin, Carolyn. *When Old Technologies Were New: Thinking About Electric Communication in the Late Nineteenth Century*. New York: Oxford University Press, 1988.

Shires, George. *Early Television: A Bibliographic Guide to 1940*. London: Garland Publishing, 1997.

Uricchio, William. "Technologies of Time." *Allegories of Communication: Intermedial Concerns from Cinema to the Digital*. Ed. Jan Olsson and John Fullerton. Eastleigh: John Libbey, 2004. 123–138.

White, Hayden. *Metahistory: The Historical Imagination in Nineteenth-Century Europe*. Baltimore: Johns Hopkins University Press, 1973.

Winston, Brian. *Misunderstanding Media*. Cambridge, MA: Harvard University Press, 1986.

Zielinski, Siegfried. *Audiovisions: Cinema and Television as Entr'actes in History*. 1989. Amsterdam: Amsterdam University Press, 1999.

CHAPTER 10

"THE END OF TV AS WE KNOW IT": CONVERGENCE ANXIETY, GENERIC INNOVATION, AND THE CASE OF *24*

TARA MCPHERSON

In March 2006, the IBM Institute for Business Value released a new study entitled "The End of TV As We Know It: A Future Industry Perspective." Replete with marketing neologisms, colorful illustrated figures, and speculative sidebars, the report maintains that the days of network television's midcentury model of "straightforward, one-to-many" broadcasting are drawing to a close, gradually to be replaced by "the growing availability of on demand, self-programming and search features," familiar hallmarks of the much-prophesied, emergent digital era. The study further predicts that, at least for the time being, the industry will be faced with two types of viewers: "While one consumer segment remains largely passive in the living room, the other will force radical change in business models in a search for anytime, anywhere content through multiple channels. By 2012, the tech- and fashion-forward consumer segment will lead us to a world of platform-agnostic content, fluid mobility of media experiences, individualized pricing schemes and an end to the traditional concept of release windows" (Berman 2006, 1). In short, this brave new world of creative consumers will crave personalized, transformable content fully available on demand, 24/7.

Given such predictions (and the recent popularity of Web sites such as You-Tube.com, with its slogan "Broadcast Yourself"), one might expect a dim future for the fifty-plus-year tradition of dramatic, narrative television, born as it was of the scheduled, broadcast model. However, one "future scenario" from the report, offered as a highlighted inset, is worth quoting at length:

My Gadget-Lover's Dream Realized

I am in digital-electronics-gadget nirvana. And, I am not afraid to boast. My home sports a fully wireless broadband (WIMAX) Internet environment, where content moves freely among the home server, several multiple high definition (HD) screens, the office PC and the mobile devices that I continually upgrade.

I regularly acquire favorite TV shows (new and old) either from Internet search engines such as Google Video, the video/telecommunications provider's on demand archive or fully-loaded Internet video destinations. I can't remember the last time I made "appointment TV," since I download or watch on replay from my multi-room digital video recorder (DVR) every important program or episode. A Bluetooth-like signal on my cell phone triggers the logon for my media center system. When ready to watch TV, I am greeted with a mosaic screen with tiles of favorite TV channels, suggested programs from the last 24 hours, season's passes and tailored on demand choices.

My home network offers different on demand pricing packages, dependent on the number of times I plan to watch, copy or download—and whether the content is a preview. When not skipping through, I am more amused than ever by advertising, particularly since it is tailored for me and comes with relevant links, add-ons and a variety of purchase options within the commercial itself. While all of these options can feel overwhelming to some, I view them as a challenge with a large pay-off. I will continue to put in the energy to be first on the block with the latest "gadget-lover's dream realized." (Berman 2006, 2).

Closely parsed, the example reveals that the traditional television series seems less at threat than the forecasted world of "self-programming" (and self-broadcasting à la YouTube) might at first suggest. Rather, the *interface* for delivering, accessing, monetizing, scheduling, and viewing such content seems to be the thing most likely to change as we move toward "the end of television as we know it." The actual programs themselves might still feel quite familiar, or, at least, exist alongside newly emergent types of entertainment. Since the heady days of the 1990s' dot-com boom, many have predicted that the ascendancy of the Internet and of computer games would foster television's demise, but the IBM report confidently observes that "[g]oing forward, analysts predict TV usage to grow by an average of 1.7 percent per annum through 2008," in part because "new technologies will allow increased control over when, how and where content is viewed" (Berman 2006, 3).

This confident prediction extends even to the youth audience, as those digital natives are apparently still watching a good deal of television. Much of the report focuses not on content or program structure but on evolving business models for delivering, extending, and repurposing extant content forms as well as on reformulating advertising models to "correct misalignment between performance and revenues" (Berman 2006, 4). The real anxiety around convergence for corporate players is not really about content at all, but, rather, about the relationship between media monopolies, particularly between telecommunication companies and traditional video providers and between "Internet content aggregators" and traditional programmers like the networks and cable channels (Berman 2006, 8).[1] Faced with competition from Internet portals such as Google and Yahoo! more traditional programmers from the BBC to Disney ABC are experimenting with new variations of on-demand content. In some ways, this also suggests that "content" matters all the more, for how better to spur on-demand, give-it-to-me-my-way success than with compelling narrative content?

The need for just such content—that is, programming that "tech-forward" consumers long to tote about on their iPods or own in pristine, collector's-edition boxed sets—works in neat synergy with what many have framed as a recent renaissance in television drama, from *The Sopranos* to *Deadwood* to *Lost* to *Buffy* to *24*. These series deploy a certain patina of quality in order to cement their status as valuable content, and their serialized format helps fuel loyal audiences. Interestingly, many of these series, especially *24*, *Lost*, and a spate of popular crime procedurals, seem themselves to be fixated on exploring just what role technology might play for humanity. In what follows, I turn in particular to *24* as a "snapshot" of transition, not only within the television industry itself, as traditional broadcast models are reworked via new modes of generic innovation, product placement, and multiplatform distribution, but also of transition within broader society as the forces of globalization and technological change reshape our notions of nation, labor, and gender.

When *24* burst onto the U.S. broadcast landscape in November 2001, it was quickly hailed as something radically new for television. Writing for the *Boston Globe*, critic Matthew Gilbert proclaimed, "Strong adjectives such as 'riveting' and 'gripping' and 'compelling' are shamelessly overused in the critical vernacular. . . . But it's time to reinvest in their stock when it comes to *24*, a riveting, gripping, and altogether compelling new suspense drama. . . . An innovative and expertly executed hour of suspense, *24* is without question the best premiere of the fall season" (Gilbert 2001, F1). Such praise was typical, and the series went on to accrue great critical acclaim, an eventually solid viewership, and no small amount of scholarly attention.[2] Thus, 24 became one of several recent series framed via a rhetoric of a new "golden age" of television quality, as a kind of benchmark of "good TV" that might also be distinguished from the ever-growing tendency toward reality programming or the recent explosion of amateur video warehoused on the Internet. In short, by infusing old-school dramatic, fictional television with a new slickness, it worked to secure a future for the medium, staving off the end of television as we know it. As a feminist who has watched the show with great ambivalence, often recoiling from its flat characterizations of women and its troubling nationalism, I am particularly interested in the way frequently voiced perceptions of the show's innovativeness and quality may serve to mask its deployment of what has long been seen as a particularly feminized form, the soap opera. Further, I aim to investigate what role this new inflection of male melodrama might play in at once fixing and troubling masculinity in the era of global capitalism and national insecurity.

This essay then considers 24 as a hybrid form, a kind of convergence parable that brings together elements of the soap opera, reality television, and "quality" drama within a formal structure that emphasizes technological innovation and change. In particular, I am interested in the ways in which the series undertakes a re-masculinization of serialized melodrama via a very particular deployment of both narrative and style. In the drama's narrative structure, a relentless focus on certain tropes of masculinity and nation works to distance criticisms that might be aimed at the program's use of a serial form that shares much with both daytime and prime-time soap operas, even as the soapy content helps secure the series' most reactionary moments. At the level of stylistic or aesthetic innovation, the series deploys technology (from the trope of liveness activated by its "real-time" countdown to the featured use of split-screen videography) to distance further the "feminine" form of the serial, reinstalling a very particular vision of the white, male post-9/11 hero. This dual strategy also serves to protect television itself (often theorized as feminine) from the perceived threats posed, first, to the industry by new media technologies such as the Internet and, second, to the "serious" or "quality" drama by reality television (itself a televisual response to the threat of digital media). I return to the question of "quality" television as this essay draws to a close, querying the work such a concept does for both broadcast television and television studies in our particular moment of convergence.

"24 IS ITS OWN ANIMAL": LIVENESS, TECHNOLOGY, AND SERIAL FORM

If critic Matthew Gilbert initially praised 24 as it premiered for being the best that television could be, by season two he was gently mocking the narrative for having "its share of Aaron Spelling moments" even as he continued to laud the show as "ambitious" (Gilbert 2002, C1). Gilbert seemed willing to call a soap a soap, a tendency many of his fellow journalists avoided. For instance, writing in the *Atlanta Journal-Constitution*, Phil Kloer described "the series' multiple plot lines" and "the sadistic way the writers keep piling stress on their beleaguered characters" while also portraying the 24 viewer as a "junkie craving a fix" (Kloer 2002, 1E). Even as he pondered whether or not "there has ever been a series that had more viewers shouting advice to the characters," he refrained from commenting on the soap-like features of the drama and from drawing references to soap operas. Still, from Teri's amnesia and hidden pregnancy in season one to the obligatory wedding scenarios of season two, 24 derives much of its narrative force and story content from terrain familiar from soap operas, even while it also draws from cop dramas and action films to prop up its investigations of masculinity.

Given its elaborate and often ridiculous plot twists and in its interlocking, ongoing narratives, 24 clearly depends on the serial form of the soap and on the conceptual terrain of melodrama, extending the ongoing serialization of prime-time U.S. television that Jane Feuer, Lynne Joyrich, and others have noted is constitutive of television since the Reagan era. As Joyrich noted, melodrama is "the preferred form for television" (1996, 46), spreading across the televisual landscape in a diverse array of forms and genres. Yet, even with this generalized diffusion of melodrama throughout television's many formats, 24 is more than simply melodramatic. Its narrative structure hews closely to the serialized form of soap operas. If many of today's television shows attempt a series/serial hybrid, allowing closure week to week while also continuing key story lines, this Fox drama deploys pure serial structure. This structure was duly noted by network executives who, hoping to allow casual viewers to drop in on the series, pressured the show's creators to move toward a more episodic structure after season two, a move the creative team resisted.

This is not to say that 24's producers were eager to have the show labeled a soap. The show's creator and executive producer, Bob Cochran, acknowledged in an interview that, while "just about every show on TV . . . has some degree of serialization . . . , serialization [on 24] is obviously much more prominent." But, even as he went on to note that his first staff job as a writer was on the nighttime soap *Falcon Crest* he maintained that the connection between his show and soaps "can be overstated. What soaps don't have that we do is time continuity . . . in that

sense, *24* is its own animal."[3] In fact, we might read the series' aggressive production techniques—including its split-screen showiness and its conceit of running in real time—as attempts to distance the show from its debased and feminized
narrative form. Thus, its trope of liveness and its technological fetishism come
together to function as a prophylaxis against the debased form of the soap while
also shoring television up against the incursions of new digital forms such as the
Internet into domestic spaces that were once the near-exclusive domain of television. The show is defended as "quality" (by its creators and most critics) precisely
because it is figured as different from soap operas, and its "quality" status is
established in the ways that it is not like debased melodramatic forms (be they soap
operas or that other form of television that now so trades in simulated liveness, the
reality television show). I return to this distinction between "quality" television and
soap opera and other forms at the close of this essay.

In her examinations of melodrama and postmodern television, Lynne Joyrich
has consistently reminded us that "sexual difference[s] in the TV melodrama . . .
invite further investigation" (1996, 46), and this is certainly true of *24*'s remaking of
the soap opera. There is a re-masculinization of television at work here, both in the
near-obsessive explorations of the twenty-first-century contours of maleness that
the show undertakes and in its hypertechnologized formal strategies, both of which
suggest an overcompensation for the series' abduction of what has long been seen
as a highly feminized form. Initially, I had (and sometimes still have) a hard time
watching the series because of its figuration of the women characters, particularly
the blondest, dumbest ones, but I have slowly come to think that this is not an
especially telling aspect of the drama. In fact, the serial form of *24* seems to demand
a certain deployment of fairly predictable representations, as form and representation reinforce one another. Its stock female characters are not that surprising
given the show's reworking of the soap opera (hence its use of delicious villainesses
and sacrificing mothers) and its deep investment in investigating masculinity
(particularly through its blend of action and melodrama).[4] Put differently, I am
not sure the stereotypical feminist critique "These are degraded images of women"
really tells us anything all that useful or surprising about *24*. A different (and, I
would say, more useful) critical project might be to explore the series' relationships
to both masculinity and technology, particularly as they interconnect via new
generic hybrids and as they speak to the shifting conditions of daily life at a
particular moment in late capitalism.

These relationships are quite complex. Many of the series' formal strategies
and production techniques pay homage to new digital forms, displaying a certain
high-tech aesthetic. When the series launched, many critics rhapsodized about the
"countdown" clock and the split-screen videography techniques, drawing explicit
connections between these devices and our own technologically mediated era.
Screens multiply across the mise-en-scène, with cell phones, computer monitors,
and surveillance devices figuring prominently in the visual field. The Web site for

the series further extends this fascination with gadgets and digital media while offering a premium on "customizable" content. The site includes a game for viewers to download to their mobile phones, a Google-powered map that allows fans to map their own locations and create their own fan page, a "24 HQ" blog, various free downloads, and a variety of "instant" polls.

Despite this recurring techno-fetishism, the story lines often enact a subtle critique of technology, ranging from faulty phone systems to frozen computer networks. In crucial moments, high technology breaks down; for instance, in the "2:00 P.M." episode of season two, Nina's spy-toy surveillance necklace gives out at just the wrong moment, leaving the agents in the lurch. Cell phones lose reception or get left at home; networks are busy and cannot receive calls. At the level of narrative, Jack's successes often derive not from a deployment of high-tech gadgetry à la James Bond or McGyver, but from individual ingenuity and courage, guts and guns. In one of the series' more gruesome moments, Jack defeats new technology with a knife, carving an embedded microchip from an enemy's flesh.[5] As likely as not, high tech fails him when he needs it most. This troubling of the status of technology recurs and intensifies across the series' development; while technology often worked on the side of "good" in season one, by season two, technology seems to be the province of the villains or to be highly unreliable. Even the vast computational powers of networked systems that might save the world remain idle without the password sequence retained in the frail, embodied human memory of girl computer geek, Paula.

Further, the series often returns to a fairly "old" technology as our most cutting-edge resource in times of trouble. The opening episode of season two features several minutes of high-tech imaging technology that allows the president and his advisers to zoom in on images of Second Wave terrorist camps in an unidentified Middle Eastern country. The Counter Terrorist Unit (CTU) offices are resplendent with computer monitors. But, despite this immersion in high-tech networks, in moments of real crisis, characters repeatedly learn about breaking news from the familiar space of television. Even at the glitzy, screen-saturated National Security Agency (NSA), the president and his team get their news from Fox TV. Perhaps not surprisingly, television here offers itself up as the most relevant and timely source of information, framing network news as the "killer app" that occupies all those big screens at mission control.[6] Thus, there is a disjuncture in the show between its formal strategies (that largely celebrate the digital and the language of screens) and a recurring narrative troubling of the value of new technologies, technologies that are as likely to advance the goals of the villains as those of Jack and the good guys. Technology is treated with a high degree of uncertainty and ambivalence in the many plot strands.

Theories of melodrama offer one way to think about this seemingly schizophrenic figuring of technology. In theorizing melodrama, critics have repeatedly noted that, in films like those of Douglas Sirk, a certain ideological leakage is made manifest in a hyperbolic mise-en-scène, structuring a visual excess that might call into question the films' neat and tidy endings. Affect and emotion get mapped over objects and settings, transferring or displacing an exploration of social relations onto material objects or visual settings that are excessively rendered. In *24*, that excess might be read as an excess of technologically slick style: the multiple-window display technique that does very little by way of servicing the story (and is typically not scripted in advance but added in post-production, like a special effect) signals that something is going on beyond the confines of the narrative. What are we to make of such excess? By reading this excess and its complicated relationship to narrative, we might begin to move beyond my first reaction to the show—a rather obvious critique of its images of women or its representations of a certain hypermasculinity—to think about what larger cultural anxieties are writ large across these figurations as well as across the frenetic spaces, style, and pace of *24*.

While the series narratively triumphs old-fashioned technologies like hero television and intrepid, lone-wolf masculinity, stylistically and formally it sculpts a loving look at the dispersion of screen languages into everyday life: as noted above, windows and screens proliferate in *24*, both in the mise-en-scène and in its formal structures.[7] Additionally, the official Web site and DVDs all capitalize on the digital technology and on glitz, illustrating once again television's well-recognized capacity to spin meaning in many directions at once and to multiply contradiction. What are we to make of this doubled, seemingly contradictory, strategy of technological embrace and containment? At one level, television's primacy—as a source of cutting-edge information that even the president turns to—is assured: television trumps new technology as the place we all go for "real-time" information in times of trouble. (Of course, in an era when the U.S. government's agenda is piped directly to Fox News, imagining that information sometimes flows the other way might also speak to our desires to have "independent" journalism once again.) On the other hand, by situating this narrative critique of new technology within a formal and stylistic embrace of digital media, the series also naturalizes a particular version of convergence, one in which television and new technologies seamlessly blend in order to offer up a particular version of the future: unidirectional broadcast and linear narrative all dressed up in an illusion of choice, multiplicity, and liveness.

Elsewhere, I have theorized several key modalities promised by new information technologies. Briefly put, one of these central modalities is a repackaging of the lure of liveness. Liveness has been central to theorizations of television's specificity, and liveness remains a key dimension of our experiences of the Internet, a medium that also promotes itself as essentially up to the minute, ideology once again masquerading as ontology, to borrow from Jane Feuer's trenchant analysis of television. But, if television traded in tropes of liveness, the forms of the Internet couple this feeling of presence to a sense of choice and possibility. As such, the

Web's liveness feels both mobile and driven by our own desires, structuring a mobilized liveness that we imagine we can invoke and impact, with a simple, tactile mouse click. This sensation is a kind of *volitional mobility*, foregrounding choice and mobile presence, creating a sensation of liveness on demand. Thus, while television insisted that it brought the world live to us, the Web weds causality and liveness to mobility, often structuring a feeling that our own desire drives the movement. The Web is in process, in motion, and under our control. In its frenetic split-screen technology, 24 hails this new form of mediated, mobile liveness. If the Web seeks to appropriate television's long-standing relationships to liveness by offering up a volitional mobility, 24 fights back from the space of the television screen, claiming this enhanced and mobile liveness for itself.

Volitional mobility is a property specific to new technologies themselves, derived from their very forms and materiality and, in some ways, independent of content. But it is also an ideological force, packaged and promoted within certain digital media as a corporate strategy and mode of address. In a sense, it is always an illusion even if also an ontological property. But this sense of volitional mobility is perhaps even more illusionary in the space of network television than on the Web, for here it morphs into pure visual effect, an effect that works to hide a championing of a unidirectional broadcast model. While the series uses split-screen technology to suggest multiple story lines and the kind of always-emergent potential promised by the interactive narratives of gaming or the Internet, the plot is, of course, tightly controlled.[8] When offered up a screen of four simultaneous story lines, we can hardly choose which story we would like to follow or pursue the story at our own pace, at least at the moment of broadcast. (That said, I did often deploy my TiVo to fast-forward through all scenes featuring Kim, particularly if they also involved mountain lions.) Even the official series' Web site offers up minimal interactivity in most of its features (like Kim's cell phone or Jack's desk). In fact, the "real-time" conceit of the series serves to heighten its tight linearity, despite its split-screen window dressing, reinstalling a strict temporal progress as the twenty-four hours rapidly tick by. This clock moves in only one direction, taking us along as it goes, reducing interactivity to the viewers' previously mentioned desire to shout at the screen as the characters endlessly get embroiled in soap-like plotlines, tragedies, and crises.

Thus, while the critique of new technologies deployed at the narrative level in 24 does make manifest some cultural anxieties about life in the digital age, the series is not defined by or contained within this critique. On the one hand, this critique simply acts as a cover story for corporate strategies of media convergence and monopoly, moving us toward a digital future that promises minimal interactivity beyond the options offered up by the DVD box sets viewers of the show eagerly purchase or by the polls that survey us on the 24 Web site. In some very real ways, 24, in its serialized form, successful exports to DVD, and new modes of product sponsorship (with Ford prominently "presenting" an entire, commercial-free episode and launching its own "sneak peek" DVD complete with Ford truck ads), is an "early adopter"—or, perhaps, an early mock-up—of the real-time, on-demand customization so many pundits now describe as the future of television. Its serialized form makes it the perfect DVD or download purchase, allowing the consumer to stockpile episodes for prolonged viewing jags, and its espionage story lines export well to ancillary products like video games. It illustrates the degree to which the industry is already experimenting with the strategies recommended in the IBM report to appeal to "gadgetiers" (who "feel great ownership over their media experiences") and "kool kids" (who "are heavily invested in media experiences") (Berman 2006, 11). Both groups are framed in the study as "revenue opportunities" (Berman 2006, 12), as on-demand media and ancillary products serve to increase the bottom line.

Of course, three decades of cultural studies scholarship reminds us that this containment or commercialization is never total: for instance, "unofficial" Web sites foster vibrant fan communities that are highly "interactive," and my own DVR-fueled viewing strategies suggest my developing desire to watch television only on my own terms. Still, all the fast-forwarding and blogging in the world will not turn Kim into a character I would enjoy, or rejigger the right-wing bias of Fox News. My ability to control my television is clearly limited. Here, the stylistic and visual excesses of melodramatic narrative seem to stitch us back into capitalism's illusions even while feeling riveting and new.

"A Man Who Knows No Limits": Masculinity in the Era of Global Capital

Even while 24 at one level might be read as a celebratory tale of convergence media, the series' reworking of gender via a technologized soap opera form also indicates a certain troubling of the contours of masculinity.[9] If the soap opera has been theorized as particularly feminine in its lack of closure and resolution, what might we make of the masculinist project of 24, a project that is deeply invested in exploring shifting patterns of maleness and manhood? I first read the series as a kind of cultural return to the hard-bodied, hypermasculinity that so characterized the first Bush (and Reagan) era. Clearly Jack Bauer's lone-wolf figuration does aim at a certain tough-guy status, but this status is never secured in the series. The drama certainly displays moments of longing for an inviolate, quick-witted, gun-toting male, but this is not the hypermasculinity of *Rambo* (George P. Cosmatos,

1985) or *Die Hard* (John McTiernan, 1988). There are both continuities and differences between Jack Bauer's tortured masculinity and the masculine projects of the first Bush regime.

Unlike the heroes of the 1980s private-investigator dramas from which *24* partially draws, Jack is less caught up in navigating the homosocial bonds of (often interracial) masculinity than in parsing the kind of familial tangles long familiar from daytime soap operas. In tracking the figuration of masculinity during the first Gulf War, Robyn Wiegman reflected on the interpenetration of masculinity and melodrama across the media landscape, arguing that the maleness this earlier Middle East conflict constructed was all about dissolving the "often accepted . . . [binaries] of masculine/public and feminine/private" (1994, 178). In such modes, there is a "narration of geopolitical crisis as private and domestic," as melodrama moves from its traditional concern with the feminine and the household to a pointed exploration of masculinity in both private *and public* realms. In many ways, the character of Jack Bauer perfectly illustrates this bleed. His workplace and familial lives consistently blur together in endless feedback loops. Other characters, such as George Mason or President Palmer, also attempt familial reconciliation and model different modes of husbandly or paternal behavior, although the series also frames geopolitical crisis as at once private *and public* occupations as various nations and ethnicities are investigated for potential enemy status.

We might push Wiegman's analysis further, thinking through why such a dissolution of binaries has a particular purchase in the 1990s and beyond, particularly in a post-9/11 United States. I would argue that that the series very much represents and responds to life in a post-Fordist economy. In their insightful article, "The Luster of Capital," Eric Alliez and Michel Feher describe the neo-Fordist economy as a shift away from the massive scale of factory production in the Fordist era toward a regime marked by a more supple capitalism. This includes a turn to flexible specialization, niche marketing, service industries, and an increasing valorization of information as the product par excellence of capitalism. The separation of the spaces and times of production from those of reproduction (or leisure) that was central to an earlier mode of capitalism is replaced by a new spatio-temporal configuration in which the differences between work and leisure blur. "Capital claims to be a provider of time" (Alliez and Feher 1987, 316), and a "vast network" emerges "for the productive circulation of information," structuring people and machines as interchangeable, equivalent "relays in the capitalist social machine."

Rather than being *subjected* to capital, privileged workers are now *incorporated* into capital, made to feel responsible for the corporation's success. Put differently, they are at the beck and call of capital 24/7, round the clock, and counting down the hours. (Indeed, the IBM report cited earlier suggests that *all* media consumers might be incorporated seamlessly into capital and encourages companies "to systematize information flow, continuous data mining and predictive modeling" through the use of technologies that encourage consumers to provide information about themselves freely to the company [Berman 2006, 14]. Providing "free user content"—but only of a "perishable" kind [such as news or late-night comedy outtakes]—can also build customer loyalty and facilitate market research without decreasing the brand's value [Berman 2006, 16]. Suddenly, the plugged-in consumer looks like the market researcher's dream.)

Jack Bauer and the denizens of 24 seem to have emerged from the pages of Alliez and Feher's astute analysis. Not only do the worlds of work and home constantly intertwine and overlap in 24 (and to a degree much greater than in earlier cop or PI shows like *McGyver* or *Miami Vice*); the series as a whole also displays an extraordinary obsession with time. From the drama's pretense of real-time structure to the frenetic pace of the plot, managing time becomes a clear goal of both the characters and the show itself. This endless focus on time hints at the heightened temporal stakes of U.S. life in the era of late capitalism when those lucky enough to be employed are tethered to the workplace by laptop computers, networked mobile phones, and increasingly ubiquitous Wi-Fi. Critics reviewing the series endlessly commented on the ways in which the characters, especially Bauer, seemed to be sleep deprived and "cranking on No-Doz" (Collins 2001), with Wendy Lesser (2002) observing that "time is the dominant character" on the series. While our fearless hero manages to beat the clock at the end of every season, we do witness the emotional toll that working 24/7 takes on his psyche. Many of the series' most sympathetic characters often seem just moments from coming undone, barely able to keep up with the pace (and anxieties) of daily life in the twenty-first century. For those with a place in the new circuits of capital, convergence may have its rewards; increased leisure time is probably not one of them.

Melodrama seems to have its greatest purchase at moments of disruption in the social order. In Peter Brooks's terms, melodrama seeks "to demonstrate, to 'prove' the existence of a moral universe" (1976, 20). In his analysis of *Miami Vice*, Scott Benjamin King highlighted our current moment of disruption as "a crisis of shifting definitions of masculinity" in postmodern times, a crisis that "is also a crisis in the concept of work" (King 1990, 286). Alliez and Feher signaled a crisis in labor as a hallmark of our post-Fordist times, a crisis heightened by the pressures of the globalization of capital and the diffusion of information across networked economies. Although Alliez and Feher wrote their analysis well before 9/11, the anxieties they analyzed have only accelerated since the twin towers fell. By calling endless attention to the stresses produced for Jack Bauer by living in our moment of convergence, particularly to his troubles on the home front, 24 seems to be pushing back against Jack's total incorporation into capital, trying to carve out a space to *be* differently.

Jack can be seen as a liminal figure of masculinity, at once inside and outside of the law and social conformity, leaving and rejoining CTU, working as both a team leader and a renegade loner. Indeed, this inside/outside status exists in interesting feedback loops with the series' blurring of private and public realms and of national and domestic contexts. Jack has a privileged position as a switching point between various domains: legality/illegality; hero/torturer; authority/individual-duality; public/private; national/domestic; and so on. Several models of masculinity are presented by the show across its multiple seasons, but Jack's position is a privileged and highly mobile one, transiting across various circuits of exchange and meaning. Other male and female characters remain more fixed, casting Jack's mobility into greater relief while also highlighting the emotional costs of such movement.

In his investigation of 1950s representations of masculinity, Steven Cohan productively examined the ways in which filmic representations of the period both reveal and manage a larger cultural crisis in masculinity at least partially brought on by new conditions of labor in the emergent cold war economy. He wrote, "[T]he discourse of masculinity crisis registered as a problem of gender what were, more subtly, social contradictions pressuring the ideological function of 'the new American domesticated male,' as *Life* named the middle-class breadwinner in confirmation of his typicality" (Cohan 1997, xix). Masculinity was perceived to be in crisis precisely because men were moving to positions of consumption from earlier labor as producers. Cohan deftly analyzed Cary Grant's Roger Thornhill in *North by Northwest* (Alfred Hitchcock, 1959), arguing that Thornhill is the prototypical "man in the gray flannel suit" of the period, working in advertising. Further, Cohan suggested that the "film's depiction [of Thornhill] . . . locate[s] masculinity in representation while revealing its place there to be highly problematic." Of course, the ad man was a perfect symbol for these shifting conditions of labor, working as he did in images at what was the very beginning of the emergent service economies of post-Fordism. At the other end of this era, when the image rules fully supreme and the information economy is in complete (if unevenly distributed) ascendancy, is when *24* unfolds. Jack's workplace at CTU trades largely in information, data displayed across the multiple screens that comprise the office setting, coursing through networks that join the global economy, but both Jack and the series at large are as ambivalent about these forces as Hitchcock's hero Roger Thornhill was about his own time. In moving from the 1950s to a new millennium, we transit from cold war global politics to a new American isolationism wrought of the Bush years, once again tracking the close intertwining of masculinity and geopolitics.

If Roger Thornhill spoke to and tried to contain society's worries over man's place in a world moving toward an ascendant middle class, that is, over his transformation into a consuming subject, *24* might be read as taking up this question for a new era in a nation strongly polarized over questions of gay marriage and urban masculinity. Social anxieties over hetero-normative masculinity are reflected in public conversations and confusion over the meaning of the metrosexual, particularly as reflected in reality television series such as *Queer Eye for the Straight Guy*. Part of the lure of the volitional mobility that so characterizes our current moment is an increasing belief in the mutability of the self. The "transformations" featured on shows ranging from *Extreme Makeover* to *Plastic Surgery Beverly Hills* (shows that also make over men) highlight the malleability of the self. Bodies become one with the bit stream, as easily morphed as a Photoshop file, as easily customized as a MySpace page. The very forms of electronic culture (and, especially, of digital culture) help naturalize this process, shifting our understandings of what constitutes the self and working in tight feedback loops with shifting modes of economic production and emergent media ecologies. The bleed between work and leisure and between old and new bodies can be seen as skilling us for the new modes of living demanded by post-Fordist economies, modes that require a new relationship to our very corporeal selves.[10]

But, if Jack is caught up in these blurred modes, his relationship to them is neither easy nor seamless. By season two, Jack emerges as a rugged alternative to the metrosexual, a decidedly unmade self whose body is constantly battered, embattled, and in need of a shave. While he is occasionally stylish, his frequent fights and physicality seem to relocate him as embodied, sexed, and gendered. Jack is not exactly hypermasculine, but neither is he easily read as an urban metrosexual. He is also more rugged and casual (and less suited) than many of his CIA counterparts and was described in several reviews of the show both as "puffy" and as an unexpected choice for a male lead, particularly because he was not conventionally handsome. One review, in the *New York Times*, remarked that Sutherland played the role with "a notable lack of vanity" (James 2002), while another mentioned his "red-gold beard" and "plaid work jacket" (Ruch 2002). Jack is never fully made over in the course of the series, staging a form of masculinity that resists the beck and call of easy transformation proffered by digital technologies and reality television. Jack may consume technology and information, but the series seems to suggest that he is less susceptible to consumption than those more feminine fellows populating reality television.

The series plays with and pushes against the temporalities and mutable selves of neocapitalism even while its formal structures, production techniques, and mise-en-scène embrace the very technologies that underwrite this post-Fordist turn. In its obsessive tracking of various modes of masculinity, *24* seems to be working through and modeling different possibilities for networked subjectivity, a condition of contemporary life for the privileged mobile subject, which means that closure and neat separations between work and leisure or public and private are no longer real possibilities. In an era of convergence, media monopolies, and diffuse networks of power, stand-alone masculinity really will not take you very far, but the series cannot quite imagine and sustain a new mode of masculinity either (even as it attempts to image more "integrated" landscapes). While America has entered a phase of retrenched isolationism, the ascendancy of globalized capital always threatens to unravel the borders of the nation-state, a reality brought home when George W. Bush defended the outsourcing of U.S. port operations to Arab nations in March 2006.[11]

The status of masculinity in the twenty-first-century United States is particularly complicated by the national anxieties spawned by 9/11 and its aftermath. The series attempts to work through these anxieties in a variety of ways, mapping its more reactionary moments alongside Jack's most sustained performances of tough-guy status. Throughout its many seasons, *24* consistently offers up rationales for torture and for operating outside the law, even as this torture is often revealed to be unnecessary, echoing our own government's game playing with the very definitions and morality of torture. Even CTU agents and their relatives are fair targets for brutality if they are thought to *know things*, adding a new level of horrifying nuance to what it means to trade in information in our post-Fordist era. If power and capital are diffuse in such an economy, so is the enemy; they must be pursued by any means necessary. Slavoj Žižek (2006) has recently written that the "depraved heroes of *24* are the Himmlers of Hollywood," commenting that their ability to perform heinous acts "while being loving husbands, good parents and close friends . . . is the ultimate confirmation of moral depravity."

In many ways, the unstable figure of masculinity that the series deploys allows Jack's relative morality to be mapped across different narrative structures and domains. His supposed humanity is confirmed by his anxiety and his familial bonds, narrative aspects most clearly tied to the serialized, soap opera format of the show. The series' action narratives figure Jack differently, as a man perfectly capable of "doing what has to be done." When newspaper critics and fans reflect at all on the series' soapiest moments, they often bemoan that such plotlines even exist, but, in the logic of the series, these moments are a necessary flip side of its lone-wolf, renegade masculinity. The two narrative threads depend on each other, wedding home and homeland security. Put differently, Jack's familial status authorizes his ability to operate outside the law (yet in its service), granting him a kind of moral authority within the series' bizarre (if hauntingly familiar) ethical universe. Still, I do not think *24* offers us a fixed ideological position on these post-Fordist, post-9/11 developments in form and meaning or gender and genre, even as its plotlines often skew reactionary and advocate "an anything-goes-in-defense-of-the-nation" mentality.[12] Rather, its masculine melodramas might be read as symptomatic of the unstable contours of masculinity in the twenty-first century and of our national anxieties over labor, security, and morality. Below Jack's scruffy exterior, one might even sense a latent longing for different possibilities, for new ways of being a man.

Finally, we can read this multifaceted ambivalence as a manifestation of (and perhaps a latent critique of) a broad cultural and individual sense of having lost control: of information, of time, of technology, of gender boundaries, of the comforts of genre, of our work lives, of our government. Such a preoccupation with the loss of control along multiple vectors in daily life may also go a long way toward explaining why we are so intent on controlling our DVRs, iPods, and desktops: if the things that really matter seem beyond our ability to change, at least we can customize our interfaces and personalize our television schedules. While the series does not articulate a progressive agenda (and often skews in quite reactionary directions), we might see beneath its slick surfaces, multiplying screens, and fascination with technology the contours of a desire to challenge the relentless pace of life and create new circuits of meaning for masculinity that can navigate the demands of both home and family. One hopes that such a desire might be mobilized differently, beyond the interface.

Some Closing Thoughts on the Work of Quality in the Era of Electronic Culture

The origin of this paper was a talk for a 2003 conference on American quality television in Dublin, Ireland, and an earlier version of this essay was published in a volume first discussed there among a number of conference participants, as 24 was the subject of several presentations that weekend. While concerns about quality may seem only tangentially related to this essay's current form, I would argue that the designation "quality" helps function to secure 24's masculinized ethos. The series is at least partially framed as "quality" because of its formal and aesthetic innovations, technological interventions that help stave off the association with soap opera that might overtly highlight the series' embrace of serial form. But rather than simply arguing that the series is a testosterone-driven revamp of a soap opera and, thus, *not* quality television, might we instead query what work the category "quality" actually performs within the series, within the television industry, and within our scholarly industries themselves, especially at this moment of convergence anxiety?

We need to examine the work that the designation "quality" performs, both within the mainstream reception of television programs and within academic publishing. Why are television executives (and media scholars) particularly interested in "quality" at this moment in time—as television (and television studies) increasingly feel at threat from new digital media? A sustained examination of a series such as 24 can help us to understand how such a term conceals as much as it reveals about contemporary issues of globalization and digital convergence, as well as about the shifting relations of gender, genre, and nation. One prominent through-line of the Dublin conference was a sustained denigration of reality television, an argument that largely worked to make manifest the binaries of the two forms of television. To defend quality television as diametrically opposed to other forms of television, like reality television, is to miss a central point about the diffusion of both digital forms and melodramatic structures across culture at large in the present moment. In fact, in their highly serialized, melodramatic nature, reality shows like *Survivor* or *American Idol* share a great deal with the serialized story lines of *24* and other examples of quality television, such as *The Sopranos*. Further, the "beat the clock" feel of *24* and its technological glitziness share formal strategies with the revitalization of the game show in the past several years, particularly in a series such as *Who Wants to Be a Millionaire*. A singular focus on (and privileging of) quality television might even serve to lead us astray, allowing us to overlook the degree to which "high" and "low" genres actually share key traits and serve to support each other, particularly in relation to cultural anxieties about new technological forms, missing the larger issues at hand in an industrial drive toward convergence.

Seeing Jack Bauer as a kindred spirit to all those guys that the *Queer Eye* fellows are intent on making over, as someone equally struggling with what it means to be a man while racing against the clock, might also help to illuminate the stakes of masculinity for our era. In many ways the reality show is a bit more straightforward in its representations of masculinity in crisis than is *24*, although each series is invested in versions of heterosexual masculinity, if differently so. As Steve Cohan observed, "a culture's hegemonic masculinity has to appear to accommodate competing masculinities" even as it attempts to secure dominant modes of maleness (1997, 35). Thus, we can more clearly understand the role of Jack Bauer's grim and gritty masculinity when we examine it in relation to other prominent representations of contemporary men. In staging a rugged maleness for Jack, *24* seems to be insulating Jack from certain crises of male labor (or male fashion) that destabilize masculinity while also protecting "serious" television from the incursions and popularity of reality television and the do-it-yourself video narratives of YouTube.

In a prescient essay on the relationship of television scholarship to broad market forces, Amelie Hastie (2007) maintained that some scholarly volumes focused on particular cult or quality television shows might be read as "fairly transparent examples of an attempt to capitalize on a show's popularity," scholarly productions that thus participate in the very consumerist nature of television at large, functioning as a kind of "tie-in." Further, the focus on "quality" series in these volumes can undergird "a hierarchical understanding of television." I think these series-based volumes and a focus on quality television also serve to insulate television studies, itself a field long struggling to prove its worth, from the ascendancy of new media studies as a field of academic inquiry. These volumes reflect a desire to conserve television as innovative (and "gripping" and "compelling") at the moment when the boundaries of television blur amid other popular elements of digital culture. Such an approach, focused on individual series, will largely fail to understand the many ways in which such programs are simply part and parcel of the larger forces shaping the future of television, forces that, as the IBM report suggests, exhibit little interest in the details of individual programs and are much more concerned with the forces of global capital and international networks of telecommunication. The luster of writing about quality television may be the very way in which it allows us to evade addressing this bigger economic picture and also to sidestep our own incorporation into ascendant forms of capital, forms that depend on knowledge production as a key form of exchange. Perhaps we find Jack such a "compelling" figure precisely because his 24/7 work habits so parallel our own working conditions, where even the leisure time of television viewing exists in tight circuits of exchange with our own scholarly labor. Jack may not be the only networked subject in town.

ACKNOWLEDGMENTS

This essay emerged from ongoing conversations with various friends about the series 24. I especially thank Rob Knaack for watching 24 with me, Daniel Chamberlain and Scott Ruston for urging me to attend the Dublin conference, and Amelie Hastie for her suggestions on an earlier draft of this essay.

NOTES

1. For a look at how the rhetoric of convergence functioned in the slightly earlier moment of the late 1990s to more securely wed the future of television and the Internet, see Tara McPherson, "TV Predicts Its Future: On Convergence and Cybertelevision."

2. The series faced cancellation after its first season, as it averaged a relatively small U.S. viewing audience of about 8.6 million viewers per week. Despite garnering critical raves and Emmy awards, it had the smallest audience of any drama picked up for renewal after the 2001–2 series.

3. This interview with Cochran was conducted via e-mail by University of Southern California graduate student Christopher Cooling on June 4, 2003. I thank Chris for so graciously sharing the transcript with me.

4. For a now-classic investigation of the pleasures of the villainess in soap operas, see Tania Modleski's *Loving with a Vengeance*. Creator Bob Cochran defends the show against accusations of misogyny by arguing that "[e]verybody on our show is duplicitous, not just the female characters. . . . They are not helpless victims or impossibly noble, any more than the men are." One wonders if Cochran actually watched the scenes of Kim and Teri in season one or read reviews like the one by Matthew Gilbert, which

summarized the Kim plotlines thusly: "See Kim. See Kim run. See the Bad Man chase Kim down the alley" (2002). (Perhaps he did, as Kim morphed into an unlikely CTU computer expert by season three.) Viewers posting to the popular Television Without Pity site took to referring to Kim as "Spawn," while another critic referred to her as "MacIdiot." Alessandra Stanley, "Countering Terrorists, and a Dense Daughter," *New York Times* (March 13, 2008).

5. This occurs in season three in the "1:00 A.M." episode; in the subsequent episode, Jack outsmarts a tracking device embedded in the chip via old-fashioned, low-tech ingenuity and smarts. I return to the role of torture in the series later in this essay.

6. The phrase "killer app" derives from the era of the Silicon Valley dot-com boom. "Killer app" was a phrase used to describe that holy grail of the moment, the software application that would fully capitalize (in all senses) on the techno-lust and rampant greed of the period.

7. "Hero television" here refers to a long history of "action" television involving detectives, government agents, and cops, a genre that often privileges tough guys who act both within and outside the law. The next section of this essay takes up some of the continuities and differences between this genre in the 1980s and 1990s and in our current post-9/11 moment.

8. This is not to say that Web site or interactive games are not themselves highly scripted; they are. But, typically, they allow a greater degree of perceived choice in terms of narrative flow than a typical television show.

9. The phrase "a man who knows no limits" comes from the promotional material for the third season of *24*. Several national magazines in the United States included a DVD of "exclusive" previews for that season, a DVD sponsored by Ford that hyped the new F-150 truck. (Ford also sponsored the first episode of that season, an episode that was presented "without commercial interruption," further cementing the series' real-time feel. The DVD packaging included the tagline "To stop a weapon that has no cure . . . you need a man who knows no limits."

10. I explored these ideas further in a piece in the online journal *Flow* (McPherson 2005b).

11. A controversy erupted in the United States in March 2006 when it was widely reported that the Bush administration had permitted Dubai Ports World, controlled by one of the United Arab Emirates' seven city-states, to purchase a company that manages the terminals at many U.S. ports. Congress immediately crafted a bipartisan plan to block the transfer, and the struggle was widely reported in the press. While it may seem that Bush's support of the Dubai company ran afoul of his often-isolationist rhetoric, it makes perfect sense given the global flow of oil and capital. For one take on the controversy, see White (2006).

12. Then again, even this qualified reading may be too optimistic, as Maureen Dowd (2006) reported that *24* is a favorite of Dick Cheney, Donald Rumsfeld, and others. She also noted that the series was feted by the Heritage Foundation in a panel entitled " '24' and America's Image in Fighting Terrorism: Fact, Fiction or Does It Matter?" Rush Limbaugh was master of ceremonies for the event, and Clarence Thomas was in the audience. Thomas also hosted a special dinner at the Supreme Court for the series' producers, writers, and three of the actors. Thanks to Robert Kolker for this reference.

BIBLIOGRAPHY

Alliez, Eric, and Michel Feher. 1987. "The Luster of Capital." Trans. Alyson Waters. *Zone* 1–2: 315–359.

"BBC Restructures for Digital Age." 2006. 19 July. http://news.bbc.co.uk/2/hi/entertainment/5194046.stm.

Berman, Saul J., et al. 2006. "The End of Television As We Know It." IBM Institute for Business Value. March 27. http://www-1.ibm.com/services/us/index.wss/ibvstudy/imc/a1023172?cntxt=a1000449.

Brooks, Peter. 1976. *The Melodramatic Imagination: Balzac, Henry James, Melodrama and the Mode of Excess*. New Haven, CT: Yale University Press.

Cohan, Steven. 1997. *Masked Men: Masculinity and the Movies in the Fifties*. Bloomington: Indiana University Press.

Collins, Monica. 2001. "Grim Themes of *24* and *NYPD Blue* Premieres are Painfully Familiar." *Boston Herald*, November 6: Arts & Life, 39.

Dowd, Maureen. 2006. "We Need Chloe." *New York Times*. June 24.

Feuer, Jane. 1983. "The Concept of Live Television: Ontology as Ideology." *Regarding Television: Critical Approaches—An Anthology*. Ed. E. Ann Kaplan. Frederick, MD: University Publications of America.

———. 1984. "On Melodrama, Serial Form and Television Today." *Screen* 25.1: 4–16.

Gilbert, Matthew. 2001. "Tight *24* Makes Every Second Count." *Boston Globe*. November 6: 3rd ed. F1.

———. 2002. "*24* Continues to Be Time Well Spent." *Boston Globe*. October 29: 3rd ed., C1.

Hastie, Amelie. 2007. "The Epistemological Stakes of *Buffy the Vampire Slayer*: Television Criticism and Marketing Demands." *Undead TV: Critical Writings on Buffy the Vampire Slayer*. Ed. Elana Levine and Lisa Parks. Durham, NC: Duke University Press.

James, Caryn. 2002. "Clock Reset, Agent Bauer Returns to Work." *New York Times*. October 29: E1.

Joyrich, Lynne. 1996. *Reviewing Reception: Television, Gender, and Postmodern Culture*. Bloomington: Indiana University Press.

King, Scott Benjamin. 1990. "Sonny's Virtues: the Gender Negotiations of Miami Vice." *Screen* 31.3: 281–295.

Kloer, Phil. 2002. "Terrorists Move in for Next 24 Hours." *Atlanta Journal-Constitution*. October 29: Home Edition, 1E.

Lesser, Wendy. 2002. "The Thrills, and the Chill, of *24*." *New York Times*. March 31: sec. 2, 27.

McPherson, Tara. 2003. "TV Predicts Its Future: On Convergence and Cybertelevision." *Virtual Publics: Policy and Community in an Electronic Age*. Ed. Beth Kolko. New York: Columbia University Press.

———. 2005a. "Reload: Liveness, Mobility, and the Web." *New Media, Old Media: A History and Theory Reader*. Ed. Wendy Hui Kyong Chun and Thomas Keenan. New York: Routledge.

———. 2005b. "Transform Me, Please . . ." *Flow* 1.8. http://flowtv.org/?p=646, accessed March 13, 2008.

Modleski, Tania. 2007. *Loving with a Vengeance: Mass-Produced Fantasies for Women*, 2nd edition. New York: Routledge.

Ruch, John. 2002. "Thrills Work Overtime in *24*." *Boston Herald*. October 28: Arts & Life, 33.

Stanley, Alessandra. 2008. "Countering Terrorists, and a Dense Daughter." *New York Times*. March 13, 2008. http://query.nytimes.com/gst/fullpage.html?res= 9B03EED61131F93BA15753C1A9659C8B63, accessed March 13, 2008.

White, Ronald. 2006. "Foreign Landscape: Non-U.S. Firms Manage Most of the Terminals at L.A.-Area Ports." *Los Angeles Times*. March 12.

Wiegman, Robyn. 1994. "Missiles and Melodrama (Masculinity and the Televisual War)." *Seeing Through the Media: The Persian Gulf War (Communications, Media, and Culture)*. Ed. Susan Jeffords and Lauren Rabinovitz. Rutgers, NJ: Rutgers University Press.

Žižek, Slavoj. 2006. "The Depraved Heroes of *24* Are the Himmlers of Hollywood." *Guardian*. January 10.

CHAPTER 11

SCREEN PRACTICE AND CONGLOMERATION: HOW REFLEXIVITY AND CONGLOMERATION FUEL EACH OTHER

JOHN T. CALDWELL

Although films and television series about films and television series now pervade most viewers' multichannel entertainment options, the stylistic practices that fuel these self-referencing genres—on-screen reflexivity, intertextuality, and critical deconstruction—were, as I have argued elsewhere, important parts of American television programming since the 1940s.[1] Although film studies and literary theory have traditionally characterized reflexivity as counter to "dominant" media, critical reflexivity now stands as a primary form of content for mainstream variants of film and television in the age of cable, the Internet, and digital media. At first glance, this connection, between increasing corporatization and reflexivity, may seem counterintuitive. Yet, the growing deregulation of media since the mid-1980s, and the steady advance of commercial consolidation through the 1990s and early 2000s into but five huge conglomerates (Time Warner/AOL, News Corporation/Fox, Viacom/CBS, Disney/ABC, Universal/NBC), has made these ostensibly progressive and resistant reflexive and stylistic practices far more prominent, rather than less so. To examine this trend, in this essay I consider together two spheres that are normally segregated in the academy: the stylistic and textual practices of television, alongside the industrial practices of contemporary conglomeration. By the 2000s, reflexive stylistic practices emerged not only as a marker of edgy programming but also as lucrative mainstream mechanisms that helped rationalize the industry as well as orient viewers to the logic and possibilities of the giant new conglomerates. How and why this happened is worth considering in more detail.

Disclosing behind-the-scenes film and video production knowledge to the public morphed into a programming obsession in the 1990s. The Viacom conglomerate (VH1, MTV, and Nick at Nite) in particular, was especially good at exploiting and promoting the "new" trend. VH1's series *Pop-Up Video* profitably mastered on-screen deconstruction as a viable mainstream genre in the 1990s, and many other shows subsequently emulated *Pop-Up*'s penchant for showcasing and deconstructing behind-the-scenes knowledge. Begun in 1985 to blunt competitors' ability to take over MTV's market share, cable network VH1 earned a reputation for on-screen blandness and managerial dysfunction that almost led to the network's demise in 1994. In that year, the network brought in hot-shot former MTV programmer John Sykes to turn things around at VH1. In 1996, *Pop-Up Video* emerged as dramatic proof that the Sykes's VH1 rebranding overhaul had succeeded. The concept was simple: take existing music videos, and graphically insert quirky and critical "thought-bubbles" that percolated onto the screen *during* the performance. What resulted was a nonstop, wall-to-wall critical dialogue and metacommentary about the video production that now displaced the original music video as the viewer's primary on-screen experience. Former VH1 executive Anthony DeCurtis noted: "That was the first time that VH1 had done something that entered the national consciousness. Everyone knew what *Pop-Up Video* was."[2]

Pop-Up Video and its descendants quickly became grist for showbiz's buzz mill, and parodies followed on everything from *Saturday Night Live* and *Star Trek: Voyager*, to *Who Wants to Be a Millionaire: VH1's Pop-Up Celebrity Editions*.[3] Almost any network could tie its content to some backstage film or television connection, as Bravo did in 2003 producing its genre deconstruction *The Reality Behind Reality* (alongside its hit *Queer Eye for the Straight Guy*), and as the History Channel did in 2004 producing its *Greatest Movie Gadgets*. But the influence was not just external. *Pop-Up Video* became the development paradigm for much of the programming that followed on VH1 as well, including VH1's flagship hit *Behind the Music*, the full-scale cultural deconstructions *I Love the 70s*, and *I Love the 80s*, and even publishing variants, such as the book *Pop This!* (which "contains 'still-lifes' of some of the biggest stars and the best pop-ups").[4] VH1's trademark "dissolution"-of-"myths" approach explicitly foregrounded screen theory and critical analysis as primary content in 2003–4's *SuperSecret TV Formulas*. Reminiscent of an undergraduate film studies course, the show uses close scene-by-scene analysis and interviews with behind-the-scenes industry veterans to "expose" recurring ideological subtexts, genre, stunt and marketing disasters, and narrative formulas like "the catfight" and "evil twin" motifs.

Current trends underscore the historical influence of *Pop-Up Video* and its sibling *Behind the Music* across the industry. Former VH1 and *Pop-Up* executive Jeff Gaspin brought the behind-the-scenes approach to NBC's Bravo, where, as chief executive, he launched *Queer Eye for the Straight Guy, Boy Meets Boy* (premiered July 29, 2003, and ran for one season), *But I Played One on TV* (developed in 2003 but never aired), and *Ready Set Van-Gogh* (pilot episode screened for press but not aired). Significantly, Gaspin and Bravo strategized all of these series in terms of their potential to generate pop-culture buzz and on-screen parodies on *other* shows and networks.[5] Similarly, VH1 and *Pop-Up* executive Lauren Zalaznick now makes deconstruction the defining programming paradigm at Universal's new cable network Trio, where she serves as chief executive. Trio's deconstructions—all involving on-screen metacommentaries—include a documentary series involving twenty-four-hour behind-the-scenes looks at film or television celebrities, *Battle of the Network Stars*, repackaged reruns about pop culture, and entire weekly schedules "programmed" by film directors such as Quentin Tarantino. Zalaznick's original concept for the network, "The Genius of the Idiot Box," eventually morphed into the network's new slogan, "Pop, culture, TV."[6] Cultural analysis and critique pervade each week's programming schedule, not just at PBS, VH1, Bravo/NBC, and Trio/Universal, but across the full network spectrum as well. These series and producer's comments situate reflexivity and the deconstruction of behind-the-scenes knowledge, not just in the increasing sophistication of audiences, but squarely in the domain of cross-promotion, multipurposing, and brand marketing by the conglomerates. Meta–critical programming of this sort only barely conceals its industrial functions as forms of intra-industry communication, self-promotion, competitor discrediting, or leveraging. Considering these "business" activities as "authoring" mechanisms requires better understanding the forms of convergence and conglomeration that set reflexive programming in motion in the first place.

Various scholars, including myself, have examined "convergence" as a confluence of technological, artistic, and audience phenomena.[7] Yet to fully understand convergence in those terms necessitates considering convergence as a corporate phenomenon as well, otherwise known by executives and stockholders (with economic interests) as "consolidation" and by critics and production workers (with public and labor interests) as "conglomeration." Conglomerates are essentially megacorporations comprised of many different smaller or more specialized companies or units, linked by common ownership. Advocates of deregulation argue that the government should get out of the business of controlling or "interfering" with the actions of free markets, and see large media conglomerates as a logical outgrowth of legitimate market forces. Proponents also argue that even though large conglomerates can greatly reduce competition (through mergers, hostile takeovers, or bankruptcies), they frequently provide better services and products more efficiently than markets comprised of many different smaller competitors. This optimistic view can be thought of as the "Microsoft principle."

When fewer and fewer conglomerates dominate a given market, however, the specter of monopoly frequently elicits restraint-of-trade accusations by critics and workers, and regulatory actions by the Federal Trade Commission (FTC). The sunny boardroom picture of market efficiency via conglomeration described above, however, seldom resonates either with the companies that are downsized, bankrupted, or vanquished, or with the laid-off or merged employees within the conglomerates. Despite the anticonglomerate precedent of the 1948 Paramount Consent Decrees, which broke up earlier monopolistic practices in favor of independent companies, by 2002 the five, giant, newly configured media conglomerates mentioned above again controlled almost 90 percent of the U.S. electronic media market. These five conglomerates do not closely resemble the pre–Paramount decree film studios, however, since the current conglomerates are horizontally diversified *as well as* vertically integrated. That is, in addition to owning production, distribution, and exhibition capacity in a single sector (feature films), they typically own such chains across multiple media sectors as well (film, television, cable, new media, etc.). Such activities can be understood in terms of the types of "integration" and "diversification" they presuppose (Table 11.1).

Table 11.1 The Flexible Media Monolith (Forms of Monolithic Reach)

Forms of Conglomeration	
Vertical Integration	Ownership/control of total process of supply, production, distribution, and exhibition *within* a single economic sector. *Examples*: Paramount Studios pre–divorcement decrees (pre-1948); Warner Bros./HBO/TheWB/Turner/WTBS/AOL (2000s)—as successive distribution "windows" *FTC restraint issues*: Oligopolies, cartels (coercion, collusion)
Horizontal Integration	Maximizing ownership of multiple competitors *across* a single market sector; sometimes known as the Microsoft principle. *Examples*: NBC, MSNBC, CNBC, KNBC, MSNetwork, Bravo, Telemundo—all simultaneously program video content *FTC restraint issue*: Monopolies (control)
Conglomerate Strategies	
Loose Diversification	Combining companies from different industries, in order to minimize risks and safeguard potential losses in a single industry. *Examples*: Gulf+Western (1960s); Vivendi/Universal (2000s)
Tight Diversification	Combining companies closely related in mission within single conglomerate to aggregate and exploit market share within niche. *Example*: Syndicated Telefilm companies as "house-companies" closely related to major studios in the 1950s

In this context, the new conglomerates are "tightly diversified" (since their properties are closely related *as* media sectors) rather than "loosely diversified" (as when petrochemical giant Gulf+Western took over Paramount in 1966 or when French bottler and sanitation company Vivendi merged with Universal Studios in 2000, both to disastrous results).[8] Nor are the current conglomerates like the classical national television networks (ABC, CBS, NBC) of the 1960s and 1970s. In the earlier period, ABC, CBS, and NBC together faced little competition from anyone else so could "mass produce" formulaic sitcom and hour dramas for a more homogenous "economy of scale." The current executive vice president of Viacom/CBS, Dennis Swanson, spoke of the earlier period in wistful terms: "You just answered the phone took the orders and then went out golfing. My gosh, that was fun." Given the predictability and sameness of programming, the executive explains "how easy" broadcast television was during the network era, since "some of the dumbest people then are now billionaires."[9] By contrast, the on-screen content of the current conglomerates since the success of cable in the late 1980s has focused on "narrowcasting" (rather than "broadcasting"). This strategy results in greater diversity of style and content, but as part of a narrower or "niche economy of scope." The working principle here is that finding and focusing on the specialized tastes of a narrow segment of the audience is more lucrative per viewer than wasting expensive production resources on vast audiences, many of whom are simply not interested in shows made for mass or "average" audiences.

Blockbuster feature films still follow a mass-produced economy-of-scale formula (expensive generic products mass marketed in order to substantially lower production costs per viewer). Yet many other, perhaps most, examples of films and series today are based on economies of scope (inexpensive "indie" products sold to specialized market sectors) since the potential financial return (per capita) from each of these ostensibly "more dedicated" viewers is higher. AtomFilms, for example, aggressively acquired short films to distribute to airlines, Web sites, malls, handheld devices, and phones.[10] By distributing a type of film that has little proven cash value to either ad agencies or box-office-based exhibitors (short animations and interactive films), AtomFilms was forced to seek out the kinds of venues where fans of this sort of content could be found, hence Atom's emphasis on the Internet, cell phones, and handheld devices. To make its business model work, however, Atom had to acquire vast amounts of cheap short-film content (more than twenty thousand titles) from independents, amateurs, and film students with little or no up-front financing or advances, and therefore no risk. After raising vast amounts of venture capital, AtomFilms ultimately failed, because although it found and cultivated a narrow niche of dedicated viewers/users, there were no realistic ways to harvest financial returns for the benefit of their thousands of indie producers, who seldom were paid in anything other than the symbolic capital allowing them to claim that "I have a film distributor." Ironically, the major conglomerates, rather than independents, have learned to make far better use of the "mobile" economies-of-scope system, since they control both content (films, programs) and distribution outlets defined by proven business models (cable, DVDs, video games). This is one of the contradictions of the scope model: niche narrowcasting works, but only if such niches are aggregated within a distribution system that has already been rationalized industrially and economically. This is why Disney/ABC is better at narrowcasting than AtomFilms.

The examples thus far suggest important interrelations between both industrial organization and on-screen stylistic practice within conglomeration.[11] The pages that follow make four general arguments: (1) that conglomerate multipurposing has changed content development, consumption, and financing through amortization and cross-collateralization; (2) that multimedia platforming optimizes marketing cross-promotion within conglomerates; (3) that conglomerate tiering based on programming taste/identity "difference" promotes multicultural diversity, which in turn helps sanction and publicly legitimize the conglomerate; and (4) that reflexivity and on-screen metatexts now serve as user guides that enable viewers to navigate the conglomerates' extensive and complicated multimedia platforms. All four of these dynamics help symbolically displace or efface the monolithic nature of the conglomerates. In doing so, they buffer the megacorporations from accusations of unfair-restraint-of-trade practice. The genius of the new media conglomerates is that their textual and industrial practices cultivate a sense of public trusteeship that the earlier film-and-television monopolies were never able to fully muster to defend themselves—even though the classical television networks were officially assigned such public trusteeship by the government.

POST-FORDIST FLEXIBILITY

The conglomerate practices examined in this essay—of multipurposing, collateralization, cross-promotion, and tiering—provide one thing contemporary industries need more than anything else for economic survival in the age of post-Fordist capitalism: *flexibility*. Since the conglomerates produce vast amounts of fairly ephemeral experiential or cultural capital rather than tangible or traditional industrial products, and since production company life spans can be incredibly brief (sometimes lasting for only the few months it takes to make a film or series), the conglomerates cannot lock up inordinate amounts of capital in assembly lines and long-term employee contracts as they did during the classic studio era. Fordism and Taylorism allowed the classical studios to segregate and regiment technical tasks, to systematically rationalize the film production process, and to minimize uncertainty in market outcomes. This resulted because the system was dedicated to finding long-term cost and labor efficiencies that come with a mass economy of scale. The idea behind Hollywood's factory-system approach, at root, was that a uniform, generic, and predictable product (like a Ford automobile or a Warner Bros. gangster film) could be marketed to buyers or viewers on a mass scale (i.e., the same product and quality in every market in the nation and world). The Fordist system's proven profitability, furthermore, inclined the studios and networks to pursue and justify vertical integration and oligopoly.

By contrast, current highly competitive, multichannel markets, along with government safeguards for consumers (in the form of fair-trade media regulations) provide far greater uncertainties in economic outcomes for the studios and networks. Since buyers are seldom fixed, guaranteed, and unchanging, and since new technologies constantly upset and alter the production process itself, studios and networks today must find ways to move quickly to adapt to any new contingency thrown their way. This problem includes rapid changes in film and television exhibition as well as consumer technologies that divert or hijack audiences to other venues outside of the arms of the conglomerate. Contingencies also include innovations in production technology that require a new kind of labor force, skills, space, and/or infrastructure. With change and uncertainty the order of the day, the new conglomerates have to seek ways to find and cultivate excessively large numbers of potential scripts and film projects on the industry's "input boundaries," for example, since most films are deemed failures and most television series are almost immediately canceled. Post-Fordism emphasizes the economic importance of flexible manufacturing, flexible capital, and flexible labor. In contradistinction to earlier corporations, which were defined and anchored by heavy manufacturing plants, studio back lots, or guaranteed network programming pipelines—typically protected by governmental regulations—the new economy rewards companies adept at a range of new corporate capabilities: quickly exploiting research and development, securing new intellectual properties, mining (and then aggregating) niche demographics, reconfiguring corporate alliances, and finding and embracing synergies at almost every level (from workplace relations to transnational conglomeration). This scheme also requires moving quickly to develop and *overproduce* new content for the industry's "output boundaries" as well (distribution, exhibition, and viewing). Post-Fordism typically entails establishing short-term labor contracts and a malleable technical infrastructure, which allows the company to continually reinvent itself and its production process, even as the brand remains the same.

The picture I've sketched here—of the vast oversupply of film and television content and the proliferation of avenues of consumption at the output boundaries—has meant two things among others. First, many mediators, or what Paul Hirsch termed "contact men" (agents, managers, lawyers, representatives, and coaches, rather than salaried studio or network employees) are needed to build relationships, negotiate serial affiliations, and manage potential content suppliers and solicitors at the fluid input and output boundaries.[12] This systematic *outsourcing of negotiation* to agents or contact men at the *input boundaries*, in turn, keeps the needed oversupply of independent producers and screenwriters at arm's length, and without any long-term security. In addition, the fluidity and ever-changing venues for viewing and consumption at the *output boundaries* mean that the conglomerates with the greatest number of multimedia distribution platforms face less risk when technological or cultural change occurs, hence the constant pressure to merge, take over, or acquire still more multimedia distribution properties.

The resulting conglomerate bears distinctive features. The studio or network of the classical era can be thought of, figuratively, as a pyramid, with a wide and solid base, or foundation, comprised of propriety production resources, a large cadre of specialized and salaried employees, and exhibition outlets, all contained within the bounds of a rigid top-down management structure and chain of command. The new media conglomerates, by contrast, are in some ways like inverted pyramids, with a narrower set of proprietary tangible properties and fewer long-term production or salaried employees at the bottom. At the top, however, the new companies use a wide rhizomic, or networked, executive management structure rather than a vertical chain of command. This organizational form allows the company to move capital quickly across units in the top strata of the conglomerate and its multimedia nodes (as the opportunity or need arises). The provisional nature of the narrow base, however, allows the conglomerate to quickly contract or affiliate with any independent production organization that circulates adjacent to the inverted point of the media brand on the ground. Given this precarious orientation, effective new media conglomerates can be thought of as shape-shifting phenomena—heavy on management activity, but fluid and selective in finding and exploiting only the production resources the company actually needs for short-term projects. In effect, the new conglomerates attempt—despite their vast holdings and precarious positions—to travel fast and light.

EXTERNALIZING RISK (AND TEXTS)

The very volatility and uncertainty of the contemporary multimedia economy means that contemporary media conglomerates place considerable emphasis on strategies aimed at *externalizing risk*. The industry has responded to the economic risk of increasingly uncertain outcomes in film and television by deploying a range of tactics designed to displace that financial risk onto the shoulders of suppliers, workers, affiliates, and buyers, rather than on the conglomerate or its stockholders. This displacement or outsourcing of risk has had a direct impact on on-screen texts, and can take place via at least seven strategies.

1. *New technologies and screen texts* (when major studios contract out costly computer-generated imagery, animation, or visual-effects work to independent boutiques, rather than buying the equipment and/or building dedicated spaces themselves). When visual-effects work shifted from mechanical to computerized methods, the major studios paid independent companies to shoulder the risks that come with any new technology development. This includes training and start-up costs in addition to technology costs. The advent and popularization of Technicolor processing in the 1930s and Panavision 35-millimeter cameras in the 1960s also helped the studios externalize the risk that came with these costly production options. Technicolor was proprietary, expensive, and beyond the parameters of the on-the-lot studio laboratories. Similarly, because Panavision cameras are so expensive and specialized, studios do not own them, and utilize them only on a rental or lease basis, thereby leaving major maintenance and upgrade costs to the manufacturer. The current shift away from film in favor of digital intermediates (DIs) as postproduction masters (even for features shot on film) also follows this logic of outsourcing as a buffer against new-technology instabilities. Using an electronic master, rather than the traditional optically printed, film-based interpositive (IP) or duplicate negative (DN), allows production companies to externalize the risk of costly and unproven new technologies onto stand-alone companies who specialize in—and stylistically exploit (sometimes intentionally, sometimes not)—the as-yet nonstandardized DI process. After almost a century in which everyone in the industry adhered to the rigid rules that made the 35-millimeter DN a consistent and universal technical benchmark for color timing and exposure, the off-loaded DI has opened the floodgates of stylistic diversity. Sometimes outsourced technical risk leads to rather uniform stylistic changes (as in Technicolor and Panavision); sometimes outsourcing technical risk produces perpetually unorthodox and uncontrolled stylistic changes (as in computer-generated imagery [CGI] and the DI).

2. *Cross-promotion and screen texts* (when major studios or conglomerates acquire television or cable networks primarily to advertise and promote their own feature films). It is generally agreed that the single biggest factor affecting the success of a feature film upon release is advertising on television. Owning a broadcast or cable network, or local stations, gives the studio in this enviable position several advantages. First, the studio can negotiate (essentially with itself) to buy and place spots in the most desirable and highly rated programming segments (with the heaviest barrage slated in the week leading up to the release). Second, the studio or network can create and encourage (well in advance of the release) intertextual references to released films or their stars within existing dramatic or entertainment series (since most studios have both film and television production arms). Third, the network can produce and program "making-ofs," and "behind-the-scenes" specials timed to spike buzz during the week of the release of a given film. Fourth, the network can air—in contiguous slots throughout the week of the release—previous films by the actors or director of a forthcoming or released film (a

common practice, as when *Born on the Fourth of July* [Oliver Stone, 1989] or *Days of Thunder* [Tony Scott, 1990] were broadcast during the week that Tom Cruise's *The Last Samurai* [Edward Zwick, 2003] was released). Fifth and finally, the conglomerate can evaluate and laud its new releases during the half-hour early-prime showbiz reports and entertainment news series that the conglomerate's stations and networks air nightly. Broadcast and cable, therefore, offer the studio and the conglomerate a marketing executive's dream—a complete package of promotional and marketing opportunities, before, during, and after a film's release. Although such tactics may look like old-fashioned, incestuous flogging, the process also shifts much of the studio's risk and the costs of a large film-marketing campaign onto the shoulders of affiliate networks and stations within the conglomerate. The conglomerate's networks also take upon themselves many of the cross-promotional forms just described, as part of their own internal programming budgets (again, taking risk away from the studios). This cross-promotional exchange, by definition, takes place through on-screen texts. The proliferation of studio and network Web sites merely extends the tried-and-true method of cross-promotion first established by studio-network synergies.

3. *Multimedia development and screen texts* (when several distribution windows in different media are launched simultaneously). This tactic essentially involves repurposing and multipurposing strategies for on-screen media content, and is regularly associated with the multimedia platforms of the five largest conglomerates, described earlier. The trades and financial columns have paid particular attention to this method of externalizing risk, since it closely mirrors the ideals of synergy celebrated in the industry. To compete critically and ratings-wise with the growing programming success of HBO in 2003, for example, NBC coproduced and broadcast the limited series *Kingpin* (a stylish and violent *Sopranos* clone about Mexican drug cartels and their Latino-American families). Hyped as must-see TV, the miniseries was simultaneously broadcast with Spanish dialogue on NBC's Telemundo network, immediately repeated on NBC's "arts" cable network Bravo, distributed on NBC's Latin American cable network Mun2, and almost immediately available on DVD as a prefabricated "cult classic." In addition, bits and pieces of the multimedia event were cross-promoted: on NBC affiliate stations such as KNBC-Burbank (which ran "special reports" on "the real" Mexican drug cartels and the confrontations that KNBC's television reporters have had with them); on numerous NBC affiliates that aired first-run syndicated showbiz report series such as *Entertainment Tonight* (produced by CBS Television Distribution) and *Access Hollywood* that featured stories on the cast and producers of the miniseries); and on NBCi (the network's Web site, which provided running visual and textual commentary on *Kingpin*). In this way, all of Universal/NBC's corporate arms were taking on the expensive *Kingpin* initiative, and the financial risks that came with it, as their own. Nowadays, conglomerates no longer bounce on-screen content sequentially down the line of the company's successive media platforms, but rather

develop that content for roughly simultaneous release on as many of those plat-forms as it can. If NBC had shouldered the costs of the *Kingpin* project alone, ad sales in broadcast would never have paid for the steep costs of this supposedly "prestige" production. Multimedia development now ensures that on-screen texts are migratory and shape-shifting.

4. *Merchandising and screen texts* (when product placement and ancillary markets allow producers to recoup income downstream from the primary film or series). Although many in the self-styled "creative community" of Hollywood still like to imagine that a recognizably artistic mission is at the heart of their enterprise, the fact is that screen-related merchandise has become an important, but seldom celebrated, prerequisite consideration for feature film and prime-time development today. Video games, which can be thought of as either multimedia or merchandise, depending on the user, have far surpassed the total box office receipts of the feature film industry since 1988. Miranda Banks has demonstrated how integrally inex-pensive toys and action figures have become in the development and success of scores of television shows in and outside of prime time. In 2000, Turner's half-hour animated *Powerpuff Girls* series on Cartoon Network—which was never intended to initiate either Emmy talk, or high ratings, or critical buzz—generated $300 million from show-related merchandising in a single year alone.[13] In essence, television-related dolls from a marginally rated "basic cable" channel *dwarf* the box-office receipts of most feature films. Yet critics, journalists, and academic scholars—obsessed with the higher cultural "prestige" of cinema—seldom ac-knowledge the determining power of merchandising in making films and series possible. I would argue that while *Powerpuff Girls* and *Buffy the Vampire Slayer* can be thought of as quintessential narrowcast or niche program forms (and therefore part of the risky post-Fordist economy-of-scope equation), the extensive flood of low-cost, show-related mass marketed merchandise directly impacts the kinds of shows that are developed, and what they look like. This flood of merchandise also allows production companies to harvest excessively large profits (following a more stable Fordist economy-of-mass-scale business model).

5. *Domestic coproduction and screen-text* strategies (as in the standard deficit-financing deals for independent companies that produce for network television).[14] Because the major broadcast networks have been in a position of influence or control since the early 1950s over what gets broadcast and when, independent program suppliers have been stuck with absorbing escalating program production costs. In this system, called "deficit financing," independent companies promise to make programs for the networks that cost significantly more than the network actually pays for them. In exchange for taking on the network's risk, the indepen-dents are offered the possibility of recouping costs on the "back end" of a program's life, in syndication (subsequent direct sales or reruns to independent stations). Historically, the system developed only because of the government-protected monopolistic position and practices of the three major networks, who could force

independents to partner in sharing the risk. Mark Alvey and Tom Schatz described another form of risk externalization in another kind of coproduction popular by the late 1950s. After the breakup of the studio system, the major film studios began to externalize their risk and economic uncertainty by shifting to a "package system" and by bringing smaller independent production companies onto the studio lot as partners in coproduction. As a result, smaller companies such as Screen Gems, Irwin Allen, and Quinn-Martin became "house companies" of the major studios Columbia, 20th Century Fox, and Warner Bros., respectively.[15] In effect, the larger majors—in their greatly reduced but more predictable roles as landlords and distributors—provide the office space, buildings, and back lots, while the smaller house companies shoulder the riskier tasks of textual content development for the big or small screen.

6. *International coproductions and screen texts* (when companies from several countries pool resources, content, and/or talent to produce a film or television show and share distribution revenues). Much of what passes for globalization or cultural imperialism today is the result of international coproduction. Media do not simply "flow" in a linear fashion from one place to another, as early versions of the "cultural imperialism" model assumed, dominating indigenous, national, and regional production as they roll across international borders. Borders are crossed in film and television today usually because of the participation of commercial entities on both sides of the border. A Universal Television executive explained the success of the studio's "Action Pack" series of first-run syndicated dramas (*Hercules, Xena*) in a quintessentially pragmatic and ideology-free American way: "Does Universal do offshore deals? Universal has two kinds of deals. We started the action business in the early nineties. We went to our key customers. And we said: 'Okay. If you can help us make these things we'll make them with you.' "[16] Yet this rarely means that there is not an imbalance of power or resentment on the part of those receiving the "help." The cheery picture of no-strings-attached U.S. dollars coming in to transform international financing into an indigenous or regionally appropriate television enterprise generates some cynicism from non-U.S. broadcasters and producers. French and British media executives in particular invoke their own "cultural exceptionalism" in the face of the lowest-common-denominator quality of programs that result from cofinancing and coproduction. Said one British television executive dismissively, "We remain a tiny Island off of the north of Europe. We are cynical about what we patronizingly consider 'Euro-Pudding' [cofinancing]."[17]

Yet major U.S. studio executives such as James Dowaliby at Paramount seem almost resigned to the fact that the rest of the world needs Hollywood's unique talent to make their own national television industries go. "I think the perception is still true that we will have a staggeringly dangerous effect on the local [coproduction] partners. There is fear and trepidation when we walk into the room. I think our goal is to make the best show that we can—in the best way that we know how. But what America does, and what our partners usually look for, is our writers, and our writing process, and our team of writers. And I probably spend fifty percent of my time setting up the writer relationships, the showrunner relationships, with them."[18] The reality is that while American blockbuster feature films travel easily across borders (usually requiring dubbing or subtitling and little else), international television distribution is a very different story. American television can no longer be dumped into international markets without considerable negotiation, not just of contracts but of on-screen content as well. In effect the only way that the U.S. studios can make the high cost of production back is through partnering and coproduction. With a smaller and smaller audience at home, and faced with escalating production costs, spreading out the pain and risk to foreign partners is now a predictable part of any new film and television development deal.

7. *New labor arrangements and screen texts* (as in runaway production that voids long-term job protections). In each case the riskier industrial phases of film and television (content development, visual effects, postproduction, union entitlements, upgraded soundstages and infrastructure, and box-office or audience consumption) are either contracted out or shared with affiliates. Toby Miller et al. have written a particularly good book describing how runaway production involves far more than a simple shift in the location of film or television production.[19] The studios and conglomerates get away with systematic outsourcing by cultivating what Miller et al. termed a complex reconfiguration of production called the "new international division of cultural labor" (NICL). In this scheme, many different companies may participate in coproductions, which always tend to have key administrative centers in the United States. That is, jobs do not simply "go away," as the popular rhetoric suggests. Instead, corporate webs cut across numerous borders, allowing the conglomerate to find efficiencies in various specialized labor niches, while at the same time calling the production in question an "American" enterprise (thus dulling claims of runaway production). Yet many in the production communities are not naive about the sophisticated ways by which labor goes elsewhere even as the production itself looks to be centered in the United States. No less than Meryl Marshall, the president of the Academy of Television Arts and Sciences (ATAS), challenges the conglomerates' tendency to take production elsewhere merely to save labor costs. "I think these companies are taking advantage of the globalization of the market. The [conglomerates] may not be as invested in their local communities. I do think there is a very serious concern here about the exploitation of expertise—which is what most of these conglomerates are engaged in. They are currently setting up production entities around the world. They are being enticed by tax incentives, tax credits, and subsidies from companies in Europe and the far east and Canada."[20]

The executives and producers draw out the implications of runaway production. "The storytelling expertise [has been] taken outside[, resulting in] the lack of current employment opportunities. Originally this happened in the animation area. Now in the movie-of-the week area . . . in the TV series area in the future. There are lots of ramifications. Both to the individual American workforce—but more important, to the storytellers here."[21] Faced with a vast trend, ostensibly out of the control of the networks and advocacy organizations such as ATAS, this producer/executive fell back on a cultural, rather than purely economic, appeal. That is, storytelling (a cultural activity) is both a defining property of America's creative industries and the victim of "the exploitation of expertise." An executive of News Corporation retorted to Marshall's appeal, "That's the world we live in. There's vertical integration. It's a global world. And we're going to sell our projects across the globe. And that's just the way it is."[22] The conglomerate's need to externalize risk trumps the production culture's appeal that the art of storytelling is a national resource whose loss will hurt America in the long run.[23]

Advocates of the U.S. creative community, like Marshall, are very good at dramatizing how conglomerates kill human creativity. But this very gambit—of making corporate practice the antithesis of creative, textual practice—obscures the fundamental ways that the new conglomerates also function as corporate auteurs. In other words, this easy caricaturing also glosses over the fairly sophisticated ways that corporate stylistic and on-screen textual practices help sanction and legitimize conglomeration. Texts matter, and for reasons that go well beyond the various permutations of farming out and risk outsourcing outlined above. Conglomerate texts resolutely cultivate the notion that the institutions that author them are anything but old-fashioned industry heavies that unfairly restrain trade. Given persistent concerns and anxieties in some sectors about why government continually green-lights corporate media consolidation, however, it is worth considering how these same conglomerates elicited such a blessing, through both business activities and on-screen texts. I argue in the sections that follow that two broad strategies—both of which involve on-screen textual practices—have been particularly effective in sanctioning and legitimizing unchecked media conglomeration. Textually, the conglomerates have been particularly effective at cultivating, first, a "responsive corporate persona" and, second, an effective "public service aura."

SANCTIONING THE MONOLITH 1: CONGLOMERATION'S "RESPONSIVE" PERSONA

Media conglomerates create formidable obstacles for any new company seeking to enter a given market with its on-screen content, as well as problems and anxieties for employees working under the umbrella of conglomeration. The wide-scale sanction given conglomeration, therefore, raises serious questions about how the new megacompanies so effectively deflect political criticism from governmental overseers of conglomeration. I suggest that media conglomerates have ably used two broad *reflexive* approaches to normalize and legitimize conglomeration. First, pervasive media marketing and public relations have transformed (and translated) the *industrial flexibility* inherent in the post-Fordist model into a broadly recognized public marker for *cultural responsiveness*. Second, the conglomerates have transformed the practices of *narrowcasting difference* and *niche tiering* by the major media brands into a public index of *cultural diversity*. This second strategy has been particularly effective in further positioning the conglomerates as de facto *public trustees* of the airwaves and media infrastructure. I am interested in these transformations for two reasons. Both tendencies humanize the conglomerates (despite runaway production, downsizing, political partisanship, and collusion) as benign. Both tendencies also extensively use reflexive on-screen texts about film and television production (promos, previews, behind-the-scenes, making-ofs, bonus tracks, and interextual programs) to achieve these transformations from economic control to cultural responsiveness and trusteeship. Texts and industrial reflexivity very much help sanction and legitimize the new conglomerates. How and why this happens is worth considering more fully.

At the heart of this textually driven legitimation process is the sense that conglomerates are not monoliths at all. At least they are not monoliths like the hardened, suspect, conglomerates of the turn-of-the-century robber barons, or of pre-divorcement Paramount, or of AT&T before it was finally broken up in the 1980s. "Affiliation," rather than outright or complete ownership, defines many relationships within and with the conglomerates. Today's five superconglomerates do not tend to coerce or domineer to achieve their ends. Instead, they act "responsively" to affiliate, bend, negotiate, horse-trade, and provide "services" to the viewing and purchasing public. As Table 11.2 suggests, continual hard or soft re-affiliation makes conglomerates a moving target whose interests seem reasonably local rather than global in design.

As a result, competence at both negotiation and relationship building have become highly valued skill sets, not just for the agents and producers who constantly broker affiliations, but also for corporate units within the conglomerate who must master continuous, serial affiliations. The "art of the deal" rules precisely because conglomerates must master responsiveness as part of their business plans, corporate affect, and branding.

Consider how these five different types of flexible affiliation operate in but one major on-screen textual "event." In February 2002, Fox and the NFL, betraying no reluctance to take the lead in government policy making, declared the 2002 Super Bowl a "national holiday." A mere five months after the national trauma of 9/11, this pronouncement launched a lengthy pregame show comprised of endless montages that melded the bared, muscular, chiaroscuro-lit bodies of pro football

Table 11.2 Conglomeration's "Responsive" Person

Hard Affiliation	Long-term contractual alliances between national parent company and network of affiliate companies in local markets. *Examples:* Traditional TV networks (ABC/CBS/NBC) and local stations; ten-year, seven-picture deal between Disney and Pixar
Soft Affiliation	Short-term contractual alliances for limited life of production project or programming season. *Examples:* Imagine Entertainment producing TV series *24* for Fox; advertising agency purchases of spot time for new broadcast season
Bet-Hedging Affiliations	When in doubt about prospects or outcomes, simultaneously buy or invest across competing companies within a specialized market sector. *Examples:* NBC simultaneously purchasing shares in TiVo and Direct TV; competitors Viacom and Time Warner/AOL each buy half of Comedy Central cable network start-up
Legacy Affiliations	Fortuitous, symbolic linkage via corporate migrations by executives. *Examples:* Terry Semel hired by Yahoo! away from Warner Bros.; Steve Jobs of Apple hired as executive for Pixar
Contingent Affiliations	Opportunistic linkages promoted by marketing/public relations operations during contingent national/industrial moments. *Example:* Fox/NFL/White House/Congress/New York City Fire Department/Pepsi/E-Trade "coproducing" Super Bowl 2002 as a post-9/11 "national holiday"

players with the sacrificial firemen and heroes of the World Trade Center inferno. A succession of former presidents from both parties then somberly recited passages of the Declaration of Independence on camera. This pantheon of elders was intercut with a succession of sports-government-society "hybrids"—including former NFL running back, Hollywood star, and urban activist Jim Brown, Vikings all-pro defensive tackle and now Minnesota Supreme Court Justice Jim Marshall, and Buffalo Bills quarterback and Reagan-Bush-era conservative congressman Jack Kemp—all of whom were swept along in the tide of a swelling Aaron Copland elegy. The televisual groundswell uncorked in this lengthy pregame show continued in each setup and break until halftime, when an ecstatic multimedia spectacle involving a cast of thousands evoked an aura of uniform political consensus. When Irishman Bono flashed an American flag as he ripped opened his leather jacket at the end of Fox's U2 halftime show, viewers had witnessed an excessively self-conscious and explicit disclosure of political commitment and collective cultural mastery by both government and the entertainment-industrial complex. The recombinant message gushing forth here fused gladiatorial masculinity, nation-building nostalgia, and political bravura with a "newfound" confidence in Manichean justice and American retribution. Of course, in American network television, even sobering political ecstasies like this rarely appear without the trappings of commerce. The Fox/NFL national holiday was no exception. Comforting commercial spots naturalized consumerism as the bedrock of an American way of life. In an update of Capra's *Why We Fight* series (1943–1945) sixty years earlier, the ad industry provided compelling evidence of the democracy-as-consumerism ideal that would soon be avenged militarily in the coming months. The cross-mediated culture industries had created a spectacular, on-screen high holiday, an unusually prominent opportunity for producers, ad executives, stars, writers, researchers, aging ex-jocks, and announcers to showcase the industry's critical acumen and intellectual stature as reluctant—but earnestly capable—historians and political scientists.

Reducing conglomerates solely to structures of control, profit, and power in moments of political "crisis" like this, however, ignores the important ways that conglomerates pursue flexible affiliation and textual nuance to forge and reinforce consensus über alles. In the Fox/NFL variant of nation rebuilding and showcased consensus, reflexive televisual forms became the very site of exchange that tied industry to culture, at least on important matters like the "war on terrorism" and professional football. Thrown into the on-screen mix sponsored by E-Trade's corporate sponsoring logo was political liberal Bono posing as flag-waving U.S. patriot. This linkage textually tied U2 and the New York City Fire Department to Wall Street as part of "E-Trade's NFL Super Bowl Halftime Show." A gyrating Britney Spears made a pastiche of the *entire history* of Pepsi's corporate brand in a succession of commercial spots, which somehow helped fuel the Bush-rebranded American as a rightous avenger poised to strike back against the "axis of evil." This eclectic textual package operated as part of the Fox network's and the NFL's joint rebranding campaign of themselves as unofficial but important and de facto parts of the U.S. federal government.[24]

Hard textual affiliations operative in Fox's "national holiday" involved the long-term, local affiliate stations that make up the Fox television network broadcasting the Super Bowl. It is important to note that many of these local affiliates are not permanent members of the News Corporation conglomerate. Several of the stations had actually been local CBS affiliates before Fox outbid CBS and won the right to broadcast NFL games in the early 1990s (a move widely seen as a way for Fox to "steal" existing stations and to build its national network). The multiyear contract between the NFL and Fox also functions as a hard affiliation and allowed Fox to shamelessly recycle the entire montage described above for use in its February 6, 2005, Super Bowl broadcast. Modifications were made to the footage in the later broadcast to make it more appropriate for the two-term Republican administration now in place. This restaged crisis mode, in effect, allowed Fox and the NFL to exploit the recent South Asian tsunami tragedy by having both former presidents Clinton and Bush in studio to solicit donations. The device worked to make Fox and the NFL bigger than either political party, and bigger than either the blue or red states.

Soft textual affiliations in Fox's national holiday include the extensive number of commercial spots sold for the highest ad rates of the year. Super Bowl telecasts are typically seen as the most important showcases for ad agency talent and corporate promotion, and 2002 was no exception. Britney Spears's "retro" emulation of the "entire" history of television ads for the Pepsi brand underscored the ad-centric nature of the spectacle, and endless news and showbiz reports during the weeks before and after the event continued to deliberate on the quality and significance of such ads. Ad purchases function as soft and temporary affiliations because they are based on a pay-to-play scheme hammered out over five decades in commercial U.S. network television. The process of cycling through thousands of ad-spot buys during a single programming year cultivates the idea in the public's mind that each conglomerate is permeable, agnostic, responsive to consumers, and nonpolitical.

Bet-hedging textual affiliations are pursued when a conglomerate is unsure about the prospects and outcomes of competition between two or more potential client companies. Such affiliations sometimes result in the simultaneous purchase of interests in competing companies. To minimize risk, management simply buys both companies, ensuring that the eventual winner in a narrow industrial sector will be within the buyer's conglomerate for the long term. Classic examples of this flexible relationship strategy occurred when NBC bought interests in both TiVo and Direct TV in 2000, thereby ensuring that whichever company eventually won the DVR wars would add value to the NBC brand. Bet-hedging flexibility also results when two competing conglomerates invest in the same media property. This ensures that if the purchased company does in fact become profitable and viable, the benefits from the co-owned property stream back to each conglomerate and are not hoarded by a single conglomerate. This scenario unfolded when competitors Viacom and Time Warner/AOL each bought 50 percent of the stock in up-and-coming cable network Comedy Central. Universal also took this approach when it co-invested with competitor Viacom in funding the start-up of the Sundance Channel, and when Disney co-invested in A&E with competing conglomerate General Electric. This result is a kind of Mexican standoff but also guarantees at least a conservative return for the investment, one that prevents competitors from running off with inordinate profits after a risky cable start-up. Fox's on-screen 2002 national holiday text incorporated several of these ambivalent affiliations and bet-hedging flourishes. This included the calculated inclusion of former presidents or their stand-ins from both parties (Jimmy Carter and Clinton as well as George Bush and Nancy Reagan). As with the in-studio appearance of both Clinton and the elder Bush in Fox's 2005 Super Bowl, professional sports superbrands (like the NFL) and their broadcast franchises (Fox) need to establish an ecumenical response to political partisanship—to appear "above the fray"—thus underscoring their commercial reach. Once again, these affiliations posture the conglomerate as fair-minded and open to the will of "all" people.

Legacy textual affiliations involve fortuitous linkages between corporations caused by the migration, departure, or arrival of executives or other instrumental figures who bring with them valuable, established reputations. Such personnel or boardroom migrations can bring to new conglomerates the brand aura of the old employer, even if such symbolic transfer is unintended. One calculated example of legacy affiliation transpired when up-and-coming Pixar animation brought in "visionary" Steve Jobs as its CEO and public face in the 1990s. This move essentially stripped off some of Jobs's wunderkind persona and Apple's aura of brand quality to help legitimize the Pixar start-up in the minds of Wall Street traders. Yahoo! pursued a similar tactic, establishing that it would survive the 2000 dot-com meltdown, when it hired former Warner Bros. executive Terry Semel to run the company in 2001. The trades marveled that "Semel's appointment continues the Internet's love affair with Hollywood and comes as Yahoo! has aggressively spent the past year trying to expand its site beyond serving solely as a portal for news and information and grow into a major entertainment player of music, movies, and other original content."[25]

Like every other dot-com, Yahoo! was in trouble. The company solved its financial decline by trying to remake itself on the lines of "old media"—the Hollywood studios. With a barrage of on-screen public relations texts to manage the union, the resulting "marriage" was largely symbolic. Yet the event did have the effect of offering dot-com stockholders an economically viable, long-standing business model tried and proven by Hollywood. By 2005, Yahoo! went further, shored up this initial legacy affiliation, and embarked on significant expansion of its industrial activities in the Los Angeles area. Fox's 2002 national holiday exploited a succession of legacy appearances in its melodramatic montage and lengthy pregame homage. Typical of most sports coverage, the on-camera reporters and commentators had journeyman career status and brought these other identities with them to Fox as the broadcast weighed in on everything from football to the nature of evil. Golden-lit shots of former football players and politicians Gerald Ford and Jack Kemp suggested that the presidency and Congress might actually have been intermediate way stations on the road to football acumen, or vice versa. Slow tracking shots of the Declaration of Independence made the gridiron a reiteration of the American Revolution. Numerous close-ups of American flags, along with tattered flags from the World Trade Center disaster, made the Super Bowl seem like a natural extension of the memorials mounted after 9/11. Legacy affiliation works by importing established identities and recognizable symbols that add value to the producing and importing companies. The kind of on-screen demeanor that results poses the conglomerate as fully aware of real-world events and full of empathy for those in the "real world" (outside of professional sports) that actually suffer. The 2005 Super Bowl broadcast embellished News Corporation as a feeling, sensitive super-empath.

Contingent textual affiliations are purely opportunistic linkages promoted by the marketing and public relations departments of the various corporate entities participating in a given media event or spectacle. Moments of local or national crisis provide particularly good opportunities for various forms of contingent affiliation and grandstanding. The violent uprising in Los Angeles in 1992, and the second American invasion of Iraq in spring 2003, provided particularly good occasions for secondary entities to make the primary conflagration part of their own institutional identity and history. Unlike legacy affiliations, which involve tangible forms of appropriation by corporations, contingent affiliations tend to erupt in more ad hoc ways, and from various directions. This is because contingent affiliations can be made by almost any entity in the spatial or temporal proximity of the event being staged, the spectacle being covered, or the crisis being managed. While Fox may arguably have real relations with the American flag, it had absolutely none with the New York fire fighters killed trying to rescue World Trade Center victims. Nevertheless, the New York City Fire Department served as on-screen iconic fodder in Fox's football montage.

But many other affiliations were rapidly asserted by entities adjacent to Fox as well. U2's halftime performance was not simply evidence of international solidarity with the United States. It was big-time mass marketing for the Irish band's recently released album. Bono was using Fox's national holiday to redefine himself as an edgy American-flag-draped patriot. E-Trade sponsored Bono's halftime show, but not just for a temporary pay-to-play affiliation with Fox. After the NASDAQ crash and 9/11, Wall Street itself was a question mark, and E-Trade was affiliating with Fox's national holiday to resuscitate and rebrand itself, and Wall Street by proxy. With her career fading, Janet Jackson exploited the frenzied 2004 halftime show televised two years later by exposing her breast to viewers nationwide. The controversy and Federal Communications Commission (FCC) fines that followed spiked interest again in her career and music, which had slowly diminished with each year's emerging teen audience.

Fox's 2002 national holiday also functioned as an extension of George W. Bush's new "war on terrorism." Fox had essentially aped and domesticated the incendiary rhetoric that Bush had been speaking since 9/11 to marshal the forces of good and patriotism to fight what the president repeatedly referred to as the "axis of evil." In this sense, the 2002 Super Bowl national holiday was not a fabrication of the Fox/News Corporation conglomerate at all. Rather, the Super Bowl spectacle, its lengthy nostalgia-infused montages and self-consciously sobered pregame shows, were actually outgrowths of a social script that had already been written by President Bush. Bush had conveniently affiliated with the morale-boosting televisual spectacle of the Super Bowl, but not by appearing live. Instead, he had chartered the very terms of a new, highly moral worldview; one with clear moral choices, and a system of good and evil that could be ably worked by the media and nonmedia conglomerates that would rush to support the coming invasion of Iraq.

SANCTIONING THE MONOLITH 2: CONGLOMERATION'S "PUBLIC SERVICE" PERSONA

The sorts of complex affiliation practices involving texts that I have just described posture the conglomerate as flexible, nuanced, and therefore responsive to changing industrial and cultural conditions. Another set of textual-organizational practices sells the public on the idea that conglomerates have a public service persona by showing that diversity of taste (and therefore of representation) are at the heart of the enterprise. Cultural legitimacy follows from this, since both screen practices and the business models that generate them pose the conglomerate as a market-driven, *quasi–public service* enterprise. The advent of new programming and delivery systems beginning in the 1980s—cable, direct broadcast satellite, pay-per-view, the VCR and remote, the Internet, and broadband—helped break the oligopoly of three-network television and opened American television screens to many more emerging companies.[26] To many, the success of HBO, CNN, MTV, VH1, Discovery, Cinemax, USA Network, BET, Nickelodeon, American Movie Classics, Lifetime, the Sci-Fi Network, Bravo, ESPN, Fox Sports Net, the History Channel, Home and Garden, and many other "networks" had splintered the mass audience into multiple niches, now somehow more responsive to divergent audience perspectives. This splintering also ostensibly disassembled the top-down control of American broadcasting in a way that publicly favored the diverse, heterogeneous identities of the American public. Fiscal conservatives in government at this time spread the mantra of the television industry and the National Association of Broadcasters: a free market—not regulation—was the only way to ensure diversity of programming. For three administrations beginning with the Reagan/Bush White House, government regulation by the FCC and FTC retreated to enable the telecommunications industry and entertainment market to work their democratic miracles. Across a broad spectrum of interests, diversity in channel choices was optimistically conflated with cultural, ethnic, and racial diversity per se.[27] Yet few looked past the hype to challenge a subsequent trend. After the multichannel market model rose to prominence, and regulatory policy withered, merger mania caught up with those in the expanding cable-television-entertainment industries.[28] While some hand-wringing greeted this renewed form of "vertical integration" long absent since the 1948 Paramount decrees (which prohibited a single corporation from owning each stage of the media cycle; from production, to distribution, to exhibition and broadcast), the new megaconglomerates such as AOL/Time Warner reestablished and legitimized vertical integration with a vengeance.[29] And they did so with the blessing of the very same government that had—in the name of public interest—aggressively abolished vertical integration five decades earlier.[30]

PROGRAMMING DIFFERENCE AND MULTICULTURAL TIERING

This reversal and sanction emerged in part because the new corporations became particularly good at "performing identity" in ways reminiscent of how "resisting" and "subaltern" subjects perform identity in critical theory and cultural studies. In some ways, multiculturalism, identity performance, and hybridity became foundational principles in media programming practice. The continuing green light given entertainment mergers and reconglomeration follows from the fact that these new vertically reintegrated conglomerates have symbolically mastered the very regime of diversity, public service, and democratic taste that regulatory limits were set in place to preserve for the past half century. However, rather than dispersing taste niches and community viewpoints across competing channels, the new conglomerates have mastered the ability to house and segregate this diverse pantheon of tastes and perspectives *within* components or tiers of the very same conglomerate. Viacom can thereby prove that it meets the needs of the youthful MTV/VH1 demographic, the African American target audience of BET, queer and lesbian viewers on Showtime, as well as the mainstream and older demographic tastes of CBS. Viacom also demonstrates to its shareholders and to governmental regulators that it is profitably diverse and inclusive, even as the industry champions its market-driven diversity.[31] As a result, economic rewards that used to follow from a program's mass audience share no longer stand as realistic corporate goals. The success of narrowcasting as a programming strategy in the 1980s is said to have ended the economies of scale that defined the network era. Media corporations now must try to master the cumulative aggregation of audiences from across the fragmented demographic niches that compromise the proliferating multichannel market.

Narrowcasting succeeded because of its ability to return lucrative, niche demographic segments of the audience to program suppliers and networks who could, as a result, charge higher advertising rates to more loyal consumers. The current media conglomerates, however, can no longer sufficiently capitalize their operations by exploiting solely this kind of limited economy of scope. Instead, large media companies seek to incorporate diversity and cultural difference (and their attendant revenues) by combining them within a single, integrated corporate structure. The dispersed flows and migrations that I have characterized above—of both texts and viewers—produces highly fragmented revenue streams. Since this kind of fragmentation is difficult to associate with single-brand identity, corporations such as AOL/Time Warner/HBO/Showtime/CNN/Turner now specialize in "tiering" numerous brand-inflected niches within the überbrand. HBO now charges cable and satellite users a gradation of premiums for no less than sixteen "different" channel "tiers." There is no need to go to Lifetime or Oxygen when women viewers have HBO Signature; no need to go to IFC, Bravo, or the Sundance Channel when cineastes and aesthete viewers can see "cutting-edge," vanguard film on HBO Zone; no need to go to the Disney Channel or Pax TV when children have HBO Family; no need to switch to BET when African Americans are sold on critically acclaimed depictions of African Americans on HBO (or its competitive brand Showtime, in series like *Soul Food*); no need to switch to general cable channels like MSNBC, either, when HBO news viewers can switch instead to Turner's CNN, an important affiliate in the HBO conglomerate. This industry loves to analyze how markets guarantee diversity: "Today's Big Five offer a stunning array of programming for just about every taste. And somehow, despite the big corporate ownership, they offer a lot of different viewpoints on a lot of different topics. To the extent those viewpoints are limited is due as much to government and public pressure as to corporate decision making. It's the gay rights groups that are driving *Dr. Laura* off the air, not Viacom."[32]

Individual media conglomerates have attempted to engineer the mannerisms of the multichannel universe *within* or inside of the branded walls of the conglomerate. Brands in the digital era are expected to function in far more extensive and complex ways than they were in the analog age. During the earlier period, a limited set of basic product and trademark names functioned as brands, whose ad agencies sponsored mass-audience television shows in the network era. Branding has now an obligatory specialization, requiring continual re-inflection as technological, market, and regulatory changes ripple through the industry. Branding markets not specific products, but rather highly individuated and easily recognizable corporate personalities. Branding is lauded if it effectively creates psychological and empathic relationships with consumers. HBO and its überconglomerate have proliferated variants of the mother brand, which invoke cultural difference without straying from the "emotional core" of the original brand. The AOL/Time Warner/HBO brand is so complicated that most Web sites within the conglomerate provide either linkages to other corporate affiliates, or schematic descriptions, maps, and user guides that help the Web user understand his or her

Table 11.3 Conglomeration's "Public Service" Persona

Diversity of Taste	Integrate racial, ethnic, cultural identity niches within überbrand. *Examples*: HBO Latino, HBO Signature, Cinemax, CNN, Cartoon Network
Diversity of Tiers	Resegregate taste/identity niches into economically graded user castes. *Examples*: Basic, Premium, Elite, HDTV packages via digital cable provider
Program Difference	Cultivate "distinctions without a difference" in programming. Find and exploit "cultural edges" in tastes and trends. Self-define economic interests and corporate power as fundamentally apolitical by definition.
Net Result/Contradictions	That massive multinational conglomerates are interpersonal in scale. That commercial market control guarantees diversity of tastes for public. That "quality" produced by conglomerates trumps safeguards as well as smaller-scale forms of media production and distribution. Size matters.

location within the überbrand. Such practices show that conglomerates have imposed and adapted flow strategies intended to work inside of their proprietary and newly aggregated worlds. Internalizing flow strategy in this way is no small task, given that viewer migrations now flow multidirectionally across potentially endless numbers of channels and niches. As a marketing and public relations goal, the proliferation of choices within the conglomerate brand demonstrates the corporation's ostensible commitment to cultural diversity and, through it, the sense that the corporation is "serving" the public (Table 11.3).

My characterization of intrabrand flows in this essay, of course, is in some ways a boardroom fantasy of corporations. What actually occurs in television network usage is that unruly users migrate in all sorts of directions that can only be loosely encouraged and facilitated with incentives, rather than controlled in any uniform sense. In comparison to the tight and heavy-handed management of flows that takes place in traditional "first-shift" programming (officially scheduled half-hour- or hour-long series on television or cable and first-run feature films screened in theaters), the looser flows of "second-shift" programming (mobile and dispersed media activities linked to the primary shows or films but accessed at times other than the primary screenings) live or die by obsessively pursuing and mastering endless forms of flexibility and nuance.[33] Online, HBO is willing to provide minimal links to its affiliates outside of HBO (with links to "free AOL service," to AOL Box Office, and to Turner's Cartoon Network, for example). Other entities try to partner and cobrand to steer users to corporations with shared economic interests—even if they are in different sectors of the economy. NBC could viably partner with Microsoft (MSNBC) but not HBO, and could create a portal with Snap.com and then ShopNBC rather than AOL. But even these alliances "leak" on the Internet. This inherent leakiness in flow management means that cable executives now strategize (and program) degrees of textual "stickiness" in the second-shift world (with stickiness being the extent to which providers can induce users to stay with a package of services). At the National Cable & Telecommunications Association (NCTA) convention on May 15, 2002, management panelists all concurred that the notion of homogenous content "convergence" is, in many ways, a myth. Chief executive officers from Time Warner Cable, AT&T cable, Charter Communications, and others asserted that viewer "churn" (the rate that subscribers canceled paid service) improved only when companies provided a package of different services within a single delivery system (video, data, telephony, enhanced TV, etc.).[34]

The CEO of Wink Communications (an "enhanced TV provider") summed up the insight that higher customer satisfaction came from packaging different services and thus "creating value on a single platform."[35] In some ways this notion (of diverse-packaging/singular-delivery) mirrors the ways that branding (in the age of digital) works by producing diversity and difference within a single über-brand. But textual dispersal and flow leakiness also mean that content providers must now learn looser forms of management to master programming in the second shift. Other interests and sites—including competing networks—can (and regularly do) pull users out of branded confines. Following the pattern established by CBS's *Survivor* phenomenon, reality shows like ABC's *The Bachelor* provided Disney with intrabrand flow and tie-in possibilities. But as each female contestant was exiled from the show, many other news and entertainment shows aired by local stations or in first-run syndication (*Extra, Entertainment Tonight*) also solicited and then showcased the banished contestants as part of their own proprietary special segments.[36]

Diversity of on-screen representation now exists in television—but only because of genre and format "ghettoizations" that the multichannel conglomerates have established and profited from.[37] The industry has been particularly good at deflecting criticism about lack of public service and diversity by arguing that it now provides greater access to a wider range of groups and perspectives than ever before. Two factors are conveniently left out of this rationale, however: first, that niche ghettoization allows the majors (CBS, ABC, NBC) to be no less appreciably white than they have been for two decades (and to be that way without regulatory pressure); and second, that the new conglomerates actually prosper by institutionalizing a regime of difference in the form of corporate-affiliate tiering. One underlying objective of each new conglomerate is to have within the walls of its extended corporate family a programming niche for every taste, culture, and social identity. Even as specific networks and studios may become more specialized and homogenous within their own narrow scope and identity; the larger conglomerates that house them are tiered as multicultural aggregations. Such aggregation deflects both claims of racism and concerned calls for new regulatory measures to enforce public service, diversity, and democratic representation. The entertainment industries have every reason to internalize and corporatize such ideals as part of a global, some would say user-driven, multimedia market.[38]

Why Industrial Reflexivity
and Critical Self-Representation
Matter to Conglomerates

Conglomeration can be productively understood by examining the on-screen critical textual practices of the film and video production industry. Contemporary media corporations deploy various forms of industrial reflexivity to pursue their goals of diversification, managerial flexibility, and synergy. On-screen representations (*of* the production world made *by* the production world) guide the viewer as he or she deciphers and navigates the many channel options available in the multimedia environment. Successful modern media conglomerates succeed not by isolating and locking onto consumers in traditional or discrete media categories. Rather, media conglomerates today are effective only to the degree that they can manage and loosely guide user-viewers in two increasingly common situations: first, as they "flow" and cycle from one multimedia platform to another; and second, as they "multitask."[39]

In a flurry of deals in spring 2006, most of the major U.S. studios and television networks had launched new media initiatives to exploit and manage this new kind of second-shift flow and multitasking phenomenon. Disney's ABC and News Corporation's Fox both developed off-network mob-casts with cell phone companies for *Desperate Housewives* and *24*, respectively. CBS loaded up its new site Innertube.cbs.com with episodes of *Survivor: Exile Island*, *Amazing Race 9*, and making-of interviews with casts of most CBS's broadcast series. Comedy Central's site motherload.comedycentral.com provides an online smorgasbord of such hits as *South Park* and *The Daily Show*, original stand-up comedy acts, and online video shorts that can be downloaded onto an iPod. Universal/NBC/Bravo's brilliantbutcancelled.com site created a second-shift strategy based entirely on programming detritus from television's first shift—resuscitating programs that choked prematurely in some other network's prime time. MTV's overdrive.mtv.com, VH1's vspot.vh1.com, and SciFi's scifi.com/pulse all stoked their network servers with backstory, minutiae, series deconstructions, and mountains of programming surplus aimed at keeping their respective fans and viewers forever preoccupied and away from some other studio's first-shift offerings. These now-obligatory business strategies underscore the importance of three related factors: first, the economic importance of on-screen textual permutation and reiteration rationalized within a system of content repurposing; second, the institutional value that various forms of textual affiliation and development flexibility play in enabling conglomerates to rapidly deploy creative resources and externalize risk; and third, the ways that industrial reflexivity and practitioner self-commentary are symptoms of adaptive behaviors generated in response to structural uncertainties. For many film and video practitioners, metatexts, demos, and reflexive rituals help workers adapt, navigate, and negotiate very real threats of industrial change and technical obsolescence. For the large media conglomerates, by contrast, reflexive on-screen content provides a different kind of adaptive behavior—what economist Arthur De Vany would call an "information cascade" needed to promote and assign "extraordinary" status for the films or series being depicted.[40] Hit films are highly extraordinary and rare. Reflexive information cascades help reduce the great uncertainty that defines the content development process. Many of the reflexive industrial artifacts that make up information cascades (studio or network Web sites, DVDs and video games spun off from films) also help the conglomerates dynamically follow or "track" the transitory, unpredictable viewer or fan.[41]

By the early 2000s, mastery of on-screen reflexivity and deconstruction became obligatory goals in content development. After a succession of reality-show successes based on audience participation in the real-time "making-of" a multi-platformed media property—like WB's *Popstars* and MTV's *Making the Band*—several series pushed the concept across the full range of multimedia possibilities.[42] *Project Greenlight/Stolen Summer* was launched as a contest for unknown but aspiring screenwriter/directors "with an edge." In an event that synthesized a lottery, the Sundance Film Festival, and gen-Y fantasies of becoming "players" in the entertainment industry, financial backers Miramax studios, Ben Affleck, and Matt Damon awarded unknown first-timer Pete Jones a million-dollar budget to produce his screenplay/entry as the feature film *Stolen Summer*. HBO (and then Bravo, in syndication) then covered every blow-by-blow of the disaster that followed "behind the camera" for its weekly prime-time series *Project Greenlight*. Far more than a "making-of," HBO scored a major hit with the on-the-set soap opera. The result: a weekly melodrama involving endless displays of production and directorial incompetence, cathartic raging, infighting, interpersonal jealousies, backstabbings, firings, and studio and executive damage control. By the time *Stolen Summer* premiered to mixed and unenthusiastic reviews at Sundance in January 2002, the lessons were clear. First, the traditional aesthetic hierarchy had been turned upside down: Time Warner/AOL's cable network HBO succeeded in making "ancillary" content (a "making-of") the *main* event, while theatrical film exhibition (of Jones's feature film) became but an afterthought. Second, the marketing and management arms of the conglomerate had effectively demonstrated their own critical competence (and their grasp of complex, multimarket media productions) to the viewing public as the production process unfolded in weekly installments. Ostensible "stars" Jones, Affleck, Damon, and others gradually faded under the shadow of the mostly offscreen higher-ups, especially Miramax's quiet but knowing executive-aesthetes who pulled strings during key story sessions, production summits, and confrontations in *Project Greenlight*. This lengthy exercise in extended self-dissection and implicitly "insightful" screen analysis supported the thrust of HBO's ever-present corporate branding motto ("It's not television. It's HBO."). Where, however, does one attribute authorship in this multimedia initiative? Is it the director of the *Project Greenlight* cable television series? Is it the director of the *Stolen Summer* film? Is it the on-camera producer who badgers and ridicules Jones in every episode of the series and every stage of production? Or could it be the director of HBO's marketing department, the designer of HBO's script solicitation and series-related Web site, or the Weinstein honchos in Miramax's executive offices? In the age of multi-affiliated, multi-platformed media content, corporate brands like HBO themselves regularly function as auteurs. Clearly, an off-screen authority has self-consciously choreographed and organized a complicated set of cross-media production registers over several years (the online selection process, the weekly televisual experience, and the cinematic spectacle) and across numerous corporate institutions.

Even as the film went down in flames, HBO provided a successful paradigm that many others would soon master. By staging a long-term multimedia experience and acting as its own critical analyst as well, HBO, much like a critic or historian, ably mined the backstory, behind-the-camera "realities," and presentational "secrets" of the developing content (the film production)—and presented this critical analysis *as* the viewer's primary form of on-screen content. Web-television-film hybrids like this, and the technologies and affiliations that animate them, now function as trading grounds not just for commerce and consumption but for industrial authorship and critical analysis as well. This symptomatic pose—the *self-critical conglomerate*—would have ill fit the network-era logic of oligopoly and dominance. Brilliantbutcancelled.com allows armchair critics to beg for the death of hated series in a show called *Make it Stop*. SciFi.com/pulse enables its viewers to give the corporation feedback on pilots the network is developing. Innertube.com programs an online second-shift series where desperate actors compete for a chance to appear on CBS's first-shift series *As the World Turns*. Comedy Central's Motherload makes viewers the judges of series pilots submitted by viewers in an *American Idol*–like Web series entitled *Test Pilots*.

In each of these cases, traditional distinctions used by media scholars have blurred. Each site and platform melds viewing, online use, critical analysis, media production, and marketing into a single hybrid entertainment experience. While the aesthetic effect is one of complex mutation, the corporate effect is clearer and more systematic. Industrial textual practices serve to publicly "rationalize" (in two senses of the term) the work worlds of media conglomeration. First, they provide a metric and logic to the industrial mode of production (ground rules that help order the volatile industrial landscape). The amortized, cross-collateralized textual economy described earlier (in which films and series are financed by dispersing production costs across numerous affiliated partners and distribution windows within the multimedia conglomerate, and in which various off- and online media cross-promote one another) helps provide this rationality. Such a scheme allows corporations and their investors to more accurately value and appraise individual projects. This, in turn, allows the companies to be more systematic in selecting and capitalizing new projects. Contractually reaggregated, newly networked affiliates within the new conglomerates provide predictability in designing marketing plans and in projecting profits—both crucial tasks in the risk-defined, failure-prone world of content development. This cross-collateralization and multimedia diversification is pushing film production further into the realm (and economic scheme) of television. After all, for five decades U.S. television has: (1) distributed production costs and risks across affiliated partners; and (2) systematically used audience and market research and analysis to produce less volatile business plans than film (this conservative scheme is based on the predictability of advertising sponsorship, merchandising, and long-term licensing fees). Long ago, television mastered on-screen programming and scheduling as a key business strategy. Programming is dynamic enough to adapt to market uncertainty, and predictable enough to build long-range plans around. Programming departments in turn enabled television to find and manage audience flow much more effectively than cinema. For these reasons, I would characterize the economic logic and less dynamic managerial system of television, in an economist's terminology, as a "mediocracy." Television stands, after all, in stark contrast to what De Vany described as the far more "dynamic behaviors" and outcome "uncertainties" that have historically defined feature film's "extraordinary" economy.

I have added a number of related distinctions to De Vany's that can be made between the economic and institutional behaviors of film and television conglomerates in Table 11.4. As feature film is gradually incorporated, disciplined, and rationalized as but a single node within giant multimedia conglomerates (which are in turn dominated by television, digital, and electronic media activities), film will increasingly emulate strategies of effective television programming to do what it needs to do to survive as film. That is, conglomerates pressure their film units to more responsively follow audiences, in order to harvest their transient financial resources. The new conglomerates, in effect, favor television's research-based industrial rationality over film's historic, personality-driven, roll-of-the-dice fatalism.

Showbiz reports, making-ofs, video press kits, ancillary digital forms, and DVDs now all (ostensibly) reveal the mode of production. Reflexive artifacts and

Table 11.4 Comparative Media Business Models: Film, TV, and Conglomeration as Managerial Tendencies and Mythoi

→Fiscal Managerial Pressures →

Film	Television	Conglomerate
Project specific	Series specific	Syndication focused
Extraordinary driven	Mediocracy driven	Predictability governed
Risk focused	Risk managed	Risk aversion
Dynamic adaptive behavior	Structured adaptive behavior	Collateralized adaptive behavior
Information-cascade method	Programming-scheduling method	Cross-promotion method
Exceptionalist creators and elites	Collective creators and teams	Outsourced creation; externalized
Intuition-based decisions	Measurement-based decisions	Cost-benefit analysis based
Charismatic management	Regulatory management	Synergistic management
Success via blockbusters	Success via longevity	Success via market diversification
Economic scope via stars	Economic scope via identity and taste	Economic scope via sub-brands
Economic scale via sequels	Economic scale via series franchises	Economic scale via merchandizing
Incremental contracts	Seasonal contracts	Cross-ownership and long-term equity
Box office	Sponsorship/subscription	Changes in stock value
Flow uncertainty	Day-part viewer flow	Intrabrand viewer flow
Appointment viewing	Habitual viewing	Affective viewer relation to brand

← Marketing Reflexivity Pressures ←

specials of the sort examined throughout this essay regularly provide charged "glimpses" of competing interests and proprietary "secrets" behind film and television content development. These mediated forms of rationality are more than simply indications of generational and educational changes in audience compe- tence (a notion assuming more media savvy, cultural capital, and aesthetic so- phistication on the part of viewers, who now somehow care about film and video production complexities). Critical, mediated, industrial "self-disclosures" like these secondary textual forms and genres function *institutionally* in several ways. First, as "critical proofs," reflexive industrial artifacts verify that some other ref- erenced or depicted primary text (film or series) is complicated, significant, valuable, or profitable. Second, as staged disclosures and "company confessions," reflexive industrial artifacts frequently demonstrate that participants in the pro- duction of films or series are ostensibly aware of the contexts, social issues, and (infrequently) political forces that impact their work worlds. Third, and finally, as "legitimating mechanisms," reflexive industrial artifacts explain and so normalize and sanction the very industrial changes outlined in this essay: conglomeration, deregulation, market segregation, branding, and tiering.

Sumner Redstone surprised Wall Street in April 2005 by promising to "split" the giant Viacom conglomerate into two megacompanies, "ViaSlow" (CBS, UPN, Infinity Radio, and Paramount TV) and "ViaGrow" (MTV, VH1, Showtime, Paramount Studios, and Paramount Home Video/DVD). The trades jumped at the chance to claim that this meant a halt in the unending march to ever-larger conglomeration. *Broadcasting and Cable* claimed that the split meant an end to "synergy, that quaint notion that companies make more money when different divisions collaborate."[43] In reality, all the split really meant was that Redstone's stock options would be more valuable under the new model, which would allow the surging value of Viacom's cable networks to complement the merely steady growth of Viacom's broadcasting and syndication arms in investor's portfolios. Far from ending, inside dealing would continue among Viacom's units even as the new Universal/NBC conglomerate achieved an even more massive scale during the very same period. In May 2005, *B&C* used the "upfronts" (the spring announcements of the fall schedule designed to lure advertisers) to argue that "vertical integration" in the television market had been "opened up" now that networks were buying some shows from other conglomerates.[44] In reality, all of UPN's new series, and two- thirds of CBS's new series came from Viacom's own Paramount Television, while the WB network bought three-quarters of its new series from sibling Warner Bros.[45] Trade news to the contrary, vertical integration was not ending; nor was inside dealing. Yet *B&C*, a tenacious antiregulatory organization for the better part of a century, used any evidence, no matter how fleeting, to establish the "fairness" of "market-driven" conglomeration. Once again, a flurry of industrial metatexts— Viacom's press campaign, the carnivalesque spectacle of the network upfronts, on- screen making-ofs, showbiz reports, and the trades, which perpetually clarify and interpret industrial events—hyped change even as they methodically legitimized the status quo. Industrial spin and on-screen reflexivity notwithstanding, the age of "de-conglomeration" is far from upon us.[46] The Viacom/VH1 and Universal/Bravo/Trio reflexive programming that opened up this essay provide far more prescient insights about conglomeration than either *Broadcasting and Cable* or Sumner Redstone.

NOTES

1. See *Televisuality: Style, Crisis, and Authority in American Television* (New Brunswick, NJ: Rutgers University Press, 1995); and "Convergence Television: Aggregating Form and Repurposing Content in the Culture of Conglomeration," in *Television after TV*, ed. Lynn Spigel and Jan Olsson (Durham, NC: Duke University Press, 2004).

2. This statement is from Kevin D. Thompson, "How VH1 Popped to the Top," *Palm Beach Post*, March 14, 1999, 1J.

3. The hybrid *Millionaire/Pop-Up* stunt aired on December 24, 26–28, and 31, 2000, on ABC.

4. Pop-Up Video Show originator Tad Low described how he came up with the idea for the show in a drunken stupor with his girlfriend, whose ex wanted to hit back at celebrity arrogance: "We set out to create a show that popped the pretense of these stars. To tell the truth behind the making of the video, who got sick, what broke. . . . And once you know the truth . . . it starts to dissolve the rock-and-roll myth." Low is quoted in Monica Collins, "Clickers: VH1 Spinoff Book Pops Up Laughs," *Boston Herald*, June 13, 1999, 5.

5. This strategy is alluded to in David Bauder, "Gaspin and Zalaznick, Once Colleagues, Now Run Their Own Entertainment Networks," Associated Press Wire Service, Entertainment News section, BC cycle, July 25, 2003.

6. See Bauder, "Gaspin and Zalaznick."

7. See Anna Everett and John Caldwell, eds., *New Media: Theories and Practices of Digitextuality* (New York: Routledge, 2003); and John Caldwell, ed., *Electronic Media and Technoculture* (New Brunswick, NJ: Rutgers University Press, 2000).

8. For a very good account of studio and network diversification in the 1950s, see Mark Alvey, "Independents: Rethinking the Television Studio System," in *The Revolution Wasn't Televised*, ed. Lynn Spigel and Michael Curtin (New York: Routledge, 1997). This account is especially useful in showing how the networks created unofficial "house companies" out of favored supposedly "independent" telefilm production companies.

9. Executive and chief operating officer of Viacom/CBS Dennis Swanson's comments were made at the National Association of Television Program Executives (NATPE) conference in 2005 and are quoted in "He Said, She Said: Barbs, Blasts, and Broadsides from NATPE," *Broadcasting and Cable*, January 31, 2005, 24.

10. Executive Mike Salmi described AtomFilm's dot-com business plan: "We focus on the short form. Because the short form is something that works very well on the internet. But we also sell to airlines. We sell to shopping malls. And we're seeing a lot of

interest now in handheld devices. And cell phones. Clearly all of these new places are experiencing entertainment—and it's a different type of entertainment." Spoken comments, NATPE Syndication Market, New Orleans, January 26, 2000.

11. Important and far more comprehensive political-economic accounts, available elsewhere, examine media conglomeration (Schiller, Aulletta, McChesney), governmental policy and deregulation (Streeter, Noriega, Holt), and globalization and conglomeration (Miller, Schwoch, Parks, and Kumar). See Dan Schiller, *Digital Capitalism* (Cambridge: MIT Press, 1999); Ken Aulletta, *Three Blind Mice: How the Networks Lost Their Way* (New York: Vintage, 1992); Robert McChesney, *Rich Media, Poor Democracy* (New York: New Press, 2000); for prescient accounts of government media regulation, see Thomas Streeter, *Selling the Air: A Critique of the Policy of Commercial Broadcasting in the United States* (Chicago: University of Chicago Press, 1996); Chon Noriega, *Shot in America* (Minneapolis: University of Minnesota Press, 2000); Jennifer Holt, *In Deregulation We Trust*, Ph.D. diss., University of California, Los Angeles, December 2003; for political-economic accounts of globalization, see Toby Miller, Nitin Govil, John McMurria, and Richard Maxwell, *Global Hollywood* (London: BFI, 2000); James Schwoch, "Global Dialogues, Paradigmatic Shifts, and Complexity: Emergent Contours of Theory and Praxis in Telecommunications Policy," *Emergences: Journal for the Study of Media and Composite Cultures* 11.1 (2000): 133–152; and Lisa Parks and Shanti Kumar, eds., *Planet TV: A Global Television Reader* (New York: New York University Press, 2003).

12. Paul M. Hirsch provided a good model for understanding the industry's "input" and "output boundaries" in his essay "Processing Fads and Fashions: An Organization-Set Analysis of Cultural Industry Systems," in *Rethinking Popular Culture*, ed. Chandra Mukerji and Michael Schudson (Berkeley: University of California Press, 1991), 313–334.

13. See Miranda Janis Banks, "Toys and Grrls: Comparing Figures in Merchandizing of Television's Action Heroine," in *Bodies of Work: Rituals of Doubling and the Erasure of Film/ TV Production Labor* (chapter in her Ph.D. diss., University of California, Los Angeles, 2006). http://proquest.umi.com/pqdweb?index=0&did=1196417971&SrchMode=1&sid=1 &Fmt=2&VInst=PROD&VType=PQD&RQT=309&VName=PQD&TS=1205150739& clientId=3507, accessed March 27, 2008.

14. Whereas the first risk mitigation strategy I referred to above dealt with farming out costly and unproven new technologies, this one focuses on ways to farm out the financing risk of on-screen content development for new films and series.

15. See especially Alvey, "Independents: Rethinking the Television Studio System" and Thomas Schatz, *Old Hollywood/New Hollywood: Ritual, Art, and Industry* (Ann Arbor, MI: UMI Research Press, 1984), 172.

16. Spoken comments by Universal Television executive at the "International Co-Production" session, NATPE Syndication Market, New Orleans, January 25–26, 2000.

17. Spoken comments by the moderator at the "International Co-Production" session, NATPE Syndication Market, New Orleans, January 25–26, 2000.

18. A showrunner is normally the executive producer, who oversees all creative aspects of a television series over a season. Most showrunners begin their careers as screenwriters, then typically advance to a writer/producer status in series television, before assuming showrunner roles. These spoken comments were made by James Dowaliby, executive, Paramount, at the "International Co-Production" session, NATPE Syndication Market, New Orleans, January 25–26, 2000.

19. See Miller et al., *Global Hollywood*.

20. These spoken comments, recorded by the author, are from television executive producer Meryl Marshall at the NATPE Syndication Market, New Orleans, January 25, 2000.

21. Ibid.

22. These spoken comments, recorded by the author, are from News Corp. executive Peggy Binzell at the NATPE Syndication Market, New Orleans, January 25, 2000.

23. This account of how conglomerates have fueled runaway production does not apply only to the international sphere (production in other countries). Runaway production is also very much a domestic phenomenon, wherein the conglomerates deftly shift production work to cheaper nonunion states and/or "down the hall" (and off the radar) to other units within the conglomerate or to nonunion contract work in Los Angeles.

24. I first examined Fox's 2002 Super Bowl coverage, described in the preceding two paragraphs, in my essay "Critical Industrial Practice," *Television and New Media*, 2006 7: 99–100. It is easy to recognize the effectivity of on-screen televisual forms and the agency of textual producers at moments of high crisis like this one. It is perhaps less easy to recognize the same kind of effectivity and agency and industrial logic in the ubiquitous flows that characterize most programming day parts. In programming outside of crisis or televised national ritual, producers and critics alike tend to compartmentalize power, industry, audience, and text into entirely different registers and public spheres. This segregation tends to be shortsighted, and blind to the industrial logics of televisual texts.

25. See Mark Graser and Jill Goldsmith, "Semel Ends Yahoo Search: Hollywood Vet Tapped to Top Popular Portal as CEO," *Variety* (April 17, 2001). http://www.variety.com/article/VR1117797226.html?categoryid=1009&cs=1, accessed March 16, 2008.

26. Before this time, during what is now known as the "network era," a government-sanctioned and regulated oligopoly in network television in the 1960s and 1970s guaranteed the NBC, CBS, and ABC corporations control of well over 90 percent of the television audience.

27. The 1934 Radio Act and the 1946 FCC Blue Book's requirements that television must implement measures to guarantee the representation of minority viewpoints, the needs of local communities, and the importance of culturally challenging, noncommercial programming now stood like no-longer-needed, archaic remnants from an earlier, less open era. In contrast to regulated public service strictures of the earlier era, the open market touted by contemporary television, along with the intensive capitalization deployed by the newer networks and start-ups, would now fulfill the earlier regulatory mandates, even as they made proprietary corporate owners wealthy. The postnetwork era was to be a win-win situation for all concerned—for industry as well as for multicultural diversity.

28. Viacom bought Paramount, which owned the *Star Trek* franchise, which fueled the launch of the UPN Network, which subsequently lost its Chris-Craft/UPN affiliate station group in a sale to Rupert Murdoch and News Corporation, which (ironically) owned and bankrolled UPN's competitor, the Fox network. Viacom, once a lowly syndication company in the 1950s but now corporate head of MTV, Nickelodeon, and VH1, also had ties to Paramount, but took over venerable broadcaster CBS in 2001. Cap Cities sold ABC to Disney, which further diversified the company by developing ESPN 1 and 2, ESPN Classic Sports, the California Angels, and Go.com. CNN merged with Time Warner, which included the Sports Illustrated programming and print franchise and the massive feature and prime-time production arm of Warner Bros., which developed and fed the nationwide delivery system Time Warner Cable—together creating a massive entertainment con-

glomerate that successfully realized the mother of all mergers: the AOL/Time Warner conglomeration of 2000.

29. In a few short years, the three-network oligopoly with a 90+ percent share of the audience fell to scores of new electronic media competitors promising program diversity. But this diverse pantheon was then reaggregated again into but five giant, multinational media corporations, which together (by fall 2000) had regained and amassed 86 percent of the audience.

30. In some cases, the individual components of the new conglomeration evidenced more hand-wringing about the effects of conglomeration than the government. The report that "UPN Executives predicted Friday that their network will continue to operate despite Viacom's new ownership of both CBS and UPN and News Corps' (parent of the Fox network) pending purchase of UPN's Chris-Craft owned affiliate stations" (Valerie Kuklenski, "UPN Brass See No Course Change Despite New Ownership," *Long Beach Press Telegram* (January 9, 2001): C6), demonstrated how precarious ownership of content had become, and how important it had become to "mark one's turf" in order to maintain one's "brand" in the confusion of conglomeration.

31. The next few paragraphs in this section are developed from ideas first presented in my essay "Convergence Media."

32. From Harry A. Jessell, "Get Set for Network II: You Do the Math—Big Five Have an 86 Prime Time Share," *Broadcasting and Cable* (October 9, 2000), 16. http://www.broadcastingcable.com/article/CA20020.html?q=Jessell+2000+Viacom+ diversity, accessed May 2, 2008.

33. These concepts of first-shift programming (officially scheduled half-hour or hour-long series on television/cable, or first-run feature films screened) and second-shift programming (mobile and dispersed media activities linked to the primary shows/films but accessed at times other than the primary screenings) were first developed in my chapter "Second Shift Aesthetics," in *New Media: Digitextual Theory and Practices*, ed. Anna Everett and John Caldwell (New York: Routledge, 2003).

34. The CEO of AT&T cable, for example, said that their churn when providing video alone was 2 percent, but that when they added telephony, the churn rate dropped almost in half to 1.2 percent (public comments on "The Future of Cable" panel at the National Cable & Telecommunications Association [NCTA] Convention, cablecast on C-SPAN, May 16, 2002).

35. Maggie Wilderotter, CEO, Wink Communications, in public comments as a panelist on "The Future of Cable" panel at the NCTA Convention, cablecast on C-SPAN, May 16, 2002.

36. The *Bachelor* ran on the ABC network starting in April 2002. Weekly installments of the series selectively culled the "most promising" of the female contestants while the bachelor banished those considered less desirable from the bevy of women. The show culminated as a sweeps-week showcase in May.

37. A recent case outlined more fully by Herman Gray in his recent book, *Cultural Moves*, underscores the centrality that programming cultural and racial difference has played as part of the networks' institutional posture. When the NAACP and others mounted a frontal attack against the networks in 1999 based on the lack of racial diversity in prime-time television, the networks and studios jumped anxiously to "blacken" or "color" many of their existing series and staffs. Subsequent analysis of network programming, however, revealed that prime time actually represented a higher percentage of

blacks than existed in the population as a whole. Yet critics pointed out that this self-congratulatory notion of adequate representational percentages masked a countervailing trend: television had resegregated itself by the very tiering and conglomeration that the new multichannel landscape had legitimized. Yes, images of color existed, but not on the still very white worlds of NBC, CBS, and ABC programming, where they were almost nonexistent. African Americans were, however, ever present on the newer networks WB and UPN, which adopted the proven start-up strategy that fourth network Fox had exploited so successfully in the late 1980s: both made extensive use of "black-block" programming to reach a young and hip multiracial demographic that the majors no longer needed. Yes, television was diverse, but many critics pointed out that this diversity is based on a caste system of genre and tiering. African Americans, that is, are diverted to the endless ethnic comedies and reality shows prevalent on UPN, WB, and Fox. See Gray, *Cultural Moves* (Berkeley: University of California Press, 2005).

38. In some ways, television now serves as a model for the new media conglomerates. That is, one key to success lies in television's ability to produce and exploit a set of quantitative and qualitative economic conditions that in turn can fuel two fundamental components in the production of a networked, globalized culture. First is the creation of branded on-screen entertainment content marked by cultural distinction, through the consolidation and intensification of capital in the entertainment industries. Second is the perpetuation and maintenance of a vast and reliable system of consumerism and global merchandising. For television, and now the electronic media conglomerates, advertising and commercialism proved to be the keys that linked the efficiencies of capital-intensive content creation (in Hollywood and network television) with the economies of scale required by broadcasting, cablecasting, and satellite distribution. As a nexus between these two worlds, digitalization and governmental deregulation have provided optimal conditions under which a range of existing institutional strategies and new formal on-screen permutations can be effectively and profitably deployed by the conglomerates.

39. "Multitasking" describes a viewer-user who simultaneously uses multiple media platforms alongside one another.

40. See Arthur De Vany, *Hollywood Economics: How Extreme Uncertainty Shapes the Film Industry* (London: Routledge, 2004), 1–6.

41. This strategy of information cascades is not unlike the ways that fashion and pop-song tie-ins helped studios track and exploit projects in the predigital era.

42. In some ways, WB's *Popstars* was the ultimate multiplatformed media property. It simultaneously provided consumers with television programming, CD and music production, Web sites, interactive media, concert venues, publications, buzz grist for *Entertainment Weekly*, and "access" and "participation" (on a worldwide basis) for aspiring *Popstar* applicants, wannabes, and participants. Other series, like MTV's *Making the Band*, followed the same formula into a third season, ostensibly allowing viewers to witness a pop-cultural phenomenon emerging (albeit prefabricated rather than "discovered") into multimedia stardom. A very good and detailed account of the interaction of the registers that make up the *Popstars*/WB phenomenon is found in L. S. Kim and Gilberto Blasini, "The Performance of Multicultural Identity in US Network Television: Shiny, Happy Popstars (Holding Hands)," *Emergences* 11.2: 287–307.

43. This quote is from John M. Higgins, "ViaSlow vs. ViaGrow: Sumner Redstone Fine-Tunes His Plan to Split Viacom," *Broadcasting and Cable* (*B&C*), May 9, 2005, 8.

44. This statement is from John M. Higgins, "It's Not All in the Family," *Broadcasting and Cable (B&C)*, May 23, 2005, 8.

45. Interestingly, in the spring of 2006, affiliates of both networks were shocked to hear that these same struggling net-lets (the smaller, newer upstart television networks of the 1990s, UPN and The WB) were closing shop and merging in order to establish a better market position. The new, resulting network, CW, premiered in September 2006.

46. After finishing a "soft" story in February 2002 that meekly questioned the impact of recent corporate acquisitions by the AOL/Time Warner conglomerate that employs him on CNN, Jeff Greenfield ironically commented that he would probably soon get a chastising call from his bosses once he was offscreen and back in his office. The on-air anchor and Greenfield both had a good laugh at the prospect. The real effect of the interchange, however, was that it served as a wink-wink, nod-nod to the audience, a supposedly comforting acknowledgment that those inside the conglomerate know well the industrial changes afoot and that they have those developments well covered and in hand. Such disclosures are now unremarkable parts of many evening newscasts, and typically appear as brief business-like acknowledgments that prove journalistic honesty and critical distance ("Meanwhile today, GE, the parent of NBC . . ."). As with making-ofs, show-business reports, and special backstory DVD tracks, such disclosures can also, however, come across like those of a used-car dealer: they intend to prove honesty and reliability—but they do so in an overdetermined, and so vaguely suspect, way.

BIBLIOGRAPHY

Alvey, Mark. "Independents: Rethinking the Television Studio System." In *The Revolution Wasn't Televised*. Ed. Lynn Spigel and Michael Curtin. New York: Routledge, 1997.

Aulletta, Ken. *Three Blind Mice: How the Networks Lost Their Way*. New York: Vintage, 1992.

Banks, Miranda Janis. "Toys and Grrls: Comparing Figures in Merchandizing of Television's Action Heroine." In *Bodies of Work: Rituals of Doubling and the Erasure of Film/TV Production Labor* (chapter from her Ph.D. diss., UCLA, 2006).

Bauder, David. "Gaspin and Zalaznick, Once Colleagues, Now Run Their Own Entertainment Networks." Associated Press Wire Service. Entertainment News section, BC cycle, July 25, 2003.

Caldwell, John. *Televisuality: Style, Crisis, and Authority in American Television*. New Brunswick, NJ: Rutgers University Press, 1995.

———, ed. *Electronic Media and Technoculture*. New Brunswick, NJ: Rutgers University Press, 2000.

———. "Second Shift Aesthetics." In *New Media: Digitextual Theory and Practices*. Ed. Anna Everett and John Caldwell. New York: Routledge, 2003.

———. "Convergence Television: Aggregating Form and Repurposing Content in the Culture of Conglomeration." In *Television after TV*. Ed. Lynn Spigel and Jan Olsson. Durham, NC: Duke University Press, 2004.

———. "Critical Industrial Practice." *Television and New Media* 7 (2006): 99–100.

———. *Production Culture: Industrial Reflexivity and Critical Practice in Film/Television*. Durham, NC: Duke University Press, 2008.

Collins, Monica. "Clickers: VH1 Spinoff Book Pops Up Laughs." *Boston Herald*, June 13, 1999, 5.

De Vany, Arthur. *Hollywood Economics: How Extreme Uncertainty Shapes the Film Industry*. London: Routledge, 2004, 1–6.

Everett, Anna, and John Caldwell, eds. *New Media: Theories and Practices of Digitextuality*. New York: Routledge, 2003.

Graser, Mark, and Jill Goldsmith. "Semel Ends Yahoo Search: Hollywood Vet Tapped to Top Popular Portal as CEO." *Variety*, April 17, 2001. http://www.variety.com/article/VR1117797226.html?categoryid=1009&cs=1.

Gray, Herman. *Cultural Moves*. Berkeley: University of California Press, 2005.

Higgins, John M. "ViaSlow vs. ViaGrow: Sumner Redstone Fine-Tunes His Plan to Split Viacom." *Broadcasting and Cable (B&C)*, May 9, 2005, 8.

———. "It's Not All in the Family." *Broadcasting and Cable (B&C)*, May 23, 2005, 8.

Hirsch, Paul M. "Processing Fads and Fashions: An Organization-Set Analysis of Cultural Industry Systems." In *Rethinking Popular Culture*. Ed. Chandra Mukerji and Michael Schudson. Berkeley: University of California Press, 1991, 313–334.

Holt, Jennifer. *In Deregulation We Trust*. Ph.D. diss. University of California, Los Angeles, December 2003.

Jessell, Harry A. "Get Set for Network II: You Do the Math—Big Five Have an 86 Prime Time Share." *Broadcasting and Cable* (October 9, 2000), 16. http://www.broadcastingcable.com/article/CA20020.html?q=Jessell+2000+Viacom+diversity.

Kim, L. S., and Gilberto Blasini. "The Performance of Multicultural Identity in US Network Television: Shiny, Happy Popstars (Holding Hands)." *Emergences* 11.2: 287–307.

Kuklenski, Valerie. "UPN Brass See No Course Change Despite New Ownership." *Long Beach Press Telegram* (January 9, 2001): C6.

McChesney, Robert. *Rich Media, Poor Democracy*. New York: New Press, 2000.

Miller, Toby, Nitin Govil, John McMurria, and Richard Maxwell. *Global Hollywood*. London: BFI, 2000.

Mukerji, Chandra, and Michael Schudson, eds. *Rethinking Popular Culture*. Berkeley: University of California Press, 1991.

Noriega, Chon. *Shot in America*. Minneapolis: University of Minnesota Press, 2000.

Parks, Lisa, and Shanti Kumar, eds. *Planet TV: A Global Television Reader*. New York: New York University Press, 2003.

Schatz, Thomas. *Old Hollywood/New Hollywood: Ritual, Art, and Industry*. Ann Arbor, MI: UMI Research Press, 1984, 172.

Schiller, Dan. *Digital Capitalism*. Cambridge: MIT Press, 1999.

Schwoch, James. "Global Dialogues, Paradigmatic Shifts, and Complexity: Emergent Contours of Theory and Praxis in Telecommunications Policy." *Emergences: Journal for the Study of Media and Composite Cultures* 11.1 (2000): 133–152.

Streeter, Thomas. *Selling the Air: A Critique of the Policy of Commercial Broadcasting in the United States*. Chicago: University of Chicago Press, 1996.

Thompson, Kevin D. "How VH1 Popped to the Top." *Palm Beach Post*, March 14, 1999, 1J.

CHAPTER 12

THE CHINESE ACTION IMAGE AND POSTMODERNITY

EVANS CHAN

Historical Man is bound up with the myths of heroic times in so far as he sometimes affirms himself by combating them, at other times by identifying with them.
— Maurice Blanchot, *The Infinite Conversation*

MARTIAL ARTS CULTURE AND NOSTALGIA

In this essay, the term "postmodernity" refers to the present era, in which the hybridization of cultural forms and aesthetics has become a commonplace phenomenon. Such a process is made possible by the heightened exchanges and interaction among nations and cultures in a world of accelerating deterritorialization and reterritorialization, driven by late capitalism's logic of consumption without end, and consumption with totally inquistive, eclectic tastes, as theorized by Fredric Jameson and Jean-François Lyotard.

The postmodern entry of Chinese action images into the arena of global entertainment has gone through a few phases over the course of a few decades: its overt phase encompassed the appearance of Bruce Lee and Jackie Chan through to the global distribution and popularity of *Crouching Tiger, Hidden Dragon* (Ang Lee, 2000), and its covert phase included the incorporation of Chinese action images in the production of recent Hollywood blockbusters such as *Kill Bill* (Quentin Tarantino, 2003, 2004) and *The Matrix* (Andy Wachowski and Larry Wachowski, 1999, 2003).

Chinese action images spring from kung fu (at times referred to generically as "martial arts"), a term, if not a practice, familiar to an international audience, as well as *wu xia*, a term and practice familiar only to China's domestic audience. While these two concepts or names may seem sufficiently straightforward on the surface, an investigation into the intricate relationship between, as well as the shifting content behind, them is necessary at this particular moment, for as Samuel Weber pointed out, in the context of Freudian repression, names may function as *screens*. They isolate rather than simply repress, "by seemingly arresting the movement of signification."[1] As I discuss later in this essay, it may seem discourteous to my Chinese compatriots for me to uncover the kernel of traumatic sentiments *repressed* by kung fu and *wu xia*, presumably among the ultimate expressions of prowess and masculinity. Yet the movement of signification traverses time and history. The full implication of the Chinese action images in postmodernity—which at this moment articulates what I call the "temptation of empire" for a resurgent China— requires a look at the genealogy of the martial arts (*wu xia*) culture, the emergence of which, in Foucaultian terms, is full of discontinuities and dispersion. More essentially, its trajectory is an interplay between the *visible* and the *articulable*.[2]

By the visible, I am referring to Chinese martial arts (kung fu) as an actual physical practice, such as gymnastics, exercises, and combative skills. Historically, the origin of Chinese martial arts has been traced back to the Shao Lin Temple in Henan, built in A.D. 497 during the Northern Wei dynasty. Legend has it that Bodhidharma (Damo in Mandarin), a South Indian or Persian monk who came to the temple in either the fifth or sixth century, felt that the Chinese monks had become too emaciated even for their spiritual striving. He therefore developed for them a regime of physical exercises that evolved into the different branches of kung fu. The popular 1982 movie *Shao Lin Temple* (Xinyan Zhang), Jet Li's screen debut, is based on the well-known Shao Lin folklore of its warrior monks' first major political involvement as they helped the would-be founder of the Tang dynasty (A.D. 618–907), fight off rivals to capture the throne. The "historical" narrative of *Shao Lin Temple*, though, is not without its mythical dimension, as the temple keeps rebuilding itself over time, developing its reputation as a haven for rebels against imperial rule. A tourist destination today, Shao Lin was famously remembered for its devastation in 1732 by the Qing armies for alleged anti-Manchu activities.

But the *articulable* aspect of the martial arts culture erupts as linguistic fantasy, above and beyond the fantastic skill anchored to human physicality. Only a couple of Chinese classical novels—such as *Outlaws of the Marsh*, about a gang of bandits, and *Creation of the Gods* (both appeared in the fifteenth century)—could be considered the forerunners of the so-called martial arts (*wu xia*) novels. They belong to China's premodernity. However, the emergence of martial arts literature as a popular literary subgenre took off during the second decade of the twentieth century, the moment China woke up to its spectacularly failed, miserable encounter with modernity.

One can argue that the fantastical realm articulated by *wu xia* literature seems to be the enactment of an imaginary bridge between a dispirited China being forced into modernity and its ancient régime—the reimagined glory of national pride and omniscience in popular fantasy and nostalgia. These popular novels depicting swordsmen, warriors, and sometimes gods, demons, and magical animals arrived with a vengeance after the conquest of the Forbidden City by the joint European armies in 1900, and the founding of the new Chinese republic in 1911. Wang Du Lu (1909–1977), one of the earliest practitioners of the genre, wrote *Crouching Tiger, Hidden Dragon* in the early 1940s in the city of Qingdao, evoking with loving detail the bygone Manchu customs and the old Beijing of his childhood. Wang also tried to be a "serious" novelist by writing non–*wu xia*, "realistic" novels, yet he was ultimately awarded posthumous fame at the millennium with the cinematic adaptation of his low-culture, subgenre, but best known work.

With the arrival of the People's Republic of China (PRC) in 1949, the *wu xia* writing tradition was transplanted to Hong Kong, the British colony at the tip of southern China. The immediate postwar decades saw *wu xia* writing's unique flowering in the hands of arguably its greatest practitioner, Jin Yong, who wrote fifteen *wu xia* novels between 1955 and 1972.[3] (Jin Yong, subject of more than one international academic conference on his work, is famous enough to have been awarded the Commandeur de l'Ordre des Arts et des Lettres in 2004 by the French government.) The idea of achieving fame as a *wu xia* writer—of being the Michael Crichton or John Grisham of his time and place—has been casually evoked by Wong Kar-wai's *In the Mood for Love* (2001), which is set in Hong Kong in the 1960s; its protagonist's favorite pastime is writing *wu xia* novels.

Wu xia novels have always evoked fights through ornate and poetical naming and descriptions of weapons and combat styles. Such writing forms a kind of self-contained semiological system. Other than the fantastical phenomena of weapons being controlled by one's mind or inner flow of energy, there is such a thing as "palm power," which is sort of a supersized version of Jean Grey's psychic power in

X-Men (Bryan Singer, 2000), meaning that supernaturally destructive energy can be unleashed through one's palm. *Wu xia* writers invent different names for sets of palm power—"Taichi Palm," "Iron Palm," or "18 Strikes to Subdue a Dragon," which features individual strikes called "A Dragon Lying," "A Dragon Appearing in the Field," and so on. Consequently, the labyrinth of literary *wu xia* fights is woven not so much with descriptions as with imaginative actions inherent with the naming of a unit of combat skills.

"Refining" the Action Image

The *wu xia* novels' popularity and movement association—newspapers often ran cartoon illustrations to accompany *wu xia* serializations—easily lent themselves to transference to celluloid images. *Wu xia* films were first made in Shanghai in the 1920s. Thus began the long process of the merging and interplay of the articulable aspect of *wu xia* culture with its visible dimension. Cinema and television conjure up the literary *wu xia* images based on their own logic as dictated by their technical development. For example, early Shanghai *wu xia* films employed extremely crude hand-drawn animation to depict flying weapons or palm power. Over time, the wildest elements of *wu xia*—such as duels between flying weapons controlled by the warriors' minds or inner energy—have been discarded in favor of a more kinetically realistic approach. Critic John Charles characterized Tsui Hark's *The Legend of the Zu Warriors* (1983) as a landmark in the history of "Chinese *fantasy* cinema" precisely because the film evokes the kind of action imagery, such as mind-controlled swords, anchored in *wu xia*'s *primitive* imagination.[4] Yuen Woo Ping's *Miracle Fighters* (1982), featuring freakish Taoist sorcery, such as two fighters with a conjoined body or a fighter whose body grows into a gigantic earthen jar, is another unique example of *wu xia*'s chaotic folksy imagination that seems almost too wacky for the genre's viability. However, such fantasy lies at the very origin of the *wu xia* films.

The genre's first important entry is reputed to be the *Burning of the Red Lotus Monastery* (Shichuan Zhang), made in 1928 and based on the novel *Legend of the Strange Heroes*, which spawned eighteen sequels in the following three years. Between 1928 and 1931, some 250 *wu xia* movies were produced in Shanghai, comprising 60 percent of the industry's total output. But the urge to protect the impressionable minds of young viewers as well as the official ideology of progress promulgated by the Republican government resulted in the passing of censorship codes in 1931, restricting works deemed to advocate superstition and the unreal. The demise of *wu xia* movies was exacerbated by the propagandist and "patriotic" films made as a reaction against the looming Japanese intrusion into China, which inevitably triggered the migration of film professionals into Hong Kong.[5] After World War II and the communist triumph in the mainland, *wu xia* film productions became entrenched in the British enclave, unmonitored by its colonial masters, thriving in its exilic and culturally peripheral status as lowbrow entertainment. (The consumption of *wu xia* literature and the consumption of *wu xia* movies were then parallel phenonomena, with only occasional exchange via "adaptations.") But until the late 1960s, most of the *wu xia* movies were very rough and basic by today's standards. They used rudimentary animation, reverse filming, and unsophisticated makeup and props.

Beginning in the late 1960s and the 1970s, the use of the trampoline was fine-tuned, enabling the staging of aerial fights, and a few action filmmakers paved the way for the international acceptance of the Chinese action image. Notable are John Woo's mentor, Chang Cheh, as well as King Hu, the first master of the genre, whose *A Touch of Zen* won a technical prize in Cannes in 1972. Chinese operas are always a combination of singing, stylish movement, and acrobatics. King Hu was the first important filmmaker to tap into the visual, theatrical, and acrobatic resources afforded by Peking opera for action choreography. The bamboo forest scene in King's *Zen*, analogous to the chase sequence in *The French Connection* (William Friedkin, 1971), remains the benchmark of Chinese *wu xia* filmmaking. (The scene's Oedipal shadow reaches as far as *Crouching Tiger* and Zhang Yimou's *House of Flying Daggers* (2004), both of which felt obliged to emulate *Zen* by shooting a fight scene in a bamboo grove.)

The first actor to bring Chinese action images to an international audience was Bruce Lee, a Chinese American actor-cum-martial-arts-master, who was so sick of Hollywood that he returned to Hong Kong to make his brand of action films in the 1970s. Some Western critics have classified Chinese martial arts films into two categories—the armed and the unarmed, swordplay and kung fu. And for them, Bruce Lee belongs to the kung fu, unarmed branch. Actually Lee also uses weapons occasionally, but his is the nakedly direct *visible* strand that showcases physicality, the hard-won virtuosity of great martial arts acrobats. After Lee's early death, his mantle was assumed by Jackie Chan in the 1980s and 1990s, and to a lesser degree by Jet Li.

The Lee-Chan-Li films are extremely actor and training focused. The camera is motivated to record the staging and thrilling execution of fantastic—but real and immediate—kinesthetic skills displayed by magnificent combatants. Critic Aaron Anderson, a practicing martial artist himself, has analyzed with relish the "rhythmic," "dance-like," "choreographic" aspects of Jackie Chan's staged fights.[6] One can see how the spectatorial pleasures associated with muscular sympathy served up by kung fu is akin to those connected with eminent athletes such as Michael Jordan and Michelle Kwan. Yet fighters of the caliber of Bruce Lee and Jackie Chan, while always in short supply, are in definite decline, as are action directors thoroughly steeped in the *visible* tradition of Chinese kung fu. Lau

Kar-leung, martial-arts-master-cum-veteran-filmmaker, whose *36th Chamber of Shao Lin* (1978) is a key creative source for *Kill Bill*, recently lamented the demise of "real" kung fu experience—the dissolution of the visceral fizz of earthbound *true* combat—in film. Sounding like an irate, grieving prophet, he berated fantastical flights and computer-generated imagery (CGI) effects.[7]

Yet, the "techno-action" films that Lau denounced have developed through the strand of the Chinese *wu xia* cinematic image that evolved through visually *articulable* techniques, notably complex wirework, trampoline-assisted movement, and editing procedures, that constitute an important legacy of Hong Kong action cinema. This is the strand, with its non–actor-specific adaptability and postmodern fluidity, that is exerting its impact transnationally. Are Lara Croft and Charlie's Angels (of the 2001 and 2003 movies directed by Simon West and McG, respectively) not Caucasian sisters of the *wu xia* woman warriors?

One can spot this non–kung fu, *wu xia* strand of filmmaking running from King Hu to *Crouching Tiger*. David Bordwell aptly pointed out that the creation of action sequences is based on the so-called constructive editing technique, along which visually *articulable* action images are fashioned through the choreographing of fights and camera movement, the development of the art of wirework—which allows more sustained horizontal flights and other stunts for the actors—as well as post-production tinkering such as slow motion and now CGI effects.[8] If these techniques allow for the fashioning of less actor-specific but still physically surreal action images, it does not mean that no physical skill is required of the cast. It is not surprising that the two big female action stars of the moment—Michelle Yeoh and Zhang Ziyi—both have dance training in their backgrounds. The end result is that this *wu xia* strand has freed the actors and the action team from having to be the best-trained kung fu practitioners.

Figure 12.1 *Wu xia*, Hollywood. *Crouching Tiger, Hidden Dragon* (Ang Lee, 2000).

Moreover, to emphasize the earthbound kung fu is to ignore the diverse models behind Hong Kong cinema's chiseling of action images. Hong Kong action films historically have been inspired by Japanese samurai flicks (Kurosawa and the cultish *Zatoichi: The Blind Swordsman* series), Sergio Leone's spaghetti Westerns, Sam Peckinpah, *The Star Wars* trilogy (George Lucas, 1977; Irvin Kershner, 1980; Richard Marquand, 1983), and other Hollywood sci-fi blockbusters—a testimony to Hong Kong action cinema's postmodern heritage. One of the key Hong Kong action choreographers, Yuen Woo Ping, is the creative force behind *Crouching Tiger*, *Kill Bill*, and *The Matrix*. And all three films are strategically located at the postmodern confluence of the Chinese action image—*Crouching Tiger*'s polish announced the fact that the Chinese action image has finally been streamlined and finessed enough for international consumption (no jarringly far-fetched palm power, freakish warriors, or mind-controlled flying weapons); *Kill Bill*'s incorporation of Chinese action image displays Tarrantino's unabashed embrace of transpacific pastiche and cool; and the Chinese action image lends exotic heroism and New Age–like fantasy to *The Matrix*'s envisioning of cyberdystopia and global redemption.

Wu Xia's Transition to Television

While cinematic trends come and go, *wu xia* films were for many years a major genre in Hong Kong cinema. (They were also a staple of Taiwan cinema in the 1970s, but few *wu xia* films were made in China during its decades of hard-line communist rule.) Before *wu xia* cinema gained international acceptance with Jackie Chan and *Crouching Tiger*, however, it had died essentially a local death in Hong Kong.

The demise of the Hong Kong film industry began some time in the mid-1990s. One major sign of exhaustion came from the tanking of so many martial arts films. Of course, one deleterious assault came from DVD/VCD piracy, which continues to sap the financial gains of local productions. (The annual output of the Hong Kong film industry has dropped from more than two hundred during its heyday to fewer than sixty in recent years.) Another assault was the brain drain of industry personnel—John Woo and Jackie Chan broke into the American markets around that time. That particular period also was seriously affected by the imminent Sino-British handover of Hong Kong in 1997, which caused much uneasiness among the middle class and professionals, who had the memory of the 1989 Tiananmen Square crackdown still fresh in their minds.

From the very beginning, *wu xia* culture has been a diversified phenomenon, even though the production of martial arts novels virtually came to a halt during the 1970s. As a literary subgenre, it largely exhausted its innovative potential, probably because of its heavily restraining formulaic nature. Some basic elements include the capturing of an all-powerful weapon, finding a master or manuscript that trains the hero into the greatest fighter so as to overcome a deadly villain and find love, while along the way some wrongs—often the murder of the hero's parents—are avenged, and some sinister plots—such as the enslavement of all the denizens of the Martial Grove—are foiled. But *wu xia* culture did not die—far from it—with the paucity of its literary or cinematic production. It saw its domestic, postmodern rebirth, or recycling, in its comic books, animation, and most important, its television incarnation, well into the twenty-first century.

As mentioned earlier, the *wu xia* image has gone through a kind of "normative" process, tied in with the technical development, or kinetic possibility, of action presentation on the movie screen. Yes, Stephen Chow's *Shao Lin Soccer* (2001) features palm power by a woman bun maker who comes to the rescue of a soccer team made up of a motley crew of Shao Lin followers in their final battle against the Evil Team. However, the staging of her palm power is anchored in tai chi, to which, alongside its New Age–like deified ability to control the flow of *chi* (breath or corporal energy), Western viewers have long been accustomed. Also, there are flying weapons in *House of Flying Daggers*, but the movements of those daggers are created with a view to convince, since they look like refitted boomerangs made of steel, which are quite different from the mind-controlled weaponry featured in *Zu Warriors* and the older *wu xia* movies. Another difficult-to-translate *wu xia* concept is *dian xue*—a skillful warrior can freeze somebody in midmotion if he can strike a certain point (*xue*) on that person's body—a fancy skill that seems vaguely connected to the principle of acupuncture. These archaic *wu xia* images (or imaginary) exhibit a more unruly brand of mind-over-matter fantasy, and they were deserted long ago in favor of the "rationalized" imaging of cinematic *wu xia* meant for export, or for an international audience, since these *wu xia* practices seem highly unconvincing for viewers unaccustomed to the convention. (One subtle, credibility-enhancing innovative touch Yuen brought to the choreographing of aerial flights in *Crouching Tiger* is to have the actors stopping occasionally to gain support before they make their otherworldly leaps, which would have been continuous, edit-constructed flights in previous films.) But such primitivism has largely stayed with Chinese *wu xia* televisuals in their untamed, unmodified, unreal, or irrational mode.

Hence, one can see that domestically, the advent of the *wu xia* action image has been experienced quite differently by the audiences of Greater China than by Western audiences. Part of the reason is that *wu xia* media culture has its roots in texts, and central to the martial arts novelistic imaginary are the fifteen books by Hong Kong author Jin Yong (which is a pen name for Louis Cha, or Zha Liangyong), who found a global Chinese audience after the softening of ideological control in the People's Republic of China (PRC), where his novels were once banned because of official suspicion that they were Mao, or simply political, satires. Today Jin Yong's novels have officially sold more than three hundred million copies worldwide, and more than one billion if one includes bootleg versions— presumably at one time privately owned presses in China gobbled all available paper to crank out Jin Yong novels so that no other books could be published for a while. Even Deng Xiaoping was an avowed fan. And if Jin Yong novels were a megahit phenomenon comparable to Harry Potter, they have also shown their staying power through their postmodern proliferation in various media. And there is no other better guarantee of continued visibility than multiple adaptations for television.

EPIC AND COUNTEREPIC

David Quint, in his book *Epic and Empire*, uncovered the imperialist ideology behind the epic poetry of Homer and Virgil. Alexander the Great supposedly carried a copy of the *Iliad* on his campaigns. And ancient Romans drew upon the *Aeneid* as their justification for imperialist expansion. Specifically, Quint examined the depiction of the Battle of Actium in the *Aeneid*, in which Virgil presents a civil war as a Roman battle against aliens—Augustus had to vanquish the Otherness of Antony and Cleopatra. According to Quint, epic belongs to the victor, since history is depicted as teleological and frozen in necessity. The victor's conquest, the crowning point of a purposive movement of people and events, is glorified by the epic, which in turn luxuriates in its literary mandate and capability of bestowing eternal fame on the "heroes" and their "heroic deeds." In opposing Augustus's triumph to the flight of Cleopatra, the *Aeneid* embodies the principle of epic poetry as well as the winner's history, which defeats time, and the feminized history, or the lack of it, of the East. Quint wrote, "Later epic poets found a normative narrative form embodied in the triumph of Augustus. *In Cleopatra's flight, by contrast, they saw a rival generic model of narrative organization.*"[9]

The emergence of *wu xia* novels as a literary subgenre and their subsequent media incarnations, we can argue, were more than expressions of mere nostalgia. They were, in fact, analogous to the flight of Cleopatra in the *Aeneid*. Here Cleopatra takes on the form of the Chinese psyche, which fled into the fantastical realm of the premodern to escape from the harsh, merciless epic of modernity and Western imperialism. Yet in the hands of Jin Yong, its foremost practitioner, *wu xia* literature was consolidated into a counterepic to rally the wounded pride of a depressed ancient civilization. Specifically, Jin Yong's *Condor Heroes* trilogy rein- scribes a fantastical literature into five centuries of Chinese history to spin a tale of restoring China's sovereignty through mythical combat. The continued popularity of these novels and their television adaptations has resulted in the feeling that Jin Yong's works have become "the only common language among the global Chinese." Following is a quick summary of the trilogy.

The Legend of the Condor Heroes (*Shè diao ying xióng zhuàn*), the first installment, was originally published in 1957. (Jin Yong has revised his novels twice—in the 1970s and 2000s.) It takes place at the end of South Song dynasty (mid-thirteenth century) when China was threatened by various nomadic kingdoms, including the Mongols. And while the novel's Chinese protagonist, Guo Jing, was raised in the great steppe of Mongolia, under the protection of Genghis Khan, he grew up to become a Chinese patriotic hero who turned against the great Mongol ruler, with whom he once went eagle hunting. (A literal translation of the title would be *The Legend of the Eagle-Shooting Heroes*.)

The Return of the Condor Heroes (*Shén diao xiá lu*), the second installment, published in 1959, was serialized for three years in *Ming Pao*, the newspaper that Jin Yong founded. This time the bildungsroman focuses on Yang Guo, the son of a traitor who was killed by Guo Jing's wife in the first installment. The goal of Yang Guo's Oedipal journey is threefold: (1) to become a superwarrior, as is the norm of the *wu xia* novel; (2) to overcome social prejudice so as to be reunited with his kung fu master, Xiaolongnü, a beautiful but older woman warrior; and (3) to overcome his hatred of Guo Jing, the original *Condor* hero, Yang's cultural father figure, so as to enter the Lacanian symbolic order, in other words, to become a patriotic hero worthy of the original condor-hunting hero.

As the action of *Return* unfolds, Guo Jing and his wife, with their uncontestable reputation and skill, rally hundreds of martial clans to defend Xiangyang, the last stronghold that stands in the Mongolians' way. At the end of the novel, Yang Guo and Guo Jing, two generations of condor heroes, join hands to repulse a Mongolian offensive against China. However, theirs was historically a lost cause; the Chinese Song dynasty would finally be conquered by the Mongols in 1279. So the final *Condor* installment, *The Heavenly Sword and the Dragon Saber* (*Yi tien tú lóng jì*), first serialized in 1961, leaps across four hundred years to find a setting at the end of the Yuan, which is now the Mongol, dynasty. In the novel, the legacy of the two *Condor* heroes enables the new protagonist, Zhang Wuji, to become not only a superwarrior, but also the head of the Chinese resistance Ming cult, which would overthrow the Yuan dynasty, ending the Mongolian occupation.

Naturally, Jin Yong's novels have been made into movies many times. The better-known iterations include Wong Kar-wai's *Ashes of Time* (1994), an idiocyncratic addendum to the *Condor Heroes* based on the biographical hints concerning two minor characters; and the Tsui Hark–produced, Ching Siu Tung–directed *Swordsman II* (1992), which is again an "unfaithful" adaptation that is known for its dazzling transgendered hero played by the screen diva Brigitte Lin, who cross-dresses to glamorize a self-castrated warrior in an *M. Butterfly* romance that is absent from the book. Given cinema's inherent difficulties in handling the longer novel form, the Jin Yong–based movies are mostly dehistoricized action spectacles. And it is not surprising that they have found a true home in miniseries. Since the mid-1970s, television producers have repeatedly mined Jin Yong's works for adaptation possibilities. According to a recent survey published by Hong Kong's *City Magazine*, seven of Jin Yong's fifteen novels have been made into serials (mostly thirty-plus hour-long episodes) a total of thirty-five times between 1976 and 2006.[10] While Hong Kong television tried its hand at *wu xia* serials early on and started adapting Jin Yong books, mainland Chinese television eventually joined the game and in time became a significant supplier of these and other programs to Hong Kong, Taiwan, and overseas Chinese communities due to the mainland's lower production costs. (Michael Curtin has pointed out that the cross-strait coproductions, starting in the 1990s, between Taiwan and mainland China favor historical drama—kung fu or otherwise—over more contemporary subject matter because of an easier, noncontroversial consensus embraced by a pan-Chinese audience.[11]) By now, the *Legends of the Condor Heroes* trilogy has been remade individually sixteen times within the past two decades, by Hong Kong, Taiwan, and PRC television corporations. (Because of the audience's familiarity with the trilogy, the remakes are not obliged to readapt all three novels into three serials consecutively, but are often produced as self-contained miniseries.)

BARDIC WU XIA

John Fiske and John Hartley, in their book, *Reading Television*, envisioned a bardic function for television because of its centrality to modern life. In this bardic role, "television functions as a social ritual, overriding individual distinctions, in which our culture engages in order to communicate with its collective self."[12]

The concept of the "bardic" posits it as a "mediator of language," which is able to negotiate among various linguistic resources, out of which "a series of structured messages" can be created to communicate to the members of that culture "a confirming, reinforcing version of themselves."[13] Over the past three decades, the bardic role of *wu xia* television, notably in its repeated transmitting of Jing Yong's *Condor* trilogy, has reinforced a consoling, uplifting counterepic narrative for a people from an ancient civilization exiled by modernity to the economic and cultural third world.

As I have pointed out earlier, the archaic imaginary of *wu xia* has been filtered out of its cinematic representation, which is geared toward a higher level of "rationality." Yet such "primitivism" remains largely intact in *wu xia*'s television incarnations. The conventions of literary imagination, even those of a subgenre, still determine the structure and plotline of a story. Rationalizing such conventions means undercutting the very foundation or identity of the cultural imaginary in question. Consider *dian xue*—freezing or immobilizing an opponent by striking a certain point on his or her body—as an example. One crucial episode in *The Return of the Condor Hero* concerns an accidental immobilizing of Xiaolongnü by a visiting warrior. While she is immobilized, her eyes are covered, so she has no idea that a man other than her student, Yang Guo, has taken sexual advantage of her. Yet when she is unfrozen by Yang Guo, she talks about becoming his wife (since premarital sex was not allowed in thirteenth-century China). This is the moment when their master-student relationship is transformed into a romantic one. Yet Yang's ignorance in regard to her hints about their sexual act infuriates Xiaolongnü, who ends up leaving her kung fu disciple in a huff, inaugurating the first in a series of separations between the lovers.

The absence of *dian xue* in any recent *wu xia* movie blockbuster reveals the producers' concern for global audiences' demand for "rational" consumption. But *dian xue*'s viability, or rationality, is never questioned in its televisual presentation. (There are factors of class and age here: cinema is created for paying audiences, whereas prime-time—dinnertime—television is seen by mostly nonpaying children and working-class and older audiences, who are more in tune with, or more accepting of, *wu xia* novels' domestic, fantasy-infested lowbrow origins.) At any rate, bardic kung fu television has reinforced the strange, unapologetic ticks of an ethnographic genre—akin to a carnivalesque make-believe—for more than three generations of Chinese audiences. The volumes in the *Condor* trilogy are not the only Jin Yong novels adapted for television, though the books are so popular that each of the *Condor* novels has been adapted more than five times in the past two and a half decades, each time a launching pad for a new generation of stars. Both Tony Leung (the key actor in Wong Kar-wai's films) and Andrew Lau (a Chinese superstar who found his long-overdue international debut in *House of the Flying Daggers*) received major boosts to their careers by playing Jin Yong heroes on television—Andrew Lau as Yang Guo in *Return*, and Tony Leung as Zhang Wuji, the protagonist of *Heavenly Sword*.

Fiske and Hartley emphasized the bardic voice as being oral, not literary, and not initiated by an individual communicator. They cited Roland Barthes's argument that the "author" is an invention of modern society, whereas in ethnographic societies, the transmission of narrative is conducted by a relator or a shaman, whose importance lies in his or her acting as a medium in brokering and channeling the languages of the collective.[14]

Jin Yong is certainly admired widely as an author in the modern sense. (He is also a remarkable former journalist and publisher whose levelheaded editorials earned him bomb threats as the Cultural Revolution's radicalism spilled onto the streets of Hong Kong in the late 1960s.) But his *wu xia* texts have become so diffusely appropriated, so thoroughly absorbed by modern Chinese culture, that they are achieving the status of collectively owned master texts that have been transmitted from print into the cyber/electronic circuits. To begin with, some of his fans disapprove of the revisions he brought to his own works. They embrace the earliest version of his novels rather than his personally revised versions, published in so-called definitive editions. The creative teams involved in the periodic television productions of his novels are participants in an intervallic revisioning of these narratives, drawing the audiences of various generations into a game in which they are invited to assess the adequacy of the latest cast as well as the merits of the latest production. Besides, the availability of these miniseries in their DVD forms has enabled the circulation of the miniseries as discreet linguistic-audiovisual fragments, not dissimilar to the functioning of the oral tradition, in the electronic village of global Chinese culture.

PRISTINE NATIONHOOD

In *Screening Culture, Viewing Politics*, Purnima Mankekar examined the effect of *Ramayan*, a hugely popular 1987 television miniseries based on the famous Hindu epic, on intensifying Hindu nationalism in India. Though refusing to draw a direct causal relationship between the success of the serial and the series of religious riots that broke out in India in the early 1990s, Mankekar did highlight *Ramayan*'s contribution to heightened hostility between the Hindu and Muslim communities. For her, *Ramayan* reified an ancient Indian/Hindu past, which is patriarchal, religious, and racialist. Such a selective view, she emphasized, "has to be recuperated from the alleged suppression of 'India' during 'Islamic invasions' and British colonial rule. . . . [T]he menace underlying the invocations of the 'glorious' Hindu/India past surfaced in the death chants of the Hindu mobs that ravaged northern India between December 1990 and 1993, in which Muslims were represented as descendants of the Moghul emperor Babar . . . and as foreigners who had to be exterminated in order for India to attain a pristine state of nationhood."[15]

Undoubtedly the "pristine state of nationhood" that Mankekar discussed carries with it a lethal purging spirit. The pristine state anchored in the heart of Jin Yong's works, as well as *wu xia* culture in general, is naturally occupied by Han Chinese. If such a racialist vision seems less touchy, less in need of being "recuperated," it is due to the fact that modern China, at least the mainland itself, though seriously humiliated, has not experienced wholesale colonial subjection as India did. Yet since the end of monarchy in 1911, the Chinese have rarely been mindful of the different outlooks harbored by the minorities within the nation. Probably, the racial others and minorities are not taken seriously because they have always *seemed* so quietly acculturated through the millennia. This vision of the unshakable Han Chinese's claim to nationhood is confirmed and reinforced in modern times by Jin Yong books and television. The Chinese father of Yang Guo, the protagonist of the *Return of the Condor Heroes*, is raised as a prince of Jin, a Central Asia minority kingdom that took over the northern part of China during the Southern Song dynasty (A.D. 1127–1279), though the Jins would be crushed by the Mongols during the latter's total sweep of China. Yang Guo's father is presented as a justly killed traitor for becoming enamored of his power and status within the Jin clan. And at the end of *Heavenly Sword*, the audience (or readers) are apprised of the imminent end of Mongolian rule. Yes, the barbarians have got to go and the collaborators must be killed. If no racist chanting mobs have ever been generated by these television serials, one can still argue that probably Jin Yong's works (as well as those by his eminent colleague Liang Yusheng) and their subsequent cinematic and televisual incarnations have created such a mythical, ethnocentric China that a sense of *exceptionalism*, not unlike that of the ideological function of the Western for America, has been surreptitiously inculcated into the Han Chinese.

The *Condor Heroes* books are counterepics for the Chinese against the West in an allegorical sense, but they are imperialist epic for China's domestic ethnic minorities in a more literal way. Is that why very little sympathy has been expressed by the Chinese toward Tibet, Inner Mongolia, and Xinjiang, three of the Chinese provinces, which have significant ethnic minority populations and are officially known as autonomous regions?[16] (And they are the largest, among the officially undercategorized fifty-five ethnic minorities in China, that dare, or find it worthwhile, to express their yearning for independence.) Tibet's cause, advanced by the Dalai Lama, Richard Gere, and other Hollywood celebrities, has enjoyed the highest exposure in the global media. But a lesser-known Pan-Mongolian movement—uniting Mongolia, Chinese Inner Mongolia, and Mongolian Buryatia in Russia—was put forward by the Mongolian Democratic Party in 1989. China seems to have been able to neutralize it by moving more Chinese into Inner Mongolia and creating economic ties with, even economic dependence for, Mongolia. Yet the Mongolian independence movement has not really gone away.

Xinjiang is the region mostly inhabited by the Uyghurs, a distinct, Turkic-speaking, Muslim minority in northwestern China and Central Asia. The Uyghurs declared a short-lived East Turkestan Republic in Xinjiang in the late 1940s but have remained under Beijing's control since 1949. Their separatist movement has been redefined as terrorism since 9/11, when China signed on to the United States' campaign against terror in order to conduct a domestic one of its own. Beijing has asserted that the East Turkestan Islamic Movement, as the separatist movement is known, has links to Osama bin Laden's Al-Qaeda. The little-known Uyghur struggle might have gained some attention over the release of five Uyghurs from Guantánamo in May 2006. (These Uyghur Chinese passport holders were not wanted by any country, including China, except Albania.) These simmering racial issues involving Mongolia and the Uyghurs are below the radar screen of not only the international community, but most Chinese, at home and abroad.

Steeped as the Chinese are in the rhetoric of anti-imperialist struggle, it rarely occurs to them that there are oppressed minorities within China itself. The Chinese vision of racial oppression has always been trained outward, obviously encouraged by the counterepic narrative of ethnocentric *wu xia* narratives. The ideological positions of *wu xia* narratives are nonetheless complex. They can even be considered "progressive." To be fair to Jin Yong's pacifist vision and sensitivity to racial politics, one must note that one of the main protagonists in his *Cycles of the Heavenly Dragon* (*Tien lóng ba bù*), a post-*Condor* novel published in 1963 that too has spawned several films and television serials, is Qiao Feng, a warrior of ethnic Khitan ancestry. (Khitan is yet another Central Asian minority group.) After Qiao's non-Han Chinese identity is uncovered, he rejoins his own kind, lamenting the bitter experience of cultural exile. He eventually brokers peace by forcing his own Khitan kingdom to withdraw from attacking the Chinese Song dynasty. But, torn by his bifurcated racial and cultural loyalties, he ends up taking his own life. In contrast to Qiao's tragic fate is Duan Yu, a peace-loving prince and the other ethnic protagonist in *Heavenly Dragon*. The book ends with him becoming the emperor of Dali, a town with great scenic and archeological beauty that still survives magnificently in Yunnan, China's southwest province with the largest number of ethnic groups.

If the racial politics in *wu xia* narratives are less than tolerant, one can argue that *wu xia* is, after all, a feminist-friendly genre that has produced the tradition of woman warriors. So the kind of stricture against women's participation in public life, as Lila Abu-Lughod has focused on in Egyptian serials, is not an issue in *wu xia* serials.[17] Huang Rong, the female protagonist of the first *Condor*, is more intelligent than her lover and later husband, Guo Jing. In *Return of the Condor Heroes*, even an intergenerational romance between a younger man and a older woman gets a nod, though the situation is soft-pedaled and normalized into a stereotypical heterosexual coupling in its details—because of Xiaolongnü's unique *chi kung* practice, this female kung fu master *looks* younger than Yang Guo, though the latter is actually younger than her by quite a few years; furthermore, Yang turns out to be a superior fighter, fulfilling the stereotypical expectation of the a strong, manly, shielding husband. (Even a woman warrior needs a stronger warrior to protect her!) Therefore, all the television adaptations have never taken seriously the master-disciple relationship on the age scale, namely that the female protagonist needs to be older than her male counterpart, in their casting decisions. Invariably, the serials solve the problem by casting a teenage version of Yang Guo when he first meets Xiaolongnü. A few episodes later, the adult Yang Guo is introduced to advance the romance in familiar grooves.

However, it must be noted that in Jin Yong novels and serials, potential racial tension is often resolved by romance, which is underlined by a naturalized power relationship between the sexes—the virgin leader of a Persian sect becomes a loyal and loving maid of Zhang Wuji in *Heavenly Sword*. Additionally, a Mongolian princess loves him so much that she risks her life to save him from her father, henceforth severing herself from her own race. In Jin Yong's mythical China, foreigners ("barbaric tribes") are either repulsed or assimilated through acculturation and seduction, in other words, romance and marriage. (Rape is too crude a means of conquest!) According to Fredric Jameson, the positional ("we" versus "they") notion of good and evil is a common characteristic shared by romance narrative, chanson de geste, and the American western. He wrote, "Such kinship suggests that this positional thinking has an intimate relationship to those historical periods sometimes designated as 'times of troubles,' in which central authority disappears and marauding bands of robbers and brigands range geographical immensities with impunity."[18] By plunging into historical periods of turmoil, *wu xia* novels and serials reaffirm the unchallenged morally superior, *good* position of the Han Chinese.

In Jin Yong's last novel, *The Deer and the Cauldron*, an atypical *wu xia* work that features more historical satire than martial arts, the Qing dynasty emperor Kangxi, though a non-Chinese Manchu, is recognized as an enlightened, benign despot who deserves the seat of power more than most Han Chinese emperors. Yet the story is told through his womanizing, "fake" eunuch Wei Xiaoboa—Tony Leung's breakthrough role in the 1984 miniseries; and a role Stephen Chow played with slapshtick abandon in *Royal Tramp*, the 1992 two-part movie (directed by Siu-Tung Ching and Jing Wong)—who returns, at the end of the novel/serial, to his mother, a harlot in a brothel of singsong girls, to inquire about the identify of his father. His mother cannot determine who among the many clients she entertained at the time was Wei's father—they included a Mongolian general, a Manchu official, a Muslim, even a Tibetan monk. Wei asks her whether any foreign *devil*, that is, Caucasian, had come her way then.

> "What kind of shameless slut do you take me for?!" came the angry retort. "Do it with one of them? With a big nose? Not on your life!! . . . If a single one of those great hairy Russians, or red-haired Dutch devils, had ever tried sneaking in here, I'd have booted them straight out the door!"
> Wei *heaved a sigh of relief*: "That's good."[19]

John Christopher Hamm observed in *Paper Swordsmen*, the first study of Jin Yong in English, that one of Jin's projects is to delineate "an essentialized and celebratory Chinese cultural identity."[20] In the scene described above, which basically marked the end of Jin Yong's career as a *wu xia* writer and has been reenacted four times between 1984 and 2000 on Chinese television, the *Chineseness* of one of Jin's best-known protagonists has, in a comic vein but with quiet violence, subsumed the identities of four major racial groups in China. (The idea of a hyphenated Chinese identity is still nonexistent today.) In the end, such a celebratory identity has to be defined, racially, as against the white man, the source of China's abject woes for a century and more.

According to Jameson's inquiry, romance, of which *wu xia* is a subgenre, contains within it a salvational perspective, or a yearning for a salvational future. There is a Marxist overtone in this idea of romance: "On this view, the oral tales of tribal society, the fairy tales that are the irrepressible voice and expression of the underclasses of the great systems of domination, adventure stories and melodrama, and the popular or mass culture of our own time are all syllables and broken fragments of some single immense story."[21] The irony is, though, that the *wu xia* culture that proliferated and in time suffused the global Chinese society took off at the doorsteps of an officially Marxist China that went to great lengths of self-laceration and flagellation. In retrospect, the "political unconscious" of *wu xia* culture, as formalized by Jin Yong, emerges as a narrative of an imaginary reversal of China's fortune, to liberate it from its subaltern status in global modernity. As experienced in television serials over the decades, such a narrative has become collective, charting the progress of the Pan-Chinese societies, partly manifesting through the growing sophistication of action images on television.

Television productions can rarely muster the kind of dedication and resources of cinema. (One famous example is the twenty-five days King Hu spent to shoot the thrilling bamboo forest combat scene in *A Touch of Zen*.[22]) *Wu xia* serials in the late 1970s relied mostly on slow-motion sequences for staged fights. Gradually, trampoline and suspension wire were introduced. Increasingly *wu xia* televisuals became more polished and ambitious. (Ching Siu Tung, one of the most important *wu xia* action choreographers and filmmakers, worked for Hong Kong television in the early 1980s, advancing the techniques of *wu xia* televisuals.) The most recent Chinese television remake of *Return of the Condor Heroes*, broadcast in China in spring of 2006, displays a post–*Crouching Tiger*, Hollywoodish epic cinema's scope and aspiration—with lavish sets and costumes, shot in stunning locations and incorporating sophisticated CGI effects. Yet, televisuals are also the index of a changing society. In this case, the *wu xia* televisuals are suffused with Hallmarkesque kitsch. Consider as an example Xiaolongnü's *dian xue* (immobolized) scene, understood to be the scene of her sexual initiation (though from the wrong man). A languorous Xiaolongnü is viewed, through a roseate filter, floating in an expansive, rippling lake—supposed to be symbolic—in a top shot. The immediate association is that of a commercial for soap, mattress, air-conditioning, or hygiene and pharmaceutical products. In short, the televisuals of the latest *wu xia* serials are a window into the onslaught of consumerism in a China with a rapidly growing middle class.

Wu Xia's Political Imaginary

Let us briefly turn to *The Heavenly Sword and the Dragon Saber* to discuss the political imaginary in Jin Yong books and serials, which, one can argue, lies at the heart of *wu xia* culture. Presumably there is a secret to the two powerful weapons in the title. Legend has it that "whoever who owns the Dragon Saber would be able to lead the world, and the only contestant to its leadership is the one with the Heavenly Sword." As it turns out, the two weapons, when striking at each other, can be broken. Hidden within the Dragon Saber is a manuscript of the best war tactics (*Wu-mu-yi-shu*) left by the late great Sung dynasty general Yue Fei. Whoever owns the manuscript will become the master of the art of war and, henceforth, the leader of the world. And hidden within the Heavenly Sword is *Jiu-ying-zhen-jin*, the most powerful martial arts manual, based on which one can train to become the world's deadliest fighter.

Undoubtedly, the paradigm as constituted by the Heavenly Sword and the Dragon Saber is also the political imaginary of premodernity: The balance of power in the world hinges on the relationship, or struggle, between the emperor and the assassin. The paradigm actually harks back to the mythical origin of the "visible" Chinese martial arts tradition as founded by the Shao Lin Temple, an enclave where fighters were reputedly trained to combat tyranny. Yet, the *wu xia* premodern paradigm, like it or not, has also survived into our postmodern world—because of the lack of a true democratic basis for the international community to resolve conflicts, as evinced by the awkward and often impotent maneuvering of the United Nations, one can easily revive *wu xia*'s naked paradigm of political struggle through that post-9/11 Baudrillardian lens: the balance of power is a tug of war between hegemony and terrorism.

While one can safely assume that these ever-popular Jin Yong novels and television serials have provided immense psychological resources to China's newfound confidence on the postmodern stage of global politics, recently one might have seen the tipping of the scales.

As discussed above, *wu xia* has been representative of a loser's reactive imaginary from the very beginning. Quint said, "[I]f the teleological epic narrative is directed to answering the question 'Who has won,' the absence of an organizing teleology proposes the answer 'Nobody wins,' which might be seen as a deep truth (or cliché) about the absurdity of war and history. The losers console themselves that in the long run empire is a no-win affair and that its conquests are bound to perish."[23]

The fact remains that most *wu xia* narratives—even Jin Yong's own besides the *Condor* trilogy—are remarkably episodic, lacking a teleological structure. Even with *Condor* itself, the third installment's triumphalist hint of the ousting of the Mongolians is tempered by the typical ending of many *wu xia* tales—the protagonist will retreat from *jianhu*, which literally means "rivers and lakes," but connotes the realm of combat, contest and struggle, that is, the realm of society and politics. To retreat from *jianhu* is to become a recluse because, yes, the hero has seen through the absurdity of war and history and strife.

While this fantasy "other" of retreat from *jianhu* rears its head at the end of many *wu xia* narratives, this could never be their propelling motor, which is about the process of acquiring supernatural power and fighting skills. Yet, among the intricate supernatural fights envisioned by *wu xia*, there is its Achilles' heel—a sensitive weak spot punctured by the Virgilian plot of imperialism, so to speak, by the fact that this ancient Central Kingdom, as it christened itself, was pried open by gunboat policy rather than diplomacy. Jin Yong and his generation, and indeed China's twentieth-century intelligentsia, all share the searing memory of Empress Dowager Cixi, in a stupendous fit of denial and indulgence, diverting 74.5 tons of silver, earmarked for naval construction, to pay for the rebuilding of the summer palace in order to celebrate her sixtieth birthday party in 1895. In fact, Cixi saw in the delusional valiant Boxers, a quasi–kung fu sect that proclaimed *their invulnerability to artillery and gunfire*, her hope of removing the imperialist threat. So she egged on the Boxers' anti-Westerner attacks by issuing defensive edicts over a chorus of protests from irate Western diplomats. The immediate destruction of those presumably ammunition-proof bodies was a symbolically significant sideshow in the towering defeat of China at the hands of the European eight-nation alliance, which stormed the Forbidden City in 1900. The self-destructive delusion of the Boxers, who are the Chinese equivalent of the Native American Ghost Dance warriors massacred at Wounded Knee, would always serve as a rude wakeup call for the mind-over-body *wu xia* fantasists.

Hence, for the longest time, despite all the fantastic power *wu xia* writers and media makers ascribe to their protagonists, a *wu xia* hero could never be Superman, meaning that he could not be *bulletproof*. (In 2006's post–Christopher Reeve *Superman Returns* (Bryan Singer), one scene highlights the man from Krypton's imperviousness to machine-gun fire. Even Superman's *eye* could crush a flying bullet.) As recently as Tsui Hark's *Once Upon a Time in China* series, made in the early to mid-1990s, gunfire weaponry, the stumbling block of the hardest edge of modernity to the Chinese psyche, is ranged tactfully at the border of the kung fu extravaganza inhabited by Jet Li's irrepressible Wong Fei Hung, who negotiates his way between rapacious Western colonists and the corrupt Qing court. The lethal punishment for kung fu's transgression against Western technology has been famously enshrined for his fans, in tragic grandeur reminiscent of a martyred third world revolutionary, in the ending frame of *Fist of Fury* (Wei Lo, 1972; known in America as *The Chinese Connection*), which shows the leaping, heroic pose of Bruce Lee frozen in midair, followed by the sound of a gunshot. As a branch of fantastic narrative, *wu xia* should theoretically allow for the most whimsical flight, so the curious question is, If the early cartoon illustration of *wu xia* novels can show a warrior, like a capeless Superman, flying through the air, why did the fantasy of repulsing gunshot seem such an unthinkable taboo? Was that a psychological threshold too paralyzing for the mind to cross? Maybe. But it is not anymore, since the threshold, after a century of *wu xia* adventure, was finally crossed in 2004: in Stephen Chow's *Kung Fu Hustle*, the audience sees the villainous warrior arrest, in close-up slow motion, a soaring bullet in midair.

Perhaps that long dance around the use of firearms denotes *wu xia*'s evasion not so much of modernity as of its own aesthetic parameter, which is its coitus interruptus, so to speak, in trying to prolong the spectatorial pleasure, the adrenaline rush delivered by the exhilarating exchange of blows. For wrestling and similar games to have sparks and fun, the organizers would have to always maintain a situation in which the opponents could never be too unequal in their prowess. Neglecting this rule probably accounts for the particularly joyless outcome of *Superman Returns*, in which Superman is either supercapable or totally vulnerable in his only hand-to-hand combat sequence with Kevin Spacey's Lex Luthor. The Man of Steel is constantly flexing his muscles, monomaniacally, as he performs various rescues—lifting various falling objects, including the broken top of the Daily Planet building and a crashing plane. The ultimate stunt at the end of the film features this one-man super–moving company lifting an entire continent into outer space. The audience may be awed, but never *thrilled*, by a mere display of digital spectacles that illustrate superprowess that seems so one-sided and lifeless when unperturbed by the friction of sparring.

Hence, the century-long banishment of flesh versus gunfire from *wu xia* probably amounted to preserving the indispensable "stupidity" of having only one ball in the soccer field for so many men to chase. Indeed when guns are used, they are distributed democratically, just like swords from *wu xia*'s arsenal, to equalize the prowess between contestants. Along that vein we see the advance of stylized gunfight action movies from Hong Kong, of which John Woo is the undisputed master. (The latest innovator in that genre is Johnny To, whose shopping mall shootout scene in *The Mission* [1999] is one for the books.) These gunfight flicks are *wu xia* films disguised in contemporary costumes. In fact, one of the bravura sequences in Woo's *A Better Tomorrow II* (1987), in which Chow Yun-fat keeps pulling his triggers as he slides down a staircase, was conceived by Ching Siu Tung, renowned *wu xia* choreographer and filmmaker of *Swordsman II* and *A Chinese Ghost Story* (1986) fame.[24]

While the scene of a naked hand arresting a bullet in *Kung Fu Hustle* can be viewed as an element in a postmodern hybridization of *wu xia* and sci-fi (Hong Kong meets Hollywood) fantasies, one can argue that *wu xia* imaginary's taming of Western weaponry is probably made possible by the trend that the Chinese action image is no longer experienced as a mere counterepic by the Chinese national ego. One prime example is Zhang Yimou's 2002 film *Hero*, which revisits the warring period of China during the second century B.C. The hero in this film should probably be understood as the first emperor of Chin, a notorious tyrant but now glorified by the film as the noble unifier of China, rather than Nameless, his suicidal assassin, played by Jet Li.

Quint noted that "[the Actium battle scene in *Aeneid*] suggests that only the autocratic princeps can hold together the Roman state and thus foster her empire. . . . [T]he very vastness of Rome's conquered territories . . . demanded consolidation both abroad and at home. Virgil's epic ideology is thus doubly 'imperial,' calling for both emperor and empire, as if neither could exist without this other."[25] One can too easily apply this epic ideology to *Hero*. Nameless, sent by other warring states about to be crushed by Chin to assassinate the tyrant, would rather have himself killed (and those states wiped out) than block the emperor's enterprise to unify "the world." It is hard not to see a parallel between the emperor and the only ruling party in China, which presides over a disgruntled rural population and restive minorities in one of the most ruthless, inhuman, mammoth capitalist transformations in recent decades.[26]

Maybe the PRC leadership is not unaware of one of the historical parallels mapped out by the *wu xia* imaginary—the Ming sect that ousted the Mongolians can be viewed as the suspicious historical predecessor of the persecuted Falun Gong, a cult with a kung fu component, which sneaked a protester into the White House during the visit of Hu Jintao, the Chinese president, in April 2006. According to CNN, the protester, appearing on the South Lawn, shouted in English, "President Bush, stop him from persecuting Falun Gong!" and though she was neither an assassin nor a suicide bomber, she also yelled, in Chinese, "Hu, your days are numbered."[27]

Kung fu battling bullets, *wu xia* allying itself with imperialist ideology—such changes underline the transformation of the Chinese action image from the imaginary of an underdog into that of a possible aggressor. The *wu xia* political imaginary now stands at a crossroads. A backward glance at its *articulable* genealogy would help us gain further perspective on its uneasy balance.

The term *wu xia* first appeared in 1903, three years after the fall of the Forbidden City, in the *New Fiction* journal, founded by Liang Qichao, one of China's most prominent intellectual reformers, who studied in Japan. Actually referring to a genre of popular Japanese fiction chronicling adventures and patriotic struggles (of Japanese against Russians, the face of Western imperialism then), the Japanese *wu xia* had become known to Chinese intellectuals admiring the island country's prescient efforts at modernization. Liang Qichao viewed specifically the Japanese samurai spirit with envy, thus emphasizing the relevance of martial arts to the Chinese civilization. His was a self-rallying cry in reaction as much to the docile Chinese body politic as to the Japanese mockery of the physical Chinese bodies corroded by opium.[28] (The Japanese called the Chinese, disdainfully, "the sick men of Asia" in the eighteenth and nineteenth centuries. This saying is notably unfurled on a banner in a scene from *Fist of Fury*, during which Bruce Lee, naturally, smashes that humiliating label.)

Strictly speaking, Japan has only "reawakened" or "reintroduced," though at a critical juncture, the concept of *wu xia* into China, a sign of the two entwining cultures' mutual influences over the millennium. In the Chinese language, only *wu* refers to martial arts; *xia* actually refers to the knight. The third-century-B.C. philosopher Hanfeizi first mentioned "the knights (*xia*) with their martial/military prowess (*wu*) trespassing prohibitions." Obviously, *xia* are warriors who use extralegal force to achieve certain ends that may not be in sync with the conventional, or legal, notion of goodness. China's first major historian, Sima Qian, whose life straddled the first and second centuries B.C., cited Hanfeizi's remark in the *Biographies of the Wandering Knights* (*Youxia lie zhuan*) section of his *Records of History* (*Shi ji*). Remarkably, Sima Qian also compiled biographies in *The Assassins*, in which swordsman Jing Ke's failed attempt at slaying the first emperor of Chin first appeared. This folklore about Jing Ke has been adapted into operas and movies many times; its most recent screen version, *The Emperor and the Assassin*, was adapted by Chen Kaige in 1998. Apparently the *xia*s in history could become casualties in their botched missions because of their less-than-perfect cool and command of martial arts skill. (Jing Ke's trembling hands alerted the emperor.) Regardless of these *xia*s' successes or failures, they had won Sima Qian's admiration, because "they had all determined upon their deeds. They were not false to their intentions. And they risked their lives." He continued with a rhetorical question: "Is it not right then, that their names be handed down to later ages?" Therefore, when Zhang Yimou replaced Jing Ke, a deified assassin in history books, with his fictional Nameless in *Hero*, Zhang was in fact challenging and revising the very historical precedent of Chinese *wu xia*, a gesture not unlike that of the official historians immediately following Sima Qian. Of course, the "reality" of Jing Ke is itself an open question, so Zhang's creative appropriation may be more complex, both aesthetically and ideologically, than the mere censuring of these wandering knights or assassins by post–Sima Qian historians, whose official role would make them eminently distrustful of these opinionated agents of societal and political change.

Maybe the political imaginary of *wu xia* is inherently unstable. What if the emperor co-opted the assassin? Or hegemony exploited terrorism in the name of national stability, self-defense, humanitarian intervention, or export of democracy? For a long time, in *wu xia* culture, a *xia* or a *dai xia*, a great knight, was idolized as a warrior with magnanimity, in the Aristotelian sense of moral superiority. In his recent *City Magazine* interview, Jin Yong repeated his own definition, which was first spelled out in his *Condor Heroes*, of *dai xia*—a great knight "who serves the nation and the people."[29] But for a China in the twenty-first century, with its decolonization completed in 1997 (the return of Hong Kong by Britain) and 1999 (the return of Macao by Portugal), with a buoyant mood of rapid economic expansion, and beckoned by the intoxicating dream of superpowerdom, how could and would the Chinese action image serve "the nation and the [Pan-Chinese] people" in postmodernity and a global capitalist system that multiplies the impact of cultural consumption as never before?

Recently, in *Iraq: The Borrowed Kettle*, Slavoj Žižek "bluntly" asked, "Do we want to live in a world in which the only choice is between the American civilization and the emerging Chinese authoritarian-capitalist one?"[30]

Žižek might have been a bit hysterical about China being the other—the non-American—face of transnational capital's transgressive globalization, but the symptomatic *wu xia* action image—literary, cinematic, and televisual—that has been accompanying China's survival in modernity and postmodernity is mutating—from domestically relished to internationally consumed, from defensively inward to offensively outward, from the dream of revitalization to the temptation of empire. How soon will it exhaust itself, surpass itself? (Chen Kaige's *The Promise* [2005] attempts, with mixed results, to steer *wu xia* in the new direction of postmodern, philosophical fable.) Has the Chinese action image arrived at its techno-aesthetic limit? (Lau Kar-leung's warning of the death of Chinese kung fu in the CGI-driven technovisual *Neverland* may not be so alarmist after all.) Has it reached a new level of ideological aggression? All these questions will be open, interesting, and at this moment, somewhat disturbing puzzles for both sociopolitical observers and media scholars to address in the coming years.

ACKNOWLEDGMENTS

My special thanks to Lynn Spigel, chair of the Radio/Television/Film Department at Northwestern University, for her advice and encouragement in the writing of this paper; to Robert Kolker for commissioning this piece; and to John Charles, Gina Marchetti, and Russell Freedman for their moral and critical support. I owe my knowledge of David Quint's *Epic and Empire* to Fredric Jameson's lecture "The Poetics of the Dialectic," delivered at Northwestern University in April 2006.

NOTES

1. Samuel Weber, *Return to Freud—Jacques Lacan's Dislocation of Psychoanalysis* (New York: Cambridge University Press, 1991), xi.

2. The formulation of "the visible" and "the articulable" comes not so much from Foucault as from Gilles Deleuze's reformulation as laid out in *Foucault* (Minneapolis: University of Minnesota Press, 1988). See the chapter "Strata or Historical Formations: The Visible and the Articulable (Knowledge)."

3. Other key *wu xia* novelists of the period include Liang Yusheng and Gu Long.

4. John Charles, *The Hong Kong Filmography, 1977–1997* (Jefferson, NC: McFarland, 2000), 1099.

5. David Desser, "The Kung Fu Craze: Hong Kong Cinema's First American Reception," in *The Cinema of Hong Kong—History Arts, Identity*, ed. Poshek Fu and David Desser (Cambridge: Cambridge University Press, 2000), 31.

6. See Aaron Anderson's "Kinesthesia in Martial Arts Films—Action in Motion," *Jump Cut*, no. 42 (December 1998), and "Violent Dances in Martial Arts Films," *Jump Cut*, no. 44 (Fall 2001).

7. "Interview with Lau Kar-leung—We Always Had *Kung Fu*," in *A Tribute to Action Choreographers*, ed. Li Cheuk To (Hong Kong: Hong Kong International Film Festival Society, 2006), 52–63.

8. David Bordwell, *Planet Hong Kong—Popular Cinema and the Art of Entertainment* (Cambridge, MA: Harvard University Press, 2000), 210.

9. David Quint, *Epic and Empire* (Princeton, NJ: Princeton University Press, 1992), 31 (emphasis mine).

10. "An Interview with Jin Yong," *City Magazine* (Hong Kong), June 2006, 146–155.

11. Michael Curtin, "From Kung Fu to Imperial Court—Chinese Historical Drama," in *Thinking Outside the Box—A Contemporary Television Genre Reader*, ed. Gary R. Edgerton and Brian G. Rose (Lexington: University Press of Kentucky, 2005), 293–313.

12. John Fiske and John Hartley, *Reading Television* (New York: Methuen, 1978), 85.

13. Ibid., 86.

14. Ibid.

15. Purnima Mankekar, *Screening Culture, Viewing Politics—An Ethnography of Television, Womanhood, and Nation* (Durham, NC: Duke University Press, 1999), 220.

16. The reaction among the ethnic Chinese to the widely publicized Tibetan protest in March of 2008 seems mostly hostile—accusing Tibetans of separatism—and xenophobic, complaining about the foreign media's bias against China and its attempts to undermine China's Olympic glory. See Jim Yardley, "Chinese Nationalism Fuels Tibet Crackdown," *New York Times* (March 31, 2008): 1.

17. Lila Abu-Lughod, "The Marriage of Feminism and Islamism in Egypt: Selective Repudiation as a Dynamic of Postcolonial Cultural Politics," in *The Anthropology of Globalization: A Reader*, ed. Jonathan Xavier Inda and Renato Rosaldo (Malden, MA: Blackwell, 2002).

18. Fredric Jameson, *The Political Unconscious: Narrative as a Socially Symbolic Act* (Ithaca, NY: Cornell University Press, 1981), 118.

19. Louis Cha, *The Deer and the Cauldron: The Third Book*, trans. and ed. John Minford with Rachel May (New York: Oxford University Press, 1997), 534 (emphasis mine).

20. John Christopher Hamm, *Paper Swordsmen—Jin Yong and the Modern Chinese Martial Arts Novel* (Honolulu: University of Hawaii Press, 2005), 79.

21. Jameson, *The Political Unconscious*, 105.

22. David Bordwell, "Richness Through Imperfection: King Hu and the Glimpse," in *The Cinema of Hong Kong—History Arts, Identity*, ed. Poshek Fu and David Desser (Cambridge: Cambridge University Press, 2000), 113.

23. Quint, *Epic and Empire*, 46.

24. "Interview with Ching Siu Tung—Wizard of Wire" in *A Tribute to Action Choreographers*, ed. Li Cheuk To (Hong Kong: Hong Kong International Film Festival Society, 2006), 96.

25. Quint, *Epic and Empire*, 27.

26. My discussion here is a comparison of only ideology, not artistic interest, between *Hero* and the *Aeneid*. For a more detailed discussion of *Hero* and Zhang Yimou's complex filmmaking career, see my essay, "Zhang Yimou's *Hero* and The Temptation of Fascism, Part Two of 'Chinese Cinema at the Millennium,' " which will be included in the forthcoming Temple University Anthology *Chinese Connections: Critical Perspectives on Film, Identity and Diaspora*, 2009.

27. See "Bush Apologizes to Hu for Protester," CNN, http://www.cnn.com/2006/POLITICS/04/20/bush.china/. Accessed March 21, 2008.

28. Okazaki Yumi, "*Wu xia* and Early Twentieth Century Japanese Adventure Romance," in *Jin Yong Novels and Twentieth Century Chinese Literature*, ed. Ming Ho (Hong Kong: Ming Ho Publishing, 2000), 211–226.

29. "An Interview with Jin Yong," 150.

30. Slavoj Žižek, *Iraq: The Borrowed Kettle* (New York: Verso, 2005), 32.

BIBLIOGRAPHY

Anderson, Aaron. "Kinesthesia in Martial Arts Films—Action in Motion." *Jump Cut*, no. 42 (December 1998).

———. "Violent Dances in Martial Arts Films." *Jump Cut*, no. 44 (Fall 2001).

Bordwell, David. *Planet Hong Kong—Popular Cinema and the Art of Entertainment*. Cambridge, MA: Harvard University Press, 2000.

Cha, Louis. *The Deer and the Cauldron: The Third Book*. Trans. and ed. John Minford with Rachel May. New York: Oxford University Press, 1997.

———. "An Interview." *City Magazine* (Hong Kong), June 2006.

Chan, Evans. "Zhang Yimou's *Hero* and The Temptation of Fascism, Part Two of 'Chinese Cinema at the Millennium.' " In *Chinese Connections: Critical Perspectives on Film, Identity and Diaspora*. Philadelphia: Temple Universtiy Press, forthcoming.

Charles, John. *The Hong Kong Filmography, 1977–1997*. Jefferson, NC: McFarland, 2000.

Deleuze, Gilles. *Foucault*. Minneapolis: University of Minnesota Press, 1988.

Edgerton, Gary R., and Brian G. Rose (eds.). *Thinking Outside the Box—A Contemporary Television Genre Reader*. Lexington: University Press of Kentucky, 2005.

Fiske, John, and John Hartley. *Reading Television*. New York: Methuen, 1978.

Fu, Poshek, and David Desser (eds.). *The Cinema of Hong Kong—History Arts, Identity*. Cambridge: Cambridge University Press, 2000.

Hamm, John Christopher. *Paper Swordsmen—Jin Yong and the Modern Chinese Martial Arts Novel*. Honolulu: University of Hawaii Press, 2005.

Inda, Jonathan Xavier, and Renato Rosaldo. *The Anthropology of Globalization: A Reader*. Malden, MA: Blackwell, 2002.

Jameson, Fredric. *The Political Unconscious: Narrative as a Socially Symbolic Act*. Ithaca, NY: Cornell University Press, 1981.

Li, Cheuk To. *A Tribute to Action Choreographers*. Hong Kong: Hong Kong International Film Festival Society, 2006.

Ming Ho. *Jin Yong Novels and Twentieth Century Chinese Literature*. Hong Kong: Ming Ho Publishing, 2000.

Mankekar, Purnima. *Screening Culture, Viewing Politics—An Ethnography of Television, Womanhood, and Nation*. Durham, NC: Duke University Press, 1999.

Quint, David. *Epic and Empire*. Princeton, NJ: Princeton University Press, 1992.

Weber, Samuel. *Return to Freud—Jacques Lacan's Dislocation of Psychoanalysis*. New York: Cambridge University Press, 1991.

Yardley, Jim. "Chinese Nationalism Fuels Tibet Crackdown." *New York Times* (March 31, 2008): 1.

Žižek, Slavoj. *Iraq: The Borrowed Kettle*. New York: Verso, 2005.

....

CHAPTER 13

WHEN CUTE BECOMES SCARY: THE YOUNG FEMALE IN CONTEMPORARY JAPANESE HORROR CINEMA

....

JOSEPH CHRISTOPHER SCHAUB

When Hideo Nakata's *Ringu* opened in Japanese movie theaters in 1998, no one could have predicted the enormous success it would have. It quickly became the top-grossing Japanese horror film of all time,[1] and inspired several foreign remakes and sequels, while effectively creating a new genre, which has come to be called J-horror. The conventions of the genre are, by now, widely known: creepy employment of communications technologies such as phones, televisions, cameras, VCRs, and computers; an emphasis on the infectious spread of evil; and most important, a young woman who becomes a monstrous killer. As a visual sign, this white-clad female ghost-killer with long stringy black hair has been especially effective at conjuring the fear and dread of the J-horror genre, which may explain why she is so often used to promote the DVDs, books, video games, and Web sites

391

Figure 13.1 Sadako (Rie Inou), the prototypical ghost killer of *Ringu*,
appears with long black hair and a white dress (Hideo Nakata, 1998).

that have become J-horror's numerous spin-off products.[2] Although the visual
roots of the female ghost undoubtedly go back centuries in Asian culture, there are
also antecedents of this particular image of femininity in the cultural products of
Japan's recent past, particularly in the cute, or "*kawaii*," style that exploded in
popularity during the height of the bubble economy in the 1980s.

At first glance, Sadako (Rie Inou) the stringy-haired antagonist of *Ringu*,
would seem to have little in common with Hello Kitty, Tuxedo Sam, Pikachu, or
any of the other smiling doe-eyed character-products of Japan's prolific and
transnational *kawaii* culture. In a thorough study of *kawaii*, Sharon Kinsella wrote,
"The essential anatomy of a cute cartoon character is small, soft, infantile, mam-
malian, round, insecure, helpless or bewildered."[3] Sadako is none of these. In fact,
she, like other various demon-women of J-horror, appears cold, wet, angular,
insectlike (in the movement of her limbs), dangerous, and utterly focused on
exacting revenge through murder. A comparison seems absurd. Yet, as several
scholars have noted, during the 1980s the human face of *kawaii* style became the
shôjo, or young Japanese female. Kinsella stated, "Young women were the main
generators of, and actors in, cute culture."[4] The question is, how and why did the
shôjo, the dominant signifier of cuteness in the late 1980s, become the dominant
signifier of J-horror in the late 1990s?

Initially, it is important to establish the context for the *kawaii* style and the
specific role played by the *shôjo* in the popular culture of the late 1980s to understand the changes that the *shôjo* image underwent in the J-horror depictions of
the late 1990s. Perhaps the best way to establish an overarching context for Japan in
the 1980s is to borrow the words of economist Akira Asada. It was the era of

"infantile capitalism."[5] In an essay published in 1989, Asada applied the term "infantile capitalism" specifically to Japan, differentiating it from the "adult" capitalism of the United States and England, and even further from the "elderly" capitalism of continental Europe. According to Asada, elderly capitalism is mercantile in origin, constrained by a transcendental value system, such as Catholicism, and dominated by vertically centralized subjects: "God, the King, the father, or, in economics, gold." Adult capitalism, by contrast, is far more dynamic and industrial, dominated by, "entrepreneurs who will invest values into the endless process of growth." Japan is relatively unique in that "there are neither tradition-oriented old people adhering to transcendental values nor inner-oriented adults who have internalized their values; instead the nearly purely relative (or relativistic) competition exhibited by other-oriented children provides the powerful driving force for capitalism. Let's call this infantile capitalism."[6]

Asada's notion of infantile capitalism is particularly relevant to a study of J-horror because Asada recognizes, as do the creators of the films I examine in this essay, the important role of the Japanese woman. In his analysis of the ideological mechanisms of infantile capitalism, Asada pointed out that "[d]espite frequent argument about Confucian patriarchy, the Japanese family is an essentially maternal arena of 'amae,' indulgence, and both the father and the children are softly wrapped in it (in other words, the mother is forced to provide that kind of care)."[7]

Asada's use of the term "amae" recalls Takeo Doi's famous theory, outlined in Amae no Kozo (translated as The Anatomy of Dependence).[8] For Doi, structures of amae, originating in the child's desire to be passively enveloped in its mother's love, permeate every level of Japanese society, from the incessant devotion a mother shows her family to the system of lifetime employment in Japanese corporations.

This tendency toward indulgence, passivity, and faith in the care of protectors—in short, the tendency toward childlike dependence—had been criticized in the immediate postwar years by prominent modernists such as Masao Murayama, who, according to Asada, believed that the evolution of a mature adult subject "that bears responsibility for himself . . . is the indispensable condition for Japan's modernization."[9] Asada, however, questioned whether Japan needs to mature into an adult phase of capitalism, or whether the infantile stage, "in a parody of Hegelian world history,"[10] is really the ultimate trajectory of global capitalism.

Certainly it was hard to argue with the success of this uniquely Japanese economic model in the late 1980s. By the end of the decade, Japan became "the world's largest creditor nation . . . and Japan's corporations bought electric companies, office buildings, and land throughout the world, with purchases in the United States stretching from Rockefeller Center in New York City to Pebble Beach Golf Course in California."[11]

In the logic of infantile capitalism, value begins to emanate from play rather than work, from software rather than hardware. Thus Sony purchased Columbia Pictures, and Matsushita bought MCA/Universal in the late 1980s as a way of securing entertainment media (software) for all of the VCRs, televisions, and stereos (hardware) those corporations had been selling for decades. This same logic leads to particular forms of indulgence at the consumer level that go far beyond acquiring a new washing machine or dishwasher to help with household chores. Just as Japanese corporations were buying global entertainment icons abroad, ordinary citizens were engaged in their own spending sprees at home, and *kawaii* style was the marketing masterstroke that encouraged them. *Kawaii* style became the dominant cultural expression of Japan's base of infantile capitalism.

Although products designed in the *kawaii* style first began to appear in the 1970s, *kawaii* reached its peak as a fashion craze during the 1980s, when cuteness raced across the media landscape like Mario across a Nintendo Game Boy screen. At first products such as stationery, clothing, and cute foods were marketed for particular consumers with greater disposable income and leisure time. "Cuteness loaned personality and a subjective presence to otherwise meaningless—and often literally useless—consumer goods, and in this way made them much more attractive to potential buyers."[12] As *kawaii* style caught on, cuteness became the emblem of the most inane household products, such as quilted toilet brush covers, and of widespread media images, such as Fuji Television's amateur talent show, *Yuyake nyan nyan* (Sunset kittens), hosted by schoolgirls with no specific talents.[13]

If *kawaii* was the dominant style of infantile capitalism, its dominant actors were the *shinjinrui*, or "new human species," as writer Tetsuya Chikushi dubbed the Generation X of Japan.[14] This was the generation born after the 1964 Tokyo Olympics, who had known nothing but economic prosperity in Japan. Their tendency to avoid hard work, to spend now rather than save for the future, and to pursue individual pleasure rather than the betterment of society prompted Chikushi to think of them as a new species, since their values seemed so different from those of the preceding generation, which had created Japan's postwar economic miracle. Media pundits also designated titles for the male and female variations of the new human species: *otaku* and *shôjo*. In terms of infantile capitalism, and the media-driven *kawaii* style, the *shôjo*—the cute, young Japanese girl—was clearly the more visible of the two.

There are probably many reasons why the *shôjo* became the human face of *kawaii* style. Certainly the traditional role of women as caretakers of the Japanese home contributed to the centrality of women's images in postwar print and broadcast media. Lise Skov and Brian Moeran wrote, in *Women, Media and Consumption in Japan*, "Women have been, and still are, key figures in Japan's consumer culture—not only because they are their country's greatest spenders, but also because they form a group which has been most carefully observed, analysed and defined in marketing discourses."[15] Since the dawn of the economic miracle in the 1950s, women had been used to advertise the products that women buy. By the mid-1980s, those products had changed from household necessities to luxury goods and services. The image that was needed to advertise this new class of products for self-indulgent consumption had to appear as far removed from the productive realm of work as possible. Young Japanese women were the obvious candidates to create the required representation to women themselves. Sharon Kinsella noted, "By virtue of their exclusion from most of the labor market, young women have occupied a relatively marginal position in society. Instead of devoting themselves to work, most young women have focused on spending their incomes from part-time and temporary employment on culture and leisure. During the 1980s in particular young women became the main consumers of culture."[16]

Clearly youth, and young women in particular, were the primary targets of advertisements employing the *shôjo*. What made the *shôjo* effective as a sign, however, was her distance from not only the productive sphere of work, but also the reproductive sphere of marriage and child raising. Susan Napier suggested that the *shôjo* makes such a perfect image for *kawaii* style because "the *shôjo* seems to signify the girl who never grows up . . . the perfect non-threatening female, the idealized daughter/younger sister whose femininity is essentially sexless."[17] This sexless femininity, the essence of *kawaii*, is what made the *shôjo* the signifier of the ideal consumer in the era of infantile capitalism. John Treat in his writings on the *shôjo* observed that "[t]he shôjo are, if you will, 'off the production line,' lacking any real referent in the 'economy' of postmodern Japan. Until they marry, and thus cease to be *shôjo*, they are relegated to pure play as pure sign. It is in the interim of their *shôjo* years that these young women (and the young men who increasingly resemble them) participate in a uniquely unproductive culture. They effectively signify sheer consumption."[18]

As the face of *kawaii* style, the *shôjo* dominated the Japanese pop-culture landscape during the 1980s and early 1990s. From pop idols like Matsuda Seiko, whose youthful looks and childish attitude landed her twenty-four straight number one singles in the decade,[19] to *Sailor Moon*, the highly successful animated TV series that Japan exported to Asia and the United States, *shôjo* were omnipresent, signifying a cute world of play and consumption where no one ever had to work, marry, or grow up. The *shôjo* was the master sign of *kawaii* style, and *kawaii* style was the dominant mode of Japan's infantile capitalism.

When the bubble burst, however, there was bound to be a backlash. And it did burst when Japan "went into recession in 1991, halting growth in 1992 and registering only small increases over the next three years. This combined with political turmoil, produced a mood of profound pessimism in Japan."[20] The voice of pessimism had always been apparent as a counterhegemonic response to the cuteness of *kawaii*. For example, Akira Asada's discussion of infantile capitalism described Japan as "a playful utopia and at the same time a terrible 'dystopia.' "[21] During the 1980s, the dystopic elements may have been visible in the margins of popular culture,[22] but in the mainstream, where *kawaii* was so closely associated with consumption, these dystopic elements would not surface until the 1990s. The longer the recession lasted, the more apparent it was that infantile capitalism was not the teleological promised land of some larger global capitalist project, but an intractable never-never land along the way. As the flaws of infantile capitalism became more visible, the critics of *kawaii* style, its conspicuous expression, became more vocal. Sharon Kinsella stated, "Anti-cute people can be divided into two social categories: young people who considered cute to be too weak and stupid, and conservative intellectuals in the academia and civil service who were appalled by the spread of new female-led youth culture."[23]

The growing criticism directed at the excessive consumption of infantile capitalism, and indignation at the marketing of *kawaii* style, found resonance in older mainstream Japanese values, in which personal consumption is considered antisocial and immoral.[24]

In addition to the recession in the early 1990s, Japan endured a string of calamities in the mid-1990s. The Kobe earthquake in January of 1995 was quickly followed by the Tokyo subway terrorism of the Aum Shinrikyo cult in March of that year. The arrest of a fourteen-year-old boy serial killer in 1997[25] only added to the utter inappropriateness of *kawaii* style in this new, uncertain era. Inevitably, Japan's recession and domestic tragedies affected the reception of the *shôjo* as a signifier, as well. At the height of *kawaii* style in the late 1980s, the *shôjo* signified consumption, utterly removed from the productive, and perhaps more significantly, reproductive, spheres of the Japanese economy, and these characteristics connotatively suggested play, endless youth, and frivolous enjoyment. However, as Akira Asada reminded us, "children can play freely only where there is some kind of protection. They always play within a certain protected area,"[26] and it is the maternal presence that provides this protected space. In the uncertain atmosphere of the mid-1990s, the *shôjo*, "the girl who never grows up," began to connote the mother who never arrives, and consequently the loss of protected space. It is in this capacity that the *shôjo* functions as a sign in the discourse of J-horror. Furthermore, characteristics of the *shôjo* that had been repressed in the 1980s came to the fore in the new anxious climate of the 1990s. As a signifier, the *shôjo* has always had an inherent tendency toward marginal identities. Susan Napier explained that "one of the most interesting trends in comics in the 1980s has been the association of women or girls and the occult."[27] In the decade following the euphoria of infantile capitalism, this marginalized expression of *shôjo* signification would gradually achieve dominance.

In the remainder of this essay, I closely examine the role of the *shôjo* in three iconic films of the J-horror genre: *Ringu*, *Audition* (Takashi Miike, 1999), and *Ju-on* (Takashi Shimizu, 2003).[28] J-horror's appearance on the heels of *kawaii* is an outgrowth of the pessimism and anxiety accompanying the economic and cultural changes affecting Japan in the late 1990s. Many scholars have noted the increased popularity of horror films during times of social upheaval, and one need only look to the numerous radioactive monster movies, beginning with *Gojira* (*Godzilla*, Ishiro Honda, 1954) to see this principle at work in Japan during the days of nuclear weapons testing in the Pacific. J-horror signals a similar period of cultural anxiety, but where the nuclear testing that brought Godzilla to the shores of Japan was externally caused by the United States and Soviet Union, the J-horror *shôjo* is a homegrown monster.

To some extent, then, these films return what was repressed by the *kawaii* images circulating during Japan's days of infantile capitalism. Where *kawaii* style employed the master sign of the *shôjo* to signal the joy of self-indulgent consumption, J-horror employs it to trigger deep-felt anxieties, surrounding not only self-indulgence, but also the loss of productive and reproductive potential that pure consumption represents. Each of these films presents a unique depiction of the *shôjo* to highlight a specific anxiety lying just beneath the surface of the Japanese cultural imaginary. However, the global notoriety that these films have received (which includes Hollywood remakes in the case of *Ringu* and *Ju-on*) suggests that these anxieties are in no way exclusively Japanese—or at least easily exploitable in the West. As a genre, J-horror seems tailor-made for a phase of late capitalism that is anything but infantile or cute.

RINGU

The film that triggered the J-horror boom, *Ringu*, also possesses one of the genre's most compelling plots. After the mysterious death of her niece and three other high school students, investigative reporter Reiko Asakawa (Nanako Matsushima) travels to an inn where the four students lodged a week before their deaths, and finds a strange videotape there. She watches the tape, immediately receives a disturbing phone call, and realizes that she too will die in seven days unless she solves its mystery. With the help of her ex-husband, Ryuji (Hiroyuki Sanada), she uncovers the murder of a psychic girl named Sadako, who was thrown into a well more than thirty years before. Just before Reiko's week is up, they find Sadako's body at the base of a well and report the incident to the police, but the next day Ryuji, who viewed the tape one day after Reiko, dies in the same way as the high school students. At this point Reiko realizes that it was not the mystery of her death that Sadako wants resolved, but the spreading of her curse through the video. Only those who copy it and show someone else, as Reiko did, will be spared.

Although *Ringu* is based on the novel *The Ring*, by Koji Suzuki, screenwriter Hiroshi Takahashi, in collaboration with director Nakata, made several important changes in the film. The first was in making the main character female, rather than male, as in the novel.[29] Thus protagonist and antagonist are *shôjo* in this film. Also, Ryuji, who is a high school friend of the main character in the novel, becomes Reiko's ex-husband in the film and the father of her son, Yoichi (Rikiya Otaka).

These changes place a fractured family at the center of the narrative, and a female character at the center of that family. The reason for Reiko and Ryuji's divorce is never made clear in the film. The fact that Reiko calls upon Ryuji to help her suggests that they are still close, and yet Ryuji does not seem to have any involvement with their son. There are no scenes of the three family members together, and in the only scene where Ryuji encounters Yoichi, there appears to be something verging on hostility between them. They pass on the street in the rain, both carrying umbrellas. They both stop for a moment; then Yoichi walks around his father without any greeting.

It is also clear that Reiko's career as an investigative reporter makes it difficult for her to properly care for Yoichi. In a later scene, Ryuji and Reiko are trying to decode the video at her TV station. Ryuji asks if Yoichi is okay at home by himself, and Reiko replies, "He's used to it." There is a subtext of neglect throughout the film concerning Yoichi. When we first see him, he is waiting alone for Reiko to return from work. He wanders off repeatedly, and, although only a first grader, walks himself to school, and waits for his mother in their apartment afterward until she returns late at night. Although Reiko knows that whoever watches the video will die in seven days, she carelessly leaves it where Yoichi can view it. Another scene suggests that Reiko must choose between Ryuji, her husband, and Yoichi, her son. When Ryuji identifies the dialect on the tape as originating in Oshima, he tells Reiko that he will go there and that she should "please stay with Yoichi." But she does not. Instead, she takes Yoichi to her father's and goes with Ryuji to Oshima. Scenes such as this project Reiko as a young woman who is ambivalent about her role as a wife and mother. In this sense she has much in common with the typical *shôjo*, who, "since the 1990s . . . simply began to reject marriage and childbearing and no longer considered the role of wife and mother as an attractive option."[30] Reiko, as long as she can have her career, also seems to want her husband (although he is her ex) and her child. But the horror in this film emanates from the impossibility of keeping all three. As in other Hideo Nakata films, the option that becomes most horrifying is the possibility that she will lose her child through her own neglect.[31]

Reiko's drive to save Yoichi makes her an interesting foil to Sadako. Since she was pushed into the well as a teenager, marriage and family were never an option for Sadako. While most *kaidan*, or Japanese ghost stories, involve a revenge motif in which the ghost haunts the person who has committed the murder or wronged the ghost in some way,[32] revenge is not what motivates Sadako. Reiko and Ryuji believe they can appease Sadako by discovering her body in the well, revealing her murderer, and giving her a proper burial. Ironically, the scene in which Reiko appears most maternal occurs when she embraces Sadako's corpse at the bottom of the well. This happens just at the point when her week is up and she should be killed by Sadako, but instead, the maternal, yet macabre, image leads us to believe that Sadako has been appeased. This scene makes Ryuji's death the following day that much more disturbing. After what appears to be the denouement, when Reiko

Figure 13.2 Sadako crawls out of the television set at the end of *Ringu*.

and Ryuji have again split up and Ryuji is working on an article he must complete, he hears the TV turn itself on, and Sadako not only violates the boundary between the living and the dead, but also the boundary between reality and representation, by crawling out of the TV screen. It is the first time we see Sadako in the diegetic world of the film, and for that reason, she is especially frightening.[33] When Ryuji is killed by Sadako, Reiko must figure out what the real motive is behind Sadako's curse in order to save her son.

While asking herself what she did that was different from what Ryuji did, Reiko sees a vision of a man pointing to a videotape. She picks it up, reads the word "COPY" in English on the label, and realizes that Sadako's motivation is the same as hers: she wants to reproduce. The difference between the two is that Reiko has chosen the socially sanctioned path by getting married and having a son. In the beginning of the film she is ambivalent about this choice, since her son seems to have cost her the marriage. By the time we see Reiko embracing Sadako's corpse at the bottom of the well, she has resigned herself to the role of mother, however unpleasant that role may be at times. Sadako, by contrast, has been cut off from the possibility of biological reproduction, and is forced to reproduce her curse mechanically. In a clever inversion of the process of biological reproduction, by which a new life is created through an interaction, in *Ringu* when someone encounters Sadako on tape and fails to reproduce the tape for someone else, a life is taken.[34]

Ringu has often been lauded for its ability to create dread and terror without resorting to blood, gore, or cheap shock tactics. Neither does *Ringu* make overt reference to what comprises the backdrop for its horror effect. In the 1990s, Japan's falling birthrate became a matter of serious concern for politicians and civic leaders. Japan has one of the lowest birthrates in the world, and unlike the United

States and other Western nations, does not have high rates of immigration to balance it out. "The trend threatens to leave Japan with a labor shortage, erode the country's tax base and strain the pension system as fewer tax-payers support an expanding elderly population."[35] The backdrop, then, for *Ringu*'s horror is cultural anxieties about a declining population, so pervasive that the Japanese coined a new word to describe them: "*shoshika*, a childless society."[36] This fear is perhaps the oldest and most deeply embedded a society can experience, the threat of cultural extinction. In the foreground, *Ringu* presents us with two *shôjo*: Sadako, who represents a horrific extreme of the late 1980s *kawaii* consumer—consuming lives without reproducing new ones—and Reiko, who comes to realize that her son is the most important thing in her life. Although the shattered family is not made whole by this realization, it shows the possibility of reforming priorities. The next film I examine also deals with a shattered family. The anxieties that it conjures stem from the dangerous pursuit of private pleasure.

AUDITION

Based on a novel by Ryu Murakami, and adapted by Daisuke Tengan, *Audition* begins with the death of the wife of the main character, Aoyama (Ryo Ishibashi). Seven years pass, and Aoyama's son, Shigehiko (Tetsu Sawaki), now a high school student, suggests that Aoyama should get married again, because he is beginning to look old. After discussing it with fellow producer, Yoshikawa (Jun Kunimura), Aoyama realizes that he would like to see many women and choose the one he likes best from among them. Yoshikawa suggests that they hold an audition for a movie they do not actually intend to produce. Against Yoshikawa's advice, Aoyama chooses Asami (Eihi Shiina), a former ballet dancer with a mysterious past. He calls her and they begin to date. Then, after a weekend getaway, during which Aoyama plans to propose, Asami disappears, only to reappear several days later to drug, torture, and dismember Aoyama. He is saved from probable death only when his son returns and, after being attacked by Asami, kicks her down a flight of steps, breaking her neck.

Audition differs from the typical *kaidan*-based movie in that the terrifying female character is not a ghost. Nevertheless, she is a *shôjo* (only twenty-four years old), and iconographically similar to Sadako in *Ringu*. When we first see Asami at the audition, she is dressed all in white, demurely bowing her head, prominently displaying her long black hair. She is most consistent with the image of the *kowai* (scary) *shôjo* when she stands on a balcony at the hotel where she and Aoyama are staying during their weekend away. Seen from behind, dressed in white, with her long black hair hanging down in the wind, she looks every inch the ghost-killer. There is also something evil about Asami that other characters, such as Yoshikawa, immediately pick up on, and she seems to have some supernatural, psychic abilities, as when Aoyama, after a hiatus of several days, finally calls her. In one of the film's most chilling moments, an extreme close-up of Asami's profile shows her long black hair covering everything but her lips, which slowly stretch into a smile as the phone rings. This marks a departure in the film that, until this point, had been shot at a disarmingly slow pace. With its many scenes depicting Aoyama alone in his study, quietly doing dishes, awake in his bed, and seated in his lounge chair, the first half of *Audition* suggests that we are watching a middle-class melodrama in which melancholy loneliness seems to be the most prominent feature. In the second half of the film, expressionistic lighting, editing, camera angles, and sound replace the melancholy loneliness of the first half with abject terror.

A fatalistic reading of *Audition* would suggest that there is no solution to the loneliness and solitude of its characters, since the attempt to remedy loneliness and solitude ends so horribly. Such a reading ignores, however, both the underlying causes of the characters' isolation and the flaws in their attempts to provide solutions for it. Early in the film, an editor helping Aoyama with a crowd scene states that loneliness is the main problem in Japan. He then turns to look at Aoyama, asking, "You too, right?" Although Aoyama is lonely, he is not completely alone after his wife's death. He and his son, Shigehiko, seem to get along amicably enough. We see them enjoying fishing and meals together. The real problem seems to be Aoyama's retreat into a particular kind of private self-indulgence that came to be associated with the *shinjinrui*, the new human species, in the 1990s. The particular type of dangerous individualism (or *kojinshugi*) that Aoyama adopts, a retreat into personal, self-centered pleasures, was widely criticized in the mid-1990s, when "social scientists suggested that the spread of youth culture and individualism through the media had produced a generation characterized by increasingly particularistic and narrow interests. Not only were youth resistant to entering society as mature adults, to becoming *shakaijin* (social citizens), but, it was observed, they had begun to lose all consciousness of affairs beyond their private hobbies."[37] Visually, Aoyama's individualism is conveyed through numerous shots of him working alone, in contrast to the group of employees who work with him. When he is not working, he is often seen seated alone, enjoying his decanter of whisky. The decanter later becomes a powerful symbol for the dangers of private self-indulgence, because it is what Asami uses to drug Aoyama before torturing and dismembering him. Nowhere is Aoyama's private self-indulgence more clearly seen than in his attempt to find a marriage partner.

It is initially worth noting that Aoyama is not seeking to get married because of his loneliness, but because his son suggested he was looking "old." A wife, then, is something he lacks, something without which he will grow older. To solve the problem, he takes the path that the era of infantile capitalism so strongly encouraged. He approaches marriage like a consumer. He wants to get the best, and the audition makes it possible for him to do so. Just before the audition, when Aoyama is looking over the applications, he tells Yoshikawa, with a mix of elation and frustration, "I don't know what I'm supposed to do. It's like buying my first car." Yoshikawa quips back, "Don't mix your car and your wife." It is, of course, too late for that. The premise of the audition has not only objectified the women who participate, but turned the process of finding a mate into a pursuit of private personal pleasure for Aoyama, like buying a first car.

Once Aoyama has decided on the object of his desires, Asami, his pursuit becomes more private, and therefore more dangerous. In numerous instances, he ignores his friends and family when they try to warn him about Asami. Following the audition, Aoyama's friend Yoshikawa suspects he has already made up his mind about Asami, and asks him to wait until he checks her out, telling him, "There's something wrong with her." Aoyama goes against his friend's advice and calls Asami that night. The same thing happens when Shigehiko asks his father to let him "take a look at her first," after Aoyama tells him he is going to propose. Again, Aoyama ignores the request. When Asami disappears after the weekend getaway, Aoyama tries to enlist Yoshikawa's help. Instead, Yoshikawa urges Aoyama to forget about her, but Aoyama vows to find Asami on his own. Even Aoyama's dead wife appears to him in dreams, telling him, "She's not right for you." Everyone, apart from Aoyama, senses that there is something wrong with his attraction to Asami, but he continues to pursue her regardless, like an addict gradually alienating anyone who could help him.

Aoyama's fate is foreshadowed in the scene immediately following the aforementioned close-up smile that we see Asami give when she knows Aoyama is calling. In what is this film's only typical horror-movie shock moment, we see a large canvas bag that had been in the background of Asami's small, sparsely furnished room suddenly jump up with a roar. Later, in what is apparently a dream sequence that Aoyama experiences after being drugged by Asami, we see that inside the bag is a man whose legs and tongue and several of whose fingers have been amputated. He is forced to eat the vomit that Asami regurgitates for him in a small dog bowl. We are led to believe that this character is Shibata (Ren Osugi), a record company executive that Yoshikawa, checking on Asami's references, had found had been missing for more than a year. Shibata's fate points to an extreme example of the dangers of *kojinshugi*. His world is confined to the canvas bag from which he occasionally escapes to be fed by Asami. The most horrifying aspect for Aoyama is that Shibata appears content with his fate, happily slurping up vomit as Asami gently pets him in a grotesque caricature of consumption and private self-indulgence.

Asami, as the agent of terror, is perhaps the most frightening *shôjo* of the three treated in this study. Her unique combination of *kawaii* demeanor and *kowai* intentions parallels *Audition*'s initial stylistic flirtation with melodrama followed

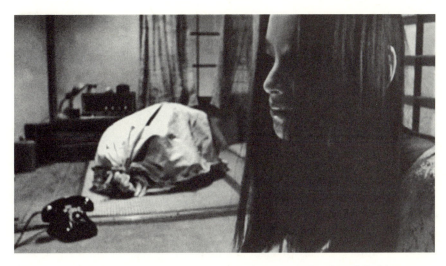

Figure 13.3 The sparsely furnished room of Asami (Eihi Shiina) holds some terrifying secrets in *Audition* (Takashi Miike, 1999).

by its rapid descent into horror. Her beauty and youth, along with her love of ballet, attract Aoyama at first, but gradually her more personal revelations (having to give up ballet due to an injury, and incidents of childhood abuse) convince him that he alone can appreciate her inner qualities. Asami also encourages, indeed demands, Aoyama's private devotion to her. During their weekend getaway she makes Aoyama promise that he will love only her. He agrees, not realizing how seriously she means, "only her." When Asami breaks into Aoyama's house and discovers that he had a wife and has a son, she sees it as a breach of his promise, and decides to take her revenge. While torturing Aoyama with acupuncture needles, she quietly, almost affectionately, reminds him of his promise to love only her. The contrast between her smiling exterior, cutely repeating *"kiri, kiri, kiri"* ("deeper, deeper, deeper") in the voice of a *kawaii shôjo*, while driving needles into Aoyama is what many viewers find so shocking about this film.

Audition has been called both feminist and misogynist. For those who see the film as feminist, Asami's torture of Aoyama is revenge for the humiliating objectification of the audition. The misogynist view sees Asami as a monstrous parody of the feminist avenger. For his part, Takashi Miike has stated that the film is neither a feminist treatise nor a misogynist attack.[38] While the film clearly implies that objectifying women through a fraudulent audition is wrong, it is interesting that Yoshikawa, who thought up the idea for an audition in the first place, is not the one who is punished for it. Instead the critique seems squarely aimed at the infantile practices that arose in the previous decade. Aoyama is punished for approaching marriage like buying a new car, and for placing his individual desires above those of his family and friends. Ultimately, *Audition* shows the terrors of a self-indulgent retreat of infantile consumers into a world of their own private pleasure.

JU-ON

Of the three films discussed in this essay, *Ju-on* is the most traditional horror movie, in terms of its basic story: the ghosts of a murdered family haunt a house, then frighten and kill anyone who comes into the house. Yet it is also the most experimental in the form that its narrative takes. The plot eschews chronology in favor of a nonlinear series of vignettes named after characters who come into contact with the house. *Ju-on* begins with an epigraph that reads: "*Ju-on*, the curse of one who dies in the grip of a powerful rage. It gathers and takes effect in the places where that person was alive. Those who encounter it die, and a new curse is born."

Following this, there is a brief montage of quick, harrowing shots: blood on cellophane, an extreme close-up of a man biting his nails, a woman's face showing just her left eye, a streak of blood running from her left temple, a small boy drawing, then crouching in a closet as if to hide, and a man's hand grabbing a cat by the neck and pulling it out of frame as it meows violently. Later we learn that this entire family died when the father went on a murderous rampage. This opening montage gives us the history of the house's curse. It also introduces us to the ghosts: Taeko Saeki (Takashi Matsuyama); his wife, Kayako (Takako Fuji); and their son, Toshio (Yuya Ozeki). The most important, and lethal, of the ghosts is Kayako, the murdered wife. Like Sadako in *Ringu* and Asami in *Audition*, Kayako is a young woman, twenty-eight at the time of her death. But unlike the other two killer women, Kayako is married and has a child. Technically, as a married woman, Kayako is no longer a *shôjo*, but her inability to leave her *shôjo*-hood behind seems to be the primary source of her rage.

There are six vignettes in *Ju-on*, each focusing on a particular character, but with no chronological connection linking them. For example, the second sequence, entitled "Katsuya," takes place the day before the first vignette, entitled "Rika," and the "Izumi" sequence takes place five years in the future. While this appears to be a thwarting of narrative convention, there is actually an established tradition for nonlinear plot presentation in Asian ghost narratives that employ the revenge motif. In her study of spectral time in ghost films, Bliss Cua Lim pointed out that "the ghost narrative has a tendency to transgress the principles of narrative linearity without becoming antinarrative (as in avant-garde and experimental films). Its fragmentation of time still lies within the purview of the spectator's narrative engagement, because the narrative (which conventionally follows the actions of a character) is merely tracing the movements of a ghost, yet in so doing follows her cyclical, spectral temporality, one that departs from linear narrative time."[39]

The disjuncture of traditional narrative temporality is one of the most disturbing characteristics of *Ju-on*, since it forces the viewer to experience the narrative from the standpoint of the ghost-killer. In her landmark study of slasher films, Carol Clover stated that one of the key features of that genre is the tendency to place the audience in the position of the stalker-killer by using subjective point-of-view shots.[40] In *Ju-on*, Takashi Shimizu has done something similar by getting his audience to experience time as the ghost perceives it, without linear continuity. The effect of this temporal identification is to get the audience to focus on the story of Kayako, the murdered wife. Although Toshio, Kayako's son, has, arguably, as much screen time as Kayako, her story is clearly the dominant one. Kayako is the only one of the three ghosts we actually see engaged in killing, and the only member of the murdered family to have a vignette named for her—the last one—so the film appears to be leading up to some revelation about her.

Kayako's appearance is usually accompanied by her signature sound, a guttural staccato utterance, which is, of course, terrifying as a sound effect, but it also serves a narrative purpose. It tells us that Kayako is making a stuttering attempt to communicate something. Were this a typical *kaidan* narrative, we might deduce that Kayako wants revenge on the person who killed her, or some suitable proxy, since her husband presumably killed himself after murdering the family. Kayako seems to want something more than revenge, however. The way she treats her victims reveals something that her staccato utterances cannot. Kayako treats unmarried women differently than other victims. We know she kills men, because we see a security guard pulled into a lavatory by Kayako's black silhouette, and later learn that he was found dead. We also see Kayako's silhouette strangling an old woman, and later she frightens a young married woman to death. In those cases the bodies of the women are found, and we do not hear Kayako's staccato stuttering. In the way that Kayako treats young, unmarried women, we see that she is trying to both communicate something to them and take something from them.

Ju-on's first vignette is devoted to Rika (Megumi Okina), a young social worker just out of college. Rika's supervisor sends her to check in on an elderly woman who has just moved into a house (the house!) with her son and daughter-in-law. When Rika arrives, she senses something is wrong. The house is a mess, and no one appears to be there except the old woman, who is nearly catatonic. But then Rika begins to hear sounds upstairs. She goes up to investigate and finds a cat and a little boy, Toshio, sealed in a closet. She tries to question the old woman to find out who the boy is, but soon the old woman is overcome with fright. She starts screaming, and Rika sees the black silhouette of Kayako, who appears to be strangling the old woman. When Kayako turns to look at Rika with bloodshot eyes, Rika closes her eyes and passes out, and the vignette ends.

Unlike most characters in *Ju-on*, Rika does not die in her initial vignette, but comes back to the house to die in the end. Her forestalling of death establishes a pattern that is played out repeatedly in *Ju-on*. It might best be expressed as "Hide now, die later." The young women in *Ju-on* invariably try to escape from Kayako, but in doing so they only postpone the inevitable. In Rika's vignette, she temporarily escapes by closing her eyes and losing consciousness. The pattern of hide now, die later is further developed in the vignette named for Hitomi (Misaki Ito).

Hitomi is the young, unmarried daughter of the old woman in Rika's vignette. The night before Rika's visit, Hitomi stops by the house to help her sister-in-law with her mother's care, but is quickly turned away by her brother, who is already in the grip of the ghosts. Hitomi's tale is among the film's most frightening, because in it we learn that the ghosts are not confined to the house. Hitomi is stalked at her job and her apartment. Kayako's ghost can also control cell phones and televisions. When Hitomi attempts to escape by ducking into a public restroom stall, she gets a call from someone she thinks is her brother, but instead of his voice, she hears Kayako's stuttering over her cell phone. She tries to run from the stall but knocks a *kawaii* teddy-bear charm from her purse and runs back to get it, only to see Kayako's smoky black silhouette stuttering out of the stall next to hers. Finally, after fleeing to her apartment and throwing her phone out into the hallway, Hitomi tries to escape from Kayako under the covers of her bed, only to find that Kayako is there, too. Kayako pulls Hitomi under the covers, and with a scream both vanish.

Kayako's haunting, and eventual consumption, of Hitomi clarifies that there is something Kayako wants to share with and take from the young women in this film. Hitomi is still very much living the *kawaii* single life, as evidenced by her teddy-bear charm, her job, and her apartment. Kayako, by contrast, was stuck in a loveless marriage to what appears to have been an older, less attractive man.[41] In addition, since the boy ghost, Toshio, always appears with Kayako, we understand that she is forced to spend eternity with this child, who performs the role of a traditional poltergeist, upsetting furniture, breaking pottery, spilling cups, and the like. When we consider that Kayako is forced to spend eternity with a monstrous child and a violent, unloving husband, it is understandable that she would want the life of a *shôjo*.

In addition to Hitomi, we see in the vignette named for Izumi (Tomomi Kobayashi) a high school student who tries to escape by hiding in her room and taping newspaper over the windows. Eventually, Kayako grabs her, though. On the one hand, this delaying of death through hiding shows that Shimizu is just adhering to good horror-movie protocol, following Hitchcock's famous dictum, "Torture the women!" In the context of J-horror, however, where the *shôjo* signifier functions as a backlash against *kawaii* style, it has particular resonance, suggesting that *shôjo* identity itself is a useless form of escapism. Despite the number of *kawaii* items one consumes, one cannot remain a *shôjo* forever.

Figure 13.4 Although her victims hide, none escape Kayako (Takako Fuji), shown here reflected in a mirror in *Ju-on* (Takashi Shimizu, 2003).

Like her victims, Kayako is unable to accept the end of her *shôjo* years. She continues to consume, like all *shôjo*, but as a ghost, she is limited to consuming other *shôjo*. We see this played out in the final vignette, named, appropriately, "Kayako." In it Rika comes back to the house because she realizes her friend is there, but she arrives just in time to see her friend's feet disappearing into the attic. She then sees Kayako crawling toward her and tries to run away. When she gets downstairs she passes a hallway mirror and notices out of the corner of her eye that the reflection in it is not hers. She covers her eyes but cannot resist looking through her fingers. She sees Kayako's reflection covering her own eyes in the mirror. Then we see Kayako's bluish fingers interlacing with Rika's, and Kayako bursting out of Rika's blouse. Rika begins to realize that Kayako has taken possession of her life, consumed her. The film's final image shows us Rika in the attic, wrapped in bloody cellophane. Her eyes are closed as the camera slowly zooms in on her bloody face. Finally, she opens her eyes, and we hear Kayako's familiar stuttering, this time coming from Rika, as the film ends, suggesting, as the epigraph tells us, that a new curse is born.

Unlike *Ringu*, which suggests that assuming the traditional role of motherhood is a way to avoid the fate (if not the curse) of Sadako, *Ju-on* presents us with two equally unpleasant choices. On the one hand, there is the choice to maintain *shôjo* identity and temporarily escape, for as long as one can, from the world of adulthood and responsibility. On the other hand, there is the choice to voluntarily end one's *shôjo* years and face the likelihood of an unhappy marriage. As a signifier, Kayako powerfully represents this dilemma. Her battered visage attests to the trauma of her unhappy marriage, and her insatiable consumption is proof that she

408   THE OXFORD HANDBOOK OF FILM AND MEDIA STUDIES

cannot quite give up the escapism of her *shôjo* years. *Ju-on* also adds an aural dimension to the *kowai shôjo* signifier. Kayako's eerie staccato stuttering is the perfect expression of her reluctance to verbally make this impossible choice.

CONCLUSION

This analysis of *Ringu*, *Audition*, and *Ju-on* makes the centrality of the *shôjo* clear in contemporary Japanese horror cinema. From it we can draw several important implications for the study of transnational popular culture. Initially, it reveals that a truly successful cultural signifier has the potential to withstand the vicissitudes of economic and political changes as well as changes in fashion and taste. The *shôjo* is clearly such a signifier. The same qualities that made the *shôjo* the master sign of carefree personal consumption and self-indulgence during the height of the bubble economy in the late 1980s guaranteed its success as a signifier for all the anxiety that accompanied the loss of productive potential in the depressed economy of the late 1990s. In the case of *Ringu*, that productive potential is a specifically reproductive impulse that has been thwarted, stagnated, mirroring the real-world problem of the declining Japanese birthrate. In *Audition,* the anxiety centers on the loneliness that results from a generation of consumers who are more comfortable dealing with machines than people. *Ju-on* conjures anxiety over the limits of escapism as well as the social problems that make escape so desirable. The success of the *shôjo* at generating dread and anxiety in these films suggests that once a cultural signifier has achieved iconic status, it requires only minor alterations to trigger entirely different responses.

This study also raises questions relevant to genre studies. While J-horror's rearticulation of the *shôjo* clearly casts the genre as reactionary against *kawaii* style, it is less clear whether that reactionary impulse is progressive or regressive. Horror is often regarded as a conservative genre, but it would be a little too facile to suggest that the depictions of the *shôjo* in J-horror suggest a purely regressive tendency in the genre. With its close associations to infantile capitalism and consumption, *kawaii* style can hardly be considered progressive, even if it did imagine and encourage new identities for Japanese women. By the same token, J-horror's depiction of its female characters shows both progressive and regressive tendencies. At times these films appear to be advocating a return to traditional roles such as wife and mother, and yet the problems with these roles, seen most clearly in *Ju-on,* are also foregrounded. What is undeniable is that J-horror's employment of the *shôjo* as both protagonist and antagonist in its narratives acknowledges that women, and women's issues, have moved from a marginal to a central position in Japanese society.

A final point that needs to be made regarding both *kawaii* style and J-horror concerns the growing international audience for Japanese popular culture. I have argued that J-horror, although it employs the same master sign, is a reaction against *kawaii* style, and as a cultural expression was more appropriate than *kawaii* for the economic and social conditions of Japan in the late 1990s. It would be misleading to suggest, however, that *kawaii* style has utterly vanished from the pop-culture landscape. *Kawaii*, while challenged in Japan by alternative representations such as those of J-horror, is still viable, and, in fact, highly marketable outside of Japan. In many cases the *kawaii* merchandise and programming that gets distributed, however, does not directly employ the *shôjo* image.[42] It is also important to note that the international success of J-horror has increased interest in Japanese popular culture in general, so that the *shôjo* in both *kawaii* and *kowai* iterations is consumed in national markets that have little connection to the economic and social realities of Japan. Although it is obviously beyond the scope of this essay to analyze the significance of the *shôjo* as a transnational signifier, a brief reference to the United States will serve as an interesting case in point.

When Dreamworks bought the rights to Hideo Nakata's *Ringu* in 2001, they decided to remake it with an American cast and director (Gore Verbinski) rather than release the original theatrically. Aside from the obvious changes of setting and actors, Verbinski's *The Ring* is very similar to Nakata's *Ringu*. One reason that the film required so little adaptation can be traced back to the influence of American horror films on this generation of Japanese directors. Anyone familiar with Wes Craven's *Scream* (1996), which opens with a high school student alone in her house getting a disturbing phone call, will see its traces in *Ringu*, which opens with two high school students alone when the phone rings. Indeed, some reviewers have attributed *Ringu*'s success to its hybridity, "marrying the vengeful ghost scenario with the sanitized teen-pitched genre revival of Craven's films."[43] Others noted the hybrid nature of *The Grudge* (2004),[44] Takashi Shimizu's American version of *Ju-on*. It can be argued that there is even less cultural adaptation in *The Grudge* than in *The Ring*, since Shimizu not only wrote and directed it, but also shot *The Grudge* in Japan with a mainly Japanese cast. One important change, however, was that the character of Rika was replaced by American actress Sarah Michelle Gellar, herself a veteran of the American horror genre as the star of the hit television series *Buffy the Vampire Slayer*. Shimizu admits to being an "eighties splatter movie kid," influenced by characters like Freddy Krueger from *A Nightmare on Elm Street* (Wes Craven, 1984) and Jason from *Friday the 13th* (Sean S. Cunningham, 1980).[45] Interestingly, Shimizu did not make his villain masculine, as is common in the American horror tradition. Instead, Shimizu, like Hideo Nakata and Takashi Miike, used the figure of the *shôjo* for both his Japanese originals and American remakes, proving that, both nationally and internationally, young female killers can be just as frightening as their male counterparts.

NOTES

1. Tom Mes and Jasper Sharp, *The Midnight Eye Guide to New Japanese Film* (Berkeley, CA: Stone Bridge Press, 2005), 261.

2. Jay McRoy's *Japanese Horror Cinema* (Honolulu: University of Hawaii Press, 2005) is a good example. It uses an image of Sadako, the ghost killer, after she has emerged from the TV set as its cover illustration.

3. Sharon Kinsella, "Cuties in Japan," in *Women Media and Consumption in Japan,* ed. Lise Skov and Brian Moeran (Honolulu: University of Hawaii Press, 1996), 226.

4. Ibid., 243.

5. Akira Asada, "Infantile Capitalism and Japan's Postmodernism: A Fairy Tale," in *Postmodernism and Japan,* ed. Masao Miyoshi and H. D. Harootunian (Durham, NC: Duke University Press, 1989), 273–278.

6. Ibid., 275.

7. Ibid., 276.

8. Takeo Doi, *The Anatomy of Dependence,* trans. John Bester (Tokyo: Kodansha International, 1987), 60.

9. Asada, "Infantile Capitalism," 275.

10. Ibid., 276.

11. James I. Matray, *Japan's Emergence as a Global Power* (Westport, CT: Greenwood Press, 2001), 24.

12. Kinsella, "Cuties in Japan," 228.

13. According to Kinsella, it was precisely the childish, frivolous (*kawaii*) nature of the show that made it popular in the 1980s. These same qualities caused its popularity to wane in the 1990s. Ibid., 235–236.

14. Patrick Smith, *Japan: A Reinterpretation* (New York: Pantheon Books, 1997), 71.

15. Lise Skov and Brian Moeran, eds., *Women, Media and Consumption in Japan* (Honolulu: University of Hawaii Press, 1996), 3.

16. Sharon Kinsella, "Japanese Subculture in the 1990s: *Otaku* and the Amateur *Manga* Movement," *Journal of Japanese Studies* 24.2 (1998): 289–316, 314.

17. Susan Napier, "Vampires, Psychic Girls, Flying Women and Sailor Scouts: Four Faces of the Young Female in Japanese Popular Culture," in *The Worlds of Japanese Popular Culture: Gender, Shifting Boundaries, and Global Cultures,* ed. D. P. Martinez (Cambridge: Cambridge University Press, 1998), 91–109, 94.

18. John Whittier Treat, "Yoshimoto Banana Writes Home: The Shojo in Japanese Popular Culture," in *Contemporary Japan and Popular Culture,* ed. John Whittier Treat (Honolulu: University of Hawaii Press, 1996), 275–308, 281.

19. Mark Schilling, *The Encyclopedia of Japanese Popular Culture* (New York: Weatherhill, 1997), 114.

20. Matray, *Japan's Emergence,* 25.

21. Asada, "Infantile Capitalism," 276.

22. Mecha-anime, such as Katsuhiro Otomo's *Akira* (1988), were particularly successful at conveying dystopic images of Japan in the 1980s, and *manga* have a history of countercultural representation that goes back to the 1920s. For more on this point, see Frederik L. Schodt, *Manga! Manga! The World of Japanese Comics* (Tokyo: Kodansha International, 1997), 51.

23. Kinsella, "Cuties in Japan," 246.

24. Ibid.

25. See Yumiko Iida, "Between the Technique of Living an Endless Routine and the Madness of Absolute Degree Zero: Japanese Identity and the Crisis of Modernity in the 1990s," *Positions: East Asia Cultures Critique* 8.2 (2000): 423–464.

26. Asada, "Infantile Capitalism," 276.

27. Napier, "Vampires, Psychic Girls," 92.

28. I refer to *Ringu* by its *Katakana* spelling to identify it with the original Japanese version released in 1998; *Ju-on* refers to the 2003 Japanese movie version (there were two prior video versions).

29. Some differences between Suzuki's novel and the screenplay are given in Mes and Sharp's *Midnight Eye Guide*, 257–258.

30. Iida, "Between the Technique," 431.

31. This fear becomes further developed in *Ringu 2* (Hideo Nakata, 1999), where Yoichi becomes possessed by Sadako, and Reiko leaves her job to try to save him, as well as in *Honogurai Mizu no Soko Kara* (*Dark Water*, Hideo Nakata, 2002), where a mother's fear that she might lose her daughter in a custody battle causes her to serve as surrogate mother for a dead child.

32. See Noriko T. Reider, "The Appeal of 'Kaidan,' Tales of the Strange," *Asian Folklore Studies* 59.2 (2000): 265–283.

33. Nakata ingeniously builds suspense by showing us subtle, incremental glimpses of Sadako on the videotape each time it is viewed. First we see just the well at the end, but the second time a hand appears. Each time after, a little bit more of Sadako arises from the well until she comes out fully in Ryuji's apartment.

34. Needless to say this is fertile ground for additional study. The use of technology for human reproduction has precedents in many cyborg narratives, such as Mamoru Oshii's animated feature *Ghost in the Shell* (1995). Additionally, the viral nature of the reproduction in *Ringu* is a concern in many other J-horror narratives, most notably in Sion Sono's *Jisatsu Sa-kuru* (*Suicide Club,* 2002), in which suicide—the ultimate antireproductive activity—becomes a fad, and young people start doing it en masse.

35. Associated Press, "Japan Deaths Exceed Record-Low Birth Rate," *Baltimore Sun*, 2 June 2006, 12A.

36. Jonathan Head, "Japan Sounds Alarm on Birth Rate," *BBC News Online*, 3 December 2004, http://news.bbc.co.uk/2/hi/asia-pacific/4065647.stm, accessed May 2, 2008.

37. Kinsella, "Japanese Subculture in the 1990s," 293.

38. Interview with Takashi Miike, *Audition,* dir. Takashi Miike, 1999, DVD (Lion's Gate Films, 2002).

39. Bliss Cua Lim, "Spectral Times: The Ghost Film as Historical Allegory," *Positions: East Asia Cultures Critique* 9.2 (2001): 287–329, 300.

40. Carol Clover, *Men, Women and Chainsaws: Gender in the Modern Horror Film* (Princeton, NJ: Princeton University Press, 1992), 45.

41. The reason Takeo becomes enraged and kills the entire family is because Kayako is in love with another man, and Takeo suspects that Toshio is not his child. This is made far more explicit in Shimizu's American version (*The Grudge,* 2004), in which Bill Pullman plays the professor with whom Kayako is in love. In Shimizu's Japanese film version, all that is explicit is that the husband believes she has had an affair.

42. For more information on this point, see Koichi Iwabuchi, *Recentering Globalization: Popular Culture and Japanese Transnationalism* (Durham, NC: Duke University Press, 2002), as well as Gary Cross and Gregory Smits, "Japan, the U.S. and the Globalization of Children's Consumer Culture," *Journal of Social History* 38.4 (2005): 873–890.

43. Mes and Sharp, *Midnight Eye Guide*, 262.

44. See Jay McRoy, "Case Study: Cinematic Hybridity in Shimizu Takahashi's *Ju-on: The Grudge*," in *Japanese Horror Cinema* (Honolulu: University of Hawaii Press, 2005), 175–184.

45. Ibid., 176.

BIBLIOGRAPHY

Arai, Andrea G. "The 'Wild Child' of 1990s." *South Atlantic Quarterly* 99.4 (2000): 841–863.

Asada, Akira. "Infantile Capitalism and Japan's Postmodernism: A Fairy Tale." In *Postmodernism and Japan*. Ed. Masao Miyoshi and H. D. Harootunian. Durham, NC: Duke University Press, 1989, 273–278.

Associated Press. "Japan Deaths Exceed Record-Low Birth Rate." *Baltimore Sun,* 2 June 2006, 12A.

Audition. Dir. Takashi Miike. 1999. DVD. Lion's Gate Films, 2002.

Clover, Carol. *Men, Women and Chainsaws: Gender in the Modern Horror Film.* Princeton, NJ: Princeton University Press, 1992.

Cross, Gary, and Gregory Smits. "Japan, the U.S. and the Globalization of Children's Consumer Culture." *Journal of Social History* 38.4 (2005): 873–890.

Doi, Kakeo. *The Anatomy of Dependence.* Trans. John Bester. Tokyo: Kodansha International, 1987.

Head, Jonathan. "Japan Sounds Alarm on Birth Rate." *BBC News Online,* 3 December 2004. http://news.bbc.co.uk/2/hi/asia-pacific/4065647.stm, accessed May 2, 2008.

Iida, Yumiko. "Between the Technique of Living an Endless Routine and the Madness of Absolute Degree Zero: Japanese Identity and the Crisis of Modernity in the 1990s." *Positions: East Asia Cultures Critique* 8.2 (2000): 423–464.

Iwabuchi, Koichi. *Recentering Globalization: Popular Culture and Japanese Transnationalism.* Durham, NC: Duke University Press, 2002.

Jolivet, Muriel. *Japan: The Childless Society.* Trans. Anne-Marie Glasheen. London: Routledge, 1997.

Ju-on. Dir. Takashi Shimizu. 2002. DVD. Lion's Gate Films, 2004.

Kinsella, Sharon. "Cuties in Japan." In *Women Media and Consumption in Japan.* Ed. Lise Skov and Brian Moeran. Honolulu: University of Hawaii Press, 1996.

———. "Japanese Subculture in the 1990s: *Otaku* and the Amateur *Manga* Movement." *Journal of Japanese Studies* 24.2 (1998): 289–316.

Lim, Bliss Cua. "Spectral Times: The Ghost Film as Historical Allegory." *Positions: East Asia Cultures Critique* 9.2 (2001): 287–329.

Lopez, Javier. The Ring World: The Most Complete Information Available on The Ring. http://www.theringworld.com/index.php, accessed February 28, 2008.

Matray, James I. *Japan's Emergence as a Global Power*. Westport, CT: Greenwood Press, 2001.

McRoy, Jay. *Japanese Horror Cinema*. Honolulu: University of Hawaii Press, 2005.

Mes, Tom. *Agitator: The Cinema of Takashi Miike*. Godalming, UK: FAB Press, 2003.

Mes, Tom, and Jasper Sharp. *The Midnight Eye Guide to New Japanese Film*. Berkeley, CA: Stone Bridge Press, 2005.

Napier, Susan. "Vampires, Psychic Girls, Flying Women and Sailor Scouts: Four Faces of the Young Female in Japanese Popular Culture." In *The Worlds of Japanese Popular Culture: Gender, Shifting Boundaries, and Global Cultures*. Ed. D. P. Martinez. Cambridge: Cambridge University Press, 1998, 91–109.

Pavitt, Jane. "A Brief History of Brands: Hello Kitty." *Guardian*, 9 July 2001. http://www.guardian.co.uk/g2/story/0,3604,518712,00.html.

Reider, Noriko T. "The Appeal of 'Kaidan,' Tales of the Strange." *Asian Folklore Studies* 59.2 (2000): 265–283.

Ringu. Dir. Hideo Nakata. 1998. DVD. Dreamworks Home Entertainment, 2003.

Rucka, Nicholas. "The Death of J-Horror." *Midnight Eye: The Latest and Best in Japanese Cinema*. 22 December 2005. http://www.midnighteye.com/features/death-of-j-horror.shtml.

Rusling, Matthew. "High Court Bolsters Japan's Anti-immigrant Image." *Asia Times Online*. 8 February 2005. http://www.atimes.com/atimes/Japan/GB08Dh01.html.

Schilling, Mark. *The Encyclopedia of Japanese Popular Culture*. New York: Weatherhill, 1997.

Smith, Patrick. *Japan: A Reinterpretation*. New York: Pantheon Books, 1997.

Shiokawa, Kanako. "Cute but Deadly: Women and Violence in Japanese Comics." *Themes and Issues in Asian Cartooning*. Ed. John A. Lent. Bowling Green, OH: Bowling Green State University Popular Press, 1999.

Skov, Lise, and Brian Moeran, eds. *Women, Media and Consumption in Japan*. Honolulu: University of Hawaii Press, 1996.

Schodt, Frederik L. *Manga! Manga! The World of Japanese Comics*. Tokyo: Kodansha International, 1997.

Treat, John Whittier. "Yoshimoto Banana Writes Home: The Shojo in Japanese Popular Culture." In *Contemporary Japan and Popular Culture*. Ed. John Whittier Treat. Honolulu: University of Hawaii Press, 1996, 275–308.

CHAPTER 14

ASIAN FILM AND DIGITAL CULTURE

GINA MARCHETTI

Asian connections with the digital have been subtly changing film culture globally. Hollywood vociferously and repeatedly decries the exponential increase in video piracy occasioned by the ease of digitally reproducing feature films on disk (particularly the cheap but technically inferior VCD, which still maintains a tenacious hold over the DVD in many Asian markets). However, other transformations in the ways in which Asia produces, markets, distributes, and exhibits its own and world cinema as well as the way in which the world views Asian film have more quietly refashioned global cinema. The Internet, for example, has dramatically altered what we see on screen from Asia, when we see it, how we see it, and how we find out about it. Frustrated by the difficulty of getting information on Asian film star Jackie Chan, Senh Duong, assisted by his colleagues Patrick Lee and Stephen Wang from Design Reactor, a Web design firm based in California, started the Rotten Tomatoes Web site (http://www.rottentomatoes.com/) to share reviews of films with limited marketing in the United States. Rotten Tomatoes stays solvent by claiming a share of the profits from DVD sales made through links to other sites (see Thompson 2006). The fact that Asian American computer professionals should take it upon themselves to carve out a place in cyberspace for fans of popular Hong Kong martial arts films provides just a glimpse of the importance of the Internet to the development of an international (Pan-Asian and non-Asian) audience for "cult" films from Thailand, Korea, India, Japan, and, of course, Hong

Kong. However, the Asian connection extends beyond the realm of Internet marketing and film reviewing.

In August 2004, George Lucas announced a joint venture between Lucasfilm Ltd. and the Singapore government to produce digital animation in the Asian city-state (see Wong 2004). This agreement highlights many of the ways in which the processes of globalization, consumer capitalism, and digital technologies have transformed Asian cinema culture dramatically. After decades of minimal film production operating under stringent censorship regulations, Singapore has reached out in recent years to global corporations in order to attempt to compete in the growing information and communication marketplace in Asia. For Western media corporations, cheap labor, a relatively educated and skilled populace, linguistic and cultural as well as physical proximity to the coveted megamarkets of China and India, a loosening of censorship regulations, and a tightening of intellectual property laws have made Singapore attractive. For places like Singapore, this influx of capital and new technology has breathed new life into dormant communications industries and stagnant film cultures. For film entrepreneurs like George Lucas, the explosion of digital culture in Asia has opened up enormous possibilities, from the sale of new technologies to investment in production initiatives, wider distribution of his products, and burgeoning profits from all quarters.

As in most parts of the world, the convergence of digital technology with feature film production has fundamentally altered film culture throughout Asia. However, the impact of digital technologies on film culture in this vast region varies considerably. Since the state of cinema culture differs so dramatically across the continent, from some of the liveliest commercial industries in Bombay and Hong Kong to countries that have virtually no film production such as Brunei, the ways in which digital/film convergences have taken place across the continent also vary enormously. In some parts of Asia, digital technology has made pirated or banned material more easily available, while, in other cases, new technologies have reduced production costs in order to make ailing feature industries more profitable. The digital revolution has been instrumental in making Asian films more readily available to global audiences (through Internet advertising, sales, and fan culture). Digital video (DV) feature films are now accepted at key Asian film festivals. As a consequence, the nature of "art cinema" in Asia has changed with the growing influence of movements like Dogme '95, which favors "low" production values and DV portability, and welcomes the novice working on a shoestring budget. Digital video has liberated marginalized communities to find a voice within the feature film world, and several "first" DV features from Asia deal with queer issues, minority politics, and other themes outside the commercial mainstream. While the Internet brings fans of anime, martial arts, and Bollywood musicals together into a global audience, it also enables dissidents to get their films into festivals, find funding, and open up a public space for debate beyond national borders. For some filmmakers, digital technology provides a way of finding a niche audience through Internet publicity and DVD sales globally, ensuring the survival of perspectives that would otherwise be expressed only locally, if at all.

BETTER FILMMAKING THROUGH TECHNOLOGY

As throughout the rest of the world, the initial appeal of digital technology for commercial filmmakers in Asia involved reducing costs and maximizing profits. Computer-generated imagery (CGI) effects, digital editing (mainly with the AVID editing system initially), and distribution on DVDs and VCDs did just that— acceptable (if not the same) results could be achieved using computers rather than optical printers, using monitors rather than flatbeds, and reaching the audience outside the theaters with video disks.

Although much has been made of the "authenticity" of Asian martial arts films when compared with Hollywood's digitized action blockbusters, Hong Kong, in point of fact, has relied on digital effects since the 1980s to create the appearance of martial proficiency where none exists or to create the illusion of lavish landscapes on studio lots. From Tsui Hark's pioneering *Zu: Warriors from the Magic Mountain* (1983), which brought together Hollywood digital innovators and Hong Kong martial arts masters, to the digitized features that followed, like *A Chinese Ghost Story* (1987) and its sequels, *Stormriders* (1998), *Shaolin Soccer* (2001), and *Kung Fu Hustle* (2004), Hong Kong has kept pace with international standards. In 1986, inspired by Lucas's Industrial Light and Magic, Tsui Hark, who went to college in the United States and has learned quite a bit from American filmmaking practices, founded Cinefex Workshop, which included, in addition to units that specialized in more traditional optical and physical special effects, a special department devoted to digital effects (Schroeder 2004, 69).

When Yuen Woo-Ping and the Wachowski brothers teamed up for *The Matrix* (1999), the Hong Kong industry was already quite adept at combining actors on wires with a wide variety of computer-generated visual effects. However, unlike *The Matrix*, which includes digital effects *and* is about cyberculture, most of the digital production work in Hong Kong (as in Hollywood) is not meant to *look* like it was done digitally and blends transparently into the overall style of the film, subordinated to the mechanics of the narrative, the allure of the characters, and the box-office appeal of the stars. Transnational Asian directors have used the mix of wire-work stunts and digital compositing with varying degrees of success (e.g., Ang Lee's *Crouching Tiger, Hidden Dragon* [2000] and *Hulk* [2003]; Zhang Yimou's

Hero [2002] and *House of Flying Daggers* [2004]). In 2004, Raj Kumar Santoshi's *Khakee* from Bollywood broke new ground when digital technology was used to change the color palette in postproduction. Japanese filmmaker Hayao Miyazaki set a new standard in animation when he incorporated digital processes into his crafting of *Princess Mononoke* (1997). In most of these films, digital effects feed a particular aesthetic vision and make no attempt at self-reflexive commentary on new cyberfrontiers for the cinema.

However, Run Run Shaw of the Shaw Brothers recognized the meeting of digital effects with a narrative about a futuristic cybersociety had enormous global profit potential when he invested in Ridley Scott's *Blade Runner* (1982), which used LucasFilm's computer-controlled Dykstraflex system to construct a vision of a cyberfuture using cutting-edge digital technology (see Schroeder 2004, 42). Peter Mak's *Wicked City* (1992), produced by Tsui Hark, blends futuristic fantasy with digital effects. Like *Blade Runner*, *Wicked City*, an allegory of the 1997 change of sovereignty in Hong Kong from British to mainland Chinese rule, owes a heavy debt to Japanese science fiction/cyberpunk (see Lee and Lam 1998). In fact, perhaps the most fecund meeting of digital technology and cybernarratives occurs in Japanese mecha-anime (see McCarter 1999, Levi 1996, Napier 2001). Mamoru Oshii's *Ghost in the Shell* (1995), for example, weds computer-assisted animation with a narrative about Major Motoko Kusanagi, a cyborg policewoman, in mortal combat with the Puppet Master, a disembodied computer program gone haywire (see Schaub 2001). While using computer imaging to create a compelling vision of the future, *Ghost in the Shell* also takes up controversies involving ethics and new technology in advanced capitalist societies, the increasingly porous borders between the human and the "posthuman," and the impact of cyberculture on notions of gender identity, personal autonomy, and power. The film marks a rare meeting of cybercinematic aesthetics with a self-conscious commentary on the implications of the digital revolution.

DIGITAL VIDEO AND NEW ASIAN NARRATIVES

The growing acceptance of DV as a means of production for feature films has opened doors across Asia to independent filmmakers who otherwise would have little chance of raising the capital for more experimental narratives, first films, or films dealing with subject matter still taboo in many places (e.g., queer Asians, youth subcultures, marginalized political perspectives, etc.). For the Sixth Generation of filmmakers in the People's Republic of China, for example, who make films outside the government-financed studio system and the transnational commercial marketplace, the lower costs, portability of equipment, and ease of operation of DV have enabled their often dissident voices to be heard globally.

Many major film festivals in Asia now allow digital features in competition, and some offer special categories for digital shorts. Beginning in 2003 and 2004, the Hong Kong International Film Festival offered a special category for Asian digital features, and the festival has screened films as diverse as Apichatpong Weerasethakul and Michael Shaowanasai's *The Adventure of Iron Pussy* (Thailand, 2003), Ning Hao's *Incense* (PRC, 2003), Amir Muhammad's *The Big Durian* (Malaysia, 2003), Tsuchiya Yukata's *Peep TV Show* (Japan, 2003), Andrew Cheng's *Welcome to Destination Shanghai* (PRC, 2003), Kim Ji-hyun's *Popee* (Korea, 2002), Hanny R. Saputra's *Tato* (Indonesia, 2002), and Doug Chan's *Love Is Not a Sin* (Macau, 2002). In fact, Hong Kong itself has produced several notable DV feature films, including Evans Chan's transnational drama *The Map of Sex and Love* (2001), Vincent Chui's Dogme inspired feature *Leaving in Sorrow* (2001), Yau Ching's story of lesbian desire *Ho Yuk—Let's Love Hong Kong* (2002), Fruit Chan's satiric *Public Toilet* (2002), and Steve Cheung's Tony Leung Kar-Fai starring vehicle *Simulacrum* (1999).

Both *The Map of Sex and Love* and *Ho Yuk* incorporate images of Internet technology (from e-mail exchanges to surfing the World Wide Web) within their narratives to explore the growing presence of queer Asian sexualities in cyberspace. Other narratives have also examined the connections linking queer sexuality, Asian gay and lesbian communities, and new technologies. Stanley Kwan's *Lan Yu* (2001), for example, draws on an anonymous novel available on the Internet in order to depict gay love in contemporary Beijing. Other films, like Shunji Iwai's *All About Lily Chou-Chou* (Japan, 2001), have looked at connections between Asian youth and cybersubcultures. Jang Sun-Woo's *Resurrection of the Little Match Girl* (Korea, 2002), for example, structures its narrative about Korean youth around the conventions of computer video games.

Shu Lea Cheang, who has produced video installations, documentaries, Internet artworks, as well a feature films, explores the connections among queer communities, computer hackers, environmental activists, community video advocates, and third world politics in her feature *Fresh Kill* (1994). Spanning the planet from New York to Taiwan's remote Orchid Island, Cheang imaginatively brings together diverse minority and progressive voices through the mediation of new technologies (see Marchetti 2001). In *I.K.U.: A Japanese Cyber-Porn Adventure* (2000), Cheang continues to subvert conventional notions of gender and sexuality by imagining new sexual identities and communities in cyberspace (see Jacobs 2003). As Jacobs has pointed out, Cheang uses digital imagining to "queer" the viewer's perspective, thereby opening up previously unimagined or unimaginable sexual identities available only within cyberspace.

ASIAN FILM FANS AND THE INTERNET

A strong connection has developed among Asian queers, New Queer Cinema, the global gay-lesbian-bisexual-transgendered community, and new technologies ranging from satellite phones to the Internet (see Berry, Martin, and Yue 2003). However, as the founders of Rotten Tomatoes knew, other communities of film viewers also gather in cyberspace to exchange information on Japanese anime, Hong Kong action films, and Bollywood features. The Asian film "fanboy," for example, is a fixture on the Internet. Conforming to the same demographic profile as the "computer nerd," the young, male, rebellious, alienated, somewhat antisocial, and often love-starved fanboy enjoys the sex and violence of Hong Kong martial arts and Japanese anime. Given the number of fans (including a number of female and older viewers) who do not conform to this profile, this view of the online Asian film fan has its limitations. Certainly, beyond the hacker fanboy, the Internet, without a doubt, has been instrumental in expanding and globalizing the market for Asian cinema beyond national borders, cultural differences, and regional divides. Web sites in English include Asian Cinema Weekly (http://www.kinoasia.com/), South Asian Cinema (http://www.southasiancinema.com/), Kung Fu Cult Cinema (http://www.kfccinema.com/), Asian Cinema Forum (http://www.acfmovies.com/board/), Asian Film Connections (http://www.asianfilms.org/), Hong Kong CineMagic (http://www.hkcinemagic.com/), Planet Bollywood (http://www.planetbollywood.com/), Korean Cinema (http://www.koreanfilms.host.sk/index.html), and Midnight Eye, devoted to Japanese cinema (http://www.midnighteye.com/), among many others. The information available through the Internet, from Listservs to Web sites, varies greatly in accuracy, quality, and depth, ranging from fan sites devoted to Asian stars to scholarly discussions of Asian cinema.

In addition to bringing fans together from outside Asia, these Internet sites often act as a means for diasporic Asians to continue to keep in touch with their homeland by following popular cinema trends. Fan sites, which often include message boards and other means of communicating electronically, facilitate global exchanges around movie stars and popular screen fictions. For NRI (nonresident Indians), for example, the Internet encourages engagement with an imagined national community revolving around Bollywood cinema (see Ciecko 2001). Many Asian stars, like Bollywood's Shah Rukh Khan and Hong Kong's Andy Lau, pay close attention to their cyberpresence (see Ciecko 2001). In the case of Andy Lau, for example, Internet information from sources other than the "official" Web site has been frowned upon and actively discouraged by the star's publicity department. While a presence on the Internet can be constructed, cyberspace is not always that easy to conquer, and fan countercultures often vie with "official" sites and commercial interests.

PIRACY AND THE DIGITAL

Given the increased ease of reproduction and transport of DVDs and VCDs (which are more widely available in Asia than in Europe or America), the fact that DVD/VCD piracy exists as a fixture in the Asian film economy comes as no surprise. Censorship regulations, import restrictions, costs beyond the reach of the average Asian consumer, and other factors, make the fact that Asian film viewers purchase pirated copies of films more understandable. When the Internet is factored in, the marketplace for pirated DVDs expands to global proportions (see Wang 2003). While most of the discussion of piracy in Asia revolves around Hollywood films and the Motion Picture Association of America's dogged efforts to get Asian governments to put a stop to illegal video trafficking, Asian film industries also suffer from pirates, who drain ticket sales and erode legitimate video profits. However, for some filmmakers in some countries in Asia, the black market provides the only means of distribution for banned films, with the Internet as the principal conduit for the dissemination of information about their work. While the shadow industries generated by the digital revolution erode legitimate profits and hurt struggling commercial film enterprises in Asia, the Internet and DVDs also expand the market to new viewers outside of Asia and enable dissident filmmakers to find a means of disseminating their work (see Pang 2004).

As digital technologies become more sophisticated, the policing of the marketplace becomes more urgent for government and commercial film interests. Streaming video, miniature DVD cameras and recorders, and an ever-expanding World Wide Web present continuing challenges to intellectual property rights and the profitability of feature film production in Asia. Part of the reason given for Lucas's choice of Singapore as a base for his operations in Asia, for example, has been attributed to that nation's newly formulated intellectual property laws and crackdown on violations of international copyrights.

DIGITAL FUTURES

Legally and illegally, motion pictures from Asia circulate globally on the scale they do because of the digital revolution. From production through distribution, marketing, and fan reception, no aspect of Asian film culture has remained untouched by digital technology. Moreover, cyberspace has created a place for the exploration of ideas and identities that challenge many traditional Asian values and beliefs, allowing the expression of queer sexualities, minority opinions, and subversive political positions. Some Asian filmmakers have even begun to critique digital culture and incorporate commentary on how the digital dream has transformed their societies. Sixth Generation filmmaker Jia Zhangke, for example, uses Flash animation in his feature *The World* (2004) to visualize the divide between the imaginary global identity and the harsh local reality of the migrant workers who fuel China's urban service economy.

During this period of enormous change, Asian film industries have suffered ups and downs related to new technologies. Hollywood has been more aggressive in the region, national governments have opened their markets under pressure from the World Trade Organization, and domestic Asian film industries have suffered. However, the Internet has made Hong Kong, Bollywood, Japanese anime, and other Asian films more widely available worldwide. The Asian diaspora has fueled interest in Asian film outside of Asia, and the Web has kept nonresident Indians, overseas Chinese, and other Asian émigrés in touch with popular culture in the region. Digital piracy hurts Asian industries as well as Hollywood in Asia, but it also brings previously unavailable films within the grasp of a wider global audience. As Asia continues to "get wired," new technologies are certain to have a continuing impact on all aspects of film culture on the continent.

BIBLIOGRAPHY

Berry, Chris, Fran Martin, and Audrey Yue, eds. 2003. *Mobile Cultures: New Media in Queer Asia*. Durham, NC: Duke University Press.

Ciecko, Anne. 2001. "Superhit Hunk Heroes for Sale: Globalization and Bollywood's Gender Politics." *Asian Journal of Communication* 11.2: 121–143.

Jacobs, Katrien. 2003. "Queer Voyeurism and the Pussy-Matrix in Shu Lea Cheang's Japanese Pornography." In Berry, Martin, and Yue, *Mobile Cultures*, 201–221.

Lee, Gregory B., and Sunny S.K. Lam. 1998. "Wicked Cities: Cyberculture and the Reimagining of Identity in the 'Non-Western' Metropolis." *Futures* 30.10: 967–979. http://www-scd.univ-lyon3.fr/externe/lee/lee_lam.htm, accessed May 2, 2008.

Levi, Antonia. 1996. *Samurai from Outer Space: Understanding Japanese Animation*. Peru, IL: Open Court Publishing.

Marchetti, Gina. 2001. "Cinema Frames, Videoscapes, and Cyberspace: Exploring Shu Lea Cheang's *Fresh Kill*." *Positions: East Asia Cultures Critique* 9.2 (Fall): 401–422.

McCarter, Charles. 1999. "2D or Not 2D: Computers in Anime." *The Online World of Anime and Manga*. http://www.ex.org/4.3/04-feature_digital1.html, accessed May 2, 2008.

Napier, Susan J. 2001. *Anime from Akira to Princess Mononoke: Experiencing Contemporary Japanese Animation*. New York: Palgrave Macmillan.

Pang, Laikwan. 2004. "Piracy/Privacy: The Despair of Cinema and Collectivity in China." *Boundary 2* 31.3 (Fall): 101–124.

Schaub, Joseph Christopher. 2001. "Kusanagi's Body: Gender and Technology in Mecha-Anime." *Asian Journal of Communication* 11.2: 79–100.

Schroeder, Andrew. 2004. *Tsui Hark's Zu: Warriors from the Magic Mountain*. Hong Kong: Hong Kong University Press, 2004.

Thompson, Anne. 2006. "World of Film Reviews Changed by Internet." *Reuters/Hollywood Reporter*, February 3. http://www.hollywoodreporter.com/hr/search/article_display.jsp?vnu_content_id=1001956859, accessed May 3, 2008.

Wang, Shujen. 2003. *Framing Piracy: Globalization and Film Distribution in Greater China*. Lanham, MD: Rowman and Littlefield Publishers, 2003.

Wong, Fayen. 2004. "George Lucas Expands Film Empire." *Reuters,* August 4. http://bun.worldonline.co.uk/news/newswire.php/news/reuters/2004/08/04/entertainment/georgelucasexpandsfilmempire.html&template=/entertainment/feeds/story_template.html, accessed May 3, 2008.

CHAPTER 15

....

POPULAR CINEMA
AND THE "NEW"
MEDIA IN INDIA

....

MANJUNATH PENDAKUR

In the last sixty or seventy years, cinema in India has been one of the principal cultural institutions despite the arrival of television, which, in the last twenty years, has made inroads into some seventy million homes. Every new technology that has been introduced into the country—broadcast television, cable television, satellite television, direct-to-home television, video tape, digital video disk (DVD), digital cinema, e-cinema, and the Internet—does not seem to dampen the enthusiasm of the audience for popular cinema.

The dominant player in the television industry is still the publicly owned Doordarshan, a central-government-controlled institution that operates twenty-one services and reaches some four hundred million viewers. In a major shift in public policy, the government of India introduced sponsored programming in 1984 and increasingly made Doordarshan depend on advertisers for revenue.[1] Privately owned corporations, some of which include transnational corporations such as Fox, Sony, Time Warner, and Disney, compete for viewers through cable and satellite channels. The cable market is one of the biggest in the world, with an estimated subscriber base of sixty million households. Privately owned FM radio, introduced in 2000 into the mix of broadcasting, is popular with young people in the cities and is allowed to play music only. The domain of radio news is still a

423

monopoly of All India Radio, the state-controlled system, which was commercialized some time ago, but is available countrywide. It is expected, however, that there will be big changes in the radio sector in the near future. An estimated thirty-eight million people were on the Internet by 2006.[2]

The vast majority of people still desire the larger-than-life images of their stars on the silver screen, and the audience's appetite for entertainment appears insatiable. Between eight hundred and nine hundred feature-length films are produced every year, and a starstruck audience is expanding both at home and abroad. The entertainment industry is expected to grow by leaps and bounds in the next ten years.

Of the approximately six million craft workers in the industry, it is not known how many of them live on the income earned solely from the film business.[3] Trade unions do exist, but they are weak and operate as advocacy groups or informal arbitrators to resolve disputes; they have no real bargaining power.[4] Little has been done by state and central governments regarding the poor working conditions of below-the-line workers in this massive industry that rides on glamour and gossip about the high-life style of its stars, producers, directors, and other above-the-line creative people.[5]

Figure 15.1 Kareena Kapoor, Hindi film star, seduces the viewer to buy Lux soap (photo by M. Pendakur).

Nothing remains constant for long, however, because larger political and economic factors have been reshaping the Indian political economy in the current historic phase of globalization, which, in turn, has produced change in the film industry. In the last ten years, representations of India in the Western capitalist media have also gone through major change. "Bollywood," for instance, has become emblematic of India and has displaced the starving, emaciated children and the mud huts that characterized India's backwardness and poverty in previous generations. The major gains made by India as it pursued a socialist path for economic and social development seldom received recognition at the time, but now India's tighter integration into the world capitalist economy and its closer but troubled collaboration with U.S. imperialism in this millennium are receiving wide coverage, often self-reaffirming the triumph of capitalism.[6]

At the same time, the "old" hangs on to the "new" in the sense that change and continuity are parallel historical processes. This essay addresses that duality of continuity and change while also addressing cinema's material fortunes as a social, economic, political, and cultural institution.[7]

INDUSTRY STRUCTURE AND POLICY

The mass-oriented cinema in India is produced in nearly twenty-five languages, and created in different parts of the country. That distinction is often ignored in the current embrace of "Bollywood" in the West, and all films from India, including those from directors of Indian origin from abroad, are too often swept together as Bollywood films. Strong linguistic and regional affinities, which often border on regional chauvinism, drive local cultural industries such as cinema. Many states in the nation have some incentive or other to boost film production in local languages. One study found that approximately 20 to 25 percent of the films produced in the country are in the Hindi language, and the rest are made in Tamil, Telugu, Malayalam, and Kannada.[8] Major production centers—Bombay, Madras, Hyderabad, Bangalore, Trivandrum—have large studios with many soundstages, some of which rival the ones in Los Angeles. For example, the Ramoji Film City in Hyderabad boasts several well-equipped soundstages and numerous gardens (even a Japanese garden) for location shooting.

Hundreds of production companies operate in different parts of the country, most of which are small, family-held units that bring capital together with talent to make feature-length films hoping to capture the box office. Adam Smith's dream of atomistic competition is almost realized in the production sector, where the more established or hallowed production companies such as AVM, RK Films, Navketan

Figure 15.2 Row of movie theaters in Bangalore showing films in different languages (photo by M. Pendakur).

International, Prasad Productions, and Yash Raj Films do not have a commanding position in the economy, although they are considered prestigious.

It is possible to have this kind of competition because of two fundamental reasons: (1) the industry is not vertically integrated as in the United States, where production, distribution, and exhibition sectors are essentially controlled by five large transnational corporations known as the majors,[9] and (2) financing of films is not controlled by banks but by capitalists of all sizes, including those who are involved in illegal trade of drugs, diamonds, weapons, and the like. As a result, there is a gigantic parallel economy in which unaccounted for or untaxed money circulates in sums equaling or exceeding the legal economy.[10]

Until 2000, the government of India did not recognize the film business as an industry, which meant that banking capital stayed out. Banks always play it safe, and the high risk involved in production was not attractive to them. They understand land, and brick and mortar, however, and as a result loans were available for constructing theaters even before changes were implemented in the central government policy regarding the banks' role in the film industry. The government of India also encouraged construction of theaters in rural areas through a subsidy scheme under the National Film Development Corporation in the 1980s and into the mid-1990s. These theaters were intended to help what policy-making circles called "good filmmakers" find their audiences.

While that appears to be changing given the neoliberal tide in the economy, banks have started financing film production, labs, distribution, and other related businesses. Venture capital and hedge funds have arrived in India's film industry, and according to one estimate, a total of $158 million went into production from institutional sources in 2004.[11] Some twenty-five new corporate players, including India's big industrial capitalists such as the B.K. Modi Group, the Sahara Group, the TATA Group, the Birla Group, and the Ambanis, have entered film production. The Swiss firm KPMG forecasted that the entertainment industry in India in 2004 was worth $1.3 billion and that the industry would reach a worth of $3.2 billion by 2010. Such predictions have drawn tremendous media coverage in India as well as in the West, where giant corporations and their allied governments are looking to expand to other markets.

The allure of huge returns that exists for black-market dealing also draws these underworld investors to the film business. Many interested parties have a stake in the telecommunications sector, which requires "content." These corporations control the coaxial cable and cellular phone industry, which has a huge appetite for sounds and images, all of which are readily available from the established film industry. In other words, the beginnings of a vertically integrated structure for the film industry may be emerging, echoing the process that has been going on in the United States ever since the 1920s. One can only speculate whether the dons of Dubai, Karachi, and Bombay who are connected in a triangular trade and have invested in the entertainment industry in India will remain interested, but given the glamour associated with film stars, the potential huge profits, the possibility of money laundering, corrupt political and police bureaucracy, and the growing popularity of Indian cinema abroad (which means earnings in hard currency), it is unlikely that the underworld influence will diminish.

The distribution and exhibition sectors are also characterized by unintegrated, privately owned enterprises. There are hundreds of distributors in various linguistic markets. New companies come and go depending on the level of risk taken and the success or failure of the films they try to market. Even Hindi cinema, which has nationwide appeal, is marketed on the basis of territories rather than in nationwide campaigns like those of the Hollywood majors, who distribute their high-budget extravaganzas in the North American market to more than three thousand screens at a time.

Derek Bose has correctly observed, "Although the industry produces films in Hindi for a pan-Indian audience, distributors have divided the country into different geographical zones, each with a distinctive cultural ethos, and taste and preference."[12] The domestic market is divided into six distribution zones: Bombay, Delhi, East Punjab, Eastern Circuit, Rajasthan, and the South. Each of these zones, however, includes different linguistic groups that cross state boundaries. For example, the category "South" includes parts of the four southern states, where Urdu and Hindi are understood or spoken historically, but also big cities such as Bangalore, where

Figure 15.3 Philips Home Theatre billboard in Calcutta (photo by M. Pendakur).

many different languages are spoken. In recent years, the expanding international market has been considered the seventh zone. In a way, Hindi cinema is increasingly becoming the national cinema of India, while its style and commercial imperatives have become the benchmark for other-language directors to follow or reject.

These zonal distributors acquire the rights to market a particular film by providing an advance and a minimum return from the distribution of that film in particular zones. In other words, the distributors assume a higher degree of risk, unlike in the U.S.-Canadian market, where vertically integrated oligopolies (the majors) dominate the market.[13] Distributors seldom acquire all six territories within the country, which means the risk is spread out among several companies and competition exists for "desirable" product. Because of the minimum guarantee, the producers are saved from any potential losses that might occur due to the highly volatile audience response to films.

Single-theater ownership was the most common feature of the exhibition sector, as national theatrical circuits controlling large number of screens did not exist until recently and distributor-owned theaters were rare in the business. The large industrial capitalists in the country—the TATAs, the Birlas, the Modis, and so forth—did not venture into the risky world of the film business. That all began to change with the arrival of commercial television in the 1980s and the expanded

Figure 15.4 Touring cinema owner and workers pose with the truck.

consumer market. The extreme shortage of theaters in a booming economy with a burgeoning population is noted in just about every report about the entertainment industry, which is now attracting investment from large corporations.

While the United States has about 31,000 screens for a population of 266 million people, India has just 12,900 screens for a population of more than a billion. This translates into a density of 8,580 people per screen in the United States versus 77,520 people per screen in India.[14] Nearly 4,000 of these screens are itinerant, "touring" cinemas, which operate mostly in rural areas of the country, where 70 percent of people still live. These touring cinemas, essentially a tent with a projector, are unable to function during the monsoon season. All in all, too many films are turned out for the too few theaters, thereby creating a huge bottleneck for market entry for those films. Exhibitors are sitting in a privileged position in this situation because they bear little or no risk, unlike the distributors and producers, who share the risk. The exhibitors collect revenue at the box office and also from candy sales, yet they share the revenue from the box office with only the distributors. Many exhibitors in rural areas or small towns simply lease their theaters to the distributors at a fixed price.

There is no doubt that Indians are avid moviegoers, though because the cinema has not yet reached all the villages due to the uneven development of the economy, most people travel by foot, bullock cart, or motorized transport to get to a small town where a theater may be located, or they must wait for a touring cinema to appear in their village. Overall, estimates of ticket sales range between eighty million and one hundred million a week, yet this cannot be verified because neither the states nor the central government keep track of such data, and because corruption is rampant in the country, no reliable statistics are kept by the exhibitors. In small cities and towns, exhibitors recycle the same tickets from the gate to the box office, suppressing the actual number of tickets sold to avoid either the entertainment tax or sharing the revenues with the distributors.

NEW VIEWING EXPERIENCES

As in the case of the advanced capitalist countries, India has also experienced new media technologies being introduced into the mix of how people receive entertainment. The entry of television, its rise to popularity in the 1980s, and its vast expansion, aided by public funds, into most parts of India by way of satellites and cable technologies have been well researched.[15] The arrival of videotape, DVDs, and the like into Indian homes, relatively slowly but still at a noticeable pace, has also meant that new ways of consuming entertainment have become possible, and related manufacturing and service industries have grown.

Pornographic cinema, which was relatively unknown to the mass audience in the Indian market, became available in the late 1980s when the government licensed video cafés, also known as video parlors. European imports of pornography began to arrive in video stores in the cities, and an underground economy began to develop. These video cafés were no more than small theaters of between fifty and a hundred seats, with a large television set and a VCR. The entrepreneurs who owned these cafes played popular movies during the day and pornographic films late at night for a male audience. Drivers of public buses coming from Bangalore to rural towns in Karnataka served as the couriers of such videotapes. The video café owner would simply spread the word among a few young men that a "special show" was scheduled for late that night.[16] Even though the video cafés are long gone, these viewing experiences changed the way cinema was being consumed in the country at the time, and served as an indicator of bigger changes to come in the 1990s.

As stated earlier, liberalization of the Indian economy, which began in earnest in 1991 and was contentious and widely debated in the country, has meant overhauling national policy regarding how much freedom capital could and should have in the market. At the heart of the debate is the question of the role of the state in an economy that is integrating quickly with global capital. The debate is also related to the question of Indian people's autonomy to pursue a path of economic and cultural development other than the one dictated by the advanced capitalist countries. On a strictly national level, the regulatory regimes that existed for more than fifty years in the postindependence period have been relaxed. For example, rules governing foreign direct ownership and joint ventures have been either abandoned or relaxed to make it easy for big Indian capital to collaborate with big capital from abroad. This has essentially meant that foreign investors can invest in all areas of the film industry.

New companies have emerged to build multiplexes, and some of the Hollywood majors have expressed a keen interest in building such theaters in India, which is considered a growth market in the international investor community. Hollywood investors were expected to build one thousand new screens in the rural

Figure 15.5 PVR Multiplex at the Forum Shopping Mall in Bangalore (photo by M. Pendakur).

areas in this decade.[17] Such speculation appears to have been on the high side, but there are clear patterns of change in the theatrical sector, particularly in the cities.

Priya Village Roadshow (PVR), in collaboration with the Australian Village Roadshow group, claims to be the largest exhibitor in the country now, with sixty-two screens in sixteen locations, all of which are in large cities.[18] It began its commercial operations in 1997 with the launch of *Anupam* in Delhi. PVR Cinemas introduced not just the multiplex concept but also a much higher standard of viewing experience, even higher than that of a typical American theater. PVR theaters are known for luxurious seating, similar to that in first class in the airline business, and high-quality audio systems, projection, acoustic treatment, lighting, and screens. They introduced the "Gold Class" area, with shiny new lobbies, a liquor bar, and food and drink brought to the seats by women dressed conservatively in skirts. Such service came with a hefty price tag. In the Bangalore theater complex, tickets with food are priced at 500 rupees. A ticket without food costs 350 rupees.[19] The audiences could choose from a selection of Hindi, Tamil, and Hollywood English-language products playing on the various screens. For the extremely class-conscious Indian middle and upper-middle class, which is bene-fiting from the neoliberal policies of the state, this is a welcome attraction. The noisy crowds that one encountered in the mass-oriented cinema halls have dis-appeared entirely from such a theatrical experience.[20] The masses throng the the-aters where admission prices are still affordable, but the "classes," as the Indian film industry prefers to call them, go to the multiplex.

Sathyam is another up-market, six-screen complex in the city of Chennai (known previously as Madras). As in the PVR Cinemas, along with the luxurious ambience provided, customers can reserve their tickets and order their food online or by telephone. Sathyam has also introduced babysitting or supervised play areas for patrons' children. The multiplex features first-run Hollywood imports as well as films in Tamil, Hindi, and other South Indian languages.[21]

To save costs involved in prints, distribution, and labor, these multiplexes are now experimenting with digital technologies, creating the new frontier for ex-perimentation in theatrical exhibition, leading the way and providing a test bed for the digital changeover that will be occurring worldwide. *Puduppettai*, a Tamil film directed by Selvaraghavan, released at the Sathyam theater in Chennai in 2006, claimed to be the first such digital release in the world.[22] The 35-millimeter film was completely digitized and encoded on QubeMaster, a patented technology by Real Image Media Technologies of Chennai, which has strategic partnerships with the U.S.-based Avid Technologies and DTS, the Belgium-based Barco Digital Cinema, and others. The data was then made available on a Qube digital cinema server at Sathyam, which in turn played it successfully on a Barco DLP Cinema TM 2K high-resolution digital projector.[23] This compressed and encrypted 80-gigabyte data file, which replaces the 35-millimeter print, can be used anywhere in the world with compatible digital delivery systems. According to one report, the technology would work as follows:

> Essentially, digital cinema is the projection of a film through a digital video pro-jection system. In a satellite-based digital cinema distribution system, the movie reel is first converted into a digital format through a process called tele-cine—the same process which enables movies to be screened on television. Subsequently, the movie is converted to a format that is satellite transmission friendly. A three-hour movie, when converted for satellite transmission, has a file size of 80 GB. The movie in the form of a file is transported using a hard disk to the satellite service provider's network operation centre (NOC). The satellite service provider uses high speed connection and streams the movie to servers installed in theaters.[24]

Real Image Media Technologies has announced that it has contracts to convert seventy-two theaters in the state of Tamilnadu, of which fifty-two are already operational. More than thirty films have played digitally in these theaters, accord-ing to media releases, and *Chandramukhi* (P. Vasu, 2005), with India's megastar, Rajanikanth, ran for more than two hundred days in such theaters. It was predicted that by March 2007, there would be at least 150 digital screens in the nation.[25]

Some 160 screens worldwide were reported to have been equipped with Qube cinema technology, but only about fifty Indian and Hollywood films were available in the Qube Master format.[26] That situation, however, appears to be changing fast, with more Indian films in local languages becoming available in the digital cinema format, encouraging exhibitors to take this proposition seriously. For example, many independently owned theaters are either considering conversion to this technology or have already made the decision.[27] The motivating factors are primarily financial, and once the variety of product available in the digital market increases, more exhibitors will certainly make the conversion.

An interesting debate is taking place in the country regarding suitable systems of delivery to fit the needs of India rather than comply with Hollywood's expectations of high technical quality of the signal. While the rollout of digital cinema in the United States has stalled over the basic question of who will bear the cost of converting the more than thirty-one thousand screens, the situation in India is different because of uneven development of the states, differences in people's purchasing power based on region, class, and caste, and the rising costs of marketing a picture on celluloid. Manmohan Shetty, the managing director of AdLabs, has made that point well:

> A big reason why digital cinema is gaining momentum in the country, is that it has emerged suitable for penetrating smaller cities where theaters get a new movie much later than their counterparts in the larger cities. . . . Celluloid prints are expensive, and these markets are too small to justify the cost. . . . It costs over $1,500 to make a celluloid print roll of a typical Bollywood film, and the industry cannot roll out more than 200 celluloid prints a time. The country has over 12,000 movie halls, so under the celluloid print mode just a couple of hundred movie halls can get to release a new movie at once.[28]

According to Shetty, Indian entrepreneurs will adopt low-quality projection systems requiring lower investments in small towns and cities, whereas in the big cities, where they can charge their customers more, the systems will be similar to those in the United States and Europe. With production budgets of Indian films soaring in the last twenty years, the big push will be to release films in a larger number of screens in order to get a quicker return on the box office and also to reduce distribution costs that involve analog technologies.

These changes on the horizon will have a great impact on the workers in the industry because the low-wage earners in the theatrical exhibition sector will need to be retrained in online delivery systems. Their expectations for a higher wage will have to be met by the exhibition sector. Due to built-in obsolescence, computer-based systems also need new hardware and software upgrades every three to five years, compared to analog projectors, which last a much longer time and do not demand the costs and technical expertise needed to maintain computer-based systems.

These economic factors will direct the industry structure in the near future toward more concentration of the industry and further integration with foreign capital. For instance, there is competition in this technology market from many Indian corporations with joint-venture relationships with foreign-owned corporations. Pyramid-Saimira Group from Chennai entered the market in a big way with the Taipei-based Delta Electronics. This collaboration deal was to bring more rugged projection systems to suit the Indian conditions at lower cost. Pyramid-Saimira Group is going after not only the Indian market but also some two hundred theaters in Sri Lanka, one hundred in Malaysia, and twenty in Singapore, and also the large market of theaters in China. Pyramid-Saimira Group's plan to encourage exhibitors to use digital cinema is to convert and lease theaters, in effect becoming an exhibitor itself. Pyramid-Saimira Group's declared goal is to create a digital theater chain of fifteen hundred screens.[29]

If the patterns of change sketched so far continue, the theatrical exhibition sector will go through a period of consolidation by way of mergers and acquisitions in which fewer, but larger, corporations will come to dominate the market.

IMAX, which owns 251 theaters in 38 countries, is another recent addition to the Hollywood film presence in India. Historically, only about 150 regular theaters in the country screened Hollywood imports,[30] but that situation has changed dramatically since the 1990s, and more and more English-language imports are on Indian screens, not just in the big cities but also in small towns. IMAX is a Canadian corporation and its eighty-foot domed theaters can be found throughout the world. The company has plans to expand into some nine hundred potential markets in the near future, of which six hundred are international. India and China figure prominently in their expansion plans. The upper classes in India are willing to pay hefty prices to see these spectacles on the gigantic screen.[31] IMAX's current strategy is not to bank on films especially produced for their theaters but to convert Hollywood blockbusters in 2-D and 3-D formats and market them worldwide to the up-market audience.

The IMAX theaters in Mumbai, Delhi, Ahmedabad, and Hyderabad have screened some of Hollywood's big-budget blockbuster films, such as *Matrix Reloaded* (Andy Wachowski and Larry Wachowski, 2003), *Harry Potter and the Sorcerer's Stone* (Chris Columbus, 2001), and *Spider-Man* (Sam Raimi, 2002). Tushar Dhingra, chief operating officer of Adlabs Cinemas, which operates the IMAX Adlabs in Wadala, a Mumbai suburb, stated, "IMAX prints have increased the business of big ticket films. About 30 per cent of the total revenue of *Harry Potter* and *Matrix Reloaded* in India came from IMAX screens. This is a substantial number even by global standards."[32]

Indian films are not yet available in the IMAX format. As Dhingra explained, "Regular 35 mm Hollywood films are converted to IMAX prints using the expensive digital re-mastering technology. And the cost is anywhere between Rs. 50 to Rs. 60 *crore*, which is nearly the entire budget of a Hindi movie like *Krrish*."[33]

According to trade figures, *Harry Potter* and *Spider-Man* grossed more than 3 *crore* (30 million) rupees in the IMAX Adlabs dome theater in Mumbai alone.

Dhingra added that he was expecting a full house over the first weekend for the IMAX version of *Superman Returns*. Mona Shah, who booked tickets for her entire family to watch *Superman Returns* said, "To see action films on an 80 feet dome screen with 12,000 watts of sound is a great experience."[34]

These new viewing experiences, all a result of the new digital technologies and the relatively "freed-up" market under the liberalization and privatization regimes pursued by the government of India since 2001, could also have an impact on Indian film production. The audience may have more choices in the marketplace, no longer limited to the "masala film," which has dominated the mass market for a long time.

Masala Film

I have argued elsewhere that the popular Indian film can be called a masala film, a metaphor that draws one's attention to the various ingredients that are used to create the mixture known as the masala in cooking.[35] By definition, these films are star driven and formulaic, irrespective of genre. Genre films in the West have internal coherence and logic; for example, spy thrillers do not have the protagonist and his love interest singing songs in a romantic scene. In contrast, a film made in any language in India, irrespective of genre, adheres to certain transgeneric codes and conventions, which audiences have come to expect. The protagonist and his love interest in a spy thriller *will* break into song. It is not that formulas do not change over time, but that the conventions of storytelling do not appear to change much. As I have noted elsewhere, "Although popular cinema remains open to outside influences, even from Hollywood, thereby appearing like a hybrid mishmash of style and content, what is borrowed is cleverly given a local 'patina.' "[36] Indians at home and abroad integrate this cinematic experience into their daily lives.

A successful masala film such as *Coolie* (Manmohan Desai, 1983) or *Veer Zaara* (Yash Chopra, 2004) tells melodramatic stories through epic style. There are stories within stories, with a parallel comedy plot that takes the audience onto a tangent, away from the narrative. The plot is seldom linear. There are many characters and events, and several flashbacks, all of which do not fit the three-act format common in the Hollywood production process. The epic style provides ample opportunities for the director to treat the audience to new heights of pleasure from visual thrills, big, colorful sets, stunts, many songs and dances, multiple costume changes within a song and dance number, beautiful, exotic locations (even in the Alps or the Rocky Mountains), moving dialogue and dramatic performances by the principal stars, and highly sexualized images of women. Audiences pay at the box office many times over to see the same dance number or their favorite song performed on the screen sung not by the actor, but by their favorite playback singer.

The dichotomy that exists in the West between highbrow and lowbrow cinema is not applicable to an analysis of Indian film because the classical and the popular have found a comfortable coexistence in film. For instance, major classical singers and musicians have performed in popular films and have also produced the musical scores for several films. The form may be kitschy, but the content may come from well-established poets, singers, writers, actors, and directors. Major novelists in different languages have contributed their work to films. Movie songs rely heavily on classical musical ragas as well as folk tunes and borrowed Western melodies and musical scores. The clever director is able to draw on that rich reservoir of culture in India (or from abroad) and give it a patina that will have the Indian look and be acceptable to the mass audience. The audience, however, goes into a theater expecting the masala but is also hoping to see how the director is able to tell the story in some novel way.

Another critical factor that affects the content and look of popular Indian cinema is that going to watch a movie is still very much a social act in which entire families participate.[37] As a result, the panoply of pleasurable "items" that constitute the masala has to be safe for the whole family. There is a great deal of playfulness in representing romanticism, which is one of the basic ingredients of the popular film, but there are serious limits to what the filmmakers can explore in terms of sexuality because of censorship, and because of the family dynamic of the audience. I return to the issue of censorship and the growing opposition to it later in this essay.

DIGITAL CINEMA PRODUCTION

Digital cinema technologies are beginning to have an impact on the production sector also. There are three important trends: (1) a new stream of production that does not fit into the broad category of masala film, (2) animation productions based on computer graphics, and (3) independent documentary film production.

India has attracted a tremendous amount of attention in media coverage and in public policy discussions in the West because of the remarkable gains it has made in the computer software and engineering sectors over the past twenty years. The outsourced jobs from all sectors of the industries in the United States that need data processing appear to have gone abroad, particularly to India, because it has one of the largest pools of scientific labor with English-language skills. A similar recent phenomenon is the outsourcing of animation work from the Hollywood majors to Indian companies in Mumbai and Chennai. Disney's *Chronicles of Narnia: The Lion, the Witch and the Wardrobe* (Andrew Adamson, 2005) was made partially by the Mumbai operation of the Los Angeles–based company Rhythm & Hues, which is also involved in 20th Century Fox's *Garfield 2* (Tim Hill, 2006). Lion's Gate Entertainment is reportedly outsourcing three features to Crest Animation, the first of which is *Sylvester and the Magic Pebble*. According to Prashant Buyyala of Rhythm and Hues, who splits his time between Bombay and Los Angeles, the 140-strong workforce in Bombay provides the backup for the critical functions carried out in Los Angeles for such films. "As of now, we are not doing any design and conceptualization work for Hollywood movies in India. Most of that work is still done in the LA facility. Once the concepts are designed, some of the execution of that work is done in the Mumbai facility."[38] Ashish Kulkarni of Anirights, a company based in Pune, compared different markets for animation production: "While Korea has the advantage as far as traditional animation is concerned, the shift to CG animation coupled with our knowledge of English helps us to stay ahead of Korea."[39]

These experiences with international corporations appear to be spawning a local animation industry that not only is competing for outsourced work from abroad but also is creating its own productions. The 2-D film *Hanuman* (V. G. Samant and Milind Ukey, 2005), a tale of Hindu mythology, has broad appeal and is available worldwide on DVD. Its success has meant that a slew of 3-D animated films based on mythological stories are expected to be on the market soon. The Time Warner Cartoon Network and Walt Disney International, which have a presence in the Indian television market, have started to produce local content to garner more Indian audiences for their channels. *Geet Mahabharata*, a musical version of the epic, and *The Little Budha*, along with *Akbar and Birbal*, are some of the projects that are being financed by Time Warner in India.

An experimental film culture may also be growing because digital production provides certain cost advantages that are not available with film. A number of young filmmakers are experimenting with styles and genres of filmmaking, and their work is showcased at events such as Cinefan in Delhi or Experimenta in Mumbai. Rashmi Dhanwani, a journalist reporting on education for a newspaper called *DNA India* in Mumbai, discussed new avenues for filmmaking: "I personally have been going to Experimenta [for] 3 years and the kind of films that are shown there are experimental in nature and give viewers immense exposure to the extent of experimentation with form. I remember watching this movie on 2 projectors and 1 screen which has absolutely no viewer appeal, was too arty farty but gave me an insight to what possibly could be done with two projectors. That film was screened on 50 projectors in some other country."[40]

Because the cost of digital production can be relatively low compared to 35-millimeter film production, films are being made in languages such as Kashmiri.

Aarshid Mushtaq, a new entrant to filmmaking in that war-torn valley, has recently completed a digital film called *Story of Love* (2006). Mushtaq's film is a period drama set in 1887, at a time when a Hindu king ruled the region. Commenting on the choice of digital versus celluloid technology, Mushtaq stated, "One of the main reasons for choosing this format, apart from money, was that there are no cinema halls in Kashmir. There is no fun to make a film and leave it on a shelf."[41] The total budget for this film was $17,000. Four days before principal photography began, the financier walked out, and the cast and crew, along with some friends, came up with the money to continue the production. Mushtaq plans to release the film on the Internet and also on DVD and View CDs, thereby making the film widely available in Kashmir and elsewhere. Niche-market experiments, if successful, can boost local production and serve an audience who would not receive attention from the major film producers, who instead are vying for profitability in the national and global markets.

In the last five years, another crop of films has emerged from Mumbai that deal with sexual issues more openly compared to the films of the last thirty or so years. *Jism* (Amit Saxena 2003), *Hawas* (Karan Razdan, 2004), *Khwaish* (Govind Menon, 2003), and *Salaam Namaste* (Siddharth Anand, 2004) all made by filmmakers in the mainstream industry, attempt to deal with sex as a central subject matter in the narrative. There are significant differences in how these filmmakers treat sex as a subject matter, as well as stylistic distinctions, but what is important for the discussion here is that such films are actually getting made and are finding audiences.

While genitals cannot be legally shown in public exhibition halls, the censorship policy in the country is slowly changing to allow for exploration of taboo subjects such as premarital sex, homosexuality, kissing, and so on. Indian cinema has always played coy with sex by using romance as a decoy for actual sex, and musical numbers as a sublimation for lovemaking. Writers and directors have developed clever ways to deal with sex on the screen by manipulating images and words through double entendre and the like in order to avoid regulation from the censorship board. Such devises, often vulgar ones, caught the attention of the audience, particularly the male audience. Digital technologies deployed in production could open this door even wider: relatively inexpensive filmmaking would allow for distribution to smaller markets, such as homes, hotels, and specialty cable channels, thereby evading the censor's eyes. If distribution systems can be set up via the Internet, for example, in order to tap into the large youth population, profits could be high, yet it would be considerably difficult for any such distribution system to succeed in India, so it is likely that sexually explicit films will remain on the margins of mainstream cinema, relegated to decaying theaters in seedy areas.

CENSORSHIP

The legacy of film censorship in India dates back to colonial times, but the national governments under different political parties have upheld the strict regulations, perhaps because the colonial elites and the Indian bourgeoisie share the same paternalistic attitudes toward the filmmakers and their audiences. Award-winning documentary filmmaker Rakesh Sharma made the following observation about the prevailing conditions in the country regarding the government's historic practice of censoring films prior to their release:

> The Government of India thinks you are stupid. I am an imbecile, indeed
> each person who steps into any cinema is an idiot. The Government is deeply
> concerned about us, which is why it has applied wise men to take care of us.
> Collectively, they inhabit this space called the Censor Board and toil day
> and night to keep us from plunging headlong into a life of sin. Their boss is
> usually a retired or out of work actor. He may have molested countless women
> on screen or she may have gyrated in a sequined bikini, but they discover
> hitherto hidden reserves of morality soon as they are appointed to the Censor
> Board.[42]

Film censorship is the jurisdiction of the central government, which administers the 1952 law through the Central Board of Film Certification (CBFC), which has branches in different parts of the country. As the states have jurisdiction over film exhibition, the board works through state governments and the local police to enforce the law. The board, however, has enormous power because all films and videos have to be subjected to censorship before they can be publicly shown in a theater. The board's policies and practices are clearly subjected to political pressures from New Delhi, and the declared policy of the government is to eliminate overt sexual representations and violence, particularly against women. Policy aside, what is practiced in these censor panels, which scrutinize every film, including documentaries and shorts, before certification, produces incongruities, financial losses, abuse of power, and lack of freedom for filmmakers, particularly those who challenge the status quo with their films.

The absurdities and the machinations of censorship in India are far too many to mention here, but one or two examples might illustrate how audiences and filmmakers in India feel about the repressive situation. Michael Moore's *Fahrenheit 9/11* was banned by the CBFC, which claimed that screening the film in India would hurt the country's "relations with foreign countries," even though the documentary was released widely in the United States in 2004. Leading independent documentary filmmakers such as Anand Patwardhan and Rakesh Sharma have had to fight every inch of the way to get their films approved. Anand fought all the way to the Supreme Court of India to get some of his documentary films shown in the country where he lives and works. The latest in his battles with the CBFC is over *War and Peace*, a thoughtful, well-researched, evocative documentary about the horrors of nuclear war and the possibilities of peace. When the CBFC banned the film in India, Anand appealed the decision, and the Bombay High Court finally cleared the film for release without any cuts in 2005.[43]

The latest blow to free circulation of ideas through films by the CBFC came in 2003 at the Mumbai International Film Festival, a biennial event showcasing shorts, documentaries, and animated works. The government clamped down by requiring that all films set to be shown have a certificate of clearance from the CBFC. This unprecedented decision to impose censorship on a film festival was met with outrage and a nationwide protest by the filmmakers. Rakesh Sharma, one of the protesting filmmakers, analyzed this policy well and indicated the negative impact it would have on the kinds of films being made in the country:

> The bureaucracy would like to retain the powers to ban "any film that affects human sensibilities." So what happens to those of us making films in the fond hope of affecting these very sensibilities? Naturally, this provision will not extend to Guddu Dhano's *Siskiyan* (of the multiple rapes fame) or to the countless dubai-se-bhai-ne-supari-diya films! Not content with butchering documentaries and sensitive narrative features at the Censor Board, the babus now want to dictate what film-makers, critics, students and international delegates can watch in a film festival space.[44]

As the protest spread widely and received media attention, the government backed off from imposing censorship on the festival but decided to ban some thirty films by claiming that they had "uncomfortable" content. These films touched on many important issues facing the Indian people, including sexuality, international relations, peace, war, and Hindu-Muslim relations. The list of films banned included *Final Solution* (Sharma, 2003), a heart-wrenching documentary on the 2002 pogrom against the Muslim minority in the state of Gujarat, in which the state bureaucracy, including the police and politicians, were implicated. But the bureaucrats came up with a clever way of preventing such films from being shown at the 2004 Mumbai International Film Festival by rigging the selection criteria. Members of the jury began to resign from the panels, expressing dismay at the government's draconian measures to eliminate politically controversial films. R. V. Ramani and Girish Karnad, both noted filmmakers, resigned from the jury panel, and Karnad wrote, "The entire atmosphere, as indeed the very purpose of the festival, has become vitiated, making it, I fear, difficult for me to be associated with it."[45] Ramani revealed more about the government's machinations behind the scenes in his letter to the media: "The selection committee had no empowerment, they never knew of the final selection, the then director had interfered with the selection process, and has even manipulated the results."[46] Several filmmakers whose films were selected for screening at the festival withdrew them in protest and in solidarity with their colleagues whose films were eliminated by the government bureaucracy.

The filmmakers did not stop at this action, but carried on with their goal of having their films shown to the public by starting their own alternative festival in Mumbai, *Vikalp*: Films for Freedom. More than fifty films were screened at a building right across from where the Mumbai International Film Festival was held in 2004. This event in Mumbai spawned a similar festival in Bangalore.

Dubbed the Campaign Against Censorship, this unprecedented collective action by filmmakers has great potential to solve not only the problems related to the untenable censorship in the Internet age but to further build a badly needed independent documentary movement in India. Filmmakers have called upon the government for an overhaul of the law regarding censorship; their concerns are echoed by Rakesh Sharma in an essay published in the *Hindustan Times* on October 22, 2005:

> Many of us believe that the main censorship law—the Cinematograph Act of 1952 itself is archaic and needs a thorough review, especially in light of rapid changes in the last decade—the spread of TV channels and Internet have led to a greater "visual literacy"; cinematic images no longer need to be treated as extra-potent images capable of influencing gullible minds and hence subject to a more stringent regulation, which for decades has been the underlying assumption behind the administration and interpretation of the Cinematograph Act both by the CBFC and the courts.[47]

In contrast, currently on display on the CBFC's Web site is the following statement, reportedly made by the Supreme Court of India, which projects the dominant view held in the circles of power in the country regarding censorship of cinema:

> Film censorship becomes necessary because a film motivates thought and action and assures a high degree of attention and retention as compared to the printed word. The combination of act and speech, sight and sound in semi darkness of the theatre with elimination of all distracting ideas will have a strong impact on the minds of the viewers and can affect emotions. Therefore, it has as much potential for evil as it has for good and has an equal potential to instill or cultivate violent or good behaviour. It cannot be equated with other modes of communication. Censorship by prior restraint is, therefore, not only desirable but also necessary.[48]

The paternalistic state is reluctant to relinquish its power over what people are allowed to see and hear. Liberalization of the economy, which began in 1991, may pose a major challenge to this dominant view because global capital demands certain cultural freedoms. Global capital, however, is also ready to accommodate the needs of local political exigencies and demands.

While successive governments since 1991 have relaxed the rules governing sexual representations on the screen, or simply looked the other way—even the forbidden kiss is becoming rather common in many popular films—repression against films that are critical of the Indian government and others is likely to continue. What will shape national policy in the years to come, however, is not so much what the external forces might want from India but what will be allowed to happen by the Indian filmmakers and viewers, a dialectical dance that has existed for decades.

CONCLUSION

Given the current phase of globalization in the country, Indian cinema is on the cusp of a radical transformation. Big capitalists in the country who resisted the temptation to enter the risky business of film production have taken the plunge because film is still the foundation of all mass entertainment in India. Due to relaxed rules governing foreign direct investment, transnational capital's presence has also grown in the Indian entertainment businesses. The foundations of vertical structures in production, distribution, and exhibition have been laid. Whether or not this will continue is difficult to predict because economics and politics are intertwined in the process. It looks as though the relaxed regime of controls over all kinds of industries is irreversible at this point because of India's ambitions to be a global player.

Indian capitalists have flexed their muscles with their large pool of scientific labor and advances made in indigenous software innovations. New media production including 3-D animation, first done in the context of outsourced jobs from the West, is creating technical expertise and experience that has already resulted in successful indigenous children's animation drawn from the Indian epics. The Indian diaspora, which is estimated to be twenty million strong, is a powerful market for these products and will drive the business into the foreseeable future.

Digital theaters and e-cinema delivered via satellite is spreading to rural areas, and it may become the standard way of delivering films to mass audiences. The biggest change is beginning to occur in the exhibition sector, due to digital technologies and policies that are promoting consolidation in the business.

Internal debates about form and content of cinema—masala films versus other kinds of cinema—are interesting, but there will almost certainly continue to be demand for both kinds of films. The large urban youth population will sustain films that may attempt to experiment with form and style, but the masses of viewers will still expect their stars to perform dances, stunts, and tricks to entertain them for three hours. The masala film, or the "family entertainer," has proved long-running success. Given that there is no shortage of unaccounted-for money for filmmakers in all languages, as well as bank financing, which has been available since 2000, big-budget extravaganzas will continue to be made. With relatively low barriers to entry into all areas of the film industry, India tends to be a better place than most countries in the world, including the United States, for starting film-makers to make their mark.

While filmmakers have had to deal with the vagaries of government policy on film censorship, organized opposition by documentary filmmakers is a promising development on that front. In the foreseeable future, the boycotts of film festivals and the creation of alternative screening venues could be very powerful methods for not only opposing repressive policies of the government but also helping to sustain an alternative, critical media culture, which is fundamental to a liberal democracy.

NOTES

1. M. Pendakur, "A Political Economy of Television: State, Class, and Corporate Confluence in India," in *Transnational Communications: Wiring the Third World,* ed. Gerald Sussman and John Lent (Newbury Park, CA: Sage Publications, 1991).

2. BBC News, Country Profile: India, 2006, pp. 4–5, http://news.bbc.co.uk/1/hi/world/south_asia/country_profiles/1154019.stm, accessed June 10, 2006.

3. M. Pendakur, *Indian Popular Cinema: Industry, Ideology and Consciousness* (Creskill, NJ: Hampton Press, 2003), p. 34.

4. Nishit Desai Associates, *Bollywood v. Hollywood. Legal & Business Practices. Comparative Analysis,* Interim Report, June 2001, p. 9.

5. Labor unions and working conditions in the mega entertainment industry in India have not been studied systematically. This is a ripe area of research for advanced graduate students.

6. See coverage in various issues of *Newsweek* and *Time* as well as major foreign policy journals; in particular, recent periodicals with front-page stories are *Newsweek* (March 6, 2006), *The Economist* (February 25–March 3, 2006), and *Time* (June 26, 2006).

7. Political economy of communication is a particular form of intellectual discourse. It is concerned primarily with structure and power in the media industries as they relate to how production, distribution, and consumption are organized in any cultural economy and their relationships to ideology. For a detailed discussion of the political economy approach to media studies see Vincent Mosco, *The Political Economy of Communication* (London: Sage Publications, 1996), and Pendakur, *Indian Popular Cinema.*

8. Nishit Desai Associates, *Bollywood v. Hollywood,* p. 1.

9. The five majors (and their parent corporations) are Warner Bros. (Time Warner), 20th Century Fox (News Corporation), Columbia/Tristar/MGM (Sony), Paramount (Viacom), and Disney (Walt Disney).

10. Pendakur, *Indian Popular Cinema,* pp. 51–55.

11. Brian Pearson, "Bollywood Makeover Takes on Big Spenders," *Variety,* March 13–19, 2006, p. A1.

12. Derek Bose, *Everybody Wants a Hit: 10 Mantras of Success in Bollywood Cinema* (Mumbai, India: Jaico Publishing House, 2006), p. 147.

13. For a thorough analysis of the changes to the motion picture industry structure and policy since the 1990s, see Janet Wasko, *How Hollywood Works* (London: Sage Publications, 2003), and M. Pendakur, *Canadian Dreams and American Control: The Political Economy of the Canadian Film Industry* (Detroit, MI: Wayne State University Press, 1990).

14. "Real Image Unveils Digital Cinema!" *Real Image-Digital Audio Film and DTS Cinema Sound*, June 10, 2006, p. 1. http://www.real-image.com/video/corpnews/11001.asp, accessed June 10, 2006.

15. See Manas Ray and Elizabeth Jacka, "Indian Television: An Emerging Regional Force," in *New Patterns in Global Television: Peripheral Vision*, ed. John Sinclair, Elizabeth Jacka, and Stuart Cunningham (Oxford: Oxford University Press, 1996), and Pendakur, "A Political Economy of Television."

16. Pendakur, Field Notes, 1988.

17. Nishit Desai Associates, *Bollywood v. Hollywood*, p. 1.

18. Wikipedia entry, http://en.wikipedia.org/wlk/PVR_%28_Village_Roadshow%29, accessed June 10, 2006.

19. Such high prices are way beyond the purchasing power of ordinary people in the country; the purchasing power of the masses of peasants and workers remains relatively low, with high inflation in food, transportation, fuel, and housing costs. The Indian rupee's exchange value was approximately 45 rupees to one U.S. dollar.

20. Pendakur, Field Notes, January 2006.

21. Ibid.

22. Such claims have to be taken with a grain of salt. *Star Wars: Episode 1. The Phantom Menace* is claimed to be the first feature-length film to be shown electronically, in 1999. A few theaters in New York reportedly screened the George Lucas film digitally. They used Texas Instruments and CineComm digital projectors for the test screening. Miramax also claimed that they exhibited *An Ideal Husband* digitally in the United States. Cisco Systems and 20th Century Fox also claim that they have digitally transmitted a Hollywood film across the United States on the Internet and digitally processed it to a cinema audience in Atlanta, Georgia. In November 2000, Real Image Media Technologies presented some scenes from the highly successful Manirathnam film *Dil Se* at an international film festival in Mumbai (www.real-image.com/video/corpnews/11001.asp).

23. http://www.chennaionline.com/film/News/2006/06sathyam.asp, accessed July 3, 2006.

24. http://www.realimage.com/digital/diginews/090502.asp, accessed June 10, 2006.

25. Estimates vary widely, and media reports appear to be driven by self-serving media releases by competing companies trying to market their digital cinema technologies. One article reported in 2005 that two hundred cinemas in India were converted to a D-Cinema format and went on to claim that the number would rise to a thousand in 2006, which has not happened. China is believed to have fifty digital screens, and a theatrical chain in Portugal was reported to be converting its twenty screens to the Qube digital cinema from Chennai (http://msnbc.msn.com/id/10682395/site/newsweek/, accessed June 10, 2006).

26. http://www.chennaionline.com/film/News/2006/06sathyam.asp, accessed June 10, 2006.

27. Vishwanath Gangavathi, Krishna Picture Palace, Hagariboomanahalli, Karnataka, India, telephone interview with the author, June 30, 2006.

28. "Bollywood Set to Embrace Digital Cinema," December 20, 2005, p. 1, http://pda.physorg.com/lofi-news-digital-film-cinema_9233.html, accessed June 10, 2006.

29. "Digital Projector Revolution," April 26, 2005, http://www.chennaionline.com/film/News/04pyramid.asp, accessed July 3, 2006.

30. M. Pendakur, "Dynamics of Cultural Policy Making: The U.S. Film Industry in India," *Journal of Communication* (Autumn 1985), 52–72.

31. "IMAX Chief Sees a Big Future in Big Screens: Conversion of Films Pays Off, Gelfond Says," *USA Today*, December 5, 2005, p. 4B.

32. Shabana Ansari, "Superman Returns to Take on Krrish," June 30, 2006, p. 1, http://www.dnaindia.com/report/.asp?NewsID=1038626, accessed July 2, 2006.

33. Ibid. A *crore* is ten million rupees.

34. Ibid.

35. Pendakur, *Indian Popular Cinema*, pp. 95–117.

36. Ibid., p. 116.

37. The exceptions are the seedy theaters located in certain parts of big towns and cities to serve an all-male audience looking for more nudity and sex. See Amit Kumar, "The Lower-Stall: A Sleaze-Sex Film Industry in India—An Introduction," unpublished manuscript, 2006, pp. 1–25.

38. Prashant Buyyala, Rhythm and Hues, e-mail correspondence with the author, July 7, 2006.

39. Shilpa Bharatan Iyer, "India Inks New H'wood Deals, Stakes Claim in 3-D Field," *Variety*, May 29–June 4, 2006, A9.

40. Rashmi Dhanwani, e-mail correspondence with the author.

41. http://www.timesleader.com/mld/timesleader/entertainment/14530744.htm, accessed June 10, 2006.

42. Rakesh Sharma. "Take the Scissors Away from the Censor Board- HT," October 29, 2005, p. 1. http://www.freedomfilmsindia.org/newsdetail.asp?NewsID=30, accessed June 10, 2006.

43. http://www.freedomfilmsidia.org/newsdetail.asp?NewsID~22, accessed June 10, 2006.

44. Rakesh, p. 2.

45. http://www.freedomfilmsindia.org/newsdetail.asp?NewsID=12.

46. Ibid., p. 2.

47. Rakesh, pp. 2-3.

48. http://www.cbfcindia.tn.nic.in/backgroundpage1.htm.

BIBLIOGRAPHY

Ansari, Shabana. (2006). "Superman Returns to take on Krrish." June 30, 2006. http://www.dnaindia.com/report/.asp?NewsID=1038626, accessed July 2, 2006.

BBC News. Country Profile: India. 2006. http://news.bbc.co.uk/1/hi/world/south_asia/country_profiles/1154019.stm, accessed June 10, 2006.

Bose, Derek. *Everybody Wants a Hit: 10 Mantras of Success in Bollywood Cinema*. Mumbai, India: Jaico Publishing House, 2006.

Iyer, Shilpa Bharatan. "India Inks New H'wood Deals, Stakes Claim in 3-D Field." *Variety*, May 29–June 4, 2006, A9.

Miller, Toby, Nitin Govil, John McMurria, and Richard Maxwell. *Global Hollywood.* London: BFI Publishing, 2001.

Mosco, Vincent. *The Political Economy of Communication.* London: Sage Publications, 1996.

Nishit Desai Associates. *Bollywood v. Hollywood. Legal & Business Practices. Comparative Analysis.* Interim Report, June 2001.

Pendakur, M. *Canadian Dreams and American Control: The Political Economy of the Canadian Film Industry.* Detroit, MI: Wayne State University Press, 1990.

———. "Dynamics of Cultural Policy Making: The U.S. Film Industry in India." *Journal of Communication* (Autumn 1985), 52–72.

———. *Indian Popular Cinema: Industry, Ideology and Consciousness.* Creskill, NJ: Hampton Press, 2003.

———. "A Political Economy of Television: State, Class, and Corporate Confluence in India." *Transnational Communications: Wiring the Third World.* Ed. Gerald Sussman and John Lent. Newbury Park, CA: Sage Publications, 1991.

Pearson, Brian. "Bollywood Makeover Takes on Big Spenders." *Variety,* March 13–19, 2006, A1.

Ray, Manas, and Elizabeth Jacka. "Indian Television: An Emerging Regional Force." *New Patterns in Global Television: Peripheral Vision.* Ed. John Sinclair, Elizabeth Jacka, and Stuart Cunningham. Oxford: Oxford University Press, 1996.

"Real Image Unveils Digital Cinema!" *Real Image-Digital Audio Video Film and DTS Cinema Sound,* June 10, 2006, pp. 1–3. http://www.real-image.com/video/corpnews/11001.asp, accessed June 10, 2006.

Sharma, Rakesh. "Take the Scissors Away from the Censor Board- HT." October 29, 2005. http://www.freedomfilmsindia.org/newsdetail.asp?NewsID=30, accessed June 10, 2006.

Wasko, Janet. *How Hollywood Works.* London: Sage Publications, 2003.

CHAPTER 16

....

DREAMING WITH OPEN EYES: LATIN AMERICAN MEDIA IN THE DIGITAL AGE

....

CRISTINA VENEGAS

Amores perros (Alejandro González Iñárritu, 2000), *Motorcycle Diaries* (*Diarios de motocicleta*, Walter Salles, 2000), *City of God* (*Cidade de Deus*, Fernando Meirelles and Kátia Lund, 2002), and 1999 Golden Globe Best Foreign Film Award winner, *Central Station* (*Central do Brasil*, Walter Salles, 1998): Latin American film is certainly not dead in the digital age. Yet how much of its recent success in the global market does it owe to the advent of new technology? Can countries such as Chile and Argentina sustain their respective "rebirths" in film? And how will film from the region survive as modern media delivery and distribution mechanisms discover and exploit life beyond national boundaries? A diagnosis of the present condition shows nothing wrong when it turns up talents like director Alejandro González Iñárritu (*Amores perros, 21 Grams* [2003], *Babel* [2006]), writer Guillermo Arriaga Jordán (*Amores perros, 21 Grams, Three Burials of Melquiades Estadrada* [Tommy Lee Jones, 2005], *Babel*), and actor Gael García Bernal (*Amores perros, Diarios de motocicleta, El crimen del padre Amaro* [*The Crime of Father Amaro*, Carlos Carrera, 2002], *Y tu mamá también* [Alfonso Cuarón, 2001]). Doubts about the impact of a digital "revolution" disappear on sight of the minimal prices for entry-level equipment, the quality of high-definition documentaries, and the increasing range of delivery and exhibition options. Yet all of these exist in national and international frameworks of policy and economics. The prognosis for Latin American film and audiovisual media in general relies on a view of the bigger picture, not of its increasing technical sophistication.

Generally, the technological advances affecting film ironically ran concurrently with a critical period in the Latin American industries at the end of the 1980s. In the 1990s, developments in digital sound and editing would contribute to larger transformations occurring in national infrastructures and policy. Legitimate and underground markets, for example, have grown up around new methods of distribution and transmission, influencing international policy. New editing and image-manipulation software as well as digital sound recording not only have proven key to the quality of production, but also have aided in the marketing of Latin American cinema worldwide. The increased polish of sound and images took Latin American film as a whole to new levels of technical finesse.

For the truly revolutionary effects of this cinema the focus is not only on a remarkable boost in output, but also on bold experimentation in look, form, and narrative. The proof of renewed life in Latin American film lies in the viewing but demands a much broader contextual frame in order to understand its larger significance.

TECHNOLOGICAL TRANSITION TO DIGITAL

Digital Technology, Access, Change, and the Bottom Line

The digital revolution rolled slowly into the Americas in the 1990s. Much as in other parts of the world, the technical advances in filmmaking would be adopted unevenly across and within different countries. Mexico, Brazil, and Argentina continued, as they still do, to be the major players in technological advancement and production. More than ten years of development of consumer equipment had begun with analog video in the 1980s (VHS and 8-millimeter video, etc.) and anticipated the reception and progression of digital technology in the 1990s. Mid-decade, as the World Wide Web became a tool to overcome barriers to cultural expression, Latin American cultural promoters, producers, and filmmakers explored the divergent needs of audiovisual media production at conferences, special seminars, film festivals, and cultural policy forums. All faced underlying structural limitations stemming from persistently poor economic conditions. Filmmakers contemplated how digital technology might deliver completed films languishing due to lack of distribution, and soon created new production networks designed to expand audiovisual markets. Changes also came to content, aesthetics, scholarship, and policies. After fifteen years, however, experience in the region brings certain "truisms" about technological innovation into question: Can developing countries really use digital technology to leapfrog the technical achievements of richer nations? Does unprecedented access actually erase boundaries, allowing genuinely democratic expression? In reality, barriers remain in the use of English as the lingua franca of the Internet, in the high cost of initial investment, in the speed of technological change, and in general limited resources.

Chances to play an advanced technical game did not produce an even playing field. Latin American film industries had to compete then, and still do now, in markets controlled by major Hollywood companies in terms of distribution and exhibition. Nevertheless, the attractions of new technology were real; digital tools were relatively cheap, lightweight, practical, and sexy. Film production at different scales, from professional to grassroots, benefited in a variety of ways: established filmmakers took the opportunity to make films differently and in some cases more consistently (Arturo Ripstein, *Asi es la vida*, *La perdición de los hombres*, 2000–2001); beginning filmmakers entered the industry at less cost (Fabrizio Prada, *Tiempo real*, 2002); and indigenous and grassroots groups such as Ojo de Agua Communicación in Oaxaca, Mexico, built cooperatives, educational programs, and traveling distribution circuits to train and promote activities with digital media, thus supporting indigenous rights, the preservation of memory, and the environment.[1]

The beneficial restructuring of the technical infrastructure required financial investment, political will, and institutional (e.g., Instituto Cubano de Arte e Industria Cinematográfica [ICAIC]/subsidies/film schools) and private sector support. Initially, investment focused mainly on acquiring nonlinear editing tools that allowed more flexibility in the editing process and opened up the traditional work flow of filmmaking. New networks and partnerships sprang up with international companies such as Avid Technologies (its products now industry standard), which began marketing its nonlinear computer editing systems to Latin America by 1995. Avid editing systems have made the process of flatbed editing almost obsolete.[2] Nonlinear editing facilitated the editing process immensely despite a steep learning curve and poor overall economic conditions. In Cuba, for example, despite the severe economic crisis and catastrophic reverberations for the film industry of the post-Soviet era, the first Avid editing system was purchased in the mid-1990s by the state filmmaking institute, Instituto Cubano de Arte e Industria Cinematográfica (ICAIC). In spite of the U.S. embargo, and with the resolution of the deep troubles of the country's once strong filmmaking community still unknown, investment in digital editing seemed an adventurous bridge to future possibilities—one the country did in fact cross successfully. Political will as well as economic investment was certainly behind this adventure. Training sessions for film professionals began immediately, introducing new ways of working. Foreign donations initially financed the professional Avid level. Shortages existed of both crucial technical expertise and electricity on the besieged island. Nonetheless, several new and established editors would eventually move over to work almost exclusively on computers. The Escuela Internacional de Cine y Televisión de San Antonio de los Baños, Cuba (EICTV), incorporated computerized editing in its curriculum with Avid and at the consumer level with Adobe Premier, and, later, with Apple's Final Cut Pro systems. In turning out the new editors of the region, Cuba's farsighted investment in equipment and training gave it a significant role in shaping digital Latin American audiovisual media. It remains, however, an example of digital advance constrained by harsh economic reality.

Computer Editing Is Real Revolution

The improvement in consumer-level editing systems such as Final Cut Pro proved highly significant, as it gave Latin American filmmakers the ability to create works not only very cheaply but mostly on their own terms. In addition, the reduction in size and cost of digital cameras and better image quality freed filmmakers from the restrictions of heavy, expensive film equipment. Improvements in the quality of image capture made all the difference for those seeking a more filmlike image, without the sharp, infinite depth of the typical digital images seen on television. Working with the new tools, available by purchase, rent, or loan, has given new opportunities to a new generation of film amateurs and professionals. Lighter-weight equipment has also influenced the look and style of camerawork, just as it did in the late 1950s, when Arriflex handheld cameras gave a new look to French New Wave films such as *Breathless* (Jean-Luc Godard, 1960). Digital sound recording has enriched sound quality; digital mixing software, such as Pro Tools, has brought multitrack sound design within reach, facilitating work at new levels of sophistication such as in the astonishing sonic complexity of Lucrecia Martel's *La ciénaga* (2001). The coproducing partnerships that increased throughout the 1990s brought high-end postproduction facilities for the first time to such countries as Cuba, Colombia, and Chile. This initiated the production of a stream of films of high technical quality, which continues today, with notable examples including *Suite Habana* (Fernando Perez, 2003), *El rey* (Antonio Dorado, 2004), and *Machuca* (Andres Wood, 2004).

Reid Burns, a high-level postproduction executive in Hollywood, captured an interesting aspect of the transition to digital cinema when he said, "I miss my Mexican and South American friends."[3] Burns has experienced a consequence of the increasing number of postproduction studios sited in Mexico, Brazil, and Argentina. These countries have been building the infrastructure to be able to complete most, if not all, the postproduction process "at home." The emergence of digital tools, either for editing, for digital intermediate, or for sound or special effects, initially sent interested filmmakers to the United States for technical expertise and training. Their systematic appropriation of the technology now keeps them in Latin America.[4] High-tech digital processing is still executed at specialty houses in Canada, Spain, France, and the United States where budgets will support this, and Latin American filmmakers continue to rely on these countries for "blowup" from digital video to 35-millimeter for final release prints. The general trend, of which Cuba was a part of in the mid-1990s, however, has been to cultivate domestic online editing and postproduction, which in turn has stimulated regional film production in general.

With digital video, exhibition venues for alternative and nonmainstream cinema have surfaced as artisan production has increased. Making a first film is no longer the biggest obstacle confronted by a new filmmaker. However, while the results are often interesting, they all too frequently show poor preparation. The scripts may not be fully developed, and when combined with low budgets, the results can be disastrous. To critics, this quick, rough method of filmmaking may have few repercussions in the broader scheme of things. However, the "playfulness" facilitated by the technology inspires a spontaneous attitude in practitioners. To a degree, this encourages a new form of practice, the roughness and self-indulgence of which are actually antithetical to notions of true practice reiterated by stylistic explorations supported by independent festivals such as Buenos Aires Independent Film Festival (BAFICI). Important innovation may yet arise from so-far undisciplined beginnings. Many young people now have access to filmmaking tools, more are making films and shorts, documentaries and features, and more are exhibited in the growing number of film festivals. The sheer volume alone has become a significant feature of filmmaking in Latin America, especially in countries such as Guatemala, Ecuador, and Nicaragua, where next to no formal production mechanisms exist. The same volume of independent production has also occurred in the United States and other countries, but, without as much necessity from a bigger economic picture to drive invention, may not hold the same potential for re-shaping creative aspects of filmmaking.

The search for fame, fortune, or simple professional or creative vocation has long been a traditional motivation for filmmakers, young and old. With the coming of digital audiovisual media, though, altruistic, community-oriented goals now find wide expression in film in Latin America, the United States, and un-derdeveloped countries throughout the world. The portability of the cameras al-lows filmmakers to document often unseen spaces, such as prison interiors, where inmates produce expressive subcultures, as in Paulo Sacramento's *O prisioneiro da grade do ferro* (*Prisoner of the Iron Bars*, 2004), a feature documentary that began as a filmmaking workshop in the infamous Carandiru Prison in Brazil; or the work of Los Angeles–based Films by Youth Inside (FYI), and Brazil's Nos na Morro group in the favelas. An international grassroots project that demonstrates the extent to which digital technology takes community education beyond national borders is the Coordinadora Latinoamerica de Cine y Communicación de los Pueblos Indigenas (Latin American Film and Communication Coordination of Indigenous Peoples [CLACPI]). CLACPI is a multination organization creating a network of indigenous media makers in Bolivia, Brazil, Chile, Colombia, Cuba, Guatemala, Mexico, and Peru. CLACPI organizes the Festival Internacional de Cine y Video de los Pueblos Indígenas (Film and Video Festival of Indigenous Peoples), now in its eighth year. The 2006 Film Festival, held in Oaxaca, Mexico, featured seventy-eight shorts, documentaries, and features, mostly produced on digital video.[5] The international reach of CLACPI also demonstrates how Latin America's use of digital production extends across various scales of production. The group plans to develop and produce a collaborative international television series with all the member countries, to be distributed throughout the region. Ojo de Agua Comunicaciones, in Oaxaca, Mexico, which is part the CLACPI organization, in contrast, provides video to members of the immediate communities. The range of application of grassroots digital media, though, rests on shared social motivation. In its aims to "increase the production and distribution of indigenous production, and develop viable financing alternatives for production," CLACPI represents the type of community goal underlying the hundreds of similar audiovisual projects across the region.[6] Digital media in particular have proven effective socialist vehicles to assist the poor, link communities, and preserve memory. These are all needs and preoccupations that have put digital tools in the service of cultural and educational functions so vital in Latin American countries such as Mexico and Bolivia, and in developing countries generally that have endured long periods of economic turmoil, civil and political strife, urban growth, and rural degeneration.

Figure 16.1 *O prisioneiro da grade do ferro* (*Prisoner of the Iron Bars*, Paulo Sacramento, Brazil, 2004).

Shooting on Film versus Digital

While "shooting on digital" and using digital postproduction processes bring economic and workflow advantages, most projects still output to 35-millimeter or super-35-millimeter prints for theatrical distribution. The reasons are simple: On the one hand, the business model of digital theatrical distribution continues to evolve since it involves highly complex issues for the major film distributors. On the other hand, few theaters are equipped for digital high-quality projection. When it comes to image capture, the relative cheapness and ease of digital video can lead filmmakers to switch from film. However, higher postproduction and completion costs may negate the lower cost of high definition or digital video because video entails conforming for output to the preferred 35-millimeter film format. Still, shooting on digital also brings relative flexibility; costs can be reduced sharply, retakes made easier, and smaller crews, less lighting, lighter-weight equipment, and shorter shooting schedules employed. However, usually for aesthetic factors, most filmmakers, given the opportunity, would still rather shoot on film.

Award-winning Argentine director Santiago Palavecino, whose first feature, *Otra vuelta* (*Another Turn*, 2004), was shot in black and white on 16-millimeter, has explained that the film could not have been shot on digital video. "The electronic image [because of lighting levels] just doesn't have the texture or density that the story required."[7] For international director Barbet Schroeder, shooting *La virgen de los sicarios* (*Our Lady of the Assassins*, 2000) on high definition in Colombia allowed him a texture that captured the "hyperreality" of the story, as well as mobility and speed, important factors given the number of locations and the dangers of shooting this type of story on the streets of Medellín.[8]

For young Latin American filmmakers, who typically work at first with minimal budgets, digital tools have meant the difference between beginning a career and not. Bolivian filmmaker Marcos Loayza, whose first feature received the Coral Prize for best first feature in Havana in 1995, reflected on the prospects for young digital filmmakers: "The looming specter of making the first project can be overcome by a small investment in a digital camera and computer editing equipment for use at home."[9] Out of the greater numbers of people producing audiovisual work, there are still relatively few who produce work that is truly reflective, introspective, or ambitiously exploring the form of audiovisual language. For Loayza the advantages of the potential freedom lie in the ability to make more personal, less commercial works. A veritable explosion of projects has resulted, particularly in documentary work, thanks to the removal of initial financial obstacles, and to the facility to work faster and more independently.

The plethora of new digital audiovisual production sits in a regional context, where the digital revolution has taken greater hold in countries with the most developed audiovisual infrastructure. This has been so even where changing economic conditions hit filmmaking hard. The increase in access due to digital tools has not generated new national film industries, nor taken fledgling film-making systems into maturity. The most sophisticated Latin American film industries are still found in Argentina, Mexico, and Brazil. Chile, Colombia, and Venezuela are expanding their industries while reforming national legislation to promote investment and project development in a wide variety of genres. Part of the aim here is to broaden the scope of production—production that already incorporates a large digital element. The 1990s renewal of the film industries of Argentina and Brazil, after their virtual collapse, has been largely predicated on state mechanisms for investment and on increases in coproductions. Filmmaking in Argentina has benefited particularly from the state's continuing support of the professionalization of filmmaking through its many film schools. The successes of the Brazilian and Argentinean film industries have, in turn, provided a boost for filmmaking in neighboring nations, through enlarged professional networks and coproduction opportunities. In 2006, for example, a Paraguayan-Argentine co-production, *Hamaca Paraguaya* (*Paraguayan Hammock*, Paz Encina) won the FIPRESCI (The International Federation of Film Critics) award in Cannes. This is an astonishing accomplishment for Paraguay which launched a national film Web site only that same year. The production crew for *Hamaca* lists Argentinian sound designers, composers, and cinematographers. Chile, which saw its film production drop to a single film in 1997, was back to making an average of fourteen films annually by 2004, again largely due to coproductions, many involving partnerships with the region's key film industry players.

The importance of regional partnerships gained official recognition with the creation in December 2003 of the Reunión Especializada de Autoridades Cine-matográficas y Audiovisuales del Mercosur (Specialized Group of Cinemato-graphic Authorities of Mercosur [RECAM]). Established by the Group of the Common Market, an organ of Mercosur, RECAM is charged with creating an institutional framework to advance the integration of the region's audiovisual industries.[10] RECAM's bulletin regarding its June 2006 conference mentions "in-creasing new audiovisual technologies in the production and commercialization of film" as only one of many topics under consideration.[11] The organization has been preoccupied primarily with establishing its own infrastructure and territorial strategies. In this way, filmmakers themselves show how they regard digital tech-nology as a component of larger concerns rather than a driving force.

The economic and technical advantages of digital production have both played a part in strengthening established industrial systems, no matter their scale, throughout Latin America. National infrastructures have been more profoundly influenced, though, by the neoliberal policies of the region in the 1990s and con-sequent mixed investment models. The trend toward coproductions has been a major result and a prop for national production, as is seen in the case of Cuba's reliance on this mechanism throughout the 1990s and 2000s.[12] Legislative reforms stemming from both economic and cultural policies have become the second strut supporting national film production in the region. Ultimately, these are the determining factors underlying and sustaining the digital revolution in Latin America.

Infrastructure, Old Habits, Young Hope

Postproduction executive Reid Burns's friends now place their postproduction work back home in Mexico, Argentina, Brazil, or even Spain. To keep costs down, they need local digital postproduction process facilities. This has led to the emergence of companies in metropolitan centers that provide postproduction options to high- and low-level producers. Such companies offer digital intermediate (DI) locally, an entirely digital postproduction process, independent of acquisition and delivery formats, at a time when the expectation in the United States is that 90 percent of the films produced in 2005–6 will use DI technology.

Latin American digital infrastructure may have adapted in this way, integrating new technology, but it retains its original geography: most Bolivians, Uruguayans, and Peruvians still have to travel to Argentina or Mexico (not Brazil, where Portuguese, rather than Spanish, is spoken) to new specialty facilities such as New Art Digital or Ollin Studios (founded in 1996) in Mexico City. Experienced Peruvian filmmaker Alberto Durant, a key player in the debates about cultural exception between the United States and Peru (who, in typical Latin American fashion, writes, directs, and produces), cites the absence of the digital scanning process in Peru as an example of the infrastructural limitations of the country. His next feature, likely to be shot on digital video, will probably have to convert back to film in Argentina or Mexico, rather than Peru.[13]

Despite new, domestic digital services, and many more new filmmakers able to practice their craft (particularly the New Cinema generation), young filmmaker Santiago Palavecino in Argentina does not have "happy things to say" about the Argentine film industry. Instead, he says, "It tends to reproduce old habits," where corrupt producers and politicians cream off state subsidies, making enough up front to abandon marketing and leave exhibition adrift in theaters in terrible condition. He describes the effervescence of the New Argentine Cinema as real, but also "a vogue," or a fad, sending hundreds of directors chasing too few possibilities to bring projects to fruition. He is not very optimistic.[14] Alberto Durant, an experienced Peruvian filmmaker, seems almost to refer to Palavecino when he counts on the persistence of the new generation: "We must expect everything from the young filmmakers; the world is theirs."[15] Less pessimistically, but like Palavecino, he observes that new and veteran filmmakers face the usual obstacles even as the digital wheels turn.

While huge investments are needed for technology at the level found in Brazil's *Cidade de Deus* (*City of God*), and the rumor persists that projects aimed at major film festivals and large markets require expensive intermediate and postproduction processes, a large technical budget is actually not essential. As cinematographer Checco Varese has stated, "the story is the most important thing."[16] In reality, the perennial factors in international success appear to remain a high-quality screenplay and, much more important, an international (i.e., American) distribution deal with effective marketing.

Distribution and Exhibition: Consumer Revolution?

Digitized delivery found quick market acceptance in the form of DVDs. Digitized piracy soon loaded up on the same chips, hacking away at markets and profits, to the chagrin mainly of the big Hollywood companies. A recent Motion Picture Association of America (MPAA) report estimates lost Hollywood revenues to the tune of $483 million in 2005 due to piracy in Mexico alone.[17] Such is the efficacy of the piracy distribution model that at least one Latin American filmmaker has placed good copies of his films in the hands of illegal distributors, thus ensuring that his films would find an audience. Profits have not followed, but the potential to create a following has. In Latin American countries, the price of a movie ticket or authentic DVD rental or purchase is beyond a large percentage of the population, one that operates in a largely cash economy where black markets thrive. MPAA companies have so far chosen not to reduce profit margins in developing nations, despite the potential for increased sales that might more than compensate for the profit foregone. Latin American distributors meanwhile concern themselves much more with the problem of reaching an audience than with piracy.[18]

The MPAA loss estimates for piracy also cover the Internet, a medium only recently experimenting with legal movie downloads. Movements such as Copyleft promote a future for intellectual property reforms, but in the meantime illegal downloading continues even as distributors test encryption in the first, highly limited Internet film releases. Consumer response, then, to Internet distribution of film in Latin America could well be a repeat of that for DVDs, with the added constraint of limited computer access.

The formal institutionalization of the Internet as a source of audiovisual distribution and exhibition will depend on the resolution of larger issues of copyright legislation, as well as security controls. These issues will link back to overarching policy issues agreed upon among nations and, primarily, the owners and distributors of media. The decisions will not be based on the advancement of a cinematographic culture in any particular nation, but rather on the controlling interests of content producers. In this realm—and not only for Internet distribution—national representation, along with consumer choice, has become submerged in the depths of corporate media ownership.

Cable and Satellite

Cable and satellite, as earlier advances in delivery systems for film and television, and therefore exhibition, had arrived on the scene in the early 1990s. The associated infrastructure, policy, and standardization evolved, then, during the period of major deregulation in Latin American countries and of increasing recognition of the importance of globalization. The three largest media conglomerates in the region, Grupo Televisa in Mexico, Grupo Clarín in Argentina, and Rede Globo in Brazil, have reconfigured the media markets. Since the 1970s, Televisa has expanded its control of Spanish-language cable distribution in Mexico, taking a controlling stake in Cablevisión, a dedicated joint-venture cable provider. Rival pay-per-view cable comes from MVS Multivisión, a telecommunications holding company. These types of operations, however, play only a limited part in television-based distribution in Latin America. The real significance seems to lie with the expansion of satellite direct-to-home (DTH).

Satellite makes sense as a dominant medium where the geographic barriers in Latin America make investment in cable very expensive. As of this writing, Televisa owned a 60 percent stake in Innova, the Mexican operator of the DTH satellite service at one point owned by News Corporation's Sky TV, only to be divested in 2004 in order to merge with DirecTV Latin America, which at that time was 34 percent owned by Fox Entertainment Group, which in turn was about 80 percent owned by News Corporation.[19] Commenting on News Corporation's sale of its Latin American Sky companies to DirecTV, market analyst Marcus Padley suggested it was making the best of a bad situation: "It had proven a difficult place in which to make a dollar."[20] This is not surprising, given the effect of economic policies that reduced the population to reliance on largely black markets for media. Against a background of revolving corporate ownership in cable and satellite distribution, MVS Multivisión has been venturing into the alternative delivery system of broadband, with profits to come perhaps from eventual dominance, or at least from a niche market.

The U.S. Spanish-language market has been served mainly by the U.S. conglomerate Univisión and its cable subsidiary, Galavisión. Galavisión broadcasts both content produced by Univisión and material purchased from Televisa. Whether satellite, or broadband, or both, will emerge as the more competitive delivery mechanism remains to be seen. That the expanding U.S. market for Spanish-language content is the focus of competition is certain. So, too, is its existence far outside the twentieth-century territorial boundaries still in place for film distribution. The astute U.S. empire-building tactics engineered by the late Jack Valenti for MPA companies have locked Latin American film distribution into subordination. In contrast, the business of home delivery of Spanish-language content is now conducted in the dizzying corporate language of global economics. Caveat emptor, consumer and owner both.

Television

Governed and operated separately from film, Latin American television can provide opportunities for domestic success without any need for product export. Nevertheless, revenues from exporting national television products are substantial, and important for the sustained growth of television conglomerates. Theatrical audiences for domestically produced films are usually much smaller than those for Hollywood films, which flood the market. Differences can be as great as two million domestic film viewers to ten for an American movie. The ever-elusive need for international distribution makes domestic exhibition space difficult to secure. Nationally produced television meets no such obstacle. In Brazil and Mexico, home, respectively, to the gigantic broadcasting entities Rede Globo and Televisa, the television industry has become an international economic force, vastly overshadowing the influence of the film industry of both despite their importance in size and scope.

In Brazilian cinemas, most of the offering is produced in Hollywood. Similarly, in Mexico on any given day, Hollywood fodder fills the screens at any of the internationally owned local multiplexes. In Argentina, American films made up 90 percent of the box-office total in 2004 and 85.4 percent in 2005.[21] In contrast, Rede Globo's enormous homegrown distribution system leads to a very different picture for Brazilian television. In the analysis of Brazilian filmmaker and scholar Heitor Capuzzo, Globo is very strong, and shows interesting characteristics. It produces 70 percent of the content it airs, meaning that Brazilians watch mainly Brazilian-made images on their sets.[22] Sharing a regional language, Mexican product broadcast by Televisa has to contend with more competition but still gains the majority of exposure, at 62 percent of total programming.

The future of broadcasting in Latin America was recast in 2006, as both Brazil and Mexico were exploding the political and legislative boundaries of their worldwide reach. The choice of HDTV standards and telecommunications legislation by these key media players affects media industries in every Latin American nation directly or indirectly. Brazil rejected the American standard (ATSC), a closed system, offered by the United States at $3 billion, which would have entailed upgrades to consumers' television sets. The European system was first offered as closed, then open, but would have cost $1 billion. The Japanese system, after a long process of negotiation among President Luiz Inácio "Lula" da Silva, the Japanese Communications Minister, and industry representatives from electronic firms, was open and free. In June 2006, Brazil adopted the Japanese standard (ISDB-T).

The resulting transition to full digital transmission will take place over the next ten years.[23] Attendant aspects should bring tremendous advantages to both parties, given that Brazil is the largest consumer market in Latin America (even though, ironically, Japan is located geographically at the opposite extreme of the globe). TV Globo supported the agreement because the Japanese standard is an open system, which is compatible with the one in place, and which allows Brazil to participate in upgrades. These points were important since Rede Globo produces the bulk of Brazilian programming and already shoots a high proportion of its production in high definition. Sets and components will be manufactured entirely in Brazil, giving the agreement economic relevance beyond the broadcasting sector. Polemic around the deal centered on the redefinition of the broadcast market in the region: Brazil would like to play a larger role in providing television content to its neighbors in Latin America; Argentina, which receives most of its television content from Brazil and Mexico, faces a strategic choice on its HDTV standard. It must ensure maximum compatibility in order for its well-developed industrial base to play a large role as a content producer in the Spanish-speaking region. It had previously adopted the American system during the Carlos Menem presidency in 1998, but this decision was later revoked by the Fernado de la Rúa administration.

In Mexico, in March 2006, congress approved and adopted Article 28 to the Federal Law of Radio and Television, known as the "Televisa Law," much to the dismay of the nation's public service broadcasters, phone and Internet providers, and filmmakers.[24] Historically, Mexico treated broadcasting space as public property, granting paid licenses for the use of assigned electromagnetic spectrum as analog channels. As a result of the new law, Televisa and a rival network, TV Azteca, were granted a license at no cost for $50 million worth of channels, which they did not have to return to the government, and from which they would be allowed to profit. Televisa could transform itself into a full telecommunications company able to provide cellular telephone and Internet services. By June 2007, those who objected argued that the new norms established for Internet transmission were unconstitutional since they eliminated existing public interest programs and prevented the entry of new competitors.[25] Intense protests erupted all over the airwaves, arguing that the law would dissolve community and educational radio networks that had evolved over decades. The Mexican Institute of Radio played cycles of songs with titles like "A Blank Check," a protest campaign that likened the Televisa Law to playing the same song repeatedly all day, and did just that. Artilce 28 of the Televisa Law, which continued to generate controversy, was annulled by a unanimous vote of congress as it was deemed to violate basic rights of freedom of expression. Stakes on the issue of state governance over digital convergence are high since control over bandwidth means more capacity for and control over HDTV transmission and satellite delivery. Those who control satellite distribution will be in a position to recast audiovisual industries in the twenty-first century, and not just in Latin America.

On the whole, digital technology along with deregulation of the telecommunication sectors has played a key role in creating and expanding markets for multinational media conglomerates. Exceptional political will is needed in order to generate new, astute policies to ensure access to new markets by smaller producers, and, indeed, to transform the entire model of distribution and exhibition.

The Box Office

The film *Bañeros III, todopoderosos* (*Bathers III, Superheroes*; Rodolfo Ledo, 2005) beat out *Superman Returns* (Bryan Singer, 2006) in the summer of 2006 on its opening weekend in its home country, Argentina. *Bañeros,* starring comedian Emilio Disi and Gino Renni, is a sequel to the 1980s versions of *Bañeros* (*Bathers*) that have become cult favorites.[26] *Bañeros,* a retro film with 1980s music, connected with audiences, who saw themselves in the film. While this situation is promising for the creation of an audience for domestic films, the real stimulus will be the continued support of a variety of producers to create a diverse moviegoing culture.

In Mexico, screenwriter and producer Guillermo Arriaga Jordán has reminded us that four Mexican movies succeeded in beating out Hollywood fare during the peak summer moviegoing seasons. They were: *Sexo, pudor y lágrimas* (*Sex, Shame and Tears*, Antonio Serrano, 1999), *Amores perros, Y tu mamá también,* and *El crimen del padre Amaro* (*The Crime of Father Amaro,* Carlos Carrera, 2000). *Amores perros* competed with *Mission Impossible II* (John Woo, 2000) and won.[27] The pattern of home-country success appears also in Brazil, where *Cidade de Deus* and *2 Filhos de Francisco* (*Two Sons of Francisco,* Breno Silveira, 2005) have set box-office records for domestic films.

While such events are not entirely new, their overall impact has not reversed the downward trend, begun in the 1990s, in box-office take. No matter the quality and appeal of a film, whether or not facilitated or improved by digital technology, Latin American cinema still suffers serious disadvantages in its industries, including a decrease in the number of theaters, increases in the price of movie tickets, piracy, and the rise of the multiplex culture. The lack of healthy exhibition conditions is compounded by poor social conditions, which have generated an increase in urban violence, which, in turn, keeps movie attendance figures down.

The Era of the Multiplex

The rise of the multiplex began around 1986 and continued through the mid-1990s. It redefined entertainment habits in a period when major American studios regained control over film distribution and began to emphasize global markets. The majority of the population in Latin America was by then resident in urban areas, as economic opportunities dried up in the rural sector as a result of failed neoliberal policies. The total number of theaters decreased as multiplexes, most foreign owned, replaced traditional movie theaters. The result has been consolidation of the dominance of U.S. films, greater U.S. control of access to foreign markets, and even less regional content than previously on exhibition in Latin America. Down but not out, Latin American film has developed alternative distribution circuits and microcinemas that barely build attendance, but which do create audiences by expanding the traditional exhibition circuits.

Alternative Distribution Circuits

In response to foreign-owned mainstream distribution, along with the rise of the multiplex, alternative national and regional distribution circuits have emerged to address the issue of dwindling film audiences, a problem whose global scope has been addressed by media scholar Charles Acland.[28] The use of nontraditional venues has multiplied, taking film into urban centers, smaller towns, churches, cafés, schools, air-conditioned tent theaters with digital projection, or a large screen playing DVDs. The concept of the microcinema is not a new one, and its potential to stabilize the overall decline in film-going numbers has yet to be realized. However, given the virtual abandonment of the countryside during neoliberal "reforms" in the 1980s and 1990s in Latin America, they may prove to be a source of culture if not alternatives to global tastes.

Microcinemas

Grupo Chaski in Peru established a network of microcinemas that has operated since 2003. The group itself was established in 1982 with the making of the documentary *Miss Universo*, contrasting the frivolity of the contest with a depressing national situation. Spurred by ideological consciousness, the group aims to provide decentralized exhibition and distribution in Peru. In alliance with various distribution circuits in other countries, including Bolivia, Argentina, and Ecuador, and with the support of a Peruvian-Swiss partnership, Grupo Chaski distributes cinema in DVD format through a network of small theaters in areas that multiplex cinemas have not reached. It also promotes cinema from Peru and from Latin America in general.[29] The value of this tactical use of media is unquestionable, even though it appears to have little impact against a dominant paradigm of foreign distribution powerhouses; it succeeds in providing an alternative and thereby increasing access.

Although ambulatory DVD clubs are inexpensive to set up, the main problem they face is not the crudely simple conditions this process entails. Rather, the limited economic setup does not allow for a proper revenue structure; this makes their existence as a community service quite precarious. But these efforts do still build an audience even while they cannot supplant mainstream distribution.

Another sign of the important role of the microcinemas is their function in establishing the community aspect in cases where videos and DVDs function as important tools of activism, education, and expression. The itinerant Film and Video Festival of Indigenous Peoples carries out such a role, alongside the main festival event, promoting a circuit of microcinema distribution among participating nations.

The late 1980s saw the rise of several independent production companies and video distributors. The idea was to aggressively carve out exhibition space for national cinema while at the same time to act as independent distributors. One such venture, Zafra Video S.A., founded by Mexican producer and distributor Jorge Sanchez, coordinator until 1988, operates as an alternative distributor of Mexican and Latin American independent films. Sanchez later founded Macondo Cine Video to produce and distribute films, and Latina S.A., focused primarily on foreign sales of Mexican and Latin American films. The results of these entrepreneurial instances can be appreciated in the work of a strong generation of filmmakers such as Maria Novaro (*Lola*, 1990 and *Danzón*, 1991) who entered international markets during this time. Cinemanía, a small chain of independent video theaters, rounds out Sanchez's broad vision of change through local ownership of production, exhibition, and distribution.

Digital Cinema, Brazil's Rain Network

Based in São Paulo, Brazil, and with offices in Rio de Janeiro, New York, and London, the Rain Network is a holding company with an aggressive digital distribution project via satellite. The company has developed Kinocast, proprietary management software using the MPEG-4 compression system, and plans to use the Embratel satellite.[30] The system addresses multiple language formats, copyright control, and online reports. Rain aims to rebuild the theatrical distribution model by connecting a worldwide network of exhibitors and distributors, and improving exhibition, distribution, and production—particularly independent—revenue. With worldwide vision, Rain has established alliances with China and has created important production partnerships in London with Buena Onda Films and in the United States with Emerging Pictures. Rain purports to prioritize security of delivery through encryption and a fifteen-number security password available only prior to screenings. Presumably it also reduces costs by decreasing middle administrative burden. To what extent this is realistic, given the domination of majors over the global distribution of film, is unclear. Its new distribution model may prove to be founded on solid business acumen. But can it reverse a perverse logic of the Brazilian film business where, as stated by critic Pablo Villaça, four hundred thousand tickets sold for 2 *Filhos de Francisco* (*Two Sons of Francisco*, 2005) is an "excellent result for a Brazilian movie, generating a box office gross of 6,000.000 reais (about $2.56 million U.S.)."[31] This presents an absurd situation in which most of the money from box-office take goes to distribution fees and to producers, who make back one or two million of the three million they have invested, and little is left for directors. And yet such a film is considered a hit. Perhaps the odds are against it, but if Rain's proposed distribution system, with its promise of increased efficiency and reduced costs, succeeds, it could significantly increase the sustainability of the Brazilian film industry.

The transition to digital cinema has begun in earnest over the last five years, with the placement of infrastructure that advances a broad spectrum of production, distribution, and exhibition issues. Some have responded almost euphorically, but a look at the bottom line suggests that caution is advisable. Cinematographer Checco Varese provided the ultimate dictum, "If you ask me, the future of the digital image lies in Wall Street."[32]

NARRATIVES AND THEMES

Three central areas of production attest to the effervescence of the cinema of the 1990s and 2000s. Despite difficult political and economic conditions and acute periods of crisis, Argentina, Mexico, and Brazil have produced a string of films that have been not only critical successes but also international box-office hits. Their respective domestic box-office takings have often beaten out competing Hollywood blockbusters. Films such as *Como agua para chocolate* (*Like Water for Chocolate*, Alfonso Arau, 1992), *Central do Brasil*, *Amores perros*, *Nueve reinas* (*Nine Queens*, Fabian Bielinsky, 2000), *Y tu mamá también*, *El crimen del padre Amaro* (*The Crime of Father Amaro*), *Cidade de Deus* (*City of God*), *Carandiru* (Hector

Babenco, 2003), and *Diarios de motocicleta* (*Motorcycle Diaries*). *El laberinto del fauno* (*Pan's Labyrinth*, Guillermo del Toro, 2006) reestablished Latin American cinema at the forefront of world cinema. As filmmakers have fought back against the effects of global economic forces with intensely local films that speak to international audiences, they have garnered more Academy Award nominations than ever before.[33]

Many successful Latin American films of recent years, however, were produced in the midst of economic and political highs and lows. As much as any of their larger counterparts, smaller industries such as those of Chile, Colombia, Cuba, Peru, and Venezuela experienced the ravages of economic upheavals. Other production sites such as Uruguay, Paraguay, Ecuador, and the Central American countries of Costa Rica, Guatemala, Nicaragua, El Salvador, and Panamá managed to produce either first features, or, through coproductions, to jump-start national production.

Together with Spain and Portugal, both large and small producing nations from Latin America joined to form Ibermedia, a pan-Ibero-American fund that facilitates coproductions. Working through international partnerships against the backdrop of regional trade pacts (principally Mercosur and the North American Free Trade Agreement [NAFTA]), nations lobbied for "cultural exception" to define new ways of integrating and building stronger culture industries.[34] On paper, the implications of trade legislation for the culture sector are not always clear; this has led groups of international media scholars and filmmakers to focus on the effects of their implementation. Mexico's case is particularly disquieting since "cultural exception" for Mexico's culture industries was not in place upon the signing of NAFTA in 1994; as a result, the audiovisual industry must abide by the same mechanisms of international trade as, for example, agriculture or automobiles. Mexican filmmaker and critic Victor Ugalde has written extensively about the disastrous implications for Mexican film production, calling it simply, "the worst crisis of our industry."[35]

In general, the close relationship of film production to state mechanisms in the region (central institutes finance, produce, and promote film production) made (and still makes) film production vulnerable to the instability of inflation, foreign debt, and the political programs and policies of changing governments.[36] From 1990 to 1993, Brazilian production experienced a familiar state of crisis, as Embrafilme and Concine, the two main government entities responsible for production, were both dissolved by the Collor de Melho government. De Melho's presidency would end in impeachment in 1992 on charges of corruption, as Brazil's foreign debt jumped to nearly US$115 billion, and inflation rose to 1,500 percent annually. Meanwhile, though, the dissolution of the state agencies brought one of Latin America's major film industries to a near standstill, with only two features produced in 1992. In addition, the "quota" exhibition system that guaranteed a space in theaters to Brazilian films had been abolished,[37] and television had consolidated its position as a global exporter of domestic content. Brazilian film was subsequently jump-started in large part due to new incentives and policies for production, financing, and exhibition promoted by new governments. The Lei Rouanet and the Lei do Audiovisual (1993) created new financing possibilities focused on the private sector.[38] Rio-based Riofilme was established to finance, produce, and distribute audiovisual content in all formats. Reversing the disastrous two previous years, Riofilme completed ninety projects between 1993 and 1994, fifty-six of which were features.

The crisis confronting Mexican cinema at the opening of the twenty-first century had begun in earnest much earlier. State policy has always affected film policy, production, and audiences, the latter through censorship. Downward-spiraling state support, along with conflicts with the film workers unions, eventually led to what, in the 1980s, Alejandro Pelayo termed the "decade of crisis."[39] In fact, it had been in order to ameliorate the state policies of the seventies through the reform of cinema policy that the Instituto Mexicano de Cinematografía (IMCINE) was created in 1983. By the late eighties, a number of independent production companies produced a cinema that was experimental, personal, and high quality. More important, the independent companies signaled that there was yet another way of making films outside the tutelage of the state. The early nineties were supposed to be a rebirth, as stipulated by the government of Carlos Salinas de Gortari, meant to find full support through the incoming policies of NAFTA. Instead, the measures set in place during de Gortari's six-year term provoked a downturn in production. Following the 1994 implementation of NAFTA, Mexico went from producing fifty-one features between 1990 and 1994, to producing only another twenty-one by 2001. More than half the number of films produced in 2001 were independent productions. Support for exhibition was eliminated, as were the state entities (Azteca Films, etc.) that had distributed films in the United States. Multiplex theaters owned by international companies, namely Cinemark, Hoyt Cinemas, and others, arrived on the scene instead. The emergence of a real independent sector in companies that produced features for international distribution proved a significant development during the late eighties and into the nineties. These companies brought multiple sources of financing: IMCINE, private companies, other state entities, and international producers. This more flexible structure facilitated the internationalization of the cinema and adoption of international financing mechanisms.

Like the Mexican weekly *Proceso*, which in a special issue examined the "Mexican Hollywood," Venezuelan film scholar Luisela Alvaray analyzed a global Latin American cinema that no longer has any references, formal or ideological, to the films of the sixties and seventies. She found that this trend is one of the consequences for production in the Americas of the growing presence of the MPA and NAFTA, and that it underscores the strategic significance of international alliances.[40] Also, with the international success of films like *Amores perros* and *Y tu mamá también,* a group of Latin American filmmakers has been integrated into the international arena (e.g., Alfonso Cuarón with *A Little Princess* [1995], Guillermo Arriaga Jordán and Alejandro González Iñárritu with *21 Grams* [2003], Fernando Mireilles with *The Constant Gardner* [2005], and Guillermo del Toro with *Mimic* [1997]), and has formed a new elite corpus with the power to mold new creative trends in film from the region.

While producers like Iñárritu and Cuarón found fame and hope for the recovery of the Mexican industry in the early 2000s, those who could find few avenues for financing had a different opinion of the recovery. The new structures of production have not brought output back to the levels of 1994. The year 2004 saw only thirty-eight films produced. Aggressive lobbying efforts by members of the film community, however, resulted in increased allocations to funding agencies, improved coproduction partnerships with Europeans, and facilitation of private investment in films. Additionally, creation of the Fondo de Inversión y Estímulos al Cine Mexicano (FIDECINE) in 2001 has made the process of project selection more democratic by opening it up to public scrutiny. Paradoxically, the level of worldwide success of the films produced during this period creates the impression that Mexico has a vigorous industrial infrastructure. The reality resembles more an infrastructure that is overcoming constant challenges.

Another sign of the improved health of the Mexican industry is the wealth of talent produced, seen also throughout the hemisphere. Thus far, this has launched the work of thirty-six new directors in Mexico between 2003 and 2005, many of them opting to work in the various digital formats.[41] The industry must still ramp itself up into more efficient production mechanisms, however, in order fully to tackle the blows dealt to it by privatizations and budget reductions.

Argentina's film industry began the 1990s producing only ten films a year, the lowest number since 1934.[42] As in other countries in the region, high inflation, foreign debt, an economy in shambles, and the 1994 reform of the Film Law to allow the infusion of new financing to the production of films galvanized an industry restructuring sufficient to overturn its languishing status. New financing revived and supported new models of filmmaking, both independent and industrial, but the film industry was again headed downward in 2001 as the economy and the political climate of the country went into complete chaos. The new mechanisms, however, along with the support of film schools in producing independent films, once again expanded the realm of production as the economy began to recover in 2004 and 2005.

Alongside exciting new trends in aesthetic style came developments in "industrial" or "commercial" cinema that also brought the first Argentine blockbusters, which attracted large national audiences. Tamara Falicov referred to 1997 as a "new watershed year for a new kind of cinema in Argentina—popular, yet in some circles (especially small director producers) it aroused skepticism and more than little cynicism."[43] New film legislation passed in 1994 facilitated the partnerships that made the blockbuster phenomenon possible by creating new means of film financing: alliances were struck between private television and the national film institute, typical big business and government arrangements that were also characteristic throughout Carlos Menem's presidency.

Smaller producing countries likewise experienced periods of catastrophe followed by renewal in their film production when similar legislative reforms spurred industry growth. The role of the state in production, financing, and distribution continues but also within the context of reformed institutions that have embraced mixed financing programs promoting a variety of tendencies, styles, and generations. Regional trade pacts such as Mercosur have helped industries such as Uruguay's integrate their audiovisual production within the common market by facilitating coproductions between Latin American and Iberian nations.[44] This also expands the market reach for each participating nation by allowing distribution agreements that encourage the circulation of the cinema in the new geography of (de)regulation and cooperation in the trade regions.

Inspired by Moments of Crisis

The filmmakers that make up the New Argentine Cinema draw for inspiration on the consequences of neoliberal policies in the nineties, swiftly enacted in the aftermath of the military dictatorships. The rising inequalities, the corruption, the piecemeal privatization of national firms, along with the total collapse of the economy in 2001, constructed the dramatic fabric of the new narratives. The resulting economic and social chaos was substance for the complex reality that emerged as people took to the streets, rebuilt their lives, and tried to plan for uncertain futures. *Pizza, birra, faso* (*Pizza, Beer, and Cigarettes,* 1998) by Adrián Caetano and Bruno Stagnaro, one of the first films to come out of this generation, became the cornerstone of newness, with an uncompromising language rooted in the streets, its slang, and its characters. Coming out of film schools and using all possible methods to shoot, often with digital tools, the filmmakers of this generation can be characterized not by cohesive aesthetic preoccupations, but by a radical diversity of styles, themes, and genres. Generally, diversity is the most important characteristic of work flowing from all over Latin America, as filmmakers of the past two decades experiment, more often merging genres than adhering to conventional distinctions. Though there is a shared experience of economic chaos, the resulting narratives and styles are highly personal and fresh, displaying a deliberate commitment to breaking away from the aesthetic canon of previous generations.

Trends in Style and Narrative

Responding to local themes, high production values, and a new emphasis on marketing, domestic audiences throughout the Americas have responded significantly to films promoted on more of a regional than international scale. Examples include *Rosario Tijeras* (Emilio Maillé, 2005), a Colombian-Mexican-Spanish-Brazilian coproduction; *La mujer de mi hermano* (*My Brother's Wife*; Ricardo de Montreuill, 2005), an Argentine-Mexican-Peruvian-U.S. coproduction; and *Bañeros III, todopoderosos* (*Bathers III, Superheroes*; Rodolfo Ledo, 2005), an Argentinean comedy. A healthy film industry must first appeal to its own domestic audience, a task not easily accomplished in a marketplace that, during the 1980s, was consolidated by the MPA member companies. In regional terms, this has led to common filmic thematic foci, including contemporary social issues, such as violence and corruption stemming from drug economies, and the mainstreaming of gay culture, as well as romance and homegrown music cultures.

Indeed, the topic of urban violence is not new to Latin American cinema. The violence depicted in the films of the 1960s and 1970s stemmed from imperialism, underdevelopment, and poverty. Luis Buñuel's unsentimental look at street kids in *Los olvidados* (1950), or Nelson Pereira dos Santos's *Rio Zona Norte* (*Rio, Northern Zone*, 1955), gave way to *Pixote* (Brazil, 1980), Hector Babenco's explicit and disturbing tale of lives lost to poverty, crime, and corrupt law enforcement. *Pixote* is indelible not only for its gritty style, but also for the fact that the film's star was the real thing: a young boy avoiding hunger by sniffing glue and surviving through petty crime. Colombian Victor Gaviria's *Rodrigo D: no futuro* (*Rodrigo D: No Future*, 1990) is a testament to the capacity of independent film to re-create the frenetic pace of lives caught up in the cycles of violence in Colombia. In constant motion, and to the pulsing beat of punk music, Gaviria's roving camera creates a visceral experience, situating the viewer in a claustrophobic embrace of endless danger. It is this same generation of disappeared young men who made a living as cheaply hired assassins that serves as the backdrop to Barbet Schroeder's *La virgen de los sicarios* (*Our Lady of the Assassins*) adapted for the screen by Fernando Vallejo from his own short story. Gaviria's other films, *Vendedora de rosas* (*The Rose Seller*, 2000) and *Sumas y restas* (*Addictions and Subtractions*, 2005), continued to explore the world of drug cartels, homeless children, and violence, defining a visual style designed to draw the viewer into the madness while still holding on to tenderness. *Carandiru* (2003), Babenco's latest film, and *Cidade de Deus* stylize violence, again to shocking visceral effect, but suspended in a strangely appealing aesthetic. *Cidade* in particular connected with a new generation of moviegoers globally, mixing music, dazzling camera techniques, and editing with depictions of intense social strife and violence.

Cidade exemplifies the way recent Latin American films have begun to give equal weight to visual style and narrative, allowing the refraction of theme and story along several planes where one can sublimate the other. Writers and directors now blur generic conventions, authoring a range of styles from popular to art cinema. Working against the less adventurous market-driven restrictions of commercial cinema (film popular with audiences), filmmakers explore local realities with the bravura of independent production. The new narrative strategies are less concerned with strict adherence to melodrama, comedy, testimonial, or pure drama, exploring instead visual and aural rhythms, multiple and minimal story lines, temporality, and most important, a rigorous attention to questioning forms of "realism."

Social Context and Aesthetic Form

A leader in the creation of new approaches, Argentinean Adrian Caetano works within an economy of style and orchestrates a restrained, deliberate pace that allows the viewer to engage slowly and fully with the action. In *Bolivia* (1999/2003), he ventured again into the gritty reality explored in *Pizza, birra, raso,* taking the audience into the confines of xenophobia in Buenos Aires. Shot in beautiful black and white, it follows an undocumented Bolivian immigrant working as a cook in a café, whose attempt at a romantic relationship is truncated by violence. The purposeful rhythm establishes the character's distance from a "legal" world limited by verbal communication among people, punctuated by spurts of aggression. The pace of the drama is slow, contained, distant, anticipating a denouement but not committed to providing one. In a similar way, Uruguayans Pablo Stoll and the late Juan Pablo Rebella revealed tremendous control of form in *Whisky* (2004), a dark comedy following the lives of three middle-aged people who communicate with one another only in abbreviated sentences and with limited emotion. The framing is absolutely still, echoing the emotional stagnation of the characters. Such films work within the well-established dramatic parameters of a central conflict and attempts to overcome it, but they are minimal, almost a denial of real dramatic action as a way to underscore a sense of alienation. Rebella and Stoll had earlier produced the Uruguayan independent slacker movie *25 Watts* (2001), which follows three aimless youths through twenty-four hours in Montevideo. With only these two impressive films to their credit, Rebella and Stoll established a personal, local style that resonated not only with regional cultural paradigms but also with international independent circuits. *Whisky* received the prestigious Sundance-NHK International Filmmaker's Award in 2003 for its script and premiered at the Cannes Film Festival in 2004. Established Argentine editor and director Ana Poliak, in *Parapalos* (*Pin Boy*, 2004), rendered in uncompromising style the life of a young man who arrives in Buenos Aires from the provinces. Winner of the top jury prize at the Buenos Aires International Independent Film Festival, Poliak's film quietly observes the life of the central character as he adapts to work in the city. Stacking pins at one of the last manually operated bowling alleys, the new arrival learns about the dangers of the ball rolling in on him, discovers the value of working quickly, and appreciates the languid pace of the wait in a doctor's office. Like Rebella and Stoll's, Poliak's style is to observe the "action" in all its stillness and silence.

In Mexico, Juan Carlos Rulfo poetically explores the rhythms of life, re-investing quotidian experience with meaning. His stunning first feature, *Del olvido no me acuerdo* (*Juan, I Forgot I Don't Remember*, 1999) is a documentary, although its style is symbolic and evocative, "an homage to time and memory," as Rulfo has said.[45] Straying from the strict boundaries of documentary, the film revolves around Rulfo returning to his father's hometown to ask the people there what they remember of the man. He decides upon a fictional device of looking for memories where they no longer exist, allowing the filmmaker to listen and recount their stories unencumbered by the formal textures of a documentary interview. Rulfo works in a tendency that has its roots in *Redes* (Emilio Gomez Muriel and Fred Zinnemann, 1934–1936) and is part of a range of unusual stylistic and thematic treatments in contemporary Mexican cinema.

Arturo Ripstein's *Así es la vida* (*Such Is Life*, 2000) reworks Greek tragedy through melodrama. Composed on digital video, Ripstein's strategy derives claustrophobic and dramatic intensity from scenes that take the viewer beyond the comfort level and reveal an abundance of dramatic information. Opposite Ana Poliak's measured observation, *Vida* is not observation but confrontation that, strangely like Poliak's film, plays out in long, deliberate takes used in this instance to increase tension.

In Ricardo Benet's *Noticias lejanas* (*News from Afar*, 2004), set in the high plateaus of Central Mexico, the director trained his camera on this evocative landscape to capture quotidian existence. In his intense isolation, Martín long dreams of moving to the city. He moves there only to return defeated, and upon his return sets in motion a series of events that have devastating consequences for himself and his family. A pensive meditation on rural isolation, the film avoids presenting any moral or ideological conflict. Instead, the narrow emotional vicissitudes of the character in his planning and his return become an instrument to convey the rhythms of an unfulfilled life lived against a backdrop of unshakable origin and disconnected future. With an observational stance sighted on a Mexican landscape rarely viewed in life or on screen, *Noticias* again captures the pace of the individual detached from mainstream life. Where Babenco makes the action hang in an artistic nonreality, Benet finds life hanging from subsistence threads against the reality of a stark, indifferent landscape. The former blends techniques with a new international audiovisual verve, while the other, like Rebella, Stoll, and Poliak,

Figure 16.2 *Noticias lejanas* (*News from Afar*, Ricardo Benet, Mexico, 2005).

lingers with a newfound sensibility afforded by a singular, but complex approach, one reliant on fewer filmic layers.

Complex Narrative Meets Minimal Style

Appearing at the other end of the spectrum are films with complex narratives or multiple storylines and that nonetheless utilize minimal style. *Amores perros* (Alejandro González Iñárritu, 2000) masterfully interweaves three distinct intimate stories, which are connected through both one violent car crash and the presence of dogs in each. The narrative freshness stems from the overlap of stories involving different social classes, with the aforementioned climactic car crash leveling the playing field. The *rock en español* sound track and gritty aesthetics set the look and feel of *Amores* apart from other Mexican productions. Its references are not to the old Mexican cinema but to a contemporary vision of urban Mexico. Not unlike the appeal of *Pizza* in Argentina, *Ratas, ratones y rateros* (*Rodents*, Sebastián Cordero, 2000) in Ecuador, or *Mala leche* in Chile (León Errázuriz, 2004), *Amores* spoke in slang and confronted contemporary social issues head-on. In *Lucia, Lucia* (Antonio Serrano, 2003), a multilayered narrative is deftly constructed around the main character's constantly shifting persona. Interestingly, *Lucia*'s multiple narrative layers mix genres effectively, as it begins the action as a thriller, unravels the plot as a road movie, and resolves the conflict as a police story. Carlos Sorin's nuanced *Historias minimas* (*Intimate Stories*, 2003) makes the smallest anecdote

Figure 16.3 *Mala leche* (León Errázuriz, Chile, 2004).

the center of three interweaving intimate stories. *Historias* features a lost dog, a guilt-ridden octogenarian, and a lonely salesman, but no car crashes. As opposed to *Amores*, it is stylistically stark, patiently observing human frailty, but still woven into a well-structured dramatic storyline.

The small story, conveniently economic for Latin American budgets, finds new meaning in veteran filmmaker Jaime Humberto Hermosillo's *La tarea* (*Homework,* 1991). Shot on VHS, the film is surprising in its economy: two actors, two camera positions, one setting. An exercise in voyeurism, the film portrays a middle-aged woman who makes seduction her object, and uses a hidden video camera to record the action. The audience becomes a voyeur in what appears to be one long take. This troubling subjectivity transforms the action and acts as yet another dramatic character in the film. Despite the minimal presentation, the film still has a three-act structure. Chilean Matías Bize's *En la cama* (*In Bed,* 2005) could have been inspired by Hermosillo's *La tarea.* Set in a motel room, the film depicts two people, who having just met up at a party, rent a room and make love throughout the night. Their pauses provide the dramatic vehicle for the development of character and story; acquaintance, familiarity, and intimacy in this case are the three stages of the drama. Hermosillo, who has been working since the 1960s, has an economy of means and audacity of approach that appear just as fresh as the newcomer Bize's. His films of the 1990s continue to challenge emotional landscapes in a cinematic register that is unabashedly independent even while embracing basic parameters of dramatic structure.

It is a move away from dramatic conventions, however, and toward abstraction that provides minimal register as structure by extracting climactic energy, such as in Lisandro Alonso's *La libertad* (*Freedom*, 2001) or *Los muertos* (2004), and Poliak's *Parapalos*, and that precludes resolution, as in *Ana y los otros* (*Ana and the Others*, 2003) by Celina Murga. This approach to narrative eschews causal plot developments, particularly in *La libertad*, *Los muertos*, and *Cómo pasan las horas* (*The Hours Go By*, 2005) by Ines de Olivera César. In *Libertad*, the main character, a lumberjack, lives alone in the woods. He works; he eats; he sells the wood he cuts. His contact and communication with others is minimal, and the film creates no expectations for a dramatic outcome, refusing to establish the expected dramatic conflict, instead insisting that the viewer experience the textures of life. In *Muertos*, Alonso goes one step further at the outset by suggesting the barest of dramatic backbones, creating a disquieting mood and a timeless narrative. We are not concerned in either film about the temporal clues, whether the film takes place in one day or two. We do notice the duration of events, eating soup by the side of the road, the slow rowing of the canoe, the detailed gutting of an animal, all increasing tension and anticipation by absence of causal narrative connections. Likewise, *Ana y los otros* begins the story with a search: Ana returning to her hometown to search for an old boyfriend. As in *Muertos*, a mood is established, uncertain, cryptic, and ultimately unsettling for its refusal to comply with any type of closure, what would be considered simply wrong in a typical Hollywood screenplay. These films demonstrate an intense focus on intimate expressive structures using minimal dramatic resources that are firmly rooted in a Latin American reality.

The same sense of unease is produced aurally in the work of Argentine Lucrecia Martel, in both *La ciénaga* (*The Swamp*, 2000) and *La niña santa* (*The Holy Girl*, 2004). These two films bring together many of the elements that are present in the work of other filmmakers mentioned thus far: experimenting with dramatic causality and minimal action. The detailed and repetitive use of sound cues creates a sense of frustration, evoking the tension of characters on the verge of nervous breakdowns. Absent is the clichéd use of music or sound to underscore a sentiment; instead the sound track is filled with the potentially grating noise of everyday life: the constant banter of children, ice cubes clinking in a glass, the constant ringing of unanswered telephones. The acoustic tapestry of Martel's work reveals the intimate lives of characters, producing a subjective sensory experience rather than adherence to machinations of plot.

Perhaps nowhere is there a more self-consciously opposite (and oppositional) stance to standard Hollywood conventions as in the work of Mexican filmmaker Carlos Reygadas. Starting in 2002 with his first feature, *Japón*, and later with *Batalla en el cielo* (*Battle in Heaven*, 2005), Reygadas followed a personal preoccupation with confounding narrative expectations and generic boundaries. Primarily the films betray a search for something essential, a search for spiritual meaning in the context of exhausted symbolic paradigms. Along with Amat Escalante's *Sangre*

Figure 16.4 *Batalla en el cielo* (*Battle in Heaven*, Carlos Reygadas, Mexico, 2005).

(2005) the films stress an emotionally detached formal approach, in which (non)actors play their roles with deadpan emotion in front of static cameras. With moral decay just below the surface, the films ponder the meaning of being human in contemporary life. Reygadas's aesthetic grows out of the tension inherent in the dialogue, with the international language of Hollywood evident in explicitly genre films.

Playing on Genres

The developing tension between working on small and personal projects and working on larger, more complex projects has already yielded interesting experiments in the area of genre films. The range and number of films working within genre conventions are daunting but worthy of mention, for they clearly function within the parameters of an "international" language of cinema. Given established audience tastes, genre films are more likely to find success at the box office. Aside from the western, no other genre is so clearly "American" as the road film, with a sturdy journey structure serving as the armature for the development of dramatic conflicts. Interestingly, the road movies coming out of Latin America express a journey across emotional landscapes, unrepresented places and moments in history, as much as they show the pleasure of the road. In Salles's *Diarios de motocicleta*, a young middle-class medical student discovers the South America shielded from him by his class privilege; *Y tu mamá también* pits two young men from opposite social classes on an apparent sexual discovery journey;

Guantanamera (Tomás G. Alea and Juan Carlos Tabío, 1995) follows an improbable cross-country funeral procession in an economically ravaged Cuba.

In contrast to the road movie, the melodrama, because of its reliance on performance and excess, is easily malleable. Arturo Ripstein's *Principio y fin* (*Beginning and End*, 1993) stands out as a monumental achievement of this example. Transposing an Egyptian novel onto contemporary Mexico City, the story reveals the suffocating structure of family life and the destructive nature of guilt and exploitation. *Filhas do vento* (*Daughters of the Wind*, Joel Zito Araújo, 2004), with the first all black cast in a Brazilian film, reworks the structure of the *telenovela* to make a statement on the legacy of racism and slavery. Marketable internationally, comedies sell while they entertain, and in doing so they facilitate the internationalization of filmmakers. Incisive and innovative comedies like Fernando Eimbcke's *Temporada de patos* (*Duck Season*, 2004) eschew the "troubled teen" formula in favor of a more sensitive, nuanced portrayal of adolescent life, thematic qualities that facilitate the internationalization of the genre. While international box-office success is relative, comedies are vehicles for working through vexing social dramas. In Cuba, Juan Carlos Tabio's film *Lista de espera* (*Waiting List*, 2000) self-reflexively expressed the cacophony of strangeness that was the 1990s. The narrative displaces a dream society onto a manageable bus station-cum-utopia. Gerardo Chijona's *Perfecto amor equivocado* (*Love by Mistake*, 2004) focuses on the intimate conflicts of relationships affected by international economies, and Daniel Díaz Torres's *Hacerce el sueco* (*Playing Swede*, 2001) follows a German tourist who passes himself off as a university professor doing research in Cuba, when in reality he is a jewel thief on the lam, hoping to hide in Cuba from the authorities.

Argentine film critic Alejandro Ricagno has suggested that the evolving tension between commercial and independent cinema has already produced fruits evidenced in a new body of work making an impact on the international market:

Figure 16.5 *Temporada de patos* (*Duck Season*, Fernando Eimbcke, Mexico, 2004).

thrillers like the late Fabian Bielinsky's *Nueve reinas* (*Nine Queens*, 2000) and *El aura* (*The Aura*, 2006), or José Campanella's *costumbrista* comedies, *El hijo de la novia* (*The Son of the Bride*, 2001) and the melodramatic police drama *Plata quemada* (*Burnt Money*, Marcelo Piñeyro, 2000).[46] The tension produces interesting opportunities for the diverse industries of Latin American countries that could be harnessed as the new mechanisms for financing facilitate the production process.

By far the most interesting work arising from the tensions between genres can be found in the documentary, where we can see formal experimentation, a boom in digital video production, and the fertile social context merging. The resurgence of the documentary amid so much economic catastrophe coupled with an available digital arsenal is appropriated most interestingly as a tool of empowerment and exploration, creating new visual languages and affective structures. Michael Chanan recently pointed out that during Argentina's recent economic collapse, "Filmmakers, many of them trained in the film schools which blossomed in Argentina during the preceding decade, and often militants of one or other political association, now in full possession of the means of production, needed no funding or commissions to go out on the streets and film."[47] The indignation at the situation is palpable in veteran filmmaker Fernando "Pino" Solanas's forceful trilogy about Argentina, *Memorias del saqueo* (*Social Genocide*, 2004), *Dignidad de los nadie* (*Dignity of the Nobodies*, 2005), and *Argentina Latente* (2007). With this trilogy Solanas returns to his earlier Argentinean opus, *La hora de los hornos* (*The Hour of the Furnaces*, 1969), which also launched the third cinema manifesto. In contrast to the production of the earlier film, the contemporary Solanas is no longer filming clandestinely, and he and his video camera are no longer marginalized from the central spheres of power. The result is fascinating.

Newcomers and established filmmakers have produced some of the most memorable documentary work seen in decades. Briefly, the diversity of styles and topics is provocative: the mixed-media explorations of the psyche in *Estamira* (Marcos Prado, 2004), a disturbing portrait of a sixty-year old schizophrenic patient over the course of several years in treatment, and the raw portrait of Mayan class C bullfighter *Toro negro* (Pedro González-Rubio and Carlos Armella, 2005), which broaches the topic of alcoholism and domestic violence with disturbing closeness. The life of fringe dwellers in the desert of San Luis Potosí, Mexico, is the topic of *Trópico de cancer* (*Tropic of Cancer*, Eugenio Polgovsky, 2005), a story of work and survival set in austere, barren lands. The people inhabiting this place survive by hunting rats, building birdcages, and cultivating cactus to sell to passing motorists. The force of this haunting look at isolation and subsistence stems from the refusal to use a slick style, revealing in its stead the ugliness of the environs and its misery. As opposed to the miserabilist style of other films that document the margins, *Trópico* eschews banal ideological commentary. The exploration of criminality and police cultures alike in Jose Padilha's *Bus 174* (2002) is also a comment on the power of television to construct events, and *O prisioneiro da grade*

Figure 16.6 *Estamira* (Marcos Prado, Brazil, 2004).

do ferro (*Prisoner of the Iron Bars*) is a fascinating counterpoint to Babenco's fictionalized *Carandiru*, and the outcome of a video workshop with interned prisoners in Latin America's largest penitentiary. Mercedes Moncada continued to work in Central America in *El inmortal* (*The Immortal*, 2005), this time staging the recuperation of war memories in Nicaragua with a family whose lives have been ravaged. Whether it is a spontaneous response to the use of different tools, to the social environs, or to something else, documentaries carry on a stimulating dialogue with the techniques of fiction and, as discussed earlier, vice versa. There is a new relationship to life as experience, to the nuances that can be captured via digital means that proportion new expressive structures. Juan Carlos Rulfo's most recent award-winning documentary, *En el hueco* (*In the Pit*, 2005), concentrates on the construction workers of the second deck of Mexico City's freeway. Focusing on the work and listening to the men in their banter renders an unforgettable portrait of life at work in one of the world's largest metropolises.

Figure 16.7 *El inmortal* (*The Immortal*, Mercedes Moncada,
Nicaragua-Mexico-Spain, 2004).

Lastly, domestic animation, which is a highly underproduced and under-exhibited genre in the region, although not for lack of talent, is seeing a revival in Brazil and in animation film festivals. Filmmaker, scholar, and director of Midi@rte, a high-tech media lab in Belo Horizonte, Heitor Capuzzo has created an analysis of the potential of animation for the future that is razor-sharp: "At present, there is no market for animation in Brazil and most of what is produced is for commercials. But between 2000–2004 Brazil has made more animation than in its entire history. It has never invested in animation before and the young generation is producing a lot."[48] Just as with live-action films, the market for animation is cornered by the U.S. majors. To maximize audiences for animated features, themes are typically family oriented and thus released during holiday and summer seasons, exhibition space that the Hollywood majors already control internationally. Capuzzo believes, however, "that Brazil's new HDTV production will benefit the production of animation since inexpensive software makes it cheaper to produce than old-style animation."[49] A look at the program for the fourteenth annual Anima Mundi Animation Film Festival, held in Brazil, reveals that the fourteen animation studios listed underscore the burgeoning industry's infrastructure. The economic support, provided under the Ley do Audiovisual from a variety of state and private sponsors, and national and international agencies, is evidence that there could be sustainability. Cappuzo may have been right when he said that "animation is an option for Latin America over live action."[50]

Which stylistic approach most typifies recent Latin American film? The answer is that the typicality lies in the range of experimentation and invention facilitated by new technology and slow improvements to the constraints of industry infrastructure.

Latin American film can now more easily seek out the rawness of experience, binding it within biography or the backdrop of a particular region, often with themes of transcendence, violence, survival, and the absurdity of life.

CONCLUSION

Unlike twenty years ago, films from Latin America today are increasingly considered de rigueur for any serious international film festival program. In 2006, the Palm Springs International Film Festival in California, touted as the biggest in the United States, included an astonishing fifty films in its Latin American sidebar. In the United States, the popularity might be explained as much by the mainstreaming of identity politics as by the remarkable output from the region. And yet, the crucible of distribution continues to marginalize even leading Spanish-language filmmakers and entrepreneurs, forcing experimentation with alternative models of distribution.

Amores perros stands as a major contemporary example of a film that ushered in a new era of films, the look and sound of which were clearly indebted to, but a radical departure from, the films of the classical period. With *Amores perros*, Mexican cinema found new life, although not without a degree of uncertainty about its future. The film's most lasting legacy is in the talents that it spawned: actors Vanessa Bauche and García Bernal, director González Iñárritu, screenwriter Guillermo Arriaga, cinematographer Rodrigo Prieto and composer Gustavo Santaolalla. Defined as transnational, they are part of a group of filmmakers no longer confined to their national identities, but who work on "local" projects that generate passion, not just professionalism and cash.

This consciously held double perspective is precisely what separates the current generation of Latin American filmmakers from their predecessors. They understand more clearly the global dimension of the work, and from this come the themes and topics that are explored. *City of God* cinematographer César Chalone's debut feature film, *El baño del papa* (*The Pope's Bathroom*, 2007), is set in a town straddling the Uruguayan-Brazilian border. Based on a real events, the film is an example of how global economies and politics affect local aspirations. Upon finding out that the pope will visit them, the town puts all its economic eggs in the tourist basket, only to be left adrift when the pope never arrives. In the manner of the newly celebrated filmmakers of the region, Chalone moves beyond apology, parody, or stereotype of Latin American culture. Like so many filmmakers of the region, he makes the art of the film itself a strong and graceful commentary on people, place, and politics.

While coproductions and regional trade pacts signal yet another era of audiovisual cooperation, speaking of Latin American cinema in a general rubric is increasingly difficult. Digital technology may have reshaped aspects of audiovisual production, but it has not brought fundamental changes in distribution. The scales of the industries, the complexities of production, distribution, and exhibition, and the enormous role of television media industries really demand closer attention and singular analysis. Some broad observations seem inescapable, though. Latin American filmmakers continue to prove their ability to work on whatever budget they can muster and with whatever technology comes to hand, yet they still have to scramble for exhibition; this, when the most powerful media industries in the region are in the business of television. Can film and television find mutual purpose in the assurance of diversity, and sustainability for their region? The answer might be elusive, but the twenty-year-old School of Film and Television in San Antonio de los Baños, Cuba, which now includes television in its curriculum and has just built a television production facility, has already placed its bet on the future direction of audiovisual narrative in Latin America.

NOTES

1. See Ojo de Agua Comunicación, Objectives, http://www.laneta.apc.org/ojodeagua/objetivos.htm, accessed July 21, 2006.

2. "Old" technology in Latin America often finds a useful afterlife in a new, but less prosperous, home. During the transition to digital at the ICAIC, for instance, flatbed editing consoles were still around. But they too will become less useful as the electronic editing process becomes more standardized.

3. Reid Burns, postproduction executive, e-mail interview with the author, July 21, 2006.

4. There are varying opinions as to whether digital technology is actually cheaper than film. The answer depends on many variables, including type of equipment, length of shoot, number of special effects, and so forth.

5. See "Quienes Somos" on the CLACPI Web site, http://www.clacpi.org, accessed March 9, 2008. Interestingly, the international umbrella organization for this group is the Smithsonian Institute.

6. Ibid.

7. Santiago Palavecino, e-mail interview with the author, July 26, 2006.

8. Barbet Schroeder, interview with Orlando Mora for *El Colombiano*, http://www.elcolombiano.com/proyectos/virgendelossicarios/detrasdecamaras.htm, accessed July 27, 2006.

9. Marcos Loayza, e-mail interview with the author, July 24, 2006.

10. See "Que es OMA?" on Observatio del Mercosur Audiovisual (OMA), http://www.recam.org/oma.htm, accessed March 9, 2008.

11. OMA, Boletín no. 9, http://www.recam.org/boletines.htm, accessed July 26, 2006.

12. For a full discussion of the role of coproductions in Cuba during the country's Special Period, see Cristina Venegas, "Filmmaking with Foreigners," in *The Special Period and the Culture of Late Socialism in Cuba*, ed. Ariana Hernandez-Reguant (New York: Palgrave Macmillan, 2008).

13. Alberto "Chicho" Durant, e-mail interview with the author, July 23, 2006.

14. Palavecino interview.

15. Durant interview.

16. Checco Varese, phone interview with the author, July 28, 2006.

17. Quoted by Reed Johnson, "Inside Mexico's Bootleg Market," *Los Angeles Times* (May 10, 2006): E1.

18. The List of MPAA companies includes Columbia Tri-Star Buena Vista Films de Brasil, Metro-Goldwin-Mayer Studios, Paramount Pictures Corporation, 20th Century Fox International Corporation, Universal Films, and Warner Bros. International Theatrical Corporation; from the MPA Latin America Web site, http://www.mpaal.org.br/es/quiensomos.htm, accessed March 3, 2008.

19. AAP, "News Corp Sells Sky Latin America Stakes," *Sydney Morning Herald* (October 12, 2004), http://www.theage.com.au/articles/2004/10/12/1097406560171.html, accessed March 10, 2008.

20. Market analyst Marcus Padley, quoted in Ibid.

21. OMA, Boletín no. 9.

22. Heitor Capuzzo, online interview with the author, July 26, 2006.

23. OMA, Boletín no. 9.

24. Alfonso Gumusio Drágon, "La ley televisa," *Bolpress*, http://www.bolpress.com/opinion.pp?Cod=2006032915, accessed July 20, 2006.

25. Ibid.

26. Charles Newberry, "Beach Pic Kicks Sand on 'Superman' Bow," *Variety* (July 17, 2006).

27. Guillermo Arriaga, "Luchar por la excepción cultural dentro de las reglas que tenemos," *Estudios Cinematográficos* 29 (February 2006).

28. Charles R. Acland, *Screen Traffic: Movies, Multiplexes, and Global Culture* (Durham, NC: Duke University Press, 2003), 17–19.

29. Grupo Chaski is quite extensive in describing the parameters of the organization. See http://www.grupochaski.org/index.php?id=576,0,0,1,0,0 accessed March 10, 2008.

30. See "Sobre a Rain," on Rain Network Web site, http://www.rain.com.br/Institucional/Pages/default.aspx, accessed March 10, 2008.

31. Pablo Villaça, "Voices Waxing Brazilian: Fighting for Scraps," *Movie City News*, www.moviecitynews.com/voices/2005/Villaca2.html, accessed July 27, 2006.

32. Varese interview.

33. Luisela Alvaray, "National, Regional and Global: New Waves of Latin American Cinema, *Cinema Journal* 47.3 (Spring 2008).

34. Tamara L. Falicov, "Film Policy under MERCOSUR: The Case of Uruguay," *Canadian Journal of Communication* 27 (2002): 33–46.

35. Victor Ugalde, "Panorama de la producción cinematográfica nacional," paper presented at Symposium on Mexican Cinema, University of California, Los Angeles, March 10–12, 2006; see also Victor Ugalde, "Desmemoria," *Etcétera* (January 2004);

"Defensa Cultural," *Etcétera* (July 2005); and "Doble Lenguage," *Etcétera* (August 2005); http://www.etcetera.com.mx, accessed March 21, 2008.

36. Despite the vulnerability that film production experiences as a result of the central role of state cinema institutes, these entities were historically responsible for the organization and promotion of cinema in individual nations. Their efficiency and efficacy, however, has often come under attack by filmmakers and politicians alike.

37. In 1982 Brazilian cinema had 140 days a year of mandatory exhibition.

38. The Lei do Audiovisual made it so that in lieu of taxes payable to the Brazilian government, foreign film companies can take 70 percent profits from distribution within Brazil and reinvest in funding Brazilian film projects. This was also true for companies and individuals and Brazilian companies and explains why funding from the oil company PETROBRAS is an advantage of the Lei do Audiovisual.

39. Alejandro Pelayo Rangel, "El cine Mexicano en los años ochenta: la generación de la crisis," Ph.D. diss., Universidad Autonoma de Mexico.

40. Alvaray, "National, Regional and Global."

41. Ugalde, "Panorama de la producción cinematográfica nacional."

42. Falicov, "Film Policy under MERCOSUR."

43. Tamara L. Falicov, "Television for the Big Screen: How *Comodines* Became Argentina's First Blockbuster Phenomenon," in *Movie Blockbusters*, ed. Julian Stringer (London: Routledge, 2003), 242–254.

44. The member nations of Mercosur (Mercado Común del Sur) are Brazil, Argentina, Uruguay, Paraguay, and Venezuela (2006). Bolivia, Chile, Colombia, Ecuador, and Peru have associate-member status. For further reading on Mercosur and its relationship to cultural policy, see Falicov, "Film Policy under MERCOSUR; and Randal Johnson, "Film Policy in Latin America," in *Film Policy: International, National, and Regional Perspectives*, ed. A. Moran (London: Routledge, 1996), 128–147.

45. Juan Carlos Rulfo, "Personal Reflections," in *Horizontes Latinos: Imagines en libertad*, 51st Festival Internacional de Cine Donostia-San Sebastian, España, 2003, 163–169.

46. Alejandro Ricagno, "Lectura de los géneros en 'el cuerpo mutante' del cine argentino," in *Horizontes Latinos*, 38–59.

47. Michael Chanan, "Latin America," in *Encyclopedia of the Documentary Film Three-Volume Set.* ed. Ian Aitken (London: Routledge, 2005), 8–9.

48. Capuzzo interview.

49. Ibid.

50. See "Annimemory 2006" in Anima Mundi Animation Film Festival Web site, http://www.animamundi.com.br, accessed July 14, 2006.

BIBLIOGRAPHY

Acland, Charles R. *Screen Traffic: Movies, Multiplexes, and Global Culture.* Durham, NC: Duke University Press, 2003.

Alvaray, Luisela. "National, Regional and Global: New Waves of Latin American Cinema." *Cinema Journal* 47.3 (Spring 2008).

Arriaga, Guillermo. "Luchar por la excepción cultural dentro de las reglas que tenemos." *Estudios Cinematográficos* 29 (February 2006).

Chanan, Michael. "Latin America." *Encyclopedia of the Documentary Film Three-Volume Set.* ed. Ian Aitken. London: Routledge, 2005.

Cumaná, Maria Caridad, and Joel del Rio. "Cronología del cine latinoamericano: 1990–2004." *Miradas* (March 6, 2005): http://www.eictv.co.cu/miradas, accessed July 13, 2006.

del Rio, Joel. "Cine latinoamericano en digital: redención esperada o conveniencia ineludible?" *Miradas* (May 18, 2006): http://www.eictv.co.cu/miradas, accessed July 13, 2006.

Falicov, Tamara L. "Film Policy under MERCOSUR: The Case of Uruguay." *Canadian Journal of Communication* 27 (2002): 33–46.

———. "Television for the Big Screen: How *Comodines* Became Argentina's First Blockbuster Phenomenon." In *Movie Blockbusters*, ed. Julian Stringer. London: Routledge, 2003, 242–254.

García Borrero, Juan Antonio. *La edad de la herejía.* Santiago de Cuba, Cuba: Editorial Oriente, 2002.

Johnson, Randal. "Departing Central Station: Notes on the Reemergence of Brazilian Cinema." *Brazil e-Journal* (November 1–April 2000): http://www.humnet.ucla.edu/spanport/faculty/randalj, accessed March 11, 2006.

———. "Film Policy in Latin America." In *Film Policy: International, National, and Regional Perspectives*, ed. A. Moran. London: Routledge, 1996, 128–147.

Johnson, Reed. "Inside Mexico's Bootleg Market." *Los Angeles Times* (May 10, 2006).

Krichmar, Fernando. "Grupo de Cine insurgente." *Miradas* (January 5, 2003): http://www.eictv.co.cu/miradas, accessed July 13, 2006.

Lopez, Ana M. "Setting Up the Stage: A Decade of Latin American Film Scholarship." *Quarterly Review of Film and Video* 13.1–3 (1991): 239–260.

Martin, Michael T. *New Latin American Cinema: Theory, Practices and Transcontinental Articulations.* Vol. 1. Detroit: Wayne State University Press, 1997.

Martin-Barbero, Jesus. "Transformations in the Map: Identities and Culture Industries." *Latin American Perspectives* 27.4 (July 2000): 27–48.

Newberry, Charles. "Beach Pic Kicks Sand on 'Superman' Bow." *Variety* (July 17, 2006).

Rangel, Alejandro Pelayo. "El cine Mexicano en los años ochenta: la generación de la crisis," Ph.D. diss., Universidad Autonoma de Mexico.

Rulfo, Juan Carlos. "Personal Reflections." In *Horizontes Latinos: Imagines en libertad*, 51st Festival Internacional de Cine Donostia-San Sebastian, España, 2003, 163–169.

Tuñon, Julia. *Mujeres de luz y sombra en el cine Mexicano: la construcción de una imagen, 1939–1952.* Mexico, D.F.: Colegio de Mexico, IMCINE, 1998.

Ugalde, Victor. "Panorama de la producción cinematográfica nacional." Paper presented at Symposium on Mexican Cinema, University of California, Los Angeles, March 10–12, 2006.

Venegas, Cristina. "Filmmaking with Foreigners." In *The Special Period and the Culture of Late Socialism in Cuba*, ed. Ariana Hernandez-Reguant. New York: Palgrave Macmillan, 2008.

CHAPTER 17

....

THE GLOBALIZATION
OF FILMMAKING
IN LATIN AMERICA
AND THE MIDDLE EAST

....

ANDREW FLIBBERT

Filmmaking has been a global enterprise for longer than most of the other major arts and industries. Not only is it situated at the crossroads of commercial and cultural production, but the medium itself has long been implicated in the intense and multifaceted interconnectedness that contemporary observers call globalization. This process has involved film production and trade beyond the United States and Europe, as the first moving pictures debuted in a host of far-flung capital cities more than a century ago. Even audiences in regions not fully in the cinematic vanguard—Latin America and the Middle East—have become connected to filmmaking's shared, if contested, social and cultural space. In both the latter places, film appeared initially as a minor novelty for resident foreign nationals and Europeanized elites, but local production and clientele followed before long, and entrepreneurs built major industries that have endured for decades. Latin America's most substantial film industries emerged in Argentina, Brazil, and Mexico, with the latter's national production asserting itself forcefully by the 1940s, propelled by developments in one of the darker expressions of global connectedness, World War II. Middle Eastern production, for its part, was dominated for decades by Egypt's "Hollywood on the Nile," having essentially no significant regional competitor other than its American counterpart.

Starting from an analytical vantage point that privileges political and economic processes, the purpose of this essay is to reveal precisely how the globalization of filmmaking in Latin America and the Middle East has unfolded over several decades. If globalization is all about the shrinking of space and time, then the long train of events in these regions should speak to the true scope, transformative capacity, and limitations of the process. Certain identifiable political and economic dynamics have been instrumental in creating a globally integrated film world, and most of these dynamics remain operative today. Changing technology has been an engine of industrial transformation, but its existence is neither apolitical nor inevitable, and it cannot be understood without reference to more fundamental forces that enable and constrain technological innovation, diffusion, and application. I begin with a discussion of the political and economic underpinnings of the industry's globalization, and then turn to regional experiences to illuminate the particular course taken by the process in Latin America and the Middle East. In these discussions, I devote most attention to the Mexican and Egyptian industries, which dominated their respective regions for years and remain noteworthy producers despite their waxing and waning successes.

GLOBALIZATION AND FILM

Observers since the 1960s have claimed that several factors are driving the world closer together through the "widening, deepening, and speeding up" of worldwide interconnectedness.[1] Popularized in the 1990s by writers such as Kenichi Ohmae and Thomas Friedman, the idea of globalization has found expression in every major academic field in the humanities and social sciences.[2] Some political economists have dismissed the concept as a fleeting intellectual cliché or "globaloney," while others have recast it as internationalization, Americanization, marketization, modernization, and a host of other large-scale social processes.[3] The idea may be subject to what Giovanni Sartori called conceptual stretching— coming to mean everything and therefore nothing—but its contested nature is unsurprising given the wide scope of its application.[4] Globalization debates show no sign of dissipating, perhaps because they speak to new international complexities facing observers in any number of areas.

Several aspects of filmmaking are implicated in the globalization process. The industry has long been characterized by extensive internationalization, with a measure of integration occurring in several areas, including markets, financing, certain technical aspects of production, and skilled labor. For decades, the film trade has witnessed the growth and development of integrated international markets, which have raised the level of competition for local producers everywhere. Major producers began exporting film early in the twentieth century, and since the 1960s, leading firms—mostly American in origin—have viewed foreign markets as equally important as domestic ones, obtaining a substantial portion of their total earnings in them.[5] The relatively low and declining cost-to-profit ratios for transporting film across the world has meant that the industry never was as constrained in exports as industries producing bulkier goods. With the low costs and high benefits of international trade in film, industry leaders had little choice but to internationalize very early on. For this reason, the U.S film industry began underwriting the integration of world markets by the end of World War I, when the film trade was still in its infancy. Accordingly, film markets for most major producers never were segmented fully by national borders.

Global integration has affected all substantial film producers. Companies in the smallest film-producing countries now compete locally with major, internationally integrated firms, while midsized, regionally dominant film producers have seen the incorporation of their traditional markets into world trade. Such changes have curtailed local exports and rendered some national industries nearly inviable, as shrinking market share has reduced profits and depleted the amount of investment capital available for continued production. Film-producing states have responded to integrative pressures in ways that have varied considerably, both from country to country among the world's many producers and over time within the same ones. On the one hand, many states have maintained liberal policies toward the film trade, and protectionist measures have not been implemented uniformly throughout the world in response to globalizing pressures. On the other hand, protectionism in the film trade has been common and substantial, even if such policies have been costly to consumers and state budgets supporting local industries.

Political Sources

The underlying impetus to the global integration of filmmaking can be traced to political and economic sources. The political sources rest principally on the power of the United States to help the major American film companies to construct and maintain global networks of integrated markets. The growth of American power in the early twentieth century enhanced rising U.S. international influence in culture, media, and the arts. In filmmaking, this influence accompanied the ascendance of modern American business. The capacity of major American film distributors to establish hundreds of overseas branches was not unrelated to the political and economic power of the United States to underwrite such endeavors. The costs of establishing systems of foreign distribution were subsidized with assistance that most other governments could not offer.

This is not to say that American policy makers served industry interests without exception or restraint. Indeed, the U.S. Supreme Court's 1948 *Paramount* consent decrees marked the beginning of the end of the studio era, and the House Committee on Un-American Activities hearings that started in the late 1940s revealed the industry's domestic vulnerability to direct political attack at home.[6] But a long-term perception of shared interests between the United States and the leading American-based film companies did facilitate the industry's global integration. While many countries aided their filmmakers domestically through the provision of subsidies or screen-time and import quotas, the American federal government assisted U.S. industry internationally through the promotion of free trade in motion pictures and by intervening on behalf of American-based companies in their disputes with host states over currency remittance, market access, and protectionism. This changed the nature of the business in profound and consequential ways, reinforcing the cultural dimension of postwar American support for a liberal international order.

U.S. government assistance to the foreign operations of American businesses such as filmmaking was driven initially by straightforward economic goals that differed from European concerns about political interests and influence in the world.[7] The growth of cold war tensions, however, broadened and politicized official American backing for its overseas businesses in a number of strategically significant locales. Evidence in the diplomatic record shows that the militarization and globalization of the containment doctrine had a cultural dimension, manifested partly by U.S. efforts to promote American films at the expense of Soviet ones worldwide.[8] In the uncompromising atmosphere of the early cold war, public rhetoric about motion pictures being simply entertainment was disingenuous at best. Policy makers saw nothing as completely apolitical in a world where the Soviets invented a cartoon character of their own—a porcupine—to counter the worrisome international popularity of Walt Disney's colorful creation, Mickey Mouse.[9]

Economic Sources

If the openly political sources of global integration were important, the economic sources were perhaps even more significant. The economic side of the story rests on a handful of the key attributes of the filmmaking enterprise, which create intense pressure to forge strong, densely connected film markets on a global basis. Two attributes of the industry are especially vital in this case: the film commodity's "nonrival" quality, and filmmaking's special needs and challenges regarding financial risk reduction. Like classic public goods—sidewalks, clean air, national defense—film has a nonrival quality because its "consumption" by one individual does not preclude its enjoyment by another.[10] Regardless of the industrial or artistic circumstances under which any film is made, production costs always are concentrated in the making of a single and unique master negative or original. From this negative, an unlimited number of prints, or digital copies, may be made at a small fraction of the original's production cost and distributed to exhibition markets. Hypothetically, such prints may be sold in an infinite number of markets worldwide without either affecting the price of the product to "rival" domestic consumers or diminishing the film's availability in home markets.[11]

If the nonrival aspect of filmmaking heightens the desirability of exports, another of its characteristics creates an even stronger incentive to trade in films: the industry is defined by exceptional financial risk and uncertainty. In terms of consumer demand, any commercial enterprise dealing in cultural or artistic production is subject to the particularly unpredictable and fickle nature of public taste. Predicting box-office success is notoriously difficult.[12] Likewise, on the supply side, filmmaking does not lend itself to easy control of labor costs. As with all cultural production, scientific management techniques cannot determine with accuracy the nature and quantity of essential labor inputs.[13] Filmmaking therefore is a risky business because human creativity defies automation while eliciting an uncertain public response, and investment decisions have to be made without reliable foreknowledge of returns.

As a result, industry strategies to reduce risk and make success more likely and predictable are a fundamental, overriding concern. They govern most other choices in the business. Such strategies have included the vertical integration of the industry and the development of star systems and genre conventions to stabilize demand, thereby bringing predictability to the flow of returns on investments.[14] For its part, wide distribution enhances the likelihood that overall returns will be sizable, since any given picture may fail in some markets but do well in others. For relatively little additional cost, especially for larger-budget commercial films, the potential benefits can be enormous. Risk reduction therefore requires that a film be exported whenever possible. Doing so is feasible because distributors can engage in price discrimination, selling their films at whatever price individual foreign markets will bear. Moviegoers in weak economies cannot afford to purchase film tickets at uniformly expensive world market prices, but ticket prices can be pegged to local economic conditions to facilitate sales and hence film exports. The incremental revenues gained from small markets worldwide often contribute decisively to the profitability of a given film, even if smaller film producers in target markets have denounced such practices as "dumping," aimed at driving them out of business.[15]

American Influence

The end result of such political and economic dynamics has been the extension of the film trade to the four corners of the earth. The vehicle for realizing this outcome has been the major film companies, mostly American in origin but increasingly ambiguous in national affiliation. Hollywood itself has been vital as an agglomeration of cinematic activity, and American-based film companies played an early, influential role as the central source of integration and dynamism.[16] When World War I forced many European producers to scale back production and export, American companies filled a void from which they would never retreat.[17] England's Prince Edward soon voiced a common European concern in business circles when he declared in 1923 that "Trade follows the film."[18] The expansion of foreign activities by the American industry was aided by the formation in 1922 of a new trade association, the Motion Picture Producers and Distributors of America (MPPDA).[19] With offices in Cairo, Mexico City, and dozens of other cities worldwide, the MPPDA created a Foreign Department to act as the trade representative of the largest American companies in negotiations with foreign governments, eventually earning the nickname "the little State Department" for its extensive diplomatic activities.[20]

Just as significantly, the American industry helped to define the film medium itself by cultivating a linear narrative style of filmmaking and by creating entertainment expectations that only large production budgets could fulfill.[21] Other viable modes of production still existed, but by the 1920s most non-American and noncommercial filmmaking was viewed as an alternative to the Hollywood norm—often entirely welcomed, but always compared to an American standard asserting itself worldwide. Certain technological elements of filmmaking that are common today were neither necessary nor inevitable. The width of film stock and the spacing between sprocket holes, for example, became a universally accepted standard that aided in the global spread of American motion pictures, even if they originated in random choices made long ago.[22]

An American-driven globalization process engendered emulative tendencies in producing countries large and small, from Egypt's "Hollywood on the Nile" to India's "Bollywood" and even English film pioneer J. Arthur Rank's decision in 1936 to call his filmmaking facility Pinewood Studios. As new national film producers came into existence, they often replicated the Hollywood style and aesthetic, as well as its organizational pattern, studio production mode, distribution methods, and star system.[23] These industries developed nationally specific forms of artistic expression, but they represented variations on a common theme. Thus, American influence—both substantive and organizational—proved to be powerfully path dependent, as early success bred later success, and the partly random events that accompanied the rise of the industry in the United States also shaped the development of filmmaking worldwide.

MEXICO AND LATIN AMERICA

Latin America has been in the direct orbit of North American power since the 1820s and the region's independence from Spain and Portugal. Major film industries developed early in the twentieth century in Argentina, Brazil, and Mexico, with the latter becoming dominant during World War II, when its political and geographic proximity to the United States enabled it to begin undermining its southern competitors for several years. The other Latin American producers generally have had more in common with European than American cinema, but their markets still became entirely integrated into the U.S.-dominated film trade. Mexico, which both connects and separates North and Latin America, played a vital role in this regard.

Mexico's close geographic proximity to the United States and its strategic position in relation to Latin American markets encouraged a greater U.S. presence in the 1920s, including the opening of distribution outlets for Universal, Paramount, United Artists, and 20th Century Fox.[24] This presence was possible only after an important early episode in motion picture diplomacy, when the Hays Office defused a crisis in U.S.-Mexican film relations in 1922. The consistently negative portrayal of Mexicans in American pictures had led to a total ban on their import, but by dispatching a representative for nearly three months of negotiations, Hays secured an agreement to lift the ban in exchange for promises of greater sensitivity to Mexican national sentiment. This encounter appears to have led Hays to broader conclusions about the importance of avoiding offense to local sensibilities, and it presaged the MPPDA's effectiveness in direct diplomacy with foreign governments.[25] By 1925, Mexico had become Hollywood's eighth-largest market by volume, accounting for 2 percent of its foreign sales.[26]

Throughout the 1930s, the consolidated American major firms experimented with varied strategies for retaining their positions in the large and lucrative foreign markets of Latin America.[27] Concerned that English-dialogue sound films would not be exportable to this and many other regions, most of the majors began filming Spanish-language versions of their pictures, drawing on actors and directors from Spain and Latin America to make 113 of them by 1938.[28] To do so, Paramount refurbished in 1930 an entire studio complex at Joinville, just outside of Paris, devoting it to making, in assembly-line fashion, as many as fourteen different foreign-language versions of its productions.[29] These films tended to fail, however, since Latin American audiences preferred seeing subtitled films with popular

Hollywood stars rather than the odd, eclectic mix of actors and accents from all over the Spanish-speaking world.[30] The U.S. industry's "Hispanic" films of the 1930s nonetheless were significant in providing technical training and stylistic socialization for filmmakers who would later become prominent in their home industries.[31]

World War II did not limit American access to the Mexican market, with U.S. producers managing to maintain an overwhelming market share of 85 to 90 percent. Unlike many European states that were cut off from U.S. sales during the war, Mexico stayed open to exports, and even before the war's outbreak, anti-Fascist sentiment on the part of organized labor and state censors from the Department of the Interior weakened Germany's trade position in film.[32] The war-related themes that rose to prominence in American pictures of this period, however, had less resonance—and therefore less marketability—throughout Latin America.[33] As a result, local Mexican producers found an opportunity to expand both domestically and abroad, and they did so at the expense of declining European production and reduced American distribution.

Just prior to the war, a resurgence in domestic production had begun with the international success of a single film, Fernando de Fuentes's *Allá en el Rancho Grande* (1936), which spawned an entire genre and convinced investors that Mexican films could be extremely profitable in Latin American export markets.[34] Growth in the film industry was possible in large part because the United States favored its pro-Allied neighbor over neutral Argentina. Aware of the propaganda power of the motion picture, the State Department's newly formed Office of the Coordinator for Inter-American Affairs worked indefatigably under Nelson Rockefeller to foster cooperation between the Mexican and American industries in technical, financial, and personnel matters.[35] Denying Argentina access to raw film stock, it assured Mexico the necessary materials, equipment, and markets to flourish.[36] Thus, the war years were instrumental in consolidating Mexico's position as the leading Latin American film producer. In 1949, Mexico was the first Spanish-language industry in the world to break the hundred-film production barrier, with a record 108 feature films.[37]

Globalization's much-heralded "death of distance" saw early expression in postwar international production in Mexico.[38] Complementing the growing use of location shooting throughout the world, American companies such as Warner Bros. and RKO initiated modest levels of production in Mexican studios in the 1950s.[39] The peso devaluation in 1954 and the availability of skilled labor and suitable local facilities enticed U.S. producers to make seven films in Mexico that year, followed by eight more in 1955, and a larger number of westerns in the north-central state of Durango beginning in 1958.[40] This trend differed from filming on location—as in Elia Kazan's *Viva Zapata* (1952)—since facilities and natural settings were rented out to make pictures that were thematically unrelated to Mexico as a place. With the demise of the Hollywood studio system by 1960 and the growing prominence of independent production companies, Mexico's less costly working conditions offered an inviting alternative to filmmaking in the United States.

The American majors in Mexico attempted to regain their market share, which had declined somewhat by the end of the war. A resurgence of U.S. exports in the 1960s was made easier by a growing crisis in the local industry, as film quality deteriorated in increasingly formulaic productions. Such a crisis may have been inevitable in light of the extent to which many companies originally were drawn into the business by the exceptionally profitable opportunities of the wartime era. In the war's aftermath, these companies turned to making quick, low-risk, cheap pictures with no export potential and limited domestic appeal. Production levels remained high at first, but a growing share of the urban middle class grew disaffected and began to abandon national productions for Hollywood and other foreign fare.[41]

Not only did Mexicans begin to lose interest in domestically produced films, but the crisis extended immediately to the industry's exports to Latin America. While Mexican films were acquiring a reputation for tawdriness, other major regional producers, such as Argentina and Brazil, were improving and augmenting their own productions and, along with Spain, regaining a more substantial place in the Latin American market through state patronage.[42] Regional instability and periodic political upheaval also took their toll, such as with the Cuban revolution's elimination of that market in 1958. From the mid-1950s to the mid-1960s, moreover, the substantial devaluation of most Latin American currencies in relation to the Mexican peso—most notably those of Argentina, Bolivia, Brazil, Paraguay, Uruguay, and Venezuela—further undermined regional exports.[43] For Mexico, the steady deterioration of exports endangered an essential source of film revenues. In so doing, it weakened the only nearby foreign market large enough to support the kinds of productions that could compete at home with American movies.[44] Without exports, the industry was virtually inviable. Consequently, the industry spiraled downward in a vicious cycle, as declining production and export cut into revenues, undermined investor confidence, and destroyed audience loyalty.

This is not to say that Mexicans stopped going to the movies, or that the global integration of the industry abated. American exports to Mexico remained dominant in the early 1970s, reportedly accounting for 5 percent of all U.S. foreign sales in 1971.[45] The U.S. hold on the Mexican market had been sliding steadily for years in comparison to Latin American and European exporters. But the United States still exerted great competitive pressure on the domestic industry by virtue of the box-office draw of its best pictures, its distribution power within Mexico, and the expectation of continually improving technical quality that its glossy productions created. Even as Hollywood passed through one of the weakest periods in its history, it bested local producers with audiences that had long since grown weary of what had become, according to Charles Ramírez Berg, Mexico's creatively exhausted and decrepit cinema.[46]

For its part, the Mexican state reasserted itself in the face of the heightened globalizing pressures of the late 1960s. Beginning in 1970, the Echeverría administration virtually nationalized the industry, causing a rapid decline in private production, from which U.S. and other exporters benefited by an opportunity to expand sales. While President Luis Echeverría had a number of objectives in intervening so extensively in the film industry, one of them was to regain Mexico's international markets by returning to the production of socially engaged, better-quality films.[47] Reflecting his aspiration to international leadership in the developing world, he sought to recapture some of Mexico's former cultural prestige and to repair relations with the country's intellectual elite, damaged immeasurably by the Tlatelolco student massacre of October 1968. Despite these efforts, the call for a quality-led cinematic renewal met with only limited success internationally. By the mid-1970s, film exports remained confined to several small countries in Central America and the Caribbean, as well as Colombia, Ecuador, Uruguay, and Venezuela. In most of Latin America, the United States held three-quarters of the market, and Mexico competed with Argentina, Spain, and a handful of other European producers for a small share of the remainder.[48]

With the return of a commercial orientation under López Portillo, foreign receipts expanded reportedly by more than a third, as production rose to 114 films in 1979, its highest point in two decades.[49] Unlike past growth in foreign sales, these were mostly low-budget potboilers in familiar genres that sold fairly well to popular classes throughout Latin America. In the early 1980s, the U.S. export boom came to an end, while Mexico also became increasingly popular among American producers as an inexpensive foreign production site, hosting such films as David Lynch's *Dune* (1984) and John Huston's *Under the Volcano* (1984).[50] American film exports followed a relatively steady course throughout the 1990s, though the production crisis accompanying Mexico's 1995 peso devaluation undermined Mexican buying power for imports. Wealthier segments of Mexican society turned increasingly to new technologies to access American films via nontraditional exhibition windows such as the satellite dish and cable television.

Aided by the growing export strength of television programming produced by the Televisa conglomerate, Mexican films also have grown in popularity in the expanding Spanish-language exhibition circuits of the American Southwest. The United States, with its more than twenty-five million Spanish speakers, represents a lucrative potential market that has been underexploited since the early 1950s. The industry's dynamics, however, highlight the dilemma for state elites faced with a choice between economically successful but culturally diminished film production on the one hand, and a commercially inviable quality cinema on the other. Most industry leaders and state officials have chosen the former, though recent critical successes such as *Amores perros* (Alejandro González Iñárritu, 2000) and *Y tu mamá también* (Alfonso Cuarón, 2001) highlight the resilience of the industry in the face of steady globalizing pressures. Still, reminiscent of the global diffusion of other purveyors of cultural influence, the Blockbuster outlets in Mexico City are virtually indistinguishable from their North American counterparts—except they have small sections devoted to Mexican cinema.

EGYPT AND THE MIDDLE EAST

The Middle East may seem like an improbable setting for a discussion of globalization and film, but the region's integration into the film trade began very early and followed a pattern repeated elsewhere. Regular exhibition of commercial motion pictures started in Cairo and Alexandria before World War I, when Egypt became the region's primary distribution hub for resident foreign nationals and colonial military forces. European and American film companies were involved in regional markets from the outset, led increasingly by U.S.-based firms that eventually played a substantial role in integrating the industry worldwide. In time, noteworthy indigenous film industries developed in several states, especially Egypt, Iran, and Israel, along with the Francophone North African countries of Tunisia, Algeria, and Morocco. The diversity of Middle Eastern cinema belies its reduction to a single set of tendencies, though important commonalities exist in the pressures to which all regional producers were subjected. Linguistic, economic, and political connections in this cultural continent justify the use of a regional lens to analyze the unfolding of global patterns.

Egypt is to Middle Eastern filmmaking what the United States is to the world: pioneering, commercially oriented, deeply influential, even hegemonic to the point of engendering resentment and resistance. Its influence exceeds its cinematic reputation, however, for there is an extraordinary disconnect between the Egyptian industry's long-standing regional visibility and its poor international image, especially in the United States. Only a handful of Egyptian filmmakers and actors, such as Yousef Chahine and Omar Sharif, have achieved international status, and the Egyptian industry has long been dismissed for its crass commercialism and perennial state of crisis. Still, not only is Egypt the oldest, largest, and most culturally prominent country in the Middle East, but its encounter with the globalization of filmmaking has been a bellwether for the experience of others, making it worth close examination. While more socially conservative countries such as Saudi Arabia have no public cinemas, let alone indigenous film industries, Egyptians have been going to the movies for a hundred years.

The Egyptian film industry was born in the shadow of Hollywood's rapid overseas expansion after World War I. Domestic production began in the early 1920s with Muhammad Bayoumi's silent feature, *Fi bilad Tout Ankh Amon* (*In the Land of Tutankhamun*, 1923), followed by a silent film called *Leila* (1927) and starring a well-known stage actress.[51] The advent of sound filmmaking provided an opportunity for local entrepreneurs in a small but expanding market, where half the movies exhibited were American films rented out to cinemas by the meter.[52] Egypt's geographic position at the crossroads of Africa and Asia magnified its significance in the film trade, since American distributors shipped films from the United States to Europe and then on to other markets via branch offices in Egypt. Universal Pictures, for example, maintained its Near East regional headquarters in Alexandria, which served as a transit point for film shipments to markets throughout the Middle East, Africa, and beyond.

Domestically produced Egyptian exports did not develop in earnest until after 1935, when prominent industrialist Mohammed Tal'at Harb built Studio Misr in Giza near the pyramids, the first modern film studio in the Middle East and Africa. The production and export of feature films grew dramatically in the 1930s and 1940s, with the Cairo-Giza area emerging as a self-styled "Hollywood of the Arab East," quickly overshadowing Alexandria as the industry's center of gravity. Entrepreneurs, some of whom were resident foreign nationals, constructed four more major studios by 1947, and the number of independent production companies quintupled from 24 to 120 by 1950.[53] Investment capital was most readily available during and just after World War II, when investors sought the quick profits of expanded production and diminished foreign competition. This was the Egyptian industry's golden age, at least financially, when moviegoing became the most popular form of urban entertainment in Egypt and much of the region.

While postwar domestic financial pressure drove Hollywood to seek more revenue from exports, it also led to more filming of motion pictures abroad. This proved to be a vital moment in the industry's global integration. Equipped with recently improved portable cameras and magnetic sound-recording tape, companies were drawn to the box-office rewards of authentic locations, the financial benefits of lower production costs, and any opportunity to put frozen foreign earnings to work.[54] In the early 1950s, two examples of this were the on-location filming by Howard Hawks of Warner Bros.' *The Land of the Pharaohs* in 1953, as well as the shooting by Cecil B. DeMille of Paramount Studios' Academy Award–winning epic *The Ten Commandments,* in 1954. Both were large-scale, expensive productions, the first using a popular new wide-screen process called CinemaScope and the second employing nearly two hundred thousand Egyptian artisans, technicians, laborers, and extras.[55] They differed in their critical and box-office successes, but both involved enough spending in Egypt to give Warner Bros. and Paramount temporary respite from their remittance problems.

Despite the cooperative partnership implied by the latter productions, competition from American exports to Egypt intensified in the 1950s, even while Egypt's own exports gained momentum and expanded. U.S. producers hoped, in Egypt as elsewhere, to recapture the market segment lost in wartime, thereby compensating for declining domestic sales and steadily rising production costs associated with new technologies.[56] As Egyptian government statistics report, the American share of imports peaked at 97 percent in 1957—307 of the 314 foreign films—after the virtual elimination of French and British exports during the Suez crisis and their drastic reduction for several years thereafter.[57] From then on, however, U.S. imports began a two-decade slide downward, with American distributors closing or consolidating their Cairo offices in the 1960s to cut costs, maintaining distribution through local agents or their own representatives stationed elsewhere.

The political impetus to globalization was on full display in postwar Egypt. The diplomatic record chronicles the efforts of American producers to defend their business interests by soliciting U.S. embassy assistance, just as it tells the story of attempts by Egyptian producers and distributors to enlist state support in the face of foreign competition. Sometimes American film companies simply found themselves caught up in regional politics: Israel declared Paramount's *Samson and Delilah* to be anti-Jewish propaganda and banned it, at the same time that Egypt delayed the film's release on the claim that it was pro-Zionist.[58] Generally, though, two international issues dominated the American government's film-related concerns in Egypt throughout the 1950s and 1960s: remittance restrictions on U.S. companies and broader cold war rivalry with the Soviet Union, the latter producing a more overtly political logic in embassy support for American film companies. Embassy officers cooperated with Hollywood representatives, even if the written record contains evidence that officials took a broader view of U.S. interests and sometimes clashed with the purely business-oriented American film companies.[59] In the final analysis, American government and business agendas overlapped sufficiently to provide a substantial net boost to the U.S. competitive effort.

With the cold war raging, American film representatives in Egypt must have been aware of these broader developments, and they may have attempted to provoke the embassy with dramatic claims of Soviet market penetration. In fact, the Soviet Union did increase its presence in the Egyptian film market, seeking indirect control over theaters by purchasing and leasing them through local intermediaries in the mid-1950s. Within a few years, the Soviets had captured 10 to 15 percent of the Egyptian market, benefiting—though not as much as their American rivals—from the post–Suez crisis diplomatic falling out, and taking advantage of Egypt's subsequent tilt to the left. An indication of the extent to which Hollywood became enmeshed in the larger political conflict of the day was the publication in 1957 of *Safir Amrika bil-alwan al-tabi'iyya* (*The Ambassador of America in Natural Colors*), a wide-ranging critique of American films and Hollywood's role in the world, written by left-leaning film director Kamil el-Tilmissani.[60]

Egyptian film exports continued to expand internationally in the early postwar years, largely sustained by the efforts of war profiteers to find fruitful investment opportunities for hundreds of millions of pounds in newly acquired wealth.[61] Still handled by individual sales agents, the majority of these exports went to markets in the Middle East and North Africa, though Egyptian films in the 1950s found their way regularly to such disparate and far-flung places as Venezuela, Hong Kong, Madagascar, Denmark, and Indonesia.[62] Closer to home, the high-water mark of Egyptian exports to the Middle East came in 1954, when Egypt shipped abroad more than £E176,000 in film, most of which went to Lebanon, Iraq, Jordan, Libya, Aden, and Syria.[63]

Just as Egypt's regional political influence grew under the charismatic leadership of Gamal Abd el-Nasser, the Egyptian film had no true rivals in the Middle East and North Africa early in this period, though American pictures continued to win the lion's share of receipts in elite-oriented theaters.[64] The official trade figures greatly underestimate the economic significance of exports by recording only nominal values for the physical reels of celluloid shipped abroad, unable to register their eventual returns from exhibition over a multiyear period. Using this crude method, film still ranked as the country's twenty-second most valuable export in 1953, out of several dozen commodities.[65] In fact, if one observer is even remotely accurate in listing gross industry revenues at £E2.7 million that year, the common assertion that film was Egypt's second-ranking source of export revenue, after cotton, may not have been completely exaggerated.[66]

These successes notwithstanding, competition in the regional market eventually reduced Egypt's foreign revenues and was instrumental in precipitating its long-term decline. A sporadic but clear downward trend in exports began halfway through the 1950s, delayed only briefly by a boom period late in the decade that film historian Samir Farid has dubbed "the second golden age for Egyptian cinema."[67] Foreign movies inundated the region, as the novelty of American color films and "spectaculars" combined with a rejuvenated European cinema led by the French New Wave. Egyptian producers and distributors faced competition unlike anything they had seen before. With the economic uncertainty that accompanied the Socialist Decrees of July 1961 and the partial nationalization of the industry that year, both production and exports trailed off for most of the rest of the 1960s. Even if opinions vary on the effects of fuller state involvement in production after 1963, clearly it meant greater thematic didacticism that was not always well received by audiences accustomed to seeing film as simple entertainment.

Exports also were subject to the vagaries of regional politics, since inter-Arab rivalry affected the availability of markets for Egyptian pictures. While Iraq had become one of Egypt's most important foreign markets by the mid-1950s, political rivalry in 1960 appears to have led Baghdad to ban Egyptian movies, at least temporarily.[68] In the polarized regional climate of the mid-1960s, the film industry joined other politically engaged mass media, such as radio's Voice of the Arabs, causing regimes in Syria, Lebanon, Saudi Arabia, and some of the other Gulf states to slash imports from Cairo. A few other Arabic-language producers such as Lebanon began making a handful of films on their own, though the greatest beneficiaries of inter-Arab conflict were the American companies and affiliated local distributors and exhibitors that filled the void created by Egypt's departure.

In the first half of the 1970s, Hollywood's presence in Egypt continued a slow, two-decade contraction, with American exports declining even more than those of other countries. The American share in the Egyptian market dropped to its lowest point in the mid-1970s, when U.S. exports were less than a third of what they had been late in the 1950s and accounted for only about half the foreign films on the market.[69] This pattern mirrored larger trends in the financial health of both the U.S. industry and its Egyptian counterpart, where the total size of the market for motion pictures had been waning since its postwar peak. The film trade also paralleled broader developments in Egyptian-American relations. Bilateral ties between the two countries had deteriorated in the 1950s after a brief, Suez-induced improvement, remaining formally correct but tense for the rest of the Nasser regime. Anwar Sadat's overture to Washington changed both regional and international equations in the aftermath of the 1973 war with Israel, and U.S. film exports rose then in a manner suggestive of the freeing of political constraints.

The 1980s were marked by a particularly erratic course of expanding and contracting foreign imports, but by the 1990s the American industry seemed to have won back some of the relative dominance it enjoyed in earlier years, partly through the decline of European production. Still, U.S. involvement was at a much lower overall level than its apogee four decades prior. With demand undermined by a shrinking exhibition infrastructure and a stagnant economy, Egypt had declined to the status of a minor foreign market for U.S. exports, with no real role as an American entrée to the regional trade for Egyptian facilities or personnel. Five decades after the famed American director Orson Welles contracted with Studio al-Ahram to shoot two different films in that studio and on location in Egypt, American producers rarely sought to brave Egypt's bureaucratic entanglements to produce there.[70]

Egypt, nonetheless, like its regional counterpart in Mexico, has become wholly incorporated into a global network of markets, images, ideas, and information. Changes in technology, such as satellite television, the digital revolution, and the Internet, have steadily eroded state capacity to limit cultural and information flows in a region suffering from persistent authoritarianism and growing social turmoil. Emerging satellite media have accelerated and deepened the region's connections to the rest of the world, providing a mechanism for information flows that are both beyond state control and not always emanating from the centers of global power. The state has attempted to strike back by building its own technological capacity in this area, but its influence is limited in a world of footloose firms and diminished control over cultural spaces.

CONCLUSION

Through international competition and market integration, globalization forces have been active in filmmaking for the better part of a century. State political leaders have responded to these pressures in widely varied ways, reflecting local and regional circumstances that themselves have evolved over the years. The film trade's early internationalization and the profound importance of foreign markets to Hollywood are difficult to exaggerate. But the worldwide integration of the industry even calls into question the very concepts of "national" and "foreign" film production and trade. Non-American markets do not simply represent additional profit to Hollywood firms; they have become integral to the entire structure of production. Without them, not only would many large-budget pictures not be made, but the industry as it is presently constituted would likely fail or require transformation.

American dominance in the film trade of the past century has seldom failed, though it has waxed and waned in particular places, both at home and abroad. In this sense, the U.S. role in motion pictures has been emblematic of the American position in the world: while the industry had the material capacity to do so slightly sooner, it emerged only after World War I; it reached its box-office pinnacle in 1946; it saw its lowest point domestically in the last days of Vietnam; by the 1980s it was undergoing a revival; and in the 1990s it began to reinvent itself to accommodate new markets and technologies. Today it is witnessing changes that will likely transform it into an important segment of a globally oriented culture and information industry. Hollywood's frequent depiction as a monolithic and omnipotent world cultural menace belies the actual financial vulnerability of many of its firms, especially since the postwar court-mandated enforcement of antitrust laws, which raised the level of domestic competition among the majors. Some of these firms have remained unaltered in name, but all have undergone transformative organizational and operational changes induced by the need to stay profitable in an extraordinarily competitive and risky business. These changes have affected film industries everywhere, as U.S. firms have been inspired by domestic competition to expand their pursuit of international markets and—especially overseas—have been empowered by the U.S. political process to do so in the collusive fashion of a legally sanctioned cartel.

Filmmakers in Latin America and the Middle East have tried to respond to globalization pressures in their home and regional markets. To compete in the home market with the most powerful of the world's producers, large-scale investments are required in both production budgets and related human and physical capital, ranging from film schools to studios and technical facilities. Such extensive investments can be sustained only by reaching larger audiences than those found in most domestic markets alone. Even in a digital era, low-budget filmmaking is difficult to undertake as a successful commercial activity due to the availability of high-budget alternatives. Cinema admission costs the same for all manner of filmmaking. Producers in Egypt and Mexico have found themselves in a perpetual state of crisis since the shrinking of their export opportunities after World War II, with even their domestic exhibition circuits contracting over time. State intervention to bear some of the costs has proved inadequate in some cases and politically unsustainable in others. Does globalization therefore mean the eventual elimination of all but the largest film productions? That is not likely, since the impulse to see recognizable images of the self will always stir the political will, rooted locally, to realize such desires through national film production.

NOTES

1. David Held, Anthony G. McGrew, David Goldblatt, and Jonathan Perraton, *Global Transformations: Politics, Economics, and Culture* (Palo Alto, CA: Stanford University Press, 1999).

2. Kenichi Ohmae, *The Borderless World: Power and Strategy in the Interlinked Economy* (New York: HarperCollins, 1990); Thomas Friedman, *The Lexus and the Olive Tree: Understanding Globalization* (New York: Farrar, Straus, and Giroux, 1999).

3. Michael Veseth, *Globaloney: Unraveling the Myths of Globalization* (New York: Rowman and Littlefield, 2005).

4. Giovanni Sartori, "Concept Misformation in Comparative Politics," *American Political Science Review* 64.4 (1970): 1033–1053.

5. William F. Hellmuth, Jr., "The Motion Picture Industry," in *The Structure of American Industry: Some Case Studies,* 3rd ed., ed. Walter A. Adams (New York: MacMillan, 1961), 410.

6. See Michael Conant, *Antitrust in the Motion Picture Industry: Economic and Legal Analysis* (Berkeley: University of California Press, 1960); Mae D. Huettig, *Economic Control of the Motion Picture Industry: A Study in Industrial Organization* (Philadelphia: University of Pennsylvania Press, 1944).

7. Ian Jarvie, *Hollywood's Overseas Campaign: The North Atlantic Movie Trade, 1920–1950* (Cambridge: Cambridge University Press, 1992); John Trumpbour, *Selling Hollywood to the World: U.S. and European Struggles for Mastery of the Global Film Industry, 1920–1950* (Cambridge: Cambridge University Press, 2002).

8. Andrew Flibbert, *Commerce in Culture: States and Markets in the World Film Trade* (New York: Palgrave McMillan, 2007).

9. Robert Sklar, *Movie-Made America: A Cultural History of American Movies* (New York: Random House, 1975), 215; see also Ariel Dorfman and Armand Mattelart, *How to Read Donald Duck: Imperialist Ideology in the Disney Comic,* trans. and rev. ed. (New York: International General, 1991).

10. Colin Hoskins, Stuart McFadyen, and Adam Finn, *Global Television and Film: An Introduction to the Economics of the Business* (Oxford: Clarendon Press, 1997).

11. Albert Moran, ed., *Film Policy: International, National, and Regional Perspectives* (New York: Routledge, 1996); Harold Vogel, *Entertainment Industry Economics: A Guide for Financial Analysis,* 6th ed. (Cambridge: Cambridge University Press, 2004); Charles Moul, ed., *A Concise Handbook of Movie Industry Economics* (Cambridge, MA: Cambridge University Press, 2005).

12. David Prindle, *Risky Business: The Political Economy of Hollywood* (Boulder, CO: Westview, 1993).

13. Michael Chanan, *Labour Power in the British Film Industry* (London: British Film Institute, 1976).

14. Aida Hozic, *Hollyworld: Space, Power and Fantasy in the American Economy* (Ithaca, NY: Cornell University Press, 2001); on star systems, see Cathy Klaprat, "The Star as Market Strategy: Bette Davis in Another Light," in *The American Film Industry,* rev. ed., ed. Tino Balio (Madison: University of Wisconsin Press, 1985).

15. Hoskins, McFadyen, and Finn, *Global Television and Film.*

16. Allen J. Scott, *On Hollywood: The Place, the Industry* (Princeton, NJ: Princeton University Press, 2004).

17. Kristin Thompson, *Exporting Entertainment: America in the World Film Market, 1907–34* (London: British Film Institute, 1985).

18. Edward G. Lowry, "Trade Follows the Film," *Saturday Evening Post* 198, November 7, 1925, 12.

19. Raymond Moley, *The Hays Office* (New York: Bobbs-Merrill, 1945).

20. Will H. Hays, *The Memoirs of Will H. Hays* (Garden City, NY: Doubleday, 1955).

21. David Bordwell, Janet Staiger, and Kristin Thompson, *The Classical Hollywood Cinema: Film Style and Mode of Production to 1960* (New York: Columbia University Press, 1985); Ruth Vasey, *The World According to Hollywood, 1918–1939* (Madison: University of Wisconsin Press, 1997).

22. Sklar, *Movie-Made America,* 216.

23. Jeremy Tunstall, *The Media Are American: Anglo-American Media in the World* (New York: Columbia University Press, 1977).

24. Paulo Antonio Paranaguá, *Mexican Cinema* (London: British Film Institute and IMCINE, 1995), 24.

25. Hays, *Memoirs,* 333–334.

26. C.J. North, "Our Foreign Trade in Motion Pictures," in "The Motion Picture in Its Social and Economic Aspects," *Annals of the American Academy of Political and Social Science* 128 (November 1926): 101.

27. Gaizka S. de Usabel, *The High Noon of American Films in Latin America* (Ann Arbor, MI: UMI Research Press, 1982).

28. Carl J. Mora, *Mexican Cinema: Reflections of a Society, 1896–2004,* 3rd ed. (Jefferson, NC: McFarland, 2005).

29. John King, *Magical Reels: A History of Cinema in Latin America* (New York: Verso, 1990), 32; Dudley Andrew, *Mists of Regret: Culture and Sensibility in Classic French Film* (Princeton, NJ: Princeton University Press, 1995), 96–98.

30. Mora, *Mexican Cinema.*

31. Carlos Monsiváis, "Mexican Cinema: Of Myths and Demystifications," in *Mediating Two Worlds: Cinematic Encounters in the Americas,* ed. John King, Ana M. López, and Manuel Alvarado (London: British Film Institute, 1993).

32. Nathan D. Golden, *Review of Foreign Film Markets During 1936* (Washington, DC: United States Department of Commerce, Bureau of Foreign and Domestic Commerce, Motion Picture Section, April 1937); John Eugene Harley, *World-Wide Influences of the Cinema: A Study of Official Censorship and the International Cultural Aspects of Motion Pictures* (Los Angeles: University of Southern California Press, 1940).

33. Thomas Doherty, *Projections of War: Hollywood, American Culture, and World War II* (New York: Columbia University Press, 1993), 299–304.

34. Emilio García Riera, *Historia del cine Mexicano* (Mexico City: Secretaría de Educación Pública, 1986), 211.

35. Emily S. Rosenberg, *Spreading the American Dream: American Economic and Cultural Expansion, 1890–1945* (New York: Farrar, Straus, and Giroux, 1982), 206–208.

36. Seth Fein, "From Collaboration to Containment: Hollywood and the International Political Economy of Mexican Cinema after the Second World War," in *Mexico's Cinema: A Century of Film and Filmmakers,* ed. Joanne Hershfield and David R. Maciel (Wilmington, DE: Scholarly, 1999); Jorge Schnitman, *Film Industries in Latin America: Dependency and Development* (Norwood, NJ: Ablex, 1984).

37. Emilio García Riera, *Historia documental del cine Mexicano,* vol. 5 (Guadalajara: University of Guadalajara and National Council for Culture and the Arts, 1992), 7.

38. Frances Cairncross, *The Death of Distance: How the Communications Revolution Will Change Our Lives* (Cambridge, MA: Harvard Business School Press, 1997).

39. *International Motion Picture Almanac, 1953–54* (New York: Quigley, 1955), 818.

40. *International Motion Picture Almanac, 1956* (New York: Quigley, 1957), 794; *International Motion Picture Almanac, 1957* (New York: Quigley, 1958), 850; Riera, *Historia del cine Mexicano,* 244.

41. King, *Magical Reels,* 129–130.

42. Randal Johnson, *The Film Industry in Brazil: Culture and the State* (Pittsburgh: University of Pennsylvania Press, 1987), 138–142.

43. Federico Heuer, *La industria cinematográfica Mexicana* (Mexico City: n.p., 1964), 86–87.

44. King, *Magical Reels.*

45. *World Communications: A 200-Country Survey of Press, Radio, Television, and Film* (Paris: UNESCO, 1975), 204.

46. Charles Ramírez Berg, *Cinema of Solitude: A Critical Study of Mexican Film, 1967–1983* (Austin: University of Texas Press, 1992), 12.

47. See David R. Maciel, "Cinema and the State in Contemporary Mexico," in *Mexico's Cinema: A Century of Film and Filmmakers,* ed. Joanne Hershfield and David R. Maciel (Wilmington, DE: Scholarly, 1999); Mora, *Mexican Cinema*; Paola Costa, *La "apertura" cinematográfica: México, 1970–1976* (Puebla, Mexico: Universidad Autónoma de Puebla, 1983).

48. *World Communications.*

49. Mora, *Mexican Cinema.*

50. Paranaguá, *Mexican Cinema,* 54.

51. Magda Wassef, ed., *Egypte: 100 ans de cinéma* (Paris: Editions Plume and Institut du Monde Arabe, 1995), 20.

52. Andrew Flibbert, "State and Cinema in Pre-Revolutionary Egypt," in *Re-Envisioning Egypt, 1919–1952,* ed. Arthur Goldschmidt, Amy J. Johnson, and Barak A.

Salmoni (Cairo: American University in Cairo Press, 2005); North, "Our Foreign Trade in Motion Pictures," 107.

53. Jacques Pascal, ed., *The Middle East Motion Picture Almanac, 1946–47* (Cairo: S.O.P. Press, 1947), 127.

54. Robert H. Stanley, *The Celluloid Empire: A History of the American Movie Industry* (New York: Hastings, 1978).

55. "Hollywood on the Nile," *Egyptian Economic and Political Review* 1.1 (September 1954): 24–25; and "The Ten Commandments," *Egyptian Economic and Political Review* 1.3 (November 1954): 12.

56. Georges Sadoul, "Geography of the Cinema and the Arab World," in *The Cinema in the Arab Countries,* ed. Georges Sadoul (Beirut: UNESCO and Interarab Centre of Cinema and Television, 1966).

57. Central Agency for Public Mobilization and Statistics (CAPMAS), *al-Ihsa'at al-thaqafiyya: al-sinima wal-masrah* [Cultural statistics: The cinema and theater], 1964–1996.

58. *Cine Film,* no. 33 (1 February 1951): 15.

59. Flibbert, *Commerce in Culture.*

60. Robert Vitalis, " 'American Ambassador in Technicolor and Cinemascope': Hollywood and Revolution on the Nile," in *Mass Mediations: New Approaches to Popular Culture in the Middle East and Beyond,* ed. Walter Armbrust (Berkeley: University of California Press, 2000).

61. Charles Issawi, *Egypt at Mid-Century: An Economic Survey* (New York: Oxford University Press, 1954), 204.

62. *Annual Statement of the Foreign Trade of Egypt* (Cairo: Statistical Department, Ministry of Finance, various years).

63. *Annual Statement of the Foreign Trade of Egypt, 1954,* 570–571.

64. See Joel Gordon, *Revolutionary Melodrama: Popular Film and Civic Identity in Nasser's Egypt* (Chicago: Middle East Documentation Center, 2002).

65. *Annual Statement of the Foreign Trade of Egypt, 1953,* 147.

66. Jacob M. Landau, *Studies in the Arab Theater and Cinema* (Philadelphia: University of Pennsylvania Press, 1958), 180.

67. Samir Farid, "Periodization of Egyptian Cinema," in *Screens of Life: Critical Film Writing from the Arab World,* ed. Alia Arasoughly (Quebec: World Heritage Press, 1996), 11.

68. *Sina'at al-sinima: haqa'iq w-arqam* [The film industry: Facts and figures] (General Egyptian Organization for the Cinema, Radio, and Television, Technical Office for the Cinema, March 1964), 14.

69. CAPMAS, various years.

70. "Echos et Nouvelles: Orson Welles va tourner en Egypte," *Cine Film* 19 (7 November 1949).

BIBLIOGRAPHY

Andrew, Dudley. 1995. *Mists of Regret: Culture and Sensibility in Classic French Film.* Princeton, NJ: Princeton University Press.

Annual Statement of the Foreign Trade of Egypt. Various years. Cairo: Statistical Department, Ministry of Finance.

Berg, Charles Ramírez. 1992. *Cinema of Solitude: A Critical Study of Mexican Film, 1967–1983.* Austin: University of Texas Press.

Bordwell, David, Janet Staiger, and Kristin Thompson. 1985. *The Classical Hollywood Cinema: Film Style and Mode of Production to 1960.* New York: Columbia University Press.

Central Agency for Public Mobilization and Statistics (CAPMAS). 1964–1996. *al-Ihsa'at al-thaqafiyya: al-sinima wal-masrah* [Cultural statistics: The cinema and theater].

Cairncross, Frances. 1997. *The Death of Distance: How the Communications Revolution Will Change Our Lives.* Cambridge, MA: Harvard Business School Press.

Chanan, Michael. 1976. *Labour Power in the British Film Industry.* London: British Film Institute.

Cine Film. 1951. No. 33 (1 February).

Conant, Michael. 1960. *Antitrust in the Motion Picture Industry: Economic and Legal Analysis.* Berkeley: University of California Press.

Costa, Paola. 1983. *La "apertura" cinematográfica: México, 1970–1976.* Puebla, Mexico: Universidad Autónoma de Puebla.

Doherty, Thomas. 1993. *Projections of War: Hollywood, American Culture, and World War II.* New York: Columbia University Press.

Dorfman, Ariel, and Armand Mattelart. 1991. *How to Read Donald Duck: Imperialist Ideology in the Disney Comic.* Trans. and rev. ed. New York: International General.

"Echos et Nouvelles: Orson Welles va tourner en Egypte." 1949. *Cine Film,* no. 19 (7 November).

Farid, Samir. 1996. "Periodization of Egyptian Cinema." *Screens of Life: Critical Film Writing from the Arab World.* Ed. Alia Arasoughly. Quebec: World Heritage Press.

Fein, Seth. 1999. "From Collaboration to Containment: Hollywood and the International Political Economy of Mexican Cinema after the Second World War." *Mexico's Cinema: A Century of Film and Filmmakers.* Ed. Joanne Hershfield and David R. Maciel. Wilmington, DE: Scholarly.

Flibbert, Andrew. 2005. "State and Cinema in Pre-Revolutionary Egypt." *Re-Envisioning Egypt, 1919–1952.* Ed. Arthur Goldschmidt, Amy J. Johnson, and Barak A. Salmoni. Cairo: American University in Cairo Press.

———. 2007. *Commerce in Culture: States and Markets in the World Film Trade.* New York: Palgrave McMillan, 2007.

Friedman, Thomas. 1999. *The Lexus and the Olive Tree: Understanding Globalization.* New York: Farrar, Straus, and Giroux.

Golden, Nathan D. 1937. *Review of Foreign Film Markets During 1936.* Washington, DC: United States Department of Commerce, Bureau of Foreign and Domestic Commerce, Motion Picture Section, April.

Gordon, Joel. 2002. *Revolutionary Melodrama: Popular Film and Civic Identity in Nasser's Egypt.* Chicago: Middle East Documentation Center.

Harley, John Eugene. 1940. *World-Wide Influences of the Cinema: A Study of Official Censorship and the International Cultural Aspects of Motion Pictures.* Los Angeles: University of Southern California Press.

Hays, Will H. 1955. *The Memoirs of Will H. Hays.* Garden City, NY: Doubleday.

Held, David, Anthony G. McGrew, David Goldblatt, and Jonathan Perraton. 1999. *Global Transformations: Politics, Economics, and Culture.* Pala Alto, CA: Stanford University Press.

Hellmuth, William F., Jr. 1961. "The Motion Picture Industry." *The Structure of American Industry: Some Case Studies.* 3rd ed. Ed. Walter A. Adams. New York: MacMillan.

Heuer, Federico. 1964. *La industria cinematográfica Mexicana.* Mexico City: n.p.

"Hollywood on the Nile." 1954. *Egyptian Economic and Political Review (Egyptian Review)* 1.1 (September): 24–25.

Hoskins, Colin, Stuart McFadyen, and Adam Finn. 1997. *Global Television and Film: An Introduction to the Economics of the Business.* Oxford: Clarendon Press.

Hozic, Aida. 2001. *Hollyworld: Space, Power and Fantasy in the American Economy.* Ithaca, NY: Cornell University Press.

Huettig, Mae D. 1944. *Economic Control of the Motion Picture Industry: A Study in Industrial Organization.* Philadelphia: University of Pennsylvania Press.

International Motion Picture Almanac (IMPA) 1953–54. 1955. New York: Quigley.

International Motion Picture Almanac (IMPA) 1956. 1957. New York: Quigley.

International Motion Picture Almanac (IMPA) 1957. 1958. New York: Quigley.

Issawi, Charles. 1954. *Egypt at Mid-Century: An Economic Survey.* New York: Oxford University Press.

Jarvie, Ian. 1992. *Hollywood's Overseas Campaign: The North Atlantic Movie Trade, 1920–1950.* Cambridge: Cambridge University Press.

Johnson, Randal. 1987. *The Film Industry in Brazil: Culture and the State.* Pittsburgh: University of Pennsylvania Press.

King, John. 1990. *Magical Reels: A History of Cinema in Latin America.* New York: Verso.

Klaprat, Cathy. 1985. "The Star as Market Strategy: Bette Davis in Another Light." *The American Film Industry.* Rev. ed. Ed. Tino Balio. Madison: University of Wisconsin Press.

Landau, Jacob M. 1958. *Studies in the Arab Theater and Cinema.* Philadelphia: University of Pennsylvania Press.

Lowry, Edward G. 1925. "Trade Follows the Film." *Saturday Evening Post* 198 (7 November).

Maciel, David R. 1999. "Cinema and the State in Contemporary Mexico." *Mexico's Cinema: A Century of Film and Filmmakers.* Ed. Joanne Herschfield and David R. Maciel. Wilmington, DE: Scholarly.

Moley, Raymond. 1945. *The Hays Office.* New York: Bobbs-Merrill.

Monsiváis, Carlos. 1993. "Mexican Cinema: Of Myths and Demystifications." *Mediating Two Worlds: Cinematic Encounters in the Americas.* Ed. John King, Ana M. López, and Manuel Alvarado. London: British Film Institute.

Mora, Carl J. 2005. *Mexican Cinema: Reflections of a Society, 1896–2004.* 3rd ed. Jefferson, NC: McFarland.

Moran, Albert, ed. 1996. *Film Policy: International, National, and Regional Perspectives.* New York: Routledge.

Moul, Charles, ed. 2005. *A Concise Handbook of Movie Industry Economics.* Cambridge, MA: Cambridge University Press.

North, C.J. 1926. "Our Foreign Trade in Motion Pictures." In "The Motion Picture in its Social and Economic Aspects." *Annals of the American Academy of Political and Social Science* 128 (November 1926).

Ohmae, Kenichi. 1990. *The Borderless World: Power and Strategy in the Interlinked Economy.* New York: HarperCollins.

Paranaguá, Paulo Antonio. 1995. *Mexican Cinema.* London: British Film Institute and IMCINE.

Pascal, Jacques, ed. 1947. *The Middle East Motion Picture Almanac, 1946– 47.* Cairo: S.O.P. Press.

Prindle, David. 1993. *Risky Business: The Political Economy of Hollywood.* Boulder, CO: Westview.

Riera, Emilio García. 1986. *Historia del cine Mexicano.* Mexico City: Secretaría de Educación Pública.

———. 1992. *Historia documental del cine Mexicano.* Guadalajara: University of Guadalajara and National Council for Culture and the Arts. Multiple volumes.

Rosenberg, Emily S. 1982. *Spreading the American Dream: American Economic and Cultural Expansion, 1890–1945.* New York: Farrar, Straus, and Giroux.

Sadoul, Georges. 1966. "Geography of the Cinema and the Arab World." *The Cinema in the Arab Countries.* Ed. Georges Sadoul. Beirut: UNESCO and Interarab Centre of Cinema and Television.

Sartori, Giovanni. 1970. "Concept Misformation in Comparative Politics." *American Political Science Review* 64.4: 1033–1053.

Schnitman, Jorge. 1984. *Film Industries in Latin America: Dependency and Development.* Norwood, NJ: Ablex.

Scott, Allen J. 2004. *On Hollywood: The Place, The Industry.* Princeton, NJ: Princeton University Press.

Sina'at al-sinima: haqa'iq w-arqam [The film industry: Facts and figures]. March 1964. General Egyptian Organization for the Cinema, Radio, and Television, Technical Office for the Cinema.

Sklar, Robert. 1975. *Movie-Made America: A Cultural History of American Movies.* New York: Random House.

Stanley, Robert H. 1978. *The Celluloid Empire: A History of the American Movie Industry.* New York: Hastings.

"The Ten Commandments." 1954. *Egyptian Economic and Political Review* 1.3 (November): 12.

Thompson, Kristin. 1985. *Exporting Entertainment: America in the World Film Market, 1907–34.* London: British Film Institute.

Trumpbour, John. 2002. *Selling Hollywood to the World: U.S. and European Struggles for Mastery of the Global Film Industry, 1920–1950.* Cambridge, MA: Cambridge University Press.

Tunstall, Jeremy. 1977. *The Media Are American: Anglo-American Media in the World.* New York: Columbia University Press.

Usabel, Gaizka S. de. 1982. *The High Noon of American Films in Latin America.* Ann Arbor, MI: UMI Research Press.

Vasey, Ruth. 1997. *The World According to Hollywood, 1918–1939.* Madison: University of Wisconsin Press.

Veseth, Michael. 2005. *Globaloney: Unraveling the Myths of Globalization.* New York: Rowman and Littlefield.

Vitalis, Robert. 2000. " 'American Ambassador in Technicolor and Cinemascope': Hollywood and Revolution on the Nile." *Mass Mediations: New Approaches to Popular*

Culture in the Middle East and Beyond. Ed. Walter Armbrust. Berkeley: University of California Press.

Vogel, Harold. 2004. *Entertainment Industry Economics: A Guide for Financial Analysis,* 6th ed. Cambridge: Cambridge University Press.

Wassef, Magda, ed. 1995. *Egypte: 100 ans de cinéma.* Paris: Editions Plume and Institut du Monde Arabe.

World Communications: A 200-Country Survey of Press, Radio, Television, and Film. 1975. Paris: UNESCO.

CHAPTER 18

COMPUTERS AND CULTURAL STUDIES

DAVID GOLUMBIA

CULTURAL STUDIES AND COMPUTERS

Arguably the most widespread and productive set of critical approaches to media in contemporary theory, cultural studies has so far been applied only partially to the world of computers. One role for cultural studies has been to look for the places in media and technology where it is possible to locate forms of social resistance and personal empowerment. Indeed, this mode is often especially important for understanding marginalized and minority cultures and cultural productions when they interact with majority and majoritarian forms. In every existing medium, we see productive examples of such analyses, and Raymond Williams insisted upon them when he showed how a technological medium like television could be constructed in socially complex ways.[1] When cultural studies looks to computers for something called *new media*, it appears to be looking for and championing just these sorts of resistant practices and forms.[2]

Yet this literature addresses only part of what is usually understood as "culture" in cultural studies. Foundational theorists such as Williams and Stuart Hall, along with Fredric Jameson, John Fiske, John Frow, and the authors in the Grossberg, Nelson, and Treichler *Cultural Studies* anthology, share a profound concern with the politics of our contemporary world, and understand cultural production, including not just media but also technical production, as part of this culture, part of us. In this mode of inquiry, cultural studies often explores the ways in which *existing* forms of power and *existing* institutions are strengthened, reinforced, deployed, and distributed throughout society. This is not simply to accuse each medium of being "complicit"; it is to say that every human product turns out, on close analysis, to reflect all the apparently political tensions of our culture.

Part of what is so unconvincing about the new media literature is that it fails so often to address real examples of digital media, and that it so often gestures—and this is particularly true of Manovich—at media that have not yet come into being, or that occupy no more than a small segment of contemporary digital practice.[3] This state of affairs exists despite the fact that Hollywood entertainment has been completely transformed by computationalist practices, from the raw calculative processes of accounting and project management to the remarkable computational transformation of special effects and no less of movie production and screen-writing. The widespread presence of the view that we are awaiting a much more significant media/technological transformation in the main run of scholarship labeled "cultural studies," while refusing in many cases to examine this real-world digital transformation, seems quite odd. A glance at cultural studies of other media would show that every new medium has come along with a rush of specifically capitalist advertisements that radically oversell the capabilities of the medium.[4] Of particular note are sales pitches that vaguely offer radical, nonspecific, transfor-mative political change. Such claims are omnipresent in the literature on elec-tricity, the telegraph, the telephone, television, and so on—and these technologies certainly did transform society, although rarely in a clearly democratic or especially benign fashion. There is every reason to suspect that recent hyperbolic claims about computers will turn out to be as misleading as they were about every other medium.[5]

Were we to put aside such claims, we would be forced to look at computers more carefully as they are—as they exist in front of us, and in the world around us. From this perspective, exploring the ways in which individuals might be em-powered via computational power seems analytically secondary to questions the literature does not seem to want to ask: How do computers aid the powerful? What does already-existing power in our world gain from massive computerization? What are the observable effects on existing human cultures of computerization? That such questions have been downplayed in a literature labeled "cultural studies" is, at least, cause for reflection. More important, we need to develop an under-standing of what cultural studies might say, and has said even if in its margins, about these questions.[6]

THE BIAS OF COMPUTATION

Questions about power relations are, in fact, typical if not characteristic of cultural studies with regard to any medium or technology: How does it enable power? What does it do for the functions of power in our society? To ask these questions requires that we look away from potential formations and toward existing ones. What is especially disturbing about the general failure to ask questions like this in the critical literature is that what is unprecedented about computers, what is characteristic of them, is the degree to which they serve the interests of power. In a critical way, computers act the role of a perfected slave in a Hegelian Master-Slave dialectic (and therefore imply a kind of perfected mastery). While this may or may not be connected with the especially American drive to computerize everything, it is nevertheless characteristic of our computers that they are strongly implicated in our contemporary experience of power and mastery. At every level, from the most miniature to the global, computers and the networks they instance appear to offer a kind of equal, distributed access to power, that on closer examination also provides unprecedented power and control to centralized and bureaucratic authorities. At a personal level, computers are very much used so as to convey to the user a sense of mastery, and users who can attain this state of mastery find themselves quickly assimilated onto paths of power and capital. These "success" stories, which arguably constitute a major part of the story of computing in our time, seem invisible when we discuss how new educational tools and online communities may empower some groups.

The slogans that are accepted today as dogma by many computing advocates—most notably, that computing and the Internet somehow lead directly to democracy—have much in common with the slogans heard during prior significant technological and media shifts. Perhaps the strong and near-uniform belief that computerization is leading toward positive political change stands as a displacement for a harder truth, the repressed inverse of the computational dogma: namely, that computerization leads directly toward *more* centralized and administrative authority, toward stratification and hierarchical distribution of power, toward centralization of resources and assets, and toward a general kind of ordering of the world that Deleuze and Guattari call "striation." Following the terminology of Harold Innis, we can think of this orientation of computation toward power and toward striation and order as a "bias," a tendency, one that we may certainly at times resist with success.[7] But in order to resist that bias we must see the existing phenomena as clearly as possible, and these include the significant (and today largely muted) absolutist heritage of computing itself.

Computational Politics

Computers provide an unprecedented level of specification and control over every aspect of human society (and the rest of our environment). Where possible, computers simulate processes from the business world, from institutional administration, and from the environment; depending on the domain, these simulations may be used either to guide human behavior or to fully govern it. In other domains, where physical manipulation is needed or where true formalization is not possible, computers control the machines and processes that produce or govern almost every aspect of society. Segmentation itself implies formalization; "perfect" processes from the computational standpoint are those which can be entirely operated through simulation and/or automation (for example, digital television recorders; CAD/CAM software and the physical models they produce; computer-generated imagery and full animation in films; nearly all accounting, investing, and banking processes). Perfectly segmented processes are found everywhere and are perhaps even characteristic of what we today understand as modernity, business, government. The most successful managers and businesses today appear to be the ones who maximize efficiency by understanding how to focus on striated objects and processes and bypass smooth ones.

The most successful managers and business are also those who focus the most power in those who have the greatest interest in success itself: the very lack of rules and promotion of individualism appear to push our society to emphasize what C. Wright Mills identified as "power elites," a tendency that seems to increase militarism, the role of imperial-style leadership (externally and internally, in government and in businesses), and indeed self-interested action on the part of the power elites.[8] Specifically, Mills worried about the intrusion of military-industrial thinking into the education system, so that "the pursuit of knowledge has been linked with the training of men to enact special roles in all areas of modern society. The military, in addition to their own schools, have used and increasingly use the educational facilities of private and public educational institutions."[9] At the very heart of the "higher immorality" that is Mills's central concern is the focused control of power by elites rather than its distribution across democratic masses.[10] This requires looking in a top-down rather than a bottom-up direction: asking not just what do computers enable the masses to do, but what do computers enable the power elite to do?

We are used to speaking of a digital divide, but we conceive of it in brute economic terms—just the terms that serve the most elite interests. If only the poor and disadvantaged had computers, goes this view, they would be saved. No doubt, if they had computers, and the rest of the economic and social benefits that go along with not being poor and disadvantaged, then they would no longer be disadvantaged.[11] But computers alone seem no more than a small part of a much larger puzzle, and an especially problematic one at that, especially if they distract our attention from much more urgent and direct problems. These include, first of all, problems of poverty, hunger, rule of force, nondemocratic states, and so forth—all of our most pressing social problems for which computers offer only the most indirect solutions. They also include the question of what computers are doing for the interests of the power elite.

It is on this score that computationalists seem less accountable. They are willing to admit to certain specific problems endemic in the computational environment—viruses, data theft, identity theft, financial theft (which occurs to a much larger extent than official statements would suggest)—but not at all willing to look at the more general outlines of computation and its usefulness to an oligarchical state. Yet the persistent deep themes of political concern in our time map uncomfortably onto the availability of computation: namely, concentration of power, unbalanced access to power and information, both in business and government, and a sense of absolute mastery and power verging on religious fervor. From this sovereign perspective, computing provides a "control-panel" view of society, an object-oriented simulation so powerful that it does not matter whether it maps precisely onto everyday material existence or not.[12] In the view from the top, the overhead view, the positionable camera angles available to simulation, (almost) all of social reality comes to appear striated, chesslike. Like every human ideology, and especially contemporary technology ones, this abstract machine is one we can become part of, or perhaps one that is already inside of us. Its power over us, its power in us, is in some sense proportional to the strength with which we believe in it.

Computational Sovereignty

Conceptually there is a powerful tie between the theory and implementation of modern political authority and the figure of computation. In the single text that might be said to most clearly define the very notion of political sovereignty in the West, *Leviathan* by Thomas Hobbes, computation figures in two precise and related ways. Both are quite well-known in their own way, but they are generally not related as tropes in Hobbes's especially tropic writing. The first occurs very famously on the very first page of the introduction to the volume:

> NATURE (the Art whereby God hath made and governes the World) is by the *Art* of man, as in many other things, so in this also imitated, that is can make an Artificial Animal. For seeing life is but a motion of Limbs, the beginning whereof is in some principall part within; why may we not say, that all *Automata* (Engines that move themselves by springs and wheeles as doth a watch) have an artificiall life? For what is the *Heart,* but a *Spring;* and the *Nerves,* but so many *Strings;*

and the *Joynts*, but so many *Wheeles*, giving motion to the whole Body, such as was intended by the Artificer? *Art* goes yet further, imitation that Rationall and most excellent worke of Nature, *Man.* For by Art is created that great LEVIATHAN called a COMMON-WEALTH, or STATE, (in latine CIVITAS) which is but an Artificiall Man; though of greater stature and strength than the Naturall, for whose protection and defence it was intended; and in which, the *Soveraignty* is an Artificiall *Soul,* as giving life and motion to the whole body.[13]

We dismiss this today largely as metaphor, wondering even what sort of automata Hobbes can have had in mind, since he is saying by his own example that watches are alive. From the citizen's perspective, the view seems metaphorical to the point of absurdity; but from the sovereign perspective it seems quite rational—indeed, it seems to justify a line of antidemocratic action on the part of the sovereign individual. The sovereign is already inhabiting the artificial soul of the people in his own being; the transubstantiation informing this exchange is fully licensed by God; the actions of the king are inherently in the interests of the parts of his body.

The parts of the body politic—in other words, individuals—the body that before was a "body without organs," and that is now an artificial animal, to be made up in the new automaton called the state, cannot themselves escape computational state administration. Very much like pieces on a chessboard, the activities of citizens are administered computationally, their own human powers essentially irrelevant to the operation of the giant machine that is equivalent, in a transubstantiative act, to the body and will of the king. But citizens cannot simply be ordered to submit, in the sense that this would deny the most fundamental principle of "natural right" that Hobbes recognized but whose satisfaction the sovereign alone can realize. They must feel it is in not just their interest but their nature to submit to the sovereign; they must have within them a simulacrum of the very mechanism that constitutes the Leviathan itself. Thus, in *Leviathan*, Chapter 5, Hobbes wrote:

> When a man *Reasoneth,* hee does nothing else but conceive a summe totall, from *Addition* of parcels; or conceive a Remainder, from *Subtraction* of one sum from another: which (if it be done by Words,) is conceiving of the consequence of the names of all the parts, to the name of the whole; or from the names of the whole and one part, to the name of the other part. And though in some things, (as in numbers,) besides Adding and Subtracting, men name other operations, as Multiplying and Dividing; yet they are the same; for Multiplication, is but Adding together of things equall; and Division, but Substracting of one thing, as often as we can. . . . REASON, in this sense, is nothing but *Reckoning* (Adding and Subtracting) of the Consequences of generall names agreed upon, for the *marking* and *signifying* of our thoughts.[14]

While by no means its origin, this passage serves as an appropriate proxy for the association in the West of the view that the mind just *is* a computer with the pursuit of political absolutism. One name we give to this view, somewhat contrary to its content but in accordance with its political lineage, is "Cartesian rational-ism," including its strong association with what Macpherson has rightly called "possessive individualism."[15] A more descriptive name for the view would be "Hobbesian mechanism." Indeed, these thinkers were lumped together at the time under the term "mechanists," as opposed to "vitalists" (who thought living matter was different in kind from mechanisms like watches), and it is the mechanists we associate especially with the rest of possessive-individualist doctrine. A more contemporary name would be "computationalism."

RATIONALISM, COMPUTATIONALISM, AND THE STATE

In Western intellectual history at its most overt, mechanist views cluster on the side of political history to which we have usually attached the term "conservative." In many historical epochs it is clear who tends to endorse such views and who tends to emphasize other aspects of human existence in whatever the theoretical realm. There are strong intellectual and social associations between Hobbes's theories and those of Machiavelli and Descartes, especially when seen from the state perspective. These philosophers and their views have very often been invoked by conservative leaders at times of consolidation of power in iconic or imperial leaders, who will use such doctrines overtly as a policy base. This contrasts with ascendant liberal power and its philosophy, whose conceptual and political tendencies follow dif-ferent lines altogether: Hume, Kant, Nietzsche, Heidegger, Dewey, James, and so on. These are two profoundly different views of what the state itself means, what the citizen's engagement with the state is, and where state power itself arises. Resistance to the view that the mind is mechanical is often found in philosophers we associate with liberal or radical views—Locke, Hume, Nietzsche, Marx. These thinkers put both persons and social groups in the place of mechanical reason, and as we all admit, tend to emphasize social and relational duties rather than "natural right."

The general tendencies of these two intellectual and political bodies are well-known, but their connection with a particular understanding of the nature of human being is something we discuss much less often today than they did in the 1650s. The immense proliferation of scientific specialties leaves most people ar-guably without even a frame from which to conceptualize a view of human nature sensitive to the vast literature on cognition. More precisely, each side of the debate continues with its tacit understanding of what is vital to human being, while technological changes subtly influence the social field out of which broad political opinion is formed. The idea that the person is somehow in essence a digital thing, especially via the sense that the mind is a computer—with no more detail than that metaphorical equation—appears to be "loose" in contemporary culture. This idea fits well with capitalist rationalism and literalist evangelical Christianity, and in some important ways meshes well with associated beliefs of both dogmas.[16] It conflicts with the traditional views of the Left, but it is intriguing enough and its contradictions are so sub rosa that many there take it up as a matter of course, where computationalism has today gained a surprisingly strong foothold.

From the historical perspective, at least, computationalism reads very much as state philosophy. It is in the nature of any philosophy that neither its progenitors nor its consequences can be said to entirely characterize its "essence"; it is contradictory on at least some readings to speak of a philosophy having an essence. But it is critical not to overlook the powerful associations of mechanism and state absolutism that appear again and again, especially in Western history.[17] "When the State creates armies," wrote Deleuze and Guattari, "it always applies this principle of numerical organization: but all it does is adopt the principle, at the same time as it appropriates the war machine";[18] "it is in State armies that the problem of treatment of large quantities arises, in relation to other matters."[19]

Just in order to take advantage of the war machine, and then subsequently as a method of social organization in general, the state uses computation and promotes computationalism. This is precisely because "the modern State defines itself in principle as 'the rational and reasonable organization of a community.' . . . The State gives thought a form of interiority, and thought gives that interiority a form of universality."[20] Interiority qua universal subjectivity emerges from numerical rationality applied as an understanding of human subjectivity, and not vice versa. This is not to reject the idea of subjectivity outside of rationalist modernity: it is rather to suggest that the particular and elaborated form of interiority we associate with present-day modernity underwrites an unexpected and radical mechanism. This mechanism does not seem radical if we associate it with a word like "rationality," because we are not accustomed to understanding rationality as a mechanical function, though that is exactly what it must be. Indeed, it is rationalists themselves who take the term most literally, seeing in the creating of ratios—of weightings, largely of the more and less powerful force—the characteristic computation of modernity. While Descartes himself did not subscribe to this particular understanding of psychology, through Hobbes in particular we associate the modern state's conception of the free individual with absolute sovereignty and natural right. Because each citizen has the power to reason (make ratios, or, in our terms, compute) for him- or herself, each citizen has access to the know-how (Foucault's *savoir*) provided by mechanical reason.[21] Each citizen can work out for him- or herself the state philosophy: "Always obey. The more you obey, the more you will be master, for you will only be obeying pure reason. In other words yourself . . . Ever since philosophy assigned itself the role of ground it has been giving the established powers its blessing, and tracing its doctrine of faculties onto the organs of State power."[22]

EMPIRES OF COMPUTATION

Computers fit into the modern story of progress, and they fit even more closely into the story of modern empire. Computers have been with us since the very idea of the state existed, as has computation. The realization of the computer in digital form propels automation in many fields where its advent had previously been unthinkable. But one fundamental law of networks is that information made available to the user may ultimately be made available for central administration. In many ways these products and projects do serve the people who use them, but they are created primarily for the use of administrators whose purpose is to govern, usually on economic terms, transactions and relations that had so far eluded human control. In economic domains such as Amazon.com, in fact, such programmatic means are often confined to economic goals, but in other parts of social experience computation can be expanded to govern much more than raw currency.

Computational Utopianism

When we talk about computers, we do well to remember the multiplicity of referents with which the term has been associated over a hundred or so years, rather than the contemporary exclusive usage. Indeed, that usage, which points most especially at personal computers and what used to be thought of as mainframe computers, ignores too much of even the digital world to be truly useful to critical thought. To this obvious designation we must add all the social systems that include physical methods of computation and calculation as well as human beings, since these together form working computational systems and not merely PCs sitting on desks. Perhaps just as intriguingly, a great proportion of the true computers used today are not captured by the PC model: these are the so-called embedded computers, essentially complete, ROM (read-only memory)–based integrated circuit computers that govern almost all contemporary electronic devices. These functions too are extremely characteristic of computer operations as a whole. Embedded computers typically striate a field that might previously have been unanalyzed or analog, identifying internal (often "soft") hierarchies that can be processed algorithmically. This information is fed back to control nodes, either preprogrammed performance measurements or human controllers who have responsibility for the object in question.

To accept the accelerating computerization of everything in society is to accept that exactly this logic benefits society. Note that in the case of the automobile, a prime but also typical example of embedded computing, despite the theoretical sense in which many different aspects of automotive performance and construction are now understood at much more detailed levels than in the past, virtually none of this knowledge is available to the user. For example, the fuel-air combustion mixture used to be managed electrochemically via spark plugs and carburetion; today, the much more efficient process of fuel injection is entirely computer controlled, and sealed in a "black box" that is inaccessible to individuals. The extremely user-friendly and convenient geographical positioning systems (GPS) included with many cars help drivers in many ways—but also locate the automobile as an object on any number of twenty-four-hour electronic surveillance networks, precisely striating what had been (relatively) invisible to these systems. This information is both specific and local (the details of the movement of the automobile) but also massively concentrated and striating, in that the master systems' GPS systems (in the "home offices," the National Security Administration, and so on) have knowledge of all the vehicles in the system, and many other objects as well. Information about and access to such mechanisms is released only very sparingly in the face of market pressures—much the opposite of what computer evangelists would suggest.[23] The consumer has not been given more democratic access to automobile technology, even if it is arguable that the automobile industry as a whole uses computerization to meet consumer needs across a broad spectrum.

To compute is to striate otherwise-smooth details, to push them upward toward the sovereign, to make only high-level control available to the user, and then only those aspects of control that are deemed appropriate by the sovereign. Computers wrap the "legacy data" of the social world in formal markup, whose purpose is to provide the sovereign with access for post hoc analysis, and secondarily to provide filter-style control. Computers can then be used, at sovereign discretion, as part of instruction, as a way of conditioning subjects to respond well to the computational model. From this perspective, it is surprising to hear prominent academics like Nicholas Negroponte suggest that the "digital age" is distinguished by "four very powerful qualities that will result in its ultimate triumph: decentralizing, globalizing, harmonizing, and empowering."[24] Without argument, Negroponte asserted that "the traditional centralist view of life will become a thing of the past," that "in the digital world, previously impossible solutions become viable," that

[t]he harmonizing effect of being digital is already apparent as previously parti-
tioned disciplines and enterprises find themselves collaborating, not competing.
A previously missing common language emerges, allowing people to understand
across boundaries. Kids at school today experience the opportunity to look at the
same thing from many perspectives. A computer program, for example, can be
seen simultaneously as a set of computer instructions or as concrete poetry.[25]

It is no surprise that Negroponte's "optimism comes from the empowering nature
of being digital. . . . As children appropriate a global information resource, and as
they discover that only adults need learner's permits, we are bound to find new
hope and dignity in places where very little existed before."[26]

These closing words of Negroponte's best-selling book completely lack exemplary support, and with good reason. Their staging of an artificial, precomputer
past where things like collaboration as opposed to competition existed seems
purely ideological, and the observation that computers alone teach a kind of per-
spectivalism instantiated in the ability to read code as poetry is nothing short of
bizarre. Indeed, "lessons" about perspective might be thought one of the main
goals of any sort of humanities education, and easily obtainable from the whole
world of cultural objects—a world which, in many worlds of education, exactly
requires no particular "missing common language," especially not the monolingual
majority languages of computing.

The Uneven Development of Calculation

Just as important, it is critical not to accept a priori the idea that "computation" as
such refers only to the operations of the particular physical objects we understand
as computers. Arguably, the major function that computers perform routinely in
our society is calculation. Calculation as such has a long history in civilization,
especially in centralized, bureaucratic administrations, and in empires. Calculation
is especially important for warfare, where it is deployed in a manner that must
be understood as simulation, even if the simulation is represented entirely via
mathematics. Turing, von Neumann, and other early developers of physical computers relied just as much on what were then named computers as they did on the
machines for which we now use that name, and warfare was their main purpose.[27]
As David Alan Grier has recently shown, along lines that have become accepted
throughout the small field of computer history, since at least since the late nineteenth century many sorts of institutions routinely employed rooms of human
calculators, very often women, and precisely enabling the exercise of administrative
power to which they lacked access.[28]

These human computers were in fact the first operators of electronic and
mechanical computers, regardless of whether they were built for analog or digital

functions. In the administrative scheme, computing acts as a slave to the powerful human master, and it is always the task of imperial administration to amplify computational power. Following historians like Crosby, and no less poststructuralist thinkers like Deleuze and Guattari, Virilio, and Derrida, we can easily see how uneven are the benefits of computational power in more aspects of their distribution than might be ordinarily supposed. This is no mere fantasy; on even cursory examination, one can easily see how many of the twentieth century's most famous and infamous institutions depended heavily on computational practices. These are the accomplishments of computing, the ones its internal advocates trumpet, today more loudly than ever, as if they were devoid of ideology. For a materialist study of computing to follow its predecessor studies, it must look not (or not only) to what computers may someday present to us, whether in the form of a genuinely "new" medium or not; it must look to what computers are doing in our world, from the implementation of widely distributed identification and surveillance to the reduction of the world's whole culture for profit.

INSTITUTING COMPUTERS

Computers present themselves as a major part of a wholesale lifestyle choice for many professionals in our world. Within large universities, both the computer science and electrical engineering departments are typically enormous, producing hundreds of graduates each year, many of whom are hoping for immediate employment after graduation, either directly within computing or in one of the many associated fields. Management practice today relies heavily on computer modeling of business systems; indeed, much of the software sold by major manufacturers such as Siebel, Computer Associates, Oracle, and other major computer companies is devoted to business process modeling (BPM), in which a variety of practices are reconfigured so as to be transportable across computing platforms or, more profitably, from the analog world to the digital world. Even more strong, and less apparent on the surface, is the pervasive use of computer models in the sciences (for example, in modeling the molecules used in drug design) and in business itself, so that many top business school graduates move to so-called consulting firms. These firms often maintain large staffs of software designers in-house, or work closely with software or hardware companies (indeed, software companies such as IBM, Oracle, and Siebel are themselves largely comprised of consultants, making both types of organization surprisingly similar).

The job of these firms is to "reengineer" corporate practices either from the analog world or from one digital platform to another. Each transaction that can be sold results in a profit for the consultant, which is the main goal of that party; each transaction is typically sold to the buyer as potentially profit generating, usually through "efficiency." Sometimes this efficiency is easy to see and specify, sometimes it is openly speculative, and sometimes it is not clear at all. Regardless, the basic operation of much business in the world today, especially the business associated with the keyword "globalization," is conducted in the name of BPM and other solutions that are focused around providing management with *simulative control of business practice*. The general thrust of this work is to reduce social process to form, ideally to the CEO's preferred computational form, which in many cases continues to be the spreadsheet.

In this sense, computational practice reflects social imbalance: we might say it is "classed." Despite the strong sense of "being cool," of being "the people who 'get it,'" and so forth, the educated elite who operate computers—whether they are programmers or accountants, administrators or assistants—are too close to the actual machine to get more than a glimpse of the abstract machine that the corporation (along with its computers) embodies.[29] But the corporation is much like Hobbes's Leviathan: it is an automaton with many parts, most of which are small and interchangeable, but like a person it has something like a "brain," and that brain controls it and seeks, as Hobbes and capitalists alike would see it, only its own self-interest. What computer workers easily miss is that their role is not the same as those of the parts of the "brain," unless the corporation is explicitly structured in that manner. The true power relation to the computer involves the raw distillation of information to a point, the ability to get a bird's-eye view (or a God's-eye view), especially if one is in the bird's seat. The spreadsheet, with its emphasis on the pure reduction of social information via computational means into numeric data, especially percentage data—ratios, that is to say, the very hallmark of rationality—provides the most direct view of "the facts of the matter" about a corporate entity.

When so-called computer geeks rise to corporate ascendancy, it is usually not through direct expertise in computer engineering. This is true throughout the computer industry, but one of the most instructive stories is also one of the most central, because it is sometimes told exactly the other way. The modern corporation resembles nothing so much as the principality we think of as characteristic of premodern states. In this sense modern government, too, shows allegiance to the apparent state only insofar as it serves the interests of the most concentrated power. Within most corporations, power is absolute, and computation is the characteristic medium for surveilling every aspect of the behavior and work of every individual contributing to the apparently corporate good. The corporate good no longer equals the good of all its members, unless such a policy is willed by the managers—thus, as in the Middle Ages, it is quite possible to have a beneficent prince who shares resources and hardships somewhat equally, but this cannot change the structural fact of the nature of political relations. They are absolute. One either is the prince or one is not; yes or no—one or zero. At least, that is the way computationalist politics, and often computers themselves, would have it.

It is tempting, and in some ways very accurate, to see the practices of companies like Apple, Google, and Yahoo! as exemplary of the computer's impact on business. Arguably, though, there have always been businesses that profit by nurturing employee creativity and distributing management power. Much writing on new media reads like it sees only the Googles, and not the way that even companies that operate like Google (such as many of the small Web companies prior to the 2001 dot-com crash) can be swallowed by more profit-driven interests. Business practices like these are the exception, and the computer plays a fundamental role in the much more normative version of contemporary business practice, such as investment banks, insurance companies, and major product companies. In each of these environments, the computer serves to focus, concentrate, and centralize power, often serving as a linchpin in profitably outsourcing corporate resources at the expense of long-term employment. For example, the computer and automation in general have played a signal role in the destruction of the U.S. auto industry, so that the highly efficient foreign manufacturing plants are in many ways entirely automated, and can use only the cheapest and often least educated laborers where human work is required.

Microsoft, IBM, Wal-Mart, Home Depot, AT&T, Cisco, Intel, Merrill Lynch, Citigroup, Nomura, Honda, Toyota: these kinds of companies, and no less the contemporary governments within which they operate, must be seen as the real exemplars of the computer revolution. WorldCom, Enron, Sprint, Merrill Lynch, Citigroup, Qwest: many of the companies accused of the most significant wrongdoing in the wake of the dot-com crash were especially devoted to selling computerization (to say nothing of the Internet companies themselves). In many cases, they are bloated, internally clashing, nonproductive bureaucracies of enormous size; some were originally much smaller and used creative strategies to displace or join their rivals (thus, today, Microsoft comes more and more to resemble the IBM it once thought to creatively destroy). Every scrap of information in these companies is computerized—every moment of the lives of many employees are available to the corporate mind. Each of the companies today makes its major profit through what can only be called striation—the capitalization of raw material, often informatic, for sale to the highest bidder who can realize more profit from informatic capitalization itself. Often the process is so literal, and so explicitly tied to the colonial project that we tell ourselves has long ended, as to be scarcely credible. But from the "suburbanization" of small-family agricultural land in the semiurban United States, to the "consumerization" of China, to "drug discovery" in indigenous South American and subcontinental Asian territories, to the "outsourcing" of electrical engineering and consumer support to metropolitan India, the computer is the central Western tool in taking for its own profit resources that often play crucial roles in existing social networks.

It is all well and good to show how computers can be used to create rhizomic connectivity and distributed decision making. At the same time, this is true of virtually every other interactive communications medium. (Many of the world's people who do not have computers do have telephones, helping to create a rhizomic, distributed network of enormous power.) Furthermore, looking for some kind of inevitable transition to something new, something coming from computers, also serves to downplay the role of human agency in all cultural and technological production. We could have a much stronger sense of human social control over computation, as we do over many other human and informational resources; we could have a much stronger sense of the human politics that informs computation as a field just as it does every other human field. To do so would not mean that we stop looking at the ways computers help us, but that we recognize that it may be just as important to focus on the ways that computers serve powerful interests.

This is not to argue that we should necessarily discard our computers, our iPods, and our cell phones. Instead, we must recognize the irreducibly human contribution to each part of the "computer revolution," and do more to bring it under responsible social oversight. From this perspective, many of the current programs for Internet research seem too much to be *about* endorsing a rationalist view of the social fabric—programs like the Semantic Web, for example, along with other plans for changing the Web's basic language from HTML to XML. These programs make it more difficult for novices to engage deeply with the Web, and help to make the contributions of novice users (for example, to projects like Facebook and MySpace) available for computation by sophisticated "power users." From a different political perspective, it seems arguable that we should be doing everything we can to simplify, expose, and clarify the Web's operations, and to make them available to anyone who wants them at the lowest economic, cultural, and linguistic cost. Such a program would make the Web "worldwide" in a sense that it just is not today, even in programs like Negroponte's One Laptop per Child (OLPC).[30] Giving the Web to everyone seems like a hard, fascinating, human, practical problem on which many of us could be working; what it would require is a change in exactly the cultural politics that many computer advocates overlook. Changing those cultural politics will mean thinking seriously about the unequal distribution of all the world's resources, the human and the physical. However welcome such a transformation may be, there is every reason to believe that computers will be neither its cultural spur nor its technological engine.

NOTES

1. Williams (1974).

2. The new media literature includes, among many other works, books such as Aarseth (1997), Landow (1991, and clearly the first iteration of a view that has grown more complex), Manovich (2001), Hansen (2000, 2004), Ryan (2000), and some of the work in collections such as Wardrip-Fruin and Montfort (2003) and Harries (2002). Hayles (1999,

2005) and Liu (2004) come closest to a kind of neutral stance on the computer revolution, and examine satisfyingly wide samples of computational culture.

3. See Manovich (2001). When pressed for an example, Manovich (2002: 209) has offered Mike Figgis's 2000 film *Timecode* as "exemplifying the difficult search of digital cinema for its own unique aesthetics," and has suggested that *Timecode* might in fact be seen "a computer game that heavily relies on cinema"—all as a way of suggesting that some new art form that is radically different from existing ones is about to emerge.

4. See especially Marvin (1988).

5. And, indeed, as they have turned out within much of mainstream computer science and philosophy, especially with regard to projects instancing so-called Strong Artificial Intelligence; Dreyfus (1992) provides a good overview.

6. The exceptions to this generalization—heterodox works from across several disciplines—follow themes developed in the nascent literature of cultural studies of computing, including Adam (1998), Chun (2006), Edwards (1996), Galloway (2004), Mosco (2005), and Robins and Webster (1999), the authors in Chun and Keenan (2003), Kolko, Nakamura, and Rodman (2000), and Herman and Swiss (2000), and often detailed reflections by cultural theorists including Deleuze and Guattari (1987), Foucault (2000), Spivak (1999), Virilio (1983, 2000), and Žižek (1997); and critical computing theorists such as Agre (1997), Dreyfus (1992), and Winograd and Flores (1987).

7. See Deleuze and Guattari (1987) and Innis (1950, 1951).

8. Mills (1956).

9. Ibid., 218.

10. Ibid., 343–61.

11. Warschauer (2003) provides an alternate and better account of the "digital divide," and begins to gesture at an alternate frame for understanding the phenomenon.

12. See Deleuze and Guattari (1987) and Liu (2004), Mosco (1982).

13. Hobbes (1651), 81.

14. Ibid., 110–11.

15. Macpherson (1962).

16. See, e.g., Mosco (2005).

17. See Anderson (1974), Mattelart (2000, 2003).

18. Deleuze and Guattari (1987), 387.

19. Ibid., 389; also see Crosby (1997).

20. Ibid., 375.

21. For the *savoir/connaissance* distinction, see Foucault (2000), especially "Truth and Juridical Forms."

22. Deleuze and Guattari (1987), 376.

23. Computers are notably hospitable to being used as "black boxes" and "closed systems," despite the focus in much contemporary writing on "open systems" (see Edwards [1996] on the heritage of closed systems throughout much of computing history).

24. Negroponte (1995), 229.

25. Ibid., 230.

26. Ibid., 231.

27. See, e.g., Campbell-Kelly and Aspray (2004), Hayles (1999).

28. Grier (2005). See also, e.g., Campbell-Kelly and Aspray (2004).

29. See Liu (2004) on "cool" in computer culture.

30. See Negroponte's http://laptop.org/ Web site for the OLPC, one from which no less prominent a computer authority and philanthropist as Bill Gates has publicly demurred, later suggesting that the existing world cell phone infrastructure would be a more hospitable computing environment (reported in Markoff [2006]).

BIBLIOGRAPHY

Aarseth, E. *Cybertext: Perspectives on Ergodic Literature.* Baltimore, MD: Johns Hopkins University Press, 1997.

Adam, A. *Artificial Knowing: Gender and the Thinking Machine.* New York: Routledge, 1998.

Agre, P. E. *Computation and Human Experience.* New York: Cambridge University Press, 1997.

Anderson, P. *Lineages of the Absolutist State.* London: New Left Books, 1974.

Bolter, J. D., and R. Grusin. *Remediation: Understanding New Media.* Cambridge: MIT Press, 2000.

Campbell-Kelly, M., and W. A. Aspray. *Computers: A History of the Information Machine.* 2nd ed. Cambridge, MA: Westview Press, 2004.

Chun, W. H. K. *Control and Freedom: Power and Paranoia in the Age of Fiber Optics.* Cambridge: MIT Press, 2006.

Chun, W. H. K., and T. Keenan, eds. *New Media, Old Media: Interrogating the Digital Revolution.* New York: Routledge, 2003.

Crosby, A. W. *The Measure of Reality: Quantification and Western Society, 1250–1600.* New York: Cambridge University Press, 1997.

Davis, M. *Engines of Logic: Mathematicians and the Origin of the Computer.* New York: Norton, 2000.

Deleuze, G., and F. Guattari. *A Thousand Plateaus: Capitalism and Schizophrenia.* Minneapolis: University of Minnesota Press, 1987.

Dreyfus, H. L. *What Computers Still Can't Do: A Critique of Artificial Reason.* 3rd ed. Cambridge: MIT Press, 1992.

Edwards, P. N. *The Closed World: Computers and the Politics of Discourse in Cold War America.* Cambridge: MIT Press, 1996.

Fiske, J. *Television Culture.* New York: Routledge, 1988.

Foucault, M. *Power. Essential Works of Foucault.* Vol. 3. New York: New Press, 2000.

Frow, J. *Cultural Studies and Cultural Value.* Oxford: Oxford University Press, 1995.

Galloway, A. R. *Protocol: How Control Exists After Decentralization.* Cambridge: MIT Press, 2004.

Grossberg, L., C. Nelson, and P. Treichler, eds. *Cultural Studies.* New York: Routledge, 1992.

Grier, D. A. *When Computers Were Human.* Princeton, NJ: Princeton University Press, 2005.

Hansen, M. B. N. *Embodying Technesis: Technology Beyond Writing.* Ann Arbor: University of Michigan Press, 2000.

————. *New Philosophy for New Media*. Cambridge: MIT Press, 2004.

Harries, D., ed. *The New Media Book*. London: BFI Publishing, 2002.

Hayles, N. K. *How We Became Posthuman: Virtual Bodies in Cybernetics, Literature, and Informatics*. Chicago: University of Chicago Press, 1999.

————. *My Mother Was a Computer: Digital Subjects and Literary Texts*. Chicago: University of Chicago Press, 2005.

Herman, A., and T. Swiss, eds. *The World Wide Web and Contemporary Cultural Theory: Magic, Metaphor, Power*. New York: Routledge, 2000.

Hobbes, T. *Leviathan, or, The Matter, Forme, & Power of a Common-Wealth Eccelsiasticall and Civill*. 1651. New York: Penguin, 1985.

Innis, H. *Empire and Communications*. Toronto: University of Toronto Press, 1950.

————. *The Bias of Communication*. Toronto: University of Toronto Press, 1951.

Jameson, F. *The Political Unconscious: Narrative as a Socially Symbolic Act*. Ithaca, NY: Cornell University Press, 1981.

————. *Postmodernism, or, The Cultural Logic of Late Capitalism*. Durham, NC: Duke University Press, 1992.

Kittler, F. *Discourse Networks, 1800/1900*. Stanford, CA, Stanford University Press. 1990.

Kolko, B. E., L. Nakamura, and G. B. Rodman, eds. *Race in Cyberspace*. New York: Routledge, 2000.

Landow, G. *Hypertext: The Convergence of Contemporary Critical Theory and Technology*. Baltimore, MD: Johns Hopkins University Press, 1991.

Liu, A. *The Laws of Cool: Knowledge Work and the Culture of Information*. Chicago: University of Chicago Press, 2004.

Macpherson, C. B. *The Political Theory of Possessive Individualism: Hobbes to Locke*. New York: Oxford University Press, 1962.

Manovich, L. *The Language of New Media*. Cambridge: MIT Press, 2001.

————. "Old Media as New Media: Cinema." In Harries (2002), 209–218.

Markoff, J. "Microsoft Would Put Poor Online by Cellphone." *New York Times,* January 30, 2006, http://www.nytimes.com/2006/01/30/technology/30gates.html, accessed February 28, 2008.

Marvin, C. *When Old Technologies Were New: Thinking About Electric Communication in the Late Nineteenth Century*. New York: Oxford University Press, 1988.

Mattelart, A. *Networking the World (1794–2000)*. Minneapolis: University of Minnesota Press, 2000.

————. *The Information Society: An Introduction*. London: Sage Publications, 2003.

Mills, C. W. *The Power Elite*. New York: Oxford University Press, 1956.

Mosco, V. *Pushbutton Fantasies: Critical Perspectives on Videotex and Information Technology*. Norwood, NJ: Ablex Publishing, 1982.

————. *The Digital Sublime: Myth, Power, and Cyberspace*. Cambridge: MIT Press, 2005.

Mosco, V., and J. Wasco, eds. *The Political Economy of Information*. Madison: University of Wisconsin Press, 1988.

Negroponte, N. *Being Digital*. New York: Alfred A. Knopf, 1995.

Robins, K., and F. Webster. *Times of the Technoculture: From the Information Society to the Virtual Life*. New York: Routledge, 1999.

Ryan, M.-L. *Narrative as Virtual Reality: Immersion and Interactivity in Literature and Electronic Media*. Baltimore, MD: Johns Hopkins University Press, 2000.

Spivak, G. C. *A Critique of Postcolonial Reason: Toward a History of the Vanishing Present.* Cambridge, MA: Harvard University Press, 1999.

Virilio, P. *Pure War.* New York: Semiotext(e), 1983.

———. *The Information Bomb.* New York: Verso, 2000.

Wardrip-Fruin, N., and N. Montfort, eds. *The New Media Reader.* Cambridge: MIT Press, 2003.

Warschauer, M. *Technology and Social Inclusion: Rethinking the Digital Divide.* Cambridge: MIT Press, 2003.

Williams, R. *Television: Technology and Cultural Form.* Hanover, CT: Wesleyan University Press, 1974.

Winograd, T, and F. Flores. *Understanding Computers and Cognition: A New Foundation for Design.* Norwood, NJ: Ablex Publishing, 1987.

Žižek, S. *The Plague of Fantasies.* New York: Verso, 1997.

CHAPTER 19

FILM AND MEDIA STUDIES PEDAGOGY

WARREN BUCKLAND

Simply teaching film or media studies in a classroom setting is not inherently radical, critical, or effective. "What is required," wrote David Lusted, "is greater attention, not just to the development of criticism in the field, but to the pedagogies that need to be inscribed within the production of knowledge . . . in order to actually effect its radical/critical intentions" (1986: 8). In this essay I reinforce the need for film and media studies pedagogy in higher education, and survey the pedagogy debates in Britain and the United States since the 1960s. In the opening section I summarize the terms of debate, which fall into the opposition between traditional and progressive media education. I then introduce the distinction between deep and surface learning, and present my own attempts to examine film studies pedagogy by analyzing film studies textbooks—both paper and digital. Does this latter distinction, marking the shift currently taking place from print to electronic technology, mean the new technology is simply making preexisting content more accessible, or is it transforming the content, thereby requiring a new form of media literacy? I address this question at the end by examining two prominent electronic film studies textbooks: James Monaco's DVD-ROM edition of *How to Read a Film* (2000) and Robert Kolker's first edition CD-ROM *Film, Form, and Culture* (1999).

BETWEEN TRADITIONAL AND PROGRESSIVE MEDIA EDUCATION

David Buckingham, in his essay on teaching popular culture, defined pedagogy as the examination of "the theories of teaching and learning which inform classroom practice" (1998: 3). He noted that pedagogy is discussed in terms of "traditional" versus "progressive" perspectives, an opposition he attempted to transcend. Traditional media education (sometimes called the "inoculation" approach) is a subject-centered, modernist project that defines media and popular culture as ideological, for they are mass manufactured and manifest dominant (oppressive) social values that are imposed on passive individuals, who are therefore perceived as victims. F.R. Leavis and Denys Thompson's *Culture and Environment* (1933) is an early example of this traditional view of the media. According to traditionalists, students need to resist this victimization by becoming active critics, a skill that media education provides. Traditional media education is a form of demystification, which involves the professor-as-expert training students in the analytical skills and techniques of media theory and analysis. Traditional media education aims to turn students into critical analysts, to empower them by enabling them to recognize, reflect on, and reject the ideology of dominant society, including its oppression and injustice. Traditional media education therefore embodies the ideal of social change, of students entering into public debate and effecting social transformation by ending oppression and social injustice. If students resist this emancipatory education, they are seen as not acting in their own interest, in which they remain passive victims mystified by the media.

Progressive media education, on the other hand, is a student-centered, libertarian project that encourages students to "find their own voice" or express their personal experiences with and through media and popular culture:

> By speaking, in their "authentic voices," students are seen to make themselves visible and define themselves as authors of their own world. Such self-definition presumably gives students an identity and political position from which to act as agents of social change. Thus, while it is true that the teacher is directive, the student's own daily life experiences of oppression chart her/his path toward self-definition and agency. The task of the critical educator thus [involves] students of different race, class, and gender positions [speaking] in self-affirming ways about their experiences and how they have been mediated by their own social positions and those of others. (Ellsworth 1989: 309)

Progressive media education celebrates popular culture as a form of resistance against or liberation from dominant culture. The students' everyday experience, active appropriation, and use of media and popular culture define them as the experts, and media education involves acknowledging this dimension of popular culture. Progressive education therefore cultivates individuality and avoids subjecting students to negative criticism, to coercion and discipline, and levels the distinction between authoritarian professor and naive student. The progressive media studies class takes students' everyday experiences of the media (not the professor's theory) as the subject matter of media education and emphasizes the media's positive and pleasurable features.

FILM EDUCATION IN BRITAIN
AND THE UNITED STATES

Historically, media education has gradually shifted from traditional to progressive assumptions. Media educators have moved away from conceptualizing students as passive victims to thinking of them as active users of media who make diverse and complex judgments. They increasingly downplay the view of media as victimizing and ideological, which in turn reduces the role of media education as demystification.

In Britain serious discussion of the media emerged from education reforms in the late 1950s, which gradually moved toward a more democratic educational system by abolishing grammar schools, replacing them with comprehensive schools, and greatly expanding higher education. (Until the 1950s, only about 4 percent of the population studied at a university.) The momentum for these reforms emerged partly from the British Left, consisting of "an older generation, many of them tutors from the Workers' Educational Association, including Raymond Williams, Richard Hoggart and Edward Thompson, [and] the generation fresh out of university, with Stuart Hall and Raphael Samuel keenly involved" (Dixon 1991: 151). The reforms not only increased access to education, but also expanded the previous narrow definition of what constitutes a liberal arts education, extending English in particular to include the press, radio, television, and film. Stuart Hall and Paddy Whannel's *The Popular Arts* (1964) represents an early and seminal attempt to address this extension of the English curriculum.

Under Whannel's chairmanship between 1957 and 1971, the British Film Institute's (BFI) Education Department initiated attempts to study film seriously. The Education Department generated curriculum development materials, held seminars, established book series (such as Cinema One, published jointly by Secker & Warburg and the BFI) and funded the Society for Education for Film and Television, which published the journals *Screen* and *Screen Education*.

The development of a traditional film studies pedagogy, which examined the ideological dimensions of film, involved two stages. The initial stage was galvanized around the concept of the auteur, which celebrated mainstream Hollywood films at a time when they were not considered to have any artistic value. Following the French critics of *Cahiers du cinéma,* Robin Wood was the first English-language critic to take Hitchcock seriously, by comparing his themes to Shakespeare's in his 1965 book *Hitchcock's Films* (Wood 1965). Wood offered the first serious study of a popular film director, but within the framework of traditional aesthetics: he did not celebrate popular culture on its own terms, but raised Hitchcock to the level of high culture by studying him with a concept of the artist found in traditional aesthetics. In its treatment of Hitchcock (and other popular Hollywood directors such as Hawks), auteurism was therefore both radical and conservative.

Although it took popular culture seriously, auteurism was too celebratory and required reevaluation. The second stage in the development of a traditional film studies pedagogy emerged from the reassessment of auteurism on the periphery of the *New Left Review* (*NLR*). Under the editorship of Perry Anderson, *NLR* introduced to a British audience continental theory such as structuralism, Althusserian Marxism, and Lacanian psychoanalysis. Continental theorists emphasized philosophy and antihumanist values, the decentering of human subjectivity in favor of language and other social structures, which overturned the British Old Left's moralism, empiricism, its privileging of individual lived experience, and its antitheoretical stance. At the *NLR,* Geoffrey Nowell-Smith, Sam Rohdie, but especially Peter Wollen employed theory to spearhead the reevaluation of auteurism. Wollen wrote standard auteurist studies for the *NLR* in the 1960s and systematized them in his highly influential book *Signs and Meaning in the Cinema* (published in the Secker & Warburg/BFI Cinema One series in 1969). In the conclusion to the third edition (1972), he rejected the standard, romantic idea of the auteur as an expressive artist and replaced it with the concept of auteur as a structure consistent across a group of films.[1]

Wollen's conclusion signals a short-lived interest in auteur-structuralism, an improbable alliance that tried to create a synthesis out of two opposed positions: the highly personal director-as-auteur approach and the highly impersonal, antihumanist emphasis on structures. In film theory (and critical theory in general) the antihumanist, theoretical approach won out, and auteurism, the founding moment of film studies' serious discussion of film, temporarily disappeared behind a study of filmic codes, structures, and ideological apparatuses.

This continental theory of film did not find its expression in the *NLR,* but in *Screen,* which followed the *NLR*'s lead and introduced continental theory to the film studies community. Under the editorship of Sam Rohdie in the early 1970s, *Screen* aimed to establish the theoretical groundwork for the development of film studies, with equal emphasis on theory and education. In 1971, Rohdie wrote a programmatic essay called "Education and Criticism," which began by asking a series of questions about education, theory, and their relation in film studies. The remainder of the essay predictably attacked auteurism, which, Rohdie argued, should be replaced with the precise and analytical methods of continental theory.

However, in overturning the antitheoretical stance of the Old Left, *Screen*'s theoretical advances isolated it from the pedagogic function it initially set out to achieve. This function was delegated to its sister journal *Screen Education*, published by the Society for Education in Film and Television between 1971 and 1982.

Both *Screen* and *Screen Education* developed a traditional pedagogic approach to film and the media. For example, during the 1970s, the contributors to *Screen* (following a broadly Marxist agenda from the *NLR* and a reinvented anti-auteurist, politicized *Cahiers du cinéma*) analyzed mainstream films to expose their hidden oppressive and unjust values—the psychical-ideological-patriarchal assumptions that implicitly inform each mainstream film. They also praised avant-garde films that attempted to break with these oppressive and unjust values and create alternative aesthetic and political messages. Len Masterman also developed a similar (although much more classroom oriented) approach to television in his book *Teaching About Television* (1980), as Manuel Alvarado pointed out in his review of the book in *Screen Education*: "Masterman adopts the notion of television messages as being *ideological* with the responsibility of the teacher being to demystify or decode these messages" (1993b: 193).

More generally, Alvarado spelled out the traditional emphasis of his—and *Screen Education*'s—pedagogy:

> Given the doubts I feel about the extent to which one can call children's culture their own I wish to argue that teachers are responsible not only for extending children's view of the world but also with challenging their perception of it as it has been constructed for them. . . .
>
> [T]he efforts of "progressive" teachers have manifestly failed to deal with the frustrations and learning problems of children or to transform an educational system that is clearly designed to reinforce and reproduce the class structure of society. (1993a: 184, 185)

The students' frame of reference, according to Alvarado's traditional view, emerges from dominant culture, not from the student's purported self-contained consciousness. The function of media education is therefore to challenge the ideology of dominant culture and turn students into critical thinkers.

In a now famous statement, Judith Williamson responded to Alvarado's traditional pedagogy in the pages of *Screen Education* (Williamson 1981–82). She represented the case for progressive education because of what she perceived as a lack of connection between ideological analysis and students' lived experiences. She argued that what is taught in the classroom is not necessarily what students are learning. In a classic example of the "inert knowledge" problem, Williamson discovered that many of her students did not appropriate the critical thinking skills taught in class; instead, they ritually reproduced—that is, merely mimicked or imitated—the skills without shifting their thinking. In class they could carry out an ideological analysis but without accepting the premises or conclusions of that analysis. They were simply "doing" media studies and confining their critical analysis to the classroom.

The auteurism of *Cahiers du cinéma* also galvanized the serious discussion of film in the United States. Andrew Sarris translated it (literally) into auteur theory by editing *Cahiers du cinéma in English*, as well as formalizing his own auteur studies in the avant-garde journal *Film Culture* (republished in 1968 as *The American Cinema: Directors and Directions*), and in his weekly columns in the *Village Voice*. More generally, film studies entered American universities primarily via the humanities (a form of auteurism modeled on literary explication), less so through the fine arts and social sciences. Dudley Andrew noted that two types of humanities film scholars emerged in the 1960s: the conservative scholars, who justified film studies by teaching adaptation (of literary classics), or by studying modernist filmmakers such as Bergman and Fellini; and the more radical humanities scholars, who studied popular films and quickly adopted the perspective of continental theory (1984: 5–6).

PROBLEMS WITH TRADITIONAL AND PROGRESSIVE EDUCATION

What we learn from Williamson's insightful paper is that traditional education "places the teacher as the bearer of 'alternative realities' which are inherently superior to the *experienced* 'realities' of one's unfortunate, deluded students" (Buckingham 1986: 88). This allows us to place film and media studies in the wider context of pedagogical theory. Buckingham implied that media educators need to privilege their students' media experiences rather than their own. He noted that "[o]ne does not need to be a wholesale progressivist to recognise the educational value of engaging with one's students' existing knowledge, or indeed to recognise the particular difficulty of starting with areas of the *teacher's* knowledge which are fairly remote from those of one's students" (1986: 88). In the next section we shall see that "deep learning" takes students' experiences as the starting point of education, but then gradually transforms that experience through the critical discourse of media education.

But "[w]hat happens," asked Buckingham in relation to progressive education, "if students use the voice they have been offered to say things which directly sustain oppression and inequality—which are, for example, racist or sexist?" (1998: 5). He asked whether the progressive pedagogy of voice is really just another form of paternalism in which students are "given" a voice to express what the professor calls "authentic" experiences. Furthermore, Alvarado wondered if only those who have direct experience of racism and sexism can talk about or analyze these oppressive, unjust experiences. He wrote, "[A]n experience of racism doesn't necessarily help one to understand, explain or fight it—and it is vital that people learn how to analyse, understand and explain in order to fight things of which they have no personal experience. . . . [I]t is necessary to construct a pedagogy that precisely does not depend upon personal experience and, in certain ways, critiques it" (1993b: 200).

Referring to progressive education in the nursery school, where most teachers are women, Valerie Walkerdine pointed out that she regards progressive education as perpetuating a liberation fantasy: "At what cost this fantasy of liberation? I suggest that the cost is borne by the teacher, like the mother. She is passive to the child's active, she works to his play. She is the servant of the omnipotent child, whose needs she must meet at all times. Carolyn Steedman suggests that such a role mirrors not the aristocratic mother, but the paid servant of the aristocracy, who is always there to service the children. His majesty the baby becomes his highness the child" (1986: 59).

Taken to the extreme, progressive education becomes an extension of the self-esteem movement, a discourse of affirmation that gives praise regardless of achievement, leading to a fragile sense of self that constantly needs reinforcement. In an educational setting, the self-esteem movement has lowered expectations and standards, while offering students excessive (unearned) praise. Jana Eaton wrote, "If self-esteem is our goal, we're making our kids feel terrific about doing less and less" (quoted in Stout 2000: 13). This can lead to students developing an exaggerated sense of self-importance, or entitlement, and consequently an exaggerated defensiveness toward any criticism directed at them. Grade inflation is the inevitable outcome, for students feel entitled to receiving A grades for all their work, and feel that their sense of self has been challenged for receiving a lesser grade. In turn they challenge the educator's authority by evoking the relativism prevalent in postmodern society, by reducing the educator's assessment of them to personal opinion rather than to educational and moral standards. To criticize the excesses of progressive education does not involve deriding self-esteem; instead, self-esteem needs to be earned to make it authentic, it must be the result of success and achievement.

Progressive educationalists view traditional education as authoritarian, too rationalist and cognitive. Traditional media education is increasingly derived for its purported authoritarian language, its institutionalized disciplinary knowledge that students are (or were) expected to imitate. Traditionalists criticize progressive education for simply celebrating the popular, for promoting relativism and subjective experience, and for conferring on students an exaggerated sense of self-importance.

Buckingham noted that current classroom practice does not clearly distinguish the two perspectives, but tends to combine them. It is therefore in the classroom that the contradictions between these two perspectives become manifest: "The emphasis on 'objective' analysis often sits uneasily alongside arguments for 'equal dialogue' between teacher and student, and for the process of open investigation. In practice, this often results in considerable tension, and even a degree of hypocrisy: much of what students are expected to 'discover' is pre-determined, and much of what passes for 'analysis' is simply a sophisticated exercise in guessing what's in the teacher's mind" (1998: 9).

Buckingham attempted to transcend the debate between traditional and progressive media education, to expose its assumptions—for instance, its reliance on oppositions such as rationalism/experience (a distancing, reflective theoretical discourse versus a celebration of the popular); active/passive (students as victims of media's ideological effects versus students as active, critical consumers); and dominant/oppositional media (the extent to which popular culture can be seen as "belonging" to the students or to dominant culture).

The crucial question to come out of this debate is, "What is the relationship between students' subjective investments and pleasures and the academic discourses and procedures of critical analysis?" (Buckingham 1998: 10). In the same volume, Carmen Luke (1998) recommended that media educators disengage from their anxieties over their own authority and power. They should choose critical analysis and educator authority over vacuous celebration of the media. Luke concluded that "a commitment to social justice and equality principles should guide the media educator's work in enabling students to come to their own realization that, say, homophobic, racist, or sexist texts or readings, quite simply oppress and subordinate others" (1998: 36).

In the following section I shift focus toward textbooks, which represent the established knowledge of a discipline. Textbooks define the discipline's boundaries by representing what is known, accepted, and legitimate. The authoritative and prescriptive function of textbooks in representing and structuring a discipline is one reason why they need to be examined closely.

ANALYZING TRADITIONAL TEXTBOOKS

Textbooks need to support instruction that goes beyond rote citation to promote reflection, problem solving, and genuine understanding. Learning that is insightful and transferable comes not from passive reading of factoids, but from engaging in the material at several levels: at the factual level, but also at

levels that lead the students to question the facts, to search for broader implications, and to connect the new information with prior knowledge so that the
student gains genuine ownership of concepts and skills. (Chambliss and Calfee
1998: 85)

What is wrong with textbooks? They typically fail to reveal to students the handful of
fundamental ideas, or underlying organizing principles, that constitute the foundations of a discipline. In place of fundamental ideas, textbooks focus on surface
information—a wealth of loosely connected facts, dates, trivia, and anecdotes. The
fundamental ideas organize facts and explain their significance and value. By ignoring a discipline's underlying organizing principles, textbooks remain on the surface,
and thereby reify, isolate, and decontextualize information. Textbooks encourage
students to memorize a surplus wealth of information rather than guide them
toward a deep understanding of fundamental ideas. In technical terms, textbooks
focus on declarative (propositional) rather than procedural (knowing how) or con-
ditional (knowing why) knowledge. Textbooks need to motivate students to assimilate and accommodate new knowledge by conditionalizing it—that is, explaining
the value for using new knowledge, how to acquire it, and how and when to use it.

A detailed examination of textbooks requires a short detour into the pedagogical theory of deep and surface learning, together with an outline of an up-to-
date, informative theory of textbooks as developed by Marilyn Chambliss and
Robert Calfee (in *Textbooks for Learning*, 1998). After outlining these theories, and
relating them back to traditional and progressive education, I illustrate Chambliss
and Calfee's work through James Monaco's *How to Read a Film*, a textbook that
helped define the discipline of film studies, before presenting an analysis of William Phillips's *Film: An Introduction*, a recent textbook that reflects film studies'
move toward progressive education.

DEEP AND SURFACE LEARNING

I use the discussions developed in The "MacFarlane Report" (MacFarlane et. al.
1992), in Van B. Weigel's *Deep Learning for a Digital Age* (2002), and in Chambliss
and Calfee (1998) to spell out the details of deep learning. The MacFarlane Report
lists the following characteristics of deep learning:

Intention to understand the material for oneself
Interacting vigorously and critically with content
Relating ideas to previous knowledge and experience
Using organizing principles to integrate ideas
Examining the logic of the argument

Deep learning is opposed to surface learning, which is characterized by:

Intention simply to reproduce parts of the content
Accepting ideas and information passively
Concentrating only on assessment requirements
Not reflecting on purpose or strategies in learning
Memorizing facts and procedures routinely
Failing to recognize guiding principles and procedures

Weigel (2002) noted that deep learning emerges from the constructivist psychology of Jean Piaget and Lev Vygotsky, and from John Dewey's focus on active learning.[2] For Piaget, learning takes place in the interplay between assimilation and accommodation. Assimilation refers to the process whereby the learner incorporates new information into preexisting knowledge, rendering the unfamiliar familiar. Accommodation involves learners bringing their existing knowledge in line with new information. For constructivists, learning does not involve simply the acquisition of knowledge, but its appropriation—interacting with and taking ownership of it. Constructivist psychology therefore directly addresses the first four qualities of deep learning as outlined in the MacFarlane Report.

Weigel defines deep learning as *"learning that promotes the development of conditionalized knowledge and metacognition through communities of inquiry"* (2002: 5). Conditionalized knowledge does not present knowledge as autonomous but emphasizes its purpose or function. Knowledge is learned only when the student discovers how to use it—how to appropriate and actively apply it to solve problems, rather than simply acquire it. From this active application, students are able to abstract general principles from their experiences. Metacognition is a reflective activity that refers to the student's ability to think about thinking, to develop self-awareness about how learning is achieved. A community of inquiry is a network of like-minded individuals studying the same discipline. A student working within a community therefore discovers that learning and carrying out research are not isolated activities, but form part of a community activity served by experts, professional institutions, and journals, all of which accumulate the insights of that learning community. Weigel's definition of deep learning—but especially conditionalized knowledge and metacognition—conforms to the MacFarlane Report's definition of the term. Moreover, the concept of deep learning cuts across the traditional/progressive division, because conditionalized knowledge conforms largely to progressive education, whereas metacognition belongs to traditional education.

In their analysis of textbooks, Chambliss and Calfee (1998) identified three primary areas of discussion: (1) comprehension, in which they argue that, to be comprehensible, textbooks should have a coherent design, present familiar material, and be interesting; (2) curriculum, in which textbooks should, more than anything else, convey the perspective of experts; and (3) instruction, in which textbooks should support student-centered learning. Although they do not use the term, Chambliss and Calfee's definition of learning conforms to the MacFarlane Report's definition of deep learning. This is evident in their discussion of curriculum as conveying the expert's perspective, and instruction needing to be student centered. Moreover, their definition of curriculum conforms to a traditional education, whereas their definition of instruction seems to combine traditional and progressive education.

In analyzing textbooks, Chambliss and Calfee examined comprehension, curriculum, and instruction by asking a key question about each one: (1) How comprehensible is the text design? (2) How well does the text design communicate the lens (or perspective) of a discipline expert? (3) How well does the text support student-centered learning? I outline each area in turn here.

Comprehension

Chambliss and Calfee identify three main text types: texts that inform, those that argue, and those that explain. Most textbooks fall into the "inform" category, which the authors divide into "descriptive text" and "sequential text." Furthermore, each is associated with particular rhetorical structures: a descriptive text can be organized as a list, a topical net, a hierarchy, or a matrix. Sequential texts can be organized as a linear string, falling dominoes, or a branching tree.

Chambliss and Calfee arranged these terms in the following way (1998: 32–37):

> List: an enumeration of objects and attributes (a primitive type of link)
> Topical net: connects via association a topic to sub-topics of details or attributes
> Hierarchy: objects and their attributes are linked by relations of sub- and super-ordination
> Matrix: compares and contrasts attributes
> Linear string: the sequential equivalent of a list; it differs from a list in that it contains a temporal dimension
> Falling dominoes: events in a falling dominoes arrangement are linked by cause and effect
> Branching tree: resembles a hierarchy, but with a temporal dimension.

The argumentative and explanatory text are not my concern here, so I shall simply offer Chambliss and Calfee's definitions: "[a]n argument presents evidence for a claim" (1998: 35) and "[a]n explanation 'fills the gaps' between a young reader's understanding of a phenomenon and the scientific explanation by presenting important information, metaphors, and analogies in tiers, or layers or sub-explanation" (33).

These three text types can be arranged in the following way:

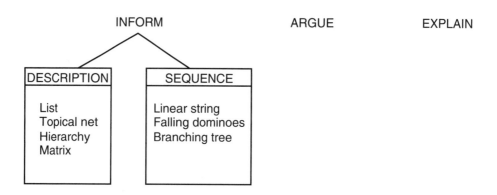

Chapter 1 of Monaco's *How to Read a Film* (1981 edition), called "Film as an Art" (1981: 1– 45), is divided into four sections. They are ordered as a hierarchy, moving from the superordinate category "Art" to three subordinate categories (performing, representational, and recording arts). Within the category of the recording arts, the chapter focuses on film as a recording art (using a matrix structure to compare and contrast it with other arts), and ends on a short argument focusing on film as a language. I analyze each subheading separately here.

"The Nature of Art" *(3–7)*. To begin a history textbook with "ancient times" may appear logical, but it is in fact the era least familiar to a student. *How to Read a Film* begins with a historical passage, with only one brief mention of film. The main aim of this section is to offer a history of the word "art." This section aims to inform and has a sequential structure—a temporal linear string. Although the section is sequential, its title is descriptive. However, the section's sequential structure is clearly indicated in the text, on the first page (and we get the one reference to film in six pages): "A review of that history [the history of the word "art"] will help us understand how the relatively new art of film fits into the general pattern of art" (3).The opening section therefore begins with the unfamiliar. It does not reflect the novice student's experience of film, but presents a long historical digression right at the beginning. The relevance of this history of the word "art" to film analysis may not be immediate to the reader (despite the brief mention of its relevance in the passage quoted above) and therefore makes assimilation and accommodation more difficult.

"The Spectrum of Art: Modes of Discourse" *(7–19)*. This complex section outlines several models that classify the entire field of the arts, together with the defining characteristics of each art form. This section is a description in the form of a matrix, since it aims to compare and contrast the arts in relation to one another.

"Film, Recording, and the Other Arts" (20– 43). This section is also a description in the form of a matrix, since it compares and contrasts film to photography, painting, the novel, theater, music, and environmental arts. Each comparison is given its own subsection ("Film and the Novel," "Film and Theater," etc.).

"The Structure of Art" (43– 45). This section aims not so much to inform as to present an argument about the nature of film as a language. This shift to argument mode is signaled in the following two sentences: "[Film] provides the first significant general means of communication since the invention of writing more than seven thousand years ago" (43). And "As a medium, film needs to be considered as a phenomenon very much like language" (44). Within this argument, Monaco used a matrix structure to compare and contrast film to natural language.

Within the overarching hierarchical structure of Chapter 1, Monaco has introduced a descriptive sequential structure (a linear string), and two descriptions organized in the form of a matrix, and ends with an argument that partly adopts a matrix structure.

Curriculum

> [T]he goal of a course of study should not be the accumulation of facts, but the acquisition of a lens for viewing experience. . . . [This] means acquiring the expert's X-ray vision, the connoisseur's sense of taste, the scholar's capacity to appraise, the scientist's ability to analyze. (Chambliss and Calfee 1998: 47– 48)

The primary challenge of traditional education is to reorganize students' existent, naive understanding toward the framework of the expert. It is unrealistic, however, to expect students to judge, evaluate, and extract useful knowledge from a discipline without guidance. The key to curriculum design is therefore to mediate between students' everyday, commonsense understanding and the expert's understanding, by means of "models, analogies, empirical reasoning, and discussion" (Chambliss and Calfee 1989: 312).

The philosopher A.N. Whitehead argued that educationalists should not teach too many subjects, and what they do teach should be taught thoroughly (1929). This is one step toward achieving deep learning, teaching the big or fundamental ideas behind a discipline—and therefore behind the experts' understanding (their critical way of knowing). This is in opposition to the attempt to simply present information, or a shopping list of facts. In writing textbooks around the perspective of an expert, we need to ask (Chambliss and Calfee 1998: 47):

What characterizes the expert's knowledge?
What can the expert do?

What is the expert's attitude toward his or her discipline?

How are the knowledge, skills, and attitudes of the expert linked?

The way to represent an expert's knowledge is not to write longer and more detailed textbooks, but to write books that teach a critical way of knowing, and a discipline's handful of organizing principles and fundamental concepts. Textbooks should not complicate the fundamental ideas in a discipline by focusing too much on details. They should link to everyday life but should move beyond the everyday and encourage students to adopt and understand the expert's perspective. Textbooks should, ideally, enable students to study in depth a discipline's principles and concepts, rather than merely expose them to a shopping list of facts.

However, as progressive educationalists note, students are unlikely to assimilate or accommodate descriptions, arguments, or explanations in textbooks that contradict their own beliefs (as William Glasser [1998] argued in his "choice theory"). They develop a natural resistance to learning a specialized perspective on the world—just as some students are alienated by film studies' defamiliarization of their everyday experience of movies. In my experience, undergraduate students' inability to adopt the perspective of the expert is evident when they copy directly into their essays or their presentations the information they gain from a textbook. Rather than understanding the information and going beyond it, they remain at the level of the information as written in the textbook. In other words, too often they passively accept what is written in the textbook and directly reproduce part of its content. Unfortunately, some students do not know how to be selective; for fear of distorting the information in a textbook, they copy down everything. This tendency to copy and be all-inclusive is a direct result of surface learning, of the student's unwillingness or, more likely, inability to take up the expert's perspective, to engage critically with the textbook's content, and to try to examine the way the information or argument is presented. But this is not necessarily the fault of the student: it is also a problem of the textbook's design, as well as its familiarity and interest to students.

How do the individual chapters of *How to Read a Film* promote the expert's specialized perspective on film studies? How does the book lead students from their commonsense knowledge to the expert's perspective? (And how do we identify the appropriate disciplinary perspective of film studies?)

Chapter 1 places film in the context of other arts in order to focus on film's specificity, a central dimension of an expert's understanding of film. But it is only in the third section of the chapter that Monaco introduced the well-known, commonsense distinctions between film and other arts. Rather than beginning from the general and moving to the specific (from the meaning of the word "art," to the spectrum of art, to film as an art, to film as a language), it may have been worthwhile to begin with these commonsense divisions, and then add a historical perspective afterward. Monaco simply followed the tradition of beginning with a general history lesson without considering its familiarity and interest to novice students, who may skip the initial section because its relevance may not be immediately clear to them.

In addition, Monaco used a wide variety of references and specialized vocabulary—the classical Trivium (4), the term "quanta" (5, 6), and reference to Horace's *Ars Poetica* (14), as well as offhand references to his middle-class lifestyle and classical education ("Having heard Mozart's Piano Concerto #23 once, having drunk a single bottle of Chassagne-Montrachet 1978" [16]), all of which may alienate novice media students (a problem I encounter in my lectures when I mention Proust's *The Rememberance of Things Past* while lecturing on the way flashbacks are motivated in *The English Patient* (Anthony Minghella, 1998), to name just one example).

Student-Centered Learning: CORE

> Effective instruction *connects* to student knowledge, *organizes* new content for the student, provides opportunities for students to *reflect* strategically, and gives students occasions to *extend* what they have learned to new contexts. (Chambliss and Calfee 1998: 54)

The first two categories of Chambliss and Calfee's CORE model overlap with questions of comprehensibility and curriculum, since connecting involves linking the expert's knowledge to the student's common knowledge, and organizing refers to the text's ability to arrange the information clearly. Once students grasp the meaning and significance of the information, they should then be able to "think and reflect, to understand and to feel, to go beyond the information given" (Chambliss and Calfee 1998: 21). Finally, students should be able to use, or extend, their new knowledge to solve problems in other areas of study.

A well-designed textbook therefore contains a coherent design and a curriculum that reflects the expert's understanding, and enables students to go beyond the information given to them by reflecting on what they have read. In other words, a well-designed textbook facilitates deep learning.

What is the learning strategy in *How to Read a Film*? Because of the initial section, Chapter 1 does not immediately connect to the reader's experience of film. It is only in the section "Film, Recording, and the other Arts" (20– 43) that the reader encounters familiar, commonsense information. This is the ideal starting point for a textbook, and only then should the specialized knowledge of the expert be gradually introduced. The text is organized in a complex way, consisting of sequential and matrix structures, plus an argument, organized into a hierarchy. Because most of Chapter 1 is limited almost exclusively to the aim to inform, the scope to reflect (as well as problem solve and understand) is limited, with the exception of the comparisons and contrasts Monaco draws between film and natural language. Finally, there is little scope to extend and transfer the information in the chapter, with the exception of the comparison and contrast between film and natural language, which students can try out on other arts forms.

Case Study: *Film: An Introduction*

William H. Phillips's *Film: An Introduction* (2002) became an immediate success after the publication of the first edition in 1999. Part of its success is due to its colloquial prose style. Phillips has been careful to write an accessible textbook that is easy for students to read. This in itself is an admirable accomplishment. Yet, Phillips has sacrificed design and especially curriculum to achieve readability. The book is full of pedestrian generic statements presenting information in a static form. There is little learning strategy embedded in the text, other than the simple presentation of "pre-established truths" for students to memorize. Moreover, the book suffers from an anecdotal way of presenting information—what I would call a "mentioning style." Phillips literally has filled each chapter with a large number of examples with minimum or no acknowledgment of the underlying organizing principles that explain the significance and value of these numerous examples. The reader is not always sure what the examples are examples *of*. Just one example is Phillips's short discussion of the techniques of continuity editing (2002: 115–17). In the main body of the text, his discussion remains on the surface, as he is content simply to list and describe these techniques:

> In narrative films and certainly in classical Hollywood cinema, continuity editing is normally used. Shots seem to follow one another unobtrusively, and viewers always know where the subjects of a shot are in relation to other subjects and in relation to the setting. Continuity editing allows the omission of minor details within scenes yet maintains the illusion of completeness. Continuity may be achieved in various ways. For example, eyeline matches may be used, in which a subject looks at something offscreen, and the next shot shows what was being looked at from approximately the point of view of the subject. . . . Continuity is also maintained within scenes if all shots show the subjects from one side of an imaginary straight line drawn between them. This is sometimes referred to as the 180-degree system. (2002: 115)

In this paragraph, Phillips has not presented the techniques of continuity editing in a systematic manner. Instead, the sentences are almost randomly strung together, with no statement of the underlying principles that regulate these techniques. The techniques themselves are simply the observable phenomena of unobservable principles (to create orientation and imaginary coherence, in imitation of Renaissance painting and the proscenium space of theater). Although Phillips mentioned these principles, they are buried in a loosely constructed text, rather than serving as the text's focal point.

Figure 3.12 (Phillips 2002: 116) accompanies this short section on continuity editing. The figure, neatly organized on one full page, analyzes eight consecutive shots from *Life Is Beautiful* (Roberto Benigni, 1998), and consists of five stills, a short description of the eight shots, and a clear and systematic commentary on how the shots are linked by the rules of continuity editing. It is more coherent than the main body of the text. This illustrates a marked difference in quality between the main text and the figures in Phillips's book. Perhaps the main text is meant to offer an informal introduction to the topic, before students read the more detailed and technical analyses in the figures. But the lack of formality in the text is too off-putting, for it is too perfunctory and leaves many questions unanswered.

Phillips has significantly revised his presentation of continuity editing from the first edition (1999: 138–40). He has compressed and reordered the text and eliminated a standard diagram illustrating continuity editing, which he has replaced with Figure 3.12. While the section gains from the addition of Figure 3.12, it has suffered due to the reorganization of the sentences and the loss of the diagram.

Phillips ended the section on continuity editing by stating that "[c]ontinuity editing is the usual way narrative films are edited, though some filmmakers choose to ignore continuity from time to time, and other filmmakers—such as the French actor and director Jacques Tati and the Japanese director Yasujiro Ozu—often reject the convention of continuity editing" (2002: 117).

There are only a few hints in the previous pages (primarily the opening paragraph [p. 115] quoted above) why continuity editing is "the usual way narrative films are edited." We do not find out why some filmmakers choose to ignore continuity editing "from time to time" and why Tati and Ozu rejected these conventions. Phillips has decontextualized the information he presented, especially concerning Tati and Ozu. It is not a matter of choosing different examples, but one of offering context and conditionalized knowledge—that is, *explaining why* these directors are important in terms of their editing, hence motivating students to learn more about them. Instead, Phillips has restricted himself to decontextualized information.[3]

Furthermore, the language is colloquial and full of what linguists call "hedges" and "attitude markers": words that qualify, reduce, and render uncertain the propositional content of sentences. In the above paragraph, "usual way," "some," "from time to time," and "often" are hedges and attitude markers. In themselves, hedges and attitude markers do not necessarily have a negative effect on writing. They sometimes express caution. But is the caution a function of the subject matter (is the subject matter inherently indeterminate?), or is the caution simply an expression of the writer's knowledge and opinion? In other words, is the caution appropriate? In the above examples, Phillips's caution simply attempts to replace his lack of explanation, perhaps in an attempt not to seem too much of an expert (which would presumably alienate his student readers). But an overcautious writing style expressed through hedges and attitude markers that downplays the writer's authority is an unusual tactic to adopt in a textbook, which is meant to represent what is known, established, and legitimate in a discipline.

To examine *Film: An Introduction* in more detail, I now analyze the design and curriculum of Chapter 8, called "Narrative Components of Fictional Films" (Phillips 2002: 261–98).

The title of Phillips's Chapter 8, "Narrative Components of Fictional Films," is descriptive and informative, for it emphasizes that the chapter focuses on the constituent elements of narrative fiction films. The chapter has five main headings that name these constituents, plus subheadings listed under each heading. The main headings are:

Narratives
Structure
Time
Style
Summary

These sections are organized as a hierarchy, with "Narratives" as the superordinate category, and "Structure," "Time," and "Style" as the three subordinate categories. The chapter ends with a clear and informative summary. Indeed, one of the strengths of the book is that each chapter has an illuminating summary at the end.

Under the heading "Structure," Phillips has included three subheadings:

Characters, Goals, Conflicts
Beginnings, Middles, and Endings
Plotlines

The section on structure is also a hierarchy, with "Structure" the superordinate category, and the three subheadings just listed as the subordinate categories. The first subheading, "Characters, Goals, Conflicts," is a topical net that names a topic ("Characters") and two subtopics associated with characters (their goals and the conflicts they experience). The second heading ("Beginnings, Middles, and Endings") names a sequence commonly used to describe narratives. "Plotlines" examines the multiple narrative strands of features films, and considers the different ways to organize them (chronological, simultaneous, intersecting).

The section on "Time" is also a hierarchy with three subordinate categories:

Present Time, Flashforwards, and Flashbacks
Chronological and Non-Chronological Time
Running and Story Times

Although the first subordinate heading, "Present Time, Flashforwards, and Flashbacks," appears to be a sequence, as with previous subheadings ("Characters, Goals, Conflicts" and "Beginnings, Middles, and Endings"), a close examination of the text itself reveals Phillips comparing and contrasting a film's representation of past, present, and future time. This emphasis on comparison and contrast makes the subsection a matrix structure. The other two subordinate sections are also matrix structures, in which the subtopics listed in each subheading are compared and contrasted.

These three sections are interrupted by two detailed figures in which Phillips has analyzed the complex temporal structure of *Run Lola Run* (Tom Tykwer, 1998) (Phillips, 2002: 282–83) and *Citizen Kane* (Orson Welles, 1941) (Phillips, 2002: 288–89). The contrast between the informally written main text and these carefully written systematic figures is again striking. The final heading, "Style," has no subheadings, and Phillips has used this term in much the same way as we use the term "genre."

Phillips's "mentioning style," in which he fills his chapters with innumerable examples, accumulates many facts, figures, film titles, and dates. He also has reproduced, in his writing style and content, the students' commonsense understanding of film, which accounts for his book's popularity and its conformity to progressive education. That is, it is popular because it does not advance very far into the expert's level of understanding. Of course, no book should *begin* with the expert's understanding. However, the crucial test for a textbook is: Can it lead the reader from commonsense understanding to the expert's understanding of a discipline? Or, How does the book mediate between the student's everyday understanding and the expert's understanding?

The expert's understanding consists of the fundamental organizing principles that constitute the foundations of a discipline, the principles that regulate the surface facts, figures, and details. Phillips has focused too much on the surface facts of film studies in themselves, rather than using these facts to examine fundamental principles. On the occasions when he has attempted to teach the principles, they become lost in the wealth of examples.

For example, the four pages of "Beginnings, Middles, and Endings" (Phillips 2002: 271–74) begin with the intended reader's (the novice student's) commonsense, everyday understanding of film. Phillips has informed the reader that a film's beginning establishes setting, the main characters, and their goals, and provides exposition (or backstory); that the middle section of a film includes obstacles; and that endings "show the consequences of the major, previous events," thereby providing closure (2002: 272). He also has drawn the reader's attention to inconsistent or improbable film endings.

In these four pages, Phillips mentioned eight different films: *Finzan* (Cheick Oumar Sissoko, 1989), *Women on the Verge of a Nervous Breakdown* (Pedro Almodóvar, 1988), *Schindler's List* (Steven Spielberg, 1993), *Unforgiven* (Clint Eastwood, 1992), *Wonder Boys* (Curtis Hanson, 2000), *Not One Less* (Yimou Zhang, 1999), *The Crying Game* (Neil Jordan, 1992), and *L.A. Confidential* (Curtis Hanson, 1997). Phillips quickly introduced these examples into the text to illustrate a principle about narrative that he has not sufficiently established. His discussion of how film beginnings introduce characters and their goals covers one paragraph and includes a discussion of two films. The entire paragraph reads as follows (notice again the hedges and attitude markers):

> Usually beginnings introduce the major characters and allow viewers to infer their goals. The events of fictional films are so intertwined that often something missing in a character's life at the story's beginning largely determines the story's ending. Early in *Finzan* (*A Dance for the Heroes*) (1990), a man wants to force his late brother's widow to marry him (Figure 8.6). *Women on the Verge of a Nervous Breakdown* (1988) begins with the main character wanting to talk to her lover. Much of the film shows her trying to connect with him, but only in the penultimate scene does she succeed. (2002: 272)

The discussion of *Finzan* is sufficiently developed in Figure 8.6 (Phillips 2002: 272), again highlighting the strength of the figures and the weakness of the main text. There is no further mention of *Women on the Verge of a Nervous Breakdown* in this section (and it is only mentioned once again in the entire book). Only the first two sentences in the above quotation (and, indeed, in the entire book) outline how characters and their goals are introduced into films. The two brief examples in the middle of the quotation are then meant to carry the weight of the discussion. But how does mentioning *Women on the Verge of a Nervous Breakdown* enrich the discussion of characters, their goals, and way they are introduced into a film, other than providing another instance of these narrative principles? These final two sentences are too vague and insubstantial to enrich the novice reader's understanding. They simply provide superficial information.

This paragraph, and many more throughout the book, does not attempt to mediate between the novice student's commonsense, everyday understanding of film and the expert's specialized knowledge. This specialized knowledge has been (deliberately?) kept to a minimum so as not to alienate the novice reader. Yet, the aim of textbooks, as I have mentioned, is to lead readers gradually from their commonsense understanding to the expert's specialized knowledge. This is a very difficult task, for it involves revealing to readers methods and procedures, and explaining how the information is generated and why it is significant. Like many textbook writers, Phillips did not rise to this difficult challenge. Rather than gradually introduce readers to the expert's knowledge and understanding, he simply presented them with information.

Textbooks (and the survey courses they serve)—whether traditional, as with *How to Read a Film,* or progressive, as with *Film: An Introduction*—rarely escape from superficial, surface learning. The sole aim is simply to cover the material:

> This sacrifice of depth for breadth is a prominent characteristic of most higher education curricula. Textbook publishers who seek to differentiate their offerings in the marketplace by adding new and more advanced topics to each successive edition exacerbate this problem. Even sensible instructors who respond to this kind of content inflation by making selective use of textbook material do not have the advantage of building out from a depth treatment of a discipline. (Weigel 2002: 7)

Because they simply aim to cover the material, many textbooks lack a consistent design, they do not always reflect the expert's understanding of film studies, and they lack a consistent learning strategy. They try to be all-inclusive rather than presenting information in a clear, rigorous, and precise manner. Film studies educationalists who write textbooks need to heed Whitehead's idea not to teach too many subjects, but to teach thoroughly what one does teach. At a time when the relevance and purpose of film and media studies is in the spotlight, we need to understand the contribution film studies can make to students' education. My response is that it must promote deep learning of fundamental concepts and skills, rather than offer a surface grasp of a very long shopping list of facts. Once media educationalists become aware of the importance of good design, of the selection criteria for the subject matter of textbooks, and of the importance of student-centered learning, they will be able to write quality textbooks that enable students to learn more effectively.

Is it too late to save the textbook? Film studies textbooks are important because they offer novice readers the core subject matter of film studies. Is the answer to be found in electronic textbooks? Do they simply make preexisting content more accessible, or are they transforming the content, thereby requiring a new form of media literacy?

ANALYZING ELECTRONIC TEXTBOOKS

Technology should enrich the experience of learning. E-learning technologies may save some costs and add a measure of convenience, but if they do not deepen the learning experiences of students, they are not worth much. (Weigel 2002: 1)

What potential benefits or added value do electronic texts offer that paper-based texts cannot? If we use e-learning technologies as merely another delivery system for traditional education, rather than creating a new, digitized learning environment, then, as Weigel has stated, such technologies are not worth much. I investigate this issue by analyzing two prominent electronic film studies texts: James Monaco's DVD-ROM multimedia edition of *How to Read a Film* (2000), and the CD-ROM that supplements Robert Kolker's paper-based textbook, *Film, Form, and Culture* (first edition, 1999). Where appropriate, I refer to my discussions of traditional/progressive education and deep/surface learning.

The bound and printed textbook is a physical, stable, tactile material object, which predetermines the sequential order and progression of information. The information is therefore usually written to conform to this linearity, even though individual readers have the potential to jump back, ahead, and so on. When I mention the printed textbook's linearity, I am referring to its design, not the way it is used.

The printed textbook promotes traditional education partly because it is based on the transmission model of communication, which involves the delivery of an intended meaning from a sender to a receiver via a physical message and stable channel of communication. The printed textbook's linearity also encourages authors to adopt an "expanded horizons" model, which refers to the traditional scope and organization of textbook content. Briefly, the "expanded horizons" model begins by presenting students with a delimited horizon on their object of study (a study of film form), and then chapter by chapter progressively expanding the horizon to include additional objects of study (such as film in its social and historical context).

The electronic text is a new writing technology that challenges the printed book. Electronic text is intangible—nonphysical, nonstable, and, at least in written form, nontactile. It exists somewhere between speech and writing. Students are encouraged to interact with the electronic text. Because it is not a physical object and does not need to be bound together, the electronic text can avoid the linearity of printed textbooks. (Of course, electronic texts can be written to remediate or simulate the printed text's linearity.) Electronic technology discourages authors from writing long, linear, sequential text, and encourages them to write small, autonomous chunks, which can then be linked hypertextually in a multithreaded or layered pattern.

A hypertext is a nonsequential, open-ended structure consisting of separate chunks of information electronically linked in an associative web. These "chunks" are no longer limited to text, but also include images, video, sound, and animated diagrams, which create a hyper- or multimedia environment that engages the reader's senses more viscerally than text alone. The links may be contained within a single location (such as a CD) or distributed globally across the Web.[4]

The hypertext therefore has a non-predetermined structure, for the reader charts his or her own path. However, some hypertext environments construct coercives to reduce the randomness of access. These coercives embody the author's expertise, including his or her preferred reading path through the hypertext. Allison Kimberly noted that many electronic textbooks "remain author-centered to such a high degree, readers' tracings cannot often create new structures that do not already exist" (2003: 189).

Although the written electronic text is nontactile, on CDs and DVDs the text can be combined with other media, creating a tactile, multimedia experience. One advantage of this multimedia experience is that it fosters concrete thinking, through which students learn about abstract ideas via visual and aural models, not simply via abstract written descriptions and explanations.

In summary, the three elements of electronic media I have examined—interactivity, associative (hypertextual) linking of information, and concrete thinking—constitute the core of electronic media competence. Electronic media require new learning methods because they utilize this electronic media competence.

From this short discussion we can begin to set up a framework, or a set of issues, critical to the design and use of screen-based electronic learning environments in film studies. I have established an inductive list of six overlapping issues with which to analyze and assess the educational potential of electronic texts.

Electronic technology:

1. Can offer genuine interactivity with the text (by means of search tools or by linking, including linking to other texts), but this raises issues of navigation and the user's potential disorientation in and random access of the text;
2. Enables learners to set their own pace and speed of learning, according to their own learning style, rather than having to follow a prescribed learning cycle; this offers them a greater potential to grasp the expert's perspective;
3. Brings into play different media (text, moving and still images, sound, etc.);
4. Links information by association (hypertextually) rather than by a single, linear structure;
5. May encourage, on the negative side, surface rather than deep learning; and
6. Presents an unstable, intangible environment and delivery system.

Case Study: *How to Read a Film,* DVD-ROM edition

How does Monaco's DVD version of *How to Read a Film* (2000) measure up to these qualities of electronic texts, and how does it handle the potential problems?

1. The guided tour to this DVD informs the user that the multimedia edition of *How to Read a Film* "is essentially the book come to life—you can read it, but it also talks to you, plays movie clips, shows the pictures, guides you to other references, and even lets you play filmmaker by making your own movie." The presence of this content on the disk is beyond doubt: one finds all this (and more) on this single DVD. The main menu for the DVD is an image map—a picture of a desktop with books, a computer, a magnifying glass, and other paraphernalia. This encourages cyclical reading patterns, prompting the user to keep returning to the same page (the homepage) before exploring the disk's other parts. This adds a center to the exploration, making it less random. To access *How to Read a Film,* the user simply clicks on the icon of the book on the desk. (Three other books are included:

Dictionary of New Media—which is cross-referenced via hyperlinks—and two comprehensive anthologies: *Reading About Film* and *Reading About New Media*.) Within each book, navigation is simplified to a few operations (back, forward, and return to main menu). The whole of the *How to Read a Film* text is reproduced, and the text layout has been well designed for maximum readability. Monaco has used Microsoft's ClearType technology to represent the text on screen, which triples the resolution of the text and creates a very smooth and pleasant reading experience. In the text's margins one finds color-coded thumbnail images or icons that function as internal markers that hyperlink to stills, photographic mini-essays, diagrams, movie clips, the author's audio notes (including Monaco's audio introduction to each chapter), virtual reality tours, sound bites, references, and a lab. These links expand the text laterally, and each can be accessed separately (for example, all the movie clips are indexed and can be accessed independently).

2. The advantages of hypertext in an educational environment are that it loosens the format of traditional teaching. But this raises the danger that a DVD can become an "electronic babysitter" in the classroom, in which students aimlessly wander unsupervised from one electronic node to the next, rather than study in a structured learning environment. Many readers of Monaco's DVD may be tempted (as I was) to bypass the linearly structured written text and simply scroll down to the next set of colored icons and view them out of context. Of course, progressive educationalists would argue that such random, nonlinear reading can lead to new, unexpected, and innovative insights.

3. Monaco has added new media to the existing textbook (he has not revised the text in presenting it in this new context). Clicking on an icon and viewing a film extract immediately after reading about it is very convenient and reinforces the text. Monaco also has used the multimedia capacities of DVD effectively and has fostered concrete thinking by animating a number of his diagrams, including one illustrating how the Maltese cross functions in a film projector. The diagram in the textbook is static, complex, and too abstract (Monaco 1981: 74). In contrast, the animated diagram on the DVD is informative, dynamic, closer to the characteristics of the subject he is describing, more explicit and explanatory (we see and hear the Maltese cross do its job), and therefore clearer than a static diagram because it does not require indirect symbols (arrows, dotted lines) to signify movement and function.[5] However, Monaco did not analyze the film clips on his DVD; we merely reexperience them. With the reproduction of Fred Astaire's famous dance routine on the floor, walls, and ceiling of his room in *Royal Wedding* (Stanley Donen, 1951), Monaco has offered the usual description of how the shot was achieved (Monaco 1981: 176). The DVD then

offers a hyperlink to the film extract. However, Monaco did not use the multimedia potential of the DVD technology to *explain* how the effect is achieved; he simply showed it. Below we shall see that Kolker's electronic textbook explains by analyzing film sequences.

4. Nonhypertext or linear text is coherent and can (potentially) offer a structured, predetermined learning environment. In transferring his book to the electronic realm, Monaco has not used the potential of hypertext to improve or transform his preexisting linear text; instead, he has simply added electronic nodes to it.

5. One criticism leveled at hypertext-based educational media is that they promote surface learning. Michael Jacobson and Anthi Archodidou, for example, pointed out the importance of mindfulness and active engagement in the process of understanding and learning. They stressed that "the very ease of traversing hypermedia environments may lead students to a mechanical or 'non-mindful' exposure to knowledge resources that have minimal learning outcomes" (2000: 157). Whereas progressive educationalists celebrate students' ease at traversing hypermedia, traditionalists despair because the hypermedia textbook with minimal coercives does not reflect the expertise of the author, who is decentered by the hypertext. Monaco's DVD continues to be author centered to the extent that the hypertextual links are carefully designed. But Monaco has not sufficiently encouraged the reader to engage with the written text.

6. Finally, humans are still attached to the physicality of books and individual pages. By transferring his book to the nonphysical realm of digital media, Monaco has traded in one tactile sensation (a physical book) for other tactile sensations (movie clips, virtual diagrams that move and have sound effects, the author's audio introduction to each chapter).

Case Study: *Film, Form, and Culture,* CD ROM

How does Kolker's CD attached to *Film, Form, and Culture* (first edition, 1999) measure up to the qualities of electronic texts, and how does it handle the potential problems?

1. The main menu for Kolker's CD (a DVD in the third edition) consists of a filmstrip down the left side of the screen. Each frame of the filmstrip represents one of eight chapters (and the ninth represents the introduction). The chapters cover the following topics: continuity editing, the long take, montage, point of view, mise-en-scène, lighting, camera, and music. To the right of the screen is a film reel that, when clicked, reveals a menu

containing four sections: "Research Tools," "Help," "Sound," and "Quit." The "Research Tools" section is subdivided into: "Glossary," "List of Film Clips" (unlike Monaco's list, Kolker's list is incomplete), "Filmography," and "Credits." The "Research Tools" section contains minimal information, suggesting that this CD is not a reference tool. When we examine each chapter, we soon realize that the purpose of this CD is to act as a tutorial in film analysis. As a result, each chapter is highly structured in a predominately linear manner, and effectively exploits electronic media's multimedia capabilities. This emphasis on linearity is built into the menu's visual design—frames on a filmstrip organized in a linear, chronological, sequential manner. Monaco's menus, by contrast, consist of an image that the user can roam across. Finally, as with Monaco's DVD, navigation on the CD is very simple: forward and backward arrows, a menu that reveals each chapter's content ("Chapter Spotlights"), or a link back to the main menu, with its film strip on the left and film reel on the right.

2. Kolker's electronic text is minimally hypertextual. Instead, each chapter presents a highly structured learning environment in electronic form. That is, the electronic technology is being used to remediate or simulate paper-based technology. As we shall see in the next section, Kolker has exploited the multimedia capacity of the electronic technology to present on the CD classroom exercises in film analysis. Moreover, students can rerun each classroom analysis in their own time and at their own pace.

3. One of this CD's strongest aspects is that it exploits the multimedia capacity of electronic technology. Unlike Monaco, who has created an imbalance between the different media by simply remediating his entire paper-based textbook in electronic form and then supplementing it with film clips and moving diagrams, Kolker has created a balance among the different media types. Each chapter consists of voice-over, film clips, film stills, animated colored lines placed over film clips, the creative use of navigation buttons, and small amounts of written text (no more than several paragraphs per chapter). These multimedia elements are combined into a highly structured environment consisting predominately of shot-by-shot analyses of short film extracts. This multimedia environment is attempting (successfully, in my opinion) to remediate classroom analysis of film extracts. It is invaluable because it embodies the expert's knowledge concerning how to conduct a textual analysis of a film.

4. As I have already mentioned, Kolker has minimized the hypertext capacities of electronic media. His information is not, therefore, primarily linked by hypertextual nodes, but follows a fairly conventional prescribed path—he simulates in electronic form the textbook's linearity and classroom practice. Navigation also follows the textbook: the forward, backward, chapter

contents, and main menu remediate paper-based textbook structure, signaling the CD's minimal use of hypertext structures.

5. One disadvantage of the CD is that the written text, taken by itself, is minimal, and gives the impression that several paragraphs are sufficient to explain topics such as continuity editing or mise-en-scène. To some extent, Kolker overcomes this limitation by packaging the CD with a paper-based textbook, which is cross-referenced with the CD. However, the cross-referencing is tenuous and indirect at best. This points to one advantage of Monaco's strategy of transferring his entire written text to DVD: the cross-referencing between text and multimedia elements is far more extensive and direct. By contrast, Kolker's textbook does not encourage the student to use the CD. At the beginning of some paragraphs, a CD icon with a chapter name is inserted. There is no further link between the two. However, I do feel that the paper-based textbook, when it is used in conjunction with the CD, goes some way toward promoting deep learning, primarily through its effective multimedia promotion of concrete thinking.

6. Finally, Kolker has tried to maintain the tactile sensations of both the physical and electronic worlds by packaging a paper-based textbook with a multimedia CD-ROM. The main problem, as I have already pointed out, is that the links between textbook and CD have not been adequately developed.

CONCLUSION

James Laspina wrote that "being digital requires designing a post-Gutenbergian *constructive* model of education through vision" (1998: 220). Neither Monaco nor Kolker has exploited electronic media's hypertextual potential. Instead, they have minimized it and exploited the electronic media's multimedia potential. Both authors have made incremental advances from the paper-based textbook, but have not inaugurated a revolution, or paradigm change. Both are still stuck within a Gutenbergian paradigm, although to different degrees. Monaco simply remediated his entire paper-based text and supplemented it with basic hypertextual links to multimedia elements. Kolker took one step forward from Monaco but also one step back: one step forward because he created an electronic textbook (rather than simply transferring a paper-based text to a new medium), and created a balance among the various media elements, whereas Monaco created an imbalance (his DVD is still too text-based). But Kolker took one step back in that he felt the need to supplement his CD with a paper-based textbook. Furthermore, in design terms, the CD remains firmly rooted in the Gutenbergian paradigm.

What would a revolution, or paradigm change, involve? In other words, what would a post-Gutenbergian film studies text look like? It would overcome the "flatland" of the printed page (which the computer screen still tries to imitate), for it would be a three-dimensional, online immersive environment that would not try to imitate the linear sequentiality of a paper-based textbook but would exploit the hypertextual as well as electronic media's multimedia (audio, video, animated graphics) potentials: in other words, it would be a hypermedia environment that subordinates verbal text to highly visual and tactile formats.

Kimberly believes this can be achieved only via Web-based textbooks, which can be continually modified and updated, not stand-alone CDs or DVDs:

> As shown by the textbook publishers' failed CD-ROM eTextbooks of the late 1990s and by the increasing demands by instructors for Web-based supplementary textbook material, the success of Web-based electronic textbooks, or eTextbooks, depend upon their ability to provide significant *added value* over their printed counterparts. *Electronic pageturners,* or digitized textbooks based on the traditional or printed book model, as Nielson suggests, will not suffice. As a result, the current trend towards Web-based electronic textbook publishing signals the need for a new rhetorical model for textbook design. (2003: 349)

That new model involves hypertext and multimedia to create a whole new learning environment, not just a repackaging and supplementation of the printed textbook, one that, as Kimberly has reminded us, fully embodies the digital structures of interactivity, connectivity, multimodality, multivocality, and non-linearity (2003: 360). Furthermore, Jacobson and Archodidou have argued that digital structures can create an effective learning environment only if the expert's knowledge controls them, which involves organizing the hyperlinks around a discipline's fundamental core concepts (2000: 187). Film studies still requires the structured environment of the expert in order to continue teaching the discipline's fundamental core concepts, and therefore still needs to promote deep learning (which cuts across the traditional/progressive divide), but those concepts need to be embedded in today's electronic environment if they are to actively engage the twenty-first-century student and continue to provide an effective learning experience.

ACKNOWLEDGMENTS

I wish to thank Sean Cubitt, Thomas Elsaesser, and Alison McMahan for their comments on an earlier draft of this paper.

NOTES

1. Paddy Whannel read Wollen's auteur essays in the *New Left Review* and invited him to work in the BFI Education Department, to edit the Secker & Warburg/BFI Cinema One series. As Wollen himself put it in an amusing anecdote (Wollen 2001), he "commissioned himself" to write *Signs and Meaning in the Cinema*.

2. These authors also inspire progressive media educators; however, the progressivists combine constructivist psychology with the therapeutic self-esteem movement, thereby distorting the psychologists' aims.

3. I have not decontextualized this paragraph from page 117. It is a self-sufficient paragraph and is followed by a new section ("Image on Image and Image after Image").

4. In analogous fashion to Chambliss and Calfee's identification of different types of written text, George P. Landow began to identify standard ways hypertext is organized (1997: 11–20). Further research is required to examine the commonalities and differences between Chambliss and Calfee's model and Landow's model, as well as the learning benefits and disadvantages of each.

5. The terms I use to compare the static and animated diagrams derive from Richard Lowe's essay "Beyond 'Eye-Candy': Improving Learning with Animations" (2001).

BIBLIOGRAPHY

Alvarado, Manuel (1993a). "Class, Culture and the Education System." *The Screen Education Reader: Cinema, Television, Culture*. Ed. Manuel Alvarado, Edward Buscombe, and Richard Collins. New York: Columbia University Press. 181–90. Originally published in *Screen Education* in 1977.

Alvarado, Manuel (1993b). "Television Studies and Pedagogy." *The Screen Education Reader: Cinema, Television, Culture*. Ed. Manuel Alvarado, Edward Buscombe, and Richard Collins. New York: Columbia University Press. 191–206. Originally published in *Screen Education* in 1981.

Andrew, J. Dudley (1984). *Concepts in Film Theory*. New York: Oxford University Press.

Buckingham, David (1986). "Against Demystification—'Teaching the Media.'" *Screen* 27.5: 80–95.

Buckingham, David (1998). "Introduction: Fantasies of Empowerment? Radical Pedagogy and Popular Culture." *Teaching Popular Culture: Beyond Radical Pedagogy*. Ed. David Buckingham. London: UCL Press. 1–17.

Chambliss, Marilyn J., and Robert C. Calfee (1989). "Designing Science Textbooks to Enhance Student Understanding." *Educational Psychologist* 24: 307–22.

Chambliss, Marilyn J., and Robert C. Calfee (1998). *Textbooks for Learning: Nurturing Children's Minds*. Oxford: Basil Blackwell.

Dixon, John (1991). *A Schooling in "English": Critical Episodes in the Struggle to Shape Literary and Cultural Studies*. Milton Keynes, UK: Open University Press.

Ellsworth, Elizabeth (1989). "Why Doesn't This Feel Empowering? Working Through the Repressive Myths of Critical Pedagogy." *Harvard Educational Review* 59.3: 297–324.

Glasser, William (1998). *Choice Theory in the Classroom*. New York: Harper Perennial.

Hall, Stuart, and Paddy Whannel (1964). *The Popular Arts*. London: Hutchinson.

Kimberly, Allison (2003). "Rhetoric and Hypermedia in Electronic Textbooks." PhD thesis, Texas Woman's University.

Jacobson, Michael, and Anthi Archodidou (2000). "The Design of Hypermedia Tools for Learning: Fostering Conceptual Change and Transfer of Complex Scientific Knowledge." *Journal of the Learning Sciences* 9.2: 145–99.

Kolker, Robert (1999). *Film, Form, and Culture*. New York: McGraw-Hill. With CD-ROM (3rd edition, 2006).

Landow, George P. (1997). *Hypertext 2.0: The Convergence of Contemporary Critical Theory and Technology*. Baltimore: Johns Hopkins University Press.

Laspina, James (1998). *The Visual Turn and the Transformation of the Textbook*. Mahwah, NJ: Lawrence Erlbaum.

Leavis, F.R., and Denys Thompson (1933). *Culture and Environment: The Training of Critical Awareness*. London: Chatto and Windus.

Lowe, Richard (2001). "Beyond 'Eye-Candy': Improving Learning with Animations." *eXplore 2001: A Face to Face Odyssey*. Ed. Neville Smythe. Proceedings of the Apple University Consortium Conference, September 23–26, 2001. http://auc.uow.au/index2.html?conf/conf01/page_7.html~mainFrame, accessed March 12, 2005.

Luke, Carmen (1998). "Pedagogy and Authority: Lessons from Feminist and Cultural Studies, Postmodernism and Feminist Pedagogy." *Teaching Popular Culture: Beyond Radical Pedagogy*. Ed. David Buckingham. London: UCL Press. 18–41.

Lusted, David (1986). "Introduction—Why Pedagogy?" *Screen* 27.5: 2–14.

MacFarlane, A., et al. (1992). *Teaching and Learning in an Expanding Higher Education System*. Edinburgh: Committee of Scottish University Principals.

Masterman, Len (1980). *Teaching About Television*. London: Macmillan.

Monaco, James (1981). *How to Read a Film*. New York: Oxford University Press.

Monaco, James (2000). *How to Read a Film*. DVD ROM multimedia edition. New York: Harbor Electronic Publishing.

Phillips, William H. (1st ed. 1999; 2nd ed. 2002). *Film: An Introduction*. Boston: Bedford/St Martin's.

Rohdie, Sam (1971). "Education and Criticism." *Screen* 12.1: 9–13.

Sarris, Andrew (1968). *The American Cinema: Directors and Directions*. New York: E.P. Dutton.

Stout, Maureen (2000). *The Feel-Good Curriculum: The Dumbing Down of America's Kids in the Name of Self-Esteem*. Cambridge, MA: Perseus Publishing.

Walkerdine, Valerie (1986). "Progressive Pedagogy and Political Struggle." *Screen* 27.5: 54–60.

Weigel, Van B. (2002). *Deep Learning for a Digital Age*. San Francisco: Jossey-Bass.

Whitehead, A.N. (1929). *The Aims of Education*. New York: Macmillan.

Williamson, Judith (1981–82). "How Does Girl Number Twenty Understand Ideology?" *Screen Education* 40: 80–87.

Wollen, Peter (1972). *Signs and Meaning in the Cinema*. 3rd ed. London: Secker & Warburg.

Wollen, Peter (2001). "From an Interview with Peter Wollen." Conducted by Serge Guilbaut and Scott Watson. http://www.belkin-gallery.ubc.ca/lastcall/current/page1.html, accessed March 12, 2005.

Wood, Robin (1965). *Hitchcock's Films*. London: Zwemmer.

···

CHAPTER 20

COPYRIGHT, FAIR USE, AND MOTION PICTURES

PETER JASZI

MOTION PICTURES AND COPYRIGHT DISCIPLINE

···

Consider the following passage, drawn from what appears to have been the first published report of a copyright infringement case involving the new art of motion pictures in the United States:

> The complainant's operator, by means of a pivoted camera of special construction, designed and owned by complainant, took in rapid succession, on a single highly sensitized celluloid film 300 feet long, 4,500 pictures, each of which was a shade different from its predecessor and successor, and all of which collectively represented at different points Kaiser Wilhelm's yacht *Meteor* while being christened and launched. From this film or negative a positive reproduction was made on a celluloid sheet by light exposure. The value of such celluloid reproduction is that by means of an appliance similar to a magic lantern these views may be thrown on a screen in rapid succession so as to give the effect of actual motion, and pictorically reproduce launching precisely as it took place. This positive celluloid sheet was sent by the complainant to the Department of the Interior, and by it copyrighted to him as proprietor under "the title of a

photograph, the title to which is in the following words, to wit, 'Christening and Launching Kaiser Wilhelm's Yacht *Meteor*.' " The complainant thereafter placed on the copies thereof issued by him a notice of copyright inscribed on a celluloid plate fastened on the front and at one end of the sheet. From the other end of one of such marked articles about one-third thereof was detached by some unknown person, and came into the hands of respondent, without knowledge on his part of its having been copyrighted. The 1,500 pictures on this part, which represented a part of the launch, Lubin photographed on a sensitized celluloid film. From this negative he reproduced a positive on a celluloid sheet, which was, of course, an exact reproduction of the copyrighted one of the complainant. These were sold to exhibitors, and enabled them to reproduce the part of the launch therein represented. (*Edison v. Lubin,* 122 F. 240 [3rd Cir. 1903] at 240)

The decision helped to establish, among other things, that motion pictures were entitled to the protection of the law even though they had not been in contemplation when the Copyright Act of 1870 was enacted. The court reasoned that "[f]rom the standpoint of preparatory work in securing the negative, the latter consists of a number of different views, but when the negative was secured the article reproduced therefrom was a single photograph of the whole. And that it is, in substance, a single photograph, is shown by the fact that its value consists in its protection as a whole or unit, and the injury to copyright protection consists not in pirating one picture, but in appropriating it in its entirety" (*Id.* at 242).

Edison v. Lubin also demonstrates another kind of truth about motion pictures—that from its inception the new medium was a radically appropriative one. Whether or not one finds Sigmund "Pop" Lubin's self-serving (and finally unavailing) representation that he was unaware of the Edison copyright believable is not to the point:[1] then, as now, the movies thrived on their ability to capture and repurpose existing material, much of it subject to prior claims of copyright protection.

Other early encounters between film and copyright deal with less straightforward appropriations from one production to another, like that involved in *American Mutoscope & Biograph Co. v. Edison Mfg Co.,* 137 F. 262 (C.C.D.N.J. 1905):

An examination of the complainant's positive film . . . shows that it contains several hundred pictures, and that the camera in which were produced the negatives from which the positive film was printed occupied no less than seven or eight different positions, the first two or three of which, it is clear from the statements of the bill of complaint, were at or near to Gen. Grant's Tomb in New York City, the others being evidently in some country district. The defendant's photograph is also a positive film, evidently printed from negatives taken by a camera located at seven or eight different places, the first two or three of which were taken near to Gen. Grant's Tomb, or to a structure strongly resembling it; the remaining places being also in some country district. That the complainant's photograph is a reproduction upon a positive film of pictures on negatives taken by a camera located at different points is confirmed by the language of the ninth paragraph of the bill, which states that "the scene prominently depicted in said photograph occurred largely at Grant's Tomb, on Riverside Drive, in New York City," and in the subsequent statement in the same paragraph that "in successive scenes the chase is depicted across the country in various situations." The title of the complainant's copyrighted photograph consists simply of the word "Personal." There is nothing in the proceedings for securing the copyright, as they are set forth in the bill, indicating that the scene depicted in the photograph "represents a French gentleman," or any other person who had "inserted an advertisement stating his desire to meet a handsome girl at Grant's Tomb." Consequently, there is nothing in the complainant's photograph, or in the title to its copyright, or in the proceedings for securing its copyright, in any wise suggestive of the title of the defendant's photograph, which is "How a French Nobleman Got a Wife Through the New York Herald Personal Columns." (*Id.* at 264–65)

Although the court was not convinced that the latter film is an unlawful derivative of the former, its opinion established the principle that infringement by wrongful adaptation (as distinct from direct reproduction) is possible under the copyright law as applied to motion pictures. That principle was underlined and extended six years later, when the U.S. Supreme Court's *Ben Hur* decision concluded that the unauthorized production of a motion picture version could infringe copyright in the underlying literary work.[2]

Indeed, down to the present day, much of the copyright litigation surrounding motion pictures has grown out controversies about the wrongful appropriation of content or imagery from one motion picture to another, or from a creative work in another medium to motion pictures. Elsewhere, I have written about this group of issues,[3] but this essay is concerned with the legal implications of another set of practices characteristic of motion picture production, to which one might apply the term coined by Bernard Edelman in a somewhat different context: the "over-appropriation of the real."[4] While much of the focus in what follows is on documentary filmmaking, I hope to indicate how the problems of copyright arise, and how the doctrine of fair use can help to resolve them, across a spectrum of media.

Motion pictures' dependence on the raw material of reality is, of course, most obvious in connection with the documentary film tradition,[5] which has its origins in early newsreels and "local views."[6] But well before 1917, it also had become an important part of the classical mode of American fiction film production, with its emphasis reliant on placing the spectator within an illusionistic three-dimensional space. Not only did actual locations come to be substituted more commonly for studio backgrounds, but as the authors of *The Classical Hollywood Cinema* noted, "whenever possible sets were build on location, so that real landscapes rather than painted flats frequently appeared outside windows in the early teens."[7] Inevitably, however, the increasing reliance of motion picture production on the appropriation of reality has given rise to tensions that have been expressed in terms of conflicts over copyright. These tensions have become more acute over time, as the "real" environment has become more and more saturated with media artifacts, and as copyright law itself has extended its domain over more and more of those media objects.[8]

Within copyright law, the tension between contemporary creators' needs for access to preexisting material, on the one hand, and the imperatives of copyright ownership, on the other, is mediated primarily by the so-called fair use doctrine. The application of this venerable legal concept, which exempts some substantial takings of protected content from infringement liability, is the subject of this essay.

WHAT IS FAIR USE?

"Fair use" has its origins in a line of judicial decisions dating back to 1841, when a federal court considered whether a biographer of George Washington should be excused for having borrowed material from an earlier published life of the subject.[9] Because it functions as a kind of "safety valve" in the copyright system, the doctrine came to be more frequently relied upon by defendants, and interpreted by the judges in their cases, in the mid-twentieth century—as the reach of copyright law increased. There have been various efforts to explain the theoretical bases of fair use, but perhaps none better than Alan Latman's 1958 summary (based on a comprehensive review of cases and other authorities):

> [A]s a condition of obtaining the statutory grant, the author is deemed to consent to certain reasonable uses of his copyright work to promote the ends of public welfare for which he was granted copyright. . . . The theory of "enforced consent" suggests another rationale which relies more directly upon the constitutional purpose of copyright. It has often been stated that a certain degree of latitude for the users of copyrighted works is indispensable for the "Progress of Science and useful Arts" [because] progress depends on a certain amount of borrowing, quotation and comment.
>
> Justification for a reasonable use of a copyrighted work is also said to be based on custom. This would appear to be closely related to the theory of implied consent. It also reflects the relevance of custom to what is reasonable. In any event, it has been stated that fair use is such as is "reasonable and customary."[10]

More recently, the U.S. Supreme Court has made it clear that "fair use" is one of the mechanisms by which copyright recognizes the principle of freedom of expression that is enshrined in the First Amendment to the U.S. Constitution; without "fair use," copyright law would be at risk of being found unconstitutional when applied to expressive activities such as documentary filmmaking (see *Eldred v. Ashcroft*, 537 U.S. 186 (2003), at 219–20).

The judge-made doctrine was codified in 1976 as Section 107 of Title 17, U.S. Code, as part of the general revision of the Copyright Act that took effect on January 1, 1978. Both before that time and afterward, the doctrine has been extensively interpreted by the U.S. federal courts, including the U.S. Supreme Court and the various circuit courts of appeals. Among other things, these courts have made it clear that, broadly speaking, fair use comes in two varieties—one relating to personal or private end uses of copyrighted material, and the other to reuses that are arguably "productive" in nature. Obviously, the dichotomy is a somewhat artificial one, since all creative practice ultimately is rooted in imitation. But the distinction is serviceable nevertheless, if only because it allows us to note that some aspects of the fair use doctrine are faring better in contemporary courts than others. Recent commentaries on case law suggest that the concept of "passive" fair use is at risk today, as new technologies continue to blur the public/private line.[11] By contrast, the "active" branch of the doctrine is thriving, in its application to fields of cultural practice as diverse as scholarship, musical parody, computer programming, and film production.[12]

Fair Use in Action

Section 107 directs courts considering whether a particular challenged use is fair (rather than infringing) to evaluate, among other things, four factors (derived, in turn, from pre-1976 judicial opinions):

1. The purpose and character of the use, including whether such use is of a commercial nature or is for nonprofit educational purposes;
2. The nature of the copyrighted work;
3. The amount and substantiality of the portion used in relation to the copyrighted work as a whole; and
4. The effect of the use upon the potential market for or value of the copyrighted work.

In recent decisions, moreover, the courts have indicated that a crucial consideration in evaluating most (if not all) of these factors is whether the use can be considered "transformative"—whether it "adds something new, with a further purpose or different character" (see *Campbell v. Acuff-Rose Music, Inc.*, 510 U.S. 569, 579 [1994]). If that is the case, the first factor can weigh in favor of fair use even if the use is "commercial" in character. Self-evidently, the second factor tends to favor transformative uses as well, precisely because they add value to the pre-existing material rather than merely repeating it for its original purpose. Moreover, if the use is transformative, courts will approve the use of a greater proportion of the protected material in connection with the third factor. Finally, and crucially, if a use is a transformative one, it is likely to satisfy the fourth factor as well, because (as the Second Circuit Court of Appeals recently recognized) copyright owners are not entitled to control the "transformative markets" for their works.

For an introduction to how fair use works today, it is instructive to examine the exceptionally detailed 2006 decision of the federal Second Circuit Court of Appeals in *Bill Graham Archives v. Dorling Kindersley Ltd.*, 448 F.3d 605. In that case, the defendant published what the court described as "a 480-page coffee table book [that] tells the story of the Grateful Dead along a timeline running contin-uously through the book, chronologically combining over 2000 images re-presenting dates in the Grateful Dead's history with explanatory text. A typical page of the book features a collage of images, text, and graphic art designed to simultaneously capture the eye and inform the reader" (*Id.* at 607). The plaintiff owned the copyrights to posters and other graphic materials associated with the musical group's historic appearances at the Fillmore Auditorium and other Bay Area venues. After a negotiation to establish license terms for the use of these materials in the book broke down, the publisher proceeded to use seven of them without authorization, and the lawsuit followed.

The court's analysis began with the first statutory factor ("Purpose and Character of Use"), emphasizing the "transformative" way in which the publisher deployed the images; the judges agreed with the trial court that the "use of images placed in chronological order on a timeline is transformatively different from the mere expressive use of images on concert posters or tickets. Because the works are displayed to commemorate historic events, arranged in a creative fashion, and displayed in significantly reduced form, . . . the first fair use factor weighs heavily in favor of DK" (*Id.* at 609). In other words, the recontextualization of the quoted material made all the difference to the determination of its transformative char-acter. Along the way to this conclusion, the court reemphasized another important point—if the user's purpose was transformative, the mere fact that it was also commercial does not bar application of the doctrine. In fact, the court noted, most fair uses are conducted for profit.

The second factor ("Nature of the Copyright Work"), which often favors copyright plaintiffs, was judged here to be inconclusive, on reasoning that echoes the language already quoted: "We recognize . . . that the second factor may be of limited usefulness where the creative work of art is being used for a transformative purpose . . . of enhancing the biographical information provided in *Illustrated Trip*. Accordingly, we hold that even though BGA's images are creative works, which are a core concern of copyright protection, the second factor has limited weight in our analysis because the purpose of DK's use was to emphasize the images' historical rather than creative value" (*Id.* at 611). The third factor ("Amount and Substantiality of the Portion Used") also was deemed a toss-up, since to accomplish its transformative purpose, "DK displayed reduced versions of the original images and intermingled these visuals with text and original graphic art. As a consequence, even though the copyrighted images are copied in their entirety, the visual impact of their artistic expression is significantly limited because of their reduced size" (*Id.* at 613).

Finally, the important fourth factor ("Effect of the Use Upon the Market for or Value of the Original") tilted conclusively for the defendant: "DK's use of BGA's images is transformatively different from their original expressive purpose [and] [i]n a case such as this, a copyright holder cannot prevent others from entering fair use markets merely 'by developing or licensing a market for parody, news reporting, educational or other transformative uses of its own creative work . . . [C]opyright owners may not preempt exploitation of transformative markets'" (*Bill Graham Archives*, at 614–615 [quoting *Castle Rock Entertainment, Inc. v. Carol Publishing Group*, 150 F.3d 132 (2d Cir. 1998), at 150]). The court continued by noting that "a publisher's willingness to pay license fees for reproduction of images does not establish that the publisher may not, in the alternative, make fair use of those images" (*Id.* at 615).

One of the most notable features of this enlightening opinion is the court's heavy reliance for precedent on some of the previous decade's crop of fair use cases involving claims against documentary filmmakers—many of which were resolved in favor of the defendants. A description of some of those decisions follows.

Motion Pictures and Fair Use by the Numbers

This important line of cases begins in 1996, with *Monster Communications v. Turner Broadcasting System*, 935 F. Supp. 490 (S.D.N.Y.), which involved no more than two minutes of clips from *When We Were Kings*, an acclaimed nonfiction feature on the Mohammad Ali–George Forman "rumble in the jungle," that had been incorporated into a TNT made-for-TV documentary called "Ali—The Whole Story." In its opinion, the court marched through the four statutory factors, finding that its status as a biography of a public figure favors fair use; that "the character [of the quoted material] as historical film footage may strengthen somewhat the hand of a fair use defendant as compared with an alleged infringer of a fanciful work or a work presented in a medium that offers a greater variety of

forms of expression" (*Id.* at 494); that the amount taken is small, both quantita-
tively and (in light of the different topical emphases of the two films) qualitatively;
and that neither the commercial reception of *When We Were Kings* itself, nor the
prospects for spin-offs (such as music videos) from the film, were likely to be affected by the existence of the TV program. Notably, the court did not address the
powerful but circular argument that copyright owners sometimes make in connection with the fourth factor: that the very loss of licensing revenue from the
defendant's use (and others like it) represents market harm. It was this argument
(apparently not presented by the plaintiff here) that the court in *Bill Graham
Archives* answered by its reference to "transformative markets." Finally, in addition
to being the first in the line of documentary fair use cases, *Monster* has the distinction of being one of the last fair use decisions—relating to this or any other
domain of practice—not even to mention "transformativeness."

For better or worse, this new metafactor rapidly came to dominate juridical
discourse. And although most documentary filmmakers who have defended infringement claims on the basis of fair use have been as successful as TNT was in
Monster, there have been exceptions to this trend—and they are instructive in
their own right. So it is useful to contrast two decisions dealing with biographical documentaries: *Elvis Presley Enters., Inc. v. Passport Video*, 349 F.3d 622 (9th
Cir. 2003) and *Hofheinz v. A & E Television Networks, Inc.*, 146 F. Supp. 2d 442
(S.D.N.Y 2001). In the first of these cases, defendants had produced a sixteen-hour
video documentary about the life and times of Elvis, which the court described as
follows:

> The biography itself is indeed exhaustive. The producers interviewed over 200
> people regarding virtually all aspects of Elvis' life. The documentary is divided into
> 16 one-hour episodes, each with its own theme. For example, one episode is
> entitled "The Army Years," whereas another—"The Spiritual Soul of Elvis"—
> chronicles . . . religious themes. . . .
>
> *The Definitive Elvis* uses Plaintiffs' copyrighted materials in a variety of ways.
> With the video footage, the documentary often uses shots of Elvis appearing on
> television while a narrator or interviewee talks over the film. These clips range
> from only a few seconds in length to portions running as long as 30 seconds. In
> some instances, the clips are the subject of audio commentary, while in other
> instances they would more properly be characterized as video "filler" because the
> commentator is discussing a subject different from or more general than Elvis'
> performance on a particular television show. But also significant is the frequency
> with which the copyrighted video footage is used. *The Definitive Elvis* employs
> these clips, in many instances, repeatedly. In total, at least 5% to 10% of *The
> Definitive Elvis* uses Plaintiffs' copyrighted materials.
>
> Use of the video footage, however, is not limited to brief clips. In several
> instances, the audio commentary discusses Elvis' appearance on a show and then,
> without additional voice-over, a clip is played from the show featuring Elvis.
> For example, one excerpt from *The Steve Allen Show* plays continuously for over

one minute without interruption. This excerpt includes the heart of Elvis' famous "Hound Dog" appearance on *The Steve Allen Show*. . . .

In the aggregate, the excerpts comprise a substantial portion of Elvis' total appearances on many of these shows. For example, almost all of Elvis' appearance on *The Steve Allen Show* is contained in *The Definitive Elvis*. Thirty-five percent of his appearances on *The Ed Sullivan Show* is replayed, as well as three minutes from *The 1968 Comeback Special*.

The use of Plaintiffs' copyrighted still photographs and music is more subtle and difficult to spot. The photographs are used in a way similar to some of the video footage: the photograph is displayed as video filler while a commentator discusses a topic. The photographs are not highlighted or discussed as objects of the commentary like many of the video pieces are. Finally, the songs are played both as background music and in excerpts from Elvis' concerts, television appearances, and movies. (*Passport Video* at 625)

As may be imagined, the court was not impressed with the defendants' fair use arguments under the various Section 107 factors. At the outset, in connection with the first statutory factor, the filmmakers' uses were deemed preponderantly non-transformative. The court pointed to some instances of transformative use where "the clips play for only a few seconds and are used for reference purposes while a narrator talks over them or interviewees explain their context in Elvis' career"; however, other "clips are played without much interruption, if any," and indicated that "[t]he purpose of showing these clips likely goes beyond merely making a reference for a biography, but instead serves the same intrinsic entertainment value that is protected by Plaintiffs' copyrights" (*Id.* at 629). With this out of the way, the statutory fair use factors begin to pile up against the defendants: Many of the works quoted were creative in nature (rather than merely factual), and too many of the defendant's uses involved unnecessarily long quotations, repetitions of shorter ones, or quotations that represented the "heart" of the copyrighted works, "in many cases [Elvis] singing the most familiar passages of his most popular songs" (*Id.* at 630). Finally, and fatally, the appeals court saw no reason to upset the trial judge's decision that, where the fourth factor was concerned,

> Passport's use is commercial in nature, and thus we can assume market harm. Second, Passport has expressly advertised that *The Definitive Elvis* contains the television appearances for which Plaintiffs normally charge a licensing fee. If this type of use became wide-spread, it would likely undermine the market for selling Plaintiffs' copyrighted material. This conclusion, however, does not apply to the music and still photographs. It seems unlikely that someone in the market for these materials would purchase *The Definitive Elvis* instead of a properly licensed product. Third, Passport's use of the television appearances was, in some instances, not transformative, and therefore these uses are likely to affect the market because they serve the same purpose as Plaintiffs' original works. (*Id.* at 631)

In short, once the battle over "transformativeness" was lost, the factoral analysis lined up neatly in the plaintiffs' favor.[13]

Hofheinz presents a very different picture. In a suit brought by the widow of one of the principals of American International Pictures, the court ruled that unauthorized inclusion of copyrighted film clips from *It Conquered the World* (Roger Corman, 1956) in an A&E *Biography* program about the career of actor Peter Graves was protected fair use because they were "not shown to recreate the creative expression reposing in plaintiff's [copyrighted] film, [but] for the transformative purpose of enabling the viewer to understand the actor's modest beginnings in the film business" (*Hofheinz* at 446–47). Once this was established, the other factors weighed, overall, in the defendants' favor. Where the fourth factor was concerned, the court held that "[t]he proper question is whether the Graves biography was, in effect, a substitute for Hofheinz's film clips"—not whether she stood to lose licensing revenue if the fair use defense was upheld. The fact that the filmmakers might have licensed the clip rather than appropriating it was not, in itself, enough: "Plaintiff may not boot-strap the specter of a fair use holding against her here, on the facts of this case, as reason why the use is not a fair use to begin with" (*Id.* at 448).

This analysis was based, in large part, on the opinion in another of the Hofheinz "trilogy," *Hofheinz v. AMC Productions, Inc.*, 147 F.Supp.2d 127 (E.D.N.Y. 2001). The discussion of *It Conquered the World*, in turn, prefigured the outcome in the last of these cases, *Hofheinz v. Discovery Communications, Inc.*, 2001 U.S. Dist. LEXIS 14752 (S.D.N.Y.), decided late in 2001, in which a fair use defense was validated in connection with the use of a clip from *Invasion of the Saucermen* (Edward L. Cahn, 1957) in a Learning Channel program entitled *Aliens Invade Hollywood*.

The copyright lawyer who experienced such a dearth of success in the Hofheinz cases returned to the fray on behalf of a different client several years later—still on the trail of unauthorized clips of Hollywood aliens. This time, in *Wade Williams Distributors, Inc. v. ABC*, 2005 U.S. Dist. LEXIS 5730 (S.D.N.Y. 2005), the grievance had to do with the use of clips from *Robot Monster* (Phil Tucker, 1953), *The Brain from Planet Arous* (Nathan Juran, 1957), and *Plan 9 from Outer Space* (Edward D. Wood, Jr., 1959) that were included in *Good Morning America* segments on the American fascination with extraterrestrials broadcast in July 1997, and intended to illustrate presenter Joel Siegel's theme that "big or small, cute or icky, alien life as portrayed in pop culture inevitably shares some humanlike traits." It is hardly a surprise, at this point, that the fact of this recontextualization was enough to demonstrate the transformativeness of the use; of additional interest is the fact that the court went so far as to specifically reject the argument that uses cannot be both transformative and entertaining! It quoted the judge in the final Hofheinz case ("does not explicitly distinguish between entertaining and serious, plausible and implausible, or weighty or frivolous commentaries, and I do not propose to engage in such subjective line-drawing") and went on to cite various heavy-duty authorities for declining to parse this illusive distinction.

A bit farther afield, but nonetheless relevant, are the results in three lawsuits brought by the Los Angeles News Service, an independent provider of news footage (including aerial footage captured from helicopters) to TV stations and other out-lets. All involved the famous footage of the beating of truck driver Reginald Denny near the intersection of Florence and Normandie during the 1992 Los Angeles riots. Two of these cases, *Los Angeles News Service v. KCAL-TV*, 108 F.3d 1119 (9th Cir. 199) and *Los Angeles News Service v. Reuters Television International, Ltd.*, 149 F.3d 987 (9th Cir. 1998), involved unlicensed broadcast of the footage while it still had considerable "hot news" value. At base, the court's skepticism about these defendants' fair use defenses reflected the fact that the footage in question was being reused to fulfill the very purpose for which it originally had been captured—to serve news reporting—rather than in some more "transformative" way.

By contrast, when Los Angeles News Service sued Court TV, some months later, for using

> a few seconds of footage from "Beating of Reginald Denny," primarily the frames depicting Damien Williams throwing a brick at Denny's head, in on-air "teaser" spots promoting its coverage of the trial [of the assailants and] in-corporat[ing] the brick-throwing footage into the introductory montage for its show "Prime Time Justice," which used a stylized orange clock design super-imposed over a grainy, tinted, monochromatic video background [that] changed as the "hands" of the clock revolved, . . . LANS's copyrighted video was in the background for a couple of seconds, one 360 degree sweep of the clock. (*Los Angeles News Service v. CBS Broadcasting, Inc.*, 305 F.3d 924 [9th Cir. 2002])

Working its way through the fair use factors, the federal appeals court con-cluded that while the quotations in "teasers" were not transformative, the more "commercially exploitive" incorporation of the footage into the *Prime Time Justice* introduction did include "the element of creativity beyond mere publication, and it serves some purpose beyond newsworthiness" (*Id.* at 938). The court went on to note that the highly factual nature of the footage pointed "clearly" toward fair use, and that the amount of material used was small, expressing skepticism that brief excerpts could be considered "the heart of the work." Finally, the court found that there was little chance that Court TV's uses (or others like them) would harm the licensing market for longer clips—which was, after all, the News Service's core business. Despite the court's equivocation on the issue of "transformativeness," what seems to have carried the day was its conviction that Court TV's uses were somehow out of the ordinary.

The *Wade Williams* and *CBS* decisions serve as perhaps the best evidence of how far the federal courts have gone to create a generally hospitable space for nonfiction filmmaking and related media activities through their application of the fair use doctrine. Even where the quotation of existing copyright content is done as much to amuse as to enlighten, or for a promotional purpose, the fact that it has been "transformed" through repurposing weighs heavily in favor of a fair use finding—at least where the quotation is not overly extensive.

In principle, at least, similar results might be expected where quotations are used in fiction films. In practice, it is difficult to be so confident. The fair uses cases involving appropriation of preexisting copyrighted elements in narrative films are fewer—too few, in fact, to form anything resembling a pattern. One decision sometimes mentioned in this connection, *Sandoval v. New Line Cinema Corp.*, 147 F.3d 215 (9th Cir. 1998), actually *avoids* the issue of fair use in assessing a copyright challenge to the motion picture *Seven* (David Fincher, 1995). Instead, the court finds that fleeting glimpses of the plaintiff photographer's images in the background of a scene in which detectives search a suspect's apartment are too trivial to constitute even potential infringements. The previous year, in *Ringgold v. Black Entertainment TV, Inc.*, 126 F.3d 70 (2d Cir. 1997), another appeals court had criticized a trial court's prior finding that an artist's poster used as set decoration in a television situation comedy constituted fair use. The main ground for skepticism was the lack of transformativeness: "Ringgold's work was used by defendants for precisely the decorative purpose that was a principal reason why she created it" (*Id.* at 78). In more or less direct contrast is *Jackson v. Warner Bros., Inc.*, 993 F. Supp. 585 (E.D. Mich. 1997), where several of the plaintiff's appropriately themed paintings decorated a set representing the apartment of a principal character in the film *Made in America*, and the court found fair use.[14]

These cases are too scattered and too disparate (in both outcome and analytic approach) to offer any real guidance, going forward, to narrative filmmakers. And while the cases involving documentary filmmaking are sufficiently numerous and consistent to suggest a pattern, a problem remains: Although the documentary cases cover a fairly wide range of different specific filmmaking practices, they by no means exhaust the list of situations in which a documentary producer might wish to rely on fair use. They illustrate a mode of analysis, and suggest a considerable judicial bias in favor of enabling documentarians' access to preexisting copyrighted material. But they leave many questions unanswered—as does any set of legal precedents applying a principle of general applicability (like "negligence" in tort or "self-defense" in criminal law) to specific circumstances.

THE CRITIQUE OF FAIR USE

The notoriously fact-specific nature of fair use analysis recently led some of the foremost advocates of greater openness in the copyright system to raise questions about the doctrine's utility. Thus, for example, Lawrence Lessig has argued that fair use does not strike an adequate balance in copyright law. The statutory formulation, he asserts, is too vague and open-ended to be relied upon effectively; its real utility is severely limited because fair use claims can be tested only after the fact of use and then only when a creator relying on the doctrine is able to retain legal counsel and is willing to expose himself or herself to considerable economic risk in the event that the defense fails.[15] David Lange, in turn, has speculated about the possibility of new legislation that would supplant fair use and lighten the burden of copyright clearance on documentary filmmakers by providing them with a special "compulsory license."[16]

But however reasonable and unthreatening proposals like Lange's may be in fact, there is little likelihood that the motion picture and music industries, which exercise considerable sway in these matters, would tolerate their enactment. Fair use, as the law summarized above now stands, actually offers filmmakers and other creators of media a considerable latitude for creative practice. But the critique of fair use—as being too vague and unreliable to be of much practical use—has achieved considerable currency, and it operates to discourage media practitioners, their lawyers, and their so-called gatekeepers (including distributors, broadcasters, insurers, and others) from relying on the doctrine. What can be done to address it, and to encourage filmmakers to take advantage of their fair use rights?

The Structural Meaning of the Fair Use Cases

Fair use challenges filmmakers, as well as other practice communities, to find ways of making this powerful but elusive doctrine more transparent and predictable. The key to meeting this challenge can be found in the passage Latman's historical study quoted earlier in this essay: "Justification for a reasonable use of a copyrighted work is also said to be based on custom." In other words, courts engaged in fair use decision making should care about evidence of what is considered "reasonable" and "customary" within the relevant practice communities. Before the enactment of Section 107, case law offered various examples of this approach.[17] These included several instances in which the customary practice was considered in deciding fair use issues involving biography, including *Rosemont Enters., Inc. v. Random House*, 366 F.2d 303, 307 [2d Cir. 1966]).[18]

Something of a shift took place in the discourse of fair use after the enactment of Section 107, and for a time the customary roots of the doctrine were obscured. Scholars sought coherence elsewhere, particularly in utilitarian economic analysis.[19] Other commentators expressed pessimism that fair use analysis, which depends on a "calculus of incommensurables," can ever be rationalized or made more predictable.[20] Although the Supreme Court, in 1985, acknowledged the connection between custom and fair use (in *Harper & Row, Publishers, Inc. v. Nation Enterprises,* 471 U.S. 539, at 550–51 and n. 4), many lower courts temporarily lost sight of this dimension of the doctrine, turning their attention instead to the factoral analysis apparently privileged by the statute.[21] And, as we have seen, their opinions came to focus increasingly on the issue of "transformativeness."

As Michael Madison has convincingly demonstrated, however, the link between fair use and custom never really was severed—only temporarily overlooked: "I suggest . . . that the contemporary focus on 'case-by-case' adjudication of fair use disputes misunderstands the properly contextual orientation of fair use decision making as it developed historically, as Congress understood it when it enacted the fair use statute, and as the statute actually has been applied over the last twenty-five years."[22]

In "A Pattern-Oriented Approach to Fair Use," his important reanalysis of historical and contemporary case law, Madison argued that as courts explore the four factors and ponder degrees of "transformativeness," they are in fact seeking to ascertain whether the challenged work fits within a privileged use category, or, on the other hand, whether an invocation of fair use is merely an infringer's attempt to dress its unjustifiable appropriations in borrowed plumage. Thus, Madison pointed out, the very first fair use decision, *Folsom v. Marsh* of 1841, involved a judicial effort to distinguish between true biographical scholarship and simple free riding. Likewise, the focus of the Supreme Court's celebrated 1994 "2 Live Crew" decision (*Campbell v. Acuff-Rose Music, Inc.,* 510 U.S. 569) was the determination of whether the allegedly infringed song was a genuine parody or a mere effort to capitalize on the fame of the plaintiff's song. By the same token, in many of the cases involving nonfiction filmmakers reviewed above, the underlying issue was whether the challenged production was actually a documentary, or merely an entertainment film in disguise. And in the handful of cases involving narrative filmmaking, a recurrent question is whether the reproductions of defendants' artistic creations were simply part of the film's decorative background— or something more. Such inquiries, although conducted these days using the vocabulary of Section 107, always involve—at bottom—a comparison between practices of a defendant and the norm or pattern of use with which he seeks to affiliate. And the best way to determine whether (in Madison's terms) a genuine "patterned" use is involved is to look, in one way or another, to common or customary practice in whatever the field of practice may be.

What, then, can we make of this central perception into the real inner workings of fair use jurisprudence? The answer, I would suggest, is that collective action offers members of various practice communities a chance to affect the way in which the law, as applied to them, is understood. The effectiveness of the approach was tested more than a decade ago by the Society for Cinema and Media Studies (SCMS). In 1993, with the help of several experts (including the present author), the SCMS developed a best-practices code for its members concerning use of stills and frame grabs from films in academic literature.[23] Ever since, this code has effectively reduced costs and facilitated publication for many film scholars. Recently, the model has been extended to the field of documentary filmmaking practice.

STATEMENTS OF BEST PRACTICES— PROCESSES AND PRODUCTS

The "Documentary Filmmakers' Statement of Best Practices in Fair Use"[24] is a testament to the power of collective self-help and accessible scholarship. Documentary filmmakers, acting through their organizations and with coordination and support from academics at American University, have asserted common principles for the application of fair use under copyright. In so doing, they have made fair use—the right to quote copyrighted material without permission or payment, under certain circumstances—far more widely available. This has made films that formerly would have been treated as too risky for broadcast— such as controversial works of social or media criticism or certain historical documentaries—available to viewers today. The filmmakers' example is one that many other creators' organizations can profit from and emulate.

Documentary filmmakers had found themselves increasingly hemmed in by ever more owner-friendly copyright law, especially as the term of copyrights was repeatedly extended. At this point, the bulk of surviving films and other works made after 1923 are copyrighted, along with practically all expression created since 1978 (including poems and grocery lists); therefore, copyright protection is the default setting. A 2004 study of current documentary filmmaking practice in copyright clearance, "Untold Stories," conducted by Pat Aufderheide of the School of Communication at American University, along with the present author, documents the creative costs of the "clearance culture." Documentary filmmakers changed the reality they filmed both during shooting (instructing subjects, for example, to "Please turn off the television!" so as to avoid incidental capture of copyrighted media) and in postproduction (when they edit sounds and images to avoid perceived copyright clearance problems). They suffered both financial uncertainty and high prices. Worst of all, they avoided topics that might involve too-complex clearance problems, including social criticism, musical documentaries, and a wide range of subjects involving historical footage. "I tell people not to make historical films," said Robert Stone (*Radio Bikini*, 1988; *Satellite Sky*, 1990; *American Babylon*, 2000; *Guerrilla: The Taking of Patty Hearst*, 2004).[25]

Of the many possible solutions to the crisis in copyright clearance, there was one that filmmakers themselves could address: fair use. As has been noted above, courts respect the views of practice communities about what constitutes reasonable and appropriate use of copyrighted materials. But filmmakers interviewed for "Untold Stories" found themselves unable to say what was appropriate because they did not know the consensus of their peers concerning what was fair and reasonable interpretation of the law. In order to help filmmakers' to establish such a consensus, Aufderheide and Peter Jaszi worked with five filmmaker organizations—Association of Independent Video and Filmmakers, Independent Feature Project, International Documentary Association, National Alliance for Media Arts and Culture, and Women in Film and Video, Washington, D.C., Chapter—to establish that consensus. In thirteen meetings, including ten small group meetings hosted by the various professional organizations, the scholars worked with veteran professional filmmakers to articulate principles, and limitations on those principles, for the application of fair use. In these conversations, documentarians wrestled first with defining what their own needs were to quote others' material without permission or payment; then they confronted what they thought would be acceptable, were someone to quote their own material without authorization.

The statement deals with four recurrent situations in documentary filmmaking practice: quotation of copyrighted material for purposes of critique; quotations of popular culture to illustrate an argument; incidental capture of media content; and the use of copyrighted material in historical narrative.[26] The treatment of the latter topic emerged out of a rich and difficult discussion among the documentarians; not only did the filmmakers respect the importance of archival activities (and understand the importance of compensating them), but they were quick to see that today's documentaries are tomorrow's archival footage! At the same time, they were outraged by (for example) C-SPAN's refusal to release some presidential and congressional material, and the arbitrary licensing practices of some private archives. The statement carefully balances these various concerns. It declares that filmmakers in general should clear historical archive material, unless it is impossible or the terms are extortionate. If it is still imperative to use the material—which is not the primary subject of the documentary—then the filmmaker must use only as much as is needed to make the point, and should credit the source.

The balanced nature of the statement, as the product of a community with stakes in both maintaining copyright and allowing for reasonable levels of access to protected material, has made the document powerfully persuasive. Following its release on November 18, 2005, the statement had an immediate effect. It was used by three filmmakers to justify inclusion of their films at the Sundance Film Festival only eight weeks later: Kirby Dick (*This Film Is Not Yet Rated*, 2006), Ricki Stern and Annie Sundberg (*The Trials of Darryl Hunt*, 2006), and Byron Hurt (*Hip Hop:*

Beyond Beats and Rhymes, 2006). In *The Trials of Darryl Hunt*, for example, the filmmakers had followed, and helped to organize, protests in a racially charged death penalty case, and then chronicled the eventual proof that the accused was innocent. Archival footage had been used with the permission of the local broadcast station, but when new station leadership saw the potential of making their own documentary, this permission suddenly was withdrawn. The filmmakers stood on the ground of fair use to use archival broadcast news footage in their film.

Within four weeks of the release, Aufderheide and Jaszi hosted a meeting with broadcast and cable executives; this meeting precipitated a decision by the Independent Film Channel (IFC) to create an internal fair use policy allowing it to clear the cablecast of *This Film Is Not Yet Rated*, which includes more than a hundred uncleared quotes from popular recent films as part of a critique of the MPAA rating system. IFC also saved hundreds of thousands of dollars by relying on fair use to reduce clearance claims for a documentary about road movies, *Wanderlust*.[27] By April 2006, the Public Broadcasting Service had accepted the applicability of fair use to *Hip Hop: Beyond Beats and Rhymes*, which quotes substantial amounts of music and video in its argument that hip-hop had become a celebration of misogyny and violence. Moreover, PBS had shared the statement with all general managers and general counsels in its network. Even insurers were in quiet conversations about accepting fair use claims.

Film professors also have become activists for the expanded freedom of expression that the statement permitted. The University Film and Video Association sponsored an award for the best use of fair use in a student and/or professor's work. Moreover, since the release of the statement, insurers who offer errors-and-omissions coverage to filmmakers are now offering to cover fair use claims.[28]

Other creator groups began to organize to emulate the best-practices model. Music educators, media literacy practitioners, and art historians began the process of assessing problems in their communities and establishing peer groups among professionals to deliberate common values.[29] In her 2006 book, *Permissions, a Survival Guide: Blunt Talk About Art as Intellectual Property*, veteran publisher Susan Bielstein warmly endorsed the potential of the best-practices approach.[30]

The "Documentary Filmmakers' Statement of Best Practices in Fair Use" has begun to change practice and expand possibility in many areas of media making and scholarship. It is part of a contemporary movement to reclaim the copyright system for the public—its original intended beneficiary. Responsibility for realizing the potential of the approach exemplified by the statement now lies with teachers, students, and practitioners themselves.

APPENDIX: EXCERPT FROM THE "DOCUMENTARY FILMMAKERS' STATEMENT OF BEST PRACTICES ON FAIR USE"

This statement recognizes that documentary filmmakers must choose whether or not to rely on fair use when their projects involve the use of copyrighted material. It is organized around four classes of situations that they confront regularly in practice. In each case, it states a general principle about the applicability of fair use and then discusses qualifications that may affect filmmakers' choices in particular situations.

One: Employing Copyrighted Material as Objects of Social, Political or Cultural Critique

Description: This class of uses involves situations in which documentarians engage in media critique, whether of text, image or sound works. In these cases, documentarians hold the specific copyrighted work up for critical analysis.

Principle: Such uses are generally permissible as an exercise of documentarians' fair use rights. This is analogous to the way that (for example) a newspaper might review a new book and quote from it by way of illustration. Indeed, this activity is at the very core of the fair use doctrine as a safeguard for freedom of expression. So long as the filmmaker analyzes or comments on the work itself, the means may vary: both direct commentary and parody, for example, function as forms of critique. Where copyrighted material is used for a critical purpose, the fact that the critique itself may do economic damage to the market for the quoted work (as a negative book review could) is irrelevant to the analysis.

Limitations: There is one—and only one—general qualification to the principle just stated. In order to qualify as a fair use, the use should be only as extensive as is necessary to make the point, to permit the viewer to fully grasp the criticism or analysis. It should not be so extensive or pervasive that it ceases to function as critique and become, instead, a way of satisfying the audience's taste for the thing (or the kind of thing) critiqued. In other words, the critical use should not become a market *substitute* for the work (or other works like it).

Two: Quoting Copyrighted Works of Popular Culture to Illustrate an Argument or Point

Description: Here the concern is with material (again of whatever kind) that is quoted not because it is, in itself, the object of critique, but because it aptly illustrates some argument or a point that a filmmaker is developing—as clips from fiction films might be used (for example) to demonstrate changing American attitudes toward race.

Principle: Once again, this sort of quotation should generally be considered as fair use. The possibility that the quotes might entertain and engage an audience as well as to illustrate a filmmaker's argument takes nothing away from the fair use claim. Works of popular culture typically have illustrative power precisely because they are popular. In analogous situations, writers in print media do not hesitate to use illustrative quotations (both words and images). In documentary filmmaking, such a privileged use will be both subordinate to the larger intellectual or artistic purpose of the documentary and important to its realization. The filmmaker is not presenting the quoted material for its original purpose but to harness it for a new one. This is an attempt to add significant new value, not a form of "free riding."

Limitations: Documentarians' fair use claims will be most unassailable if they assure that:

- The material is properly attributed, either through an accompanying on-screen identification or a mention in the film's final credits.
- To the extent possible and appropriate, quotations are drawn from a range of different sources.
- Each quotation (however many may be employed to create an overall pattern of illustrations) is no longer than is necessary to achieve the intended effect.
- The quoted material is not employed to avoid the cost or inconvenience of shooting equivalent footage.

Three: Capturing Copyrighted Media Content in the Process of Filming Something Else

Description: Documentarians often record copyrighted sounds and images when they are filming sequences in real-life settings. Common examples are the text of a poster on a wall, music playing on a radio or television programming heard (perhaps seen) in the background. In the context of the documentary, the incidentally captured material is an integral part of the ordinary reality being documented. Only by altering and thus falsifying the reality they film—such as telling subjects to turn off the radio, take down a poster, or turn off the TV—could documentarians avoid this.

Principle: Fair use should protect documentary filmmakers from being forced to falsify reality. Where a sound or image has been captured incidentally and without prevision, as part of an unstaged scene, it should be permissible to use it, to a reasonable extent, as part of the final version of the film. Any other rule would contradict the fundamental purposes of copyright: to encourage new creativity.

Limitations: Consistent with the rationale for treating such uses as fair ones, it is important that documentarians should be careful that:

- Particular media content played or displayed in a scene being filmed was not requested or directed.
- Incidentally captured media content that included in the final version of the film is integral to the scene/action.

- The content is properly attributed.
- The use is not so extensive that it calls attention to itself as the overall scene's primary focus of interest (or if the scene has been included primarily to exploit the incidentally captured content in its own right).
- In the case of music, the content does not function as a substitute for a synch track (as it might, for example, were the captured music to be used after the filmmaker has cut away to another sequence).

Four: Using Copyrighted Material in a Historical Narrative

Description: In many cases the best (or even the only) effective way to tell a particular historical story is to make selective use of words that were spoken during the events in question, music that was associated with them, or photographs and films that were taken at that time. In many cases, such material is available, on reasonable terms, under license. On occasion, however, the licensing system breaks down because of the copyright owner's disapproval or simple greed.

Principle: Given the social and educational importance of the documentary medium, fair use should apply in some instances of this kind. To conclude otherwise would be to deny the potential of filmmaking to represent history to new generations of citizens. Properly conditioned, this variety of fair use is critical to fulfilling cultural mission of copyright. But unless limited, the principle also can defeat the legitimate interests of copyright owners—including documentary filmmakers themselves.

Limitations: Before concluding that a use of this type is fair, one must be satisfied that:

- The film project was not specifically designed around the material in question.
- The material serves a critical illustrative function, and no suitable substitute exists.
- The material cannot be licensed (or cannot be licensed at a price consistent with the budget of the filmmaker).
- The use is no more extensive than is necessary to make the point for which the material has been selected.
- The film project does not rely predominantly or disproportionately on any single source for illustrative clips.
- The copyright owner of the material used is properly identified.

The four principles just stated do not exhaust the scope of fair use for documentary filmmakers. Inevitably, actual filmmaking practice will give rise to situations that are hybrids of those described above or that simply have not been anticipated. In considering such situations, however, filmmakers should be guided by the same basic values of fairness, proportionality, and reasonableness that inform this statement. Where they are confident that a contemplated quotation of copyrighted material falls within fair use, they should claim fair use.

NOTES

1. For a firsthand account of Lubin's questionable duping practices, see Fred J. Balshofer and Arthur C. Miller, *One Reel a Week* (Berkeley: University of California Press, 1967), 7–8. Balshofer also noted that "[b]esides duping and occasionally making a picture, [the Philadelphia studio] faked championship bouts by using matched doubles for the boxers and staging the round-by-round action from the newspaper accounts," and describes the production of an ersatz newsreel of the San Francisco earthquake using cardboard cutouts of buildings (9).

2. *Kalem Co. v. Harper Bros.*, 222 U.S. 55 (1911).

3. Peter Jaszi, "When Works Collide: Derivative Motion Pictures, Underlying Rights, and the Public Interest," *U.C.L.A. Law Review* 28 (1981): 715.

4. Bernard Edelman, *Ownership of the Image: Elements for a Marxist Theory of Law*, trans. E. Kingdom (London: Routledge & Kegan Paul, 1979).

5. Patricia Aufderheide, *Documentary—A Very Short Introduction* (Oxford and New York: Oxford University Press, 2007).

6. Charles Musser, *The Emergence of Cinema: The American Screen to 1907* (New York: Scribner, 1990), 266.

7. David Bordwell, Janet Staiger, and Kristin Thompson, *The Classical Hollywood Cinema: Film Style and Mode of Production to 1960* (New York: Columbia University Press: 1985), 217.

8. In documentary practice, the tension has been further exacerbated by the rise of the cinema vérité style, reliance on which increases the likelihood that copyrighted works will be captured incidentally in the course of filming, and by the increasing inclination of some filmmakers to take the media environment itself as a subject.

9. *Folsom v. Marsh*, 9 Fed. Cas. 342 (C.C.D. Mass. 1841).

10. Alan Latman, "Copyright Office Study No. 14, Fair Use of Copyrighted Works," *Studies Pursuant to Senate Resolution 240*, 86th Cong., 2d Sess., 1960 (Comm. Print), 7.

11. Rebecca Tushnet, "Copy This Essay: How the Fair Use Doctrine Harms Free Speech and How Copying Serves It," *Yale Law Journal* 114 (2004): 535.

12. Paul Goldstein, "Fair Use in a Changing World," *Journal of the Copyright Society of the U.S.A.* 50 (2003): 133.

13. Another recent example of a nonfiction filmmaker who may have gone "over the top" and forfeited the ability to rely on fair use can be found in *Video-Cinema v. Lloyd E. Rigler-Lawrence E. Deutsch Foundation*, 78 U.S.P.Q.2d 1538 26302 (S.D.N.Y.) 2005, where the defendant's Classic Arts Showcase program for public television consisted of a miscellaneous collection of clips showing famous performances by musicians, dancers, and so forth, intended to whet viewers' interest in the fine arts. Included among the quoted materials were excerpts from a movie, *Carnegie Hall*, that the plaintiff company licenses for TV and home video distribution. Finding that the inclusion of the clip was "nontransfomative," the court then made relatively short work of the remaining statutory factors.

14. The outcome appears to have been influenced, in some degree, by the fact that the plaintiff's objections to the use were primarily ideological rather than economic. Fair use also provides a secondary rationale for the court's finding of noninfringement

in *Amsinck v. Columbia Pictures Indus., Inc.* 862 F. Supp. 1044 (S.D.N.Y 1994), where the plaintiff's children's mobiles were used as set décor in the film *Immediate Family*.

15. See generally, Lawrence Lessig, *Free Culture* (New York: Penquin Press, 2004). These themes are developed at greater length in Lessig's *Testimony on "The Digital Media Consumers' Rights Act of 2003" (H.R. 107)*, before the Subcommittee on Commerce, Trade, and Consumer Protection, U.S. House of Representatives, May 12, 2004.

16. See the Webcast of the April 2, 2004, legal panel from the "Full Frame" conference, http://www.law.duke.edu/framed (follow link "Culture on the Legal Cutting Room Floor"), accessed March 21, 2008.

17. See generally, Harry Rosenfeld, "Customary Use as 'Fair Use' in Copyright Law," *Buffalo Law Review* 25 (1975): 119.

18. In 1973, the U.S. Court of Claims held that handwritten copies of text materials by scholars represented fair use since they were "customary facts of copyright-life." *Williams & Wilkins Co. v. United States*, 487 F.2d 1345, at 1350.

19. Wendy Gordon, "Fair Use as Market Failure: A Structural and Economic Analysis of the Betamax Case and Its Predecessors," *Columbia Law Review* 82 (1982): 1600; William W. Fisher III, "Reconstructing the Fair Use Doctrine," *Harvard Law Review* 101 (1988): 1559.

20. Lloyd Weinreb, "The Donald C. Brace Memoral Lecture: Fair Use," *Fordham Law Review* 67 (1999): 1291.

21. That this trend may have run its course is suggested by the discussion of custom in a 2006 Ninth Circuit Court of Appeals decision, *Wall Data Inc. v. L.A. County Sheriff's Department*, 447 F.3d 769, at 778.

22. Michael J. Madison, "A Pattern-Oriented Approach to Fair Use," *William and Mary Law Review* 45 (2004): 1525, 1587.

23. Kristin Thompson, "Report of the Ad Hoc Committee of the Society for Cinema Studies, 'Fair Usage Publication of Film Stills,' " *Cinema Journal* 32 (1993): 3.

24. Association of Independent Video and Filmmakers et al., "Documentary Filmmakers' Statement of Best Practices in Fair Use" (2005), http://www.centerforsocialmedia .org/resources/publications/statement_of_best_practices_in_fair_use, accessed March 3, 2008. Excerpts from the statement appear as an appendix to this chapter.

25. Patricia Aufderheide and Peter Jaszi, "Untold Stories: Creative Consequences of the Rights Clearance Culture for Documentary Filmmakers" (2004), http://www .centerforsocialmedia.org/resources/articles/untold_stories_creative_consequences_of _the_rights_clearance_culture/, accessed March 13, 2008.

26. Of course, as the statement itself makes clear, the articulation these consensus principles is not intended to foreclose the assertion of fair use by filmmakers in other situations.

27. Elaine Dutka, "Legendary Film Clips: No Free Samples?" *New York Times*, May 28, 2006, sec. 2, 16.

28. See Center for Social Media, "Success of the Statement of Best Practices," http:// centerforsocialmedia.org/files/pdf/success_of_the_statement.pdf, accessed May 20, 2008.

29. See, for example, Renee Hobbs, Peter Jaszi, and Pat Aufderheide, "The Costs of Copyright Confusion for Media Literacy" (2007), http://www.centerforsocialmedia.org/ files/pdf/Final_CSM_copyright_report.pdf, accessed May 20, 2008, at 21–22.

30. Susan Bielstein, *Permissions, a Survival Guide: Blunt Talk About Art as Intellectual Property*. Chicago: University of Chicago Press, 2006.

APPENDIX 1

EVOLUTION OF
MODERN-DAY
INDEPENDENT
FILMMAKING

TOM BERNARD

There was a time when landline phones where the only means of communication in the film industry. There were no indie trade organizations or studio specialty divisions, HBO had just been born, cable television was a luxury, videocassette machines cost between five hundred and seven hundred dollars, and foreign-language films were the main source of alternative cinema. In the late 1970s, some alternative American films, such as *Between Time and Timbuktu* (Fred Barzyk, 1972), *Coming Apart* (Milton Moses Ginsberg, 1969), and *Pink Flamingos* (John Waters, 1972), began creeping out of crevices and were being shown outside the system.

The venues for such films were independent campus film series, cinema classes, and local repertory film houses, which would mix in some of the emerging American underground films with foreign fare and finally spearhead the new American wave of film making.

The first organized event to showcase these films exclusively took place in, of all places, Salt Lake City, Utah. In 1978, a local Mormon, Sterling Von Wagam, and his sidekick, Lori Smith, created a film festival that would be devoted exclusively to films made in the United States outside the studio system. They called it the United States Film Festival. The films they found for the first year were *The Whole Shootin' Match* by Eagle Pennell, *Joe and Maxi* by Joel Gold, *Girlfriends* by Claudia Weill, and *Martin* by George Romero.

Why were so few films available for this pioneering festival? The studio system had made it incredibly difficult for someone to make a feature film outside of studio lots. But the roadblocks that were put up by the studio system actually worked to shape the style and content of the early indie films. Because they did not have access to studio facilities and did not have to hire union labor, early indie filmmakers were forced to wear many hats in the filmmaking process. John Sayles, Jim Jarmusch, Joan Silver, Robert Young, Rob Nilsson, and Gus Van Sant would write, direct, edit, carry lights, run the camera, and at times act. Money was scarce, and the lack of cash had a big effect on locations, actions, actors, and the actual look of the film—the grainy quality of 16-millimeter blown up to 35-millimeter. There was no money for shooting permits, so guerrilla-style sets were the norm. The cameras of choice were 16-millimeters, as they were available through college campuses or pawn shops. Friends and neighbors would be cast in key roles; the family home or local town would double as location. Limited takes resulted in changes made on the fly, the script often rewritten to save time or as new opportunities arose.

Equipment rental houses did not want to do business with fly-by-night productions. There was only one lab that would even deal with this new breed of filmmaker as a credible artist, DV-Art, based in New York City. Its owner, Irwin Young, is the godfather of modern-day independent filmmaking—he took risks with this new breed of artists that fostered the careers of many of the early pioneers.

This seat-of-the-pants filmmaking created unique styles that emerged from the intense, personal energies devoted to all aspects of the process, and out of this chaos in the late seventies came a groundbreaking new breed of cinema unlike anything that had been done before in the United States—films like *Eraserhead* (David Lynch, 1977), *Northern Lights* (John Hanson, Rob Nilsson, 1978), *Return of the Secaucus 7* (John Sayles, 1980), and *She's Gotta Have It* (Spike Lee, 1986).

Suddenly, it was a boomtown. There were new indie distribution companies—Atlantic Releasing, Island Alive, Circle Releasing, the Samuel Goldwyn Company—creating new outlets for these films. Critics were starting to take notice; studios were creating divisions of alternative cinema. A new breed of entrepreneurs emerged who wanted to live outside of the studio system. These companies collaborated with the filmmakers, creating guerrilla marketing tactics, playing films in rogue cinemas—independent like the films themselves— and keeping the integrity of the director's vision in the release plans.

UA Classics was the indie branch of the venerable United Artists, staffed entirely by people under the age of twenty-five. They were cinephiles who had come out of college film schools, where they ran film series. This unit was the worst nightmare of the old-school distribution world. They took the skills they used to run bare-bones college film series to the marketplace. They did everything in-house, including postproduction and publicity; they had their filmmaker friends work with them on creating trailers; they sold the films to renegade art houses instead of powerful movie chains. It was the beginning of big changes in the old-school system. Hollywood took notice. In 1982, the indie company Island Alive received the Best Actor Oscar for William Hurt in *The Kiss of the Spider Woman* (Hector Babenco) and Best Actress for Geraldine Page in *Trip to Bountiful* (Peter Masterson). All in all, during the 1980s about two hundred indie companies came and went.

In the 1980s, technology began to have a tremendous influence on the independent movement. Artists who had started their careers with Super 8 and 16-millimeter, moved to Super 16-millimeter. The trick was always how to blow up these formats to 35-millimeter, which was the only format that theaters had to project films at the time. DV-Art labs pioneered again. If you look at the 16-millimeter blowups in the early eighties, you could barely see the picture through the grain of the print. The process improved every year.

Videocassettes and pay cable emerged as new revenue sources for the studios in the 1980s. The studio system tried to keep these new distribution channels closed to the indie movement. The power brokers who controlled these markets were not interested in programming indie films or selling them in the video marketplace. The video world was mass market, commodity driven, and the distributors had no interest in opening venues for alternative cinemas because they did not think there was an audience for them.

But the emergence of director-centered films that made money began to change people's minds. Francis Ford Coppola's *Godfather* (1972) and Steven Spielberg's *Jaws* (1975) are films with artistic vision and a unique cinema style made by directors who had worked their way into the studio system. Most important, the films made a great deal of money. Doors opened.

Big business, even Hollywood big business, is not happy if it is not getting a piece of the pie, and so things began to change in the indie world. As the nineties approached, many of the boomtown companies had gone bust. They had grown, and the businessmen and their accountants took the reins and pushed these indie companies to go public, changing their structure, making them more dependent on films that made big profits—studio films and exploitation films as well. If the films failed, the company could easily go bankrupt.

The United States Film Festival began as the Woodstock for indie cinema. Filmmakers gathered there in the late eighties to exchange ideas and recommend nonunion personnel to work on films, while union cameramen, editors, and other professionals took their vacation time to go to this festival to see some of the mothers of invention on-screen. New movies were born out of informal conversations on the streets. Then something happened that, for better or worse, changed the indie movement forever: the festival moved to Park City, Utah, and Robert Redford's Sundance Industry wanted to push its brand name further in the mainstream marketplace, so it bought the United States Film Festival. This changed the dynamic of the festival, which had become the center of the American indie world. Many Hollywood people owned condos in Park City, so that during its first year, people from Arnold Schwarzenegger to studio heads to other Hollywood businessmen started to invade the streets of the indie world. The machine had started to find its way into the mainstream.

Hollywood agents descended on the festival to sign up new talent. Some indie directors started to aspire to break into Hollywood, and a low-budget film accepted to be screened at Sundance would help them get to the next level in the studio food chain. Christopher Guest best tells this story in his film *The Big Picture* (1989): a story about a young idealistic film director who wins a short film contest and is swallowed up by Hollywood and spit back out. Not all filmmakers were being seduced by the headlines from the festival, which rapidly turned into a commercial marketplace, where money and distribution deals became more important than who received honors for filmmaking. In many instances, success at Sundance became the invitation to Hollywood dreams. *Sex Lies and Videotape* (1989) put Steven Soderberg on the fast track to studioland. More and more followed in Soderberg's footsteps. The eighties came to an end.

Indie film still faced many of the same challenges. Union employees still could not work for independent productions. A number of nonunion techies moved like migrant workers from indie film to indie film. The blowups were looking better. Slowly the ancillary markets were letting pictures through the crack in the door. Still the video and cable dollars for those films were dismal compared to their potential. And the unique style each film had in the eighties started to conform to what was quickly becoming a genre, the indie film.

By 1990 one only specialty studio division remained, Orion Classics. But in 1991, its parent company went bankrupt, and the door was finally closed on the entrepreneurs of the eighties. Most of their personnel had started to be absorbed by the studios or found other lines of work.

Events were put in motion for changes indie world. Only a few indie companies survived the attack of the studios—Samuel Goldwyn Co., New Yorker Films, Miramax—but these were on the ropes. Sony, under Peter Guber, decided to resurrect a studio specialty division, and the people from Orion Classics came over. The first film they released was *Howard's End* (1992), produced by Ismail Merchant and directed by James Ivory. The film did $25 million at the box office (a big number at the time), and the studio machines smelled the money. The next year Disney bought what was left of Miramax, and Universal put together a joint venture with Polygram Records to form Gramercy Pictures. The game was on again for the indies.

Around this time there occurred one of the most significant events to affect the indie movement. The studios were withholding productions in New York City to try to break the union's request for pay increases. Many of the rank and file were desperate for paychecks, and the craft unions cut a deal with the indies to keep their members, even if it meant working for less pay. The "East Coast Contract" reduced wages for movies. This changed the indie world for good. Now almost anyone who had the cash could make a movie with studio production values created by studio technologies.

Big-name actors felt more confident taking a chance on indie films now that they were assured of quality production values. Studio money and private investors became more available. Equipment rental was easier with people from the system running the films. Bond companies became involved. The indie world became "the off-beat studio film." Now a studio or television director could try to revive a career without the obstacles that were part of the eighties independent scene.

Agents started to move talent who needed a career boost into indie films for cheap rates. This in turn got the attention of the Academy chiefs. With name stars, indie films moved even farther into the main stream. Recognizable names in the films created bigger value in the ancillary markets. Cable and video could generate more revenue. The Oscars started to recognize a number of indie films every year. *Howard's End* won best actress for Emma Thompson, best art direction, and best writing. Sundance became the unofficial marketplace to sell indie films for piles of cash and then integrate the directors into the studio system.

The nineties became the studio specialty division decade. Most of the indie companies had been squeezed out of the marketplace. Cable networks like Bravo sprang up devoted to specialty products. HBO included indie films in its deals with studios and its specialty divisions: Fox Searchlight, Warner Independent Pictures, Lion's Gate, and Paramount Classics joined Sony Pictures Classics as "independent" branches of big studios. As mentioned, Bob and Harvey Weinstein sold Miramax to Disney and have formed their own production company. The steady move from film to high-definition video has made production easier and cheaper without sacrificing visual quality. Filmmaking itself is in the process of moving into and out from the online world, where film companies are now scouting for new talent. The indie world may be captured by the studio machine, but the spirit of independent filmmaking remains.

APPENDIX 2

....

THE DIGITAL
REVOLUTION

....

LEE BERGER AND
RICHARD HOLLANDER

Today's visual effects are dominated by digital solutions. Oddly enough, the introduction of the computer was not the key to the beginning of the digital effects world. Very sophisticated computers were already in use in motion-control technology. Digital scanning of the negative, digital printing back to the negative, and software for the industry were the driving forces that launched the digital revolution. The computer was absolutely necessary, but software, or the lack of software, was the real limiting factor. Once all three technologies came to a certain level of maturity, the industry took off. There seemed to be no end to what could be done. There still seems to be no end in sight.

Usage of digital solutions is broad and cannot be confined to a single domain in the effects industry. It is clear, though, that the optical printer function has been replaced entirely by digital compositing techniques. Many, if not all, of the limitations of the optical printer were gone, as the rules that applied to the digital world dictated an almost unlimited set of solutions for compositing, with no regard to "generation loss," or limitations of layers or complexity, that were tremendously faster as well.

Compositing was not the only process that took off. The actual process of creating realistic virtual imagery that ranged from spaceships and stormy waters to creatures that have and have not been seen before has become commonplace. The digital techniques have no bounds, and year after year we see the results on the motion picture screen.

THE DIGITAL SCANNER

Digital scanning, the process of converting the imagery, in this case many frames of negative, into a computer-readable digital form, was a necessary component to launch the digital effects world. At the time that the digital scanners were being developed, almost all effects originated from film, negative to be specific, and needed to end up on film, again negative, for the motion picture industry. Early digital scanners varied and were very experimental. Almost all of them had a film-transport mechanism that carried the negative and some kind of illumination system/sensor system. In the early days, they were all custom built, and it was not until the technology matured that a few companies, and only a few companies, began to commercially manufacture digital scanners.

A key aspect that has always been important for a digital scanner is to ensure that the information in the negative is fully retained in the digital form. This can be characterized by having enough pixel resolution and enough color dynamic range and resolution. Other important aspects are speed of the digitization process, consistency over time, and ease of use.

Although scanners took on different forms in the early stages, using such technologies as the flying spot scan, a technology well known in the video industry, and the early solid-state sensors, primarily developed for use in spy satellites and observatory telescopes, today's commercial scanners all use solid-state trilinear array sensors and provide fast, accurate, and efficient digital scan data.

THE DIGITAL PRINTER

The bookend component to the digital scanner is the digital printer. The digital printer imprints the digital data back onto the film negative. As with the digital scanners, this technology started with home-brewed prototypes that were manufactured by individuals and small companies. The gas-laser scanning/illumination systems and cathode-ray-tube (CRT) phosphor systems were the basis of the first digital printers. In time, the later solid-state laser systems virtually replaced all other technologies.

All these systems had the same goal, which could be described in the following simple test. Start with the original negative of some test shot with lots of good shadows and highlights. Digitally scan this information into the digital form. Then re-create the negative using the digital printer. Create a print from both of these negatives using the same exact process at the same exact time, and visually evaluate the results. It should be obvious that the goal is to have them at least look the same. A further test is to rescan the new digitally fabricated negative and mathematically analyze the two images for their differences. The more they are alike, the better the scan/reproduction loop and thus the quality of the imagery.

Today's commercial digital printers are dominated by systems that incorporate three solid-state lasers capable of putting out the colors red, green, and blue. Up until about 2002, short-lived and not easily maintained gas-tube lasers dominated the market. Before that, there were CRT systems. But it was the introduction of the "blue" solid-state laser in the 1990s that allowed the current systems to come down in cost and complexity, resulting in highly reliable designs.

Given the ability to digitally scan the original negative and to produce a negative from digital data, the basis for the digital revolution was set. Manipulating and creating the imagery became synonymous with using computers, a virtually limitless universe from which to work. The process of programming the computers and creating application software to perform the specific tasks began slowly and then exploded, as witnessed every year with mind-boggling papers and imagery delivered for the industry's premier conference, SIGGRAPH (Special Interest Group in Graphics), sponsored by the Association of Computing Machinery (ACM).

THE DIGITAL TOOL SET

This limitless void was not easily filled. Application software does not come easily. Software is the set of instructions created by a programmer to run on a computer. Usually software is written to satisfy some function, whether it is your accounting program or the word-processing program that was used to write this document. All these programs have had teams of software engineers creating the final application.

From the beginning, individual visual effects houses wrote their own programs. As the whole field matured, giving way to a base of general knowledge and standards, individual vendors made attempts to write software applications that would be used by more than one company.

To write your own applications requires quite a roster of individuals for the visual effects industry. First you have to know what you want, or know what the function of the software will be. The digital age of visual effects has certainly been one of discovering exactly what is needed, building those tools, and then, of course, reestablishing the new needs and goals and again building the new tools on top of the older ones. This circle of discovery and application building has not stopped and probably never will. One of the most interesting aspects of visual effects in the digital age is that there seems to be no limit to the discoveries for new technologies.

In addition, to write your own applications, you must have computer scientists, software engineers, and knowledgeable people in the fields of physics, biomechanics, mathematics, and more. The applications to date have spanned a broad set of functions from modeling, animation, lighting, and effects software, to name a few.

THREE-DIMENSIONAL AND TWO-DIMENSIONAL APPLICATIONS

The digital tool set can be categorized into two somewhat distinct sets based on the type of data that is handled by the application. The two-dimensional, or 2-D, applications use and typically output only images, that is, an array of pixels of an arbitrary bit depth with an arbitrary number of layers. The remaining applications fall into the three-dimensional, 3-D, type, which typically use 3-D objects in some form to produce either more 3-D data or 2-D data.

2-D Applications

For the visual effects industry, the most important applications are those that composite imagery. This is the heart and soul of the digital revolution. Digital techniques were able to replace the function of the optical printer with these compositing packages. Not only was the entire function of the optical printer replaced, but also the new tool allowed for the field of summing imagery to be expanded well beyond what could be done with the state-of-the-art optical printer.

The following list is not complete but samples most of the established tasks that are in use today within a single application package.

- *Simple A-over-B compositing.* The summing of two pictures while controlling the resulting opacity of the B layer.
- *Unlimited multilayer A-over-B compositing.* The summing of multiple pictures; unlike the optical printer, the digital compositing programs do not have a significant limit on the number of layers that can be summed into the picture.
- *Double exposing.* Full control of how layers are treated in the summing process.
- *Matte extraction for multicolored backgrounds.* Process that replaces the photo/filter matte extraction process of the optical printer with very sophisticated software routines specifically tailored for different extraction problems.
- *Grain removal.* The ability to reduce the amount of grain in a photographic image.
- *Grain addition.* The ability to add grain to make the photographic image match normal film characteristics; usually added to pure computer-generated objects that when rendered do not include the simulation of the grain.
- *Animation 2-D.* Moving layers around in the image.
- *Shape alteration, animated.* Changing the shape of an object; step needed for the "morph" effect.
- *Color correction.* The ability to fine-tune the color palette of a series of images.
- *Color animation.* The ability to color correct over time.
- *Rotoscope.* A process of tracing live-action things, most commonly humans or animals, to retrieve that realistic movement into an animation.
- *File conversions.* The ability to convert a 2-D data file into one of the many available in the digital world; most packages allow for input and output to these different formats.

- *Blurring effects.* Altering the image in many different ways to fake rack focus or motion blur.
- *Time domain alterations.* Slowing down or speeding up the imagery.
- *Semi-3-D image plane projection, animated.* The ability to project imagery on a 2-D plane that is placed effectively in a 3-D environment and rendered to a 2-D image.
- *Painting.* Adding color to imagery.
- *Scripting.* The ability of the user to remember and re-create the actions of the composite perfectly each time through scripts, which can take many forms but are usually graphical in nature, thus allowing for an easier convergence to the solution than the optical printer. (Desperately missing in the optical printer age was the ability to list the exact steps involved with a composite and the machine that operated on the list without failure. This is exactly what was provided by the digital revolution.)
- *Viewing solutions.* The user's ability to see the results of the work in various forms before the imagery is processed to its final output form, whether that be a low-resolution result or some other abbreviated test.

As important as the list of techniques above is the human interface of the application. All of these techniques are housed within a construct called the applications interface (or user interface). Work flow, speed, and the artistic execution of the work are dominated by this user interface design. The single most important development in today's 2-D software is the human interface; it cannot be ignored.

The impact of the 2-D digital world has not yet reached its apex. The whole film postproduction process is being restructured due to the success of the past ten years of 2-D digital techniques. Witness the current trend to either digitize an entire film or shoot the entire film digitally, bypassing the use of the negative altogether. This step allows the previous postproduction steps of color timing, and editorial additions such as fades, to be completed in the digital medium. All these changes are a direct result of the progress of the 2-D digital world and continue to blur the line between digital visual effects and the post-process for a motion picture.

3-D Applications

The digital visual effects world did not just liberate the practitioners from the optical printer but opened up another world, a 3-D world, of tools and applications. Instead of building a miniature spaceship, practitioners could create one on the computer, and it could then be flown (animated) on the computer and finally composited on the computer. Instead of building a large dinosaur and using stop-action photography, practitioners could build, animate, and render one on the computer. A new menu of solutions awaited practitioners.

In a simple world, 3-D computer graphics can be roughly broken down into the following phases: building, prelighting, rigging, animating, and lighting-rendering, followed by a reintegration into original photography, that is, the composite. Like all things in visual effects, all these phases actually overlap, and thus one must plan from the start how the design will affect all these phases.

Building

"3-D" was given this name because most things inhabit a world of three dimensions, typically assigned the nomenclature x, y, and z of the Cartesian coordinate system. Within this system, objects must be described in these three dimensions. This is sometimes called the "model-making" phase and specifically relates to how the object takes up space. There are applications that allow the user to easily build fairly complex systems much in the same way as a computer-aided design (CAD) program does. The end results are usually a list of polygons or a list of mathematical entities called nonuniform rational B-splines (NURBs), which define the surface in three dimensions.

These technologies that are based on CAD-like systems all do a wonderful job of putting together a class of relatively solid objects such as aircrafts or buildings. There are limitations for the general packages, though. Usually when something more organic needs to be built, say, the shape of a special rock or a person's face, there are two approaches. One is to just sculpt the shape on the computer using application tools that allow this to happen. This requires great patience and, of course, a great sculptor. Other technologies have come to light that can digitize the objects, even the face of an actor. These "3-D digital scanners" all have a mechanism that allow them to deliver a cloud of points in space, that is, a big list of points in 3-D space that sample the surface in some rigorous fashion. These points are then delivered to other application software that convert the large list to the more convenient representations of the polygon or NURB form, not a trivial step at all.

There is even a third type of object that pushes the boundaries even further. Suppose the object exhibits the even more organic look of a tree. Again, because we are in the remarkable world of computer graphics, there are applications written to produce 3-D representations of such objects that are convincingly real. Anytime that a program is used to create, in this case, a 3-D description of an object, the process is termed "procedural."

Prelighting

Once the object is built so that it describes how it fills 3-D space, another process is begun that will describe how it will look to the human eye. The space-filling information does not tell us whether the object is red, shiny, bumpy, or clear, for instance, and it is this step, the prelight step, that defines just what physical characteristics the model will have.

This step utilizes theories of how light interacts with different surfaces and the corresponding computer programs that are used to compute and simulate the final look of the object within a defined lighting configuration. The process of creating, that is, computing, the final look is sometimes called "rendering."

The prelighter is tasked with the problem of assigning the needed characteristics onto the surface of the object. A simple and incomplete list includes diffuse color, ambient color, specular color, subsurface color and characteristics, isotropic or anisotropic surface characteristics, specific shading math to simulate iridescence, transparency, reflectivity, wetness, wrinkles, bumps, and about a thousand other items. One item, a class in itself, should be mentioned, and that is hair. Hair is also defined in this step. The qualities cover at least the following: color as controlled by length and placement over model, thickness of color, transparency of hair, types of curls, hair density at skin level, hair clumping, and hair shadowing, to name a few.

The field is huge. Every year some astonishing new technique is developed. Almost all the lighting programs written are approximations of the real solution, where the real solution usually will take enormous computing power to create. So the art is in finding the approximation that will satisfy the look needed. Lighting techniques will continue to develop for some time. The visual effects industry will always be looking at advancements to provide a new sense of realism to motion picture images.

RIGGING

While prelighting is the definition of how light will react with the object, rigging is the process of defining how an object will change shape and the establishment of the proper controls, for the animator, to do so. A corollary to this goal is to provide relief to the animator from having to animate small repetitive actions such as skin folding and jiggling.

Some objects are not rigged. For instance, a solid-body object such as a building may not be rigged. Any object that will change its shape must be rigged to some degree, however. Creatures are a good example of objects that need to be rigged. Even an aircraft needs to be rigged to simulate the movement of the flight-control surfaces and the bending and flexing of the wing surfaces.

The act of rigging is defining just how an object will move and how to control those movements. Imagine a three-boned creature. Each bone is connected end to end with the first bone's free joint, which is connected to the ground. There are different ways to move the bones. They can be rigged such that the animator actually controls the angle that bone 2 makes with bone 1 and bone 3 makes with bone 2. (Remember, since this is in 3-D there are really two such angles.) Another rig might be one where the animator is allowed to just "grab" the last and open end of bone 3) and place it where it is needed. The computer is used to find at least one solution for the rest of the joints, to solve for the final "grabbed" position.

Usually the process of rigging restricts movement. The elbow joint does not move in every direction, and even the directions of freedom have limits. These details can be implemented in the rigging step to help the animator move the character properly.

For characters, the process of rigging is further defined as controlling the actual 3-D volume the creature takes on as a function of the movement. As the elephant walks, his skin moves over his muscles, which in turn flex and move over the skeletal system. These complex details are approximated in the rigging step. Although many techniques have been developed to simulate this animation process, most of them try to define basic structural elements such as the skeleton, muscle, skin, and fat.

The solutions for exactly determining the final form the skin will take run the gamut from pure sculptural (done by human) solutions to incredibly detailed procedural (all done by computer calculations) methods. As the elephant places its leg on the ground, there may be some fat jiggle resulting from the impact of the footfall. Even this aspect can be rigged; in this case the procedural software will model the fat layer as a network of springs and weights. Most visual-effects facilities make use of all these methods.

Animating

Grabbing the real model in your hands and placing the model in the exact location it needed to be was the straightforward approach of the stop-motion animator. Today, this process is done on the computer, and although it has been abstracted to the computer screen, the animator can animate, finesse, and see the results almost in real time, an advantage that was unheard of in the stop-action world.

It is the animator's job to bring to life the movement of the object, whether it be an aircraft or a character. The animator uses application software, to visualize the environment, the object he or she is animating, the control structure as provided by the riggers, and a visual playback system to evaluate the work.

Animation over the years has become more and more sophisticated with the addition of many new techniques. One of the most visible new techniques is the process of "motion capture" as used in the Warner Bros. film *Polar Express* (Robert Zemeckis, 2004). Motion capture is a process by which the motion of a human or animal is extracted in a computer-readable form. This procedure is done on a special stage. The subjects whose action will be recorded wear special retro-reflectors attached to their bodies. A large multicamera system, which "sees" the performers, detects and records the movement. Computers and software resolve all the data and determine exactly where the markers were located in 3-D space for every single frame. Those markers and the knowledge of where they were placed on the human subjects further allow this data to drive the animation of the desired computer-generated character. Thus, the actor or performer usurps the animator. For the motion picture *Polar Express* Tom Hanks through his performance became the animator for many of the characters in the film.

As techniques for modeling the true dynamics of physical systems come into play, sometimes the animation may be driven by a procedural solution. For example, the actual flight path of a jet aircraft may need to be as real as possible, thus calling for systems that would be faster at finding the solutions than a human animator.

Other procedural animation solutions have recently been visible. Imagine having to animate an army of fifty thousand warriors, as was done in the *Lord of the Rings* trilogy (Peter Jackson, 2001–3). This task could have taken years and years to produce if each character were to be individually animated. Instead, an application called Massive was created to allow a small number of individual operators to control and train a small number of "agents" how to behave under the circumstances of their environment. These few agent rules were then automatically applied to the fifty thousand characters in the scenes and resulted in distinctive animation for each character. Such systems, sometimes called "artificial intelligence," truly capitalize on the power of the computer to apply large amounts of detail to the animation.

Lighting-Rendering

The prelighters have defined the look of an object. They have set it up such that if light were to land on its surface it would reflect back light in a very specific and desired fashion. But where is that original source of light coming from? It is the job of the lighter to create the final look of the object for use in the composite. This usually means defining just what kind of lights will be used in the scene and where they will be placed, and then feeding all the information to the program that performs the final rendering.

Since lighting and rendering in today's digital-effects world is just an approximation of the real world, this step can be a delicate enterprise. If it were possible to describe the object thoroughly and then render light as it really is understood in the physical world, this would be a conceptually simple, albeit tedious, process. But the computational speed of today's computers is not sufficient to allow for this approach, nor will it be for some time. Consequently, the digital community resorts to the approximation and embraces the issues that come with it.

There are two types of lighting situations. One is where the practitioner has a scene that has been shot to film and is trying to imitate the lighting conditions of the original physical environment at the time of the filmed exposure. The other is when the entire scene is completely generated on the computer and thus has no reference to any physical situation.

When dealing with the former case, the lighter will always want to know exactly where and what the physical situation was in order to simulate the lighting on the computer. Doing so will allow the lighter to illuminate the object that is being synthetically added to the scene in a way that will produce a final image that looks like it belongs in the scene. If the lighter, for instance, had the main key light illuminating from the wrong direction, there would be something wrong with this object; in other words, it would not be responding to the light like all the other objects in the scene.

In today's digital world, the process of simulating real-world illumination is aided by a series of photographic processes that help record the environment. Typically these systems capture a full spherical representation of the environment—sky, ground, objects nearby, and so on. Rhythm and Hues has developed a special high-dynamic-range-imagery (HDRI) digital camera that is essentially six digital cameras mounted on the faces of a cube. Each camera automatically exposes many frames, each with a different exposure time, effectively covering a wide range of exposure. Given this digital information from the HDRI cameras, a digital process is run on the computer that extracts the needed lighting that will be required to accurately illuminate the computer-generated objects in the scene.

In the case where there is no reference to "real" imagery, it is still important to place or define the lights consistently throughout the scene; although in this situation they are usually defined by someone whose task it is to artfully create the entire environment, usually the production designer.

DIGITAL EFFECTS

A very important aspect of visual effects is the ability to re-create natural phenomena such as water, fire, snow, rain, fog, dust, smoke, clouds, cracking earth, shattering glass, heat, cloth, flowing hair, and so on. In the past, these effects, especially those involving water because of its notorious ability to resist scale changes, were very difficult to create. Over a period of time, many of these obstacles have been successfully surmounted using digital solutions. A very good example is the recent Fox production *The Day After Tomorrow* (Roland Emmerich, 2004). Almost all of the natural phenomena depicted in the movie employed digital-effects solutions.

The whole field is very eclectic. Usually a facility will have people dedicated to development of software to solve parts of these problems. Topics usually covered by such research fall into the fields of biomechanics, rigid-body dynamics, physics, numerical solutions, simulations, artificial intelligence, and behavior animation, to name a few. Usually if a problem cannot be given to an animator or lighter, it will be delivered to the digital-effects artist to find a solution. The solutions usually are very sophisticated and usually cross boundaries of other areas, such as lighting, rigging, and animation.

Putting a Shot Together
in the Digital World

"A reptilian creature with hands similar to a human's is having a tug-of-war with an actor over a small toy" is the screenplay description of the next example. The shot will be an interior, with wide-angle lens, in the bedroom set. It is the job of the visual effects (VFX) supervisor to determine what is supposed to happen and exactly how it will be executed.

For this example the VFX supervisor will evaluate methodologies such as creating the reptilian creature as a prosthetic costume versus creating it synthetically on the computer. Assuming there is some overriding reason to not create the costume, for example, the creature has proportions that would never support having a human in the costume, the VFX supervisor determines the creature will be created on the computer.

The next, very important, step is to define what the creature looks like and how it will behave. Usually the VFX supervisor and director will resort to the age-old technology of 2-D pre-visualization, or in other words, utilizing an artist to produce drawings. Studies are created and discussed for the static look. Even studies that try to suggest different poses for the creature are explored. Once an agreed-upon set of drawings is found, the VFX supervisor can begin the next step in the process of defining the creature.

This preplanning phase is very important. It is less costly to change a drawing at this stage than to change the character at a latter time when great energy has already been spent in building it. Ideally, this preparatory work occurs before the commencement of photography for the specific shot.

It is even better if the facility that is creating the creature is able to create a facsimile of the creature to help define just how it will behave for the specific shot. With regard to the current example, will the creature have poor footing and skid on the floor of the room? How strong is the creature? How do all the joints move? Does the creature drool during the tug-of-war? Any preparation that can be done will help sell the creature. More planning usually results in higher-quality work.

At this point in the preparation of the shot, not one frame of film has been shot. The facility has begun to build the final creature, and studies have been performed to give the director and VFX supervisor a pretty good idea of how the creature will act.

One more step can be included in the planning phase. It is called pre-visualization (pre-vis), a simple computer animation that tries to simulate the struggle between the human and the creature, with the inclusion of the room, objects in the room, and a simple animated human. The pre-vis will help define any gags that might be necessary to rig before the shoot and will give the director a good idea of the millimeter and placement of the camera lens. Again, another step in the planning process will only make the actual shoot day go that much more smoothly, and that rapidly translates to a less expensive shot.

The toy is a plastic duck. The VFX supervisor determines that the human, during the actual shoot, needs to interact with something tugging on the duck; otherwise, viewers will not be convinced that the reptilian creature is actually there. A plan is devised to mount the duck at the end of a very long stick. A person will hold the duck/stick device and will pull and push on the stick while remaining offscreen. The actor will hold onto the duck and struggle with it. This methodology will produce more convincing action, especially for the actor. It will have an artifact, though—that being the stick that will be in the frame during the struggle.

The VFX supervisor determines that the stick will be removed later in postproduction using what is typically called a "rig" removal technology, a 2-D image manipulation.

The plan is set. It is shoot day. Stick and duck and actor are ready. The footage is shot. All works to plan. (This is not usually the case, but for this case an optimistic approach will be taken to move this example along.)

The VFX supervisor still has work to do on the set. To facilitate the 3-D work to come, data needs to be gathered about the particular aspects of the shoot. For instance, the lighters will want to know everything about the lighting on the set. The animators will want to know exactly the geometric 3-D nature of the set and the duck and the stick.

There have been many techniques used to document the lighting of a particular scene. In the beginning, simple notes about the types of lights used and their approximate location on the set were created. More recently, additional information is obtained by actually filming within the specific set lighting a series of approximately one-foot-diameter balls with coatings that are flat white, flat gray, and highly reflective. Even more sophisticated are special cameras that allow a technician to record the environment either onto film or straight to digital form. These cameras are capable of imaging the full view of the set, more than a 360-degree panorama, in that the top and bottom of the environment image are included, to create a sort of spherical picture of the environment. In addition, the cameras capture the full range of energies from all the light sources, something that cannot be represented on just one frame of film. This data is delivered later in the postproduction to the lighter for the specific scene and will contribute greatly to the look of realism.

The goal is to put a computer-generated creature back into the scene. To achieve this end, the creature has to be re-created on the computer under the same circumstances that were present for the live action. The creature must be on the floor and must appear to be rendered with the same millimeter lens and same camera position as the live-action footage. The process of determining the exact path of the camera and the millimeter used on the lens throughout the shot is called camera tracking. It is a postproduction task; that is, it is done at the facility after the film has been shot.

Camera tracking can be aided by more physical information about the set. The VFX supervisor is responsible for obtaining as much 3-D information about the shot as can be determined. The VFX supervisor engages individuals whose specific task is to "measure" all the objects and the room. This process is called "digitizing." There are many methods to obtain the information, including photo methods, regular survey methods, and more recently, the LIDAR method. LIDAR stands for "light detection and ranging" and can produce a very accurate and rapid sampling of the environment, whether it be the bedroom set of the example or a city block of buildings.

The last thing the VFX supervisor will obtain from the set before moving on to the postproduction phase of the sample shot is the duck/stick device. As the shot is animated, it will be a requirement that the reptilian creature have its hands on the duck during the struggle. To assist this process, the duck/stick device will also be digitized and brought into the computer. Once 3-D camera tracking is accomplished, that is, once the VFX supervisor knows where and how the camera moved during the shot, another individual will perform what is called "match moving," on the scene. This is the process of finding out exactly where the duck/stick unit was during the shot, frame by frame. This is accomplished by taking the digitized duck/stick object and moving it around until its position is the same as that in the actual movie image, frame by frame within the shot. This will allow the animators to know exactly where to place the creature's hands and how to place them around the object so that the final computer image created will not "swim," or appear to be disconnected.

With the duck/stick unit in hand, the process moves to the postproduction phase, which is outlined below.

Postproduction Phase for the Sample Shot

- Digitize the duck/stick for match move.
- Digitize the film negative on the film scanner.
- Input the digitization of the set plus all notes into the computer system.
- Begin camera 3-D tracking.
- Finish modeling, rigging, and prelighting the creature.
- Input the on-set lighting information in preparation for lighting the creature.
- Once 3-D tracking is complete, begin match move of the duck/stick.
- Once the match move is complete, begin animation blocking and first-pass lighting.
- As a separate and independent step, remove the stick ("rig removal") from the scene, frame by frame.
- In a recursive process, refine the lighting, the animation, and the composite.
- Assuming the goal is reached, output the imagery to create the final negative.

The struggle over the duck example shot is only the beginning. The overall complexity is low by today's standards but still represents the thought processes that must occur no matter the size of the problem.

The Visual-Effects Facility

In order to accomplish these digital feats there has to be some infrastructure in place to do the work. While we have given much attention to this point to writing the software required for this process, there are also backbone infrastructural pieces of hardware that are typically needed to do this work. They include, at least, computer workstations for the artists, render farms to calculate imagery off line, massive disk systems to hold imagery, backup systems to store data securely off the more expensive disk systems, a network capable of handling large amounts of data and traffic, playback display devices including HIDEF and film, editing equipment, and, of course, the film scanner and printer.

Probably the most notable difference between this list and that of, say, some ten years ago is the idea of a special-purpose supercomputer for all large computational needs. Today, with the power of the commercial consumer computer being so high and the price so low, the supercomputer has been replaced by the idea of using many of these smaller processors—thousands—to satisfy the computing needs of a facility. Not only is it significantly cheaper, but it is easily scalable in size and, most important, resistant to the rather depressing fact that the lifetime of a computer is only a few years. Given Moore's law, computers are almost obsolete the day they are installed. Thus, a large array of computers allows the facility to retire and update portions without starting with a whole new computer.

The industry is changing rapidly with the advent of the digital intermediate (DI) in film production. Production companies that specialize in the handling of the postoperation phases of film production are now more likely to handle all the film scanning and printing of a motion picture. Thus, facilities will not need to house the hardware for the scanning and printing of film negatives.

General trends in the price and performance of hardware—that is, faster, better, and cheaper—have made it much easier for start-up facilities to hit the ground running. Today's start-up's biggest issue is in hiring the artist and the support team to execute and support the system. Couple the advancements in hardware with the commercialization of software for the effects business, and the result is a small explosion of facilities around the world producing high-quality work.

As previously noted, the rapid advance of technology has given the creative process new tools with which to tell the cinematic story. Accordingly, this has affected the filmmakers' approach to moviemaking in both an artistic and a fundamental business sense.

For example, the screenwriter's palette is ever expanded in his or her ability to describe environments, characters, and situations. In the past, when the writer wrote, "The cavalry charged the castle," the filmmaker had to keep in mind the logistics and the cost associated with dressing an army of human extras with horses in period costumes in a location that had an actual castle. Now one can imagine almost everything in that scenario to be computer generated. Of course, there is still a cost associated with these visual effects that the producers of the film have to deal with, but the writer now knows that his or her perhaps expansive vision is quite capable of being brought to fruition.

The directors of these films also understand that previous limitations to the approach of designing and photographing their films are quickly and continually evolving. Films such as 20th Century Fox's *The Day After Tomorrow* or computer-generated character films such as Warner Bros.' *Scooby Doo* series (Raja Gosnell, 2003, 2004) could not have been made as they have been without the state-of-the-art visual effects applications used. Keep in mind, as stated earlier, that in this day and age almost all films, not just the big "tent-pole" blockbuster studio films, contain some type of visual effects work. Bringing a visual design approach into the storytelling narrative can now be part of the director's vision and storytelling tool set. In 2004's *Eternal Sunshine of the Spotless Mind* (Michel Gondry), for example, the story was integral to the design of the visual effects approach.

The director can now arbitrarily change the color, the balance, or the design of any object in the frame to add to a scene's impact. This often occurs without the audience even being aware that they are watching a postproduction process. The director is now directing not only the actors and the camera, but also the tapestry of textures and elements that compose every shot.

On the business side of the equation, the producers of a film are those individuals who are responsible for the financial aspects of the production. Often they are the ones caught between their fiduciary responsibility to the sponsoring studio or investors of the project, and the creative appetites of the director, the cinematographer, and the writer. When this dialectic comes to the subject of visual effects, it is the producer's responsibility to find the capacity and wherewithal to apply the correct fiscal balance to the film. This can be a huge task on a big effects film for which the effects budget alone may comprise half or even more than half of the budget for the entire film. The scope of the financial variance may run the gamut from millions of dollars to a few thousand, but it is an endemic problem for the producer to find where that money is coming from and how it is to be applied. This theme of having new tools that can be used that also must in the end be accountable to the budget and resources available will no doubt continue as new tools are created and applied to the filmmaking process.

Accordingly, as the technology has become more efficient and user friendly, and with the related diminishing cost of software and hardware, even low-budget independent filmmakers now have access to using effects in their films. The software has become such that many rudimentary yet applicable effects can be created by individuals on their laptop computers while sitting in the comfort of their living rooms.

For the larger studio films, where there is clearly much at stake, there is still the dilemma of how the visual effects are done. Directorial choices, studio executive input, financial restrictions, and hard deadlines with release dates make the visual effects process more changeable and thus more challenging.

At the outset of the computer era, post *Star Wars*, there were only a few fledgling companies that led the foray into visual effects films. George Lucas's Industrial Light and Magic was the main player in the field. However, other offshoot companies came into being in the early 1980s. Apogee Productions, Boss Films, and Bob Abel & Associates were among the earliest. These days there are multitudes of visual effects companies scattered around the globe. The Internet and satellite transmission has made it possible for a director to edit the film in Los Angeles while effects for the film are being created in Mumbai, London, and Vancouver. However, there are still only a handful of large companies, including our own Rhythm & Hues Studios, in existence that can turn over hundreds of highly crafted visual effects shots for a single film.

So how do the filmmakers decide how and where to get the actual computer effects work done? John Swallow, the vice president of production technology at Universal Studios, told us that he "casts the company, not unlike casting an actor. Some companies are good at one thing and not another, so I go where it seems like I will get the appropriate work done with people I trust. And part of the casting process is talking through the tool sets you can use to accomplish what you want." Some directors or producers take work to facilities where they have personal relationships and trust built up with certain supervisors and executives, and where there is a sustained and proven pipeline to get the work done. Also, as we have pointed out, cost is a driving factor. Effects work is normally bid out to multiple facilities in order for the studios and producers to get the best price. Work sometimes goes to other countries, where the government subsidizes film budgets for dollars spent in their labor pool. Australia, the European Union, Canada, and New Zealand are all currently involved in tax-rebate situations.

So who actually does the work? Visual effects and animation facilities such as Rhythm & Hues Studios that focus on doing digital effects for the feature film business are home to an assortment of individuals whose skill sets range across the board in terms of applications and technologies. Animators, lighters, matte painters, compositors, match movers, and rotoscope artists all can be employed to work on a single shot. These artists are intertwined with a gaggle of visual effects producers, coordinators, pipeline support managers, software and hardware technicians, and systems engineers. It is no small task to create and deliver hundreds of high-end visual effects shots for a single movie with a hard, immovable delivery date.

The infrastructure and computing power of the company must be both robust and flexible in order to take on the ever-changing landscape of the postproduction process. Preview screenings of a film have put additional stress on both the studio and the director to accommodate audience criticisms before the movie is released. Visual effects, being one of the last tasks finished on a film, are routinely excised or added right up until the last moment before the prints are struck for theater distribution. It can be a taxing and labor-intensive procedure for all involved. As technology has made the imagery more sophisticated, it has also allowed it to be implemented faster, thus fostering an ability to work up to the very last moment.

As long as writers and filmmakers imagine stories that go beyond the boundaries of what can be filmed as reality, there will be a need for visual effects. The trend since the beginning of filmmaking indicates that there is no limit to new ideas that will require the assistance of visual effects.

The absolute underlying methodologies of telling stories in the motion picture form will radically change in the future. These changes will go hand in hand with the increased capabilities of the visual effects industry. Based on trends of today, those activities that have been solely categorized as "visual effects" have already transcended their original definitions. As evidenced with the motion picture *Sky Captain and the World of Tomorrow* (Kerry Conran, 2004), the visual effects augmented the story, providing the entire environment around which the human actors performed for the whole film. The techniques used to create a computer-generated character in *Lord of the Rings* became the dominant technique that replaced cinematography in making other motion pictures such as *Polar Express*. It seems that not only environments for whole pictures but principal characters of whole films are and will continue to be an option for computer-generated effects.

Visual effects must satisfy the sophisticated viewer in the future. Viewing an old motion picture with visual effects such as *The 7th Voyage of Sinbad* (Nathan Jeeran, 1958), today's viewer will note the somewhat odd, unrealistic nature of the skeleton battle created by Ray Harryhausen using stop-action techniques. At the time, however, viewers had no problem looking at this effect, which was something they had never seen before. As the viewer becomes more and more visually sophisticated, however, old techniques will not satisfy the visual effects requirement of suspending disbelief long enough for the story to be told. For many films to come, the future of visual effects will be dominated by technologies that will contribute to the creation of either absolutely photo-real imagery to maintain that suspension of disbelief, or new "looks" or unreal worlds that the audience has never seen before.

On a more pragmatic level, the future of visual effects can be examined as a continuous evolution of ideas in the fields of lighting and material definitions, animation, natural phenomenon simulation, and the cluster of effects falling under the category of image touch-up, such as rig removal, simple compositing, and so forth. All of these changes will be directly linked with the further development of the software that humans use to perform effects work.

Animation is ripe for change. One of the desirable aspects of using motion capture to acquire the animation of a character, as was done, for instance, in *Polar Express,* is the fact that there is only one actor working with one director to create the performance. One difficulty of producing a non–motion-captured animated character is the fact that many people are used to animate the single character. That means they must all have the ability to express the same character, a process difficult to achieve. One of the future advances of animation will be the ability for one person to set up the "characteristics" of the character so that many people can implement those "characteristics" across many scenes. Further in the future, perhaps a single individual could animate a character in an entire film by not only describing the "characteristics" of the character, but also allowing more semiautomated processes to animate the lower-level behavior of the character (walking, running, dealing with inanimate objects). Whatever software is developed in the future, it will embody the goals of creating a consistent preprogrammed behavior of the character while reducing the labor to do so.

Motion capture, the process of recording human or animal movement to act as a basis for animation, will undergo further development. Although the process is widely used, further improvements in accurate recording of the face and eyes are required. Software still needs to be developed to allow faster and more efficient editing of the motion-capture data. And finally, character retargeting, the process of using motion-capture data to animate a character that is very different from the original recorded subject, for example, a human driving a two-thousand-point, fifteen-foot giant, will have to evolve with new methodologies.

The process of lighting computer-generated elements is one of those technologies that will always strive to make the results look perfectly real. As mentioned earlier, lighting requires the visual effects practitioners to render the imagery they produce by the skillful management of a set of approximations. The further reduction of those approximations and the increase in computer speed will have a tremendous effect on the world of lighting and thus on all visual effects. Having a more accurate solution will mean more realistic rendering of the desired environment and the ability to rapidly find the desired "look." The process could be compressed into the simple practice of artful production design—"build these sets using this wood, steel, and velvet"—and artful photography direction—"put these kind of lights here." Modeling and building infrastructure that ties the synthetic world closer to what we really see and experience will certainly be a trend.

The simulation of natural phenomena will become more and more sophisticated with further research and development. Even though we have witnessed exceptional computer-generated water in a series of films over the years, it is still very difficult to create realistic computer-generated images of water, whether it is in a glass, a river, or an ocean. The same goes for fire, dust, explosions, clouds, and so on. As in lighting, the tools used to solve these problems produce approximations. With further software development and the ever-increasing capacity of the computer, the imagery produced will be executed using more interactive techniques and will result in flawless representations of natural phenomena.

The future of visual effects becomes a little blurry as the future of film postproduction techniques is considered. With the advent of the digital revolution, the whole postproduction process is changing rapidly. Films have been edited digitally for some time, but at resolutions and quality comparable to video, accompanied by a postconformation of the negative to produce the film. Now the digital world allows the combining of the editorial, color timing, and other operations at film-quality levels. Since the film is carried throughout the postprocess in a digital form called the digital intermediate (DI), which is adequate for motion picture representation, some tasks will have to shift. Operations once common to the visual effects studio will be done within the postproduction editorial unit or the color-timing unit. The blurring essentially means that there will be more options in structuring the work for postproduction.

When talking about the future of visual effects, it is difficult to avoid the concept of fabricating the human form. It is easy to say it will not be long before a very convincing synthetic human appears in a principal role in a motion picture. We have already seen computer-generated humans in motion pictures. They are used primarily when it is too dangerous or impossible to place a real human in the circumstances of the film production. These synthetic characters are called computer-generated stunt doubles. They provide a solution to a problem, such as the fist fight in the *Matrix* trilogy (Andy Nachowski and Larry Wachowski 1999, 2003), in which the creation of a computer-generated Agent Smith allowed the filmmakers to have many copies of him present in the fight, as well as the execution of the shot where Smith takes a fist direct to his face in ultra-slow motion, something that did not easily lend itself to a real human solution.

Duplicating the human form for a principal part in a film will probably happen soon, but it will not be complete. The development will continue beyond the first day one appears in a movie. There are many issues and challenges, mostly old technologies that will require major evolutionary steps of improvement. The list includes but is not limited to:

- Hair geometry and lighting
- Shadowing of the hair onto itself and the skin and other surfaces
- Hair dynamics, hair touching hair, hair touching skin or other objects, hair influenced by air
- Skin lighting and detail, including further work on subsurface scattering, bone and cartilage lighting influences, changing blood flows, and so on
- Fluid flow and dynamics into the eyes
- Bone-, organ-, muscle-, tendon-, fat-, and skin-simulation advances
- Clothing simulations
- Body dynamics, including further understanding of walking, hiking, climbing, running, and the like
- Expression control for face and body
- Refinements for motion capture for body and face
- Retargeting refinements from motion capture to character target
- Semiautonomous animation software

Each and every item listed exists today in some form at various facilities. The future of visual effects is tightly coupled to how these young technologies develop and relate to one another in a way that produces perfect solutions at prices that filmmakers can afford.

Probably the most interesting issue about having a synthetic human form in a movie is the reason to have one. Assuming you are not using the synthetic human for stunt purposes, why have a photo-real synthetic human? What are the conditions that would require a synthetic human? One theory is the idea of creating a character, much like the animated character Shrek, for which the lifetime of the character is not at risk. The synthetic human character will not grow old and will cost the same each time it is used; in other words, it will not demand more and more money if it becomes famous. The creators of the synthetic human character will own all the rights. Undoubtedly someone will create the need, and it will happen.

Ten years ago the dominant prediction about visual effects was that they would become digital and dependent on the speed and price of computers. Even though Moore's law has it that the performance of computers consistently doubles every eighteen months or so, the utility of the programs used for working in visual effects has not followed the same curve. Software has always lagged behind hardware in the fast-paced computer industry. Even though faster computers and better graphics-display hardware will be a big boost to the future of visual effects, the dominant required growth will be in software. There will be advances in the science of calculating the images as well as the equally important human interface application software that will have to support more real-time solutions with more intuitive interfaces. Software development for the next ten years will focus on closing the software-hardware gap.

Jon Landau, producer of 20th Century Fox's *Titanic* (James Cameron, 1997), when talking about the future of film stated that "[p]eople will always want to go to the cinema. If for nothing else, for the social experience." Given that assessment, visual effects, which have had a fundamental effect on the motion picture industry from the very beginning, are tied closely to the cinematic experience. Accordingly, it seems obvious that with a quick extrapolation, visual effects are here to stay and will provide story support for motion pictures that will entertain us deep into the future.

INDEX

....

Curriculum, deep and surface learning and, 536, 539–41
Curtin, Michael, 271–72, 375
Customary usage, copyright and fair use, 569–70
Customer satisfaction, media conglomeration and, 351
"Cuteness." *See kawaii* style
Cut scenes, 30
Cybernarratives, 417, 418, 419, 421
Cycles of the Heavenly Dragon (Jin), 379

Daguerre, Louis Jacques Mandé, 162, 291
Daguerreotypes, 162
Dallas, 156n75
Dances with Wolves, 269
Dark Water (Nataka), 411n31
Daughters of the Wind, 475
David, Jacques-Louis, 167
Dayan, Daniel, 65
Debord, Guy: documentary films and, 129–30, 133–35; European radicalism and, 117; photography and, 168, 179–80; spectacle and, 73
Decentralization, society and, 517–18
Declarative knowledge, 535
Decolonization, China and, 386–87
Decontextualization, textbooks and, 543
DeCordova, Richard, 195, 198
DeCurtis, Anthony, 328
Deep and surface learning: about, 537–39; case study, 542–47; comprehension and, 537–39; curriculum and, 539–41; electronic textbooks and, 550, 551, 554; student-centered learning (CORE), 541–42
Deep-focus, long-take filmmaking, 60, 88
Deep Learning for a Digital Age (Weigel), 535
Deer and the Cauldron, The (Jin), 380
Deficit financing, 337–38
Defining genres, film genre theory and, 228–29
Definitive Elvis, The, 564–65
Delaroche, Paul, 182n24
Deleuze, Gilles, 50, 72, 73, 388n2, 515
DeLillo, Don, 108
Delluc, Louis, 50
DeMille, Cecil B., 495
Democracy, computers and, 510, 513
Denny, Reginald, 567
Deregulation, of media. *See* government regulation
Deren, Maya, 76n53, 96
Derrida, Jacques, 40
Descartes, René, 514, 515
Descriptive texts, 537, 538
De Sica, Vittorio, 9
Determinations: of apparatus theory, 72; of the concept of television, 287
Détourne, of images, 134
Deutschland im Herbst (Kluge), 130, 138–39
Devil Finds Work, The (Baldwin), 210
Dewey, John, 536
Dhanwani, Rashmi, 437

Dhingra, Tushar, 434
Dialectical materialism, 54, 57
Dialectic of Enlightenment (Adorno and Horkheimer), 13–14
Dialects, sound techniques and, 57
Diamond, Hugh, 165
Dian xue effect, 376
Diarios de motocicleta (Salles), 474
Diasporic cultural identities, 273
Diaz Torres, Daniel, 475
Dick, Kirby, 572
Dick, Philip K., 105
Dictionary of New Media, 550
Die Hard, 235
Die Patriotin (Kluge), 130
Digital animation, 415
Digital cameras, portability of, 71
Digital delivery systems, 244
Digital divide, the, 511–12, 523n11
Digital installation art, 30, 34
Digital intermediate (DI) technology, 455
Digital intermediates, 335
Digital media: Asian film and, 414–21; aura and, 33–35; *caméra-stylo* and, 72–73; convergence and, 17; Eastern and Central European revolution and, 145; European radicalism and, 117, 118; externalizing risk and, 335; film distribution and, 444n22, 444n25; film theory and, 70; future of filmic narrative and, 21–36; globalization and, 500; Indian cinema and, 431–32, 436–38, 442; Latin American media and, 447–48, 448–55, 479–80; media celebrity and, 213; medium specificity and, 70–71; photography and, 158–80; piracy and, 420; postmodernism and, 106; "quality television" and, 322–23; technological advances and, 289; television and, 109, 458–59; transparent representation and, 28–31; visual narratives and, 25–26; volitional mobility and, 314
Digital theory, 70–71
Digital video (DV) films, 415, 417–18
"Digital World Picture, The" (Geuens), 70
Dignity of the Nobodies (Solanas), 476
Direct adaptations, 239–40
Direct cinema, 117
Directors, 9–10, 11, 56, 197
DirecTV, 344, 457
Disclosures, stages, 357
Discord, sound techniques and, 57
Disdéri, A.A.E., 162, 163
Disney/ABC, 327, 344
Distance, television and, 288
Distinct properties, new media and, 239
Distribution, new media and, 148–49; Abu Ghraib images and, 151–52; Eastern and Central European revolution and, 145
Distribution, of films. *See* film distribution
Distribution, of images, 176, 179
Distribution systems, 339
Diversity, cultural. *See* cultural diversity